Manual of Crime Scene Investigation

Over the past several years, myriad manuals on crime scene investigations have been published with each focusing on select, or partial, aspects of the investigation. Crime scene investigation, done right, is a multi-faceted process that requires various forms of evidence to be collected, examined, and analyzed. No book available has addressed procedures to present global best practices by assembling a collection of international experts to address such topics.

Manual of Crime Scene Investigation is a comprehensive collaboration of experts writing on their particular areas of expertise as relates to crime scenes, evidence, and crime scene investigation. This book outlines best practices in the field, incorporating the latest technology to collect, preserve, and enhance evidence for appropriate analysis. Various types of forensic evidence are addressed, covering chain of custody, collection, and utility of such evidence in casework, investigations, and for use in court. The approach, and use of international contributor experts, will appeal to a broad audience and be of use to forensic practitioners and the forensic science community worldwide.

Key features:

- Assembles an international team of contributing author experts to present the latest developments in their crime scene field of specialty
- Examines global best practices and what are consistently the most reliable tactics and approach to crime scene evidence collection, preservation, and investigation
- Provides numerous photographs and diagrams to clearly illustrate chapter concepts

Manual of Crime Scene Investigation serves as a vital resource to professionals in police science and crime scene investigations, private forensic institutions, and academics researching how better real-world application of techniques can improve the reliability and utility of evidence upon forensic and laboratory analysis.

Manual of Crime Scene Investigation

Edited by
Anna Barbaro and
Amarnath Mishra

CRC Press
Taylor & Francis Group
Boca Raton London New York

CRC Press is an imprint of the
Taylor & Francis Group, an **informa** business

First edition published 2022
by CRC Press
6000 Broken Sound Parkway NW, Suite 300, Boca Raton, FL 33487-2742

and by CRC Press
4 Park Square, Milton Park, Abingdon, Oxon, OX14 4RN

CRC Press is an imprint of Taylor & Francis Group, LLC

Library of Congress Cataloguing-in-Publication Data
Names: Barbaro, Anna, editor. | Mishra, Amarnath (Forensic scientist), editor.
Title: Manual of crime scene investigation / edited by Anna Barbaro and Amarnath Mishra.
Identifiers: LCCN 2022012872 (print) | LCCN 2022012873 (ebook) |
ISBN 9780367653071 (hardback) | ISBN 9781032315553 (paperback) |
ISBN 9781003129554 (ebook)
Subjects: LCSH: Crime scene searches. | Criminal investigation. | Forensic sciences.
Classification: LCC HV8073 .M25543 2023 (print) | LCC HV8073 (ebook) |
DDC 363.25/2--dc23/eng/20220604
LC record available at https://lccn.loc.gov/2022012872
LC ebook record available at https://lccn.loc.gov/2022012873

ISBN: 978-0-367-65307-1 (hbk)
ISBN: 978-1-032-31555-3 (pbk)
ISBN: 978-1-003-12955-4 (ebk)

DOI: 10.4324/9781003129554

Typeset in Sabon
by MPS Limited, Dehradun

Dedicated to Aldo Barbaro

Contents

Editors

Dr. Anna Barbaro holds a BSc in biological sciences, a diploma of postgraduate school of specialization in applied genetics (University of Rome La Sapienza, Italy), a MSc in psychological and behavioral techniques of criminal investigation (University of Rome LaSapienza, Italy), a PhD in forensic genetics (University of Santiago de Compostela, Spain). She has also a Diploma of Expert in Criminal Investigation, a diploma in Intermediate Crime Scene Investigation, and a diploma in Criminalistics: Specialized in the Crime Scene.

She has also experience as director of the Forensic Genetics Dept. at Studio Indagini Mediche e Forensi (SIMEF) in Italy and as a post-doctoral researcher at the University of Alcalà (Spain).

She is professor of forensic genetics in degree or post-degree courses about forensic science and expert consultant for Italian Penal and Civil Tribunals.

She is the president of the Worldwide Association of Women Forensic Experts (WAWFE), honor member of several international associations, and author of more than 100 papers, serving also as an editorial board member and reviewer for some international scientific journals. She is an organizer of courses and conferences about forensic science and lecturer about CSI and DNA topics in national/international conferences/courses.

Dr. Barbaro has previously edited the book *Manual of Forensic Science* (2017) published by CRC Press/Taylor & Francis; the *Manual of Criminalistics and Criminology* (2020) published by Tébar Flores (Spain), and the *Manual of Criminalistics and Criminology* (2021) by Ecoe Ediciones (Colombia).

She is co-author of the *Manual Technical Evidence in the Criminal Trial* (2016) published by Key Editore (Italy). She is also the author of the chapter on SNPs technology: approach and applications in the *Manual Forensic Genetics Research Progress*, Novapublisher (USA), 2009; author of the chapters: STR Typing and Available Multiplex Kits Including Validation Methods and of the chapter DNA Databases (2020) in *Forensic DNA Typing: Principles, Applications and Advancements*, published by Springer Nature (Switzerland), and author of the chapter Challenges in DNA Extraction from Forensic Samples (2021) in *Handbook of DNA Profiling* by Springer (Singapore).

Dr. Amarnath Mishra has been working as Associate Professor (Forensic Science) at the School of Forensics, Risk Management & National Security, Rashtriya Raksha University, (An Institution of National Importance) (Pioneering National Security and Police University of India), Ministry of Home Affairs, Government of India, Gandhinagar, Gujarat, India since July 2022. Prior to this, he worked at Amity Institute of Forensic Sciences, Amity University, Noida, Uttar Pradesh, India, Department of Forensic Science, School of Humanities, Arts & Applied Sciences, Amity University Dubai Campus, United Arab Emirates, Department of Forensic Medicine & Toxicology, Tribhuvan University, National Medical College, Birgunj and Department of Forensic Medicine & Toxicology, Kathmandu University, College of Medical Sciences, Bharatpur, Nepal. He has 14+ years of experience in Research, Academics, and Administration.

Dr. Mishra has been awarded with a PhD degree in Forensic Science with specialization in Forensic and Analytical Toxicology from the Sam Higginbottom University of Agriculture, Technology & Sciences, Prayagraj (Formerly SHIATS, Allahabad) in collaboration with the Central Forensic Science Laboratory, Chandigarh, MHA, Govt. of India. He has completed his M.Phil. degree in Biochemistry with specialization in Forensic Biochemistry from Vinayaka Missions University, Salem, Tamilnadu, India. He has completed his M.Sc. degree in Forensic Science with specialization in Forensic Serology & DNA Fingerprinting from the Sam Higginbottom University of Agriculture, Technology & Sciences, Prayagraj (Formerly AAIDU, Allahabad) in collaboration with the Central Forensic Science Laboratory, Hyderabad, MHA, Govt. of India. He has worked as Research Scholar (May 2007 – July 2008) for the pilot study on "Non-registration of F.I.R." at Police Stations conducted by the Bureau of Police Research and Development (BPR&D), MHA, Govt. of India. He has qualified UGC-NET Exam. June 2007 for Lectureship in Forensic Science. He has completed his B.Sc. degree in Chemistry, Botany and Zoology from Deen Dayal Upadhyay Gorakhpur University, Gorakhpur, Uttar Pradesh, India.

Dr. Mishra has published 7 books, 20 book chapters, and more than 45 research articles in reputed peer-reviewed national and international journals and presented around 25 papers in national and international conferences, and has attended more than 55 conferences, seminars, workshops, FDPs, and refresher courses. He has delivered more than 17 invited talks at various national and international events. He has granted/awarded 4 national & international patents. He has taught at various Institutions like the Department of Forensic Science and Criminology of Babasaheb Bhimrao Ambedkar University (A Central University), National P.G. College, University of Lucknow, India, etc. He is supervising four PhD candidates in the area of issue and prospective of DNA application, analysis of anesthetic drugs, analysis of fire accelerants in arson cases, and drugs of abuse respectively in which two PhD students have already submitted their PhD thesis. He has guided more than 120 undergraduate and postgraduate students in various programs i.e., B.Sc., B.Tech., M.Sc., M.B.B.S., and M.D for their major projects and dissertations.

Dr. Mishra is a Technical Assessor for NABL, India. He is a paper setter and an external examiner for various academic institutions and recruitment agencies. He is an editorial board member in different reputed National and International journals.

Dr. Mishra has organized several events like One-Day International Web-Seminar on "Role of Forensic Science and Law in Safety of Women & Children" (A dialogue dedicated to the Mission Shakti: An initiative of U.P. Government, India), International Conference of Biotechnology Society of Nepal on "Biotechnological Revolution in Environmental, Agricultural Technologies and Healthcare (BREATH)", Seven Days Online Faculty Development Program on "Recent Advancement in Forensic Science and Technology" (Crime Scene to Court Room), 15 Days Online Refresher Course on "Emerging Trends & Challenges in Interdisciplinary Research & Teaching in Science, Technology and Intellectual Property Rights", 2nd Seven Days Online Faculty Development Program on "Current Trends in Forensic Science Research and Teaching" (Classroom to Expert Witness Box) and One Month Online Certificate Course on "Cyber Crime Investigation, Digital Forensics & Cyber Security".

Dr. Mishra is a Freelance Forensic Expert and Medico-legal Consultant for the Court of Law under section 45 of the Indian Evidence Act 1872. He has also contributed his knowledge and experience in TV and Radio programs as a Forensic Expert. He is the founder of Aspire Forensics and Amar Educational and Social Welfare Trust. In addition to his above assignments, he is serving many professional bodies along with lifetime membership.

Contributors

Anna Barbaro
Worldwide Association of Women Forensic
    Experts (WAWFE President)
Studio Indagini Mediche E Forensi (SIMEF)
Reggio Calabria, Italy

Amarnath Mishra
Worldwide Association of Women Forensic Experts
    (Regional Coordinator WAWFE-India)
School of Forensics, Risk Management & National
    Security (SFRMNS)
Rashtriya Raksha University (An Institution of National
    Importance)
Lavad-Dahegam, Gandhinagar, Gujarat, India

Adrienne Brundage
Maples Center for Forensic Medicine
University of Florida
Gainesville, Florida, USA

Alan Diego Briem Stamm
Worldwide Association of Women Forensic Experts
    (WAWFE-Argentina)
Unidad Académica Odontología Legal
Universidad de Buenos Aires
Argentina

Almir Olovčić
International Commission on Missing Persons (ICMP)
Sarajevo, Bosnia-Herzegovina

Carlos Muñoz Quezada
Iberoamercan Association of Medicine and Forensic
Veterinary Sciences
Chile

Chintan Singh
Amity Institute of Forensic Sciences
Amity University
Noida, Uttar Pradesh, India

Dalia Al-Saif
Worldwide Association of Women Forensic Experts
    (WAWFE-Caribbean)
Dammam Center of Forensic and Legal Medicine
Saudi Arabia

Ekta B. Jadhav
Government Institute of Forensic Science
Aurangabad, Maharashtra, India

Esther Espejo Alvim
Experimental and Comparative Pathology Program of
    the Faculty of Veterinary Medicine and Zootechnics
University of Sao Paulo; Brazilian Association of Legal
    Veterinary Medicine
Brazil

Gonzalo Germán Miguez Murillas
Scientific Police Division of Comodoro Rivadavia City,
    Argentina; Estudio Pericial GV
Argentina

Gregory J. Williams
Worldwide Association of Women Forensic
    Experts (WAWFE-Caribbean)
University of the West Indies, Mona Campus Jamaica
Royal Police Force of Antigua and Barbuda
    Police Headquarters
St. Johns, Antigua, Caribbean Association of Forensic
    Sciences (CAFS)

Harshita Tara
Nextechno Gen Private Limited
Patparganj, Delhi, India

Hillary Mullings-Williams
Worldwide Association of Women Forensic
    Experts (WAWFE-Caribbean)
Institute of Forensic Science and Legal Medicine
University of the West Indies, Jamaica
Caribbean Association of Forensic Sciences

Jyoti Singh
Amity Institute of Forensic Sciences
Amity University
Noida, Uttar Pradesh, India

Jason Byrd
Maples Center for Forensic Medicine
University of Florida
Gainesville, Florida, USA

Kapil Parihar
Department of Forensic Science
Vivekananda Global University
Jaipur, Rajasthan, India

Leggie L. Boone
Polk County Sheriff's Office
Keiser University Florida
Sherlock Institute of Forensic Science (SIFS) India Pvt. Ltd.
Editorial Board of Fashion and Law Journal
Legal Desire Media and Insights
Worldwide Association of Women Forensic
  Experts (WAWFE-US)
International Association for Identification
Florida Division of IAI
Generation ForSciTe, LLC
Lakeland, Florida, USA

Lerah Sutton
Maples Center for Forensic Medicine
University of Florida
Gainesville, Florida, USA

Mahipal Singh Sankhla
Department of Forensic Science
Vivekananda Global University
Jaipur, Rajasthan, India
and
Department of Forensic Science
Institute of Sciences
SAGE University
Indore, M.P., India

Maram Al-Farayedhi
Worldwide Association of Women Forensic Experts
  (WAWFE-Caribbean)
Dammam Center of Forensic and Legal Medicine
Saudi Arabia

Mohammad A. AlShamsi
Head of Firearms and Toolmarks Section
Gen. Dept. of Forensic Science and Criminology
Dubai Police, Dubai, UAE

Mohammed Naji
Senior DNA Analyst, Dubai Police – General
Department of Forensic Sciences and Criminology
UAE

Prashi Jain
Amity Institute of Forensic Sciences
Amity University
Noida, Uttar Pradesh, India

Rodrigo Marcos
Chilean Association of Criminalists (COLCRIM AG);
  Forensis SpA
Chile

Samar A. Ahmed
Worldwide Association of Women Forensic Experts
  (WAWFE-Egypt)
Ain Shams University
Cairo, Egypt

Swaroop Sonone
Department of Forensic Science
Dr. Babasaheb Ambedkar Marathawada University
Aurangabad, Maharashtra, India

Vaishali Omi
Amity Institute of Forensic Sciences
Amity University
Noida, Uttar Pradesh, India

Victor Toledo González
International Scientific Working Group of Animal Forensic
  Sciences (ISWG-AFS); Worldwide Association of
  Women Forensic Experts (WAWFE)
Spain

CHAPTER 1

Crime Scene Management

Gregory J. Williams

Worldwide Association of Women Forensic Experts (WAWFE-Caribbean), University of the West Indies, Mona
Campus Jamaica, Royal Police Force of Antigua and Barbuda Police Headquarters St. Johns, Antigua, Caribbean,
Association of Forensic Sciences (CAFS)

CONTENTS

DOI: 10.4324/9781003129554-1

FIGURE 1.1   Cover photo for chapter.

INTRODUCTION

Crime scene investigation is regarded as the gateway to forensic science. Forensic science is defined as science used for the resolution of legal disputes in the courts of law. The management of a crime scene requires the proper handling of human resources and the ability to recognize and identify potential evidence. The integrity of the crime scene is paramount and the ability of the first responding officers (FRO) forensic officers (FO) or the crime scene investigators(CSI) must be of high quality to be able to recognize, identify, examined, document, collect, and preserve physical evidence. These stages in crime scene processing can impact the entire investigation and can cause forensic evidence to be tainted and may later become inadmissible in the judicial system. Once a crime is committed and proper documentation and collection is done, the chain of custody will come into effect as the evidence recovered will have to be handed over to other forensic experts where varied examinations and analyses will take place; therefore, the chain of custody will be established to maintain the integrity of the evidence. In instances where a crime has been committed, law-enforcement officers will be the ones to respond and collect evidence and will have to maintain a chain of custody, but a chain of custody must be extended beyond the law enforcement because they are not the only one who must maintain the integrity of the evidence; the forensic analyst at the lab also must maintain a chain of custody (Figure 1.1).

Integrity of the evidence cannot be a task only for law enforcement but for all other persons to include forensic experts who might have been in contact with the evidence. Proper handling, collection, preservation, and recovery of physical evidence along with proper management of human resources and the scene as a whole will provide the chances for better forensic analysis that will aid the judicial system. Management principles of the crime scene should not change but adapt to suit the situation at hand as all crime scenes are never the same.

THE CRIME SCENE

What Is a Crime Scene?

A crime scene can be defined as any place or location where a crime has been committed. A crime scene is any building occupied or unoccupied; any person who may be a victim, suspect, or even a witness; or any form of transportation whether motor vehicle or skateboard and any area of land or body of water. Each incident under investigation will normally have a minimum of at least two crime scenes – the victim or venue and the offender. Based on the Locard Exchange Principle, "Every contact leaves a trace" evidence can be transferred between victim and suspect, victim and crime scene, and suspect and crime scene. Crime scenes can be primary or secondary. The primary crime scene is the exact location where the crime has been committed and the secondary crime is the location or space that is directly related to crime but not the exact location where the crime was committed.

As Williams' recognition principle states, "A good eye don't miss anything," the ability to recognize forensic evidence with probative value on the crime scene is very important in crime scene management and investigation. As the Locard exchange principle states that "every contact leaves a trace," however, to recognize that trace the investigators and forensic officers must have a good eye to be able to see and identify physical evidence and be able to distinguish between relevant and non-relevant items of evidence than can add value to the investigation at hand and for the successful processing of the scene with a good eye for details brings a successful investigation.

What Is Crime Scene Management?

Crime scene management is the accountability and supervision of evidence that may be found at the scene of a crime and the application of the techniques used for the recovery and collection of that evidence. Crime scene management requires a senior investigator be delegated to coordinate a major crime scene whereas in a minor scene a junior investigator can be given the task to coordinate the scene. Once a crime is committed, a crime scene manager is appointed to manage the proceedings

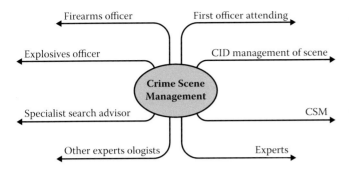

FIGURE 1.2 Showing crime scene management structure.

and must be knowledgeable in both forensic investigation and crime scene investigation. In crime scene investigations, the coordination and control of the criminal investigation combined with the forensic investigation are very important stages in the criminal investigation process. In investigations, we either have individuals or the evidentiary items. A crime scene investigation team consists of police officers, first responding officers, detectives, crime scene investigators, medical examiners, and specialists or experts, as seen in Figure 1.2.

In crime scene management, there are several key components that must be taken into consideration:

a. Information and communication management
b. Manpower management
c. Technology management, and
d. Management of logistics.

These key management components are mainly based on the ongoing communication skills of the persons receiving and passing on the information.

Information Management

When information is received about a crime, the relaying of information is very important. That information can be passed on using different means of communication equipment as technology is developed at a rapid rate. The management of that information is very vital to the outcome of the investigation. The information received from the first responding officer allows the crime scene manager and their team to set out a plan in responding to the scene where the crime took place. That information helps to prepare necessary equipment and set the stage for the investigation. The crime scene itself provides valuable information that can link an assailant to a crime scene, can confirm or refute a witness alibi, and can develop leads that can build and strengthen the investigations. This information can be in different forms: oral, written reports or statements, documents, pattern evidence (present or missing), or physical evidence located on the scene. The faster the information can be acquired, identified, or recognized, collected, stored, preserved, and

distributed can increase the solvability rate of the crime. So that information must also be used properly.

Different information, when managed properly, can improve crime solving; it can help to identify the victim and suspect, carry out background checks, help to trace and inquire about victim and suspect whereabouts, and their belongings during and after the crime. Obtaining information before the crime occurs for e.g. 24 hours before the crime or a week before the crime, can establish an information database to provide intelligence to aid in investigation and be preserved for later use in court.

Upon receiving the information, one must be able to communicate it properly to avoid flaws within the investigation. The wrong communication can ruin the investigation and can cause injuries to investigators and officers.

Manpower Management

In crime scene management, manpower is very important. It is the organization or institution that you are attached to or work for that is responsible for manpower. The head of the crime scene department or forensic unit makes his or her request for the personnel needed to carry out investigative needs of the organization. It takes team effort to carry out the investigation and processing of the crime scene. So, if the crime scene team is not staffed properly, it can create or cause an adverse effect on the crime scene processing time, the evidence collection, and the management process as a whole. The crime scene manager will have a difficult time managing the personnel on scene; he/she must ensure all staff is properly trained. Untrained or improperly trained staff lacking experience and knowledge can create overload or overworked personnel who will not be able to adequately carry out the professional work and maintain the daily working hours.

Manpower planning consists of putting the right number of crime scene investigators (CSIs), the right kind of CSI at the right place, right time, doing the right duties for which they are best suited to achievement of goals of the department, unit, and organization on a whole. Manpower planning has an important place in the management of the crime scene investigation. Manpower planning needs to be a team approach and is carried out in a set procedure. The procedure is as follows: analyzing the current manpower portfolio, making future manpower projections, developing investigative skills and programs, and implementing and designing training programs.

Technology Management

In managing a crime scene, the information received must be managed properly with the increase in technology. As technology improves, state-of-the-art equipment is developed, which will also aid in the proper processing of the crime scene and the proper handling and sharing of information. The crime situation in every country should be properly assessed that will allow the heads of department or officers in charge to properly allocate resources for purchasing and upgrading relevant equipment necessary for serious and minor crime processing by the crime scene team or forensic unit. Relevant training must be made available for the CSI teams/units in the use and understanding of the new technology and new equipment. Technology can help to solve many crimes and must be managed carefully.

Equipment Can Be in Different Categories

Crime scene vehicles: specially designed for crime scene and forensic investigations.

Two-way radio communication: cell phones, computer, and tablet via Internet connection.

Forensic light sources, metal detectors: used for searching.

Crime scene kits: latent print kits, trajectory reconstruction rods and accessories, casting kits for tool marks and footwear impressions.

Chemicals reagents: blood print enhancement reagent, latent print developers, etc.

Portable instrumentation: night vision equipment, portable laser, radar, etc.

Evidence packaging materials and related forms.

Management of Logistics

Logistics issues ought to be appropriately managed through good organizing and efficient allotment of resources. In crime scene management, logistics are the activities carried out by the different forensic companies or agencies for the physical distribution of forensic equipment or supplies. This equipment must be transported from the distributors and suppliers and finally to the purchaser who is the organization or police forces which will then be distributed to the crime scene, forensic, or investigative unit who will be the end user. When looking at logistics, a wider view must be taken because it does not just cover transportation. In crime scene management, there's different activities which are done daily. Different organizations have varied logistical activities that may be established early in the investigation. When equipment is received it must be appropriately logged and inventory must be kept and recorded for accountability. The crime scene manager or officer in charge must also make sure that crime scene or forensic supplies are handled properly and professionally in the appropriate manner and the conditions in which they were delivered must be recorded and the equipment returned to dealers, etc. must be logged and recorded so it is accounted for.

In the management of logistics, these functions should be considered.

Order Processing for a Crime Scene

In some police forces or agencies, the logistic activities start from the procurement and order processing that may be the work of the crime scene department, storeroom keeper, or the procurement department which your organization has in place.

Crime Scene Equipment Handling

Equipment and evidence handling is the movement of the crime scene tools and evidentiary materials within the department. It involves handling the equipment in such a way that the department or unit can access items easily and efficiently in time of response and ordering of new equipment.

Storage of Equipment and Exhibits

Storage plays a very important role in logistics within the crime scene or forensic department. Storage of equipment for proper forensic use on scene and storage of exhibits for proper preservation for use in court is important.

Inventory Control

The crime scene department manager must know the amount of material or equipment at hand and must pay attention to the volume of crime in order to make the right purchase of materials needed to avoid over- or under-purchasing. This in turn will save the organization and the crime scene or forensic department unnecessary spending.

Transportation

Transportation is one of the major logistic activities that is one of the heaviest revenue segments of the department of logistics. It can be costly in relation to fuel and is highly used up in different crime scene activities, so proper control and management of the crime scene transportation system is very important.

Packaging

The packaging of equipment and exhibits is very important. Equipment and exhibits must be packaged properly to prevent damage during movement from one scene to the next, which will avoid breakage and contamination.

Who Is a Crime Scene Manager?

A *crime scene manager* is a term given to a senior crime scene investigator who manages the entire crime scene and conducts the plans necessary for the successful processing of the crime scene. He or she also leads a team of crime scene investigators (CSIs) and specialist forensic investigators who will conduct or carry out the roles necessary to conduct the scene investigation and helps with the management of the crime scene and criminal investigations. The crime scene manager's team must be competent and highly skilled.

Planning and Preparation

Pre-scene attendance responsibilities: a crime scene manager's responsibilities start from the call that is received from the first responding officer informing the crime scene team or the crime scene manager about a crime. In response to the alert, the crime scene manager organizes the crime scene team, first briefing for the successful management and processing of the scene. The manager is also responsible for supervising the preparation and collection of equipment and materials needed to process the crime scene.

Crime scene processing Protocol

The Interview

The interview of the first responding officer is the first process of the crime scene processing protocol. The crime scene manager will effect the crime scene protocol. That protocol should be used at all crime scenes no matter the size of the scene. Applying the crime scene protocol will assist the crime scene manager to control the scene and effectively delegate duties to their CSI team. There are different types of crime scenes e.g. house break-ins, burglaries, and homicides that can contain multiple scenes. The crime scene manager or the crime scene investigator will conduct an interview with the first responding officer or officers who arrived on the scene and secured the scene. If a victim is present, he/she will be interviewed to assist the investigating team with a plausible theory of the events of the case, what transpired, what crime took place, and how it was perpetrated. Information given may not always be true but will create a platform or give the investigative team a base to start the processing of the scene. The CSI will also dialogue with the FRO to get a clear assessment of what he/she did on the scene, what actions the FRO may have taken to prevent onlookers from entering the scene, the route the FRO took to enter and exit the scene, and if anything was moved or how many scenes may be involved. As the interview is completed, the crime scene manager will then carry out scene assessment and conduct the walk-through.

Scene Assessment

The crime scene and its surroundings must be properly assessed not only by the first responding officer but by the crime scene manager and the CSI team. This allows the crime scene team to develop a plan for the coordinated recognition, identification, collection, and preservation of physical evidence and identification of witnesses. It also allows for the exchange of information among law enforcement personnel and the development of investigative strategies. Scenes of Crime Officers must initially assess the scene to ascertain the major features, any cadaver (deceased person), weapon, implement, footprint, shoe print, fingerprint etc. Consideration must also be given to the weather and lighting condition as this may affect the sequence of evidence collection. SOCO's or CSI's should wear protective clothing (ppe) to prevent and reduce contamination throughout their activities on the crime scene and for their personal welfare.

CRIME SCENE INITIAL WALK-THROUGH

At the crime scene, after the briefing with the first responding officer, the crime scene manager (CSM) and their team of CSIs will conduct a walk-through of the scene. The crime scene manager will decide who will do the walk-through of the scene, which may include the photographer, whose role is to photograph the scene during the initial walk-through, which helps to document and maintain the integrity of the scene. During the walk-through, the scene manager will make notes while observing the crime scene. The notes made will allow the crime scene manager to better coordinate and conduct a necessary plan for the proper documentation and collection of evidence. During the observation, the CSM will make their own notes, identifying key items and conditions of the scene that will later enable him/her to properly delegate duties to his team who will later process the crime scene. The CSM will also use information from the first responding officer who may have altered the scene in an emergency circumstance or during the arrival of emergency personnel who may render first aid to the victim present on scene and show signs of life. This information is important because the investigators may not arrive before or during the time of the medical intervention.

Another importance of the initial walk-through of the scene is for the investigators to identify physical evidence of value and get it first time (GIFT), other experts may be called in if necessary, for specialized processing of the forensic potentials at the scene.

ASSESSMENT AFTER WALK-THROUGH

After the walk-through of the crime scene, the crime scene manager or investigators will make the final assessment and to do this the manager should assess the need for additional personnel just in case of multiple scenes, multiple victims, numerous witnesses, or other circumstances. The forensic needs of the scene should be assessed by the crime scene manager or senior investigating officer and call in the forensic specialists to the scene for expertise and/or equipment in relation to the crime at hand. Detailed descriptive notes of the scene must be made in the process. Some of the specialists that may be called include a forensic pathologist, pathologist, or medical doctor to pronounce life extinct, and a forensic odontologist to provide dental examination of badly burnt, decomposed, or damaged body, body with no fingerprint or ridge detail for identification purposes. A forensic anthropologist will examine bones to determine gender and examine bones found in mass graves, a forensic entomologist will examine the insects to determine time and place of death, and a forensic firearm examiner will conduct firearm examination and collect firearms and spent shell casings from the crime scene. Upon completion, an action plan must be laid out.

ACTION PLAN

To process a crime scene, an effective action plan should be formulated. If the crime scene consists of both inside and outside scenes, processing of the crime scene should commence from the outside and progress to the inside. If the scene is outdoors and a body is present, the scene around the body should be processed first, leaving the body for last. If the body of a victim is present within the scene, it should be treated as a separate and complete entity. The body at a homicide scene can provide a great deal of evidence that may lead to the perpetrator and it can help to identify key evidence areas and help to establish point of entry and exits from scenes. These specific areas, sometimes referred to as the "ingress" and "egress" points, are extremely useful to the CSI or scene of crime officers (SOCO) because they are sometimes the only places where it is certain the offender has had definite contact.

CONTAMINATION ISSUES

In managing the crime scene, contamination issues are a big concern and it must be managed and controlled properly. To prevent and control contamination and cross contamination at single or multiple crime scenes, it is essential to maintain the safety of personnel and the integrity of evidence. The crime scene manager (CSM) in charge shall require all personnel to follow procedures to ensure scene safety and evidence integrity is always maintained. A secure area must be designated as secure for trash and equipment control and handling.

PERSONAL PROTECTIVE EQUIPMENT (PPE)

The CSM is also tasked with the responsibilities of making sure that the crime scene team is fully protected, and all clothing is right for processing the scene and the prevention of contamination from person to evidence, evidence to evidence, evidence to person, and person to person. Personal protective equipment (PPE) is used to prevent contamination of personnel and to minimize scene contamination, as seen in Figure 1.3.

PPE includes:

- Nitrile gloves
- Latex gloves
- Disposable biohazard suits
- Disposable shoe covers
- Dust mask/respirator
- Safety goggles
- Coverall

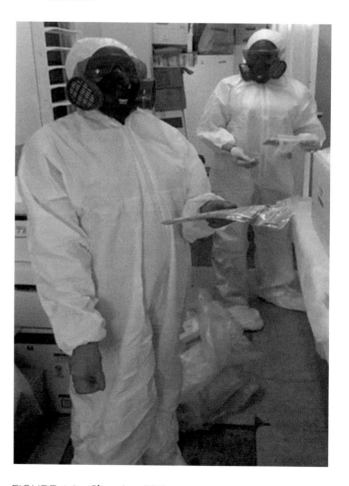

FIGURE 1.3   Showing PPE.

RISK ASSESSMENT

Risk assessment is a serious component in managing the crime scene. The CSIs, when processing the scene, must take into consideration the risk that is associated within the crime scene in relation to health and safety. A CSM must always ensure safe methods are devised to recover physical evidence in places that would pose risks to safety (e.g. footprint/shoe print, fingerprints on rooftops, ledges, tall poles at/near point of entry). Proper PPE must be worn to protect self and others from possible diseases that can be contracted when handling biological fluids.

Examine the Crime Scene

In the processing protocol, examining the scene is the second step. The scene should be examined to establish if the "theory" of the case is authenticated by what the CSI observes. The scene must be examined to identify possible items of evidentiary value, identify point of entry, and point of exit, and mainly to get a general layout of the crime scene in relation to the crime. The CSI, on examination, must assume control on the scene, evaluate initial scene boundaries, determine the number and size of scene(s), and prioritize which scene should take precedence and safety issues that may affect all personnel entering the scene(s) (e.g. blood-borne pathogens, hazards). A secure area should be established within proximity to the scene(s) for the purpose of consultation and equipment staging where a command post can be created.

Documenting the Crime Scene

Documenting a crime scene physical attributes before the collection of evidence provides vital information and gives a pictorial view of the investigations. When a crime scene is well documented, it strengthens the integrity of the scene and brings credence to the investigation, thereby creating a permanent record for later examination and forensic analysis. If a crime scene is not documented properly, it can disrupt the integrity of the scene and can negatively impact the keys areas of scene investigation and later forensic analysis. Some areas that can be affected are court proceedings, crime scene reconstruction, and forensic case review. In documentation, all pertinent information must be recorded before any removal, collection, recovery, alteration, and walk-through of the crime scene.

Documentation of the crime scene will include the following: notes, sketches/plans (not to scale), photography (color, high resolution, digital, or standard), video, metrology, computer modelling, or 3D scanning. The assessment of the scene will determine what documentation is best suited for a scene investigation.

NOTES

Notes are very important in the documenting of the scene, whether it is a serious or minor crime, and must be taken continuously throughout the scene investigation, starting from the first responding officer to the crime scene investigators as soon as possible after their arrival on the scene and just before the initial walk-through. Notes should start during the observational stage, noting whether it is an outside or inside scene. During the observational stage, the scene should be recorded as it appears at first sighting, with all aspects of the scene documented without attention made to potential evidence type. The overall notation of the scene should include time of arrival, lights on/off, curtains drawn/open, windows open/closed or if it is a building, heating on/off, appliances on/off, smells (odors), date, location, transient evidence, sounds, weather, and temperature. Notes must also be taken during the processing of the scene and when the processing is over and also documenting the handing-over process. Any distraction on the scene must be documented, the use of audio may also be used which can complement the notes which can be converted to text. In the Caribbean region, documenting of notes is done on different booklets or logbooks. A logbook is designed to record notes from the crime scene manager, crime scene investigator, and first responding officers. That logbook can later be used in the courts of law as an official documentation book.

SCENE PHOTOGRAPHY AND VIDEO

Photography is the third step in the crime scene processing protocol.

Crime scene photography plays an important role in crime scene investigation and helps to improve the documentation process. Even if a video camera is used on the scene, still photographs must always be taken. Also, if a video camera is not present on the scene, still photography becomes the number-one process of documentation. A crime scene must be photographed as seen with all items present, whether it is of value or not. This helps to give a true perspective of the scene as first seen by investigators. Digital still photography of the crime scene is used to illustrate the scene, its items, and the condition of both. Still photographs of victims and/or suspects should be taken to document their appearance and condition. Photographs are usually taken to provide overall, mid-range, and close-up images of the crime scene and any evidence identified on the scene. The scene must be photographed before any modifications occur. These modifications may include the placing of evidence markers, flags, scales, or tents. It is recommended that close-up images of evidence be taken with and without a scale.

When documenting pattern or impression evidence, specialized photographic techniques may be applied (e.g. tire tread marks, foot and footwear impressions, friction ridge skin, toolmarks impression, etc.).

Photographs taken at crime scenes are considered as exhibits and should be logged properly in a photo log (Table 1.1). That photographic log will be used for the courts and its integrity must be maintained and established from the crime scene to court; this is achieved by maintaining detailed photos of scene photographs to include a sequential listing of each image, time, location, or description of each image as well as any changes made to the scene to facilitate the taking of the photographs. The images obtained in photography should never be deleted from the camera or from any other media on which it may be stored. Media used for storage of images must be able to provide effective long-term storage of the original images. Working copies of the images must be made to facilitate enhancement and processing of the images while securing the integrity of the original images.

The following are recommendations that can be used when photographing a crime scene: The scene should always be photographed as you see it; the photograph should always be taken in the perspective as general to specific; photographs should always be taken in the order of overall view, mid-range view, followed by close-up view; and photographs should be linked.

VIDEOGRAPHY

Videography is an additional form of scene documentation that is used to note the crime scene, its contents, and the condition of the contents. Videography is a complement

TABLE 1.1   Showing Photographic Log

CRIME SCENE PHOTO LOG

Type of Crime: _____ _____Case Number:_____

Exhibit Number: _____

Location: _____

Agency:_____ Photographer:_____

Investigator(s): _____

Date:_____ Time:_____

Log maintained by:

No.	Description of Photographs	Date	Flash	Special Lighting, Tool, or Technique

Name... ....   Signature... ....

                                                               PAGE No... ... . of ... .

for photography and should not be used as a replacement for it. Videography begins before any changes occur on the crime scene, and it records the scene location, scene contents, and any item that is considered evidence. Videotaping should follow the same trend as photography, where it is taken in three different stages: overall view, mid-range view, and close-up view. It is recommended that the task of a videographer is assigned to one CSI whose sole responsibility is to plan and record continuous, synchronous, and methodical video of the crime scene. Original videos or files should not be edited or deleted, and a working copy can be created to facilitate editing or enhancement of images. Videos should be stored in a secure area and, when presented to court, must be properly submitted with a video log. If a secure digital (SD) card is used in a digital recorder, the same process must be followed in securing and protecting the exhibit.

SKETCHING THE CRIME SCENE

A sketch can be a diagram or bird's-eye view showing the relative position of objects or evidentiary items of interest at the scene. The sketch is the last stage in documenting the crime scene. Once the potential evidence is located and identified, the sketch or diagram can be made. The first sketch should be a rough sketch that is not drawn to scale and should be done freehand and can be used to locate evidence and objects within the scene. A rough sketch should be drawn for all serious and major crimes and must be legible enough for later use by the investigator who may later need to use the data to produce a drawn-to-scale sketch for court purposes. The main purpose of the sketch is to allow the crime scene investigator (CSI) to show the location of items in relation to other items of evidence on the scene. It can also assist the investigators and the courts. Visual aids complement photographs, videos, and notes, and help refresh your memory and enhance professionalism. A sketch must always show the direction of the north arrow at the top of page with a title set in block letters at the lower right of the page, showing a key or legend explaining numbers or letters in the sketch. The offense, address, date of sketch, case number, and by whom sketch made should be completed.

There are different types of sketches.

An **overview sketch** mainly comprises a bird's-eye-view or floor plan of the scene. This is the most common type of sketch and consists of items on the horizontal plane.

An **elevation sketch** portrays a vertical plane rather than a horizontal plane. Examples include bloodstain patterns on vertical surfaces such as walls and bullet holes through windows.

A **perspective sketch** depicts the scene or item of interest in three dimensions. It is the most difficult sketch to create and requires some artistic skill.

An **exploded view or cross-projection sketch** consists of a combination of the first two (overview and the elevation sketches). It is like a floor plan, except the walls have been laid out flat and objects on them have been shown in their relative positions; see Figure 1.4.

In crime scene documentation, sketching is the final task to be performed in documenting the crime scene. Obtaining and recording accurate measurements is a critical part of the crime scene sketching, as seen in Figure 1.5. No other forms of documentation record the scene with regards to actual size, measurements, and its physical evidence, whereas sketching the crime scene allocates units of measurements and puts evidentiary items and the entire scene into perspective and shows the relevance of the evidence within the scene. Sketching cannot be done without measurements. There are many different types of measurements that can be done to show the items in position on the scene. The common types of measurement utilized in crime scene sketching include the following:

Triangulation method: method by which an imaginary line is formed by measuring the distance between two fixed points and an item of evidence. It is the most versatile of the methods and can be used both inside and outside the scene.

Rectangular method: classes as the simplest method for indoor scenes and where there are four walls in a rectangular form used with right angle walls, e.g. north wall, south wall, west wall, and east wall.

Baseline method: measures from a spot on an established straight line and at 90-degree angle spots on two established spots on a stretch are used as reference points. This method is ideal for long buildings and roadways (Figure 1.6).

The global positioning system (**GPS**) settings can be used in outdoor scenes where there are no reference points creating or pinpointing a location where that incident occurred. If a crime took place at sea, GPS tracking or mapping will be the best method in locating where that crime occurred. It is a very important tool in forensic investigation and can be used to reconstruct a crime scene.

CRIME SCENE SEARCHING TECHNIQUES

A crime scene search is an integral part of crime scene investigation and the key to collection of physical evidence from the crime scene. A crime scene search is done to identify evidence before documentation begins and to highlight evidence that may be missed. Once the scene documentation is carried out, upon completion, a thorough search must be executed to assist in evidence location based on the type of scene encountered where

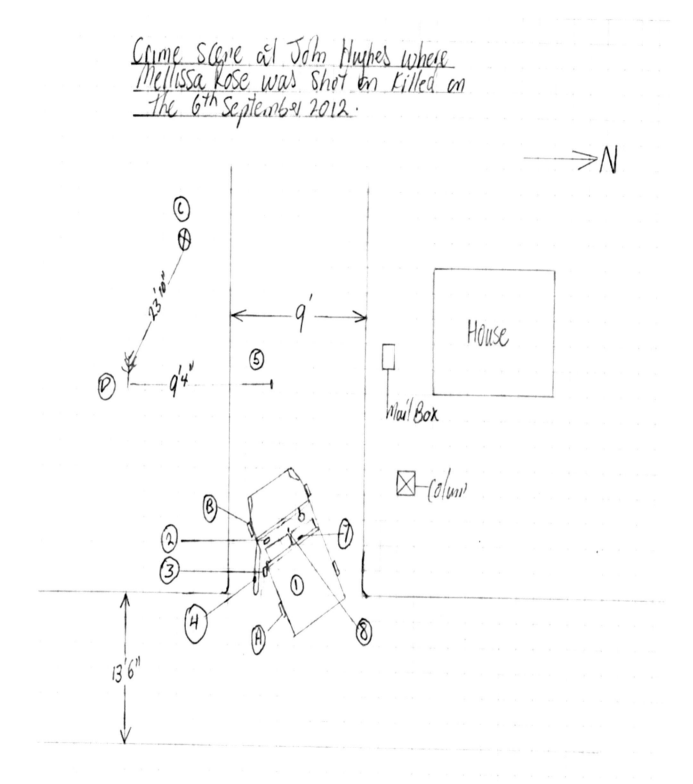

FIGURE 1.4 Rough sketch of crime scene.

the lesser or minute evidence may be overlooked. This search is done after the scene is documented and before the evidence is collected. After the scene is documented and the evidence collected, a further search may be necessary where the same documentation procedures as mentioned before will be carried out.

Crime scenes searches should be conducted in a systematic and organized manner. The main aim of a

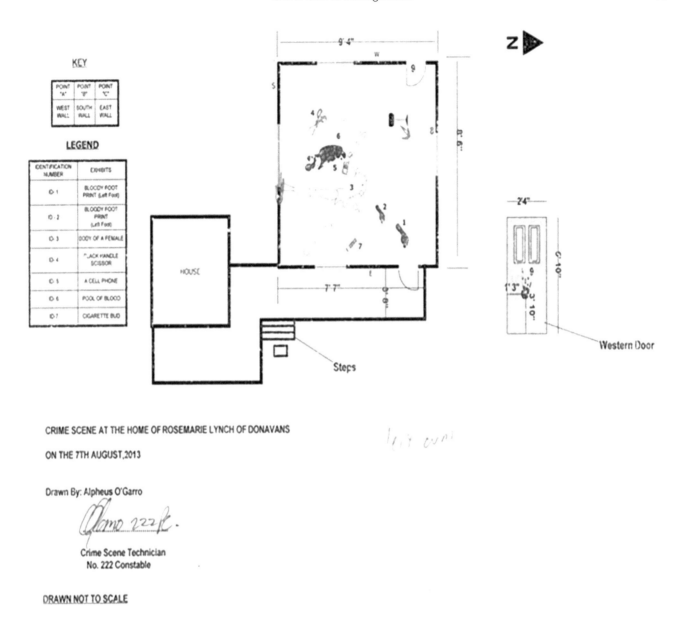

KEY

POINT "A"	POINT "B"	POINT "C"
WEST WALL	SOUTH WALL	EAST WALL

LEGEND

IDENTIFICATION NUMBER	EXHIBITS
O-1	BLOODY FOOT PRINT (Left Foot)
O-2	BLOODY FOOT PRINT (Left Foot)
O-3	BODY OF A FEMALE
O-4	"JACK HANDLE SCISSOR
O-5	A CELL PHONE
O-6	POOL OF BLOOD
O-7	CIGARETTE BUD

HOUSE

Steps

Western Door

CRIME SCENE AT THE HOME OF ROSEMARIE LYNCH OF DONAVANS

ON THE 7TH AUGUST,2013

Drawn By: Alpheus O'Garro

Crime Scene Technician
No. 222 Constable

DRAWN NOT TO SCALE

FIGURE 1.5 Finished sketch of crime scene.

search technique is to make sure that no evidence is missed or left behind as a result the investigators or the CSI must use the GIFT (get it first time) approach. In searching the crime scene, there is no single type of search method that is applied to a particular scene. The crime scene team or the crime scene technicians will apply or adapt the best search method based on the type of scene and the experience of the crime scene technicians or investigators. Without the proper experience and knowledge base on the search patterns, investigators can miss vital or key evidence types "as a good eye doesn't miss anything." While searching, if evidence is found, it should be flagged and noted.

In searching the crime scene, these major search methods are often used: spiral search, zone or quadrant search, grid search, strip or line search, and the wheel search. The searches mentioned have their advantages and disadvantages, as not all search patterns are suitable for inside and outside searches.

Figures 1.7, 1.8, 1.9, 1.10, and 1.11 are summaries of the different types of search patterns. A crime scene briefing is done with the search party that will conduct the search, informing them of what is expected during the search, with clear instructions. When an item of evidence is found, nothing should be touched, moved, or handled. When a piece of evidence is found, it should be signaled by the person finding it and bringing the search party to a stop. At this time, no evidence must be handled by anyone in the search party. The finder will utter the word "flag," where a flag will be placed next to the

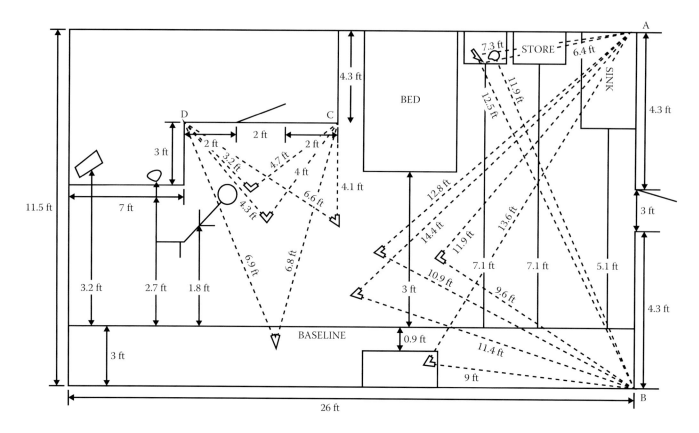

FIGURE 1.6   Rough sketch showing measurements of triangulation and baseline.

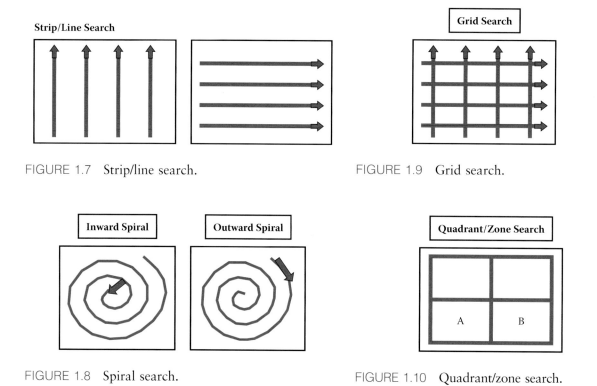

FIGURE 1.7   Strip/line search.

FIGURE 1.9   Grid search.

FIGURE 1.8   Spiral search.

FIGURE 1.10   Quadrant/zone search.

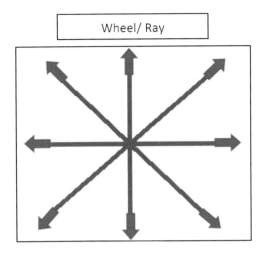

FIGURE 1.11 Wheel/ray search.

exhibit for continuation of the search and it is still done today, which will help in coordination of the search. Evidence that is found during the search will be documented before it is moved or collected. The area or scene must also be documented after the search and collection of evidence to show the before and after. The flagger of the evidence may not be the collector; as a result, the chain of custody will become effective.

Search methods or techniques require a hands-on approach that is highly practical and may involve all search methods. Different enhancement techniques may be used during the search, in cases where impression and biological evidence may be recovered. Crime scene procedures must always be followed when conducting the search. Also, searchers may be limited based on the type of scene to ease overcrowding and evidence damage and to protect and preserve evidence.

The **line search** is an appropriate search method for an open field or elongated areas like a ditch or a road. One or more searchers work shoulder to shoulder from one known point to another known point extending along a straight or nearly straight line.

Spiral search: inward and outward spiral is recommended with limited manpower and works well in the field and underwater. Start at the center and use a stick and rope.

Grid search: like the zone search, but is usually confined to a smaller area, for smaller objects, and anthropology.

Quadrant/zone search: often used to concentrate on a specific area. More than one group can conduct the search (e.g. one group can be searching "A," while another searching "B").

Wheel/ray search: starts from the center and movs outward and can be used on circular crime scenes.

The last step in the protocol is to process the crime scene. The CSIs or the crime scene technicians will process the crime scene for evidence, mainly for physical, trace, and testimonial evidence. It is the responsibility of the crime scene technicians to identify, evaluate, and collect physical evidence from the crime scene for further analysis by a forensic or crime laboratory. The main purpose is to try and link the perpetrator to the scene and the scene to the perpetrator. For this to happen, the integrity of the evidence must always be maintained in a systematic and secure way in collecting, packaging, storing, and transporting the physical evidence. In doing this, personal protection will take precedence. The amount of protection needed will be determined by the actual scene. The crime scene technicians should be fully dressed if body fluids are involved, or overcoat, gloves, masks, and possible shoe covers should be worn if required.

PPE plays a dual role. It both protects the crime scene investigators from airborne pathogens, dust, powder, chemicals, and the spread of possible diseases by carrying it on shoes, clothing, and gloves, etc. It can also be carried to cars, offices, the next scene, and home. PPE also protects the crime scene investigators from contaminating the scene (e.g. sweat, hair, fingerprints, footprints/shoe prints, on objects) or in the scene.

In crime scene processing, two phases are involved: non-destructive to destructive. Non-destructive includes photographing and collecting visible physical evidence, without having to add anything to the scene. Please note, constant documentation must be done throughout the processing stage of the crime scene.

PHYSICAL EVIDENCE

Physical evidence is any item or material that has evidential value, and that may be used to establish the nature of the offense or the identity of the perpetrator and which may be presented to the court for its physical assessment. Properly presented physical evidence may serve the same purpose as taking the court to the scene of the crime and reconstructing the events that led to the commission of the crime. A thorough understanding of physical evidence, its protection, preservation, and examination is important. All the items that are important in solving a crime would be impossible to list. Mostly anything on the crime scene can be physical evidence. Physical evidence can be twofold, or indoors and outdoors, so it's best to process the scene from the outside first, collecting all physical evidence and then moving to the inside and collecting physical evidence. This must be done by taking the environmental conditions into consideration (e.g. rain, snow, and heavy wind). All physical evidence must retain the number of the evidence marker it was highlighted and photographed with. This number must not be changed or altered at any time.

COLLECTING AND PACKAGING EVIDENCE

Fragile evidence is collected right after being photographed. Tape lifting, hand picking, and vacuums are used for trace evidence such as fiber, dirt, glass, and hair. Plaster or dental stone are used for footprints and tire tracks. Fingerprints, shell casings, firearms, body fluids, bite marks, and tool marks all have specific methods of removal. Evidence found at crime scenes can fall into seven major groups: weapons, blood, imprints or impressions, tool marks, dust and dirt traces, questioned documents, and miscellaneous trace or transfer (Weston and Lushbaugh, (2003).

Trace evidence is never removed from any object that is carrying it; the whole object is bagged. If two or more similar objects are found, they should go in separate bags, even though they are similar. Blood-stained material should be air-dried and placed in separate paper packaging that can breathe. They should then be stored in an area with good ventilation. Charred debris should be placed in an airtight container to prevent evaporation of petroleum residue. Guns/knives can be collected in gun boxes; spent casings in paper folds (numbered) or paper bags/envelopes; blood/suspicious fluids on sterile swabs (allow to air-dry then individually package in envelopes) stored in the exhibit fridge if not submitted to the laboratory the same day; shoe print (2D) should have detailed photographs and then lifts; shoe/tire impressions (3D) should have detailed photography and then cast with dental stone; tool marks (3D) should have a detailed photo and then cast with silicone materials; gunshot residue (GSR) should have sterile stubs or swab packaged in individual sterile containers and then envelopes. Evidence should be stored in the exhibit fridge if it cannot be submitted to the forensic laboratory the same day.

Obtaining control or "known" standards is important. When "unknown" samples or specimens are collected that are believed to belong to or have been transferred by the suspect, a "known" sample must be collected so forensics can determine if the "unknown" is different from the "known" specimen. With hair, samples are collected from the victim and other persons lawfully present at the time of the crime. This can be done at a hospital. With paint, "known" samples are collected from "known" surfaces. With blood, samples are collected from victims and other persons lawfully present at the time of the crime. This can be done at a hospital. With soil, "known" samples are taken from areas around the area in question that contain the "unknown" substance. With fingerprints, elimination fingerprints are collected from the victims and other persons who are lawfully in the area of the crime.

Once all known evidence has been collected and packaged, and all other information has been collected from the scene (photographs, diagrams, and notes), a decision must be made on maintaining the crime scene or terminating the crime scene. This decision will be based on an assessment by the lead investigator and crime scene manager after reviewing the evidence collected and estimating the likelihood of anything else of investigative value being present. If there is doubt, the police will maintain the perimeter with an officer present to ensure integrity. Once the decision has been made to release the crime scene, all equipment and reports are collected and finalized, and all evidence is transported to the evidence unit and/or crime lab.

REFERENCES

FBI Handbook of Forensic Science. *Collection, Identification and Shipping Index (with modifications)*. Washington, D.C.: Federal Bureau of Investigation, 1992.

Fisher, B. A. J. *Techniques of Crime Scene Investigation, 5th Edition*. Boca Raton, Florida: CRC Press Inc., 1993.

Saferstein, R. *Criminalistics: An Introduction to Forensic Science, 6th Edition*. Englewood Cliffs, N.J.: Prentice-Hall, 1998.

Weston, B. P., & Lushbaugh, C. (2003). *Criminal Investigation: Basic Perspectives*. Upper Saddle River, N.J.: Prentice Hall.

Weston B.P., & Lushbaugh, C. (2003). *Criminal Investigation: Basic Perspectives*, 9th ed. Upper Saddle River, N.J.: Prentice Hall.

CHAPTER 2

Crime Scene Reconstruction

Gonzalo G. Miguez Murillas

Scientific Police Division of Comodoro Rivadavia City, Argentina; Estudio Pericial GV, Argentina

CONTENTS

INTRODUCTION

Crime scene investigation involves a broad and complex set of activities focused on the study of physical space[1] where a criminal act has occurred, as well as all the elements contained therein, and especially the relationships between them. This space is known as a *crime scene* since its legal, police, and scientific investigative approach always begins on the premise that it has been committed by or it is directly the result of a criminal act in any of its phases (planning, execution, disposal, etc.). Its format is variable, as seen in the first chapter of this book ("Crime Scene Management," by Gregory Williams), accepting the traditional closed, open, mixed, movable, and underwater spaces until now, that the clothing and the corpse are crime scenes themselves. In all of them, its value to the criminal investigation is given by the richness of *indicia;*[2] it contains potential information that, through a scientific study, will make it possible to obtain *evidence* that together will provide reconstruction *pieces* of the incident, providing evidence to judicially define whether it was an accident, a homicide, a suicide, a natural death, etc.

The purposes of the investigation of the crime scene involve the detection and gathering of various indicia and the contextualized analysis of the results that the respective laboratories obtained from them, and thus establish the sequence of events prior to this incident, that concatenated in a logical way, explain how it happened, why, and who was involved. According to the different jurisdictions and criminal systems of each country, the intervening actors are the police force, the prosecution,

DOI: 10.4324/9781003129554-2

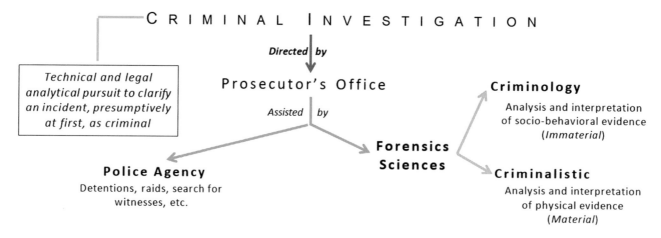

FIGURE 2.1   The main organizations involved in a criminal investigation in an adversarial criminal system, according to Fernández-Sánchez, (2009). The so-called forensic sciences are criminalistics and criminology, differentiated due to the type of indicium they analyze.

detectives, and the forensic experts (Fernández-Sánchez, 2009). (Figure 2.1)

We can infer that there will be a scientific analysis of each physical indicia detected at the crime scene, and a *meta-analysis* of the respective results, consisting of essential parts of a reverse analysis engineering: starting from a result (or effect), it is sought to establish its causes (what, where, when, and how it occurred) identifying each associated and binding factor (what and who participated), based on the marks, traces, and vestiges that according to their nature will be analyzed, as colleagues will describe, respectively in the chapters of this book.

This *backwards reasoning* – as it became known in detective adventure literature[3] – includes the reconstruction of the crime scene. The Association for the Reconstruction of the Crime Scene (ACSR) conceives the activity as the *"use of scientific methods, physical evidence, deductive and inductive reasoning, and their interrelationships"*[4] to understand the series of events that led to the committed of a crime. This analytical process combines observation, experimentation, and interpretation of all data collected by the application of scientific methods on physical objects, in order to describe the development of actions and circumstances of a particular incident.

EPISTEMOLOGICAL UBICATION: SCIENTIFIC NATURE OF CRIMINAL RECONSTRUCTION

Among different professions and even among different colleagues still persists a sort of debate about recognizing whether the criminal reconstruction is a science itself, a specialty of forensic sciences, a technique or a discipline.

From epistemology we observe that the so-called forensic sciences, in fact, comprise the conjugation of both

criminology and criminalistics sciences. Criminalistics falls within the factual-natural-applied sciences, while criminology falls within social factual sciences. This is clear from the nature of the elements they study: material/physical and *im*-material/behaviorist indicia. The first are characterized from the concept of matter from physics, as any body that occupies a place in space-time, which means sensitive and tangible elements, like a firearm, a fingerprint, a bloodstain, pollen particles, and so many, etc. The immaterial/behaviorist ones are perhaps more complicated to define since they are not exactly immaterial, because it expresses itself indeed in material elements, but they exceed them since they imply a socio-behavioral-emotional charge in their use, production, causality, and purpose. A particular view may emerge from those lines, departing from what is understood by criminology, especially in the Latin American legal field (García Pablos de Molina, 2003).

Let us think again about the firearm in a certain case, why a pistol was used and not a knife, even if both elements were present at the scene, why the money that still remains in the victim's pockets was not stolen and his ring was; that unnecessary attention to detail and the way to carry out a cutting injury in this specific anatomical portion after the death of the victim; that the victim is brunette with long and straight hair; that the sexual abuse is committed at a certain time and date, and so on. All of these circumstances point to questioning *why* the aggressor and the victim acted in a certain way and not another, a response that leads to analyzing the lifestyle, idiolect, culture, level of education, economy, profession, or occupation of the person. These whys can be answered by criminology, which has a systematized body of knowledge about deviant behavior, victims, aggressors, and social control, using forensic psychology, psychiatry, sociology, and anthropology.

In this way, and taking into account the definition of the ASCR, it comes off that the reconstruction of the crime scene is essentially a criminalistic reconstruction, as it will analyze the physical evidence, so the criminalistic professionals are the ones in charge to direct the studies, the planning, and the experiment's execution needed to accomplish it. Reconstructive analysis is also a holistic study of the indicia in context; that is, interrelated with themselves and with the scene, such is the holistic approach (Chisum & Turvey, 2013), which require that among all the criminalistics professionals – fingerprint, chemists, ballistics, arson experts, etc. – the *forensic generalist* will be the one who can direct the studies and applications of reconstructive techniques. Indeed, a single discipline cannot face reconstruction by itself, since each type of evidence must be linked to another and to the context; while a forensic generalist, being sufficiently trained in the knowledge of other disciplines, in their techniques and foundations to understand their scope and limitations, and then the reports that originate from such, related to each type of evidence, she/he is empowered to make this interpretation of evidence in context, and therefore, proceed to the criminalistic reconstruction of the case in hands.

Then, it is clear that this analytical integration of the evidence that constitutes the reconstruction of the crime scene is within the field of natural factual sciences, and one of them in special: criminalistics. The object of study lies in the physical indicia, in its analysis and interpretation, in order to provide relevant, objective, and well-founded information to the investigation of an incident assumed first like criminal or deviant, being the main goal the maximum *eureka*, rebuilding or *recognizing it* (Aldaraca-Ramírez, 2019). As forensic ballistics is a discipline that explains and provides information regarding the caliber, type of weapon, and trajectory of the projectile that hit the victim, the reconstruction of the crime scene is a discipline that explains and provides how those ballistic data are linked sequentially with the victim-perpetrator position, with the DNA found on the grip of the revolver, with the footprint, and the vehicle.

Indeed, though this criminalistics reconstruction is achieved through the application of the scientific method, peer reviewable, and implies a body of ordered knowledge shaped by theories and scientific principles, to achieve the *status* of science, yet it remains the construction of an empirical body of scientific principles and fulfillment ensures at least a quantifiable degree of certainty of the result – reconstruction – achieved.

This important limitation meets an interesting analogy with solving a puzzle game. Quoting an archaeologist named Stephen Dean, in an interview he gave about the archeology of which he says that "[...] *the most interesting part is the detective element. Archeology is like a jigsaw puzzle, except that you can't cheat and look at the box, and*

not all the pieces are there" (Marsh, 2013); and it could be added that many pieces are not only missing, but there are others belonging to another different puzzle game. This analogy is the one that best outlines the reconstructionist's duty of caution. And indeed, each item that one preserves, records, and collects at the crime scene does so based on the suspicion that it is related to it: getting evidence, an analysis may confirm – getting evidence – or not such link, and from the obtained meta-analysis of the entire body of evidence, only some of the event segments will emerge to be correlated and sequenced, without ever being able to access the entirety of the complete image and without any possibility of having a reference that verifies whether this analysis is giving close sequences to reality or not, the actions of this incident to be reconstructed are so dynamic that even having the fact videotaped it may not be completely understood (Bevel & Gardner, 2008). We will hardly have a case that we can fully clarify in all its dynamics through the interpretive analysis of the material evidence in context; it will be possible to complete a little more than another frame of the film integrating criminological techniques, but even so, scientifically, the challenge – and the demonstration – of looking backwards, totally reconstructing the mechanics of the events is highly improbable. The maximum that we can achieve, at best, is a certain probability, which will depend on the quantity and quality of the material evidence analyzed.

This impossibility of reference standard is not salvageable with the confession of the suspect either from the criminalistic point of view, nor even in the legal systems that use that kind of declaration in the criminal prosecution, since they constitute immaterial elements, testimonies, observations, and stories made from a perspective contaminated with individuality and subjectivity of the being itself, without offering the demonstration that is required to scientific conclusions; and this, regardless of the observations and questions that can be objected to the reasons for it (for example, covering someone up for money, honor, acquiring guilt due to psychological pathology, confusion, etc.). Similar objections remain to the statements of eyewitnesses, and though there are conflicting opinions among colleagues, the immaterial nature within do not allow it to be included in the subject matter of criminalistics; therefore, it shouldn't be used for crime scene reconstruction or any other discipline of criminalistics, since this science lacks any incumbency to analyze them under scientific rigor.

CRIMINALISTIC PRINCIPLES FOR RECONSTRUCTION

Everyday experience shows that any event or incident – including a crime or an accident – is caused in some way by physical agents who produce effects as a result of their actions on a spatial and temporal scene, as on the body of the victim and the aggressor or perpetrator. These results are known as *silent witnesses* in Latin American criminalistics literature, that Dr. Paul L. Kirk (1902–1970) identifies as those who do not forget and do not get confused with the excitement of the moment: the physical evidence cannot be wrong, cannot harm itself, and it is never totally absent (cited in Chisum & Turvey, 2013). These physical indicia are classified according to different criteria regarding to their nature, their connection, and their causality, but they all consist of elements that have been produced or are a result of the modification in the condition, position, or state of the elements already present at the crime scene and on the protagonists of the incident, and/or those elements that materialize on them. To mention some examples: a vase that falls and breaks on the floor during a fight produces material indicia consisting of glass fragments on the floor and on the clothes of the *criminal couple* (change in condition from a pre-existing element: intact to broken vase); that fight also produces a drop of a chair which then leans against the wall (change in the position of an element pre-existing at the scene: chair in normal position then leaned on the wall); a firing shot produces a projectile and remains deflagration (new elements on the scene and on the protagonists); in a fire, the heat melts the plastic insulation of a cable (change of state of the plastic: solid to fluid); and as many etcetera as the imagination can offer us and reality constantly shows us in each case we investigate.

This circumstance is what expresses the principles of criminalistics in general, and the crime scene reconstruction in particular, which synthesize the consequences of the interactions whose effects we must observe, record, and interpret for the purposes of association and indicia-linked with the causes that we seek to establish with the analysis: the identification of things (projectiles with weapons, fingerprints with people), the sequencing of events (first the wound, then the bleeding, then the footprint), and the degree of certainty that it is possible to reach in the conclusions of the analysis. The summary of these principles are listed below (Figures 2.2 and 2.3).

- *Principle of exchange*: attributed to the distinguished French professor; Dr. Edmond Locard (1877–1966) states that in the contact of two or more elements there is a reciprocal transfer of matter from one to the other (Guzmán, 2010). This forces us to search even the smallest detail because it could indicate the contact interaction with which elements involved in it, depending on the intensity of that interaction, in what way they were transferred,

FIGURE 2.2 *Principle of exchange:* This tire came into contact with the asphalt and, specifically, the double yellow divider line. In this violent interaction, there was a transfer of material from the black rubber to the asphalt, producing the mark we see; and some of the yellow paint was transferred to the tire. We can infer then a moment in the vehicle accident.

FIGURE 2.3 *Principle of correspondence of characteristics:* The front of the block, where the firing pin peeks out, has a grooved solid metal design. When the gunshot occurs, the gases generated by the combustion of the gunpowder propel back the fired case, punching the block, and in that sudden contact, a transfer is produced of those characteristic grooves. We can compare whether the same gun fired a set of fired cases by confronting those macro- and microscopic designs, especially on the primer.

which will allow linking them mutually (e.g. paint traces in a vehicular collision, fibers of a carpet adhered to the sole of a shoe, etc.). Likewise, criminological techniques have revealed the transfer of *psychological traces*, applying this principle also in the analysis of immaterial evidence, especially in victimology, as we will see later.

- *Principle of correspondence of characteristics*: it is also attributed to a French criminalistic, in this case to Pierre Fernand Ceccaldi (1917–2006). This principle indicates that from the interaction of two or more elements, there is a transmission of macro- and microscopic characteristics that reveal that interaction. Again, we see an attempt is being made to establish a link between the effect and the cause, and this determination will be more accurate as long as the cause-element possesses greater quantity and quality characteristics, and in a greater quantity and quality these characteristics are captured on the element where the effect is observed. At the same time, nothing prohibits within the same interaction that could be indicia produced and explained by this and the previous principle, it is actually difficult to occur in isolation; for example, a trace of footsteps on mud transmit designs and patterns of the shoe sole, but it can also leave adhesions that had the sole already, on the footprint, taking simultaneously geological material from the mud surface, complementing evidence for linkage between a certain footwear and the footprint. Considering the lines above, the more and the better the characteristics that the footprint presents, the better the certainty in the analytical link with the footwear can be obtained. In the same way, the *strial structure*[5] on the projectile forcing zone of its body link that projectile with the barrel of the weapon that fire it and, also, during this forcing passage there will also be material transfer, especially from the projectile to the barrel, leaving metal remnants from its own body or from its metal hedge.

- *Principle of phenomenon's and event's reconstruction*: completed monitoring and application of the principles above, which act as a guide in the testing and verification study of the isolated indicia, obtaining evidence, the criminalistic task can now be directed to the reconstructive stage. This principle postulates that from the analysis of the evidence in context may be found the dynamics of its relative production, certain actions, segments of events, and events that then could be sequenced. For example, we have a footprint bleeding at the foot of the couch, sitting trace and hair on the sofa, glass with latent partial palmar print revealed with *amido black*[6] and *cheiloscopic trace*.[7] This footwear, hair, palmprint, and lip print corresponded to the same person, and the blood, to

the victim, so it can be stated with high probability that this person is involved with the victim's injury, explaining that after injuring or murdering the victim, sat down and drank from the glass on the table in the living room. Note that a possible action is also to help the victim, and later sit down and drink from the glass, a hypothesis that must be corroborated with an intervention of criminology, since it will be the science that could examine the conduct that we cannot criminalisticly establish. For simplifying subsequent exemplification, allow us a *police suspicion* by assimilating that person as the aggressor.

Currently, and especially the appearance of sequencing of events, this principle has been broken down into the following three (Gardner & Bevel, 2009; Houck, 2013):

a. *Principle of lateral continuity*: the indicia is produced and deposited on the scene, the victim, and the aggressor without finishing abruptly, but with a development and ending according to their nature; and conversely, on the surface where it is produced or deposited, an alteration in the continuity of that surface will result. In this way, a concatenation of actions and events can be established by reading this continuity-interruption contrast, observing which elements presented a change through a certain action, and which did not suffer any alteration due to the absence of that same action. This principle allows the explanation of the *circumstantial voids*[8] (Figure 2.4). Following the previous example, the sitting trail on the sofa is an obvious disruption of the surface of its own.

b. *Principle of horizontal superposition*: closely related to the previous principle, indicia do not escape the temporal dimension, so their respective production and deposition on the scene, the victim, and the aggressor allow inferring a relative antiquity among them being the most recent, which needed less time to form, then indicating relative order. This is most evident when the elements are deposited one on top of the other: the top is the most recent, the last to be deposited. Following the previous example, the fact that the aggressor's palmprint on the cup and her/his footprint was found, both with the victim's blood, indicate an order: 1) the victim bled, 2) the aggressor stepped on the blood – touched the body, 3) the aggressor stood at the foot of the sofa – sat down – touched the glass cup. Note the dashes that

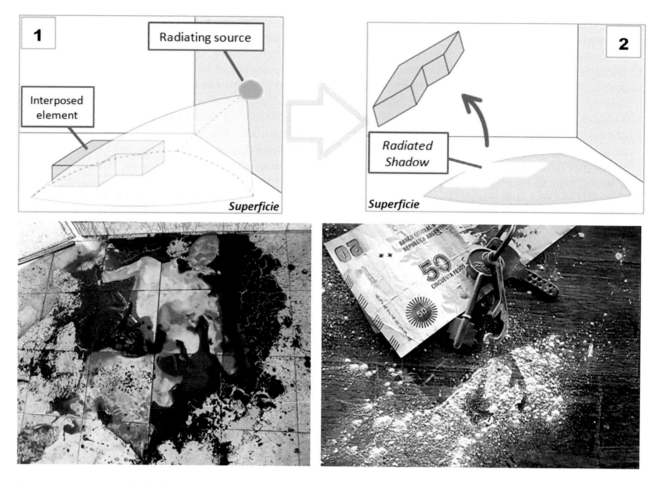

FIGURE 2.4 *Radiated shadow's mechanism:* When an element gets in the way of a fluid or energy or solid particles irradiated from a source, masks with its body, a part the surface. Removing that element will discover its own shape by a lateral discontinue of the surface's texture, color, state, chemistry, or physical proprieties; in other words, its specific characteristic, lateral continuity, and manifesting the pre-existing element when the radiation occurred. This is very valuable in criminalistics, especially when with blood, heat, or dust. This general indicium is called by the author of this chapter, a radiated shadow.

indicate not being able to specifically establish the order of actions based on these evidences, as well as the conciseness of the assertions that can be scientifically proven, far from a fictional story.

c. *Principle of chronology*: refers to the characterization of time in absolute assumptions (exact date and time) against a relative assumption, that is, in relation to another element. The problem of time in criminalistics includes many related forensic sciences (documentology, forensic medicine, ballistics, forensic chemistry, and so on), and relative time is the most preferred, concluding in a dimension of antiquity of one element linked to the antiquity of another. For example, impact A was subsequent to impact B, the handwritten line settled before the mechanical writing. We don't address the exact time or date, just which element was produced first.

- *Principle of probability*: from the point of view of epistemology it is not humanly possible for us to obtain an assertion with absolute truth, for which scientifically we can only obtain truths with a certain approximation to this ideal, through a level of confidence and certainty based on empirical verification, experience, and casuistry. However, it is in the probability discard where the result could be considered as absolute, for example, in a correspondence of height make it to *probably* to be the same person; the disimilarity of the fingerprint pattern discards it absolutely. This principle invokes caution in the conclusions, in reconstruction analysis, it recalls that given the dynamism of the factors involved as we reported in the preceding paragraphs, the scientific validity is to conclude in assertions of relative likelihood, being low, medium, or highly probable certain sequence. In the same way, we cannot quantify this probability, but we can rather describe based on the test, what is proven by physical evidence: the footprint was produced in high probability after the victim's bleeding, since it is made up of a transfer-type bloodstain pattern whose DNA is from the victim (the nature together with the DNA of the footprint proves this conclusion), and it is a probability, because it is still possible, based on this mere presentation of data, that a person made contact with a shoe in the blood and then placed it on the floor, as a print (Figures 2.5 and 2.6).

These are the criminalistic principles that most of the authors agree on, including those who postulate the existence of nine or even ten, and even calling them criminalistic *laws*. Without going into an epistemological discussion – for which a recommended study of the deconstructions of the work of recent new edition (Ramírez-Aldaraca, 2019) – we tried to describe those principles that serve as practical utility for the purposes of criminalistic reconstruction, as it is known in Latin American bibliography (Montiel-Sosa, J., 2010; Bertone & Fenoll, 2012; Nuñez, 2016), which is kept in tenors on the international bibliography (Inman & Rudin, 2000; Gardner & Bevel, 2009; Houck, 2013).

To achieve the solution of a certain problem, a scientist elaborates a hypothesis and develops a series of previously organized and planned steps to test it,

FIGURE 2.5 *Principle of horizontal superposition:* We can see very easily a bloodied palmprint, probably from the right hand on a wall. Although the photograph is not ideal, we can infer through this principle something that may be very obvious: there was a bleed previous to a hand that touched that bleeding. In this particular case, the victim doesn't have blood on his hands, so with identification by papiloscopy we might get the identity's aggressor!

carrying out checks and experiments, recording their results and then interpreting them, to finally draw well-founded conclusions about that hypothesis, and then submit their work to discussion and review with the rest

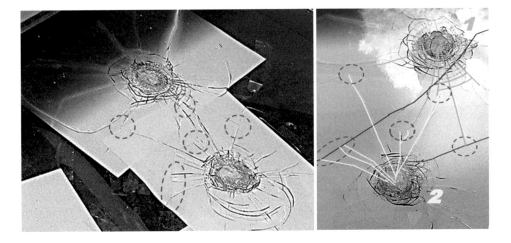

FIGURE 2.6 *Principle of chronology:* When we say relative age, we mean that the temporal reference of an element is the event of another element that shares a proximity in temporal space. The closer both elements interact, the easier it will be to set the relative age. In the image, we see an order of bullet impacts in the car's windshield: the interruptions of any of its fractures (radiant or concentric) with the fracture of the other impact indicates that the impact with uninterrupted fractures occurred before the other one.

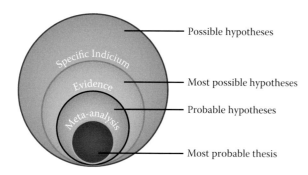

Possible hypotheses

Most possible hypotheses

Probable hypotheses

Most probable thesis

FIGURE 2.7 The evolution of the crime scene reconstruction or criminalistics reconstruction hypothesis starts with a set of ideas that requires a very open mind and holistic view as possible: that ideas are the first set of possible hypotheses. When you get into the crime scene, the physical indicium eliminates some of those and offer more support to other ones. Getting the results from the different forensics laboratories, the physical evidence now proves some of that most possible hypothesis and transformed it to probable. In this part, some prosecutor offices tend to leave and try to offer a reconstruction by themselves (like a person who tries to perform surgery on him/herself without being a surgeon). Finally, the most probable thesis resides in this still large group of probable hypotheses, and only when analyzing in context and the relationships between all this, evidence emerges events and its sequence: the most probable thesis of the criminalistic reconstruction.

of the colleagues in the scientific community. These lines briefly describe the scientific method. In the case of criminal investigation, forensic analyses such as criminal reconstruction, to be scientifically valid, will also require the application of the scientific method, involving a series of systematized steps specifically designed for reconstruction.

SYSTEMATIC METHODOLOGY

That is to say, systematic methodology is the recipe of the ordered steps whose fulfillment guarantees a reliable result. Scientific knowledge is nurtured and enlarged through the application of the scientific method, which synthetically consists of the recognition of a problem, the formulation of an idea to resolve it (hypothesis), and the experimentation that contrasts it. In criminalistic problems, the general method is the same; it is the scientific method, but different procedures and techniques are presented according to the nature of the criminalistic problem in question: ballistic problems – method to link the serving case – weapon, to establish its aptitude and operation, to establish the caliber of the projectile and type of weapon that fires it, etc.; problems in papiloscopy[9]

– development or enhance techniques, methods of confrontation for their identification; documentological problems – techniques to establish the age of the writing, the identification of the signature, the technology on the printing machine, authenticity on paper money, etc., and so on. In all of these examples there is a single scientific method with procedures according to the element in hand to investigate.

And the importance and value of an ordered procedure-method not only consists of the uniformity of the scientific community to solve a certain problem, but also to supervise and control that the results obtained are not biased by the investigating subject, and the reached conclusion manifests the logically valid interpretation and reasoning from those results. That transparency is the characteristic that the different legal systems impose when regulating the admissibility and evaluation of expert forensic opinions, again in the search of being able to verify that objectivity, that the conclusions are the product of logical derivation from the results obtained, and that these are data objectively obtained, without intervention of the will of the operator, but of the procedure only.

So, considering the need of verification, demanded by science, and visibilization[10] by the judicial system, the criminalistic reconstruction will require a structured procedure or method consisting of a series of sequential steps that respect the inherent execution of the technical inspection at the crime scene, that apply reverse engineering for inference the causes from effects, and be aligned with the chronology of the indicia obtained and evidence produced. Certain hypotheses of how the incident occurred will be discarded at each analytical step, approaching the final conclusion of the sequence of events.

With this figure in mind, imagine as an example the approach to an incident of a violent death (Figure 2.7). The possible hypotheses of etiology are relatively few, just three: homicide, suicide, accident; adding that natural death may still be feasible. However, within each etiology, assumptions of how this death happened are infinite – by gun fire, stabbed, poisoning, etc. – producing a huge variety of hypotheses, all *possible*. The arrival at the crime scene of the incident is when these hypotheses are filtered by the presence of specific indicia – expelled shells and victim with injuries compatible with firearm projectiles, eliminates the hypotheses of death by knife injury, and then a shooting involved emerges as *hypotheses are more possible*. When these indicia are studied at the laboratory and their respective analyzes begin to offer results, a new sieve is produced that leads us to another, though large, set of *probable hypotheses* (proven by evidence). With a meta-analysis of this evidence there will be obtained a smaller group, in which the *most probable* are found. In this last group, and through the last steps of this method, will be found the thesis or explanation that, linking all the interpretations and technical checks of the material evidence, explains a flow of events that describe how the investigated incident occurred: the scientific explanation that best adapts to the information extracted by each evidence for each indicia interrelation, that is, the intended reconstruction.

Now, in the criminalistic literature, a gap has been observed in this regard, especially in the Latin American bibliography. An attempt to approach the presentation of a pragmatic method for criminalistic reconstruction so pointed out by Snyder (1977), is by the author of this chapter (Miguez-Murillas, 2016), which presents within the essence that Prueger (2018) recovers from the natural sciences as *meta-analysis*, and which could be integrated into the case management of Graff (2016) and in the *revolver system* of Nuñez (2017). On the other hand, and for almost a decade, Bevel and Gardner (2008 and 2009) presented their *analysis of events* for the crime scene reconstruction[11] and in recent years Gardner synthesizes the basis of the reconstructive analysis under his *qualitative theory* formed by *12 axioms* (Gardner, 2016). All the aforementioned authors agree with regard to the factual limitation regarding the scope of the reconstruction, according to the aforementioned analogy with archaeological work and which is a direct function of the quantity and quality of evidence to be analyzed, a circumstance that recently reached a logical expression in the structural formulation under *Aldaraca's Law* (Ramírez-Aldaraca, 2019).

As mentioned, this pragmatic methodology described below, makes the entire process of reconstructive analysis transparent while guiding the analyst in this process, allows the supervision of another colleague in its development, and allows an orderly presentation of the findings and the reasoning to arrive at reconstruction. The systematic methodology presented below allows achieving these objectives, and includes the steps seen in Figure 2.8.

It can be seen that the proposed methodology also follows a development based on the great criminalistic aphorism that reads *from general to particular*, which, as mentioned, is commonly applied in photographic records and the inspection technique at the crime scene. Indeed, the reconstructive analysis begins with the most general elements, which locate in time and space the context of the entire incident to be reconstructed, such as the police inspection records and their graphic records. From there, each particular indicia will be analyzed by the respective forensic expert, and then the reconstruction will examine how each evidence that was obtained interacts into that context, starting with the most relevant evidence of criminalistic and legal value in cases of violent death – such as the corpse – and then proceeding with the analysis of the rest of the indicia that was collected in the different crime scenes (primary scene, in the house of a suspect, the victim's home, etc.). Subsequently and gradually, these indicia will be correlated next to the scene by applying the corresponding *interpretive techniques* (Nuñez, 2017) that correspond according to the nature of the evidence present in the case.

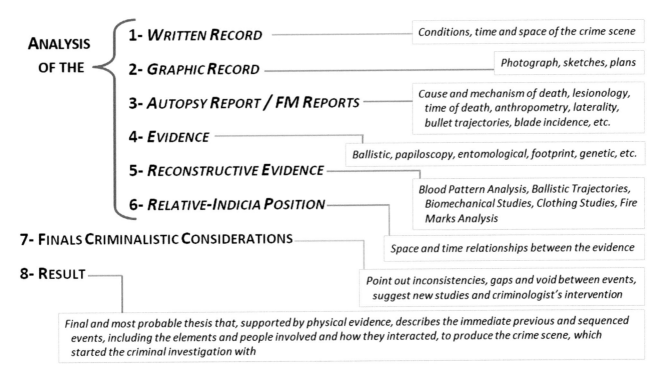

FIGURE 2.8 Graphical synthesis of the methodology as described (Miguez-Murillas, 2016).

Let's develop the steps of this methodology:

Analysis of the Written Record: these are generally the first documents available at any criminal investigation kick-off, drawn up by the first responders – belonging to the police forces – and by the expert agency that coordinates the management of the crime scene. The first ones, the acts performed by police intervention, fire department, and/or emergencies services, should have the details of the exact place of intervention, with date and time of the receiving of the call, and arrival date-time, equipment used, the record of environmental conditions, preservation measures adopted, as well as the assistance provided to forensic technicians, tours of the technical inspection, manner and time of detection, and collection of each indicia. At the forensic agency, a coordinator elaborates and notifies a report, which describes in detail the date, time and place of arrival, the inspection route, the marking and registration of the indicia collected, as well as the techniques applied for their respective survey.

In the consciousness of the goal of the criminal investigation and especially criminalistics reconstruction, it is convenient that this report has the respective potential information to each indicia collected and its subsequent forensic study suggested in order to potentiate the maximum criminalistic exploitation of it (Figure 2.9).

Following the above, here is the moment when the first filter happens, of possible hypotheses into more possible ones.

Analysis of the Graphic Record: the freehand sketch and the plan based on it, reproduced at a convenient scale, describing the location, situation, and direction of the indicia surveyed with geopositional reference at crime scene. It is highly recommended the performance of general, particular, and detailed plans, both in flat view and in perspective as required or demanded by each case. In the same way, the photographs taken must be described individually in terms of what they record and in terms of their shooting condition (type of lens, filter, and location on the scene), following the same general-detail guidelines, adding the record of *curious;*[12] the types of photographs must be and presented as a route, marking an arrival sequence, being satellite, panoramic, general, approximated, indicia-linked, and in detail or metrics views.

It is extremely useful for reconstructive purposes, both for the analyst and for the client, to have the assembly of graphics composed with the plane and detailed photographs of each indicium detected. It will be very convenient for the sixth step of this analysis (Figure 2.10).

From this point each data and relevant information obtained will be correlated and linked with the data obtained to immediately preceding analytical step, with the scene and the victim and or perpetrator. Let's see an example, in the next step.

Analysis of the Autopsy Report/ML Reports: As we mentioned, the main and fundamental evidence in any legal-criminal investigation of violent death is the corpse of the person who is the victim of the incident. This report, as well as everything that has to be seen on material evidence, must keep the technical and legal aspects for its admissibility and forensic utility. In the particular case of the autopsy, it must be carried out in a *complete* way – which analyzes the corpse from head to feet, carrying out its external-cadaveric-traumatic-internal examinations, at all its *times,*[13] samples of any emerged indicia of interest,[14] correct documentation[15] of each finding, and then evaluating them correlatively with the radiological shots, histological, toxicological and anatomic-pathological studies, and in the context of the respective clinical history and environmental conditions of the crime scene – *methodical* – the studies should be in a detailed and orderly presentation, following accepted protocols – and duly *illustrated* – using 2D graphics and diagrams of the body with anatomically located, situated, and oriented findings, together with a photographic annex with general, close-up, relational, and detailed shots of each wound and finding. Let us remember that its objectives are to establish the *noxa* element or pathological condition – *cause* – that triggered the pathophysiological events that led to death – *mechanism* – and post-mortem interval (*IPM*); current acceptance that an opinion can only be issued regarding the etiology – *form* – only in cases where it is of interest and/or evident findings are observed, always aligned on subsequent correlative and holistic meta-analysis of evidence, which is, reconstruction. See that a broader task emerges for a forensic medical expert than the mere description of an injury (Echazu, 1973) (Figure 2.11).

As mentioned in the previous analysis, some consideration from the analysis of this step can and should begin to tie in with what was examined; for example, asking if there is a link between specific wounds to the probable causative element at the crime scene, evidenced by their typology, production mechanism, morphology, and relative location according to the body-scene position.

Here, the most possible hypotheses are filtered again in this sieve, beginning to coexist together with probable hypotheses (proven by the evidence that emerges in the autopsy).

Analysis of Evidence: This consists of a meta-analysis of the results obtained by specialized forensic colleagues, seeking to rescue their reconstructive aspects, continuing the search for the link with previous data – autopsy, scene graphics, etc. – but under a critic review with a falsifiability perspective in similar terms to what Turvey calls *equivocal forensic analysis* (Turvey, 2008).

Item Nº	Nature	Position on scene	Suggested forensics tests	Probable data within
1	(02) *Quilmes* beer cans	ICNº1 – Exterior of the house, at kitchen window level	Fingerprints and DNA	Probable victim's ID
2	Bloodstan swab	ICNº2 – Access door	DNA	Probable victim's ID
3	Bloodstain swab	ICNº3 – Edge of the counter, near to access door	DNA	Probable victim's ID
4	DNA touch swab	ICNº3 – Knife kitchen blister	DNA	Probable murderer's ID
5	Knife kitchen blíster	ICNº3 – Knife kitchen blister	If it corresponds to knife blade (ICNº10-3) and knife handgrip (ICNº5)	Reconstruction
6	Bloodstain swab	ICNº4 – On window, near to Access door	DNA	Probable victim's ID
7	Knife handgrip swab	ICNº5 – On living floor, between sofa and coffee table	DNA	Probable murderer's ID
8	Knife handgrip	ICNº5 – On living floor, between sofa and coffee table	If it corresponds to knife blade (ICNº10-3) and blíster knife (ICNº3)	Reconstruction
9	Manuscript note	ICNº6 – On dinner table	Fingerprints and documentology	It says: *"The one who tells it the one who participates in the story or story"*
10	Bloodstain swab	ICNº7 – East wall, next to the bathroom door frame	DNA	Probable victim's ID
11	Bloodstain swab	ICNº8 – Bathroom handwash	DNA	Probable victim's ID
12	Red fiber	ICNº9 – On mainroom door	Physical and chemical ID	Probable murderer's clothes
13	Bloodstain swab	ICNº10-1 – On mainroom south wall	DNA	Probable victim's ID
14	Bloodstain swab	ICNº10-2 – On mainroom south wall	DNA	Probable victim's ID
15	Knife kitchen blade	ICNº10-3 – On bed, west side, next to civtim corpse	If it corresponds to blíster knife (ICNº3) and knife handgrip (ICNº5)	Reconstruction
16	DNA tocuh swab	ICNº10-4 – Knife blade	DNA	Probable victim's ID or victim's partner
17	(02) cellphones: *LG* and *Samsung*	ICNº10-5 – On bedside table, west of mainroom	Cyber forensics	Motive, Schedule, persons involves. Reconstruction. Last 24hs of the victim
18	(01) Pair of sneakers *Topper*	Voluntary surrender of the victim's father	Footprints ID	Probable presence of victim's father on scene
19	(01) Subungual swabs	Of both hands of the victim	DNA	Probable victim's ID, no evidence of fighting
20	(01) Hammer	ICNº10-6 – Inside the last drawer of the closet	Fingerprints and DNA	Probable victim's or murderer's ID
21	Fingerprints traces (A, B and C)	ICNº1 (Inner side and above kitchen window), ICNº3 (knife blíster), ICNº4 (Livingroom window frame), ICNº6 (TV)	Fingerprints	Probable murderer's ID

Scientific Police Division
Comodoro Rivadavia City
Chubut, Argentina

FIGURE 2.9 This table is a very useful way to summarize and describe to prosecutors the work done at a crime scene about the indicia collected, with detail of the nature and quantity of items, exact place of recovery, the order in which forensic study was applied for maximal exploitation, and probable contributors for the criminal investigation. *ICN°* stands for *Indicium Card Number*.

In each analysis of the individual forensic results there will be a review of these as well as a link to where each one of them was initially collected, to later analyze the possible cause-and-effect relationship that will allow reconstruction. For example, .22LR caliber pistol fired from projectile 2 collected at the autopsy, caliber .22L or .22LR from the B-12 fired case – from the scene – John Doe contributor of the fingerprint A-3 – at the crime scene – and of the DNA in the bloodstain B-5, Nike shoe size X collected in house Z linked to footprint C-1 – crime

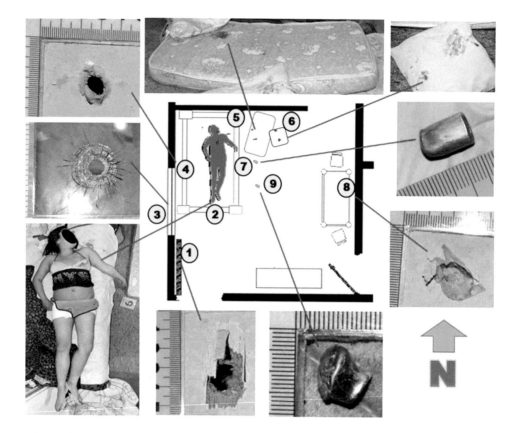

FIGURE 2.10 *Infographic:* The spatial relationships between all indicia collected at a crime scene is more clear if we took the photos and put them together on the crime scene's plane. It is very useful for the client and for the reconstruction process itself, especially for the sixth step of the methodology described.

scene – and to blunt footprint 5 on the victim corpse – autopsy – and so on.

We highly recommend reading the various chapters of this work, in which you will find the potential information within various biological and non-biological evidence, as well as adequate preservation, survey, and analysis by forensic experts in the respective forensic fields.

Culminating with the analysis of all the individual evidences, an update of the previous infographic, a new infographic containing this new information, along with its respective spatial and/or relational linkage between evidences, is convenient for illustrative purposes.

Analysis of Reconstructive Evidence: As stated, reconstruction pursues the search for causes based on the relationship of the evidence, since these consist of the effects of the cause. Most of the elements that are produced in and due to an incident present a hierarchical/ancestral, diffuse or direct link with the cause that produces them.

When the indicia may be caused by one series of achain cause-effect, that is, the cause is the effect of an earlier case, it is known as an ancestral/hierarchical link. This allows the linking of effects with actions that may not be clearly manifested at first. Generally this link is in the range of probabilities.

Linkage is diffuse when more than one cause can produce the same effect. For example, a positive result (MEB-DRX[16]) of gunshot residue (*GSR*) on the hand of a suspect could indicate that this hand fired a weapon or it was in those moments and close enough when a fire shot occurred, or because it manipulated a recently fired weapon. There is no direct link to the action of firing the weapon.

And it is direct link when the effect admits a single possible cause or of many, it is clearly manifested. An example might be the excoriation wounds of surrounding projectile inlet on the victim's corpse due to its location and position in the crime scene, is linked directly with slivers of wood by violent detachment by projectile impact, as we see in Figure 2.12. Another, perhaps more direct link is between a latent fingerprint and a digit (Figure 2.13), considering the pertinent studies to corroborate that it was chemically composed of sweat and did not present evidence of a planted or apocryphal trace.

Finally, there is some evidence that makes it possible to build such a structure of the incident that fixes the positions and possible sequences of the elements and participants in the incident pretty well, providing a lot of reconstructive information by themselves. Examples of

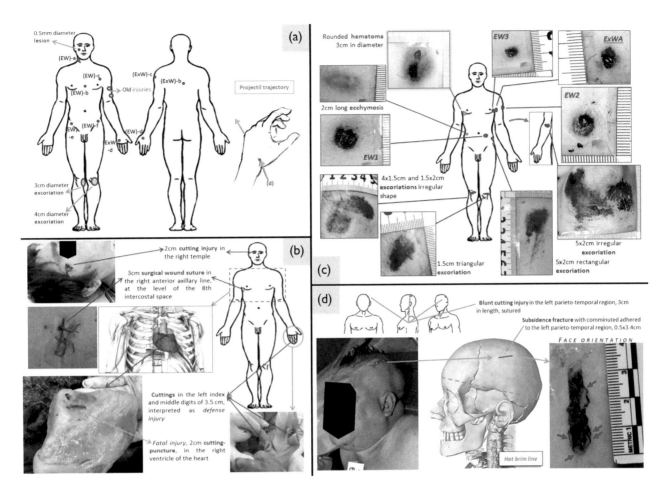

FIGURE 2.11 Four examples of adequate graphics of autopsy reports. (a) Simple 2D diagram of the human body with front and back views with drawings of wounds; (b) photos of lesions linked to the same drawings in the 2D scheme; (c) internal 3D scheme with photos of wounds added to the 2D scheme; and (d) photograph, 3D scheme and detail of the fatal blunt-force wound. The 2D scheme is always necessary and requires care and clarity to be understood and correctly interpreted, consistent with the entire report and attached photographs.

these are bloodstain patterns, ballistic trajectories, clothing, fire marks, biomechanical studies, car body deformation, as well as others whose reconstructive contribution requires other circumstances, like a bloody footprint. Note that individual studies of this evidence actually involve correlation analysis among other evidence (BPA requires wounds, chemistry, and crime scene data; for bullet trajectories, we need to know the weapons, ammunition type, and impacts measurements; in biomechanics, studies of the probable elements of potential injurious entity and of the wound type itself, and so on). Indeed, a bloodstain can exhibit a pattern that indicates how it was produced; a projectile trajectory will show a relative position between impact and shooter at a specific moment; the violence expressed in the clothing shows the type, form, and direction in which it occurred; the fire marks will indicate the location of the area of origin, where there was greater heat transfer and how the fire spread through the scene; the

deformation of the car structure can indicate the speed of the vehicle as well as its position at the moment of impact; video recordings allow reducing the victim's time of death, duration of the attack, if not all the mechanics itself, identification of the participants, the role adopted by each one of them, location and time of the incident, as well as developing ballistic acoustic studies to a set number of shots and shooter locations, etc. Consequently, we can hardly depart from a certain bloodstain pattern analysis (BPA) or a ballistic trajectory, since the characteristics of these determinations are that they can show an event segment or even an event, a specific and sequential cause-effect.

It follows, then, that all these evidence are extremely important due to their great reconstructive contribution, which is why they must be correctly detected and registered at the crime scene of the incident and in the respective laboratory for subsequent meta-analysis. Although some of them are described in the chapters of

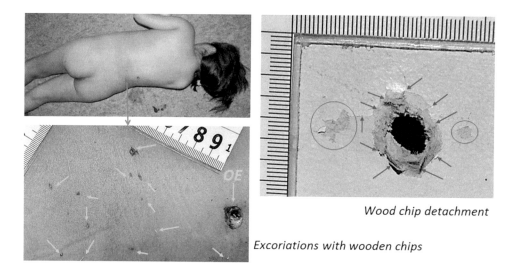

Wood chip detachment

Excoriations with wooden chips

FIGURE 2.12   Near the entry bullet wound, tiny abrasions and wooden chips at the victim's back are observed. At the crime scene, there is a bullet exit hole in a wall, 62 cm from the floor, near the middle part of the victim's bed, when she was found. That bullet hole presents wooden chips detached in same color as ones incrusted in the victim's back. With the bullet trajectory established at the autopsy, we can link with a high probability the victim's position lying down on the bed, sideways with her back near and against the wall when the fatal shot occurred.

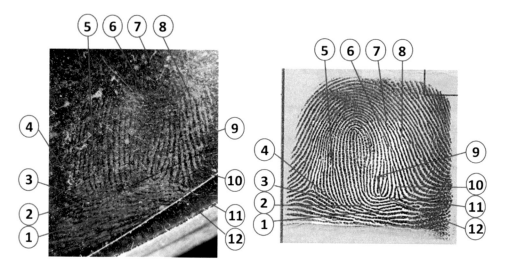

FIGURE 2.13   Positive identification between a fingerprint trace revealed and collected at a crime scene and a known print; example of an indicia with a direct link cause-effect. Notice the application of the numerical criteria in the papiloscopy ID method, used in most Latin American countries.

this work, it is considered advisable to give them a little more development, with the autopsy report, in the next section with a focus on their reconstructive contribution.

As a corollary to this stage, it is worth highlighting something curious that usually happens: the case *is assembling itself*. Indeed, as the data extracted from each analysis is being related with the previous one it seems that each frame of the film that we seek to reproduce is clearly forming itself, the image of the puzzle becomes increasingly clear. However, the work is not over yet, and

the following steps seek to verify that this *automatic assembly* has not been influenced by a cognitive bias. Actually, in this step what has been made is a preliminary of what will be one or more *event segments* (Gardner & Bevel, 2009): a segment of a bullet trajectory, two by BPA, another by biomechanics, etc. What follows is to see in what order or sequence these segments are related. And precisely, a sieve of hypotheses is formed that begins to delimit which of all the probable ones become stronger and more sustained by physical evidence.

Analysis of Indicia-Relative Position: This step shows the convenience of the infographics formed above, since it allows us to observe and examine the locations, orientations, directions, and movements of evidence, counting now with the information that each evidence individually offers and how they relate spatially and therefore begin analyzing how they are temporally associated (Miguez-Murillas, 2016).

Indeed, here the movement of the participating elements, the effects of their interaction, the concentration of the violence exerted, and the focus or intensity of the energy delivered begin to manifest when the linkages and inter-linkages are examined under logic and critical thinking (Figure 2.14).

The graphic support at this stage is convenient, since it allows us to order the frames that we have been able to establish, especially in the previous steps of analysis of reconstructive evidence, and based on them, begin to link the other evidence, analyzing whether or not there is

factual coherence to be placed before, during, or after one or another set of frames. It follows that this sequencing will be possible in proportion to the quantity and quality of available evidence, and it begins to assemble the temporal plan, applying the reconstructive principles of superposition, parallel continuity, and chronology described above.

A simple way to start drawing is transcribing assertions concluded in each step of each analysis of the respective evidence. Then, link each one according to the linkage analysis carried out, and finally order them according to their time or relative chronology with reference to the date and time most supported and proven by the evidence available (like a videotape, arrival at crime scene by the first respondent, the time of death, etc.). A similar illustration is what Gardner and Bevel call a *flow chart* (Gardner & Bevel, 2009).

Final Criminalistic Considerations: At this point, the description of the reconstruction – how the incident

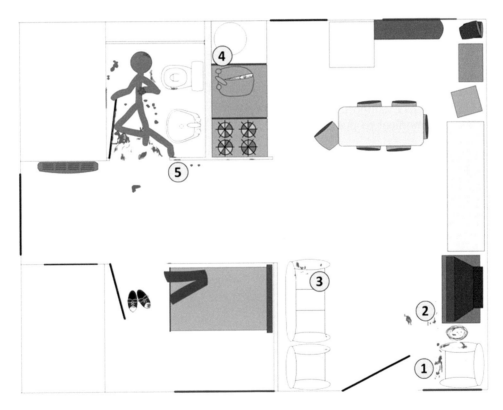

FIGURE 2.14 *Indicia-relative position*: the infographic made before can offer valuable information about the position of every indicia-evidence registered and collected at the crime scene. That value relies on a graphical crime scene registration for all criminal investigation's members, and the spatial relationships between the indicium-evidence that allow the time relationships, manifesting the reconstruction principles described for reconstructionists. In this example, knowing just that all the bloodstains are from the victim (DNA's evidence proved) and that he was stabbed to death, we can infer that all the violence starts in the bathroom or at the entrance hall, on the couch, and then the victim moving from one point to another with or without any help; adding more data from the evidence obtained (bloodstains patterns, types and manner of the knife injured the victim, footprints, etc.), we then can establish the direction specifically and how the victim moved across one point to the other.

happened, the relative positions between victim and aggressor, the sequence of when and how the binomial was found, what type of interaction happened, and how the victim is eventually found and the aggressor fled – it is now *almost* ready, clear, and sharp ... except for interest voids into the sequence that cannot be established with certainty. We have already seen why this emptiness happens: the natural limitation of this meta-analytic process will never be able to establish a complete reconstruction since only the physical evidence is analyzed, and these may be scarce due to the incident itself or may have been lost due to the passage of time, or – worst scenario – haven't been properly observed or registered. Sometimes the necessary technology may not yet exist to analyze other indicia that, consequently, we cannot even recognize them.

This stage of the method consists of the instance in which the experience, training, and professional skills of the analyst are counted in order to appreciate and propose possibilities, to formulate further research questions, suggest further studies or experimentations, and to request the intervention of others scientists, especially criminologists (Figure 2.15). And also, to explicitly state those inconsistencies that attempt against explanations by the logical reasoning of events established those segments and evidence that are constantly conflicting and require an explanation, perhaps unsupported by physical evidence: it is precisely the moment to point it out and suggest its search.

Result: In this last step, the reconstruction is concluded, describing the concatenated sequence of events that led to the incident and ends with the crime scene that initiates the criminal investigation. This description that develops in the relative chronology relates all the evidence and indicia analyzed that sustain it; it is convenient that as it is narrated, it is illustrated by *storyboards*,[17] combining or not with photographs of the scene and three-dimensional simulations/representations by computer (Figure 2.16).

In the application of this systematic methodology, the criminalistic reconstruction of the incident is developed through a constant audit of the evidence obtained. Indeed, following the order from the general to the particular, where the initial conditions of the scene are first set as they were at the time of initiating the criminal investigation and the forensic technical inspection, the physical and temporal framing of the incident is fixed by the confrontation in logical coherence of the various records of the crime scene – written, graphic, and film records –we begin to analyze and correct any errors in it. These errors in processing or recording may require a new visit to the crime scene at the same or different time, with certain specific instruments or applying a particular reagent to confirm or discard any observation or conclusion drawn in this analytical step.

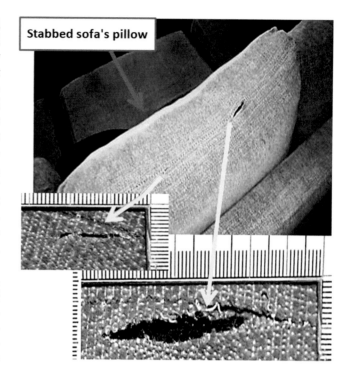

Stabbed sofa's pillow

FIGURE 2.15   Consider this example of an immaterial indicium. This sofa was aligned with its back with the left wall of a corridor that leads to the room where a stabbed female was. That pillow shows two stabs, without any trace of blood. The bigger one is near the victim's room. Knowing the high probability that they were produced by the same kitchen knife that was used by the murderer to kill the victim (bloodied and consistent with the wound, collected at dining room, near that sofa) tells two things: probably the murderer was left handed, and the stabs on the sofa's pillow were produced before stabbing the victim. The one thing criminalistics can't establish is *why* he/she did that, what thought or emotion drives him/her to do it. Only criminology could, by applying a behavioral analysis.

If we follow the analogy of the puzzle game, these first two steps would be equivalent to the orderly assembly the limits or the frame of the final image to assembly. We start with the limits since they are the easiest pieces to recognize: the four corners and the sides. However, unlike the puzzle game, these steps do not limit the final image: first, because we already specified that we will not seek to put together an image, it would rather be a movie; and second, because these limits are consequently not sharp or strict, they are pretty fuzzy. The recognizable pieces that primarily delimit the incident to be reconstructed consist of setting the place and time of occurrence: if something can be in absolute security, excusing the exaggeration, it is that the incident did not occur after the technical forensic inspection. From this point, the reverse engineering process begins.

FIGURE 2.16 A storyboard generated by computer software. In this case scenario, it's illustrating a violent death with high probability of a suicidal manner. It helps a lot to communicate to the client and the jury the reconstructionist's conclusions achieved, but a storyboard in any format (2D, 3D, dramatized, etc.) by itself can't and it must be presented as the reconstruction on it own. We described the scientific foundations and methodology; there is a great amount of knowledge to sustain the storyboard, and it must be according to that knowledge. The storyboard is just an illustrative tool.

Placed these pieces, fixed this point, the application of the following steps seeks not only to locate each indicium and evidence obtained, but also if they have been obtained logically and in coherence with that temporal context. The beginning with the analysis of the corpse and the injuries is based on the natural duty of social and human haste in ordering the delivery of the body to the relatives for burial, being therefore the first evidence to be *consumed*; the corpse will follow its thanatosemiological process, and the assumption accepted by forensic medicine is that the greater the thanatological evolution, the less quantity and quality of evidence can be obtained. It follows, then, that if any omission is observed or any corroboration is required that requires a re-examination of the corpse, this must be attended to as quickly as possible to reduce the risk of losing eventual evidence. This is the same observation as a living person: the healing process will erase every wound or potential evidence.

The fourth step, although it was presented in a generic way, governs the same criteria as regards the incidence of the time factor on the quantity and quality of the indicia or evidence; the available ones being categorized and analyzed in decreasing priority. That is, having a firearm, a bloodstain, or a projectile from the corpse, the bloodstain is the most labile of this set, so it must be analyzed first. Although the documentary stage, which is the conformation of the final criminalistic reconstruction report, like any other forensic report, must be carried out in accordance with the development of the analytical and experimental operations carried out, in the judicial role of reporting by the entrusted study, the analysis of the evidence of this step, again following the general to the particular. This is especially convenient for the reading of the non-expert in these sciences, in the cases of evidence that resulted from sampling other evidence, for example, of GSR sampled during the ballistic examination of a firearm, or traces of DNA from its grips: it is not incorrect, for the practical purposes of the report, to place the analysis of the results of the ballistic experimentation of the weapon first, then the GSR analysis result, and then the DNA result. Finally, in this step, each piece of evidence will be audited again, observing if it was obtained technically and legally, if the conclusions are logically coherent with the results obtained, and if they present a proper record. If any inconsistency is observed, a review will be requested by a colleague or a reexamination of the evidence if possible. Again, this is an auditing on each piece of evidence or a critical analysis of the evidence (Turvey, 2008).

With the fifth step, the first analysis of the relationship or linkage of evidence begins, using the interpretive techniques (Nuñez, 2017) of the reconstructive indicia, as explained. In carrying out these analyses, both by independent colleagues and by the reconstructionist him/herself, evidence will be correlated with each other and with the scene and the corpse, according to the type of reconstructive evidence – patterns of bloodstains, ballistic trajectories, etc.– which consequently will imply the examination of concordance and coherence between those pieces of evidence. The conclusion provided by each reconstructive evidence, in turn, should also be located in the large image or dynamic puzzle that is being formed from the previous steps, and as it consists of an incidental link included, it really consists of more than one piece of the puzzle; it is better to be a set of pieces.

The final analysis of each reconstructive piece of evidence as well as the rest of the evidence obtained regarding its link with all the evidence, with the corpse and with the crime scene corresponds to this step, where the relative evidence position is examined. Here, again, there is an audit, but specially attended in the return to the scene: the results obtained from each *indicium* raised at the scene and on the victim, are they logically consistent and coherent with the space where they were collected? This step not only allows further support to the intrinsic relationships between the pieces of evidence, but also allows demonstrating indications of voluntary contamination – simulations, *forensic awareness*[18] or also known as the staged scenarios – or involuntary contamination – in police preservation, due to neighbor access, relief and security maneuvers.

A systematic methodology emerges then to address any incident that is intended to be reconstructed that analyzes the isolated evidence and in relation to the others, with the crime scene, with the victim, and with the aggressor, constantly challenging that its insertion within the image or final film is consistent with its internal coherence and linked to the rest, maintaining a constant review of the evidence and the scientific principles that guide criminal work in general and criminalistic reconstruction in particular. Likewise, it allows peer review and judicial evaluation, consolidating the scientific character through verification. Understanding the constant progress and scientific becoming, the above is considered as a way of approaching a perfectible systematic study criminal reconstruction, open to falsifiability and debate by the scientific community of criminal sciences.

RECONSTRUCTIVE ASPECTS OF SOME EVIDENCES

Framing the following considerations in the previous section would have resulted in an extremely broad development of the methodology with the natural and fatal consequence of losing the thread of its exposition and foundation. Because of it, it was considered convenient to highlight some criminalistic evidence and its disciplines that provide enormous reconstructive information in a differentiated section; however, in the systematic application of the method, and according to the case of research and available evidence, should release its full development.

Next, we will highlight some points of interest, and the valuation and limitation with the reconstructive analytical task. We will start with the evidence that indicates dynamism, setting a structure in the mechanics and movements of the elements involved, and then briefly rescue the evidence that marks space-time, which will not be deepened since there is plenty of experience and technique offered by colleagues in the chapters of this work.

DYNAMIC INDICIA

Ballistic Trajectories

Determining the ballistic trajectories is one of the most important analyses to carry out in every case where firearms are fired, and especially when some of the targets hit consist of human or animal bodies. The physics defines the trajectory of the path traveled by a projectile through a fluid; in forensic ballistics, that fluid is normally air, and the path always forms a parabolic line due to Earth's gravitational force. However, and only in cases where the shootings occur in urban or suburban scenes, given the short distance between them – for more concentration of buildings, vegetation, poles, billboards, people, furniture, etc. – it is accepted to consider the trajectories of projectiles fired as linear, which simplifies calculations from counting two points, phenomena, and/or indicia to link in one ballistic trajectory.

The key indications from which this determination can be made consists of the impacts and deviations of trajectories (the commonly called *ricochet*[19]), the projectiles, and the fired cases to be found. Regarding the first ones, it is important to consider the entry and exit holes and deviations with respect to the nature of the impacted material, which will provide more information – such as distance, estimated caliber, energy transferred, and relative age – through experimental checks with the same material and similar ammunition, but especially to show the direction, and with respect to it, the impact angles. We live in a three-dimensional world; therefore, as it may seem obvious, on the impacts we must obtain, the angle on the horizontally and vertically planes, perpendicular to it. While the first indicates the lateral position where the shot was fired, the second, the vertical one, and the most probable shooting distance at which it was made by applying simple trigonometry calculations (Mattijssen & Kerkhoff, 2016), and therefore the target/victim-shooter positions, results in mathematical approximations that can be taken quite close to empirical checks (Figure 2.17).

However, it is ideal to have more evidence to support this approach. The fired cases ejected in each shot of some types of firearms also allow inferring the location of the weapon after each shot as long as it is considered the type of soil that receives those fired cases. It will not be the same if they fall on concrete, asphalt, or dry earth. To fall on grass, mud, or sand, for the first case, the rigid surface will cause uncontrolled rebounds and bearings that will randomly move away from the position of the shooter, while on the soft surface it will capture each ejected case and keep it in the place where it fell or in minimal proximity.

Finally, the projectiles involved may present deformations and material adhered to their surface as a result of their interaction with the contact surfaces of the target reached (remember the principles of transfer and correspondence of characteristics), which with analysis and verification, can indicate and corroborate the impacted surfaces.

Autopsy Reports

On the animal corpse – forensic veterinary – or on the human corpse, the corpse of the victim and the intracorporeal trajectories should also record the impact angles in both planes of three-dimensional space, complementing the findings and evidence of close-up shots on clothing, skin, and/or bone. In this way, the positioning the victim at the time of the shooting is achieved, correlating it with the evidence recorded at the crime scene, previously described by applying trigonometry (Figure 2.18).

For this, it is a fundamental requirement that the autopsy report be carried out in a complete manner, as described in the previous section; duly illustrated, in 2D graphics, *two* angles are shown, and a description of all tissues injured during the passage of the projectile (Figure 2.19).

This description of angles of incidence is equally important in the cases of knives, adding in this case the depth of the lesion measured in consideration of whether or not the possibility or impossibility of *the accordion effect*[20] exists in that specific body region. This would

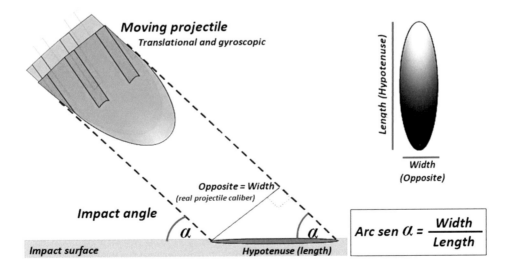

FIGURE 2.17 *Oval method:* Consists of the application of trigonometry to a bullet hole or bullet effect observed in an impacted surface to calculate the impact angle of that bullet/projectile. Above we can see how the bullet's caliber is expressed in the width of the mark, and its length will be the hypotenuse of a rectangle and triangle, both data that can be obtained by direct measurement on the mark. Applying the width-length quotient arcsine, we get an impact angle that we can extrapolate to a bullet's trajectory that is never exact but has a great approximation.

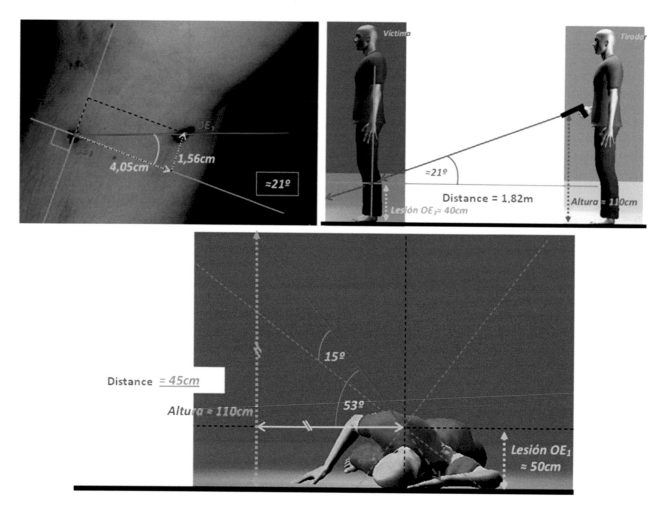

FIGURE 2.18   The shooting distance is not only determined through the interpretation of the signs observed on the victim in its planes of the clothes, the skin, and the bone, but also in conjunction with the determination and extrapolation of intracorporeal trajectories, which are essential to take the appropriate measurement of the angle of that trajectory. Adding this value we can test the hypotheses of the victim's position, at what height the firearm that fired at the victim would be, and, thereby by trigonometry calculations, establish a good approximation of the shooting distance.

make it possible to discard suspicious knives, according to the length of the blade, supported by a DNA sample on it. Likewise, the cutting directions in cutting injuries, the number of edges in the sharp injuries, orientation of the edge, its vitality, and the relative vitality between various injuries are essential data that can indicate the possibility of self-injury, laterality of the aggressor, the order of the injuries and thus their position at the time of attack, the type of injurious element, and as many others as the case may be (Figure 2.20).

In cases of heat burns, the type of burn based on its intensity – A, AB, and/or B – the probable way in which the heat was transmitted – radiation, convection, or conduction – will be important for fire and arson reconstruction. Its direction – orientation towards the heat source – is important, paying special attention to any *heat shadows*.[21]

The graphic record must necessarily consist of diagrams and photographs in the same sequence that are taken at the crime scene – general, approximation, linkage, and in detail – and with radiographs in different body planes that optimize the illustration of such angles and the details that may become decisive for the case.

In the case of blunt injuries, the direction, orientation, and intensity of the blow; the presence and shape of production of the abrasions, bruising, ecchymosis, and impact injuries; and a deep and careful study and registration of fractures –again, using diagrams and photographs – allow for more in-depth analysis of the *biomechanics* of their cause, the possibility of linking the injuries with the potential or damaging entity of the element, and even their identification through the confrontation of the transferred pattern. Remember the

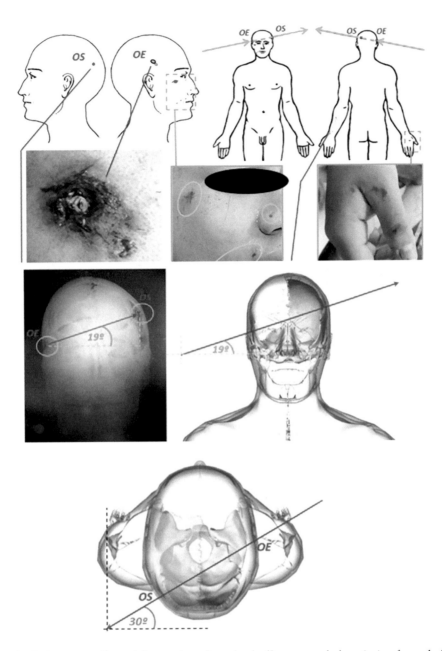

FIGURE 2.19 Very little is a contributed by saying that the bullet entered the victim from behind, slightly from above, and a little from left to right. Scientifically, it is valid to ask how much is slight, and how much is little. This must be quantified. And it is easily obtained by measuring an approximate angle with a protractor, in the vertical and horizontal planes of the placed stylet on the cadaver or the imaginary junctions of the entry-tissue-exit lesions on radiographs or photographs. With these angles, we can then provide more elements that more accurately estimate the shooting distance and, with it, the victim-shooter positions, as illustrated in the previous figure.

principle of correspondence of characteristics. We will see a more in-depth study that complements this topic.

An autopsy procedure and its consequent report are complete when, in addition to an exhaustive external and internal examination, all the samples that the case deserves were carried out, whether or not they are required by the judicial authority, since the intention is to provide data to the criminal investigation by preserving eventual evidence: sub-nail sampling of digits, larvae and insects, hair, gastric contents, epidermal gauntlets, etc. Likewise, it's complete when lesionological and pathological findings were analyzed in conjunction with the victim's medical history, with environmental data from the crime scene – especially humidity, pressure, and temperature conditions – and with the results of histopathological, toxicological, and biochemical tests.

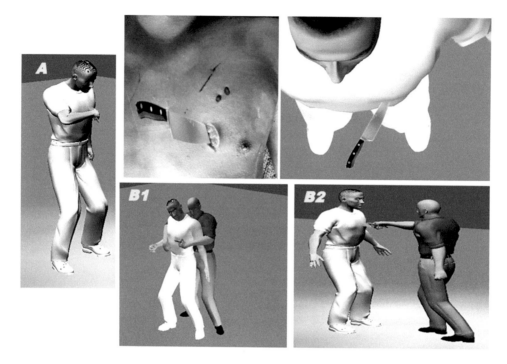

FIGURE 2.20   The angles at which a dagger was used to injure are as important as the ballistics trajectories of firearm projectiles: they can provide the probable laterality of the aggressor, the relative position with the victim, or, as in this case, whether or not self-harm was possible. Criminalistically, we will reach a point, as it is in this case, to place the different hypotheses in which the fatal puncture-cutting injury occurred, but they are measurable, physical data that may offer an enormous contribution to the criminologist's intervention. If the victim is known to be left handed, how likely is hypothesis A?

Only with the set of all of these data can it be adequately assessed how the victim's corpse –unique in itself with its intrinsic and particular characteristics referring to its previous health, pre-existing pathologies, and bone-muscular development – has physically responded to the aggression suffered in life, how it evolved through cadaveric transformations, and how the damaging mechanisms that generated the external and internal lesionological findings described and registered on the corpse have been produced. Thus, it will be possible to achieve greater probability and certainty in the conclusions referring to the cause and mechanism of death, as well as the determination of the time of death, the identification of the victim, the identification of the harmful weapon, and the calculations corresponding to the positions of the victim, aggressor, and scene; information that will clearly contribute beyond the criminal reconstruction if not to the entire criminal investigation.

Biomechanical Studies

If we pay attention to the previous paragraphs, a continuity is observed in the relationship of the subject of ballistic trajectories with the autopsy report. Again, we repeat the scheme for this topic, since biomechanical studies help to determine the probable mechanisms involved in the production of certain lesions.

Biomechanics consists of a science that combines physics with biology, studying the forces and accelerations that act on living organisms. In the automotive, medical, industrial, occupational, and biological engineering bibliography there are a variety of studies and empirical investigations concerning biomechanics, mostly with the objectives of establishing the safety conditions for the physical and healthy integrity of the human being, considering the structures, materials, and ways of handling objects to minimize injury.

Applied to criminalistics, it allows providing information regarding the mechanisms, intensity, direction, and meaning of lesionological findings, both internal and external, especially but not exclusively in the case of fractures. Indeed, they make it possible to verify the energy required to produce a certain fracture, by means of experimental checks and careful extrapolation of the results. They manage to verify or discard certain hypotheses about its production, as mandatory application in cases of head trauma, falls from heights, assaults, death by blows with blunt elements, and traffic accident cases.

Another application corresponds to the relationship with anthropometry and footprints, providing valuable scientific support to the identification of a person through the pattern of their act of walking, both recorded in videotapes and in the portrait of the passage through a series of footprints.

BPA or Bloodstain Pattern Analysis

It is not intended to develop this subject in depth because Dr. Jyoti Singh among others will dedicate a whole chapter to it in this same work, with the accurate and proper finished development of it. We simply highlighted the great reconstructive potential obtained from the analysis of patterns of bloodstains by the steps of the protocols of the IAPBA[22] this is regardless of the information on identity through DNA studies this fluid contains.

Indeed, these studies allow us to obtain important data regarding the location and concentration of the violence, the possibility of survival of the victim, height and movement of the source – whether it can be of the injury or of a bloody weapon – the minimum number of blows suffered by the victim, identification of the damaging element, victim-aggressor-scene positions, among others, through the correct registration of bloodstains, their biochemical identification – blood nature first, and genetic afterwards – and their correlation with the lesionological data contributed by the forensic medical study (Figure 2.21).

The methodology applied at the crime scene begins with the appropriate photographic record and

FIGURE 2.21 *Bloodstain pattern analysis:* At this corner of a kitchen was the victim of a robbery followed by a homicide. The bloodstains not only showed the region where the greatest violence occurred, but moments of survival of the victim: when touching the wall (blue arrow) and even getting up for a certain time, lying on his side resting his head against the door (arrow green-magnification), producing bloodied finger, hand, head, and back transfer.

corresponding position on the planes of all the present bloodstains, and a corresponding sampling of them, in order to corroborate their hematic nature. This is essential and scientifically required for further studies of the pattern classification based on the *identification key*[23] (Esperança, 2018) since the morphology in consideration of the support where they have been deposited depends on factual verifications and studies of fluid mechanics on blood (Attinger et al., 2013). If it's not known and it turns out that the reddish stain observed isn't blood, we cannot apply BPA, because the fluid that produced that stain may behave completely different than blood, and then, acts and stains totally different.

Once it has been established that the stain is blood, it is necessary to categorize the typified patterns, which contain information inherent to their mode of production. Normally, and depending on the case in question, we will find that the stain accepts more than one category or cannot be classified more than in a general typology. The situation can be saved with the information from forensic medicine, in terms of the lesionology present in the victim and in the aggressor together with the DNA test identification analysis.

It is not uncommon that, even in the integration of these data, the production mechanism is still not explicit or well defined, admitting more than one possibility. That is why it is understood that this study is simply one more – or more than one – piece of evidence for the reconstruction, and why an analysis of bloodstain patterns, although providing extremely valuable and essential information to establish how the incident happened, is just one more part of the whole analysis team in a criminal investigation (Figure 2.22).

Forensic Clothing Analysis

Another element that provides great information to the reconstruction is offered by the clothing, both of the victim and of the aggressor of the incident, since they are an intermediate plane of both corporality, capturing, and transferring various indications – to mention a few, stains of blood, GSR, hair, pollen, textile fibers, attached hair, dirt, and previous stains – as well as absorbing and expressing effects of heat, the incidence of knives, firearm projectiles, blunt blows, etc.

In some jurisdictions, there is still a discussion about whether the clothes should be removed at the crime scene or during autopsy operations, contrary positions that seek to indicate the ideal, more orderly and clean moment to carry out the task of preservation, registration, and analysis, especially in cases with those deceased. Based on this, it is argued that the best thing is to extract them in the morgue, since there they will not be contaminated with other elements, due to the weather or that will not

(a)

(b)

FIGURE 2.22   (a) and (b). Two detailed photographs of the scene depicted in Figure 2.21.

produce cleaning of other nearby indicia – acquiring fibers, pollen, and dirt from the scene. On the contrary, it has been observed that some indicia transfer on clothes dressing the corpse inside the death bag are lost or masked, making some evidence unrecoverable, such is the case of bloodstains, whose patterns are lost in transfer by diffusion and absorption given to movements, no matter how careful it is applied during transportation.

In analogy to the preference of a forensic identification method,[24] it is the opinion of the author of the present chapter, that the best moment of preservation of the clothing will be determined by the specific case and the crime scene that is presented to us, preferred is the extraction in the same place where the corpse is found with the maximum care possible and under constant photographic and or film registration. As mentioned, in the cases of firearm shots that produce bleeding, the analysis of the pattern may indicate what the position of the victim was like before, during, and after the shooting, while chemically we can collect GSR, so carefully removing and preserving the clothing will

ensure that this evidence is not lost. In other cases, the clothes could not present obvious signs of interest, but this also requires an adequate and thorough search so that if some stains or marks are to be produced during transport, these are wrongful interpreted as a product of the incident instead of a product of that transportation.

Related to clothing, the pieces or cuts found at the crime scene are of special interest. In a homicide case that the author of this chapter had to analyze, both at the scene and later in its reconstruction, a piece of cloth was found, an irregular short-sleeved cutout from a white T-shirt underneath the victim's corpse; subsequently, the arrested suspect had a white shirt with short sleeves, one of which was cut by traction and, by comparing the cut profile as well as the fibers, it was possible to demonstrate a common origin and, therefore, an impossibility of separating the suspect from the homicide (Figure 2.23).

Finally, it should be noted that textile products offer a good capacity to register and allow distinctions in terms of expressive violence on them, expressing different patterns for the same type of fabric and according to weft and warp, if a cut was produced by scissors, by a cutting element, orientation of the edge, direction of the cut, firearm projectile, heat transmission mechanism, among others, which contribute a lot to the correlation analyses between clothing, weapons, or injurious elements, and lesionology present in the victim and perpetrator, highly reconstructive data (Taupin, 2011). One more question consists of the study of fibers that can be transferred in violent interactions, a topic that will also be addressed in one of the chapters of this work and we suggest to not miss reading it (Figure 2.24).

Fire Marks

Once again, we do not pretend to more than to comment on superficial aspects, being an exciting topic that will be developed with the depth it deserves in two closely related chapters in this work. Fire cases are usually presented as scenes of difficult reconstruction given the great material destruction that it exhibits, but precisely this combustion process, the influence of ventilation, and heat transfer is what produces most of the indications that will be used for the reconstruction analysis (Chisum & Turvey, 2013). Among others, at the scene of the fire incident, the most interesting evidence is the marks of fire.

Fire marks consist of the visible and measurable changes produced by the effect or set of effects of the fire, that is, the observable or measurable changes in or on a material as a result of its exposure to heat, flames, or smoke from the fire. Mainly there are two groups of fire marks: intensity and movement marks. The first ones are those effects that are produced by the amount of transmitted heat and cached by a material, also dependent on

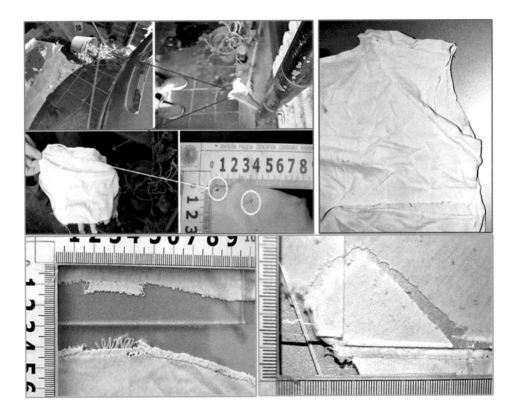

FIGURE 2.23 Under an overturned plant, broom, and mop, close to where the head of the victim's corpse was oriented, a piece of white fabric is registered and collected. One of the suspects in this homicide presented at the time of his arrest, a white short-sleeved T-shirt. The cutting profiles produced by violent traction of both pieces fit together perfectly like puzzle pieces, demonstrating that they had formed the same clothing product, broken in the moments immediately close to the death of the victim and, therefore, that this suspect was involved in this homicide case.

the nature and quantity of that material available. The second ones are made up of generally superficial effects that indicate the way in which the fire has spread.

Another way to categorize the effects are surface deposits, where there are no irreversible effects on the material; thermal effects on the surface – burns, discoloration, melting; and surface charring, deep charring, and consumption – complete destruction of material. These fire marks indicate the intensity and duration of a material's exposure to heat and, in general, the intensity marks will be found in the same place as the fire source; that is, in the area of origin indicated by those movement marks. However, the relationship is not so direct, and the interpretive analysis of them must be carried out with rigor and scientific method, in conjunction with laboratory analysis with the samples that are preserved at the fire scene, and especially of the materials that contain those marks, to analyze the nature and properties – like ignition temperature, range of inflammability – and behavior against heat (DeHaan & Icove, 2012).

Other highly relevant evidence is the eventual casualties, whether human or animal, who also express heat-related lesions on their corpse. Their proper registration, description, and location in the autopsy is

essential, as mentioned above. This medical forensics analysis must be extreme in these cases due to the possible behaviors of concealment or destruction of evidence related to the incident and/or related to the identity of the victim-aggressors through the fire.

These elements, together with the laboratory analysis of the samplings carried out at the fire site, together with the mathematical modeling, chemical theory, and dynamics of fire and the empirical tests with standardized methodologies of re-created rooms and under controlled conditions, an adequate reconstruction of the fire incident can be accomplished.

Fixing Evidence of Space-Time

This group of elements is really big because it essentially involves most of the indicia and evidence analyzed in isolation: the bloodstains allow identification trough the DNA from the source person when the context can be inferred as described in previous paragraphs, a firearm projectile contains information related to its caliber and type and identification of the weapon that fired it, in addition to the fact that it may have material attached

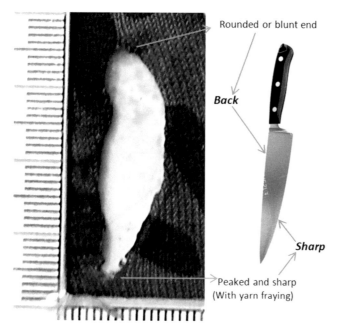

FIGURE 2.24 Note how the shirt worn by the victim in this case offers bonding characteristics to the type of element that produced this sign, evidencing the participation of a cutting-edge knife, and where that edge was heading. These data were not provided by the autopsy report; the clothes were the only indication that pointed to this important element of the homicide.

and or deformed to its body that allows the impacted materials to be established and linked to a trajectory, and various et cetera.

This does not mean that in the reconstructive analysis they should be analyzed in the context of the rest of the evidence; precisely, that examination will often allow greater endings in the resolution of its conclusions. For example, the determination of the time of death is expressed in a time interval with expression on hours range: gaze it this conclusion with the results of an entomological study or a security tape, a decrease in the time of death can be inferred, approaching increasingly smaller intervals as more evidence is linked.

Evidence of space-time is, among others, GSR, the cadaverous fauna and flora, the geological material, stains of paint, semen, footprints, papillary traces, lips, hair, and fibers, elements analyzed by *verification techniques* (Nuñez, 2017) and supported by the principles of exchange and correspondence of characteristics, establishing the presence of an element or person in the interaction with the crime scene, with the victim and or with the aggressor. These analyses will then be evaluated in the fourth meta-analytical step of the previously described systematic method, allowing the extraction of more information that these pieces of evidence manifest by themselves, linking them in context and to others.

This requires an adequate record and correct preservation of each indicium detectable at the crime scene, using all the technology available for such purposes and within the legal framework and chain of custody to validate them legally. A lot of these types of evidence and the techniques to study them, will be described in this book; don't miss them.

RELATIONSHIP WITH CRIMINOLOGICAL TECHNIQUES

Once it has been established how the incident happened from the analysis of the material or physical evidence, in other words, from the application of the criminalistic reconstruction analysis, the holistic approach to criminal investigation demands the criminological analysis, examining the behavioral evidence of the incident. Through this study, generally, parts of the frames or pieces that could not be established through the analysis of the physical evidence may be defined or approximated, and especially those pieces that refer to the motives of the aggressor, to the typology of the victim, to the locations and times where the crimes were committed, to the instrumental and expressive violence manifested (Disanto, 2006). Likewise, the behavioral study makes it possible to further consolidate the conclusions observed in the cases of staging, allowing the explanation of any eventual evidence that, in isolation, falls outside the reconstructed sequence and shows signs of being a voluntary and false production.

In the seventh step – final criminalistic considerations – of the described method, the need that arises is to offer the limitations of the reconstructive analysis, to indicate what could and could not be established, as well as the suggestion of in which points, aspects, or indicative links it could refer to a criminological analysis. It is imperative that the criminalistic reconstruction is carried out before the criminological analysis, since they will give the necessary elements for the adequate examination of the crime scene, the background and actions of the victim, and the apparent conduct and actions taken, carried out by the aggressor.

Mainly, the intervention of the criminologist in a criminal investigation is usually requested to be issued in relation to the psychological state during the incident, analyze the motivation, check the linkage of cases, analyze simulated or rigged scenes – to protect the aggressor or the victim – and carry out the psychological autopsy (Jiménez-Serrano, 2012). Depending on the criterion that was offered for the distinction of the criminalistic-criminological sciences, within the criminology the intervention of forensic linguistics would be. We will describe a brief conceptualization of each of these techniques, and will conclude with a discussion of their respective links with criminalistics reconstruction in the conviction holistic or generalist approach that a reconstructionist must know in aiding a criminal investigation.

CRIMINAL PROFILING

It is the criminological discipline that aims to study the personality of known aggressors – cases solved – and estimate that of unknown aggressors – crime case in progress – seeking to complement the comprehensive clarification of the incident by determining the motivation, answering the *why* of the crime, based on the material and behavioral analysis of the crime scene, social and psychological characteristics of the victims – *victimology* –, criminalistic findings, the study of geographic behavior – *geographic profile* – and analysis of the testimonies obtained, in order to identify or define a type of person who could commit the incident and thus, guide the criminal investigation. Likewise, in addition to providing the characteristics of the aggressor that help to recognize him/her in the cases of ongoing investigation (Rodríguez, 2011), it also aims to offer relevant information on the possibility of her/him acting again, the probable locations of future action, the probable location of residence or comfort zone where she/he usually moves, and what probability exists that one case and another are linked (Climent Durán et al., 2012). It is clear from the above that there are different types of profiles, based on different approaches, currently being unified in the contributions of diagnostic evaluations – psychopathological and psychiatric, psychologic; academic research – statistics; and casuistry through the analysis of the crime scene of clarified incidents (Jiménez-Serrano, 2012).

In the context of a criminal investigation, the profiling includes the following analytical stages (Garrido-Genovés & Sobral-Fernández, 2008):

- *Analysis of behavior through the crime scene*: includes the characterization of the scene in terms of its size, how it is reached, who attends it, what activity is carried out there, who has access, how many entry and exit routes, and finally how the scene is linked with the victim and the aggressor – not only through the criminalistic evidences that set the criminal binomial position, but also, if the crime scene itself, as a non-neutral space has some special meaning for someone of them. This makes it possible to analyze the approach method –surprise or deception; the attack method – verbal threat, use of force with or without a weapon, and combined; the control method – using force, under verbal threat and/or with presence of arms; and the aggressor's acts of precaution.

- *Categorization of the information*: the incident, the motivation, the risk of the aggressor, and the victim are classified together with the time and space factors. Organize all of this data that is obtained so far to move on to the critical analysis of the evidence and direct attention to obtain more information.

- *Examination of the criminalistic reconstruction*: which is to analyze the material support that establishes the identification of the elements and participants to see how they are related and the concatenated sequence of the scientifically determined events of the incident. Its consistency is examined, paying special attention to those jumps or gaps between events; that is, to those segments that could not be determined criminalisticly. Specifically, those actions or behaviors that deviate from the need to commit the incident, referenced in the criminalistic report.

- *Determination of the modus operandi, signature, and conformation of the geographic profile*: synthetically, the *modus operandi* (MO) consists of the set of behaviors carried out to achieve the crime, protect the identity of the criminal, and to facilitate the escape. This MO is not static and can evolve or regress depending on the aggressor's learning or mental or physical deterioration, which allows discovering the intellectual characteristics about a skill, profession, or work; about his possible relationship with the victim; and his familiarity with the crime scene. For its part, the *signature* consists of those behaviors that infer from the final motivation to commit the crime, evidencing the psychological or emotional needs that the criminal intends to cover with the conduct, generally assuming extra time for its development on the scene, being unnecessary by themselves to achieve the criminal act, they are more visceral and less rational, and they usually involve acts of communication between the aggressor-victim or the aggressor with another person. In the analysis of the case, categorizing the actions in signature or MO is essential and not always so clear. The *geographical profile*, on the other side, aims to discover the movements, areas of action, and the possible location of residence or anchorage area of the aggressor.

- *Analysis of the surviving and/or deceased victims (victimology)*: the background of the victim and its lifestyle, how was her/his last 24 hours, the characteristics that will allow her/him to be categorized into a compliant type of victim are examined, and linked to the crime scene to correlate victim risk and MO risk. The basic

FIGURE 2.25   This is a transfer-drag of a hand stained with excrement on a wall in a burglary case. More excrement was found in the dining room of the house. Defecating could be explained by the nerves of the perpetrator at the moment of the incident, but their location –both excrements and this transfer, far from the bathroom – do not seem so according to this. This action was obviously unnecessary for the robbery itself, right? Mockery to the police, contempt for property, style of marking the work …?

premise and purpose of its analysis in criminal profiling is that by knowing the victim, the aggressor can be known as well.

- *Determination of the evolution or criminal escalation*: based on the data obtained in the previous stages, especially how the risks that the aggressor may take are related, and how his MO is developing based on this, to the confidence that he is gaining in the succession of crimes that it produces, and in the time intervals that occur between them, establishing how their criminal conduct evolves.
- *Elaboration of the aggressor profile*: in writing, the relevant information is gathered and organized with logical inferences based on the evidence collected, presenting it to the manager of the criminal investigation. The final stage of profiling is to evaluate and test the effectiveness of the profile, feeding it as new evidence appears (Figure 2.25).

PSYCHOLOGICAL AUTOPSY

Technically, it's a retrospective bio-psycho analysis performed on a deceased or missing victim, being an indirect process of collecting and analyzing information about the behavior that reconstructs the psychological profile and his/her mental state before the death, with the aim of getting closer to the understanding of the circumstances of their death (García Pérez, 2007).

It is carried out through a series of retrospective, indirect, and postmortem investigations. It emphasizes the cognitive capacities, tendencies, and behaviors of people who have died to establish causal relationships or

explanations of doubtful deaths. It is based on the victim leaving psychological evidence at the scene of death, in the spaces she/he inhabited, and in their work.

During the criminal investigation, it provides information that enables the elaboration of a victimological profile, to project its results into a probable profile of the aggressor/s. Also, the psychological profile of a person who disappeared, to deal with possible cases of forced disappearance of persons, and the profile of kidnapping victims, to plan capture strategies (Blanes Cáceres, 2011). In later stages of the incident, during the prejudicial stages, it helps in the classification of the crime, in the etiology and the responsibility determinations.

The current integrated psychological autopsy method (MAPI) created in 1990 in Cuba and applied with emphasis in Latin America (García Pérez, 2007) consists of the following four steps:

- *At the crime scene (physical and psychological evidence)*: removal and collection of psychic traces; technical inspection of the crime scene; review of the evidence material –criminalistic reconstruction; categorize and analyze the information – emotional, behavioral, and core psychodynamic indicators.
- *Interviews*: preferably it should be carried out three months after the death occurred, due to the grieving process that affects relatives, but before a year and a half, so that the data obtained is not distorted – misrepresentation and forgetfulness – by cognitive natural processes.
- *Collective discussion*: reconstruction of the profile, description of the personality, lifestyle, ideologies, beliefs, hobbies.

- *Conclusions*: conformation of the report where the family, personal, and medical antecedents are established. The biographical data of the deceased, a development of life in its psychological aspect of the last two years; the methodology – MAPI and genogram – used; the elements of judgment – documents, testimonies, belongings, readings; the assessment of suicide risk factors; heteroaggressive or accidental; from conflict and motivational areas; a psychogenesis of behavior; if there were signs of presuicidal conduct; if such a state existed; and the state of mind before death.

FORENSIC LINGUISTICS

Synthetically, forensic linguistics consists of a multifaceted discipline that studies the interaction between communication and the law. It has three sub-technical branches; we will develop the central aspects of the one oriented to criminal investigation and criminalistic reconstruction.

The forensic linguistic analyzes the linguistic matter at different levels – phonological-phonetic, morpho-syntactic, lexical-semantic, pragmatic-discursive, etc.– settled in manuscripts, printed mechanics, voice recordings, video, and those like gestural or body language; and its evidence value in judicial processes. The linguistic evidence presented in court cases can be outlined in a simple and general way based on a basic distinction widely used in applied linguistics between the comprehension and production of texts, whether they are spoken or written (Santana Lario & Falces Sierra, 2002).

Its main foundation is that there are not two people who can speak or write in the same way; each one uses a style of idiosyncratic speaking or writing. This style is called *idiolect*, which can be defined as the individual choice of each speaker of some linguistic form – phonetic, phonological, morphological, syntactic, pragmatic, discursive – determined from the repertoire offered by the language, depending on their personal, cultural, social, geographical, and temporal characteristics. Although there is no linguistic imprint, each person has a style, a unique and unrepeatable idiolect that remains fairly stable over time.

In the field of criminalistics, forensic linguistics experts have established new perspectives for studies in documentology, human identification through voice, and forensic computer science. In the first, within the expert studies that are carried out on documents or written in handwritten form, such as those made with a typewriter, printer, photocopier, or any other printing system, always mechanical and forensic linguistics revalue the traditional *determination of the typist* or author of the typed writing through what was known at its time as layout or style analysis (Albarracín, 1969; Alegretti, 2007); that style is idiolect, and this analysis is currently the responsibility of an expert in forensic linguistics.

Regarding identification through the human voice, the skills aimed at identifying the speaker are carried out through the application of two types of studies: one is aural, in charge of a speech pathologist who reports on the anatomical and physiological component of each sound that conforms to the doubtful voice; and a spectral one, in charge of a spectrographic technician that detects and measures the intensity and temporal evolution of the *speech formants*. For the identification of the author, forensics computer science can provide text messages and chats on various platforms, especially given the freedom of the linguistic conventions that give a significant difference in the idiolectual style that can be analyzed to identify the author. For both, this science can provide the linguistic profiling of the speaker and sender of the message, in terms of linguistic features that are characteristic at a certain age, gender, religion, and cultural or idiosyncratic region.

Valuable information is revealed regarding the incident to be reconstructed from the analysis of the immaterial or socio-behavioral evidence, by observing how the exchange principle also occurs at the psychological level: in the interaction of one person with another and in the decision and execution of a behavior, part of the emotional motivations and psychological needs are transferred reciprocally – between people – and can be expressed on a material level, indicia that accounts for that interaction through a scientific analysis from the criminological disciplines, checking the personal and particular significance that behavior applies to the person.

And only a few have been mentioned, the main ones, focusing on the encounter with criminal investigation and especially with criminalistic reconstruction. This discipline, framed in a criminal investigation, feeds on material and on immaterial components, analyzed through criminalistic reconstruction and criminological analysis. An intimate relationship complements their reciprocal contributions, offering a more perfect image of the puzzle to be put together, of the film of the incident, that the criminal investigation pursues to clarify.

BIASES IN CRIMINALISTIC RECONSTRUCTION

We previously described that in a moment of the reconstructive analysis there is a sensation that the incident is like assembling itself. In the application of interpretive techniques while analyzing evidence of great reconstructive potential, such as bloodstains patterns and ballistic trajectories among others, what happens is that a small segment of an event is clarified. By continuing with another piece of evidence or that one segment consolidates it or clarifies another segment, or even manages to position it in the concatenated sequence of events that indicate how the incident occurred.

Inquiring is valid if at that time there is no any idea or belief in the minds of the reconstructionist who is directing *involuntarily* the results obtained from the analysis of evidence, to give a sequencing of events in accordance with this idea or belief. This systematic error of involuntary targeting is a type of cognitive bias, a phenomenon that cognitive psychology defined as an error in the reasoning, evaluation, recall, decision or another cognitive process that usually occurs by maintaining an idea based on preference and own beliefs, independently or contrary to the information or data to be analyzed (Kahneman & Tversky, 1972). We highlight the involuntary quality, totally aliened, being an automatic brain mechanism that escapes control, and is only linked to the ethical issues of the profession in terms of being aware of its occurrence and adopting measures to counteract them (Dror, I. 2013).

The most common types of biases in criminal investigation, and specifically in forensic sciences, are essentially three, appearing already at the very beginning, in the inspection of the crime scene. With the information and feedback that researchers and first responders were able to gather regarding the etiology of the incident – alleged homicide, alleged suicide, alleged accident – the coordinator and the forensic experts of the intervener agency may be influenced unconsciously for *selection bias*, looking for and detecting more indicia that favors any of the supposed etiologies, thus making it difficult to find other indications that contradict it.

This error can become perpetuated in the laboratory, when the respective analysts tend to seek to obtain results that coincide with the information submitted regarding the etiology, probable identity of the author, or *how* the events occurred – the latter, reconstruction, all of which characterize the *confirmation bias*: the tendency to seek, interpret, or favor information in a way that confirms one's own preconception (Jiménez-Serrano, 2012). This type of bias is very common in forensics analysts of the government agencies – from the police, prosecution, and defense – producing what some authors have called *paradigm sides* (Chisum & Turvey, 2013), where the analyst tends to confuse their role and relation to the agency where she/he works, believing that is their duty to provide proof coincident or aligned to the hypothesis that the agency has on certain evidence, suspect or defended, respectively, taking sides and believing in the guilt or innocence according to the theory of the case carried out by her/his agency, even reaching conclusions of a legal nature – with terms referring to guilt, innocence, victim, homicide, accident, etc. This bias is closely related to another known as the *experimenter's bias*, occurring in the forensic field at the time of making scientific verifications and experimentations, documenting and focusing on those observations and circumstances that best fit the expectations of the acting expert.

Apart from these types of biases, in criminalistic reconstruction analyses, a very common logical fallacy is the attribution of a cause-effect relationship to two events that occur in a very close time interval, or that two or more events are causally linked, by simply succeeding together.[25] Certain indicia allow a very obvious logical causal link – for example, the fired shot cases have a very direct causality with a previous shot – but even in such cases, one must be cautious and corroborate this causality together with other evidence – determining if that previous shot corresponds to the incident under investigation or not. Likewise, other evidence presents a very diffuse causal relationship. In this regard, remember the examples offered in the fifth step of the methodology developed for the criminalistic reconstruction.

While the specialized bibliography is divided into the fact that the expert who carries out the inspection and gathering of evidence at the crime scene must be the same one who carries out the laboratory analysis – to the point that an example in the field of forensic medicine goes so far as to say that the crime scene represented two-thirds of the autopsy (Lacassagne & Martin, 1921); an axiom that has been interpreted with the fact that it is the same doctor who checks the corpse at the scene and examines it in the morgue, or at least counts with *all* the information gathered at the crime scene – this fatally implies a great risk of falling into confirmation bias. Similarly and perhaps under the same interpretation of the previous axiom, some authors prefer that the reconstructionist who performs the technical inspection is the same one who performs the reconstructive analysis as well.

That axiom must to be interpreted in the historical context when forensic science began to emerge and the criminalistics and criminology were mixed, without being fully defined without specific academic training, so in many cases the same medical examiner performed the criminalistic and or the criminological task, made some ballistic determinations, in fingerprints, in documents, and reconstructions; examples of this are found in the first books of legal medicine and persist in some contemporaries, as well as in the training of great teachers and criminal precursors in various disciplines, including criminal reconstruction. Consequently, at that time in which there was a small number of professionals specialized in the study of the respective indicia and specific forensic determinations, the same professional was in charge of several of them. Currently, due to the advancement of science, and now with the contribution of cognitive psychology, we observe that this does not result in good practice, since it implies a great risk of incurring involuntary errors due to these cognitive biases.

There are several solutions proposed to counteract the bias, especially the confirmation *bias* – also called *contextual bias* – provided by specialists in cognitive psychology (Kassin, Dror, & Kukucka, 2013), but it must be understood that any solution simply mitigates this risk, analogously to the documentary security measures against forgeries and adulterations. for example, on money paper, they will not prevent counterfeiting or adulteration; they will only be able to make it more manifest, reducing the risk of their occurrence. And precisely, this is the first proposal to solve the problem of bias: the accepting that it exists, that no one is exempt from it, and the need of constant training in this problem.

Most of the proposed solutions collide with the capacity and resources of each forensic agency and jurisdiction. Indeed, a *blind peer review* or *verification* of each forensic analysis carried out in every discipline would be ideal, but implies at least a duplication of human resources and a slowdown in operational capacity.

Another interesting solution is the addition of *false indicia* in the items collected at the crime scene. For example, adding fired shots cases from a known weapon that haven't any participation or relationship in the incident under investigation, together with fired shots cases that were collected at the crime scene. Likewise, in a papiloscopic identification, in addition to the suspect's file, add other files from other people, omitting the names of all the files. In both cases, the respective forensic expert, in the proper application of the analysis, will arrive at a positive or negative identification – of fired shots cases served/of the suspect – discarding the added elements, or *bait indicia*. Again, the question lies in resources, time, and the legal aspect that such control would require, which would depend on each jurisdiction. And whatever the strategy is, it is reiterated, none will be 100% effective; humanly, we can only reduce the risk.

The author of this chapter applied some of the strategies to counteract contextual bias. In charge of the case manager incoming at the Scientific Police Division of the city of Comodoro Rivadavia, Chubut, Argentina, he applied the proposal to take over direct communication with the various prosecutors that required forensic analysis. Using the data provided on each case, by applying a grid of required information, he advised on the analyses to be carried out and in what order. Later, such analyses were entrusted to each forensic colleague of the division, only providing the controversial points and the elements offered and needed for the forensic examination. This limited the contextual information of the case, reducing the risk of confirmatory bias. In some cases, that had special relevance; it was also added an informally comment to the forensic in charge, information related to the case, but irrelevant for the analysis and false, within potential influence in the interpretation of the colleague. For example, the ballistics expert was told that in the case of homicide, there were witnesses who indicated the presence of a shooting between two people, being then two different weapons of the same caliber that produced the fired cases to be analyzed, information totally invented and supported by other evidence – a filming of a security camera, where a person shooting was clearly recorded. If the ballistics expert concluded that the fired cases corresponded to two different weapons, the confirmation bias was clearly evidenced, the study has to be invalidated, must be repeated, and the acting expert must be re-trained. Fortunately, in the few times that the author could apply this cognitive *tramp*, the acting expert reprimanded him with great enthusiasm arguing that the witness – false – was lying about it.

Likewise, and in accordance with the appropriate interpretation of Lacassagne's axiom, previously described, it was customary among the reconstructionist colleagues of the aforementioned division, that one carried out the technical inspection at the crime scene of a case, and another colleague carried out the analysis of criminalistic reconstruction, and we rotated that role. It is understood that the scene and its technical inspection are the fundamental sources of the entire reconstructive process, but tended to be what fatally implied contamination by close contact with other actors in the criminal investigation, and then more information that facilitated the contextual bias was filtered through the analytical performance of another colleague. Unfortunately, this strategy could not always be applied because not always are enough reconstructionist personnel available.

Finally, peer verification was also applied, but given the small size or operational capacity of the division, where we were a just a few of colleagues, it could not be applied *blindly*. What was applied was the critical verification of the colleague's analysis, adopting a counterpart's expert position – or *devil advocates* – looking for the error in the report and in each step of the reconstructive method, analyzing each valued element. In some cases, we were forced to review the whole case; in others, we contributed some very valuable observations that allowed us to practice for the eventual oral debate in a trial. Ergo, that peer review was a guaranteed success: either corroborating and reviewing the conclusions and the analysis itself, and at the same time that it produced a criminalistic discussion of great professional richness for all the colleagues involved.

The problem of cognitive biases is not exclusive to criminalistic reconstruction in particular, nor to forensic science in general, but to the entire science. And therefore it is an ethical duty of each scientist to be trained in this problem that seems not be extinct in the near future, and far from being discouraged, training, strategies, and resources should be reinforced to reduce their incidence as much as possible. When this knowledge is applied to judicial cases, such as criminalistic and criminological reconstructions frequently, our intervention as a scientist must be with extreme rigor and caution possible, since our conclusions will be evaluated to define or prove responsibility on a person, applying a certain penalty or position that our purpose is precisely to contribute to the criminal investigation; and the less aware we are of the problem, there is no doubt that the more frequently we fall into bias, and thus into error, therefore, serious consequences can fall wrongly on an innocent or guilty person.

CONCLUSIONS

Criminal reconstruction is an exciting topic due to the varied types indicia and disciplines it draws on, some as small as DNA, as subtle as a positional relationship of fired cases, and as intangible as a signature or words that a person uses, details that, through proper registration and preservation, and scientifically analyzed in their particularity first, and linked in context secondly, demonstrate *how* the incident occurred, or in judicial terms, the materiality of the incident and authorship that the criminal investigation seeks to establish.

They all have been interesting topics that really demand a complete book, many of which have been referenced, and have fueled the training, theory, and the casuistry of this ambitious chapter, and much as other issues addressed in a superficial way related to the essential analysis of different evidences, which are covered by specialists in this work. As it has been suggested in these lines, the reader will be able to perfectly survey at the crime scene to the respective analyses and interpretations of the laboratory results in the following chapters of this work, by the great experience of all the forensics colleagues.

It is expected that in this interesting study of criminalistic reconstruction, its characterization and scientific foundation, and the criminalistic principles as they are formulated especially in Latin American countries, a systematic method of the cases of presumed homicide/violent death, but extrapolated to other cases that present material evidence, could have been achieved for your knowledge and debate. Likewise, how this criminal discipline is related to criminological scientists forms a more holistic criminal reconstruction, providing a description and a clearer image with the pieces that have remained of the criminal puzzle. And finally, we have referenced one of the problems that has mobilized forensic science in general, especially since the publication of the criticized report by the National Institute of Justice (NIJ, 2009), and we have seen its impact on reconstruction, as well as some of the strategies that cognitive psychology provides us to counteract it.

As a discipline, it still requires greater experience to rise to the degree of science, and this entire chapter as well as the entire work has the objective of both disseminating knowledge, benefits, and limitations, as well as receiving contributions, comments, and inquiries, in the belief that this is the most fruitful way of contributing to the growth and evolution of these forensic sciences.

NOTES

1 Nowadays, computer forensics brings the paradigm of the *virtual* space. In this chapter, we will focus on its traditional physical concept.

2 Notice that the author highlights a difference between physical indicia and evidence. The first are the elements at a crime scene that the investigator and the forensic scientist *thinks* were produced by the crime or incident (in a change of its nature, position, condition, or form in it). The second is the same element with scientific results that validate that production relationship: evidence it's the next level of the indicia after scientific analysis applied to it and the result is a *confirmation* of that previous assumption.

3 Activity defined by the most famous detective in fiction literature, *Sherlok Holmes*, by Sir Arthur Conan Doyle.

4 Website https://acsr.org

5 The embossing that is created and transmitted in the body of the bullet while passing through, in a high friction and abrasion mechanism, by the grooved barrel of the gun during the firing shot.

6 Reagent solution that allows revealing and enhancing papiloscopic prints contaminated with blood, through a chemical reaction where the proteins of the compound are colored.

7 Mouth lip print. Its study for identification is the task of *cheiloscopy*.

8 In bloodstain pattern analysis, one of the types of patterns is known as a *void*. *Heat shadows* are known in fire investigations. In both, an interruption of the pattern that blood and heat produce is observed, due to the interposition of an object between the source (of blood, heat) and the surface. The author of the present conjugates both phenomena in a so-called *radiation shadow*.

9 In Latin America, known as the *papiloscopy* or *lofoscopy* science, it is applied as a method of classification and identification of fingerprints created by Don Juan Vucetich, in 1891 and the variations of it. Papiloscopy is the science that pursues the identification of a person studying the papillae drawing or dermatoglific on fingertips, palms, and soles.

10 In the majority of the juridical procedural codes, it is required that expert's opinions have an admissibility criteria that includes the description and the results obtained from the operations carried out, which is nothing more than the description and the results from the method followed.

11 Notice that the term, as the ASCR agreed, is not totally accepted by the author. Reconstructing the crime scene is not the task, the real goal is to reconstruct the events and *how* the persons and elements involved interacted between them, resulting in the crime scene. The crime scene is the

picture that we already have, the picture we start the investigation with. We must pursue previous pictures and in their adequate sequence, the film that caused it; that's what we have to reconstruct. There is, also, another lingüistic debate based on the law system about *crime scene*: in Argentina, we called it very generic as *place of the event* (we don't konw until doing the reconstruction, if there is a crime or not; scene is also problematic, because it is related to *staging* (again, in Argentina), concept that will have a proper development in another chapter of this text.

12 In some cases, it is possible not only to find eventual witnesses, but even the authors of the incident themselves, present motivation by a personal delight, enjoying observing their work – example of arsonists and some serial aggressors – behind the police cords of preservation.

13 Or stages: cervical, thoracic, abdominal, and pelvic.

14 Of interest for the case, remembering that the goal of criminal investigation is to reconstruct the whole incident: entomological samples, epidermal gauntlets, adhered substances and elements, projectiles, among a variety of et cetera.

15 Each finding – stain, wound, mark – must be fully described – metrical and anatomical located and oriented. Regarding the wounds, indicating their typology, relative vitality, and production form.

16 Electron scanning microscope coupled with X-ray diffraction is the most widely accepted and currently supported technique for determining the presence of gunshot residue (GSR).

17 The illustration of the sequence by an animation is not recommended, rather that it is a better practice to perform a succession of images, graphics, illustrations, and/or with photographs, since it finds an especially greater coherence with the scientific and verifiable result that can be achieved.

18 Conduct by any of the participants in the incident with which it is intended to divert the correct course of the criminal investigation by modifying or eliminating evidence or even planting false ones.

19 It is not considered technically correct since a ricochet involves sudden contact in a completely *elastic* collision, in which the elements are not permanently deformed; the kinetic energy and linear motion are conserved without mass exchange between the elements. This clearly does not happen in the interaction of a firearm projectile against any surface.

20 It consists of the production of a deeper wound, larger than the length of the blade of the knife, due to affection on an anatomical portion that deforms under pressure, returning to its normal shape once that pressure is removed; for example, when it affects the lower part of the thorax or the buttocks.

21 One of the forms that integrate the group called by the author is irradiation shadows.

22 *International Association of Bloodstain Patterns Analysts.*

23 Designed by Phillipe Esperança, it consists of a flow diagram that is developed from the morphology adopted by the stain under study, through a series of increasingly detailed issues regarding the characteristics of that stain, discarding a pattern type until it achieves a specific type or group of type patterns.

24 It has been taken as an axiom that the best identification method is the one that provides identity information in a faster and simpler way depending on the particular case, and not a specific one applicable to every case. Fingerprinting is the most practical, simpler, and cheapest method, but we cannot apply it on a skeleton, can we?

25 Fallacy known as *cum hoc, ergo propter hoc.*

REFERENCES

Albarracín, R. *Manual de criminalística*. Argentina: Editorial Policial de la Policía Federal Argentina, 1969.

Alegretti, J. C. *Escrituras manuales y mecánicas*. Argentina: Editorial La Rocca, 2007.

Association of Crime Scene Reconstructionist. Official website https://acsr.org

Attinger, A., Moore, C., Donaldson, A. Jafari, A., & Stone, A. (2013). Fluid dynamics topics in bloodstain pattern analysis: comparative review and research opportunities. Published on *Forensic Science International*, Elsevier, Volume 231, Issues 1–3, 2013, ps. 375–396, [Retrieved 02 October, 2020, from 10.1016/j.forsciint.2013.04.018].

Bevel, T., & Gardner, R. M. *Bloodstain Pattern Analysis, With an Introduction to Crime Scene Reconstruction*. 3rd edición, Florida, EstadosUnidos: Editorial CRC Press, 2008.

Bertone, F. M. Y., & Fenoll, A. M. *Criminalística y criminología. Implicancias prácticas de la Investigación Criminal*. Argentina: Editorial Advocatus, 2012.

Blanes Cáceres, S. A. *Manual de Evidencias Científicas II: Cuestiones Psicojurídicas*. Argentina: Editorial Sello Patagónico, 2011.

Chisum, W. J., & Turvey, B. E. *Crimereconstruction*. 2da edición, California, Estados Unidos: Editorial ElsevierAcademicPress, 2013.

Climent Durán, C., Garrido Genovés, V. Y., & Guardiola García, J. *El informe criminológico forense: teoría y práctica*. Valencia, España: Editorial Tirant lo Blanch, 2012.

DeHaan, J. D., & Icove, D. J. *Kirk'sfireinvestigation*. 7° Edición, 7th Edition, Estados Unidos: Editorial Pearson, 2012.

Disanto, L. A. (2006). *Fenómenos de serialidad criminal: una cuestión "psi-juridica"*. Publishedbythe Asociación Latinoamericana de Psicología Jurídica y Forense (ALPJF), [Retrieved 02 October, 2020 from http://psicologiajuridica.org/].

Dror, I. E. (2013). Cognitive Forensics and Experimental Research About bias in Forensic Casework. *Elsevier Science and Justice*, 52(2012), 128–130.

Echazu, D. *Investigación de la muerte*. Buenos Aires, Argentina: Editorial Policial, 1973.

Esperança, P. (2018). Clave de Identificación de Patrones de Manchas de Sangre. *Minerva, saber, arte y técnica*, Año 2, Volumen 2, ps. 24–35.

Fernández-Sánchez, J. I. *Investigación Criminal: Una Mirada Innovadora y Multidisciplinaria del Delito.* Barcelona, España: Editorial Bosch, 2009.

García Pablos de Molina, A. *Tratado de Criminología: Una Introducción a Sus Fundamentos Teóricos.* Madrid, España: Editorial Tirant lo Blanch, 2003.

Gardner, R. M., & Bevel, T. *Practical Crime Scene Analysis and Reconstruction.* EstadosUnidos: CRC Press, 2009.

García Pérez, T. *Pericia en Autopsia Psicológica.* Argentina: Editorial La Rocca, 2007.

Garrido Genovés, V. Y., & Sobral Fernández, J. *La Investigación Criminal: la Psicología Aplicada al Descubrimiento, Captura y Condena de los Criminales.* España: Editorial Nabla, 2008.

Gardner, R. M. (2016). A Qualitative Theory for Crime Scene Analysis. *Association Crime Scene Reconstr, 2016*(20), 45–55.

Graff, G. W. (2016). Case Managment: The Foundation for crime scene reconstruction. *Association for Crime Scene Reconstruction, 2016*(20), 35–43.

Guzmán, C. A. *El Examen en el Escenario del Crimen. Método Para la Reconstrucción del Pasado.* Argentina: Editorial BdeF, 2010.

Houck, M. M. *Forensicfingerprint.* Estados Unidos: Elsevier, 2013.

Inman, K., & Rudin, N. *Principles and Practice of Criminalistics.* EstadosUnidos: CRC Press, 2000.

Jiménez-Serrano, S. Y. Col. *Manual Práctico del Perfil Criminológico.* 2nd Edition, España: Editorial Lex Nova, 2012.

Kahneman, D., & Tversky, A. (1972). Subjective probability: a judgment of representativeness. Academic Press, *Cognitive Psychology*, 3, 430–454.

Kassin, S. M., Dror, I. E., & Kukucka, F. (2013). The Forensic Confirmation Bias: Problems, Perspectives, and Proposed Solutions. *Elsevier Journal of Applied Research in Memory and Cognition*, 2(2013), 42–52.

Lacassagne, A. & Martin, E. *Précis de Médecine Légale.* Francia: Editorial Masson et Cie, 1921.

Marsh, S. (September 6, 2013). Being a council archaeologist is 'like being a detective'. *The Guardian.* [Retrieved 15 September, 2020 from https://theguardian.com/local-government-network/2013/sep/06/being-a-council-archeologist-like-being-a-detective]

Mattijssen, E. J. A. T., & Kerkhoff, W. (2016). Bullet trajectory reconstruction methods, accuracy and precision. *Forensic Science International* [Retrieved 18 September, 2020 from 10.1016/j.forsciint.2016.03.039].

Miguez-Murillas, G. G. (2016). La posición indiciaria relativa en la pericia mecánica del hecho. en *Revista Digital Visión Criminológica-Criminalística* N°13, Año 3, ps. 49–64, del CLEU, México.

Montiel-Sosa, J. *Manual de criminalística: tomo 2.* 2° edición. México: Editorial Limusa, 2010.

National Research Council, Strengthening Forensic Science in the United States: A Path Forward. Estados Unidos, 2009.

Nuñez, P. M. (2016). *Técnicas interpretativas en la criminalística moderna.* en Revista digital Skopein: la justicia en manos de la ciencia, Año 4, N°11, ps. 41–47, Argentina.

Nuñez, P. M. (2017). Sistema revólver para la investigación de homicidios. *Revista TEMA'S de Criminología y Seguridad*, N°42, Año 6, ps. 84–97.

Prueger, E. *Criminalística aplicada.* Neuquén, Argentina: Editorial Neuquén, 2018.

Ramírez-Aldaraca, R. C. *Criminalística: Nuevos paradigmas. Una visión epistemológica y científica.* Edición 2°, México: Flores Editor y Distribuidor, 2019.

Rodríguez, J. R. (2011). La perfilación criminal como técnica forense en la investigación del homicidio intencional con autordesconocido. *Revista de la Escuela de Medicina Legal*, Cuba. [Retrieved 10 October, 2020 from https://dialnet.unirioja.es/servlet/articulo?codigo=4370212].

Santana Lario, J. Y., & Falces Sierra, M. (2002). *Introducción a la lingüísticaforense: "Any Statement You Make Can be used against you in a court of law".* Editorial Universidad de Granada, pp. 267–281. Publicado en el sitio de la Universidad de Granada, España [Retrieved 10 October, 2020 from http://ugr.es].

Snyder, L. (1977). *Investigación de homicidios.* Editorial Limusa, traducción de Avila de la Torre, E. y revisada por GilbonMaitret, M., México.

Turvey, B. *Criminal Profiling: An Introduction to Behavioral Evidence Analysis.* California, Estados Unidos: Editorial Elsevier, 2008.

Taupin, J. *Scientific Protocols for Forensic Examination of Clothing.* EstadosUnidos: CRC Press, 2011.

CHAPTER 3

The Role of the Medical Examiner in the Crime Scene Investigation

Dalia Al-Saif, Maram Al-Farayedhi, Ghada Al-Shamsi, and Marwah Al-Bayat

Worldwide Association of Women Forensic Experts (WAWFE-Caribbean), Dammam Center of Forensic and Legal Medicine, Saudi Arabia

CONTENTS

Dealing with a crime scene can be intimidating to the unexperienced medical examiner. There are so many aspects to take into consideration that may become overwhelming at times. The two most important rules to follow once arriving at a crime scene are to be systematic in the examination, and to remember to adhere to proper police protocol as the medical examiner does not have full jurisdiction over the scene. Investigating a crime scene is a joint task that involves professionals from different specialities, so adhering to police procedure and respecting the boundaries set by other investigating professionals will allow for smoother work flow. Solving the crime is a team effort, it is not a competition and there are no so-called "turf wars," so relaying information and good communication of data is key. After all, the main goal for attending a crime scene by all of these people is to help each other locate significant evidence, form logical theories and motives, and to establish the sequence of events leading up to the crime or death (Shaler, 2011). Therefore, it is wise to try to restrict contact to the body and its immediate surroundings to avoid tramping all over the scene and disrupting evidence or even inadvertently introducing false evidence. This small mistake can cause the integrity of the whole case to be questioned. In the end, everyone's main goal is to conduct a comprehensive examination of the scene, the body. and the collection of evidence (Fonneløp et al., 2016).

Attending the crime scene allows the medical examiner to see the full picture, and to fully appreciate some findings. A good medical examiner is wise enough to realize that their main concern is not just the body of the deceased; they must also meticulously examine the surrounding scene and the clothes because they can all give valuable clues. For example, examining the body of a

DOI: 10.4324/9781003129554-3

victim that died in a small space due to positional as-phyxia in the morgue is not the same as actually seeing how the body was initially seen in that small space. The medical examiner should be able to correlate between the findings on the body of the victim and the findings in the surrounding scene, a patterned abrasion, or a distinctive bruise seen on the body can be matched up to a potential weapon found at the scene or with any other object that could have inflicted such a specific appearance. In some cases, the crime scene can be much more im-portant than the body of the victim when it comes to answering investigative questions. Victims of electrocu-tion may not show any physical signs of electrocution, but the crime scene may show the body lying in a bath tub with the radio or hair dryer inside with it. Other examples are cases of smothering where the pillow and bedding may hold more solid evidence than the body, or even in cases of SIDS (sudden infant death syndrome). Having the opportunity to observe the body with respect to its sur-roundings is crucial for the medical examiner not only to be able to have a better understanding of the cause of death, but also to be able to determine the manner of death and the circumstances leading up to the death. For example, in an elderly man who was found dead in his home due to a drug overdose, it is important to look for all medication bottles at the scene and do a pill count. Keep in mind that not everything is always as it seems, some crime scenes may be staged in an attempt to disguise a homicidal death as an accidental one. The same goes for a victim with multiple gunshot wounds to the chest. The manner of death may be suicidal and not homicidal (Hejna et al., 2012, de la Grandmaison et al., 2008).

An important point that needs emphasis is that when attending the crime scene and examining the scene, the clothes, and the body, any thoughts or impressions formed are considered preliminary conjectures. An in-clusive report cannot be formed without considering the information gained from the police investigation, the results of the evidence, and most importantly the find-ings of the autopsy. Again, solving a death is a combined effort. Speculations can be made but a medical examiner should never insist on an opinion based on what had been seen at the crime scene.

The first thing to consider when arriving at a crime scene is safety! The medical examiner should first and foremost follow safety regulations. Personal protective equipment such as masks, gowns, shoe covers, gloves, and face shields should be used whenever possible. Wearing plastic shoe covers and gloves is not only es-sential for avoiding cross-contamination of the scene and the body, but they are also important for the med-ical examiner to avoid contracting an infection of any kind. When it comes to safety, the scene should always be taken into consideration. Could this area cause harm in any way? For example, in cases of suspected carbon

monoxide poisoning, it is important to make sure the proper authorities have closed off any gas valves or re-moved the source of the carbon monoxide. Another example is cases of electrocution; the power should be turned off, especially when attempting to examine the suspected source. If the body was found in an old house with unstable walls or roof, the body and the area should be photographed and removed as quickly as possible. After the scene has been deemed as safe, cau-tion should always be taken when handling the body. There may be a number of concealed sharp objects that can be potentially harmful or even lethal at times. Lastly, upon leaving the scene of a crime, it is extremely im-portant to adequately dispose of all the personal pro-tective equipment that was used.

Obviously, not all dead bodies are conveniently found lying in bed in their homes. They can be found practically anywhere. That is why, when attending the crime scene and the body is out in an open and exposed area, the rules change. Each scene dictates how it should be handled. It is ridiculous to assume that one can ex-amine a body in the daylight in a house in the same manner as that found in a ditch in the woods at night in the pouring rain. Many points should be taken into con-sideration. Lighting is one of the most important things. Optimal lighting should be available to thoroughly ex-amine the scene and the body to avoid anything being overlooked. Another point to take into consideration is that if the body was found near the shore of a beach and the tide was rising, in this scenario the scene and the body should be photographed and documented and profes-sionals should attempt to work at a faster pace than usual to avoid the loss of any potential evidence.

One crucial step that cannot be stressed enough is sufficient documentation. The scene should be photo-graphed as much as possible and paying special attention to the body. This does not mean to only document the positive findings because sometimes the negative or lack of findings are just as important (Gill & Pasquale-Styles, 2009). One of the most important reasons for such ex-tensive photographic and written documentation of the scene and deceased is to be able to re-study and correlate them at a later time after gaining more information from the autopsy. It is also known that some evidence may change over time (such as bruises that may become clearer, abrasions that become darker in color due to drying, the degree of decomposition) or even be lost due to environmental changes, or induced while transferring the body in or from the scene (Spitz, 2006).

The clothes and the body should be photographed in the exact position found; then, additional photographs should be taken after moving the body to allow for better examination. The clothes should be photographed in detail, especially for an unidentified body; the photos (or notes) should depict the hygiene of the clothes, any tears or cuts found in the fabrics, if the clothes fit properly, if the buttons were done up correctly, if they are appropriate to the current season, and any jewelery or watches should be mentioned.

The body should be photographed in respect to the surroundings, and then further photographs should be taken of close-ups of the body and any particular findings, such as wounds, bloodstains, personal items, signs of medical intervention, signs of injection marks, paint or other odd findings, any nearby objects such as tools, medications, and drug paraphernalia, weapons, etc. In short, one should take as many photographs as possible. A video walk-through of the scene can be very helpful to take in the bigger picture. As helpful as photographs are, detailed notes about the whole scene are also very important to the medical examiner. Any particular finding should be written down and described using exact measurements for the dimensions and reference points for their location in relation to the surroundings.

Asserting the time passed since death is an important issue. Both the scene and the body can give many clues to determining this or at least making a close approximation. It is difficult to talk about the body alone and the scene alone, because many issues are overlapping or must be taken into consideration together. In regards to the body, post-mortem changes are crucial in determining the time of death. The presence or absence of insect activity is also a significant clue that needs to be considered.

There are many important things to look for at the scene of death that can give indications as to the circumstances surrounding a death. It is important to remember that the presence of blood at a crime scene does not necessarily mean a traumatic death. Some causes of natural death can result in a bloody scene such as that resulting from esophageal varices (Dolinak, 2005). Remember that the initial appearance of a scene can be deceptive. A victim may have suffered a severe crush/burst injury to the internal organs causing massive internal hemorrhaging, but externally the body may show insignificant bruises on the abdoKnight's forensic pathologymen (Van den Eeden, 2016).

The scene should be carefully examined for any peculiar findings such as signs of a struggle, drag marks, and anything out of the ordinary. Special attention should be given to the findings on the body that do not match up with the surrounding scene; for example, if the clothes of the victim were damp but the victim was found inside a room with no signs of a water source. Or if there was evidence of tire marks on the clothes of a victim whose body was found in the woods half buried. This can also be vegetation and grass stains that have no obvious source in relation to the surrounding scene (Spitz, 2006). In these cases, a clue should be given to the investigating team that the body was removed from the original crime scene to a "dump site."

POST-MORTEM CHANGES

One of the well-known tasks of the medical examiner at a crime scene is the determination of post-mortem interval (PMI), which is the period of time from death to the examination of the body by the medical examiner. It is significant because a suspect can be clearly ruled out or included in the investigation of death and also it can help in narrowing the list of missing persons. Although it is perceived through media that this period can be given by exact minutes, this is not applicable in reality; with advanced techniques, one can reach a narrow range of time. Another very important task of a medical examiner is to determine whether the body was transferred from one place to another after death.

Post-mortem changes are changes in the human body that start at the moment of death. They progress with time while the body is transferred to the morgue, and hence a good observation at the death scene is very important. These changes of the body are mostly used in determining post-mortem interval. They can provide a wide range of time that can even reach years, as in bone remains. Some of them can also help in deciding whether the body position was altered after death. Hypostasis, rigor mortis, putrefaction, mummification, and adipocere are among post-mortem changes that will be discussed.

HYPOSTASIS

Hypostasis, or lividity, is stagnation of blood in the blood vessels due to the effect of gravity. It results from the absence of active blood movement. The blood circulation can be sluggish even before death in a recumbent patient as in brain deaths and this should be taken in consideration in determining the time passed after death.

Stagnation of blood gives discoloration of the skin in dependent areas of the body in relation to gravity. In bodies found lying on their back, it mostly appears in the back of the body, while in suspended bodies it would appear in the lower limbs. Determining post-mortem interval by describing hypostasis is a subjective method as it can be affected by several factors, and can be divided into stages. The stage of beginning followed by confluence, maximum expansion of intensity, incomplete shifting after turning the body, and non-displacement. The last stage results from hemoconcentration as fluids are lost through the vessel wall (Henssge et al., 1988). Hypostasis starts half an hour after death and becomes fixed in 8–12 hours (Saukko, 2004).

Moving the body can shift part or all of the blood to new body areas, depending on the time the body was moved. Hypostasis that is located in different body areas gives a clue that the body was moved within a certain time (less than 8–12 hours). Once it is fixed, any change in the position will not affect the location of hypostasis in the body. Therefore, having the hypostasis in a body area that is not corresponding to gravity indicates that the body was moved after passing the time of fixation.

RIGOR MORTIS

The skeletal muscles in the living are always in a state of partial contraction; to release this contraction, there is a need for energy in the form of ATP (adenosine triphosphate). ATP is needed to break actin-myosin bonds in muscle cells. As there is a depletion of ATP after death, stiffening of the body in its antemortem state of contraction appears in the form of rigor mortis that starts to appear 2–3 hours after death. Stages of rigor mortis include the stage of beginning, full development that stays for a period of time till it reaches the stage of complete resolution with the start of putrefaction (Henssge et al., 1988). It starts to appear within small muscles in 3 hours and maximizes in 8 hours and can be re-established after breakage in 2–8 hours but can reach up to 20 hours (Henssge et al., 1988) (Crostack et al., 2017). The development and progress of rigor is influenced by several factors, including body exertion before death, diseases, drugs, and body temperature. All should be taken in consideration while evaluating rigor to determine post-mortem interval (Saukko, 2004).

The use of rigor mortis as an element in determining time passed after death is subjective and based on vague factors as there are no experimental data and it only relis on literature. Knowing the fact that it can be re-established after breakage (with forceful movement of the limb over the joint to overcome stiffness) makes its use in determining PMI more complicated and can only be used with other clues at the scene.

Rigor mortis can help in telling whether the body was moved after death. This is possible once full rigor is reached, as stiffness of the body will keep it in the same shape when rigor reached full development. For example, if the body passed through stages of rigor reaching its full development while sitting on a chair, moving the body to the floor will clearly tell that the location of the body has been changed after death.

PUTREFACTION

Human decomposition is a complex, biological, and chemical process that involves enzymes, bacteria, fungi, and protozoa (Cockle & Bell, 2015). It is influenced by several factors including the state of burial, temperature, humidity, acidity, clothing, scavenger activities, and geographical area (Cockle & Bell, 2015) and thus it can't be applied constantly to the human body to determine post-

mortem interval over the world. Putrefaction marks the end stage of both hypostasis and rigor. It starts when the bacteria inside the body starts acting upon tissues. Blood components disintegrate and stain vessels, leading to marbling of the body by making the vessels more visible externally. Putrefaction includes autolysis of tissues and hence disappearance of muscle stiffness. The sequence of body decomposition is unified while the time each stage takes is variable across different regions. It starts with greenish discoloration of the lower abdomen, marbling of vessels, followed by abdominal distention by gases, burging of fluids, and infestation with flies at different stages. Total body score (TBS) is established for visual observation of the head, torso, and limbs and it is directly related to the post-mortem interval (Dabbs et al., 2016, Suckling et al., 2016).

A study of human decomposition has set three stages, including a fresh stage (0–7 days) with insect activity, hypostasis, and rigor. Early decomposition (3 days–2 months) hapenns with skin color changing from pink to grey to green to dark brown; leathery, bloating, skin slippage, and hair loss with moderate maggot act; bullae of upper limbs trunk and thighs; and bulging of the rectus. Advanced stage (3 days–2 months) happens with extreme maggot act, moist decomposition with thick black liquid, and the start of drying up into mummification (Parks, 2011).

ADIPOCERE AND MUMMIFICATION

Body decomposition could be retarded by other changes of the body depending on the environment (Ubelaker & Zarenko, 2011). As the process takes longer, the range of time is wide and even more complicated than the previously mentioned changes. Both adipocere and mummification are post-mortem changes that can either occur solely in the body or as a combination.

Adipocere is a bacterial enzyme–produced change in the body fat where hydration and oxidation of fatty acids lead to insoluble saturated fatty acids (Takatori, 1986). This gives an appearance of hardening and saponification of body fats, with a soft, greasy appearance. Moisture is a key in the adipocere formation, warm temperature, mildly alkaline pH, and anaerobic conditions all contribute to its formation (Ubelaker & Zarenko, 2011). It starts a few days after death, becomes apparent after 3 months, and extensive in 5–6 months. It can be degraded in months and years by gram-positive bacteria, air, and fungal growth. However, it was found in a dead body dated 600 years from the late Romans.

In contrast, mummification includes drying of the body and requires a hot, dry environment and 3 days–9 months to form. While it can involve the whole body in some cases, in other bodies, the moisture that is used to form adipocere in parts of the body leads to dryness of other parts and, hence, mummification appears. That makes estimation of the time past death using these body changes very vague and inaccurate. However, these changes can give a clue to the season and location of the body when such changes developed, depending on the preference of each change.

TEMPERATURE-BASED DETERMINATION OF TIME PASSED AFTER DEATH

The nomogram method (temperature-based death time estimation) is a graphical tool that is a gold standard in determining early post-mortem interval (Potente et al., 2017). It includes mathematical calculations with factors including rectal temperature, ambient temperature, virtual body weight in kilograms and hours since death (Potente et al., 2019), and it uses body cooling as the main indicator of timing. It is based on deep rectal temperature with a model of rectal cooling curve (Mall et al., 2005). However, this calculation is expected to be applied on standard cooling conditions where the body is naked, supine, on a thermally indifferent surface with no airflow, solar irradiation, or dampness. This typical situation is not the case in the majority and thus correction factors are applied when making calculations (Potente et al., 2019). It is obvious that all information should be taken at the crime scene as movement of the body will make this method useless. Flaws to this method include that it is based on a constant environmental cooling while in reality, nobody can tell exactly what the temperature was and its changes before finding the body (Mall et al., 2005).

The clothes worn by the victim can also give an idea about the time of death; for example, if a body was found wearing heavy clothing in the summer season, it gives an important clue. The medical examiner should make note of any articles found that may give an idea about the time passed after death such as newspapers, receipts, clock/watch, calendars, and expiration dates of food (Saukko, 2004).

CSI IN ASPHYXIA DEATHS

Asphyxia could occur in different forms as suffocation, smothering, hanging, strangulation, or choking. Death by asphyxia could be accidental, suicidal, or homicidal. The purpose of attending the scene by the medical examiner has many folds, mainly to provide insight into the cause and the manner of death. Scene investigation is essential in asphyxia cases to rule out a homicidal manner of death. By examining the body at the scene with the viewing of its surroundings, the medical examiner would be able to interpret specific findings that could be found in the autopsy, such as a patterned imprint on the neck of the deceased or a unique post-mortem change as an appearance of the hypostasis in the head and upper chest only. Also, it may enable the examiner to evaluate the circumstances, whether it is more consistent with natural death or with injury, and to advise the investigators on specific evidence collection. Usually, in cases with suspected homicide asphyxia, the medical examiner should examine the body before being moved or removed from the scene. In some occasions, scene investigation is more important than autopsy. Complete work in the death scene leads to the proper diagnosis of the cause and manner of death, especially if correlated with autopsy findings (Taktak et al., 2015).

A medical examiner who performs autopsy in a doubtful case of positional asphyxia needs to know information about when, where, how, and under which circumstances the body was found. Not attending the death scene is a significant mistake that a medical examiner would make. The scene description and photographs are essential in deaths because physical circumstances and body posture are the most critical findings that need to be documented, as the autopsy findings may not give any helpful results in such cases. It would be convenient for the medical examiner in the interpretation of an autopsy's finding if they attended the death scene before the body was removed or changed in position.

Bodies that are found in a cramped position or crowded area that could compromise breathing might have died due to traumatic or crush asphyxia. Crush asphyxia is attributed to the circumstance where an individual has become trapped with significant weight over their body or crushing their body so they are unable to breath. This leads to squeezing or compression and splinting of a chest wall that prevents chest movement. The scene here may show the body under a car being crushed by the vehicle slipping off a jack (Byard & Woodford, 2008).

Child accidental asphyxia usually results from unsafe circumstances, mostly sleeping in a bed or play area. Accidental hanging in infants and toddlers can occur by being suspended from their clothing or ropes near them when they get out of their beds. Also, choking with food fragments or any foreign body may occur in infants and toddlers commonly while moving or talking during eating, or when a child plays and tries to put what comes to their hand inside their mouth. Examination of the deceased in such cases should be done at the death scene. With all circumstances around, a medical examiner can identify the causal factors of the accidental asphyxia and may clarify the cases that resemble accidental death (Byard & Jensen, 2007).

Even though most hanging cases have a suicidal background, the medical examiner could be the discriminator in regards to the manner of death. In hanging cases, it is critical to see if body suspension occurred before or after death. Dribbling of the saliva for example is considered a significant marker in support of death due to hanging. Also, a crucial thing is to determine whether a crime was committed in that scene, like if the body contains any trace evidence that is not from the scene location; for example, mud, grass, or seed found on the shoes, clothing, or the body of the deceased. Post-mortem examination of a hanging case in a death scene may provide important information, such as finding multiple injuries or defense wounds on the body and if there are signs of violence at the crime scene that raise suspicions where further investigation is required.

The medical examiner at the location can do little but should document much more. They should note the position of the body concerning nearby objects and establish the plan of the premises if indoors. Injuries may present in cases of suicidal hanging; an injury may result from striking an adjacent object during suspension or due to attempts of suicide before it was done by hanging. It may come from handling of the corpse during or after the release of the suspended body or can occur with resuscitation procedures. The deceased's location relative to objects, with the accurate measurements of the distance between them, within site, is essential to mention in the hanging case, to help in the interpretation of injuries on the body that could result from objects that present in a scene. An expert medical examiner evaluates almost everything, such as a little bruise, abrasion, fingernail marks and underneath nails, and does not focus on a major injury only.

The basic processes in documenting a scene of asphyxia death that must be followed are taking photos and video, writing a note, and sketching the scene. By taking pictures of the scene and the body before moving or removing anything around it, and by the description of the scene location and weather, conditional evidence of the site (entry and exit doors or windows), structural evidence of activities (bottles, cans, papers, trash, etc.), furniture, and weapons if present (Dogan et al., 2010a).

In dealing with an asphyxia case, evaluate post-mortem hypostasis and rigor mortis at the death scene should be done before moving the body from the discovered position because it may give useful feedback to answer the question about if the position of the body changed after death or not. Furthermore, this is critical to identify if the discovered location is the original death/crime scene.

Due to the post-mortem settling of the blood by gravitation, hypostasis appears externally as a red-purple discoloration at the lowest point of the body and its location and state of fixation are significant findings in a hanging. Fixed postmortem hypostasis remains the same color when the examiner applies pressure on it, opposed to an unfixed one that blanches white when moderate pressure is applied. Suppose hypostasis manifests on the parts of the body does not belong to the discovered position. So, the forensic medical examiner at the scene should concede the possibility that somebody transferred a deceased after death because, after the fixation of the hypostasis, it will not change the area of its appearance with movement. Otherwise, if the body was moved before fixation, the hypostasis will change its site on the body. Post-mortem hypostasis in the hanging is unique and seen in the legs, forearms, and hands. Assessing the appearance or absence of rigor mortis and stiffness of the body at the scene can support the information of the person and location when found if it is the original death location or not.

It is vital in the hanging case to examine the body while it is suspended before releasing the ligature from the neck. For example, fractures of the cervical vertebrae do not happened regularly in suicidal, homicidal, or accidental hangings, unless the body has dropped from a high distance. Additionally, the suspending body from a high point leaves marks on the neck like an inverted V, not run around the full circumference of the neck. This can be used to distinguish a hanging case from manual strangulation. However, in the hanging from a low point, the marks tend to be horizontal and may resemble characteristic of manual strangulation. That way the forensic medical examiner should note critical information such as the type of hanging (complete or partial hanging), knot position (typical or atypical hanging), and the ligature material. A complete hanging is when the body is entirely suspended by a ligature, with the feet off the ground. On the other hand, partial hanging is when any part of the body is in contact with the ground. In a typical hanging, the knot is situated on the midline of the occipital region over the neck nape, while any other position of knot is an atypical hanging. The ligature is the object used to suspend the victim from the neck, and usually it is reachable at the location. Ropes, belts, clothing, and electric wires are among commonly used ligature elements in hangings. The critical factors for the decapitation are the height of fall, the strength of the neck tissue, and the width and flexibility of the ligature (Hejna & Bohnert, 2013).

The ligature mark is the most specific sign of the hanging. The medical examiner is expected to compare between the ligature mark and a given ligature at the scene and should take in consideration the composition of the ligature as a soft fabric might not leave any mark on the neck of the victim.

Asphyxiation can be caused by carbon monoxide poisoning. Carbon monoxide (CO) is a light, colorless and odorless gas. It is an incomplete combustion product of hydrocarbons and found in fuel-burning: cars, engines, gas stoves, fireplaces, and heaters. At moderate to high levels of concentration, it can cause death. Although deaths from CO poisoning in the vehicle are usually suicidal, such deaths can be accidental. Death scene examination and investigation in a suspected cases of CO poisoning are critical. Suicide method includes sitting in a vehicle while the engine is working in a closed-door parking area or garage and could be bypassing the exhaust-gas into the vehicle cabin by a tube or hose.

On the other hand, accidental CO toxicity may happen when CO affect drivers of a moving vehicle, usually due to a defective exhaust system. Another cause is with the leakage from the heat exchanger in vehicles that use a direct air supply from the heater. Also, it is usually occurring with inadequate ventilation in a closed room with coal- or charcoal-burning inside. That emphasizes the importance of crime scene attendance by the medical examiner to look for any evidence of CO gas sources, like finding a heater in the vehicle or closed home, burned charcoal, fireplace in a closed room, defect on the vehicle exhaust, or fire in the building. The external body examination usually shows congestion and cyanosis of the face, cherry-red lividity, and the clothes or body of the corpse may have burned (Demirci et al., 2009).

Mechanical occlusion of the respiratory orifices is another form of asphyxia, generally caused by placing a plastic bag around the head and securing it around the neck with a rope, choking on food or a foreign object, or by a pillow on the face. Suicidal smothering is a rarer method and, in such cases, it may be challenging to establish whether a suicide or homicide has occurred. From here, we see the importance of the presence of the medical examiner at the crime scene in asphyxia, to avoid the difficulty of analyzing autopsy results. Unfortunately, sometimes the death scene of asphyxia does not give any clues to the cause of death, and the autopsy findings are nonspecific (Di Vella et al., 2002).

Autoerotic asphyxia is a subcategory of sexual masochism indicated by self-strangulation to the point of loss of consciousness to enhance sexual arousal. Though a person who does this action could die accidentally by hypoxia, commonly, it is used to enhance orgasm by strangulation, hanging, or suffocation with plastic bags. By the examination of the body in the crime scene in an autoerotic asphyxia case, usually the body is found naked. In male cases, one might find intimate female clothes, and the zipper of the pant could be found open or without underwear. By investigating the death location, there could be props or things that are used for sexual/pain stimulating, such as pornographic magazines or DVDs, mirror, ropes, chains, locks, condoms, and anesthetic elements (Idota, 2019).

FIREARMS

When it comes to violence, shootings are a very common occurrence in every society. Determining whether they are accidental, homicidal, or suicidal is crucial, rendering the crime scene or the scene of death very important. A thorough investigation of the scene includes collection and preservation of forensic evidence, and the interpretation of any and all findings (Shaler, 2011).

When assessing the scene of a shooting, the forensic pathologist must have a basic knowledge of certain elements regarding ammunition and their chemical components, the effect it has or can leave on the victim or any other nearby object (i.e. bullet holes), and distance and range of the projectile (Shaler, 2011). This should obviously be in addition to knowing how to duly conduct oneself in a crime scene.

Once you have been called to the scene of a shooting, many questions will come to mind, so moving in a systematic manner is key to avoid missing anything and making sure no aspect of the scene is missed. It is also very important to keep in mind that some of these interpretations can be considered as preliminary at best; they can be debated later. One should always keep an open mind when collecting information/data/evidence and attempt to formulate and educated opinion but never jump to conclusions. Remember, the scene investigation is a joint effort between many professionals of different specialties and therefore good communication is essential to collect all the significant data to produce satisfactory answers to solving the puzzle. Some of this data may not be readily available at the scene and will come to light as the investigation continues forward. For instance, the forensic pathologist may be called to the scene of a burn victim, the body may have second- and third-degree burns and the room may be burned, but upon closer examination a gunshot wound to the head is revealed (Türk, 2004).

There are many different aspects when it comes to investigating a shooting scene, such as identifying the assailants and their numbers, retrieving the bullets or any other firearm evidence, and collecting trace evidence. Not to mention the importance of observing the surroundings and noticing signs of a struggle, blood spatter on the floors or walls, and the presence of a suicide note along with all the other important evidence. This section will concentrate on the body of the victim.

The first thing to be done on arrival at the scene is to document the findings in detail by making notes about the surroundings and the condition of the body. An important task that every medical examiner must not neglect is photographic documentation of the crime scene and the body, even if there appears to be no specific findings (Gill & Pasquale-Styles, 2009). This is done with diagrams, a written report, and abundant photographs. Photographs are also an indispensable tool to meticulously document the scene, the body, and the evidence. With the current advancements in digital technology, it is easy to take as many pictures as needed.

The body should be photographed in the exact position and place it was found, the photographs should also include pictures of the body in relation to the surroundings. If there was anything covering or obscuring the view of the body, there should be two sets of photographs, ones before removing the obstructions and ones after removal. Finally, there should be close-up photographs of the body including the face, hands, clothes, and all injuries. It is also important to be sure that the photographs of the injuries should be taken in relation to a prominent anatomical site, as well as using a scale to convey its measurements and its exact location on the body. All the photographs taken at the crime scene are important to the medical examiner to have the chance to go over again before and after the autopsy (Gill & Pasquale-Styles, 2009).

This, of course, must all be in addition to any handwritten records detailing any and all important details worth noting, in regards to the clothes, the body, and the surroundings.

The clothes of the victim (if any are found) can give an idea or clue as to the circumstances surrounding the death, as is the case with the body. After photographing the clothes (without removing them from the body), they should be examined as thoroughly as possible given the many limitations of working at the crime scene. Usually the first thing that is spotted is the presence or absence of blood. The site on the clothes where the bloodstains are located typically indicates the site of injury; for example, bloodstains on the groin area of the pants most likely means there is an injury in that area of the body. The effects of gravity on the blood should also be kept in mind during examination; for example, in the case of a gunshot wound in the head, one would probably find bloodstains on the top of the shirt around the collar and on the front or sides of the shirt, depending on the position of the body (if it is lying on the back or on the side). Whether the blood found on the clothes is completely dried or not is a very important factor in estimating the time the shooting occurred and to corroborate the story of any possible suspects or even witnesses. Another usually obvious thing on the clothes is the presence of damage to the fabric of the clothes, though sometimes it may be concealed by blood. These defects usually correspond to either entrance or exits wounds found on the body of the victim. Some of these defects in the fabric may have a characteristic appearance such as those left by shotgun pellets. In these situations, the holes are multiple and scattered around one particular area on the clothes and body of the victim. It is very important to pay close attention to these "holes" or defects left by the bullets as they can give information about many things, such as the trace evidence left by the bullet and its metal coverings or jackets and GSR (gunshot residue). It may even help determine the caliber of the bullet used (Shaler, 2011). For a medical examiner, these defects are an important indicator for the distance between the victim and the firearm. If burning or singeing is found around the defect, it means the gun was held close enough for the flame igniting from the barrel of the gun to have burned the fabric. If there was no evidence of burning and only soot or carbon was found around the defect, it means that the gun was held at an intermediate distance from the victim (Dolinak, 2005, DiMaio, 1999). Some of these signs are major indictors of entrance holes for the bullet (Cvetković et al., 2018). When dealing with any crime scene, it is important to operate in a systematic way and examine everything accordingly. While the bullet holes or defects are very important, a good medical examiner must also note the presence or absence of any other defects in the clothes that may indicate a struggle, for example tearing around the collar of the shirt or a front pocket. This may help formulate an idea of what happened prior to the shooting and how many people were involved.

Many of the major points to look for in the body of a shooting victim are quite similar to those we look for on the clothes of the victim. When examining the body at a crime scene, the medical examiner must use the utmost precaution as not to disturb any evidence left on the body or the clothes. This fact alone allows for many limitations in the process. It may be wise to examine the body after a forensic scientist or the police have collected all or any trace evidence such as dirt, grease, or metal particles from the bullet seen on the clothes and the body and especially around the wounds. Foreign material such as clothing fibers may be embedded in entrance wounds covered by the victim's clothes. The body should be photographed and all particular features should be documented in detail, as previously mentioned. The body should be thoroughly examined to look for any other injuries and wounds that may give a clue as to the manner of death, such as signs of past suicidal attempts like scars from cuts on the wrists, or even signs suggesting a homicide, especially injuries found on the palms, wrists, and forearms that may give a clue as to the occurrence of a struggle or fight or even signs of attempts at defense prior to the shooting. A common injury seen in victims of gunshot wounds is called pistol whip injuries. These occur when the gun itself is used to inflict blunt force trauma instead of just for firing bullets. These injuries are usually found on the head of the victim and can carry the distinctive features of the gun itself. Graze wounds can be seen on any part of the body. They are superficial gunshot wounds where they only graze the skin of the victim without entering the body. A key feature in graze wounds is the presence of skin tags; the direction of the skin tags always points towards the direction of the gun and the shooter. This gives an idea as to the orientation of the shooter and the victim. The hands should always be carefully examined for any gunshot residue or soot and even blood spatter, which may hint to the shooting being a suicide or even accidental rather than a homicide. When examining the head, close attention should be given to try and identify any gunshot holes that may be covered by hair. A clue to the presence of a fracture to the base of the skull in cases of gunshot wounds to the head is a bilateral false bruising around the orbits (periorbital area), called raccoon eyes. Also, if upon examining the body we only see one bullet hole wound in the skull that carries the features of an exit wound, it should be a clue to attempt to examine the mouth for an intra-oral entrance wound or evidence of injury or gunshot residue to the teeth and mucus membranes of the mouth and lips, though this may be difficult to do at the crime scene and is best done during the autopsy after removal of the tongue. It is important to note that the presence of multiple gunshot wounds on the victim does not necessarily mean a homicide or the presence of several perpetrators. It has been documented that victims may commit suicide by self-inflicting several shots to themselves, and these self-inflicted wounds may not always be found on the areas of the body containing vital organs (Hejna et al., 2012, Grandmaison et al., 2008).

Gunshot residue found on the skin around the gunshot holes is a crucial piece of evidence as it can help answer some questions about differentiating between an entrance wound and an exit wound and can even help in determining the distance between the muzzle of the gun and the victim (Plattner et al., 2003). A rule of thumb in distinguishing between entrance and exit gunshot wounds is that the edges of an entrance wound are usually inverted while the edges of an exit wound are usually everted and may even be ragged. In an ideal setting, when the muzzle of the gun is held perpendicular to the victim, making the angle between them zero, soot would be seen in a circular pattern around the entrance hole. This appearance changes based on the angle between the muzzle of the gun and the victim; the soot residue seen takes on a more elliptical appearance. Studies have shown that the shape in which the residue is seen around the entrance wound may indicate what direction the gun was held in relation to the victim (Plattner et al., 2003).

Another important factor to consider is the distance between the muzzle of the gun and the victim (Table 3.1). In close contact shots, soot from the smoke of the gunshot is seen around the entrance wound, but when the muzzle of the gun is held close to the victim, a seal is created between the gun and the skin upon firing; thus, little or no soot is visible around the entrance wound, and instead it can be found imbedded in the tissue underneath the wound. Close contact wounds where the gun is pressed hard against the skin of the victim have characteristic marks around the entrance wound that imitate the configuration of the muzzle of the gun. These marks are called muzzle imprints. Another key feature of an entrance wound in hard contact wounds when the gun is held up

TABLE 3.1 Estimating the Range of a Discharge

Distance of Shooting	Characteristics

Tight Contact	• Over Soft Tissue:
	   • Muzzle imprint
	   • Circular entrance wound surrounded by a collar abrasion
	   • Possible bruising
	   • Little or no burning
	   • Little or no soiling
	 • Over Bone:
	   • Stellate and lacerated entrance wound
	   • Bruising
	   • Little or no soiling

Distance of less than 15 cm	• Circular entrance wound • Abrasion collar • Burning signs • Soot soiling • Some powder tattooing
Distance between 15 cm and 30 cm	• Circular entrance wound • No soot soiling • Powder tattooing • Rarely burning signs are seen
Distance more than 40 cm	• Circular entrance wound • Abrasion collar
Far distance	• Large, irregular entrance wound

against a bony part of the victim's body (especially the skull) is the presence of laceration at the wound. It may even take up a satellite shape, due to the buildup of gases between the gun and the tissue of skin over bone (Buyuk et al., 2009). Also, burning or singeing, blackening of the skin, and clubbing of the hair is usually seen in close contact entrance wounds due to the heat of the gases and the flame expelled upon firing the gun. The use of a silencer attachment (a sound suppressor) not only decreases the distinctive noise created by shooting a gun, it also decreases the flash of flame and smoke released from the muzzle, thereby diminishing some of the characteristic features of a close contact wound. This should always be kept in mind and should keep the medical examiner from giving a definitive statement about the range of shooting at the crime scene because more accurate information can be found at the time of autopsy (Brożek-Mucha, 2017). If a body is found without any clothes (or without any clothing covering the wounds) and the wound seen has the features of an entrance wound of close contact but lacks the presence of soot, it may be inferred that the soot was deposited on the clothes that have been removed. At a crime scene, not everything is as it seems, so one should always tread carefully and take everything into consideration. Entrance wounds resulting from an intermediate distance or range of firing are characterized by powder tattooing, which is stippling marks left on the skin that are actually just tiny abrasions that are caused by the gunpowder hitting the skin. There would be minimal to no soot seen due to the increased distance between the gun and the skin, and because the propellant particles can travel a longer distance than the soot made by the smoke that is expelled from the gun. Powder tattooing should not be confused with pseudo stippling, which are artifactual abrasions created by insect bites, other trajectories such as broken glass, or even from a fragmented bullet. Abrasion collars are created around entrance wounds due to the friction created between the bullet and the skin and their width depends on the distance of firing. When examining abrasion collars, it should be kept in mind that, upon drying, this abrasion becomes dark in color and thus produces an important artifact. It can then be misconstrued as soot and thus give a false impression as to the distance of firing. Another special injury usually found on the skull is the keyhole injury; this occurs when the bullet enters the skull but then exits from the same hole or exits from a hole very close to the entrance wound, thus creating a distinctive appearance resembling that of a keyhole. Here the wound can carry both features of an entrance and an exit wound. Not every entrance wound is met with an exit wound, especially when examining the body at the scene where there are many limitations in manipulating the body (Saukko, 2004).

Typical exit wounds have everted and even ragged edges with none of the characteristic features of entrance wounds such as soot, burning, tattooing, etc. Exit wounds may not always be larger than entrance wounds. Shored exit wounds look like lacerations and may be surrounded with some degree of abrasion. This occurs when the bullet attempts to exit a body that is supported by something hard such as clothes, a wall, or even furniture (Dolinak, 2005, DiMaio, 1999).

It goes without saying that the medical examiner should never under any circumstances insert a probe into gunshot wounds at the scene of the crime in an attempt to reproduce the angle of trajectory, because in doing so the integrity of the hole and the bullet track may be manipulated and valuable evidence may be lost (Denton et al., 2006). Needless to say, if the body of the shooting victim was found to be decomposed, the interpretations of some of the findings around the bullet holes become somewhat of a moot point.

In cases of multiple gunshot wounds, things become rather difficult, but the same basic concepts still apply. Photographs and written notes about the details of the body still apply, and should be done without any haste; the wounds should be denoted with numbers or even letters. It is not wise to try and match entrance wounds to their so-called exit wounds at the scene of the crime because it would be absolutely erroneous since the bullets can have very different pathways within the body, not to mention the possibility that some wounds may be due to fragmented bones or split bullets. Some wounds may even be due to two or more bullets passing through it. It should be kept in mind that many cases of multiple GSWs are due to both perpetrators and the police, so taking a thorough statement from the authorities as to where the police were involved in the shooting in relation the victim is very valuable.

ENTOMOLOGY AND CSI

When arriving at the crime scene and after locating the dead body or the remains, all evidence should be collected; anything situated on, underneath, and inside the body/remains should be collected. Live adult flies flying over the dead body should be caught personally by using a net. The ante-mortem colonization of insects should be distinguished from post-mortem colonization at the crime scene. Both can be found simultaneously at the crime scene, especially in cases like poor nursing care. Genuine collection and handling of entomological evidence will aid in the investigation (Mona et al., 2019).

When arthropods are discovered at a crime scene and on the dead body, they help in various forensic investigations. This is because they deliver the required information, especially about time since death, season at death, initial crime scene, and movement and concealment of the remains after death. Furthermore, the use of trauma sites found on the dead body can indicate various drug abuse and are found on neglected children and the elderly (Viero et al., 2019). However, even though arthropods are very informative at crime scenes, they are believed to have the possibility of changing and modifying it.

The interval between the time the body is believed to be found and the time when the insects colonized the body can be calculated using entomology as the minimum post-mortem interval (min-PMI). Through the look at the necrophagous insects, the blowflies (also called *Diptera calliphoridae*) are believed to be the first flies to be detected and then colonize the body. However, even though the blowflies have evolved to detect the various odors that result in decomposition, specifically within the little time of death, the situation or time of year can postpone their arrival at the cadaver (Beutler, 2020).

The foreign entomological clock is believed to have two observable parts that play a unique role in the investigation and general use of forensic entomology. The parts include the period of insect isolation and the time since the insect started colonization. The period of insect isolation is believed to be the time of the insect's invasion, which eats flesh, specifically on the dead matter. Insect colonization is believed to be the developmental stage for the insect species found at the crime scene. The insect grows in different developmental stages right from the larvae to the stage of increase in their weight, length, and shape. During this period, the feeding larvae isolate themselves from the dark places where they convert into the pupae. The last stage of cracking the larvae, finally the adult insect emerges. (Mona et al., 2019).

Insects, carnivores, and even scavengers are responsible for flesh removal that causes various types of macroscopic changes/artifacts on the body. These changes should be kept in mind when evaluating the dead body either at the crime scene or during the autopsy. It should be noted that differentiating between ante- and post-mortem findings on the body could be challenging. (Viero et al., 2019) As many adult flies openly consume the existing body fluids, they try to defecate the ingested foods on the surfaces or nearby the crime scene. Therefore, this creates a unique stain of fly artifacts that contain human fluids and bloodstains. Fly contaminates are not confined to the main crime scene. False secondary crime scenes originate as a direct result of scavenging activity on the cadaver. The issue with fly artifacts are emphasized by the fact that human bloodstain is very difficult to be distinguished from fly regurgitation and defecation (Rivers & Geiman, 2017).

The medical examiner should be aware of such findings on the body and should be able to interpret them based on the insect growth that is seen in the death or crime scene.

CSI IN FALL FROM HEIGHT

The manner of death in falls from height can be very challenging. While suicide is the most common manner, an investigation could be initiated to exclude other manners including accidents and homicides. In order to differentiate, you have to examine the cadaver and inspect for any defensive wounds that have specific distribution over certain areas of the body and examine the crime scene to see if there are any signs of a struggle indicating a malicious act.

At the crime scene, the medical examiner should give special consideration to the location of the fall, height, and the objects that the victim might hit while falling, which might give us different patterns of wounds; examples are suspicious wounds that look similar to stabs. These can take the investigation to an entirely different direction, while a good observation of the death scene reveals that objects that are located in the way of the body while falling are the cause (Shaw & Hsu, 1998, Töro et al., 2006, Türk et al., 2004).

CSI IN SUDDEN INFANT DEATHS

In some circumstances, the medical examiner is the one who demonstrates the importance of death scene investigation and could ask legal personalities to initiate one. Information that a medical examiner gets from death scene could be the best support of their final decision on the cause and manner of death.

Death in infancy is an example of such scenarios where a sudden death cannot be taken lightly and certified as a natural death without a full investigation. Sudden unexpected death in infancy is identified as the sudden death of an infant under 1 year of age that remains unexplained after a thorough case investigation, including performance of a complete autopsy, examination of the death scene, and review of the clinical history. Several hypotheses are postulated to explain such a death, including intrinsic (neuroregulation and cardio respiratory function) and extrinsic factors (prenatal exposure to tobacco smoke, prone sleep, loose bedding) that lead to asphyxia in a vulnerable infant (Goldberg et al., 2018). Data from the autopsy and ancillary investigations (histopathology, microbiology, radiology, toxicology, metabolic, blood chemistry, and genetics) together with a full structured scene investigation would be of vast importance to reach the real cause of death (Erck Lambert, 2016).

A detailed scene investigation can explore or exclude a malicious act. A structured death scene investigation is followed by several countries and it consists of digital recordings with video or photography, doll re-enactment, and personal communication with care providers (Erck

Lambert et al., 2016). Data inquired can help determine the position of the infant when left asleep and when found dead, including bedding and amount of clothing, ventilation and heating, and sharing of the bed surface (Palusci et al., 2019).

This information helps the medical examiner give an interpretation for the findings on the body. For example, the location of lividity on certain body parts can easily be explained and correlated with the position of the body at scene. Unexplainable marks on the body can be explained by objects found near the body. Such data can help determine the position of the body and, hence, the possibility of asphyxial death or hyperthermia as a cause of death, but more importantly excluding any suspicious act surrounding death.

CSI IN SUSPECTED CASES OF CHILD ABUSE AND NEGLECT

Burn Cases

In cases of hot water burns of a child in a bathtub or a sink, a diagnosis of non-accidental manner cannot be reached without full investigation, including crime scene examination. History from the care giver, physical findings on the body of the child, and information from the scene can all help determine the true scenario. Information that is needed from the scene includes tub water temperature that must be taken at different time intervals to determine the initial and peak temperature. The dimensions of the sink or tub and distance between the water faucet and the floor of the tub, together with the rate of water flow, are all important. The construction material of the tub is also important. Using a doll to demonstrate how the child was found in the tub and comparing it with burns on the body is significant. This information, together with information from the caregiver in regards to the time interval from putting the child in the tab until the burn, are vital in deciding whether it was an inflicted burn or an accidental one. General observation of the scene can reveal vital information about the living situation that can point to elements of child abuse and neglect (Feldman, 2007) (Knox & Starling, 2010).

Fall Injuries

Whenever a fall is used as an explanation for a child injury, a well-structured investigation of the scene is needed. A plausible explanation for the injuries should be reached after obtaining detailed information from the scene. Description of the surfaces where the fall occurred, any impacted object during the fall and dimensions of the objects, all need to be documented in sketches and photographs. The position of the child after the fall should be obtained from witnesses. All of this is needed to correlate between body injuries and the alleged fall with the main goal of excluding non-accidental trauma. Skin injuries, head injuries, and more importantly bone fractures can all be used to determine if the witnessed fall explains the injury from a biomechanical point of view (Knox & Starling, 2010).

SEXUAL ASSAULT

Assessing the crime scenes in a sexual assault can be requested after the medical evaluation of the victim. A detailed history of the incident that is taken by the assessing physician is needed to direct investigators to areas of the crime scene that should be well examined. There is a good literature support of collecting evidence from the crime scene in cases of child victims of sexual assault rather than collecting it from the body of the victim. Bed linens, clothes, and other articles are the objects to look for (Knox & Starling, 2010), (Alsaif & Frasier, 2007).

Examining the crime scene is vital in case proceedings if used to support a history from the victim describing details of the site where the crime took place. Collaboration between the assessing physicians and crime scene examiners is crucial, as some information given by a child victim might be considered a fantasy until a careful inspection reveals the true existence of strong evidence.

TRANSPORTATION INJURIES

Transportation injuries represent an example where information from the death scene could be vital to the medical examiner. Most of the time, crime scene investigators will provide the medical examiner with a detailed documented description of the scene. Solving a critical question can all rely on this information.

One important piece of information is the site of the victim in the vehicle, whether an occupant or the one in control of the vehicle. In some situations, the victim site in the vehicle changes for several reasons. However, the site of injuries on the body and biological evidence in the vehicle can both be used to locate the victim in the correct place at the time of the accident.

Full understanding of the controls of a vehicle, especially in small plane accidents, is needed by the medical examiner to interpret some injuries. Limb injuries and fractures can be used to determine the position of the victim and whether they were in control of the vehicle or not (Wolf, 2005). A visit to the death scene is needed to understand it.

In pedestrian victims of road traffic accidents, an autopsy of the body with radiological examination can reveal important information that helps in the reconstruction of the event. Specific features of lower limb fractures can help determine the direction of the impact and add vital information to those collected by scene investigators (Kharoshah, 2020). They can provide the medical examiner with the types of suspected vehicles to determine the possibilities of their involvement in the accident in hit-and-run accidents.

The importance of death scene investigation in transportation injuries is emphasized in scenarios that involve questions about the cause of death. An example is a firearm incident where the victim tries to escape the location using their car. A traffic accident could occur and inquiry about the true cause of death, whether from a firearm injury or injuries that resulted from the accident. In this case, a full and detailed investigation of the death scene can solve the case. One example is failure to spot tire marks on the road, which indicates that the victim either lost consciousness or died before the accident and, hence, death can be attributed to a firearm injury.

REFERENCES

Alsaif, D., Almadani, O., Almoghannam, S., Alfarayedhi, M., & Kharoshah, M. (2018). Teaching Children About Self Protection From Sexual Abuse: Could it be a Cause for Source Monitoring Errors and Fantasy? (two case reports). *Egyptian Journal of Forensic Sciences*, 8(27).

Alsaif, D., & Frasier, L. (2007). Child sexual abuse. In A. Barbaro (ed.), *Manual of forensic science; and international urvey* (pp. 200–201). CRC press.

Beutler, M., Hart, A., & Hall, M. J. R. (2020). The Use of Wing Fray and Sex Ratios to Determine the Origin of Flies at an Indoor Crime Scene. *Forensic Science International*, 307, 110104.

Brożek-Mucha, Z. (2017). A Study of Gunshot Residue Distribution for Close-range Shots With a Silenced Gun Using Optical and Scanning Electron Microscopy, X-ray Microanalysis and Infrared Spectroscopy. *Science Justice*, 57(2), 87–94.

Byard, R. W., & Jensen, L. L. (2007). Fatal Asphyxial Episodes in the very Young: Classification And Diagnostic Issues. *Forensic Science, Medicine, and Pathology*, 3(3), 177–181.

Buyuk, Y., Cagdir, S., Avsar, A., Duman, G. U., Melez, D. O., & Sahin, F. (2009). Fatal Cranial Shot by Blank Cartridge Gun: Two Suicide Cases. *Journal of Forensic and Legal Medicine*, 16(6), 354–356.

Byard, R. W., & Woodford, N. W. (2008). Automobile Door Entrapment–a Different Form of Vehicle-related Crush Asphyxia. *Journal of Forensic and Legal Medicine*, 15(5), 339–342.

Cockle, D. L., & Bell, L. S. (2015). Human Decomposition and the Reliability of a 'Universal' Model for Post Mortem Interval Estimations. *Forensic SciInt*, 253, 136.e1–9.

Crostack, C., Sehner, S., Raupach, T., & Anders, S. (2017). Re-establishment of Rigor Mortis: Evidence for a Considerably Longer Post-mortem Time Span. *International Journal of Legal Medicine*, 131(4), 1039–1042.

Cvetković, D., Živković, V., Juković, F., & Nikolić, S. (2018). Double Suicidal Gunshot Wounds to the Heart. *Forensic Science, Medicine and Pathology*, 14(2), 248–250.

Dabbs, G. R., Connor, M., & Bytheway, J. A. (2016). Interobserver Reliability of the Total Body Score System for Quantifying Human Decomposition. *Journal of Forensic Sciences*, 61(2), 445–451.

de la Grandmaison, G. L., Fermanian, C., Aegerter, P., & Durigon, M. (2008). Influence of Ballistic and Autopsy Parameters on the Manner of Death in Case Of Long Firearms Fatalities. *Forensic Science International*, 177(2–3), 207–213.

Demirci, S., Dogan, K. H., Erkol, Z., & Gunaydin, G. (2009). Two Death Cases Originating From Supplementary Heater in the Cabins of Parked Trucks. *Journal of Forensic and Legal Medicine*, 16(2), 97–100.

Denton, J. S., Segovia, A., & Filkins, J. A. (2006). Practical Pathology of Gunshot Wounds. *Archives of Pathology & Laboratory Medicine*, 130(9), 1283–1289.

Di Vella, G., Neri, M., & Belviso, M. (2002). Unusual Suicidal Smothering by Means of Multiple Loops of Adhesive Gummed Tape. *Journal of Forensic Sciences*, 47(3), 645–647.

DiMaio, V. *Gunshot Wounds: Practical Aspects of Firearms, Balistics, and Forensic Techniques*. 2nd edn. Florida, USA: Charles C. Thomas Press Taylor & Francis Group, 1999.

Dogan, K. H., Demirci, S., Erkol, Z., & Gulmen, M. K. (2010a). Accidental Hanging Deaths in Children in Konya, Turkey between 1998 and 2007. *Journal Forensic science*, 55(3), 637–641.

Dogan, K. H., Demirci, S., Gunaydin, G., & Buken, B. (2010b). Accidental Ligature Strangulation by an Ironing Machine: An Unusual Case. *Journal Forensic Science*, 55(1), pp. 251–253.

Dolinak, D., E.W, M. and E.O., L. *Forensic Pathology: Principals and Practice. Massachusetts*. Massachusetts, USA: Elsevier Inc, 2005.

Erck Lambert, A. B., Parks, S. E., Camperlengo, L., Cottengim, C., Anderson, R. L., Covington, T. M., & Shapiro-Mendoza, C. K. (2016). Death Scene Investigation and Autopsy Practices in Sudden Unexpected Infant Deaths. *The Journal of Pediatrics*, 174, 84–90.e1.

Feldman, K. (2007). Burn Injuries; case studies. In R. C. Alexander (ed.), *Child fatality review, an interdisciplinary guide and photographic reference* (pp. 297–310). St Luis: GW Medical.

Fonneløp, A. E., Johannessen, H., Egeland, T., & Gill, P. (2016). Contamination During Criminal Investigation: Detecting Police Contamination and Secondary DNA Transfer from Evidence Bags. *Forensic Science International: Genetics*, 23, 121–129.

Gill, J. R., & Pasquale-Styles, M. (2009). Firearm Deaths by law Enforcement. *Journal of Forensic Sciences*, 54(1), 185–188.

Goldberg, N., Rodriguez-Prado, Y., Tillery, R., & Chua, C. (2018). Sudden Infant Death Syndrome: A Review. *Pediatric Annals*, 47(3), e118–e123.

Hejna, P., & Bohnert, M. (2013). Decapitation in Suicidal Hanging–Vital Reaction Patterns. *Journal of Forensic Sciences*, 58(Suppl 1), S270–S277.

Hejna, P., Safr, M., & Zátopková, L. (2012). The Ability to Act–Multiple Suicidal Gunshot Wounds. *Journal of Forensic and Legal Medicine*, 19(1), 1–6.

Henssge, C., Madea, B., & Gallenkemper, E. (1988). Death Time Estimation in Case Work. II. Integration of Different Methods. *Forensic Science International*, 39(1), 77–87.

Kharoshah, M., Alsaif, D., Albayat, M., Alshamsi, G., & Alsowayigh, K. (2020). Images in Forensic Thanatology. In G. L. R. A. A. M. M. C. Cattaneo (ed.), *Radiology in Forensic Medicine*. Springer, Cham: Springer Nature Switzerland.

Knox, B., & Starling, S. (2010). Abusive burns. In C. Jenny (ed.), *Child Abuse and Neglect; Diagnosis, Treatment and Evidence* (pp. 233–235). Reverport Lane: Elsevier.

Mall, G., Eckl, M., Sinicina, I., Peschel, O., & Hubig, M. (2005). Temperature-Based Death Time Estimation with only Partially Known Environmental Conditions. *International Journal of Legal Medicine*, 119(4), 185–194.

Mona, S., Jawad, M., Noreen, S., Ali, S., & Rakha, A. (2019). Forensic Entomology: A Comprehensive Review. *Advancements in Life Sciences*, 6(2), 48–59.

N, I., M, N., H, T., H, I., K, S.-I., & H, I. (2019). Autoerotic Asphyxia Using a Plastic Bag Loosely Covering the head over a gas mask. *Legal Medicine*, 38, 69–72.

P, S. & B, K. (2004). *Knight's forensic pathology*. 3rd edn. London, U.K.: Hodder Education Publishers, 57–59.

Palusci, V. J., Kay, A. J., Batra, E., Moon, R. Y., Corey, T. S., Andrew, T., Graham, M., Neglect, C. O. C. A. A., Prevention, S. O. C. D. R. A., Syndrome, T. F. O. S. I. D., & Examiners, N. A. O. M. (2019). Identifying Child Abuse Fatalities During Infancy. *Pediatrics*, 144(3).

Parks, C. L. (2011). A study of the human decomposition sequence in central Texas. *J Forensic Sci*, 56(1), 19–22.

Plattner, T., Kneubuehl, B., Thali, M., & Zollinger, U. (2003). Gunshot residue patterns on skin in angled contact and near contact gunshot wounds. *Forensic SciInt*, 138(1–3), 68–74.

Potente, S., Kettner, M., & Ishikawa, T. (2019). Time since death nomographs implementing the nomogram, body weight adjusted correction factors, metric and imperial measurements. *Int J Legal Med*, 133(2), 491–499.

Potente, S., Kettner, M., Verhoff, M. A., & Ishikawa, T. (2017). Minimum time since death when the body has either reached or closely approximated equilibrium with ambient temperature. *Forensic SciInt*, 281, 63–66.

Rivers, D., & Geiman, T. (2017). Insect Artifacts Are More than Just Altered Bloodstains. *Insects*, 8(2).

Shaler, C. R. *Crime Scene Forensics: A Scientific Method Approach*. 1st edn. Florida, USA: Charles C. Thomas Press Taylor & Francis Group, 2011.

Shaw, K. P., & Hsu, S. Y. (1998). Horizontal Distance and Height Determining Falling Pattern. *Journal of Forensic Sciences*, 43(4), 765–771.

Spitz, W. and D., S. *Clark R. Spitz and Fisher's Medicolegal Investigation of Death*. 4th edn. Illinois, USA: Charles C. Thomas Publisher Inc, 2006.

Suckling, J. K., Spradley, M. K., & Godde, K. (2016). A Longitudinal Study on Human Outdoor Decomposition in Central Texas. *Journal of Forensic Sciences*, 61(1), 19–25.

T, T., N, I., H, T. and H, M. (1986). Microbial Production of Hydroxy and Oxo Fatty Acids by Several Microorganisms as a Model of Adipocere Formation. *Forensic Science International*, 32(1), 5–11.

Taktak, S., Kumral, B., Unsal, A., Ozdes, T., Buyuk, Y., & Celik, S. (2015). Suicidal hanging in Istanbul, Turkey: 1979–2012 Autopsy results. *J Forensic Leg Med*, 33, 44–49.

Töro, K., Szlávik, N., Mészáros, A., Dunay, G., Soós, M., & Keller, E. (2006). Jumping and Falling Death in Children, Adolescents, and Young Adults. *Journal of Clinical Forensic Medicine*, 13(3), 129–134.

Türk, E. E., Anders, S., & Tsokos, M. (2004). Planned Complex Suicide. Report of Two Autopsy Cases of

Suicidal Shot Injury and Subsequent Self-immolation. *Forensic Science International*, 139(1), 35–38.

Türk, E. E., & Tsokos, M. (2004). Pathologic Features of Fatal Falls From Height. *The American Journal of Forensic Medicine and Pathology*, 25(3), 194–199.

Ubelaker, D. H., & Zarenko, K. M. (2011). Adipocere: What Is Known After Over Two Centuries of Research. *Forensic Science International*, 208(1–3), 167–172.

Van den Eeden, C. A. J., de Poot, C. J., & van Koppen, P. J. (2016). Forensic Expectations: Investigating a Crime Scene With Prior Information. *Science Justice*, 56(6), 475–481.

Viero, A., Montisci, M., Pelletti, G., & Vanin, S. (2019). Crime Scene and Body Alterations Caused by Arthropods: Implications in Death Investigation. *International Journal of Legal Medicine*, 133(1), 307–316.

Wolf, D. (2005). Motor Vehicle Collisions. In D. Dolinak, E. Matshes & E. Lew (eds.), *Forensic Pathology, Principles and Practice*. San Diego, California, USA: Elsevier Academic Press.

CHAPTER 4

Archaeological Evidence Collection

Almir Olovčić

International Commission on Missing Persons, Sarajevo, Bosnia-Herzegovina

CONTENTS

INTRODUCTION

Since the dawn of humankind, human interactions led to conflicts sometimes decimating entire cities, even countries; in conflict, rules are frequently broken, and atrocities emerge, leaving countless victims in their wake. Numerous archaeological and historical accounts exist on this topic, allowing us to examine the types and scales of the crimes which are often regarded as genocide, a term coined by Raphael Lemkin in his 1944 book *Axis rule in occupied Europe: laws of occupation, analysis of government, proposals for redress*. Although there are many definitions of genocide, in short terms, it is defined as destruction of a nation or an ethnic group in phases or by immediate actions which result in mass killings of a large number of persons during a short period of time (Lemkin, 1944). During 20th century, mankind had witnessed some of the most brutal and inhumane mass killings, such as Armenian Genocide (1914–1923), The Holocaust (1941–1945), The Cambodian genocide (1975–1979), Rwandan genocide (1994) and Srebrenica (1995). Srebrenica was classified as genocide in trials, prosecutions and verdicts conducted by ICTY (The International Criminal Tribunal for the former Yugoslavia), against high level army officers of Vojska Republike Srpske (VRS, eng. Army of the Republic Srpska) (ICTY, 2010; ICTY, 2017).

In this chapter, the focus will be on experiences from forensic archaeology excavations in Bosnia and Herzegovina (BiH) and activities of The International

DOI: 10.4324/9781003129554-4

Commission on Missing Persons (ICMP) archaeologists and anthropologists aimed at documenting and investigating crimes against humanity during 1992–1995 conflict. Initial excavations and recoveries of human remains were conducted in 1996 and have been ongoing till the present day. Since 1996, ICMP has played a central role in the efforts to account for the missing persons in the former Yugoslavia, especially in Bosnia and Herzegovina's, with helping to develop institutional capacity to address this issues in a non-discriminatory manner, designing legislation to safeguard the rights of families, introducing systematic forensic methods, including the use of DNA, upholding rule of law-based processes that have ensured the provision of evidence to domestic courts and the ICTY, and facilitating the active engagement of the families of the missing. Most of the evidence was collected from a numerous mass graves, scattered around the country.

Technical definitions of a mass grave are abundant (Mant 1987; Schmitt, 2001; Jessee & Skinner, 2005), but maybe the best definition is the one by Skinner (1987), who defines mass grave as containing "at least six individuals, usually placed indiscriminately and tightly together with no reverence for the individual". The objectives of mass grave investigations fall into three broad categories: humanitarian, legal and historical, all of which can contribute significantly to the reconstruction of societal safety, especially to reestablishing trust in societal institutions (Juhl & Olsen, 2006).

Bosnia and Herzegovina is characterized by diversity of natural landscapes and since the wartime activities happened all over the country there are multitudes of different forensic contexts. Eastern parts of the country are characterized by mid to high mountain ranges with dense forests and inhospitable terrain, which were used by refugees as an escape routes to free territories and that is where most of the surface human remains were found. Southern and western parts of the country are characterized by karst landscape, with numerous caves, caverns, pits and deep holes, used for disposal of human remains, not only during recent wartime atrocities, but also during WWI and WWI. Remains from the various historical contexts can be mixed at the same site, usually in the same cave or pit. Evidence and artifacts found during human remains recovery have been of the great importance in differentiating between forensic contexts predating 1992 and the later ones. Beside evidence, archaeological stratigraphy of the excavated graves and locations played great role and contributed to the important conclusions, such as sequence of events. Most large-scale mass graves, such as Tomasica and Kevljani (both in the old iron mines), Gorice (Brcko municipality) and numerous Srebrenica mass graves were found in northern and eastern parts covered in low to mid-range mountains and plains.

A great number of experts from various fields participated in these processes, providing expertise and advice on proper archaeological techniques, evidence collection, documentation/filing, analysis and interpretation of results, which as a result had convictions against individuals or groups responsible for crimes. On numerous occasions, evidence collected during these excavation campaigns had a major role during trials, providing crucial evidence linking perpetrators, victims, crime modus operandi and locations of execution and subsequent burial of human remains.

First excavations and forensic investigations of exhumed human remains in BiH were carried out by then ICTY and PHR (The Physicians for Human Rights), and later on by ICMP, which still provides technical assistance – exhumation and anthropological examination - to BiH local institutions, primarily MPI BiH (Missing Persons Institute of Bosnia and Herzegovina). A component of ICMP's tasks has been the provision of assistance to local institutions, which includes forensic assistance to identify the missing, with the use of state of the art DNA technology, on a large scale (ICMP, 2014). Technical assistance in the field (reconnaissance of locations that could potentially contain clandestine graves and exhumation of human remains) and in the mortuary (anthropological examination of exhumed human remains and sampling for DNA analysis), together with DNA-led process are major components of the forensic framework provided to local institutions.

FORENSIC ARCHAEOLOGY DEFINITION AND ITS USE IN THE MEDICO-LEGAL CONTEXT

Forensic archaeology is defined as the discipline that incorporates archaeological methods and principles within a legal context (Groen, Márquez-Grant and Janaway, 2014). Data collected by archaeologists provides detailed documentation about the stratigraphic sequence of the crime that happened, from killing, burial, and possible post-burial disturbance of the grave, and recovering of evidence and artifacts can help in identifying of the dead and sometimes even the perpetrators (Steele, 2008).

Excavation is the archaeological approach to the field work which includes locating, exhumation and documenting human remains and the connected forensic evidence, where evidence can be artificial (manmade) or natural in its origin. Exhumation is the anthropological contribution to the uncovering of human remains from natural (pits, caves, crevices, holes) or artificial (mass graves) locations. Not every excavation is an exhumation, but every exhumation is an excavation, meaning that a comprehensive archaeological approach is necessary in order to recover human remains.

Archaeologists involved in forensic excavation need to have skills in pre-excavation planning, location assessment, a certain degree of knowledge of hard science-based applications (geophysics, chemical analysis, geology), logistic requirements, and proper excavation methodology; furthermore, they need to know how to report and present results in a clear and concise manner, and if needed, to be attend court proceedings as an expert witness. Precise archaeological excavation techniques are needed:

- to avoid misinterpretation of observed alterations to the recovered body that occurred as a result of lifting and moving the individual;
- to avoid confusion about the relationship of 'evidence' to the body (Blau & Skinner, 2005);
- to recover physical evidence that will allow a reconstruction of the temporal sequence of a single event, usually in a buried context (Hanson, 2004).

A skilled forensic archaeologist must be familiar with stratigraphy of the site that is excavated, soil type and changes occurring over time upon deposition of remains and with differentiation between human and non-human bones (Haglund, 2001). Quite often authorities receive a call about bones that are found and need to be assessed. Upon arrival at the location, authorities may find he remain of a barbequed lamb/pig/cow that had been thrown into a meadow or shallowly buried in the soil. It may be considered surprising how often this happens in BiH, where barbecued lamb is a traditional delicacy, and not surprisingly, many times a whole team of police, crime scene investigators, prosecutors, and archaeologists/anthropologists had been summoned to the site, just to find out that the discovered bones are non-human.

In order to validate a forensic claim about the past, there must be a clear chain, linking crime scene and perpetrator or human remains and the missing persons (Crossland, 2013). Establishing connections between the suspect, the victim and the crime is of vital forensic importance, and that is why forensic archaeological deposits

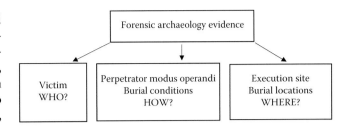

FIGURE 4.1 Diagram representing relationships in forensic archaeology contexts.

must be analyzed in relation to other deposits, either on the same location (primary burial) or other, distant locations (secondary, tertiary, etc. burial) (Moreno & Maita, 2020).

This can be easily illustrated by a scheme as in Figure 4.1.

Unlike indoor crime scenes, outdoor crime scenes are more susceptible to a number of environmental and anthropogenic factors, leading to crime scene contamination, which can also greatly affect evidence, the resultant quality of evidence collection, and subsequent interpretation. A proper recognition and documentation of the effects of natural or man-made environmental processes is important for understanding what happened to the remains and evidence from the point when they have been deposited at the location (Dirkmaat & Cabo, 2016). A summary of this factors is given in Table 4.1.

Sometimes families of the missing and government officials are impatient to discover the truth about the fate of their relatives; pushed by the perceived lack of progress, they take matters into their own hands. Unfortunately, families of the missing and government officials are not trained in proper excavation techniques and forensic methodology, and they contribute to crime scene contamination in a way that can make any subsequent forensic identification impossible, thus greatly delaying the process and extending grief and pain of the living relatives (Stover, Haglund & Samuels, 2003; Blau & Skinner, 2005).

Most modern scientific approaches employ interdisciplinary methods and strategies, resulting in time- and cost-saving benefits, while yielding more accurate

TABLE 4.1 Most common factors involved in the crime scene contamination

Environmental	Anthropogenic
Weathering (rain, snow, sun, landslides)	Agricultural works including use of fertilizers
Animals (scattering, gnawing, insect work)	Construction works
Botanical (plant and tree roots)	Industrial works (open mining, quarries)
Soil and geology (dry, wet, frozen, clay, sand, silt, peat, chalk, loam, combination of soil types)	Family of victims excavating graves in an inadequate manner, undeliberate destroying possible forensic evidence and context
Presence of microorganisms	Deliberate actions of perpetrators (incineration, heavy machinery crushing, robbing of primary graves, use of chemical fluids, such as acids, limestone, etc.)
Physico-chemical (pH, temperature, moisture, electrochemical properties, oxygen content, salinity)	

TABLE 4.2   Science-based applications in forensic investigations

Science	Methods	Sample type
Geology	Auger probe, direct-push probe, XRD	Soil, rocks
Chemistry	Spectroscopy (UV-Vis, FT-IR, Raman), crystallography, thermal analysis, chromatography, C-14 dating	Soil, fibers, various artifacts (cartridge cases, bullets), organic material
Physics	Optical microscopy, electronic microscopy, X-ray microscopy	cartridge cases, bullets, fibers
Biology and medicine	DNA analysis, palynology, entomology, osteological methods, pathology	Bones, pollen samples, botanical samples, insect samples, human tissues

results. Forensic archaeology is no exception: it pulls from knowledge bases of physical anthropologists (as the most important player/factor in the excavation together with archaeologists), biologists, chemists, geologists, physicists, experts in methods of DNA analysis, criminal law and crime scene investigation (CSI) experts. Table 4.2 summarizes the most common applications of science-based methodologies in forensic investigations. Often, the distinction between methods is not that clear and one or more techniques are intertwined.

Final goal of a forensic archaeology project is the collection and interpretation of evidence in such a way so as the resultant record can be found to be reliable and admissible in court; for this to be achieved, certain steps prior and during excavation need to be fulfilled. Archaeological methods employed in forensic archaeology mostly overlap with the ones used in commercial/traditional archaeology, and closely follow well-established archaeological best methods and practices used worldwide (Barker, 1977; Harris, 1979; Evis et al. 2016). The most frequently employed in steps forensic excavations which result in the best possible recovery of human remains and associated evidence are summarized in the following section.

LOCATION ASSESSMENT PRIOR THE EXCAVATION

Like in any endeavor worth undertaking, good preparation is half the work; archaeological work is no exception, especially considering the destructive nature of excavation, and the legal necessity of proper evidence collection at crime scenes. Planning will be informed by the results of the location assessment; however, before any assessment is initiated, it is advisable to define the boundaries of the area to be assessed and excavated, with the help of geographic and topographic maps and aerial photography (Dupras et al. 2006). Basic planning and assessment of sites of potential forensic interests includes:

I. review of available documentation on the site history;

II. visual assessment of the location that includes:
- slope of the terrain
- Ease of access
- visible site disturbances
- previous use of site (open field, farm field, orchard, forest, gravel pits, industrial, open mining, etc.)
- present day situation at the site
- potential need for works prior the excavation (site clearing from trees, shrubs, etc.; making an access path if none exist; facilities needed (toilets, security, storage of equipment, etc.)

III. physical assessment of the location (Auger probe, cadaver dogs, ground penetrating radar, electric resistivity and magnetic testing, soil analysis, test trenching);

IV. risk assessment (natural and anthropogenic factors, such as poisonous animals and plants, unexploded ordnances (UXOs) and land mines, underground electric and gas lines and water pipes, subterranean waters);

V. total station survey of the site to document changes prior to the excavation works, with the production of an accurate plan of site if any additional future works are needed;

VI. report writing/conclusions/recommendations.

EXCAVATION STEPS

After all the necessary prerequisites for the site are made and the approval from the authorities involved in the investigation is granted, the excavation process can start and it includes:

I. plans, photographs and sketches of location prior the excavation;

II. cleaning the area and preparing for excavation;

III. top soil stripping;

IV. excavation of the area and recovery of human remains and evidence;

V. mapping the spatial distribution of remains and evidence;

VI. collection, documentation and transport of human remains and evidence;

VII. additional work, including soil sieving, metal detecting, sampling of soil, entomological and botanical sampling;

VIII. writing a report of the excavation,

IX. presenting in court of law, if required.

Professionally conducted archaeological recovery and documentation plays a critical role in an overall investigation process that involves many potential disciplines for various purposes such as:

- anthropological analysis and autopsy of human remains in mortuaries;
- scientific analysis of collected samples;
- criminological processing of evidence (cartridge cases, bullets, tire and machine marks)

HISTORICAL BACKGROUND OF THE ARCHAEOLOGICAL CONTEXT. ARCHAEOLOGY OF THE COUNTRY/REGION

Archaeological context – simply the place where the artefact was found - is probably one of the most important archaeological concepts. An unbroken association of the artefact to its archaeological context gives the artefact its legal authenticity and archaeological significance (Ford, 1977); context can also inform on the site formation processes. Archaeologists working on a forensic site need to obtain a broader insight into the historic processes of the area, as well as a deeper knowledge about material culture of the modern era. All kinds of modern objects must be recognized in the fragments found in forensic sites, which can include not only the archaeologist's own culture, but that of others who might be encountered in the grave (Scott & Connor, 2001); this knowledge is crucial when establishing the forensic (in) significance of artefacts.

During forensic archaeology work, investigators often come across archaeological and historical remains at the location, from the time periods predating the one which is the main focus of our work. Such findings must be properly evaluated, documenting chronological sequences, to avoid possibility of excavation of remains that have no humanitarian or forensic significance (Moreno & Maita, 2020). This is why it is important to gain as much information as possible about historical context of the location of forensic interest, but also about local burial customs and archaeological findings of the area, before deploying to the field. In general, modern and legal funerary contexts contain dressed bodies and the disposal box, which colloquially is known as casket, where additional clothing such as improvised pillow for stabilizing

the head of the deceased and lining material are also present inside (Moreno & Maita, 2020). Next, orientation of human remains can be useful in determining of historical or forensic context. If the grave was created under normal circumstances and not as a result of atrocities, then it will probably have proper orientation based on the most common religious practices; Christian graves will be oriented East-West and Muslim ones North-South. In Balkan Eastern Orthodox Church adherents, when they are buried, it is a custom to put a small coin in a mouth or inside casket and which are often found when excavating graves, leading to a conclusion that we are dealing with a historical, regular burial. Persons who are buried in a hurry or as a result of violent crime will not have respectful burial and often are found just wrapped in blanket, without proper orientation. Additionally, ligatures and blindfolds on the body, with few personal artefacts are also found in non-funerary, criminal context burials (*ibid*). Sometimes even bullets or bullet cartridges are found inside grave.

All of these factors mentioned above can help in differentiation between historical and forensic burials, but the final decision on exhumation or re-interment should be made in agreement with all the participants in the process.

ARCHAEOLOGICAL EVIDENCE COLLECTION AND CHAIN OF CUSTODY PROCEDURE

Skinner (1987) advocates four types of physical evidence that could be found inside mass graves:

- evidence of identity of victims;
- evidence on the time of death;
- evidence of antemortem traumas and
- evidence on the cause and manner how victim died (evidence on perimortem traumas)

For Juhl (2005), there are two types of evidence: *hard evidence* provided by physical anthropologist and odontologist and *soft evidence*, provided by forensic archaeologist. As it is case with the evidence in the everyday homicide investigations, evidence collected during forensic archaeology excavations must be obtained in a manner admissible in court (Connor, 2007). A simple flow chart as in the Figure 4.2 shows the pathway of evidence from collecting to final result.

The custody procedure plays a major role. By following the path of evidence within the forensic/legal system, from the initial in situ discovery to the final presentation in the court of law, the chain of custody warrants the admissibility of evidence. (Melbye & Jimenez, 1997). It is important that the chain of custody pathway is unbroken at any point of time, otherwise the

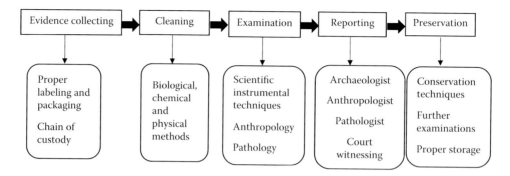

FIGURE 4.2   Evidence pathway from the collection of evidence to final result.

use of the evidence may be compromised in the investigation or legal proceedings. Traditional archaeologists are mostly unfamiliar with providing the level of security necessary to maintain the chain of custody required in forensic investigations, since most of the artifacts that archaeologists work with (before engagement in forensic work) has no or little commercial value (Melbye & Jimenez, 1997; Crist, 2001). Therefore, when classically-trained archaeologists enter the medicolegal work context, they have to be extensively trained in the chain of custody procedures and the consequences of failure to follow them.

Special attention needs to be addressed to circumstantial evidence. This is a very common type of evidence, found inside graves, and can include clothing, identification documents, photographs or other specific personal items (jewelry, amulets). But use of this type of evidence is an unreliable sole identifier of the victim (or victims, in the case of mass graves and commingled human remains) and reliance on it must be avoided. On the other hand such evidence sometimes can be used for linking specific location and victims, like in the case of Ovčara mass grave in Croatia. Victims from Ovčara were identified as patients and hospital stuff because of the presence of bandaged limbs or limbs in plaster casts and slings, broken crutches, a pelvis with catheter swinging from it and hospital apparel (Juhl, 2005; Juhl & Olsen, 2006). In the forensic archaeology cases, circumstantial evidence can only be used to aid the personal identification process, but the formal identification remains in the hands of a forensic pathologists authorized to issue the death certificate (Juhl, 2005) and the proper archaeological recovery and documentation of evidence can play a very important role in the identification process. With the advancement of scientific identifier technologies such as DNA, odontology, distinctive medical records, fingerprints (if available), possibility of comparison of blood samples of living relatives with the DNA samples from victim and from ICMP's long term experience with this methodology, DNA reports should be the only reliable scientific identifier of the victim's identity.

The spoil left after the creation of the grave, dropped artefacts (bullet casings), footprints and vehicle tracks, broken vegetation and subsequent taphonomic alterations are examples of the stratified physical evidence in an environment associated with the formation of the grave, and that altogether represents the sequence of events within the forensic landscape (Hanson, 2004). Important evidence left at a devastated site might include a grave feature, as well as residual items such as clothing, hair and ballistics evidence, and are frequently found at the primary grave site, providing us with valuable evidence that can help in resolving questions such as formation of site, and sequence of events regarding the persons recovered from a particular body mass (Jessee & Skinner, 2005).

All these findings need to be documented in logs and in chain of custody procedures. Sometimes procedures have to be amended, in compliance with the state laws and in line with archaeological best practice. This can only be done with the agreement of all the participants in the exhumation process, documented in an activity log, and supported by a detailed description of the reason for the change, the nature of the change, and the expected outcome. Evidence collection from individual and mass grave sites differs to some extent: in individual graves, a total evidence collecting approach is used, since it is not known what can become evidence, during the course of investigation (Wright et al., 2005).

Evidence that was recovered will be examined in light of pertinent questions:

i. how was the grave created – in what manner and by which means;
ii. was the grave digging quick or slow;
iii. is there evidence that the grave was left open prior the burial of body;
iv. is there any evidence supporting a more precise estimation of the post-mortem interval?;
v. is the burial the result of criminal activity or archaeological finding;
vi. is there any evidence on the cause of death;
vii. who is the victim;

TABLE 4.3   Labeling and documentation options for the evidence collection in the field

Type of label	Labeling options
Case number	Combination of letters and numbers. A good idea is to incorporate geographical determinant, i.e. recovery location three letters acronym or any other letter combination. For example Sarajevo01 would be SAR01 or SRJ01
Sample number	Combination of letters and numbers that also includes case number.
Exact location of sample	Can include grid number or coordinates of micro location
Name of the collector	Can also include all the other persons in the field chain of custody procedure
Color and sample dimensions	Dimensions: volume (in sieved samples), weight, size
Date and time of collection	Additionally can include weather conditions during collecting

viii. was any material transferred from the perpetrator to the grave or victim;

ix. is there any foreign material inside the grave and how did it get there (Hunter & Cox, 2005).

Mass graves are mostly large-scale criminal sites and total evidence collection approach is meaningless - everything and anything can become evidence. In this case, time and storage will be limiting factors deciding against the total collection approach, but closer inspection of the surrounding waste will be enough to identify objects which are out of character, lying within the waste in the grave itself (Wright, Hanson, Sterenberg, 2005). Archaeological approaches to the mass graves excavations can also affect quality of the evidence collected. Currently, two of the excavation methods are in use, arbitrary or pedestal method and stratigraphic. Each method has (dis)advantages, but experimental archaeology demonstrates that the stratigraphic approach should be favored, as it yields better quality, consistency, and accuracy of recovery of humans remains and artefacts (Tuller & Đurić, 2006; Evis et al., 2016). Results presented by Evis, Hanson and Cheetham (2016) show that by stratigraphic approach average of 71% percent of all evidence is recovered, as opposed to average 56% recovery rate of arbitrary method

The procedures for collecting archaeological forensic evidence is not significantly different from the collection, labeling and handling of evidence from recent criminal activities (a summary of labelling evidence is given in Table 4.3). All evidence should have assigned a unique number, which will be used for tracking the evidence through all stages of evidence recover, analysis and interpretation. Evidence information should include a jurisdiction order, case number, date and location information. All evidence should be photographed in situ where possible, with an evidence number card visible, scale and north arrow. The evidence should be mapped using a theodolite, total station, GPS or in the absence of these, a mobile phone with some of the preinstalled geotagging applications. The evidence, photography and

survey log, together with notes provide the main record of the evidence. Once everything has been recorded, the evidence item can be removed and placed into an evidence bag and sealed.

In the end, a mass graves is a complex archaeological and environmental system where intrinsic and extrinsic factors greatly contribute to the preservation of human remains and evidence. Depth of burial, number of cases of human remains and their distribution, presence of clothing, type of soil and its porosity, geology of the micro and macro area and subsequent actions of perpetrators are all of the factors which, when combined, make each mass grave specific and thus evidence preservation site specific.

TEXTILE AND CLOTHING EVIDENCE

Textile evidence is one of the most abundant types of evidence that can be found in archaeological contexts of forensic interest. For the past few decades this is even more so due to the extensive use of synthetic fibers in manufacturing of clothing and associated accessories made of synthetic rubber, polyester, nylon and acrylic. Understanding patterns of fabric degradations could be helpful in estimation of time since deposition of human remains, and may eventually lead to a standard being created whereby unusually high levels of damage to fibers can be recognized (Mitchell et al., 2012).

Identification of textile type may be helpful in investigation, since it can correlate with the clothing reported in victims' files (Lowe et al., 2013). This is maybe true when dealing with individual or double burials. But, in the case of multiple burials and mass graves, situation is not that straightforward and a broader generalization or conclusions cannot be made; presumptive individual identification should not be carried out based solely on clothing and the positive identification should only be made through DNA matching reports.

Clothing can be used to bring together two pieces that share some properties and are found within same grave context. This was used in Srebrenica mass graves, where clothing was used for reassociation of body parts commingled within the same grave, either by matching up the characteristics and unique patterns of paired clothing (pairs of socks) or by matching the tears in clothing, such as sides from the same pair of trousers (Jugo, 2017). Also, in the beginning of the investigation of mass graves in Srebrenica, there were some attempts to use clothing as an identification tool *(ibid)*. But, when DNA-led procedure started to be incorporated into identification process, it was shown that that only some 15% of the clothing recognized by family members in fact belonged to a missing relative, indicating that clothing recognition is an unreliable means for positive identification (Yazedjian & Kesetovic, 2008).

The passing of time and human memory are often very important factors that need to be taken into consideration. As with any material, textile is subject to degradation, depending on the burial factors and the type of material. On the other hand, human memory about events that occurred 10, 15 or 25 years ago is ever-changing and information gained about the type of clothing the victim was wearing when it was last seen changes during the course of time. Also, during war time, people often changed clothing or had multiple layers of clothing during escape, which also makes any conclusions about type of clothing found in mass graves and its original structure and especially color unreliable. In an experiment by Was-Gubala and Salerno-Kochan (2000), it was found that soldiers' woolen uniforms structurally decomposed after five to six weeks, in the biodegradable soil and nothing of textile had been left. They also found that the rate at which fibers and fabric were decomposed was dye dependent and the brown colored fabric degraded much quicker than the blue one. Sometimes damage on the fabrics can corroborate or dismiss specific scenarios of the event and how the victim died (Mitchell et al., 2012; Hemmings et al., 2018). In one case, ICMP was involved in re-exhumation of victims of violent event from 1992. Bodies were buried in a local cemetery and information was that one particular victim died from gunshot wounds and had three bullet holes in the chest area. Upon exhuming bodes, it was discovered that clothing buried with one of the victims had three bullet holes on the sweater and underlying garment. They were in the chest area and in identical places, when superimposed over each other (Figure 4.3).

Synthetic materials are more durable, due to their chemical properties and as such are very often found in contemporary crime scenes, including mass graves. As for the natural materials that have tendency for durability, leather is the most important material, usually found on crime scene in the form of belts or shoes. Interestingly, leather is best preserved on the opposite

FIGURE 4.3 Holes in the chest area, corroborating witness information (image provided by the courtesy of ICMP).

sides of the environmental spectrum – either in very dry or very wet climate (Stuart and Ueland, 2017).

A degree of preservation for different types of fibers depends on the variety of environmental factors, most important being soil pH, climate and presence of different microorganisms. In the acidic soils, animal fibers are better preserved than the plant ones (Rowe, 2010).

Naturally occurring soft fibers like cotton, wool or silk are very prone to degradation. This process can be inhibited if the burial environment is dry, cold and contains metal inhibiting ions, such as chromium and copper are present (Rowe, 2010). Metallic ions are in some instances toxic to microbes and can lead to a localized condition of inhibited microbial activity, which in turn results in better than usual preservation of textile, leather and wood (Carter & Tibbet, 2008). This antimicrobial activity of certain metallic ions is known from everyday life, with examples of copper ions being used as fungicide in a form of blue copper sulfate pentahydrate or well-known antibacterial and antifungal activities of silver ion. Table 4.4. summarizes textile types found in forensic sites in BiH and their preservation condition.

Graves are microenvironments where chemical balance between environmental and man-made factors is established during a certain time period. Excavations can disturb that balance and contribute to the potential degradation of the remains and evidence. Clothing material should not be placed into a plastic bag because of possible degradation and cross-contamination and if it is wet or damp, it first must be left to air dry (Evans and Stagner, 2003). In this way gradual establishment of the newly formed micro environmental chemical balance between material and its new ambience is enabled, diminishing chances for material degradation. If there is still a small amount of moisture left, then clothing should be put into a sealed bag and then into a larger

TABLE 4.4   Textile/clothing types and preservation condition found on sites of forensic interest in BiH

Material	Garment type	Condition
Leather	Belts, shoes	Excellent
Cotton	Sweaters, trousers, undergarment, shirts, T-shirts	Poor to moderate
Wool	Socks, sweaters,	Moderate to very good
Polyester	Jackets, track suits, blankets	Moderate
Rubber	Boots, gloves	Excellent
Nylon	Body bags	Moderate

paper bag, leaving the second bag with top open (*ibid*). Long-term storage can lead to degradation from the storage packaging and consideration should

be given to the use of museum type products such as acid-free card and bags (Hemmings et al., 2018). If only plastic bags are available and there is a short amount of time to collect evidence, then a good idea is to put clothing into such a bag and leave it partially open, either on the top or by making a number of small holes, so that air circulates around evidence. As soon as the opportunity rises to remove the clothing from the bag, for a longer time period (in storage facility, morgue or police station), it is advised to do so.

METAL DETECTING, CARTRIDGE CASES AND BULLET EVIDENCE COLLECTION

When someone mentions a metal detector, everyone's first thought is running around with the device, headphones on their head, searching and finding gold and silver coins. Well, the truth is a bit more complicated. It is not that easy to differentiate between signals that promise fortune and the ones giving us disappointment. The person that is in charge of this work must be familiar with the instrument used and the response of the detected signal.

Metal detecting can be useful to find bullets, cartridge cases or firearms, and can be used as a rapid screen to indicate the presence of graves that the metal objects are associated with. In many violent crime scene scenarios, the occurrence of ammunition on the forensic sites is linked with the manner of death of individuals or group of people. Before any search is undertaken, it is very important to ensure that the work is systematic and detailed, so for this purpose a grid system should be used. Knowledge of the geology of the area should additionally be taken into account, since some ores and rocks can give false positive signals. In most cases those are iron (hematite, magnetite and limonite) and copper bearing minerals. To avoid this, it is always a good idea to perform a calibration of the site, to get acquainted with the natural type of signals to be expected. In addition to regular metal detectors, handheld detectors are

also useful to pinpoint source of signal more accurately. Regular and handheld detectors can be used in combination: with the regular one artefact is searched for and once there is a good signal, the hand held detector is used for pinpointing the exact location of the signal. This is a very effective way of work and it has been used in practice on the locations in BiH. In one case (location Zecovi) investigators were able to detect a pattern of cartridge cases, described by the witness, precisely as he had told that the event happened. Figures 4.4 and 4.5 show the systematic approach used in the Zecovi, where team searched for promising signals and after detecting one, flags were used to mark the locations, which were later subsequently checked for cartridges (Figure 4.6).

At the second location, a garbage dump at Kozluk, uncovering of large number of cartridge cases was successful among the pile of bottles, aluminum cans and corroded iron objects. Since the previous information provided targeted this location as a place of execution and the cartridge cases are mostly made of copper, the metal detector used was set up to detect only copper signal and ignore all the others. During this process over twenty cartridges of different caliber was recovered (Figure 4.7).

FIGURE 4.4   Systematic search for the cartridge cases on the Zecovi location (image provided by the courtesy of ICMP).

FIGURE 4.5 Flagged locations of the detected cartridge cases with the assigned case numbers (image provided by the courtesy of ICMP).

FIGURE 4.6 Cartridge case with the assigned case number (image provided by the courtesy of ICMP).

FIGURE 4.7 Cartridge case from the machine gun recovered during metal detecting of the location (image provided by the courtesy of ICMP).

Metal detecting was successfully used at the location of infamous El Mozote Massacre in El Salvador, where large amount of ballistic evidence was found in most of the burial sites, together with personal belongings, such as coins, belt buckles or hair clips (Egaña et al., 2008).

Bullet casing analysis, carried out by US Bureau of Alcohol, Tobacco, Firearms and explosives (ATF) found connections between different locations of forensic interest in BiH. Kravica warehouse was connected to the secondary mass grave Zeleni Jadar 05; the Lazete 02 primary mass grave was connected to Hodzici Road 02, Hodzici Road 03, Hodzici Road 04 and Hodzici Road 05 secondary mass graves (Jugo & Wastell, 2015). The analysts from ATF also managed to link bullet casings collected from the surface around primary graves, areas where executions happened and the same secondary mass graves (*ibid*). Bullet casings analysis from the WWII mass grave found and excavated in Ukraine in 1990 proved that the execution was done by Nazis, not the Soviets, because casings were manufactured in Germany in 1941 (Blewitt, 1997).

Evidence collected in this way should be treated as any other evidence found which means properly photographed, described, surveyed by total station, collected in appropriate bags and labeled. On large sites, there is no need to photograph them *in situ*, unless their position is such that it can be considered significant (ie. pointing out manner of death, inside skull or body part) then *in situ* photographing is mandatory (Donelly et al., 2013). The bags used for this purpose should be clean and dry since the presence of moisture can lead to corrosion and potential loss of valuable information from the evidence material.

PERSONAL ITEMS AS EVIDENCE MATERIAL

Throughout historical archaeological practice, artifacts found with deceased persons were always considered one of the most important findings in buried context. The situation is not much different when dealing with forensic cases and personal items found, especially in mass graves, with personal items treated as evidence and proper procedures followed. A personal effect is any item that belonged to a specific person such clothing, jewelry, wallets, photographic or identification documents and, while not definitive, can be helpful to establish presumptive identification. But, with this type of evidence everyone should be extremely cautious and not give rise to premature conclusions, for example in assuming that proximity of personal items is a strong indication of association to nearby human remains.

Artifacts can be designated as isolated and non-isolated. Isolated artifacts are those without a direct relationship to specific human remains and non-isolated are those for which there is a proof of direct relationship with specific human remains. For example, eyewear (glasses) or rings found near the human remains are isolated artifacts; while a ring found on a metacarpal or hand phalange, or a mirror or razor found inside clothing can be considered non-isolated artifacts and can be linked to individual human remains that are in turn directly related to clothing they are found in. In the case of BiH mass graves, both types of artifacts have been used as criminal evidence in court trials related to war crimes and as a reconstructive element of events, for identification of victims and perpetrators (Jugo, 2017). In other cases, it is only possible to make general identification regarding religious or national affiliation. Italian nationality of soldiers from WWI mass grave in Veneto Mountains (Italy) was confirmed based on the military vaccination badge and religious medals (Gaudio et al., 2013). Religious items such as Koran verses or amulets found inside mass graves in Srebrenica and in other mass graves (Figure 4.8), different types of crosses, Bibles or other religious artifacts were used to establish religious identity of victims as Bosniaks (mostly Muslims), Serbs (mostly Eastern Orthodox) or Croats (mostly Roman Catholic), respectively (Juhl, 2005; Tuller, 2012; Jugo, 2017).

Sometimes inside mass graves personal items can be found, which can be used as an exact chronological indicator of the date and time when the crime was committed and the grave was created. In BiH, during one year, a total of ten self-winding watches were found. All of these watches had date/time window function. They all stopped working between 36 and 48 hours after last winding and based on that it was concluded that executions most probably happened on July 14th (which was Friday) and eight out of ten watches had stopped on either Saturday 15th or Sunday 16th (Wright et al., 2005). All of the watches were still working during the time of excavation, and only needed a little shake to start moving again. If their dials had not been photographed at the time of discovery, but left to subsequent examination, the critical day/date combinations would have been lost (*ibid*). Wrist watches were also found on victims from Tomašica, the biggest primary mass grave in BiH, during the third excavation campaign in the fall 2013. Watches have stopped working at the time of the executions and a significant number of watches had engraved inscriptions, as an anniversary gift from local companies to its employees; these watches aided with targeted DNA testing (Begic et al., 2019).

SURFACE REMAINS EVIDENCE COLLECTION

Very often wartime activities have as a result a displacement of local population, either deliberately by perpetrators, or voluntarily in order to escape and get to the safe environment. Such movements of smaller or larger groups of population are frequently followed by crimes and executions, where perpetrators target these groups, following them and making ambushes in suitable places. The outcome is that there is a huge number of victims and their remains scattered over large area. The best approach for the search and recovery of the surface-scattered remains and associated evidence is to focus on the spatial distribution of the evidence through precise mapping procedures in order to understand how the remains were scattered and which taphonomic agents (e.g. gravity, slope wash, animals, humans) were most responsible for the moving, removing, and alteration of the evidence (Dirkmaat & Cabo, 2016). If the area is too large to be covered by precise total station mapping, then a handheld GPS can be used, to accurately map the scattering of remains and evidence. New generation GPS devices have accuracy within the 1 m. Data collected either by total station or GPS can be entered into GIS program (such as ArcGIS or QuantumGIS), analyzed, interpreted and results can be used in further planning of search for the remaining skeletal remains or evidence.

When searching for remains and evidence on surface, it is important to know that environmental conditions may have a great impact on preservation of bones and artifacts. Surface remains can be roughly divided in two groups:

- remains directly exposed on the surface;
- remains that are few centimeters below surface, often covered with leaf litter.

FIGURE 4.8 Prayer beads of Islamic provenance recovered from the mass grave (image provided by the courtesy of ICMP).

This distinction can have major role in the preservation and ability to spot the remains when searching for them. When the remains are directly exposed on the surface, they are subject to heavy weather conditions, with seasons changing regularly, making a huge impact on the preservation of bone and DNA inside it. Constant rain-sun-snow-wind combination is stressful to bone structure and it can lead to cracks, fractures and loss of bone material. Clothing exposed directly to the Sun tend to pale with passing of time and belt buckles and metallic buttons corrode, ultimately leading to the degradation of original material. As for the bones, substantial exposure to UV radiation and other environmental conditions, leaves only the mineral portion of bone, hydroxyapatite, naturally white in color (Dupras & Schultz, 2014). This is the reason why most of the surface bones, found after long time is white in color.

In general, when dealing with surface remains and evidence, it is best to use a system of grids, baselines or quadrants and do the systematic search and recovery inside these predetermined areas, with flagging the remains and evidence, photographing them, assigning case numbers and collecting (Cheetham et al., 2013).

EVIDENCE COLLECTION USING SIEVES

Sieving, as a very helpful archaeological method, is used when there is a need for recovery of very small artefacts or fragmented human remains. Layer or "spit" sieving ensures identification of these small items within particular parts of the grave (Hunter, 2014). These fragments are more than usual missed during excavation, and sieving is used after the deposit has been cleared from the larger evidence and human remains; sieving can also be used at the end of the excavation process.

Sieving can be dry, i.e. by sifting through mesh of different sizes, or wet by using water jet to break thick soil through the grid. Which technique will be used depends on the type of soil (is it more clay or more gravel), and the type of soil impacts the density of uncovered finds (Lorenzon, 2018). How much soil will be sieved depends on the excavation strategy and there are instances where sieving has a specific purpose, like search and recovering of bullets from the soil underneath bodies (Wright et al., 2005). Sometimes, only a portion of grave fill can be sieved (*ibid*). This is a good idea when excavating mass graves, since it is impossible to sieve all the material, so a strategic partial approach can be used. In circumstances where presence of bullets or cartridge cases, or small or burnt fragmented human remains is suspected, sieving is highly recommended operation (Figure 4.9).

If the dry sieving method is going to be applied, then the soil needs to have a low moisture content, allowing soil to split in small fragments that can reveal items of forensic interest (Cheetham et al., 2013).

FIGURE 4.9 Fragment of bullet recovered during the sieving operation (image provided by the courtesy of ICMP).

TOOL MARKS AS FORENSIC EVIDENCE

Understanding the mode of grave construction can offer useful insight into the planning used for grave preparation. Was it dug by hand? Or maybe machinery was used for its construction? If so, what kind of machine was used? Front loader, backhoe loader or excavator? Were they used in combination? These are all the questions that can be answered by careful examination of tool marks left in the soil. When a grave constructed with access ramp method is dug, the machine used for construction leaves bucket tooth marks and wheel tracks inside grave, forming compressed impressions in the new surface; upon subsequent forensic excavation of the grave, these impressions became visible (Hanson, 2004). Figure 4.10 shows marks left by machine in the course of creating mass grave. Clay and silt soils readily retain tool marks, unlike sand and gravel soils which are too coarse

FIGURE 4.10 Machine bucket tool marks left during the creation of a mass grave and exposed during the recovery of the remains (image provided by the courtesy of ICMP).

and dry to hold the imprint needed for evidence collection (Dupras et al., 2006).

No matter how subsequently grave is opened and archaeologically excavated, either by machine or manpower (hand tools), care should be taken to prevent contamination and destruction of imprints during the archaeological excavation process. This is especially important when the archaeological recovery of human remains is done my machine. Depending on the soil type, different types of machine buckets are suitable. For hard soils, like clay, excavator bucket (with protruding teeth) is better choice. For soft soils, like gravel and sand a use of ditching bucket (without teeth) is recommended. The best option is employing the backhoe loader, with interchangeable buckets. An excavating bucket is used on the beginning of excavation process, removing soil carefully, in order to reveal the forensically important layer. When this layer is reached, the bucket is switched for a ditching one and excavation is continued. In this way, time and equipment are used most efficiently, producing the best possible results.

After reaching the level below the layers containing tool marks, it is advised to continue cleaning with hand tools and brushes, in order to carefully expose the marks for photography and casting (Dupras et al., 2006). The archaeologist's role is to document any evidence of vehicular activity of the gravesite that may relate to the original construction (e.g. heavy machinery), the method of depositing the remains (e.g. impressions of wheeled vehicles), and evidence of any backfilling or sealing sequences (Dupras et. al, 2006).

A quite detailed sequence of perpetrators action can sometimes be discerned. In the case of one secondary mass grave in BiH, each of the forensic deposits (soil and bodies) was separated by a surface interface, represented by vehicle tracks pressed into the soil fill. A reconstruction of events showed that as each deposit was dumped into the ramped grave, a front loader machine would drove into the grave, with soil and human remains being moved towards the far end of the grave and the machine would then back out in reverse (Hanson, 2004). In this way, the next deposit sealed the surface created by the vehicle track, creating a total of four episodes of dumping and bulldozing the remains.

Other than machine work evidence, it is also possible to document traces of hand tools like mattocks and spades, whose impression quality varies, depending on the composition of deposits through which the grave was cut (Cheetham et al., 2013).

SOIL, BOTANICAL AND GEOLOGICAL EVIDENCE

Soil and pollen analysis were used for linking different points of forensic interest in BiH. Zeleni Jadar 05

secondary mass grave was linked with robbed primary mass graves in Glogova and Lazete I and II mass grave locations were linked to Hodzici Road 02, Hodzici Road 03, Hodzici Road 04 and Hodzici Road 05 series of secondary mass graves (Brown, 2006). A link between Branjevo Farm primary grave and secondary mass graves originating from it was found through presence of hay on these locations (Jugo & Wastell, 2015). Plant material, including pollen can survive inside mass graves, in a way that it becomes trapped inside the grave when it was created or because it was already growing in places such as pits or quarries (Cheetham et al., 2013). At one an execution site in a shallow gravel quarry in Bosnia, a few species of flowering plants growing at the time of the killings were recovered flattened underneath the bodies, a strong indication of grave being created in high summer season. Human remains had a function of stratigraphic layer, thus protecting the plants lying on the ground surface, and the interface layer between grave surface and fill revealed point where plant roots were cut off when the grave was created, preventing also growth of the plants (Hanson, 2004).

Botanical evidence should never be put into plastic bags, since the risk of mold formation is high, which can lead to sample decomposition very quickly, with sample losing its characteristics used for identification (Dupras et al., 2006). The best is to use paper material, between sheets of newspaper or a catalog (Hall, 1997; Dupras et al., 2006). Use of paper bags is also possible, but there is a risk of crushing of dried plant material if they are smashed. For large pieces it is advisable to use pasteboard boxes (Hall, 1997).

Linkage by geological evidence comparison was successful in the case of Petkovci Dam (primary burial site) and Liplje 2 (secondary burial site), where greenish clay specific for the primary site was found at the secondary location, together with the evidence of human remains being removed by heavy machinery (Jessee, 2003). Also, a striated clast of serpentinite from secondary grave Hodzici road 03 was matched to the geological signature of primary site Lazete I (Brown, 2006). In general, all the Srebrenica 1995 primary and secondary mass grave sites can be linked by lithology, mineralogy and pollen evidence found inside them (*ibid*).

OTHER EVIDENCE COLLECTION

When the Ravnice mass graves were excavated, ICTY investigators uncovered plaster, concrete, and other building materials, identical to the material from the execution place in Kravica warehouse, the Glogova 01 and Glogova 02 primary mass graves and the secondary mass graves in Zeleni Jadar 05 and Zeleni Jadar 06 (Janc, 2013). Of the specific interest was finding of pieces of colored polystyrene found in Ravnice 2, which

FIGURE 4.11 A deposit containing fragments of green glass bottles (image provided by the courtesy of ICMP).

FIGURE 4.12 Ligatures photographed *in situ* (image provided by the courtesy of ICMP).

was identical to foam lettering from the outside façade wall of the Kravica warehouse (*ibid*). This was the direct link of execution point and mass grave, that contained victims detained as prisoners in the warehouse.

Evidence from construction elements was also helpful in finding victims executed by KGB, between 1944 and 1947, in Vilnius (Lithuania). There was information that they were executed in a former garage (later demolished), as the ground there was less frozen and easier to dig. Exhumations in 1994, 1995 and 2003 located this garage and the indication for its location was preserved stone pavement (floor) and parts of foundation (Jankauskas et al., 2005). In this case, the approach based on the collection of *pre-event data* (information about location) and *post-event data* (evidence excavated) proved to be very important part of the investigation that yielded the best possible results.

A link between Kozluk primary mass graves at the Drina river bank and the Cancari Road 03 secondary grave has been made through occurrence of fragments of green glass bottles and bottle labels, originating from the "Vitinka" bottling factory, near the Kozluk mass grave (ICTY, 2001; Wright et al., 2005). A deposit showing fragments of green glass bottles is represented in Figure 4.11. In one case from BiH, parts of black plastic pipe found in secondary mass grave HZ 5 matched to those on a water pipe that intersected the primary grave site Lazete II (Brown, 2006).

Ligatures and blindfolds are common findings inside graves excavated in BiH. Finding of these items is a definite proof that killings and victims were not result of the battle actions, as the legal defense of the perpetrators sometimes tried to represent (Hanson, 2004). When excavating, it is important to pay attention to skull and forearm/feet regions, since these are the spots where blindfolds/ligatures are found. Careful work around these areas must be done, since it is of great importance to

locate these artifacts *in situ* and document them with total station and taking detailed photographs (Donelly et al., 2013). Figure 4.12 shows *in situ* occurrence of ligatures inside mass grave. Only after proper documenting it they should be removed and put into evidence bags. Sometimes, based on the type of clothing used and knotting mode on the ligatures, it is possible to link two sites, as was the case for Branjevo Farm (primary) and Cancari Road (secondary) (Jugo, 2017).

CASE STUDIES

Yugoslav Army in the Homeland case

In 2015, during the construction of *hair cesma* (Turkish word for a type of drinking fountain, usually constructed by Muslims as a way of honoring a family member), in eastern Bosnia, near Zvornik, the local population found the human remains. As soon as the bones were seen, construction work stopped and the police were informed. The location was on a small slope, in a forest area, just below the main regional road Tuzla-Zvornik. Since a number of missing persons were expected to be found from that area and the near proximity of a series of Hodzici Road mass graves that were discovered and excavated in the past, it was agreed that exhumation should take place as soon as possible. ICMP representatives were engaged in the recovery of human remains from the start. Forensic archaeologists and pathologist uncovered a total of sixty cases of human remains, with distinctive male characteristics and cartridge cases from various types of weapons. Everyone at the site was convinced that a large mass grave was found, most likely from 1995. However, as soon as the first artifacts started to emerge, it was clear that this might not be the case. Coins that circulated during WWII time period were found (Kingdom of Italy 20 lira from the 1940 and

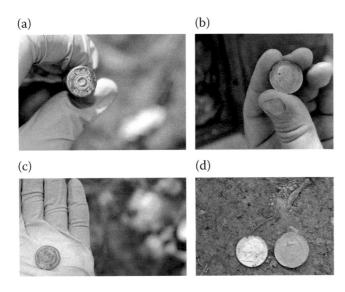

FIGURE 4.14   Image showing location before the draining operation (image provided by the courtesy of ICMP).

FIGURE 4.13   Artifacts recovered during exhumation of WWII cases; (a) cartridge case from 1943; (b) a button from the 1944 and inscription JFS; (c) silver coin from Kingdom of the Yugoslavia; (d) coins from the Italian Empire, circulating during WWII (image provided by the courtesy of ICMP).

Kingdom of Yugoslavia 20 dinar from the 1936) and red Bakelite box of the German origin containing a tooth cleaning powder used in the WWII. Investigation showed the cartridge cases were produced 1936 and 1939 and some buttons with inscription JFS from 1939 were also recovered. All this indicated that the human remains found were not from the 1992–1995 time period and most probably were the members of Yugoslav Army in the Homeland. A final proof that remains were indeed from the WWII period was when on a third day of excavation, a local Orthodox priest visited the site and told that before 1992 there was a wooden cross on the location, marking the spot where Partisans executed a large number of members of the Yugoslav Army in the Homeland and that until 1992 a regular Orthodox religious rites were performed annually. Figure 4.13 shows some of the artifacts found at the location.

WWII German soldiers' case

In 2012, ICMP representatives were part of the exhumation team in eastern Bosnia, on the location Brdine, Rogatica municipality. The location was in waterlogged mountainous terrain, where local cattle came to drink water. Based on the information provided to us, it was expected to find a small-scale mass grave, with the victims from surrounding villages. Since the exact location was waterlogged (Figure 4.14), it was decided to make a channel to drain the basin.

After this procedure was successfully applied, excavation started. Soon, numerous disarticulated human remains started to emerge and preliminary anthropological assessment showed they were all adult males. Some coins were found, but since they were dirty and with green patina they were cleaned with water and paper to reveal the dates on them. The coins had an eagle on one side and coin value on the other side, with the year 1940 engraved on it. Further inspection revealed inscription in the German language. Other artifacts were also recovered: a red case from material resembling hard plastic, a silver knife without a handle, a dog tag, buttons, a ring and even a part of army truck chassis. Some of the artifacts recovered are shown in Figure 4.15. A detailed inspection of artifacts and checking revealed that they were:

FIGURE 4.15   Artefacts recovered from the location (image provided by the courtesy of ICMP).

- red bakelite made decontamination pill case from 1936, containing Losantin. It was a skin protection and decontamination agent, calcium hypochlorite (Ca (ClO)$_2$, issued to German WWII soldiers;
- a stainless-steel knife, with the inscription GOTTLIEB HAMMESFAHR. Subsequent check confirmed it was Gottlieb Hammesfahr's Solingen Foche 2 knife type;
- a dog tag that had inscription 6.LW.EIS.BATL. XIII 137. Based on a brochure of German military abbreviations, issued by Military Intelligence Service, War Department, Washington, from the April 12, 1943 it most probably belonged to Sixth Luftwaffe Field Engineer Company, which was in charge of construction works on the Eastern Front.

All of this evidence suggested that the remains and artifacts are historic ones, belonging to soldiers in WWII German Army, deployed in the Yugoslavia during WWII actions.

A case of human remains from a cave

Commingled human remains were found in cave, in Western Bosnia. They were located at the bottom of the cave, at the depth of 60 meters. ICMP archaeology and anthropology staff were requested at the location, to provide assistance in the assessing the situation and providing expert opinion, based on the stratigraphy, context and taphonomy of human remains. This was due to the fact that the wider area was known to have many caves and pits, where atrocities were happened in the past, during WWI and WWII, when whole villages were wiped out and people were thrown, alive or dead, in those pits. A great number of them are still venerated annually by Eastern Orthodox or Catholic Church, depending on the nationality of the victims. After carefully descending to the cave bottom, it was discovered that it contained a pile of truck tires, with dates predating 1992 and vehicle registration plates, with a design from the Socialist Federal Republic of Yugoslavia period. Human remains were found underneath this pile, suggesting that they predate 1992 and later events. Together with the human remains, a number of artifacts were also found, further supporting idea about historical context of these remains. Two artifacts were especially interesting:

- Ring with ruby red rock inside, with letters FR engraved, next to floral motif. Ring had greenish patina at some parts, suggesting it is not pure 24 K gold, but some cheaper 14 K version, with copper/brass admixtures. Online search revealed

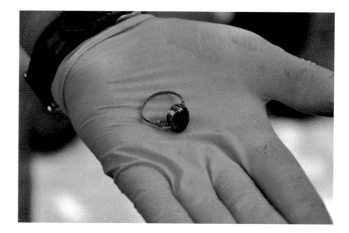

FIGURE 4.16   A ring with the ruby red rock and engraved FR and floral motifs (image provided by the courtesy of ICMP).

that FR initials on rings are monograms for Fritz Rossier, a prominent German jeweler during Art Noveau and Art Deco periods (roughly between 1890 and 1939). They were known to use 14 K gold to make their rings and floral motifs were very often used during Art Noveau period (Figure 4.16)
- Praying book (fragmented and burned). Heavily fragmented book, written in Latin script. Although in bad condition, lines and paragraphs were readable and it is written in some archaic form of Slovenian language. Online search afterwards revealed that it was possibly book entitled *Skrbi za dušo. Molitvena knjiga za pobožne Slovence*, by Karol Čigon (roughly translated as *Care for the soul. Praying book for the pious Slovenians*). It had couple of editions between 1889 and 1911.

Additionally, the taphonomy of the remains suggested that they were older than it would be case if they were 1992 onwards victims. Besides that, the observed rock material was native to the cave, not brought by trucks from quarries, as was claimed by information acquired by investigation.

Based on the all information gathered: a location and chronology of historical events, artifacts found, stratigraphy of cases, geology of the cave and taphonomy of human remains, it was recommended to treat these findings as historical ones and close the case.

CONCLUSION

In the end, archaeological evidence collection from sites of forensic interest is not different from collection of evidence from everyday criminal sites. The biggest challenge when dealing with archaeological evidence is that it is mostly found in an outdoor environment and as such is prone to contamination by weather conditions and diverse deliberate human factors. A great deal of care needs to be taken when collecting this type of evidence, with an emphasis on chain of custody, and the preservation, documentation and proper subsequent storage of evidence. No one wants to have his evidence destroyed, since when the mass grave or any other forensic location is closed and location returned to the previous state, there is no turning back. All the evidence collected during forensic archaeology excavations must be obtained in a legal manner, following strict chain of custody procedures, recommended by local, state and international laws. In the end, each and every excavated location is different in its construction and deposition type, so depending on intrinsic and extrinsic factors evidence preservation and excavating strategy will be site specific.

ACKNOWLEDGEMENTS

I would like to extend my sincere thanks to Thomas Parsons, former ICMP Director of Science and Technology, for his invaluable support, insightful suggestions and advices when preparing this chapter. Thanks should also go to Sandra Sostaric, Forensic Coordinator for Western Balkan for providing me with useful advices regarding chapter structure and constructive ideas for sentence structure.

Special thanks go to Marijana Kandic for reading draft versions in English and her useful comments regarding not writing in first person and to reduce the use of pronouns. I'll have this in mind when preparing future papers.

And many thanks to my wife Almira, who supported me while I was stumbled between chapter parts and without ideas how to proceed further. Merci!

REFERENCES

Barker, A. P. *Techniques of Archaeological Excavation.* New York: Universe Book, 1977.

Begic, M., Ramic, S., & Alisic, Z. *Tomasica-mass grave (Monograph).* Sarajevo: American University in Bosnia and Herzegovina, 2019.

Blau, S., & Skinner, M. (2005). The use of forensic archaeology in the investigation of human rights abuse: Unearthing the past in East Timor. *The International Journal of Human Rights,* 9(4), 449–463. 10.1080/13642980500349857

Blewitt, G. T. (1997). The Role of Forensic Investigations in Genocide Prosecutions before and International Criminal Tribunal, *Medicine, Science and the Law,* 37(4), 284–288.

Brown, A.G. (2006). The use of forensic botany and geology in war crimes investigations in NE Bosnia. *Forensic Science International,* 163, 204–210; 10.1016/j.forsciint.2006.05.025

Carter, D. O., & Tibbet, M. (2008). Cadaver Decomposition and Soil: Processes. In: M. Tibbett & D. O. Carter, (eds), *Soil Analysis in Forensic Taphonomy: Chemical and Biological Effects of Buried Human Remains* (pp. 29–52). Boca Raton, FL: CRC Press.

Cheetham, P., Cox, M., Flavel, A., Hanson, I., Haynie, T., Oxlee, D., & Wessling, R. (2013). Search, location, excavation and recovery. In: M. Cox, A. Flavel, I. Hanson, J. Laver, & R. Wessling, (eds.), *Scientific Investigation of Mass Graves* (pp. 183–267), Cambridge University Press, Cambridge, UK (paperback edition).

Connor, M. A. *Forensic methods. Excavation for the Archeologist and Investigator.* Lanham, MD: AltaMira Press, 2007.

Crist, A. J. T. (2001). Bad to the bone?: Historical Archaeologist in the Practice of Forensic Science. *Historical Archaeology,* 35(1), 39–56.

Dirkmaat, D. C., & Cabo, L. L. (2016). Forensic Archaeology and Forensic Taphonomy: Basic Considerations on How to Properly Process and Interpret the Outdoor Forensic Scene. *Academic Forensic Pathology,* 6(3), 439–454.

Donnelly, S., Hedley, M., Loveless, T., Manning, R., Perman, A., & Wessling, R. (2013). Scene of crime examination. In: M. Cox, A. Flavel, I. Hanson, J. Laver, & R. Wessling, (eds.), *Scientific Investigation of Mass Graves* (pp. 148–181), Cambridge University Press (paperback edition).

Dupras, T. L., Schultz, J. J., Wheeler, S. M., & Williams, L. J. Forensic Recovery of Human Remains: Archaeological approaches: Boca Raton, FL: CRC Press, 2006.

Dupras, T. L., & Schultz, J. J. (2014). Taphonomic Bone Staining and Color Changes in Forensic Contexts. In: J. T. Pokines & S. A. Symes (eds), *Manual of Forensic Taphonomy* (pp. 315–340). Boca Raton, FL: CRC Press.

Egaña, S., Turner, S., Doretti, M., Bernardi, P., & Ginarte, A. (2008). Commingled Remains and Human Rights Investigations. In: B. J. Adams & J. E. Byrd (eds.), *Recovery, Analysis, and Identification of Commingled Human Remains* (pp. 57–80). Totowa, NJ: Humana Press.

Evans , M. M. , & Stagner , P. A. (2003). Maintaining the chain of custody-evidence handling in forensic cases. *AORN Journal, 78(4),* 563–569; 10.1016/s0001-2092(06)60664-9

Evis, L. H., Hanson, I., & Cheetham, P. N. (2016). An experimental study of two grave excavation methods: Arbitrary Level Excavation and Stratigraphic Excavation. *STAR; Science & Technology of Archaeological Research,* 2(2), 177–191, 10.1080/20548923.2016.1229916

Ford, R. I. *Systematic research collections in anthropology: an irreplaceable national resource.* Cambridge, Mass: Peabody Museum for the Council for Museum Anthropology, 1977

Gaudio, D., Betto, A., Vanin, S., De Guio, A., Galassi, A., & Cattaneo, C. (2013). Excavation and study of skeletal remains from a World War I mass grave. *International Journal of Osteoarchaeology,* 25(5), 585–592.

Groen M. W. J., Márquez-Grant N., & Janaway C. R. (2014). Introduction. In: Groen M. W. J., Márquez-Grant N., & Janaway C. R. (eds.), *Forensic Archaeology: A Global Perspective* (pp. lii - lxvii), Hoboken, NJ: Wiley - Blackwell.

Haglund, W. D. (2001). Archaeology and Forensic Death Investigations. *Historical Archaeology, 35(1),* 26–34.

Hall, D. W. (1997). Forensic Botany. In: W. D. Haglund & M. H. Sorg (eds.), *Forensic Taphonomy: The Postmortem Fate of Human Remains* (pp. 353–363). Boca Raton, FL: CRC Press.

Hanson, I. D. (2004). The importance of stratigraphy in forensic investigation, pp. 39–47, In: K. Pye & D. J. Croft (eds.), *Forensic Geoscience: Principles, Techniques and Applications. Geological Society, London, Special Publications 232.* The Geological Society of London; 10.1144/GSL.SP.2004.232.01.06

Harris E. C. *Principles of Archaeological Stratigraphy.* Academic Press, Cambridge, MA: 1979.

Hemmings, J., Carr, D., & Robertson, J. (2018). Textile Damage Interpretation. In J. Robertson, C. Roux, K. G. Wiggins (eds.), *Forensic Examination of Fibers,* Third edition (pp. 61–87). Boca Raton, FL: CRC Pres.

Hunter, J., & Cox, M. (2005). The recovery of forensic evidence from individual graves: case studies 14–29. In J. Hunter & M. Cox (eds.), *Forensic archaeology: Advances in theory and practice* (pp. 96–136). New York, NY: Routledge.

Hunter, J. R. (2014). Human Remains Recovery: Archaeological and Forensic Perspectives. In C. Smith (ed.) *Encyclopedia of Global Archaeology* (pp. 3549–3555). New York, NY: Springer.

ICMP (2014). Bosnia i Herzegovina: Missing persons from the armed conflicts of the 1990s: A STOCK-TAKING, https://www.icmp.int/wp-content/uploads/2014/12/StocktakingReport_ENG_web.pdf, accessed 17 November 2020

ICTY (2001). *Judgment, Prosecutor v. Radislav Krstic (IT-98-33-T),* (https://www.icty.org/x/cases/krstic/tjug/en/krs-tj010802e.pdf), accessed 10 October 2020

ICTY (2010). Popovich et al., Srebrenica (IT-05-88), https://www.icty.org/x/cases/popovic/cis/en/cis_popovic_al_en.pdf, accessed 17 November 2020.

Janc, D. (2013). https://srebrenica.sense-agency.com/assets/exhumations/sg-2-08summary-eng.pdf, accessed 10 October 2020.

ICTY (2017). Judgment, *Prosecutor v. Ratko Mladic (IT-09-92),* http://www.icty.org/case/mladic/4, accessed 17 November 2020.

Jankauskas, R., Barkus, A., Urbanavièius, V., & Garmus, A. (2005). Forensic archaeology in Lithuania: the Tuskulènai mass grave. *Acta Medica Lituanica,* 12(5), 70–74.

Jessee, E. (2003). Exhuming Conflict: Some Recommendations for the Creation of a Series of Experimental Mass Grave and Mass Grave-Related Test Sites. Master of Art Thesis, Department of Archaeology, Simon Fraser University, Canada, 141 pp.

Jessee, E., & Skinner, M. (2005). A typology of mass grave and mass grave-related sites, *Forensic Science International,* 152, 55–59.

Jugo, A., & Wastell, S. (2015). Disassembling the pieces, reassembling the social: the forensic and political lives of secondary mass graves in Bosnia and Herzegovina. In E. Anstett & J. M. Dreyfus (eds.). *Human Remains and Identification: Mass Violence, Genocide, and the 'Forensic Turn'* (pp. 142–174). UK: Manchester University Press.

Jugo, A. (2017). Artefacts and personal effects from mass graves in Bosnia and Herzegovina: Symbols of persons, forensic evidence or public relics? *Les Cahiers Sirice,* 19(2), 21–40.

Juhl, K. *The Contribution by (Forensic) Archaeologists to Human Rights Investigations of Mass Graves.* Stavanger: AmS-NETT 5, Museum of Archaeology, 2005.

Juhl, K., & Olsen, O. E. (2006). Societal safety, archaeology and the investigation of contemporary mass graves. *Journal of Genocide Research,* 8(4), 411–435.

Lemkin, R. (1944). Axis Rule in Occupied Europe, Laws of Occupation, Analysis of Government, Proposals for Redress. *Chapter IX: Genocide Washington: Carnegie Endowment for World Peace,* p. 79–95 (http://www.preventgenocide.org/lemkin/AxisRule1944-1.htm), accessed 22 October 2020.

Lorenzon, M. (2018). Screening Methods in Archaeology. In C. Smith (eds.), *Encyclopedia of Global Archaeology.* Cham: Springer. 10.1007/978-3-319-51726-1_2520-1

Lowe, A.C., Beresford, D.V., Carter, D.O., Gaspari, F., O'Brien, R.C., Stuart, B.H., & Forbes, S.L. (2013). The effect of soil texture on the degradation of textiles associated with buried bodies. *Forensic Science International*, 231, 331–339; 10.1016/j.forsciint.2013.05.037

Mant, A. K. (1987). Knowledge acquired from post-war exhumations. In A. Boddington, A. N. Garland, & R. C. Janaway (eds.), *Death, Decay and Reconstruction: Approaches to Archaeology and Forensic Science*. Manchester: Manchester University Press.

Melbye, J., & Jimenez, S. B. (1997). Chain of custody from the field to the courtroom. In W. D. Haglund & M. H. Sorg (eds.), *Forensic Taphonomy: The Postmortem Fate of Human Remains*. New York, NY: Taylor and Francis.

Military Intelligence Service War Department (1943). German Military Abbreviations, Special series No. 12, Washington.

Mitchell, J. L., Carr, D. J., Niven, B. E., Harrison, K., & Girvan, E. (2012). Physical and mechanical degradation of shirting fabrics in burial conditions. *Forensic Science International*, 222, 94–101.

Moreno, F. E., & Maita, P. (2020). Forensic archaeology and humanitarian context: Localization, recovery and documentation of human remains. in: R. C. Parra, S. C. Zapico & D. H. Ubelaker (eds.), *Forensic science and the humanitarian action: Interacting with the dead and the living* (pp. 171–182), Volume 1. Hoboken, NJ: John Wiley & Sons Ltd.

Rowe W. F. (2010) Forensic Hair and Fiber Examinations in Archaeology: Analysis of Materials from Gravesites at the Home of Samuel Washington. *Technical Briefs in Historical Archaeology 5*, 43–51.

Scott, D. S., & Connor, M. (2001). The Role and Future of Archaeology in Forensic Science. *Historical Archaeology 35*(1), 101–104.

Schmitt, S. (2001). Mass graves and the collection of forensic evidence: genocide, war crimes, and crimes against humanity. In: W. D. Haglund & M. H. Sorg (eds.), *Advances in Forensic Taphonomy: Method, Theory, and Archaeological Perspectives* (pp. 278–291). Boca Raton, FL: CRC Press.

Skinner, M. F. (1987). Planning the archaeological recovery of evidence from recent mass graves. *Forensic Science International*, 34, 267–287.

Steele, C. (2008). Archaeology and the Forensic Investigation of Recent Mass Graves: Ethical Issues for a New Practice of Archaeology. *Archaeologies*, 4, 414–428; 10.1007/s11759-008-9080-x

Stover, E., Haglund, W. D., & Samuels, Margaret (2003). Exhumation of Mass Graves in Iraq. *JAMA*, 290(5)663–666. 10.1001/jama.290.5.663.

Stuart, B. H., & Ueland, M. (2017). Degradation of Clothing in Depositional Environments. In: Schotsmans, E. M. J., Márquez-Grant, N., & Forbes, S. L. (eds.), *Taphonomy of Human Remains: Forensic Analysis of the Dead and the Depositional Environment* (pp. 120–133). JohnWiley & Sons Ltd.Hoboken, NJ; 10.1002/9781118953358.ch9

Tuller, H., & Đurić, M. (2006). Keeping the pieces together: Comparison of mass grave excavation methodology. *Forensic Science International*, 156, 192–200.

Tuller, H. (2012). Mass Graves and Human Rights: Latest Developments, Methods and Lessons Learned. In: D. C. Dirkmaat (eds), *A Companion to Forensic Anthropology* (pp. 157–164). Hoboken, NJ: Blackwell Publishing Ltd.

Was-Gubala, J., & Salerno-Kochan, R. (2000). The biodegradation of the fabric of soldiers' uniforms. *Science & Justice*, 40, 15–20; 10.1016/s1355-0306(00)71928-9

Wright, R., Hanson, I., & Sterenberg, J. (2005). The Archaeology of Mass Graves. In: J. Hunter & M. Cox (eds.), *Forensic archaeology: Advances in theory and practice* (pp.137–158). New York, NY: Routledge.

Yazedjian, L., & Kesetovic, R. (2008). The Application of Traditional Anthropological Methods in a DNA-Led Identification Process. In: B. J. Adams & J. E. Byrd (eds.), *Recovery, Analysis, and Identification of Commingled Human Remains* (pp. 271–284). Totowa, NJ: Humana Press.

CHAPTER 5

Biological Evidence Collection

Anna Barbaro

Worldwide Association of Women Forensic Experts (WAWFE-Caribbean), Studio Indagini Mediche E Forensi (SIMEF), Italy

CONTENTS

DOI: 10.4324/9781003129554-5

INTRODUCTION

A crime scene is any location associated with a committed crime. Edmund Locard published the *Manual of Police Technique* where he formulated the basic *principle of* forensic science: "Every contact leaves a trace" (Locard, 1923). This means that when two items come in contact, a transfer of material occurs. For example, a perpetrator or a victim can leave traces of their activity (e.g. biological fluids, prints, hairs) at crime scene and inversely they can take something with them (e.g. blood on the body or on clothes). Generally, the process is mutual; in a few cases, the transfer is or appears to be one way. In all cases, there is always a direct relationship between all the elements at the scene, the victim, and the perpretor. Physical evidence can link a suspect with the victim or with other items; it can also be useful to connect different crime scenes. Because of this, physical evidence is a record of the interactions between the victim, the perpetrator, and the environment.

Therefore, the main objective of the crime scene investigation is to recognize, collect, preserve, and analyze all physical evidence that may be useful to reconstruct the event and that can help the investigator to answer the following fundamental questions: **what** (what crime happened?), **why**, (why it happened), **who** (who was the victim?), **when** (when the crime occurred), **where** (where it occurred), and**how** (how it happened?).

Each crime scene obviously is different from the others and it has its own peculiarities. This is because each person may act differently during a criminal event.

Because of this, crime scene investigation is an activity that must be carried out by specialists, with adequate preparation and in accordance with international standardized protocols.

Due to the relevance and complexity of crime scene activity within the judicial system, the European Network of Forensic Sciences Institutes (enfsi.eu) established a crime scene working group (ENFSI Scene of Crime Working Group), with the aim of facilitating the standardization of crime scene examination procedures. It developed a protocol in accordance with the requirement of ISO/IEC 17020 for assessing all steps of this activity, from the the first officer arrival at the scene to the preparation of the final crime scene report (ENFSI, 2012).

CRIME SCENE INSPECTION AND EVIDENCE SEARCHING

Crime scene inspection consists of a meticulous observation of the crime scene finalized to a careful and exhaustive search of all the areas, avoiding evidence losing or contamination (Lee et al., 2001).

Since crime scenes are very different each other, investigators can choice the most appropriate searching method, depending on the scene type, location, size, in order to perform a systematic and effective inspection without leaving unexamined areas.

The most commonly used methods for searching evidence are the following:

- Line or Strip Method
- Grid Method
- Spiral Method
- Zone or Quadrant Method

Line/Strip Method

The line/strip method is generally used for large areas in open fields, but it can also be useful in closed fields. The scene is traversed in a linear manner, advancing from an extreme to the opposite one and then returning in parallel without leaving any unexamined area (comb).

Grid Method

The grid method consists of dividing the area into squares, assigning a number or letter to each of the squares. It allows a very detailed search, but it is very time consuming. Because of this, the method is recommended for small areas like bedrooms.

Spiral Method

The spiral method consists of an inspection from the center of the scene to its periphery or in the opposite direction, making a circle from the inside to the outside, or vice versa (spiral). This method is recommended for open areas or where there are no physical barriers.

Zone/Quadrant Method

In the zone/quadrant method, the scene is divided into small zones or quadrants. Each zone/quadrant is assigned a letter or a number and within it other search methods are applied. This method is recommended when several investigators are available at the scene.

Wheel/Ray Method

In the wheel/ray method, the investigator moves from the center straight to the boundary (outward) or vice versa from the boundary straight toward the center of the scene (inward).

This method is used in limited cases such as small or circular scenes.

EVIDENCE CLASSIFICATION

Evidence can be considered as all the physical elements and immaterial data that lead back to the author of a crime or to the victim. Hence, evidence is any material or not material elements able of indicating the occurrence of an event (Fisher, 2012). According to their general nature, evidence can be classified as physical (e.g. cartridges, firearm, plastic, glass), biological (e.g. blood, saliva, semen, hairs), or chemical (e.g. drugs, explosives). The relevant evidence are those generated during the event, but often other evidence produced after the event or due to contamination may be found (e.g. by family members, first rescuers). Occupational traces are classified those produced before the event by subjects not involved in the crime and therefore not related to the crime. Evidence plays a fundamental role because, if they are effectively recognized and properly collected/handled, they can provide reliable informations useful to rencontruct a crime. Anyway, evidence localization is a very difficult issue as well as the identification of any potentially missing sample. Investigators must have technical knowledge and adequate experience to investigate the crime scene. In addition, they must have all the necessary tools for evidence searching and collection.

EVIDENCE SEARCHING

At the crime scene, visible evidence and evidence that cannot be identified with naked eye is found. Some examples can be seen in Figure 5.1.

The searching strategy is established after the initial scene observation, taking into consideration the type of the crime, the context, any possible alternative scenario,

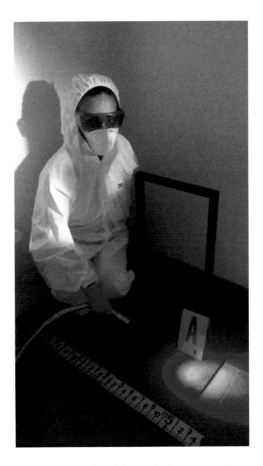

FIGURE 5.1 Example of forensic lamp use for evidence searching.

and especially the surfaces where potentially evidence may be placed.

Searching method includes the inspection with naked eye and white light as magnifier but also the use of special forensic lamps at a variable wavelength or the use of chemical reagents.

Personnel at a crime scene must wear protective equipment (PPE) either to avoid any direct contact with potential pathogens than to prevent evidence contamination. PPE items include disposable coats, masks, gloves, and shoe covers (Table 5.1).

Forensic Lights

Forensic light sources consist of special lamps that emit visible, ultra-violet, and infrared lights.

They allow the enanchment of latent evidence by absorption, fluorescence, or oblique lighting.

The technique is safe and nondestructive and forensic lamps are relatively simple to use.

Generally, forensic light lamps are portable xenon devices that emit light within, below, and above the visible

TABLE 5.1   Examples of common biological evidence (according to NIST, NIJ, 2013)

Evidence	Possible Biological Material
Bottle, glass, can, chewing gum, cigarette, toothpick, envelope, stamp	Saliva
Bite marks	Saliva, skin
Facial tissues, mask	Saliva, mucus
Hat, bandana, mask, scarf	Sweat, hair
Eyeglasses	Sweat, skin
PC Mouse, keyboard, phone	Sweat, skin
Clothes	Sweat, skin, blood,sperm
Underwear	Sweat, skin, blood, sperm, vaginal cells
Pillow, sheets, blanket	Sweat, skin, blood, saliva, sperm, hairs
Condoms	Sperm, vaginal or rectal cells
Fingernails	Blood, sweat, tissue
Gun, rifle, knife, baseball bat, or similar	Blood, sweat, skin, tissue
Cadaveric remains	Bones, teeth, muscle, tissue

spectrum; that is, from 380 to 750 nanometers (nm). The light color changes according to wavelength change.

Depending on the sample to be searched, for its enhancement and photography, it is necessary to choose the right wavelength and the correct filter, as shown in Table 5.2.

Some body fluids (e.g. saliva, sperm), organic materials, and fibers emit fluorescence under exposition to the light source, while other materials such as blood, gunshot residue, and some inks absorb blue light and they appear dark under the light source.

The use of forensic lamps provides more sensitivity than traditional methods since it permits the investigator to identify the specific locations of a stain for its collection, especially when testing large surfaces (e.g. carpet, floor, clothes) to uncover evidence, as illustrated in Figure 5.1.

Anyway, when searching evidence, it's necessary considering that many background surfaces glow under UV light even in absence of any biological trace and therefore it's relevant to eliminate the background interference. Several types of forensic lamps are commercially available: some of them are quite simple, containing only some principal light bands; others are complete multiple color light source. Obviously more powerful and with more multiple tunable color bands is the forensic lamp, the more evidence are found.

Hair and fibers may be found using a strong white light with oblique or parallel lighting of a surface (e.g. clothes, floor, carpets). Some hair and fibers also glow under UV. Hence, examination with white and UV light should be performed to increase the chance of collecting the maximum number of evidence.

Forensic lights are useful also for the examination of the victim, for searching biological fluids or hairs/fibers on the body but also for reveling bite mark or shoe mark that are invisible under normal white light illumination. Different wavelengths penetrate to different depths within the skin and therefore it's necessary to vary the color band of the lamp. Deep wounds, for example, require infrared illumination to get enough skin penetration. Most biological fluids are detected at 450 nm using orange filters/goggles, even if other useful combinations are 415 nm/yellow for biological stains on dark-colored

TABLE 5.2   Example of forensic lights use for evidence searching

Wavelength (nm)	Color	Filter	Application
	White	n/a	General inspection
365	Black	UV filter	Bitemarks, pattern wounds, bruise
415	Violet	Yellow	Bloodstains
450	Blue	Yellow or Orange	Saliva, sperm, urine, biological fluids stains
500	Cyan	Orange	Latent fingerprints, Rhodamine 6G, DFO
525	Green	Orange or Red	Fibers, Ninhydrin
590	Amber	Red	Samples on a fluorescent background
630	Red	n/a	Hairs, questioned documents

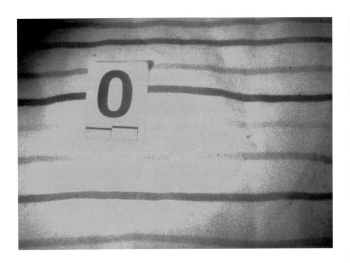

FIGURE 5.2   Semen stain search at 450 nm/orange filter.

surfaces and 505 nm/red in order to decrease background emission (Vandenberg & van Oorschot, 2006). At 450 nm/orange, biological stains appear white: vaginal and saliva stains are quite similar with white-thin edges, seminal stains have thick edges (as shown in Figure 5.2), and urine stains appear the most intense. The type of substrate where the stain is located (nylon, cotton, plastic) and its color affect the stain's appearance. For example, saliva or seminal stains on clear substrate (i.e. spink nylon) may be difficult to detect. In addition, sometimes background surfaces may show brightness due to detergents or fabric conditioners. The most used wavelength for bloodstain searching is 415 nm with yellow filters. The stains appear typically solid and dark brown in color. This is very useful because the enhanced contrast allows to revealing details of bloodprints. Although the luminol test has a greater sensitivity than a forensic lamp in detecting bloodstains, forensic lights may have a particular application in cases of painted bloodstains that at 415 nm/yellow appear detectable under a substrate or a painted surface.

Chemical Methods

To identify the most valuable evidence, the crime scene personnel may conduct initial screening tests (presumptive tests) directly at the scene. These tests are useful in determining the possibility that a specific biological fluid is present.

The most common presumptive tests used at the scene are chemical methods for blood detection, such as Kastle-Meyer test or phenolphthalein test, the Adler test or the Benzidine test, Leucomalachite green, and the Luminol test.

The Kastle-Meyer test was named by the American chemist Joseph Hoeing Kastle (1864–1916), who

invented the test in 1901 and by the German chemist Erich Meyer (1874–1927), who modified it in 1903. It is based on the chemical oxidation of phenolphthalein (PhTh) that is a colorless reagent that turns bright pink in presence of blood, due to the peroxidase-like activity of the hemoglobin.

A drop of phenolphthalein and a drop of hydrogen peroxide are put onto the presumptive bloodstain: if blood is really present, the trace turns pink rapidly. It's relevant to consider that after 30" the sample may turn pink naturally due to air oxidation. The Kastle–Meyer test sensitivity for blood is generally reported as about 1:100,000 (Kastle & March Shedd, 1901; Meyer, 1903).

Leucomalachite green is an organic reagent used as a catalytic test for blood detection. The reaction is based on the peroxidase-like activity of hemoglobin, that in presence of hydrogen peroxide, catalyzes the transformation of leucomalachite green from its colorless reduced form to the blue-green oxidized form. Leucomalachite green has long been the favorite field reagent because of its high sensitivity (1:300,000) and cost/time-effectiveness. It's toxic after a long exposition at high doses.

The Adler test was named by the German physician Oscar Adler (1879–1932), who first utilized benzidine for blood detection. Since its discovery in 1904, the benzidine test has had a great diffusion.

Benzidine (3,3′, 5,5′-tetramethylbenzidine o TMB) is a colorless reagent that turns dark blue in the presence of blood due to the peroxidase-like activity of the hemoglobin in blood. It requires hydrogen peroxide for the activation (Adler & Adler, 1904). Sensitivity of the Adler test is quite variable, generally reported as about 1:300,000.

The Benzidine test for blood screening was used by forensic laboratories during many years, but when its carcinogenic effect was discovered, it was replaced by other methods.

The luminol (5-ammino-2,3-dihydro-1,4-phtha-lazindione) test is used to enhance minute amounts of blood or washed blood. Like the other reagents, luminol reacts with the hemoglobin producing a blue chemiluminescence when oxized by the peroxidase-like activity of the hemoglobin (Huntress et al., 1934). Hydrogen peroxide or sodium perborate are usually used as luminol activators.

Blue chemiluminescence lasts only a few seconds and it requires total darkness to be seen by the naked eye. Because of this, special precautions and measures are necessary to be able to document the blue glow (e.g. long-exposure photography). The intensity of the blue glow does not indicate the amount of blood present, but it only indicates the possible presence of trace amounts in that area, as illustrated in Figure 5.3. Luminol is highly sensitive and it is reported as capable of detecting bloodstains dilutes up to 1:500,000–1:1,000.000.

FIGURE 5.3   Traces of blood detected by luminol on a washed floor (Author's property).

Luminol doesn't interfere with any subsequent DNA testing that may be carried out in the laboratory.

Reagents for presumptive tests are available in various commercial preparations that can be easily brought to the scene, as shown in Figure 5.4.

It's important to remind that all types of presuntive tests are not specific to blood, because they can react with substances other than blood. For example, oxidizing agents such as sodium hypoclorite (bleach), some detergents, metals, and plant peroxidases produce false positives. In addition presumptive tests cannot

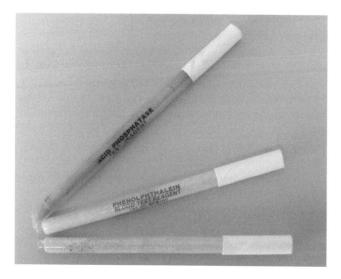

FIGURE 5.4   Example of rapid leucomalachite green, phenopthalein, and luminol rapid field test (Author's property).

distinguish between human and animal blood and they produce the same reactions with both types of samples. Presumptive tests are useful as preliminary screening because they help the investigator to assume that the substance in question could be blood and therefore to proceed with the evidence collection. This allows to reduce the quantity of evidence that is submitted to the lab including only the most important items. Since presumptive tests reaction is not specific to human blood, subsequently a confirmatory test is required. Generally presumptive tests for the other types of fluids (semen, saliva) and confirmatory tests are carried out directly at the laboratory. Confirmatory tests are able to identify a substance with a lowest chance of a false positive. Immunocromatographic assays are the most common confirmatory tests, that allow rapid, reproducible, and highly sensitive analyses. They are based on the use of monoclonal anti-bodies specific for the material to be identified such as anti-human hemoglobin (for blood detection), anti-human α-amylase (for saliva detection), and anti-human PSA (for sperm detection). This permits simultaneously to establish the sample nature (blood, saliva, semen, etc.) and the specie (human or not), using only small quantities of samples. Several tests are commercially available, as shown in Figure 5.5.

BIOLOGICAL EVIDENCE COLLECTION PROCEDURE

A crime scene must be isolated and protected, as quickly as possible, in order to prevent any alteration and to preserve evidence. Evidence collection must be carried out after the observation, fixation, and detailed inspection of the scene and only after having marked the evidence in a unique way (with a number or letter), having photographed it with and without a metric reference, and having written notes and made sketches. Improper evidence collection can lead to its destruction or contamination, if the necessary precautions are not observed. In addition, priorities in evidence collection must be decided to avoid any degradation or alteration of the sample. Biological evidence should be the first to be collected. As biological evidence is intended as all biological material samples (e.g. blood, saliva, semen, bones, teeth) or any physical evidence containing biological material. This type of evidence is frequently used to link or to exclude someone to/from a crime event. Biological evidence can be of different types and they can consist of fluid materials; traces of transportable or non-transportable objects; on porous or non-porous surfaces; there are specific procedures for the correct collection and handling of each type of evidence, biological or not (NIST, NJ

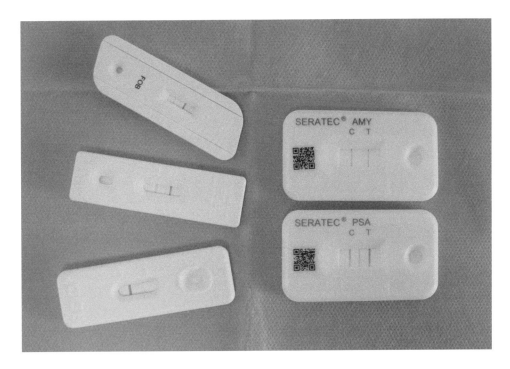

FIGURE 5.5   Example of immunological confirmation tests for blood, sperm, and saliva (Author's property).

2013). For example, the Spanish and Portuguese Group of the International Society of Forensic Genetics (GHEP) has developed recommendations for the collection and shipment of biological samples for genetic identification purposes. (ghep-isfg.org)

Evidence at Crime Scene

Trasportable Objects

If the biological sample is on a transportable surface, such as small objects (an example is illustred in Figure 5.6), it's required to collect the entire evidence and to introduce it

FIGURE 5.6   Example of bloodstains on transportable object (Author's property).

separately into appropriate containers to be transported to the laboratory. Wet evidence should be put into paper bags or air-dried before packaging into apposite containers. In the case of a soft surface (e.g. clothes, sheets), it's necessary to avoid folding wet evidence on itself.

Non-Transportable Objects

Non-Porous Surfaces   Non-porous surfaces are mainly smooth surfaces (e.g. plastics, porecelains, metals, glass, varnished wood), without pores, so liquid moves through them or flat on them. If the suspected biological evidence is on a non-transportable surface such as a floor (see example in Figure 5.7), the evidence should be recovered using a swab in order to absorb as much as possible of the substance. For dry surfaces, the swab should be moistened with 1–2 drops of sterile, distilled water. Multiple swabbings should be carried out when a large quantity of biological material is available. If the available stain is very small, it's suggested to collect it by concentrating the material on the tip of the swab. Each swab must be placed into a separate container. Swabs should be air-dried before being packaged. Using the same procedure, it's convenient to collect a control sample by swabbing a clean area.

Special swabs are commercially available for the collection of biological samples at crime scenes or from non-living individuals. These swabs maximize sample recovery and they are coated with antimicrobial agents that preserve the integrity of nucleic acids without the need of air-drying them.

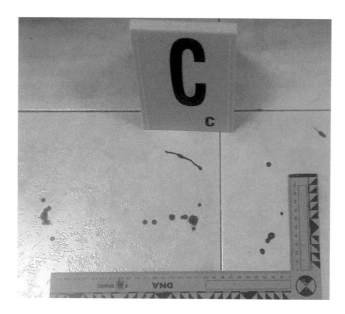

FIGURE 5.7   Example of bloodstains on non-transportable porous surface (Author's property).

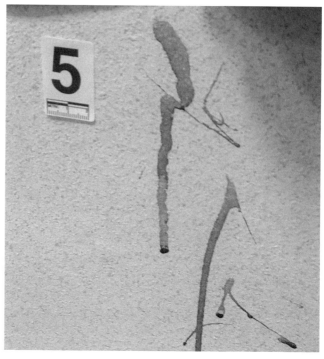

FIGURE 5.8   Example of bloodstains on non-transportable non-porous surface (Author's property).

Porous Surfaces   Porous surfaces (e.g. fabrics, sponge, untreated wood, paper, cardboard) have pores and they allow the biological samples to penetrate into them. In these cases, the most appropriate method consists of cutting a part of the stain with a disposable steril scalpel or scissors. The evidence should be air-dried before being packaged. Figure 5.8 shows an example of bloodstains on a non-transportable surface. It's suggested to collect a control sample by cutting an unstained area using the same technique.

If using a tape for evidence collection, it's recommended to apply it repetitively to the suspected superficies (e.g. on clothing or other support) in order to get as much as possible of the sample.

Biological Liquids

If the evidence is in a liquid state (blood, saliva, sperm), it may be collected by swabbing or by disposable plastic pipettes. Collected material must be than transferred into a sterile tube or another suitable container.

Several items are commercially available for sample collection at a crime scene, as illustrated in Figure 5.9.

Evidence from the Body of the Victim

Evidence (skin cells, saliva, semen) can be found on the body of the victim as well as in the mouth or in the anal or vaginal regions, under fingernails, or on the clothes worn by the victim.

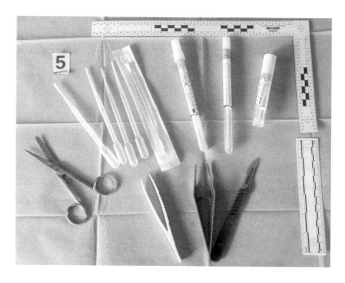

FIGURE 5.9   Example of items commonly used at a crime scene for evidence collection (Author's property).

Stains of Blood, Semen, or Other Biological Fluids

The stain should be collected using a sterile swab moistened with distilled water, cleaning the entire area by pressing gently.

Saliva in Bite Marks

The stain should be collected with a sterile swab slightly moistened with distilled water. It's suggested to clean all the areas delimited by the mark left by the teeth in a circular way.

Nails

It's suggested to pick up with tweezers the hairs or fibers on the victim's hands and nails and to cut the upper edge of the nails. Nails from both hands should be collected separately in appropriate containers (e.g. tubes, paper or plastic bags) or, alternatively, carefully wrap into a paper folder that must be inserted into small paper bags.

Hairs

Hairs must be collected with tweezers and then placed separately or as a group of hairs in paper bags. Alternatively, they may be placed on a small paper that must be folded carefully and then stored in a small paper bag.

In the case of sexual assault evidence or samples inside a victim's body, they should be collected by a physician or sexual assault nurse examiner. In addition, a medical examination should be conducted immediately after the assault to detect any injuries and to test the victim for sexually transmitted diseases.

In sexual assault cases, typically the vaginal cavity, mouth, anf anus may have come into contact with the assailant. Because of this, it's recommended to take swabs in each typical area, as follows.

Oral Cavity

Any semen traces should be collected with sterile swabs, passing them with care and without rubbing, under the tongue, around the teeth, and the palate.

Oral swabs should be taken as soon as possible because in the mouth the semen disappears speedly.

Body Surface

It's recommended to search for semen stains or saliva as well as for possible bites using a Wood lamp. Use sterile swabs to collect any possible biological fluids detected.

Pubic Area

Use a comb or tweezers to collect hairs into plastic/paper bags or over a paper that should be folded carefully and then placed in a small paper bag.

Cervix, Vaginal Cavity, and Vulvar Region

Collect two cervical swabs, two vaginal swabs, and one swab from external genitalia gently swabbing the surfaces.

A vaginal washing must be carried out after swabbing. For washing, use physiological saline sterile (about 10 ml) and collect it in a tube or plastic bottle.

Anal Samples

Using sterile swabs, carefully take two samples from the anorectal canal and one from the anal margin, respectively.

The clothes worn by the victim at the time of the aggression must be carefully collected by putting them into separate paper bags.

Cadaveric Remains

The collection of cadaveric remains is conditioned by the type of remains found at the scene.

Bodies in Good Conditions

A blood sample (10 ml) is collected in a tube containing an EDTA-type anticoagulant.

Putriefied Bodies

Bones (preferably long bones like a femur) and teeth (preferably molars) must be introduced separately in paper bags, small or large depending on the size of the samples.

If the bones have putrified attached remains, it's necessary to remove them before to introduce the bones into the appropriate containers.

Muscle tissue from the best preserved areas must be introduced in plastic containers with a wide mouth and screw cap without fixing liquid.

Carbonized Bodies

It's suggested to take fragments of skeletal muscles from deep areas or from cardiac muscle because they are the most resistant to putrefaction. Additionally, it's advisable to extract four teeth (preferably molars and premolars).

It is essential to collect samples separately, placing them in jars or wide-mouth containers without fixing liquid (if samples will be processed for DNA typing).

It's known that the use of formalin or paraffin may compromise further DNA extraction from fixed or embedded tissues since they damage DNA, producing highly degraded samples with variable quality.

REFERENCE SAMPLES COLLECTION

Reference sampling in living persons (suspect or victim) should be done with judicial authorization. Individuals should sign a document (informed consent) for giving their consent to the sample collection exclusively for specific test purposes (i.e. DNA typing). Informed consent is an ethical and legal requirement for any test involving human participants according to the legislation about privacy that may be variable in different countries.

Blood, saliva, and hairs are commonly used as reference samples.

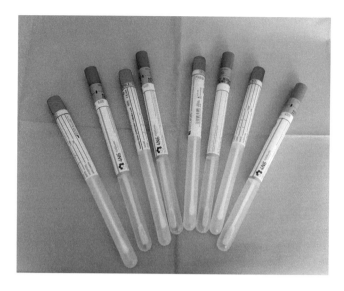

FIGURE 5.10 Example of swabs commonly used for saliva collection from living persons (Author's property).

Blood

Venous Puncture

A blood sample (about 5–10 ml) is collected in a tube containing an anticoagulant-type EDTA.

Finger Puncture

The fingertip is punctured using a needle or surgical lancet. Around 3–4 drops of blood are deposited on a blotting paper and then they are dried at room temperature in a protected place. A commercially available chemically treated filter paper is designed for the collection and preservation of blood (e.g. Whatman FTA) for forensic puroposes. It allows long-term storage of biological material at room conditions.

Saliva

Saliva and buccal epithelial cells should be collected by rubbing the inside of the oral cavity with a steril cotton swab. It's suggested to use swabs (see example in Figure 5.10) for rubbing the surface of the right cheek and another one for the left cheek. Swabs must be dried at room temperature before introducing them into the covers since bacteria may proliferate rapidly with moisture, producing DNA degradation. Several cards with chemically treated filter paper are commercially available (e.g. Whatman FTA) and allow long-term storage of saliva at room conditions (as shown in Figure 5.11).

Currently, saliva samples have become the first-choice sample due to the easy collection.

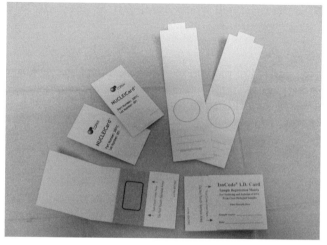

FIGURE 5.11 Example of chemically treated filter paper for biological material collection (Author's property).

Hairs

Around 10–15 hairs with root should be collected with tweezers and then placed in paper bags or on a small paper that must be folded carefully and then stored in a small paper bag.

In cases of sexual assault, it is necessary to also take 10–15 pubic hairs of the victim.

Transfused Subjects

If a person has received a blood transfusion, it is appropriate to use saliva or hairs with roots as a reference sample since in the blood, the DNA of the donor or a mixture between the donor and recipient DNA may be detected, expecially in a short period of time after the transfusion.

EVIDENCE PACKING

Once collected, the evidence must be packed properly in order to avoid breakage, contamination, alteration, or changes and to ensure sample integrity (ENFSI, 2012) Obviously the choice of the package (e.g. paper or plastic bags, envelopes, boxes, etc.) depends on the type of the evidence (e.g. porous, non-porous). It is necessary to use disposable material for the collection and once the collection is finished, it is important to throw all used material (gloves, masks, papers, etc.) in appropriate containers, without leaving anything at the scene. Each piece of evidence must be uniquely labeled and individually packed. It is necessary to avoid any contact between different pieces of evidence and between the evidence and the reference samples.

Biological evidence exists in several different forms and it may easily undergo degradation, so special precautions are required during packaging. For example, wet samples should be placed in a waterproof, non-porous container. In the case of wet evidence, plastic bags are not recommended and they can be used only temporarily, due to the possibility of bacterial and fungal growth that degrades the sample. Breathable plastic bags can be used for wet evidence and swabs. For a good preservation, however, before packaging it is preferable to dry the wet evidence in a protected place, on a clean surface. Dry evidence (cigarettes, fibers, etc.) can be stored in paper or plastic envelopes. It is important to avoid any rubbing between the sample and the container to limit the loss of biological material. Plastic tubes or bottles are used for liquid biological samples. Hairs and fibers can be packaged in various containers such as paper envelopes, plastic or glass vials, or bags.

Generally, to ensure correct preservation, three types of packaging are used:

Primary: it is the container that is in direct contact with the evidence.
Secondary: it is the container used to transport the primary packaging.
Tertiary: it is the container used to simultaneously contains several secondary-type packaging.

It's necessary to seal the evidence container to ensure that evidence will be not lost or altered.

This can be done by using security bags, tamper-evident tapes, and non-removable tape marked with the date and initials of the person who collected the evidence, in such a way that any improper access is detectable. Some examples of containers used for evidence collection are shown in Figure 5.12. Each package must have a label containing all the informations relevant to the efficient sample processing and useful to documenting when and where the evidence was collected at the scene (NFSTC, 2013).

They include:

- case identifier
- brief description of the evidence
- classification of evidence
- date, place, time of collection
- name of the person who collected the evidence.

All of these annotated data are important because they allow the certain identification of the evidence, guaranteeing the correspondence between the evidence indicated on the packages and the items contained inside it.

SCENE RELEASING

Since the possibility of returning to a crime scene is unlikely, before leaving a crime scene it is necessary to review everything to find out if any evidence has been inadvertently forgotten and to make sure that all areas of the scene and all evidence have been properly measured and documented (NIJ, 2000; ENFSI, 2000). In this perspective, the following actions should be performed:

- a meeting between the technicians who performed the inspection to review the activity carried out
- tracking the scene through each of the previously analyzed areas
- checking that no evidence or other items of interest have not been collected and that all evidence is properly packaged for transport
- checking that all instruments/materials are not forgotten
- taking away the container with the used material (e.g. gloves, masks, disposable material)
- taking final photographies or video registrations of the scene, to document its final state before releasing it.

EVIDENCE TRANSPORTATION

Once the evidence is appropriately collected (e.g. adhesive tape, tweezers, swabs) and packed (e.g. bags, containers), adequate conditions must be used for the transportation from the site where the evidence was collected to the forensic laboratory or to any intermediate location. Correct transportation of the evidence is a crucial step to prevent the evidence from being damaged or altered prior to the examination (NFSTC, 2013). In fact, to be useful for the analysis, the evidence must be transported to the laboratory ensuring the maintenance of its integrity and

FIGURE 5.12 Example of forensic containers for evidence collection (Author's property).

identity. The use of adequate transportation conditions avoid evidence alteration. For example, the transport conditions of biological evidence must guarantee protection against heat, humidity, and sunlight to avoid the degradation of the sample.

Limited and secured access during transportation helps to prevent any unauthorized access and any possible alteration of evidence. If a critical piece of evidence is missed or improperly preserved, the investigation will be compromised.

In addition, appropriate documentation is necessary to clearly demonstrate in which situation the evidence was collected and the modality of the transfer from an officer to another or to the forensic laboratory. It is also necessary to document the storage conditions of the samples before shipment to the laboratory and inside the different areas of the laboratory. Onto each document must be placed the signature of who has handled the evidence and also date, place, and time of handling. When choosing the transportation modality and the place where to relocate and store the evidence, it's necessary to evaluate also the costs, distance, timeframe, and any eventual incompatibility between evidence and transportation modality. The relocation of physical evidence such as drugs and firearms, must be also done in accordance with local legislations.

EVIDENCE STORAGE

For an optimal preservation of the evidence, requires not only proper collection, packaging, and transportation procedures, but also storage at the right environmental conditions that are essential to protect its integrity (NIST, NIJ, 2013). It is important to observe the necessary precautions to prevent the evidence alteration or degradation if it is not properly conserved according to its own nature. These precautions should include evidence protection from heat, sunlight, moisture, and its storage in areas with controlled temperature and humidity in order to avoid the risk of extensive degradation. In fact, it's well known that environmental factors, such as heat and humidity, provide a good environment for bacteria growth that can accelerate the degradation of DNA.

According to international guidelines (NIST, NIJ, 2013), depending on the type of evidence and eventually on the type of analysis that will be conducted, it's suggested to store biological evidence in one of the following conditions:

- *Room temperature:* temperature is equivalent to the environmental one. In this case any temperature and humidity control methods may be absent.

- *Refrigerated:* temperature is between 2°C–8°C(36°F–46°F) and humidity is maintained less than 25%
- *Frozen:* temperature is at or below –10°C (14°F)
- *Temperature controlled:* temperature is between 15.5°C–24°C (60°F–75°F) and humidity is maintained less than 60%

Biological evidence can be stored in refrigerators or freezers with controlled temperatures and humidity depending on whether it is temporary or long-term storage.

Depending on the type of evidence and management process, it is necessary to choose a temporary or a long-term storage location. This latter represents any location area where evidence is stored for more than 72 hours.

Evidence should be stored in designated areas, tightly closed, with limited access by personnel, and in such a way to avoid mixture or contamination. They cannot be stored in unauthorized areas.

A physical or digital inventory of the evidence must be kept including information on the evidence classification, storing location, date, time, and the identity of the person who stored the evidence.

Furthermore, it's necessary to record, if applicable, any information about the identity of the people who have reviewed the evidence or had it in custody for a limited time during the storage, the reason, the date and time when it was taken, and the return date and time.

CHAIN OF CUSTODY

Chain of custody is intended for all the documentation (notes, photographs) that accompanies the evidence. It allows the identification of all persons who had in custody the evidence and of all locations where the evidence has been kept in chronological order from the collection at the crime scene to its elimination. Because of this, the chain of custody is as an unbroken link between all the evidence investigation phases (collection, transfer, custody, elimination of the evidence). It serves to demonstrate the integrity and identity of the evidence, ensuring correct handling of the evidence during all steps, from the crime scene to the laboratory (NIST, NIJ, 2013). This ensures that the evidence analyzed is the same that was found at the scene, confirming the authenticity of the evidence and the validity of the results obtained from its examination. Because of this, any break in the chain of custody can result in unhelpful critical evidence at the trial. Chain of custody documentation may be recorded using an electronic system, a paper system, or both. All records should report the following information:

- unique case identifier (e.g. case number)
- description of the evidence

- location where the evidence was collected
- location where the evidence was stored
- who collected the evidence
- who become in possession of the evidence and for what reason (e.g forensic analyst)
- what was done to the evidence (e.g. analysis)
- place, date, and time of any activity

Records must be kept for a period of time, variable depending on countries, even in case the evidence has been already destroyed or lost. Although a tight chain of custody may be established, the evidence may have been altered previously or during the scene investigation, if correct procedures were not performed. In other words, the chain of custody alone cannot be the only element on which to base final conclusions. The reliability of the results must be guaranteed by a rigorous quality management program that refers not only to the documentary phase necessary for the maintenance of the chain of custody, but also and, above all, to the scientific methods used for the execution of the analysis. In recent years, many automated laboratory management systems (LIMS) have been developed that enable the lab to track evidentiary items through their examination life cycle from the crime scene to the elimination. They allow electronic chain of custody immediately upon evidence collection and they accurately document all activities for every evidence. These systems are also able to alert the investigators when highly sensitive evidence is transferred to the laboratory. In addition, they use a barcode for the identification of cases and evidence, increasing the efficiency of monitoring the evidence and allowing more efficient and accurate processing of large volumes of evidence than than manual methods. Several softwares are specifically designed for all aspects of the forensics activity and are commercially available (e.g. CLIMS, STARLIMS).

COMMON ERRORS

The purpose of crime scene investigation is to discover useful physical evidence in order to reconstruct how a crime has occurred. Therefore, crime scene investigation represents the most critical phase that (if not accurately done) that could compromise all subsequent laboratory analysis and the investigative process. It is an unrepeatable activity that must be carried out with patience, attention, precision, and experience. Due to the criticality of this activity, it must be performed by experienced and adequately trained technical personnel in accordance with international protocols and, if possible, with quality certification (ISO/IEC 17020) for crime scene investigation.

The most common errors during evidence collection at a crime scene include:

- Image distortion during evidence photography or videography
- Absence of any metric and or identifying reference
- Difficulty in discovering or locating the evidence
- Difficulty in understanding if evidence was photographed before or after the scene manipulation
- Inaccuracy during the collection, packaging, transport, and storage of the evidence (this may produce loss, contamination, or degradation of the evidence)
- Recovery of only visible evidence that may result in losing relevant evidence
- Incomplete documentation that results in an altered chain of custody and in challenged evidence not useful during the trial
- Indiscriminate evidence recovery that may complicate laboratory analysis and may compromise the investigation

In fact, a bad common practice is to collect everything that could have theorically an evidentiary nature. Collection of irrelevant items results not only in a waste of time and resources, but it could potentially cause legal and investigative issues; if every object at a scene is collected and submitted for the examination to the forensic laboratory, this latter will be overcharged. In addition, it is likely that some of the evidence analyzed will have no real probative value. Furthermore, the analysis of materials unrelated to the crime will waste time and money and may lead to identify as a suspect the the wrong person (Table 5.3).

CONTAMINATION

The potential impact of biological evidence contamination is a relevant issue due to the sensitivity of current forensic analytical methods such as DNA typing (NIJ, 2000, NIST, NIJ, 2013).

Evidence contamination can occur, at crime scene, in different situations, such as during the evidence collection, packaging, or transportation to an intermediate location or to the forensic laboratory.

Altough it's impossible to completely eliminate crime scene contamination, the use of precautions and of accurate collection and preservation procedures strongly reduce the risk of evidence contamination.

The use of PPE reduces the risk of contaminating the evidence; for example, by touching it, sneezing, coughing, or talking over it.

TABLE 5.3   Example of best practices (according to NIST-NIJ 2013)

Best Practices Summary (according to NIST-NIJ 2013)
Avoid indiscriminate evidence recovery
Collect evidence appropriately depending on the type of evidence
Air-dry evidence thoroughly before packaging
Use paper bags, envelopes, cardboard boxes, or similar porous materials for all biological evidence
Use plastic bags only with dry evidence. Don't use plastic bags in the case of wet evidence to avoid fungal or bacterial growth
Package each evidence separately. Avoid contact between evidence and between evidence and container
Label each evidence container with a unique identifier, the name of the person who collected the evidence, the place and date of collection.
Seal evidence container to avoid damage, loss, or contamination of the evidence
Use evidence security bags or seal each package with evidence tape or other seals that allow checking for alteration
Transport the package, as soon as possible, to the laboratory or to an intermediate storage location in adequate conditions
Store the evidence in designated areas, with limited access by personnel and in adequate conditions according to the nature of the evidence
Accurately maintain the chain of custody

Unfortunately, also the equipment used during crime scene processing may be a source of contamination, because often examiners travel from one scene to another with the possibility of transferring material. This risk can be reduced using disposable PPE, changing equipment, or decontaminating it before and after every crime scene examination.

Indequate collection and packing can contribute to the evidence contamination. Evidence must be collected using disposable items and they must be packed separately using new containers free of contaminantes. For some evidence, it's necessary to use sterile containers. Containers must be properly marked for identification and sealed to avoid manumission, alteration or damage. Separate packaging avoids cross contamination between samples. (e.g. adventitious transfer of biological material from a sample to another).

In addition, it must be considered that, sometimes, before the arrival of the examiners, the crime scene may have been altered by rescuers, family members, or those curious who can adventitiously leave their traces, contaminating irremediably the relevant evidence.

- at the laboratory: during the analysis, contamination may occur with the biological material of the analysts or between samples.

Contamination with biological material of the personnel may be avoid wearing personal protective equipment such as such as gloves, safety glasses, and lab coats. Separate PPE should be dedicated to different laboratories areas. In addition, in the laboratory, separate work areas for the different activities must be available.

In order to reduce the risk of introducing contaminants (e.g. extraneous DNA) into the working areas that can affect samples, access to the different laboratory areas must be restricted only to the authorized personnel according to the specific activity performed in those areas.

DNA laboratories should have a DNA elimination database including DNA profiles of laboratory personnel and of all contamined profiles found by the laboratory during the analysis. These profiles are used to detect any instance of contamination.

Cross contamination with other samples is more difficult to detect and the laboratory must develop specific strict procedures for reducing and monitoring it. Contamination between samples must be avoided by using accurate handling and storage conditions. Use of disposable material and cleaning procedures for equipment and instruments, as well as procedures to minimize contamination for reagents and consumables are necessary. Replicate analyses and reaction controls are helpful in determining whether and whenever a contamination has occurred. The use of automated workstations may reduce the risk of contamination from the analysts and between samples.

Mantaining physically separated evidence and reference samples and processing them separately and in different frames (before evidence and after reference sample) may help to reduce contamination.

Even if stringent protocols are applied, unfortunately, contamination may occur and especially in case of DNA analysis is often difficult to distinguish a contamined sample from a true mixture of DNA templates. Invisible cells are easily transferred with the contact so that touch DNA is considered the most insidious form of contamination.

Crime scene personnel and laboratory staff should receive training on protocols useful for the detection and minimization of contamination.

The identification of contamination events prevents their further occurrence and it allows reducing false

TABLE 5.4 Example of Precautions for Preventing Evidence Contamination (according to NIST-NIJ 2013)

Precautions Summary (according to NIST-NIJ, 2013)
Wear PPE and change them often
Not touching evidence or sneezing, talking, coughing over it
Not touching face, nose, or mouth when collecting evidence
Use disposable items for handling evidence or sterilize them before and after their use
Avoid touching the area where biological material can be placed
Air-dry evidence thoroughly before packaging
Use paper bags for wet evidence
Package each evidence separately
Use new containers to package the evidence
Avoid contact between evidence and between evidence and container

positive results, to avoid errors that may change the final outcome of an investigation (Table 5.4).

REFERENCES

Adler, O., & Adler, R. (1904). Über das Verhalten gewisser organischer Verbindungen gegenüber Blut mit besonderer Berücksichtigung des Nachweises von Blut. *Hoppe-Seyler's Zeitschrift für physiologische Chemie*, 41(1–2), 59–67.

ENFSI Scene of Crime Working Group (2012). ENFSI Scenes of Crime Best Practice Manual.

Fisher, B. *Techniques in Crime Scene Investigation*. USA: CRC Press, 2012.

Grupo Español y Portugués de la International Society For Forensic Genetic (2000). Recomendaciones para la recogida y envío de muestras con fines de identificación genética.

Huntress, E., Stanley, L., & Parker, A. (1934). The Preparation of 3-Aminophthalhydrazide for Use in the Demonstration of Chemiluminescence. *Journal of the American Chemical Society*, 56(1), 241–242.

ISO/IEC 17020. (2017). Requirements for the operation of various types of bodies performing inspection.

Kastle, J. H., & March Shedd, O. M. (1901). Phenolphthalin as a Reagent for the Oxidizing Ferments. *American Chemical Journal*, 26 (6), 526–539.

Locard, E. *Manuel de technique policière*. Paris: Payot, 1923.

Lee, H. C., Palmbach, T. M., & Miller, M. *Henry Lee's Crime Scene Handbook*. San Diego, CA: Academic Press, 2001.

Meyer, E. (1903). Beiträge zur Leukocytenfrage. Fermente der Leukocyten. *Münchener Medizinische Wochenschrift*, 50 (35), 1489–1493.

Technical Working Group on Biological Evidence Preservation (2013). The biological evidence preservation handbook, National Institute of Standards and Technology (NIST, NIJ).

Technical Working Group on Crime Scene Investigation. *Crime Scene Investigation: A Guide for Law Enforcement*. USA: National Forensic Science Technology Center (NFSTC), 2013.

Technical Working Group on Crime Scene Investigation. *Crime Scene Investigation: A Guide for Law Enforcement*. USA: National Institute of Justice (NIJ), 2000.

Vandenberg, N., & van Oorschot, R. A. H. (2006). The Use of Polilights in the Detection of Seminal Fluid, Saliva, and Bloodstains and Comparison with Conventional Chemical-Based Screening Tests. *Journal of Forensic Sciences*, 51(2), 361–370.

CHAPTER 6

Bloodstain Pattern Analysis

Amarnath Mishra[1], Jyoti Singh[2], Chintan Singh[2], and Ayushi Dwivedi[2]

[1]Worldwide Association of Women Forensic Experts (WAWFE-Caribbean), School of Forensics, Risk Management & National Security (SFRMNS), Rashtriya Raksha University, Lavad-Dahegam, Gandhinagar, Gujarat, India
[2]Amity Institute of Forensic Sciences, Amity University, Noida, Uttar Pradesh, India

CONTENTS

INTRODUCTION

Physical evidence is well-defined as any and all materials or items associated with a crime scene that by scientific evaluation helps to establish the elements of a crime and provides a link between the crime scene, the victim, and the assailant and blood is one of the most significant and commonly encountered types of physical evidence at scenes of violent crimes. Bloodstain pattern evidence is often present at delinquencies of violence. The shape and distribution of blood droplets can assist in reconstructing how the crime occurred. The bloodstain interpretation should be incorporated into the organized approach for crime scene examination. Bloodstain explanation is part of the complete investigation, which includes the documentation, collection, and assessment of all physical evidence. The information provided by bloodstain interpretation should be evaluated in unification with evidence provided by the post-mortem examination of the victim and analyses performed by the crime laboratory.

The examination of blood offers vital information to the forensic scientist in many areas of criminal

DOI: 10.4324/9781003129554-6

investigation. Information is gained from blood by the forensic pathologist, toxicologist, serologist, and crime scene analyst. Blood is studied by the forensic pathologist to assist with the diagnosis of various diseases that may relate to the cause of death. Blood is examined by the forensic toxicologist in concurrence with other body fluids and tissues to determine the presence or absence of alcohol, drugs, and poisons. The forensic pathologist also utilizes blood evidence during the external examination of a victim before post-mortem. The forensic serologist scrutinizes blood collected from crime scenes to establish that the substance is, in fact, blood and differentiates human from animal blood. After that, the blood may be typed within the ABO group and other antigenic systems, isoenzyme systems, DNA typing, or other individualization systems (Eckert, 1997). Annotations of bloodstains have been used since prehistoric man tracked wounded animals, just as modern hunters do today.

Bloodstain pattern analysis (BPA) is the systematic assessment of the visual patterns of bloodstains at crime scenes based on the physics of fluids. Bloodstain pattern analysis is well-defined as "the scientific study of the static consequences resulting from dynamic blood shedding events" (Hulse-Smith et al., 2005). It is an important is a forensic discipline that deals with the physics of the blood and assesses bloodstains discovered at a crime scene using visual recognition and observation. The analysis of bloodstains at a crime scene gives clues on how blood travels through a given space due to bloodstains encountered on a surface.

When bloodstains are studied with respect to their geometry and distribution on various surfaces, they can impart valuable information for the reconstruction of events that produced the bloodshed.

- Origin(s) of the bloodstains
- Remoteness between surface and origin at time of bloodshed
- Nature and direction of impact
- Object(s) that produced particular bloodstain patterns
- Number of blows, shots, etc. that occurred
- Location and movement of victim, assaulter, or objects during and after bloodshed
- Support or contradiction of version of events given by suspect or witnesses
- Additional criteria for estimation of time of death
- Correlation with other laboratory and pathology findings relevant to an investigation. Bloodstain pattern interpretation uses the sciences of biology, physics, and mathematics.

The shape and appearance of bloodstains and smears can also give useful information about the crime.

In 1971, MacDonell published his classic work on bloodstain pattern evidence and outlined several general rules regarding bloodstain evidence:

1. Spots of blood may be used to determine the directionality of the falling drop that produced them. Their shape frequently permits an estimate as to their velocity and/or impact angle and/or the distance fallen from source to the final resting place.
2. The diameter of a blood spot is of little or no value in estimating the distance it has fallen after the first 5 or 6 feet. Beyond this distance, the change is too slight to be reliable.
3. The edge characteristics of blood spots have absolutely no meaning or value unless the effect of the target surface is well known. This is especially true when attempts are made to estimate the distance from the so-called "scallops" around the edge.
4. The degree of spatter of a single blood drop depends far more upon the smoothness of the target surface than the distance the drop falls. The coarser the surface, the more likely the drop will be ruptured and spatter. A blotter, for example, will cause a drop to spatter to a considerable extent at a distance of 18 inches, whereas a drop falling over 100 feet will not spatter at all if it lands on glass or other smooth surfaces.
5. No conclusion as to the cause of a very small bloodstain should ever be drawn from a limited number of stains. Very fine specks of blood may result from an overcast or cast-off satellite from a larger drop or droplet. In the absence of the larger drop, however, when hundreds of drops smaller than 1/8 of an inch are present (often down to 1/1000 of an inch in diameter), it may be concluded that they were produced by an impact; the smaller the diameter of the drops is, the higher the velocity of the impact that produced them. The difference between medium-velocity impact, such as an axe or hammer blow, and high-velocity impact, such as a gunshot, is sufficient for differentiating the two, provided an adequate sample is observed by someone thoroughly familiar with bloodstain pattern reconstruction.
6. Directionality of a small bloodstain is easily determined, provided the investigator recognizes the difference between an independent spatter and a castoff or satellite thrown from a larger drop. Small independent stains have a uniform taper resembling a teardrop and always point toward their direction of travel. Cast-off droplets produce a tadpole-like, long narrow stain with a well-defined "head." The sharper end of

these stains always points back toward their origin. Because these satellite spatters travel only a very short distance, the larger drop can almost always be traced.

7. The character of a bloodstain, made by drops or smaller droplets or by larger quantities of blood up to several ounces, may reveal movement at the moment of initial staining or later if a body or other stained surface is moved from its original position.

8. Depending upon the target and impact angle, considerable back spatter may result from a wound. The range of back spatter is considerably less than that occurring in the same direction of the projectile, however. This is especially true with exit wounds when expanding-type slugs are used.

9. Blood is a very uniform material from the standpoint of its aerodynamics. Its ability to reproduce specific patterns is not affected to any significant degree by age or gender. Likewise, because blood is shed from a body at constant temperature and is normally exposed to an external environment for such a very short time, atmospheric temperature, pressure, and humidity have no measurable effect on its behavior (Fisher, 2004).

HISTORICAL DEVELOPMENT

From the earliest of mankind, human hunters developed and utilized the knowledge and skills associated with the analysis of bloodstains and patterns in order to provide valuable information about their prey (Dutelle, 2010). The hunters, by the help of bloodstains and patterns, were able to gather information relating to how an animal was injured (by another animal or if the animal was being hunted), the direction traveled by the injured animal, and possibly the time in which the injury took place. Dutelle also discovered that there are Biblical passages that relate to bloodstains with injury and with mortality; such reference helps as signs that humans have been analyzing bloodstain patterns for years. Bloodstain pattern analysis is perceived as a new forensic science. It is used on a frequent basis to assist in the investigation of violent crimes (Sferstein, 2015). Herbert Leon MacDonnell as the historian for the International Association of Bloodstain Pattern Analysts (IABPA), has found literature references to bloodshed characteristics dating back to the 1500s. In 1895, Dr. Eduard Piotrowski published an article on his experiments to examine bloodstain patterns resulting from head wounds. In 1939, Dr. Victor Balthazard presented a paper at the 22nd Congress of Forensic Medicine concerning his research associated with bloodstain pattern analysis.

Blood spatter analysis, as a forensic discipline is credited to Dr. Paul Leland Kirk of the University of California at Berkeley. Dr. Kirk (1952 to 1974) explained the benefits of BPA and its applications within crime scene analysis in his book entitled *Criminal Investigation* and the chapter "Blood: Physical Investigation," subsequent to his research. Kirk's research and conclusions on BPA stood strong in the 1955 case involving Samuel H. Sheppard who was suspected to have murdered his wife in their dwelling. Dr. Sheppard, a prominent doctor in Bay Village, Ohio, was convicted of the beating death of his wife, Marilyn Sheppard. Dr. Kirk examined the bloodstain patterns at the crime scene and did scientific research that he used to formulate his opinions concerning the bloodstain patterns on the walls of the Sheppards' bedroom. This is considered to be the start of bloodstain pattern analysis as a forensic discipline. In 1966, Dr. Kirk appeared as an expert for the defense during Dr. Sheppard's second trial, in which he was acquitted of beating to death Marilyn Sheppard. In 1971, Herbert Leon MacDonell's *Flight Characteristics of Human Blood and Stain Patterns* was published. This publication was a compilation of Mr. MacDonell's research that was sponsored by a funding from the Law Enforcement Assistance Administration (LEAA). In 1973, Mr. MacDonell developed a training program and instructed the first of many bloodstain institutes. In the years that followed, interest in bloodstain pattern analysis grew rapidly. Many publications and books can be found concerning this forensic discipline and several professional associations have been created. The International Association of Bloodstain Pattern Analysts, founded in 1983, is dedicated to advancing bloodstain pattern analysis as a forensic science. The International Association of Bloodstain Pattern Analysts publishes an online journal quarterly and hosts an annual training conference that is attended by bloodstain analysts from around the world. In the late 1990s the International Association for Identification began offering a bloodstain pattern analyst certification program. In 2002, the Federal Bureau of Investigation hosted the first meeting of the Scientific Working Group for Bloodstain Pattern Analysis (SWG Stain). SWG Stain was tasked with addressing current issues that affect the forensic sciences and the impact of those issues on the discipline of bloodstain pattern analysis. SWG Stain was also tasked with developing recommended guidelines for training, quality assurance, and research in bloodstain pattern analysis.

BLOODSTAIN PATTERN ANALYSIS SIGNIFICANCE

Bloodstain pattern analysis provides significant forensic information about the crime under investigation; it tells what happened. Bloodstain patterns appear in several discrete categories, each revealing a piece of the crime scene riddle. The most important functions of bloodstain pattern analysis to substantiate or corroborate witness statements and laboratory and autopsy findings. For example, if the medical examiner determines the cause of death is blunt force trauma to the victim's head, the pattern and volume of blood spatter should be consistent with a blunt tool striking the victim one or more times on the head. On the other hand, if the spatter appears that seen in expired blood spray, the expert will check the medical examiner's reports for injuries that can cause the presence of blood in the nose, throat or respiratory system of the victim. The analyst may be able to exclude expiration as the possible cause of that spatter pattern if blood is not reported in these sites. The significant uses of bloodstain pattern analysis include:

- The reconstruction of the events of a crime or accident.
- To differentiate between homicides, suicides, and accidents.
- To corroborate or disprove statements of witness, victim, or suspect.
- To bring about some certainty in cases where there is doubt as to involvement in a crime.
- For the identification of areas with a high possibility of offender movement for the prioritization of DNA samples.

BLOODSTAIN PATTERN ANALYSIS PRINCIPLE

One must understand the basic properties of blood to understand how experts interpret bloodstains. Blood contains plasma and serum as liquid and red blood cells, white blood cells, platelets and proteins as solid. Blood can be characterized as a fluid consisting of cellular components and plasma which circulates under pressure through the arterial and venous systems of the body. Blood behaves according to the laws of fluid dynamics because of being a liquid. Its physical properties (viscosity, specific gravity, surface tension, and the forces) acting on blood outside the body determine the size, shape, directionality, and location of bloodstains on different surfaces. When blood is exposed to the external environment, it is subjected to various forces and will behave in a predictable manner based on the laws of biology, physics, and mathematics.

Bloodshed occurs internally or externally or both when the circulatory system is disrupted by trauma or disease. Biologically, the clotting and drying process of blood will be initiated. Experiments performed with human blood subjected to various external forces including gravity have confirmed that blood follows the principles of fluids in motion. Blood droplets are formed when small masses of liquid separate from a larger mass outside the body. The separation of these drops from the source of blood is caused by gravity and/or impact to the blood source exceeding the forces of surface tension and viscosity of the blood. Surface tension is the result of the molecular cohesive forces that cause the surface of a liquid to resist penetration and separation. Viscosity is the resistance of a fluid to flow or to change form or the position of its molecules due to the attraction of the molecules to each other. As a drop of blood is falling through air, the surface tension of the liquid will minimize its surface area; this will cause the drop to assume a spherical shape rather than the teardrop shape often used by artists.

The occurrence of blood clots in bloodstains can point to that victim was bleeding for some time after the injury occurred or the attack was prolonged. Observation of the degree of clotting and serum production and extent of drying of blood at a scene may help estimate the time since bloodshed occurred.

Categories of Blood Stains

There are three general classes of bloodstains; everyone is characterized and portrayed as far as the force required to form the pattern that is observed as shown in Figure 6.1:

1. Passive
2. Transfer
3. Projected

Again, we should depict the forces acting on bloodstains and not simply the bloodstains themselves. Along these lines, passive bloodstains will be bloodstains shaped by gravity as the external force acting up on the bloodstain. Truly, all passive stains are a combination of gravity and attachment with the resulting bloodstain framed by the blood sticking to the contact surface. Passive bloodstains include drops, trickles, clots, and pools.

Transfer bloodstains are made when the principle acting force to cause the stain is adhesion as it were. In the event when object experiences something bloody, blood will pass between the two objects through the cycle of grip. Move stains contrast from passive stains by having no gravity segment to their formation. Transfer stains can be additionally partitioned into contact dying, swipes, smears, wipes, or smudges.

Projected stains are caused when a force or power applied more prominent than gravity acts to create the bloodstains. Projected stains can be additionally partitioned into spurts, cast-off stains, and impact stains.

Wonder 2007).

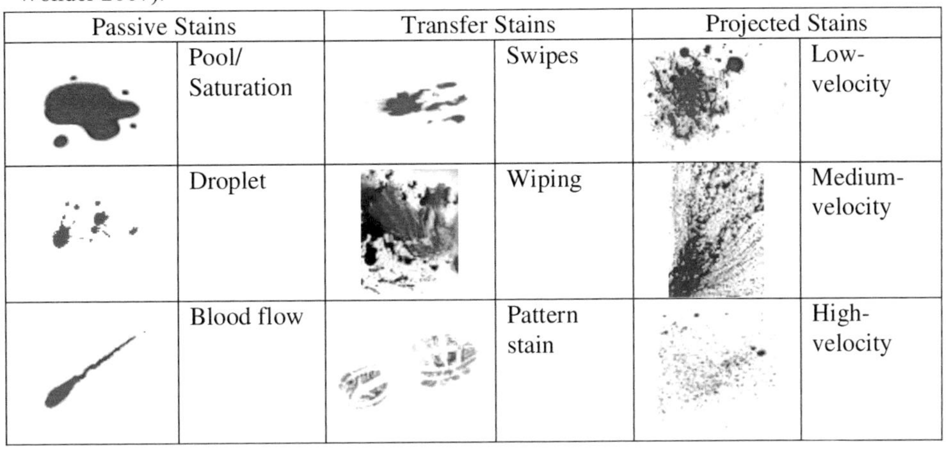

Passive Stains		Transfer Stains		Projected Stains	
	Pool/ Saturation		Swipes		Low-velocity
	Droplet		Wiping		Medium-velocity
	Blood flow		Pattern stain		High-velocity

FIGURE 6.1   Different categories of bloodstains.

PRESUMPTIVE TESTING AND CHEMICAL ENHANCEMENT

The definition of "presumptive" according to Merriam-Webster.com (Presumptive, n.d.), is "giving grounds for reasonable opinion or belief." Therefore, when conducting presumptive testing either on scene or in the laboratory, a positive result does not mean that the suspected stain/sample is, in fact, blood. A positive presumptive test gives the analyst grounds for reasonable belief that the substance is blood and that he or she can continue with the investigation as if it were blood, pending confirmatory or DNA testing.

Historically, the chain of testing was as follows: presumptive → confirmatory → species determination → DNA. Today, however, it is very common that the intermediate steps are not performed, and a sample is sent for DNA testing after a positive presumptive test is obtained. There are a number of presumptive tests available: catalytic color tests, such as phenolphthalein (PTH) (also known as Kastle-Meyer or KM), leucocrystal violet (LCV), Hemastix, leucomalachite green, tetramethylbenzidine (TMB), as well as chemiluminescent and fluorescent preparations. Hexagon OBTI is currently the only presumptive test available that can make the analyst more confident that a suspected sample is, in fact, human blood. While false positives have occurred with some primate blood samples, it did not react with blood from common domestic and farm animals.

It is good practice to collect two swabs of a stain and utilize one for presumptive testing and one to submit for DNA testing, as many of the color tests can render the sample useless for DNA testing. Catalytic color tests are testing that function by utilizing a chromogen solution (color) that is oxidized, usually by a 3% hydrogen peroxide, which is catalyzed by the presence of hemoglobin, and results in a visible color change. These tests should be read within a few seconds of the completion of the application of solutions to the swabs, or the results are not reliable.

Examples of tests that produce light instead of color are chemicals such as Luminol, BlueStar Forensic, and Fluorescein, that are luminescent (Luminol, BlueStar) and fluorescent (Fluorescein), respectively. These chemicals are typically used to identify areas of bloodshed after a cleanup or to enhance bloodstains that may be on a substrate where visualization of bloodstains is difficult. When photographing chemiluminescent or fluorescent reactions, it is preferable to use a technique that reveals both the reaction and the surrounding location. This can be achieved by either "painting with light" or rear-curtain sync techniques. Some agencies will take a photograph of the area in normal light conditions, followed by the chemical enhancement of the same area (that typically looks like areas of light on a black background) and then layer the two photographs in a photo-editing program. While this technique is not impermissible, there are a few steps that should be taken to ensure admissibility. First, once the image of the "normal" lighting conditions is obtained, a tripod must be used. Second, a scale should be placed for the normal light conditions, photographed and left in place for the chemical reaction photographs. The scale will serve as proof that the camera was not moved from its original position and provide an "anchor" to utilize when the photos are layered in the photo-editing program. Unscaled photos, or one scaled photograph with one unscaled photograph, should not be used for layering purposes. Additionally, each step in the photo-editing process should be documented, whether within the software program, in writing, or both, so that the composite image can be deconstructed and reconstructed following the documented steps, by a third party.

Luminol (Additional Searching Technique): Since 1930 luminol has been utilized as an additional technique to recognize shrouded and hidden bloodstains (Benecke & Barksdale, 2003). Luminol (3-Aminophthalacidhydrazide) shows chemiluminescene within the sight of blood, when blended in with a proper oxidizing agent (H$_2$O$_2$ and NaOH). The iron found in hemoglobin catalyzes the synthetic response, leaving a striking blue glow, which goes on for around 30 s.

The most popular guidelines on the best way to make luminol-arrangements are via Carter (Carter, 2001) and Lytle and Hedgecock (Lytle & Hedgecock, 1978). The formula by Weber is more delicate and is delivered with three arrangements:

- 8 g NaOH in 500 ml Aqua dest.,
- 10 ml of a 30% H$_2$O$_2$-arrangement in 490 ml Aqua dest.,
- 0.354 g Luminol in 62.5 ml 0.4 N NAOH-arrangement, Aqua dest. add 500 ml.

On the off-chance that the H$_2$O$_2$ isn't more seasoned than about two months, these norm luminol arrangements are steady for a while and exceptionally delicate for 8–12 weeks.

Luminol is utilized to distinguish minor, unnoticed, or covered-up bloodstains diluted to a degree of up to 1:106 (1 micro liter blood in 1 liter of arrangement). The blended substances are straightforwardly sprayed into suspected areas, typically in a totally dark environment. If the response is positive, the chemiluminescenic response can be shot while the glowing regions are stamped to research them once the light has blurred, as shown in Figure 6.2.

Luminol has a high affectability for blood, particularly for more seasoned, totally dried blood (Pex, IABPA News 2005). Lamentably, the luminol response isn't set off by blood alone, and a rather wide range of environmental and pharmaceutical substances substances, for example, cleansers, a few metals, and vegetables can impact the cycle (Grodsky et al., 1951). Since there are a number of substances meddling with the luminol response, furthermore, conceivably prompting wrong conclusions, it is fundamental that the scientific analyst knows about these disadvantages (Peschel et al., 2011). Experienced examiners can perceive visual contrasts, depending upon chemical reaction with luminol.

Aside from luminol, there are different substances that are ready to recognize hidden blood stains, for instance Blue Star. This arrangement, monetarily created in France, shows a more grounded visual response with blood at high blood fixations, yet has a minor affectability at lower blood focuses. The two substances, luminol and Blue Star, normally permit a dependable DNA-examination after the application (Klein et al., 2007).

Symptoms of luminol have not yet been completely inspected. There are mucocutaneous aggravations of the eye, skin, and gastrointestinal parcel with loose bowels and heaving. Because of this, it is fitting to guarantee natural air flow in the wake of having utilized luminol. There is no proof concerning persistent impacts (Barni et al., 2007).

All presumptive tests are subject to some false positive results, which is a positive reaction from a substance other than blood, such as vegetable peroxidases and chemical oxidants. There are several studies available that examine the specificity (how likely the test is to react to materials other than blood) and sensitivity (how low of a concentration of blood will the test detect). For color tests, if there is an apparent color reaction before the addition of the oxidizing agent, this is also considered a false positive.

Apparent partial prints in blood may be enhanced to further reveal either ridge or tread detail for potential comparison. Some commonly used chemicals for this purpose include amido black, Hungarian red, aqueous leucocrystal violet, and Coomassie Brilliant Blue. There are advantages and disadvantages to each, and the method should be chosen based on the substrate and the potential probative value (Presumptive, 2015).

Positive and negative controls should be performed immediately prior to use in casework to assure that the chemicals are functioning properly. It should be noted that this is a very brief overview of presumptive testing to acquaint the reader with some of the commonly used chemicals. A great deal of literature exists that covers additional testing and enhancement methods (Sears, 2002; Secomb, 1991).

EVALUATING A BLOODSTAIN CASE

A bloodstain pattern analyst may be asked to conduct an analysis at various points in the criminal justice process

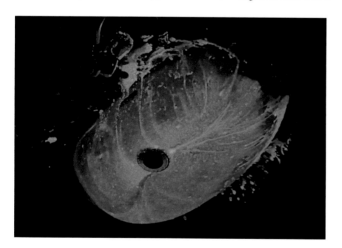

FIGURE 6.2 Image showing luminol reaction with blood and forming chemiluminescence.

from responding to a fresh crime scene to evaluating a cold case. This section will also be an overview of some of the most important issues to consider when evaluating a bloodstain case, regardless of where it is within the process, rather than a comprehensive reference manual.

When examining a crime scene, or physical evidence, proper personal protective equipment (PPE) should be utilized. All biological material should be considered infectious and handled accordingly. Additionally, the scene and evidence must be protected from contamination by the analyst. At a fresh scene, a preliminary walk-through should be conducted, initial observations noted, and assessment of what PPE, equipment, and personnel will be necessary.

The reconstruction of a bloodstained scene requires the input from other disciplines and information sources, such as the autopsy report, hospital records, witness statements, DNA, and other laboratory testing.

Initially, patterns should be identified and described based solely on their size, shape, distribution, and location, without attempting to attribute a specific event that created the pattern; this will be done later. For example, a pattern consisting of small, round stains, between 1 and 3 millimeters in diameter, is located on a wall approximately 12 inches above the floor. The "differential diagnoses" based on this information could be impact spatter, satellite spatter, or expired bloodstains. If there is no pooling of blood nearby, nor evidence that one was cleaned up, or that an object onto which dripping may have occurred had been removed, satellite spatter may be ruled out. After review of EMS, hospital, autopsy reports, scene, and autopsy photographs, there is documentation of blood in the nose, mouth, airway, airway injury, or positioning of the victim such that an expired pattern is possible (such as breathing into a pool of blood), then expired bloodstains may be ruled out. This would leave impact spatter and the most likely pattern and would then be correlated with the injuries.

Once DNA testing results are obtained, it may be possible to place individuals in their respective positions. This is especially important when multiple victims are involved.

Each case will have different information available for review. It is important to note that the analyst may find him- or herself in the position of not having sufficient information on which to base an opinion, or many overlapping, complex, and/or altered patterns that make rendering an opinion difficult or impossible. It is critical that the analyst recognizes this and reports only conclusions that can be supported by the available evidence.

Several examples of worksheets are available to ensure that examinations are systematic and thorough, whether it is of a scene, clothing, vehicle, or other items of evidence. It is not uncommon for a defense of an accused to be something like, "Look at all the blood at

this scene. No blood was found on Mr. Jones' person, clothes or vehicle. Mr. Jones could not have been involved in this crime and not gotten any blood on himself!" Research by MacDonell and Kish has coined the axiom in blood- stain pattern analysis that "absence of evidence is not evidence of absence." This means that simply because a suspect has little or no blood on his or her person or clothing does not mean that he/she was not involved in the incident. There are a number of factors that determine whether or not an assailant becomes spattered with blood, as mentioned earlier, including but not limited to the following:

The nature of the weapon (length, mass, arc of swing) utilized
Direction of the blows or sharp force trauma
The number of wounds and if covered by clothing or hair
Duration of assault
The assailant discarded clothing worn during assault and cleaned him- or herself up
Assailant committed the assault while naked, subse quently cleaned up
Assailant utilized outer protective clothing

Different Classes of Blood Stains

Blood patterns classes are such categories that are affected by just gravity, or transfer stains, where a blood-bearing object transfers blood onto another surface. Spritz or spatter of blood incorporates a way, for example, the crime happened, including beating or shooting; also called satellite scatter and projected patterns. Projected models or patterns are those which are followed up on by a power more prominent than that of gravity and happen from some different option from sway, for example, blood vessel spouting and expired bloodstain designs. Adjusted bloodstain patterns are those that have gone through a type of physiological, physical/mechanical, or substance change, like weakened bloodstains, or examples made by bugs. While "modified" may appear to infer a negative or purposeful change to beguile implication, that isn't what is implied by its utilization in bloodstain order. While designs in this classification can incorporate purposeful changes to the bloodstains, in this specific circumstance, it just implies that there has been some change. These classes will be inspected in more detail and described below.

Flow Patterns

Flow patterns occur when a drop of blood is unable to attach itself to its surface and, under the influence of gravity, such blood drops start to move towards the downward slope, which further makes it flow and hence forms flow patterns. The object topography and gravity play vital roles in movement of flow patterns. These patterns help to find out the victim in a crime scene. At the point when a flow design is as yet wet, a streamline's heading will change with the position of the body/object. For example, if flow designs are recognized on a person's leg with directionality from the knee to the foot, yet the individual is discovered resting on the ground, it very well may be resolved that the victim was in a situated or standing position.

Blood Pool

A pool of blood occurs when blood collects in a level (not sloped) and undisturbed place. Blood that pools on an absorbent surface may be absorbed throughout the surface and diffuse, creating a pattern larger than the original pool. Figure 6.3 shows a real crime scene image of a blood pool pattern in which we can see non-uniform deposition of blood further characterized on the basis of wet and dry blood pool pattern.

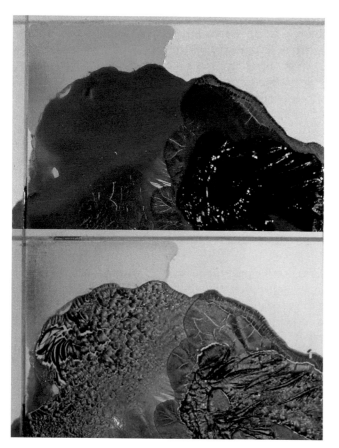

FIGURE 6.3   Real image of blood pool at a crime scene.

Impact Spatter Stains

The old characterization of bloodstains depended on the speed at which the blood source was affected and the size of the bloodstains that came about.

Impact spatter stains that are reliable with a beating or wounding will in general have the dominance of bloodstains with a breadth of around 1–3 mm. In any case, there can be a wide variety from 1 to 3 mm, dependent on sort of weapon, measure of uncovered blood, and a few different variables. The speed of the power that impacts the blood source is by and large somewhere in the range of 5 and 25 feet/second. There should be blood uncovered before it tends to be scattered. This implies that without something like a devastating head blow, it would not be astounding not to perceive any blood splash coming about because of a solitary hit to the head. People who oversee a beating or cutting could possibly get scattered with blood themselves.

There are numerous components that decide if an aggressor gets scattered with blood, some of which include the dimension of weapon i.e. length, weight, and shape of the weapon; from which direction the force was applied; how many blows were made; and relative movement, posture, and position of both the victim and criminal.

Cast-off Projected Stains

There are two kinds of cast-off, not to be mistaken for wave cast-off. The primary kind is cessation cast-off stains. Cessation cast-off stains are formed when a grisly item arrives at an abrupt pause, which is held by hand and blood is projected due to sudden stop in movement of the weapon, due to which blood falls off. Oftentimes, cessation cast-off is darkened by sway scatter and might be troublesome, or unthinkable, to separate.

The second kind of cast-off is normally essentially alluded to as "cast-off." This sort of cast-off alludes to blood that is delivered from an object because of its movement. This is usually found in beatings and stabbings on walls and roofs when the item is swung vertically. In the event that the object is swung in an even way, as in a baseball swing, cast-off might be available on walls in a flat configuration. Cast-off is recognizable by its straight nature and changing directionality through the curve of the swing. Figure 6.4 shows the mechanism of formation of a cast-off bloodstain pattern and Figure 6.5 shows a cast-off stain pattern on a roof.

Expired Bloodstains

Expired blood stains are formed due to air pressure. This might be because of blood in the nose, mouth, or

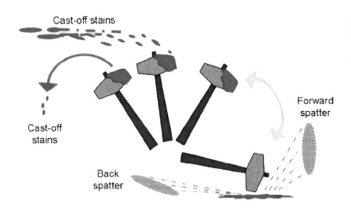

FIGURE 6.4   Formation of cast-off blood pattern.

aviation routes; air mixed in with blood in the chest or stomach wounds; or situations of casualty, for example, with his/her head in and breathing into a pool of blood. The size of such bloodstains varies incredibly, as it will rely upon how powerfully the blood was removed. As found in sway scatter, the more noteworthy the power, the more modest the bloodstains. Accordingly, expired patterns might be mistaken for impact spatter, either that which is seen with a beating/cutting, or what is seen with gunfire wounds.

There might be a few attributes that permit separation of the patterns. For example, air pockets might be available. The presence of air bubbles is basically indisputable and there is a type of aviation route injury. Nonetheless, the shortfall of air bubbles doesn't imply that the example cannot be expirated. There are a few factors, for example, the starting point of the expirated blood (from mouth, nose, wound), the idea of the injury causing the dying, the idea of the objective surface, and the power with which blood is expirated that may influence whether air pockets might be

available or potentially seen. At times, when blood with air bubbles dries, there are bubble rings that remain. An air pocket ring is the layout inside a bloodstain that remains where the air pocket had been before it burst and additionally dried. While the portrayal may sound like that of a perimeter stain (talked about in the segment on changed bloodstains), they are outwardly unique in relation to each other. The diagram of an air pocket ring might be thicker, accordingly making what resembles little vacuoles or pits, where the border stain is by and large level and is the framework of a stain that has been cleaned through before it was dry. Figure 6.6 shows the formation of an expirated stain resulting from air pressure present in the mouth of a victim.

Clotted Bloodstains

At the point when an individual endures a bloodletting injury, there is a mind-boggling coagulating course that happens to stop the draining and forms a scab. Nonetheless, blood will clot when it is outside the body also. This can be noticed rather rapidly (in no time) in a blood tube that doesn't have an anticoagulant in it when one has blood drawn for clinical testing; an image representation is shown in Figure 6.5. When coagulating happens in a pool of blood, serum partition can be seen. The period of time needed for thickening and serum detachment is influenced by numerous factors. These incorporate the underlying volume of blood, temperature, dampness, substrate on which blood is found, and wellspring of blood. The wellspring of blood is significant in light of the fact that injuries that include the head or in any case penetrate the spinal waterway may bring about the blending of cerebrospinal fluid (CSF)

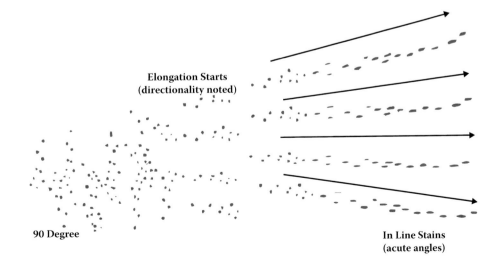

**Elongation Starts
(directionality noted)**

90 Degree

**In Line Stains
(acute angles)**

FIGURE 6.5   Cast-off blood stain on a roof.

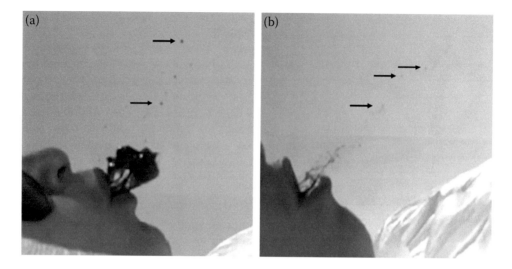

FIGURE 6.6   Expirated blood stain due to air pressure present in the mouth.

with the blood, which is known to altogether speed up the coagulating cycle.

Generally, when fresh blood is spattered, it will dry before a clot can frame. Accordingly, whenever clotted splash is seen, this may give a sign of how long an attack proceeded, which, in certain regions, might be a factor in what charges are looked for against a respondent. The length of an attack can likewise be a critical factor in condemning, especially in regions that have the death punishment, when the arraignment is endeavoring to show the especially terrible, abominable, and cold-blooded nature of the attack (Figure 6.7).

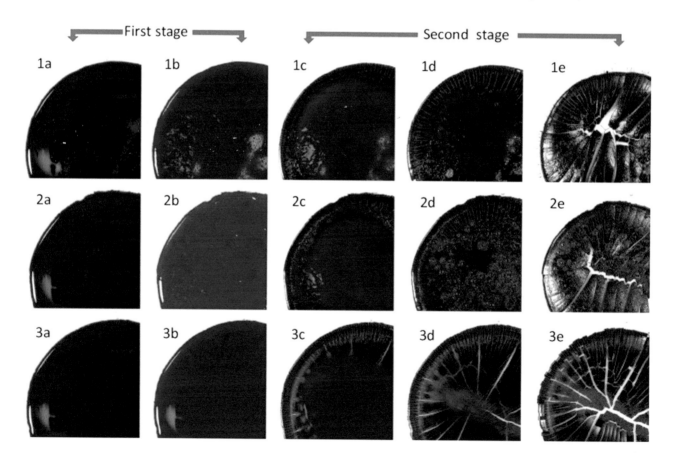

FIGURE 6.7   Different stage of clotting of blood.

Diluted Bloodstains

Diluted bloodstains are those that have been modified by expansion of a fluid. This might be natural, like snow or downpour; physiological, like tears, sweat, or salivation; or purposeful, for example, found in cleanup endeavors.

Diluted blood is by and large more obscure around the fringe.

Bloodstains that are generally found in crime scenes are affected by an adjustment in temperature/mugginess, like a stroll in a cooler, ought to be managed first and completely captured (be certain photos are adequate), and hypothetical testing finished, if important, preceding allowing a huge change in the climate (for example, inviting delayed time frames).

Dried Bloodstains

As has been examined already, ecological variables, target surface, and measure of blood are significant while considering the drying seasons of blood. Under "room temperature" conditions, little scatter stains, thin/light exchange stains, and stream patterns with a little volume of blood can dry within a couple of moments on non-permeable surfaces. Bigger volumes of blood will take more time to dry, and surfaces that can be soaked (e.g. cover, bedding) as a rule take longer than a similar volume of blood on a non-porous surface.

For the most part, drying time is diminished with raised temperature and lower mugginess. Alternately, drying time is increased with lower temperature and increased stickiness. Increased wind current, for example, delivered by fans, winds, and breezes from open windows, will influence drying times. Casework will frequently introduce highlights of both of the previously mentioned over-simplifications. For instance, in regions nearer to the equator, one may find a circumstance with increased temperature and increased moistness. Experiments may should be acted in situations where drying times are a critical issue. In these cases, the size of the bloodstains, temperature, moistness, target surface, and wind current ought to be re-created as intently as could be expected. Bloodstains dry from the outskirts toward the middle. At the point when the fringe edge is intact, however, the focal point of the stain has been removed. It is alluded to as a skeletonized stain, or a border stain. This drying principle remains constant with a wide range of stains, pools, immersion, stream patterns, and so on.

In certain instances, the focal point of the stain may dry and begin to drop away. This is frequently seen on smooth and stained sort surfaces or on surfaces with an oily film. Dried bloodstains on various kinds of skin may show up totally different from each other. Blood in a uniform layer that has dried moderately rapidly and without unsettling influence, may have a "crazed" or broken appearance. This marvel can be seen on a few different kinds of target surfaces too. Blood that is kept in thicker, more modest drops or scatter can show up "puckered." Still others may show up additionally, as the vast majority without experience in the discipline may expect, fairly a "crusty" appearance.

Note that the kind of skin (identity, age, ailments, and so forth) notwithstanding the utilization of items on the skin, alongside the standard natural factors, can influence the presence of the bloodstains.

Splash patterns and expired patterns exhibit directionality that may remain intact on hands, arms, or other body zones that may help with positioning in recreation, if necessary. The aging of bloodstains (meaning, when was the blood kept?) has been a subtle assignment. As of late, there has been work distributed using hyperspectral imaging in the aging of bloodstains that may be more prominent than past aging endeavors. It is regularly believed that bloodstains obscure, from red to a corroded sort tone to dark, as they age. While bloodstains do in general obscure as they age, attempting to assess the age of a bloodstain by its tone, without experimenting with duplicate conditions specific to that case, isn't logically faultless. Bloodstains stored on a piece of glass and a piece of wood simultaneously and in this manner examined seven days after the fact may show surprising outcomes. The one on the wood may show up a lot more obscure, while the one on glass may in any case seem red because of the light that is sent through the glass. Consider bloodstains on two indistinguishable lights in lights with blood stored at something very similar time. One light was rarely turned on, while the other remained on for an hour prior to being closed off. When the law requirement shows up, in the two instances, the bulb will be cool; however, the stains on the two lights may look altogether different. Depending on when law implementation shows up, the measure of blood kept, temperature, and so on, the bloodstains on the bulb that was never turned on may in any case be "tacky" or even wet, while the bloodstains on the bulb that had been on might be dry, more obscure and maybe in any event, starting to piece off. Missing case-explicit experiments (whose evaluations should in any case be traditionalist, as a few out of every odd variable can be reproduced), it is ideal to be moderate, assuming the blood was as yet wet upon appearance, it tends to be reasoned that it was as of late kept.

Assuming the blood is dry upon appearance, it tends to be presumed that some time has passed since it was saved. Epstein and Laber, in 1983, distributed information in *Experiments and Practical Exercises in Bloodstain Pattern Analysis*, taking into account a few ecological elements, surface qualities, and volumes of blood up to 10 mL that can be utilized as an overall guide/reference.

Diffused/Capillary Action

Diffusion is defined as the net development of a substance from a region of high focus to a zone of low fixation. Capillary activity alludes to the capacity of a fluid to stream in little/limited spaces in rebellion of gravity and without the help of outside powers. This happens when the cement powers, which are the powers between two disparate substances, between the fluid and the container, are more prominent than the firm powers within the fluid. Strong powers are powers between like substances. Thus, if the firm powers are more noteworthy than the glue powers between the fluid and container, an opposite stream will happen. It is capillary activity that is the principle at work when using paper towels or wipes when cleaning up a fluid shows diffusion and capillary activity. A few individuals might be acquainted with the expression "wicking," which is regularly used to portray capillary activity. The rate at which this marvel may happen is profoundly subject to the surface, weave, or "grain" involved, notwithstanding the glue forces. Capillary activity is the principle at work in thin layer chromatography, where there is a strong and versatile stage. In bloodstain cases, the versatile stage is the fluid part of the blood and the strong stage is the permeable material on which it voyages. Alert ought to be practiced while evaluating bloodstains/splash patterns identified with directionality determinations, as the weave of the texture can misshape the state of the stain—what was dropped at a 90-degree point and ought to show up round, may show up to some degree curved, and the other way around, a circular stain may show up more adjusted. Furthermore, for certain textures, it tends to be very hard to determine on which side of the texture the blood was saved. The green dividing line isolates the stains that were saved on one side from stains stored on the contrary side. A basic visual examination may not be adequate to make the determination. This creator has seen this issue in a few sorts of material. Experimentation might be needed on irregular or new materials. Insects (and other animals) Not extraordinarily, a casualty or casualties, regardless of whether by manslaughter, self-destruction, unintentional, or common passings, are most certainly not found until they are essentially into the decay interaction. Indeed, now and then the principal indication of a dead body might be broad fly action around the trunk of a vehicle, for instance, or vultures circling in an outside territory. Parasites can ingest up to around 95% of a weight, who will at that point transform into flies. Flies can make little stains that might be confusing to the investigator at a scene where other little stains might be available, like a beating or shooting. The presence of these ancient rarities may vary from arch molded, accordingly of the sucking activity of their proboscis (in

some cases portrayed as "lappers and suckers" rather than "biters" like a horsefly), to a swiped appearance because of poo, or moved from walking through fluid blood.

These stains are frequently seen concentrated around light sources, windows, and ceilings and may likewise be found on an assortment of surfaces, including on the expired's body and clothing. One of the defining highlights of these "patterns" is that there is no pattern; there is no defined region of assembly.

Note the void between the ring of stains and the base of the light. In like manner, it isn't unexpected to see bloodstains all around an uncovered bulb, however not on the actual bulb, if on. Note the variable appearance of the stains notwithstanding the irregular evident "directionality." Some extra things to consider while evaluating if the stains are identified with the instrument that caused passing are as per the following:

- Is there an absence of edge qualities that would be normal on a given surface?
- Is there proof of fly action (alive or dead flies present)?
- Are there stains in different rooms that don't seem, by all accounts, to be associated with the incident? Contrast stains in different rooms with those close to the body.
- Do they look like known fly relics?

Sequenced Bloodstains

It isn't extraordinary to find various as well as overlapping bloodstain patterns at the location of a demise or attack. This may happen for an assortment of reasons, from an injured gathering just moving around, to a delayed battle or attack to staging endeavors. Some of the time, the grouping of pattern testimony can be ascertained and, accordingly, can be used to assist with corroborating or discredit articulations.

By examining the edge attributes of the swipes, the request for testimony might have the option to be determined; see the numbering on photograph for request of statement. The "newest" swipe will upset the edges of the recently saved swipe in the event that it is still at any rate part of the way wet. Another guide to consider is a scene where a cleanup was endeavored and the body present at the scene. In the event that the body doesn't disturb the wiping pattern, it may very well be reasoned that the body was put there after the wiping happened. Further, with a lot of blood, if no upset coagulations are available, this would indicate that the wiping happened while the blood was still very new, which may help affirm or discredit suspect or witness explanations concerning a timeline of occasions.

There are a few additional sorts of sequencing stains that might be seen that can answer various kinds of inquiries; the preceding figures are a couple of models. When determining grouping from photos, the investigators ought to be moderate, on the grounds that in certain conditions.

Voids Patterns

The current acknowledged definition of a void pattern is "a shortfall of blood in a usually continuous bloodstain or bloodstain pattern." Voids can assist with placing objects or potentially individuals within a scene.

There is a general void where the casualty's head was situated during the administration of the beating.

The objective paper was set behind the correct side of the tennis shoe and a blood-doused wipe was set on the left side and was along these lines shot into with a .22-type pistol. The void made by the shoe, whose left side intercepted a segment of the bloodstains, can without much of a stretch be seen on the objective paper. A void may uncover a conspicuous pattern, or it just shows that something obstructed the testimony of blood in that specific zone. Voids are usually seen in the middle of move patterns on the limits of a casualty, which may help with casualty positioning. In like manner, voids on the clothing of suspects or casualties may indicate how it was worn (e.g. secured or unfastened), collapsed, or wrinkled at the hour of blood affidavit.

The effect of bloodstain patterns result when static pools of blood are hit. The energy of the effect is moved to the blood, making it separate into beads which are impelled through the air. In the event that the drops of blood hit a middle surface before the energy that puts the blood in light can disperse to a level where gravity dominates, particular blood patterns will result. The presence of these blood patterns is influenced by the forcefulness of the effect, the volume of blood affected, the surface attributes of the blood source, the qualities of the surface the blood is kept on, and what is affecting into the blood to place it in flight. Effect bloodstain patterns will have round bloodstains in the segment of the pattern which is nearest to the blood source. As the distance between the blood source and the bloodstains increment, the length of the stains increments and the width diminishes. These bloodstains will likewise show the heading the blood drop was voyaging when it affected the objective surface. These stain attributes make it conceivable to remake these patterns and decide the area of the blood that was affected. The quantity of stains in the pattern, just as the size of the stains, relies upon the forcefulness of the effect. Most of the little stains will be near the blood source, while the bigger stains will in general be longer good ways from the

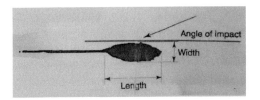

FIGURE 6.8 Measurement of the blood drop to determine angle of impact.

blood source. The quantity of stains in the pattern is subject to how hard the blood was hit. Patterns which result from low-power impacts have a low number of stains, most of which are huge and have distances across more noteworthy than 3 mm. The patterns will have a more modest surface region than patterns coming about because of high-power impacts. High-power sway patterns have more bloodstains in the pattern and most of the stains that are near the blood source will have widths of 1 mm or less. The size and state of the bloodstains and their conveyance on the objective surface make it conceivable to decipher bloodstain patterns and decide, inside a healthy level of logical conviction, the degree of power used to affect the blood source (Figure 6.8).

Cast-off Bloodstain Pattern Analysis

At the point when fluid blood covers the outside of an item that is being swung, the blood will be hurled from the article's surface because of the radial power of the tune the blood is stored on an objective surface, the subsequent pattern is known as a cast-off pattern. The alliance in cast-off patterns line up with each other giving the pattern a linear appearance. The bloodstains in the pattern that are nearest to the beginning of the swinging movement will be round, while those at the terminal finish of the pattern (cast-off toward the finish of the swinging movement) will be oval. On the off-chance that the pattern is stored on various surfaces that are arranged diversely to each other; for example, a comer where two dividers meet, the shape of the stains in the pattern will be round any place the curve of the swing was opposite to the objective surfaces. The width of the cast-off pattern is a factor of the width of the surface the blood is constrained from.

The outward presentation of the pattern can be influenced by the surface attributes of the article, just as like the movement and speed of the swing. Cast-off patterns typically happen just during the back-swing away from the blood source. At the point when a blood-covered item is swung powerfully, the majority of the blood will he cast-off during the back-swing. The impacts of inactivity as the swing switches bearings will drive any leftover blood to be cast off before the forward movement starts. Hitting a blood source a few times can create covering cast-off patterns, Since it is implausible that each swing will go along a similar circular segment, the covering patterns can be checked to show the quantity of hits after the bloodstream started. Cast-off patterns may display a slight bend along the length of the pattern. Under certain conditions, this arch can be utilized to show if the swing was left or right. Since cast-off patterns are not difficult to misjudge, it is imperative to be wary while assessing these patterns for the quantity of hits or whether the swing was correct or left or right.

Projected Bloodstain Patterns

Projected bloodstain patterns result when the blood is moved forward against an objective surface (Figure 6.10). In the present circumstance, the power that put the blood in flight is going a similar way as the blood pushing it from behind. The activity is like that of water spurted from a spurt weapon. The most widely recognized reason for these patterns is blood vessel injury. Blood moves through our bodies in a shut arrangement of veins and courses. At the point when a supply route is harmed, blood will be constrained out of the injury with each beat of the individual's heart. The blood leaves the conduit under high tension. In the event that the blood strikes an objective surface while the pressing factor or power is as yet raised, the subsequent pattern will have an extremely unmistakable appearance. The focal point of the pattern will normally be one enormous bloodstain, or a few huge bloodstains. As the blood impacts into the objective surface, the blood is separated into many beads which are sprinkled outward at an intense point to the objective surface, making many auxiliary bloodstains that are exceptionally long and spindly in appearance. With each progressive beat of the heart, more blood will be siphoned out of the harmed supply route; however, the pressing factor under which it is constrained out diminishes because of blood misfortune. The patterns that happen later won't hit the objective surface as strongly, and the auxiliary scatter bloodstains lose the spindly appearance. These lower-power projected patterns can likewise happen when the projected blood ventures an all-encompassing separation from the blood source to the objective surface. As the blood flies through the air, the energy that propels it forward will diminish until the speed the blood is going at has eased back down to the draw of Earth's gravity.

Huge Volumes of Falling Blood Patterns

Patterns that happen from huge volumes of falling blood will ordinarily have a huge focal stain where the blood first affects the objective surface, with various optional scatter stains emanating out from the affected site. Bloodstain patterns that happen from enormous volumes of falling blood will change in appearance because of the impact of the distance the blood tumbles to the objective surface. Enormous volumes of falling blood fall because of gravity. As blood falls, its speed increases. The speed of the falling blood will keep on expanding until it arrives at a max speed, 9.8 ms^2, the descending draw of gravity. Studies done by MacDonell on 0.05 ml drops of falling blood showed that maximum speed would happen when the drop falls 25.1 feet. There is a quick speed increase of the falling blood in the initial 48 creeps of the fall, after which the speed increase is continuous until maximum speed is arrived at. Blood that misses the mark distance impacts the objective surface at a low speed, causing a less intense sprinkle and less auxiliary splash. As speed builds, the blood will affect the objective surface all the more strongly, the optional scatter will vary, and the bloodstains may begin to turn out to be long and spindly. It is workable for bloodstain patterns from falling blood to be mistaken for projected bloodstain patterns. As the blood falls, its speed increases until it impacts an objective surface or arrives at max speed. The speed of projected blood diminishes until it impacts a surface, or it arrives at max speed. In the event that the distance went by the blood in these two circumstances is adequately long, the two volumes of blood will go at a similar speed when they sway the objective surface and the subsequent patterns will seem comparative.

DOCUMENTATION

It is not uncommon for a bloodstain pattern analysis to be performed "remotely" from photographs and other case documentation. Sometimes the conclusions that the analyst can reach regarding the significance of particular bloodstains is compromised as a result of incomplete or not appropriately gathered documentation.

Photography is critically important. Photographs should be taken with the standard overall, mid-range, and close-up (preferably macro, where very small stains are involved) protocol. After initial "as found" scene photography is complete, markers may be placed to assist in showing the orientation of the pattern in a particular photograph. This may be accomplished in many ways, depending on the nature and size of the area being photographed. Photographs should be taken in a manner such that the close-up photographs can be easily related to the overall scene. Some methods utilized are gridding off a large area, such as a wall, with either painter's tape, stick-on scales as seen in Figure 6.1, or markers. Individual stains may be circled, as in Figure 6.9, to show the overall

FIGURE 6.9   Bloodstains on a wall circled by a marker.

Videography is also useful in documenting the spatial relationships among objects and stain patterns that may be difficult to discern from two-dimensional photographs.

Written documentation should accurately describe the overall pattern as well as the size, shape, distribution, and location of individual stains. The condition of the blood should also be described; for example, wet, dry, partially dry, crazed, and so on. Areas of bloodstaining can also be indicated on the scaled scene diagram using measurements from triangulation.

Collection of items with bloodstain patterns of interest, or that may be difficult or questionable should be collected in their entirety when possible. When considering bloodstaining on flooring, both a bloodstained sample and a control sample (without visible bloodstaining) should be collected. If carpeting, the carpet and padding should be collected and notation made as to the underlying surface (e.g. hardwood, cement). Additionally, these samples should be labeled so as to indicate what their positions were within the carpet/flooring. Compass directions and measurements via triangulation may be useful in achieving this. The control sample(s) should be sufficient so that both prosecution and defense analysts have adequate material on which experiments can be conducted if necessary. Each person maintains their floors/carpets differently, so the best way to carry out case-specific experiments as closely as possible to the actual conditions is to use flooring from that particular scene. If flooring cannot be collected for logistical or storage reasons, it should be described as thoroughly as possible (e.g. marble tile with apparently sealed grout,

distribution from a distance. For better results, scales should be utilized when photographing bloodstains, and they should be photographed at 90 degrees from the surface whenever possible to minimize any distortion, as shown in Figure 6.10.

Bloodstains on clothing may be highlighted in different ways as well. Some methods include ring reinforcers (with the paper backing still on), stick-on arrows, triangles created from masking tape, and so on. Clothing should be photographed prior to the placement of any marking devices. Consideration must also be given if there is going to be, or is likely to be, DNA testing.

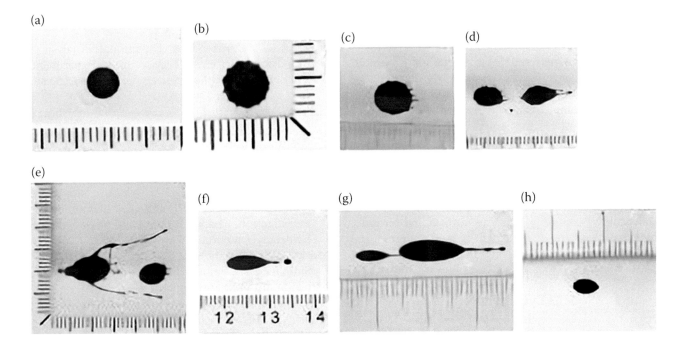

FIGURE 6.10   Scaling of different patterns of bloodstains.

linoleum with a hazy appearance). This will allow experts to reconstruct as closely as possible if the case requires a reconstruction. Swabs of wet or dry stains (collected with a swab wet with sterile water) should be collected from a representative sample of each discrete area of bloodstain patterns and from those stains which appear "out of place" (e.g. a passive stain on the back of a single victim found face down) for presumptive and DNA testing to assist in placing participants in their relative positions in reconstruction efforts, if necessary.

Multiple documentation methods should be utilized to thoroughly document a scene. There may appear to be some overlap in documentation, but it is better to have redundancy instead of a gap that may turn out to be critical. When documenting a scene, the investigator should ask him- or herself, "Could someone unfamiliar with this scene review my documentation and reconstruct this scene?" If the answer is "no," then there must be a gap in documentation that should be revisited.

PRESERVING EVIDENCE

Actual proof on hard, unfaltering items is for the most part moved and made sure about by standard subatomic organic strategies. The technique which is utilized to gather proof relies upon the sort of proof and the area from where it is being taken. The best type of protection is first to photo the region being referred to and afterward take the proof with the necessary technique to forestall defilement with different substances. Contingent upon the significance of each blood stain, it is once in a while important to safeguard entire items to dissect them later under controlled lab conditions.

For legitimate reasons the examination of blood stain, its origin, significance ought to be carried by measurable pathologists. Their clinical foundation gives them a more prominent information on different conceivable injury systems that could conceivably prompt the current outcomes. Preferably, the forensic pathologist who played out the post-mortem likewise takes part in the crime scene examination and the investigation of the bloodstain pattern.

However, the understanding of bloodstain patterns and their interpretation is a part of medical and forensic knowledge, chiefly based on experience and requires consistent hypothetical and practical training and knowledge.

CONCLUSION

Bloodstain pattern examination can be a significant analytical tool. If investigating officers and medical practitioners partake in an essential bloodstain pattern analysis, while it won't make them moment "specialists," it will help them in distinguishing, understanding, and preserving important bloodstains for assessment by a specialist that may somehow or another be ignored and lost. Legal documentation is basic for a valuable bloodstain pattern analysis.

It ought to be recollected that bloodstain pattern examination ought to be used as another "instrument" in the analytical tool stash. Since a few stain examples can seem like each other, despite the fact that brought about by various systems, one ought to be reproachful of an investigator or expert who infers that a given example might have happened exclusively by one specific instrument.

Finally, this chapter on bloodstain pattern analysis is not all inclusive, but meant to assist with understanding some of the basic tenants, procedures, and challenges that exist in this discipline.

REFERENCES

Barni, F., Lewis, S. W., Berti, A., Miskelly, G. M., & Lago, G. (2007). Forensic Application of the Luminol Reaction as a Presumptive Test for Latent Blood Detection. *Talanta*, 72(3), 896–913.

Benecke, M., & Barksdale, L. (2003). Distinction of Bloodstain Patterns From Fly Artifacts. *Forensic Science International*, 137(2–3), 152–159.

Brodbeck, S. (2012). Introduction to Bloodstain Pattern Analysis. *SIAK-Journal – Journal for Police Science and Practice*, 2, 51–57, Online: 10.7396/IE_2012_E.

Carter, A. L. (2001). The Directional Analysis of Bloodstain Patterns Theory and Experimental Validation. *Canadian Society of Forensic Science Journal*, 34(4), 173–189.

Dutelle, A. *An Introduction to Crime Scene Investigation* (p. 238). Wisconsin-Platteville: Jones and Bartlett Publishers, 2010.

Eckert, W. G. (1997). Introduction to Forensic Sciences, Chapter 10 Bloodstain Pattern Interpretation 2nd Edition, Page 176–241.

Fisher, Barry A. J. (2004). Techniques of Crime Scene Investigation, Chapter 8 Blood and other Biological Evidence, 7th edition, Page 220–240.

Grodsky, M., Wright, K., & Kirk, P. L. (1951). Simplified Preliminary Blood testing–An improved technique and a comparative study of methods. *Journal of Criminal Law, Criminology and Police Science*, 42, 95.

Hulse-Smith, L., Mehdizadeh, N. Z., & Chandra, S. (2005). Deducing Drop Size and Impact Velocity from Circular Bloodstains. *Journal of Forensic Sciences, 50*(1), 1–10. 10.1520/jfs2003224

Klein, A., Feudel, E., Türk, E., Püschel, K., & Gehl, A. (2007 Jun 1). Lumineszenz nach Luminolanwendung. *Rechtsmedizin, 17*(3), 146–152.

Lytle, L. T., & Hedgecock, D. G. (1978 Jul 1). Chemiluminescence in the Visualization of Forensic Bloodstains. *Journal of Forensic Science, 23*(3), 550–562.

Peschel, O., Kunz, S. N., Rothschild, M. A., & Mützel E. (2011). Blood Stain Pattern Analysis. *Forensic Science, Medicine, and Pathology, 7*(3), 257–270.

Presumptive. (n.d.). In Merriam Webster online. Retrieved from http://www.merriam-webster.com/dictionary/presumptive (Accessed July 5, 2015).

Sears, D. W. (2002). Overview of Hemoglobin's Structure/ Function Relationships. *Biochemistry and Molecular Biology Education, 30*(3), 208.

Secomb, T. W. 1991. Red Blood Cell Mechanics and Rheology. *Cell Biophysics, 18*(3), 231–251.

Sferstein, R. (2015). Criminalistcs: An Introduction to Forensic Science, Chapter 4 Crime Scene Reconstruction: Blood stain Evidence, 11th Edition, 93–116.

CHAPTER 7

Collection of Botanical Evidence

Ekta B. Jadhav[1], *Kapil Parihar*[2], *Mahipal Singh Sankhla*[2,3], *and Swaroop Sonone*[4]

[1]Government Institute of Forensic Science, Aurangabad, Maharashtra, India
[2]Department of Forensic Science Vivekananda Global University Jaipur, Rajasthan, India
[3]Department of Forensic Science Institute of Sciences SAGE University Indore, M.P., India
[4]Department of Forensic Science, Dr. Babasaheb Ambedkar Marathawada University, Aurangabad, Maharashtra, India

CONTENTS

INTRODUCTION

Forensic botany is a field of applied science where plant evidence is used in a court of law. Forensic botany encompasses several subdisciplines such as plant anatomy (the study of cellular features), limnology (the study of freshwater ecology), palynology (the study of pollen), dendrochronology (the study of dating tree growth rings), plant ecology (plant succession patterns), lichenology (the study of lichen communities), mycology (the analysis and the identification of fungi), bryology (the study of bryophytes), and plant systematics (identification of species and taxonomy) (Bock and Norris, 1997). Bryophytes occur in every type of environment, even those unable to host vascular plants and other organisms. Therefore, they are one of the most vulnerable

plants over every type of crime scene and majorly utilized during forensic investigations. Moreover, the previous studies conclude that fragments of bryophytes can easily remain attached to clothes and shoes, and even if the plant has been fragmented, their DNA can be analyzed (Virtanen et al., 2007). Botanical trace evidence can be a significant clue for criminal investigation. But the lack of knowledge or awareness about botanical evidence and challenges arose during identifying this trace evidence among investigators, evidence collection teams, and even forensic botanists, the botanical evidence remains under-utilized during the forensic investigation (Coyle et al., 2005). The evidence collection team may not necessarily see the importance of botanical trace evidence found on the scene as well as ignored during the collection of evidence of the crime. First responders and investigators are also sometimes unaware and careless about the potential of botanical evidence and its proper collection, which can provide linkages between crime scenes and individuals. Sometimes they may simply not know about collection protocols and who to contact for this job. The improper handling, as well as inadequate collection of the botanical evidence, consequently impact its later analysis, which may lead to false results or unable to draw a conclusion even after thorough analysis.

Typically, experienced botanists use plant population databases from a large number of plant species during forensic casework. Usually, they also used to collect the plant samples surrounding the crime scene as reference samples for the positive identification of evidentiary samples (Figure 77). While in the case of the unknown or undetected crime scene, the plant population databases and herbariums are considered as a reference collection (Hall and Byrd, 2012). Furthermore, forensic botany has a wide range of potential applications from the recognition of plant materials over clothes, hair, body, or vehicle of individual involved in the crime to the identification of vegetable matter present in gastrointestinal tract contents, faces, or vomit of an individual (Bock and Norris, 2007). This chapter deals with a major part of forensic casework i.e. proper collection and packaging of botanical evidence including all possibilities and types of the crime scene and location of evidence.

FORENSIC BOTANY

The use of plants and plant-related materials in criminal investigations is defined as "forensic botany." In other words, it is defined as a branch of forensic science that applies plant sciences to the legal process (Robertson et al., 2016). The detailed examination of plant materials or remains collected at a crime scene and utilizing them to solve crimes or other legal problems is the main aim of this field. During the past century, due to unawareness regarding the value of botanical evidence and lack of trained specialists in the same area, forensic botany remained under-utilized and very limited in criminal or civil cases as well as forensic practices. Moreover, academic or specialized centers for training botanical experts are almost absent. But later on, the potential of botanical trace evidence in criminal cases has been enlightened and it is permitted as suitable scientific evidence by the courts of many countries because the ubiquitous presence of plant species makes forensic botany useful for many criminal cases. Although forensic botany has been underused in criminal investigations over the years, now the initiatives of resourceful and trained investigators and forensic botanical experts bringing them into focus (Wiltshire, 2009; Margiotta et al., 2015).

Forensic botany has many applications in criminal casework and it involves gathering clues from plant evidence including its trace materials that assist to solve serious crimes like the cause of death, time of death, kidnapping, murder, illegal drug trafficking, etc. It is a multidisciplinary area of applied science, which encompasses traditional botanical classification of species, plant material evidence (trace and transfer evidence), crime mapping, geo-sourcing, and DNA fingerprinting (Coyle et al., 2001) (Figure 7.1).

Significance of Botanical Evidence

The branches of forensic botany have been very efficacious for various forensic scenarios, such as in determining the difference between accidental, suicidal, and homicidal death, as well as in verifying an alibi. Botanical evidence significantly helps in forensic investigations by linking objects and places, locating hidden human remains and provenancing of objects, estimating temporal aspects of deposition of remains, differentiating murder scenes from deposition sites (Wiltshire, 2009). These types of evidence also assist identification of specific locations of kidnapping victims (Bever et al., 2000; Brinkac et al. 2000) (Figure 7.2).

Diatoms, pollens, and spores are considered significant evidentiary materials in drowning cases. Moreover, diatoms can provide information about the manner of death whether homicidal or suicidal drowning. The technique of quantitative diatom-based reconstruction developed to confirm drowning as the cause of death and localize the site of drowning (Horton et al., 2006; Armstrong and Erskine, 2018; García-Mozo et al., 2021; Liu et al., 2021). Illegal logging and trading of plant materials are also investigated under the discipline of forensic botany (Dormontt et al., 2015). Furthermore, botanical evidence can significantly contribute to law enforcement by biological identification of illegal drugs, poisonous plant substances, dangerous agricultural weeds, and exotic species known to invade and destroy native habitats. The botanical evidence can be found on any type of crime scene including death scenes or scene of sexual assault and play a major role to link that scene with the culprit (Hall and Byrd, 2012). Forensic botany, however, can be used to calculate the time of death by pollen analysis or analysis of stomach contents (Coyle, 2004). Botanical evidence can be any plant material particularly, pollen, leaves, fruit, petioles, stems, seeds, and roots. The plant evidentiary matter can be present in every type of crime scene but mainly found and informative for outdoor crime scenes. The botanical evidence like vegetable matter can be obtained from gastrointestinal tract contents or fecal matter, wood from a weapon or from a tree embedded in the undercarriage of an automobile or its illegally logging, stains or trace evidence from clothing,

FIGURE 7.1   (a, b) Outdoor crime scene where plant material is used as a modus operando; (c) grass rope as ligature material.

FIGURE 7.2   Plant material (guava fruit) found at the crime scene. The bite marks present on this fruit are significant to verify a suspect's alibi.

hairs, or shoes as well as toxic material in a deadly overdose or related to drug trafficking from the medical examination of an individual or postmortem analysis of deceased (Ladd and Lee, 2004).

Role of forensic botany in a criminal investigation, where botanical materials are involved as modus operandi or associated with a crime as evidence, to determine (Hall and Byrd, 2012; Chandra and Sharma, 2014):

a. The manner and cause of death, suicide, or homicide
b. The time of death
c. The scene of violent crimes, such as sexual assault and vehicular accidents
d. Primary or secondary crime scene
e. Geographical location or point of origin
f. Species and origin of poisonous plant material and drugs
g. Plant succession and clandestine graves
h. The point of entry and exit of the culprit
i. The path traveled by the culprit

BOTANICAL CRIME SCENE ANALYSIS

Searching for Evidence

Professional forensic botanists have detailed knowledge of where to search for botanical evidence. In some challenging cases, they may take the help of trained cadaver dogs or sensors for searching evidence (Bock and Norris, 2016). The common places to search for botanical evidence are (Lee et al., 2004):

a. Suspect's clothing including pockets, cuffs, and textile seams (Figure 7.3).
b. Suspect's shoes, shoelaces, and shoe seams (Figure 7.4).
c. Suspect's or deceased victim's hairs.
d. Body orifices of a deceased or live victim.
e. Internal and external parts of vehicles used for committing the crime, mainly undercarriage, chassis, wheel wells, trenches on and around the forward-facing bumper and heater.
f. Annual rings of plants rising over, through, or near to a body, skeletal leftovers, a graveyard, or item at a crime scene, the rings can be measured and gives a time period.
g. Damage to the plants and huge twigs could be done by a vehicle driving into a tree, a vehicle parked on the root, soil placed onto the segments

FIGURE 7.4   Plant material embedded on the bottom of a suspect's shoe. Identification of this evidence can connect a suspect to a specific site.

of roots, submerging, covering of the greenery, uncommon temperatures, and other illnesses.

h. Gastrointestinal tract contents, injured skin surface, hairs, and nails of deceased during postmortem analysis.

Photography and Documentation

Taking pictures is a brilliant technique to use for the documentation of the bodily features practical at the crime scene prior to the gathering drying process starts. As with almost all kinds of physical evidence, appropriate shooting is important. The phytologist will be required to regulate the documentation of the flora and conduct a trial by breaking alike twigs. By inspection at consistent intermissions, a phytologist will be capable to regulate the comparative period it takes the juice and/or wilt to match that exposed in the pictures. The period of activity can be identified using other plant features. A wrecked branch typically will wilt. The quantity of wilt can be determined empirically if the object is snapped and gathered appropriately. The time for sap to dry after a branch is broken or bark is nicked can also be determined by experimentation. Foliage wilt can also occur when plants are displaced or the root schemes are harshly supplied. Determining the estimated time the sap has been collected or the leaf wilting will be contingent on having a phytologist at the scene rapidly. As with all kinds of bodily evidence, the proper taking of pictures is essential (Hall and Byrd, 2012).

To assist identify the pollens originating in a control sample, the flora at a site of curiosity should be carefully plotted and snapped by a botanist or palynologist. The body of the target/victim must be carefully observed and documented before sample gathering. Label and drawing/picture the site of any likely wound, trace evidence, or

FIGURE 7.3   Plant material remains stuck to the suspect's clothes. Identification of this evidence can connect a suspect to a specific site and verify an alibi.

dyes on the targets. Note all the probable cut marks, contusions, scrapes, and anything else. All trace evidence, counting blood and body liquids, patterns, soil, hairs and fibers, pollen, plant wreckages, and dyes, should be snapped in place before gathering and packing. All the botanical materials found in biological fluids, content, or injuries of the deceased should be photographed during autopsy (Ladd and Lee, 2004; Bock and Norris, 2016).

COLLECTION OF BOTANICAL EVIDENCES

Anything related to an illegal or civic forensic case may denote vegetal material as evidence that may be significant for case investigation (Milne et al., 2004; Wiltshire, 2009). Botanical evidence can be found on any type of crime scene such as indoor, outdoor, or conveyance, which may be related to underwater, premeditated burials, poisoning, and illegal drug trafficking crimes (Wiltshire, 2015). Therefore, their collection methods are depending on the type of crime scene. The critical evaluation of botanical evidence found on the crime scene or victim's body and establishing the plant's origin may significantly help investigators by linking that scene with the suspect, identifying the sources and trafficking details of poisonous and psychotropic plants and related products or drugs (Coyle et al, 2005). The accurate results depend on the primary stage of crime scene investigation, which is the proper collection of evidence and its suitable preservation. Because improper collection techniques and negligence result in the contamination of the evidence (Bock and Norris, 2016).

Essential Equipment for Collection and Packaging

The essential equipment for the collection and packaging of botanical evidentiary material can be easily obtained from any general store. Some basic equipment that commonly carried by the forensic botanist for searching evidence, noting, and capturing observations during the collection of botanical evidence and their instant packaging are described below (Hall and Byrd, 2012) (Table 7.1).

Plant presses for collection and temporary storage of plant samples. The plant press consists of a stiff-slatted panel containing layers of newsprint, blotter, or cardboard, and this frame is strongly destined with adjustable bands to put evidence even and display its feature as plant sample dries. In the absence of these formal plant presses, presses are designed by placing the sample between newsprint covered with two cardboard pieces on both sides and tightened with string or tape or simply by keeping the sample between the pages of magazine or phone directory (Figure 7.5).

Collection and Packaging Methods for Botanical Evidence

The potential identification of relevant evidence at the crime scene and its proper documentation (photography, note-making, etc.) is prior to their collection and preservation. The appropriate collection and adequate preservation are followed by maintaining a chain of custody, transportation to the forensic testing laboratory for scientific examination, identification and individualization of

TABLE 7.1 Essential Pieces of Equipment for Collection and Packaging of Botanical Materials

Equipment	Application
Digital SLR camera	Photographic documentation of sample plants on the scene of a crime
Hand lens on a string around the neck	Scene observation of the plant and its primary recognitions and handheld GPS to record the exact location
Bound notebook, graphite pencils, or indelible ink pens	Note-making
Hand pruners, knives, or scissors	Cutting and sampling of leaf and twigs from woody trees or shrubs
Garden spade or archaeological trowel	A sampling of a whole herbaceous plant with its roots
Labeling materials such as flags and tents	Labeling collecting bags and boxes with the proper name or initials, dates, and a specific sample number that is registered in the book
Collecting bags, paper grocery bags, or cardboard boxes	Storage of evidence based on its size. Big paper grocery bags or cardboard boxes are used to store whole herbaceous plant samples and branches. Paper bags are preferred over plastic bags. Paper stamp and coin envelopes for tiny plant samples or fragments.
Wax-coated paper	Collection of fleshy and sticky fruit samples and other wet botanical evidence to avoid its adherence with paper while drying
Tamper-evident tape	Sealing of the collection bags
Plant presses	Collection and temporary storage of plant samples
Over-the-shoulder (field) bag	For keeping all above-listed equipment together

FIGURE 7.5   Collection of botanical evidence simply using forceps: (a) Dried leaf, (b) thorny fruit, (c) thorn, (d) flower.

plant samples, recording testing reports, and their admissibility and use in the court (Coyle, 2004; Coyle et al., 2005). Forensic botanists should identify and enlist as possible as plants observed at the crime scene. If it looks significant for further investigation, they should collect evidence such as whole plants (alive and dead), fallen fruits, leaf, and clutter, and any allochthonous vegetal solid. Botanical evidence shall preferably be collected in paper bags rather than plastic bags (Wiltshire, 2015) (Figure 7.6).

Whole herbaceous plant evidence (alive or dead) with its roots should be uplifted from the ground using a garden spade while in case of the collection of plant parts present on the live plant should be facilitated using a hand pruner or knife (Hall and Byrd, 2012). General botanical evidentiary materials such as plant flowers, fragments, seeds, fruits, and leaves found on the scene of the crime should be picked and collected by hands covered with gloves. In the case of a crime scene involving the vehicle for committing criminal activity, the vehicular evidence is seized for further investigation. All possible botanical evidence materials such as leaves, lichens, twigs, and seeds found inside and outside the motor vehicle (into wheel wells, on and under floor mats, under the carriage, vents, trunk, inside the engine compartments, foot pedals, and on windshield wipers) should be collected with hands. After examining the whole car for plant fragments and confirming the collection of all fragments, a vehicle is vacuumed for collecting microscopic trace evidence. However, in murder cases, where the plant material is buried or dragged with the body to conceal evidence, the plant fragments are collected using a trowel and fork. In the mortuary, the macroscopic botanical evidence over the hairs of the body can

- **Step 1 - Setting up a field or botanical press**

| Newsprint or other cheap absorbent paper should be folded over each sample. | Evidence tags should be used | Quality paper should be used collect to wet samples | For larger samples grocery bags should be used |

- **Step 2 - Collection of plant material around and in the scene should include at least 10–12 samples of different plants around the scene to document local vegetation.**

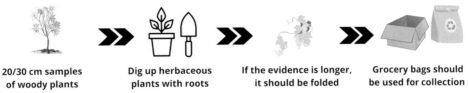

| 20/30 cm samples of woody plants | Dig up herbaceous plants with roots | If the evidence is longer, it should be folded | Grocery bags should be used for collection |

- **Step 3 - Each item of evidence should be photographed before and after it is collected**

FIGURE 7.6   Stepwise and general guidelines for collection of botanical evidence. **Step 1:** Collection of plant material from the crime scene. **Step 2:** Collection of reference samples in and around the crime scene. **Step 3:** Documentation and photography before and after collection and packaging.

be easily removed using comb or forceps and collected inadequate collection bags (Wiltshire, 2006; Wiltshire, 2015). The collection methods of botanical evidentiary materials may slightly be varied depending on their types and sources, setting, and motives for gathering, with commonsense dominant. For example, botanical leftovers require preparation like herbarium specimens on card or paper and dried flat, whilst sediment samples for pollen or diatom revisions would be gathered into poly pots or bags and stored in a fridge or freezer (Miller, 2017).

Palynological Samples

Palynology, the study of microscopic and not visually obvious entities of the plant such as plant spores, fungal spores, pollen, and other microscopic entities, is the most vulnerable source of botanical evidence on any type of crime. Most of the botanical entities from a crime scene might be yielding pollen and spores. Therefore, the knowledge of its presence and identification on a crime scene would help interpretation of palynological data related to seasonal details, geological location, and also the timing of deposition and to date the burial of skeletal remains in a mass grave (Coyle, 2004; Coyle et al. 2005; Bryant, 2009; Wiltshire, 2009). The collection of macroscopic evidence is not a very challenging process, but for the collection of palynological evidence, it is necessary to critically search and handle the scene, and collect the microscopic evidence using proper collecting methods. Also, it is necessary to keep a record of the plants growing in and around the crime scene from

where pollen has been collected. The pollens are trapped and found in soil, dust, leaves, moss, and other plant fragments. Some cloth fabrics, particularly wool, are capable of sticking with plant fragments including spores and pollens, and pick them up. Moreover, slight brushing of clothing and foot coverings against a flowering shrub led to deposit them directly over clothes and shoes. These pollen grains are searched in welts, shoelace holes, laces, and any soil residues on soles, especially the upper part of the shoe should be treated to obtain pollen and spores. The upper part and lower part of cloth may be deposited with pollens of different profiles depending on the surface of contact at the crime scene. The palynomorphs over cloth can be picked up using a tape-adhesive method (Wu et al., 2006). A forensic botanist should be competent to recognize complex profiles and separate irrelevant findings from those critical to the case. As the soil and loose materials adhered on footwear and clothes may dislodge from their original locations during evidence transportation, the trace samples from these items should be collected prior to the items being sealed in evidence bags. In the case of illegal trafficking drugs derived from plant parts and pollen grains are considered as significant evidence for locating the origin and racket of trafficking. These pollen evidentiary samples found in small or trace amounts over the primary or secondary crime scene, or location of interest (Ladd and Lee, 2004; Hall and Byrd, 2012; Wiltshire, 2015).

The improper collection and handling of pollen evidence may contaminate it or make it useless for investigation (Bock and Norris, 2016). During the autopsy, the pollen may be found in nails, hair, skin, orifices, and other body injuries. In such cases, the microscopic evidence can be collected by washing skin and hairs, scraping nails, swabbing vagina, and body injuries. The process of swabbing is facilitated by cotton, nylon, or sponge (Wiltshire, 2006). Sometimes the pollen grains inhaled by the culprit or victim over the crime scene may be found with traces of pollen lodged in his/her nasal cavity and turbinate bones. The retrieval of these pollen traces is a very critical process of collection and done by flushing a nasal cavity with the help of a mortuary technician or pathologist using a simple, non-invasive swab-and-tube sampling kit (Wiltshire and Black, 2006; Hall and Byrd, 2012). In the case of a crime scene involving vehicular evidence, the microscopic evidence found on the interior of the vehicle should be collected by brushing and scrubbing entities with tiny brushes or vacuuming it using powerful handheld vacuum machines. Direct sweeping the interior of the vehicle may lose the evidence. The exterior vehicle entities such as wheel arches and tires may not be able to provide significant evidence. However, marks on bodywork and fascia boards should be rubbed with a moistened swab to retrieve palynomorphs deposited on that part. In the case of homicidal offense and concealing evidence by burying the body using different digging tools, the palynological profiles can be obtained from digging implements that have provided links between them and victims' graves (Wiltshire, 2015).

During all of this process of collection, samples should be handled with disposable gloves, collected using clean sampling tools (whichever suitable for the case) such as spatulas, teaspoons, and small brushes, or swabbed with the moistened swab, stored in clean containers or small grip lock bags, and finally sealed into tamper-evident bags for their transport to forensic laboratories for further examination, identification, and individualization. The case itself decides the number of samples to be collected for forensic analysis. In a case of drug trafficking, for the investigation of the country of drug origin one or two samples may be sufficient. However, in the case of the presence of a dead body, a vehicle, as well as a crime scene, the collection of several samples from each item may be necessary. The forensic palynologist could attend the crime scenes to assist evidence collection teams. But in the case of their absence, the type and number of samples to be collected can be discussed with them by the collection team using the telephone/internet. With the pollen collection of samples from a crime scene, it is also essential to maintain a record of the plants growing surrounding the crime scene. This aids to relate the pollen in the sample to the vegetation at the crime scene (Hall and Byrd, 2012). Spore and pollen reference material in a good collection will contain examples taken from different anthers/sporangia, different plants, and different places at different times for each species; and to be competent, a palynologist requires access to an authenticated and comprehensive reference collection of pollen, plant spores, fungal spores, and other microscopic entities (Wiltshire, 2009; Adams-Groom, 2012).

Diatoms from Water Bodies

Diatoms are considered as one of the most crucial evidentiary materials for solving criminal cases regarding drowning as it helps to decide the type of case whether antemortem or post-mortem drowning (Horton et al., 2006; Singh et al., 2006). During the collection of diatom samples, all collecting equipment and containers should be clean and ideally sterile to avoid cross-contamination. Diatoms found in both aquatic and damp or sedimentary habitats. The collection of diatoms from the submerged or underwater crime scene facilitated by taking about a liter of a water sample using sterile bottles or glass jars. At the time of discovery of the body or as soon thereafter as possible, the sample of drowning medium or water should be collected from the scene (Hall and Byrd, 2012). However, for the collection of samples from sedimentary areas, it is advised to take a volume of a few cubic centimeters of sediment sample using a spatula or short surface corner and samples over stones should be collected by brushing or scrapping it. In case of doubt about the drowning site, then water samples from the putative site of drowning can be collected and analyzed to determine the similarity of different species of diatoms in the water and the body. In case of suspicious transfer of diatom-containing substances from the crime scene to the culprit, the collection of samples at the scene should be performed in small vials or bags. If there is a large time gap between collection and examination of samples, that should be preserved in formalin or alcohol (Cox, 2012).

Clothing is an appropriate recipient surface to examine diatom transfer due to its frequent presence at a range of crime scenes (Bull et al., 2006). For the collection of diatoms from cloth samples, the cloth should be dipped into sterile plastic containers containing deionized water or 70% ethanol or treated at each location using 30% H_2O_2 digestion in a water bath (Scott et al., 2014).

The diatoms will enter the lungs if the person is still alive while entering the water as a person inhales water and drowns. These diatoms are transported via circulation to various body parts such as the brain, liver, kidneys, and bone marrow. Therefore, samples of lungs, brain kidney, liver, and femur marrow should be sent to laboratories for isolation and detection of diatoms (Krstic et al., 2002; Rohn and Frade, 2006). For investigating the presence of diatoms in the bone marrow to determine the type of drowning whether antemortem or post-mortem, the putative drowning medium samples from the scene of body recovery should be collected and the bone marrow of an intact femur of the body should be removed during autopsy. These femurs are then washed with distilled water and longitudinally sectioned using a clean band saw. The bone marrow, about 50 g, is collected using a clean spatula and kept in a boiling flask (Pollanen, 1998; Verma, 2013). After collection, processing for examination typically involves the concentration of the diatoms via centrifugation and acid digestion (mainly using nitric acid) of the pellet. The repeated washings with distilled water and centrifuge-mediated concentration of the diatoms are followed by acid digestion. Then these treated diatom samples are mounted over a microscope slide for examination under compound light or scanning electron microscopy (Hall and Byrd, 2012).

Sample Collection for DNA Analysis

Recent advances in genetic analyses of plants show promise for plant DNA-based forensics and it can tell the incredible complexity of the stories behind the scene (Bock and Norris, 2016). The DNA-based analysis provides species identification, the population indication of origin of a sample, and evidence of genetic identity between two samples and consequently aid to solve the case. If morphological and anatomical features are not sufficient for comparison due to damaged or small amounts of diagnostic characteristics in plant evidence, then the species identification can be done accurately on the basis of DNA sequences (Gitzendanner, 2012). Plant DNA-based forensics facilitates the identification of a population of origin, individualization of plants, geographic origin, testing narcotic plant, patented cultivar, poisoning plant, tracking genetically modified plants, and investigating the origin of drug trafficking using random/anonymous markers or microsatellites of DNA (Coyle et al., 2001; Gressel and Ehrlich, 2002).

As various plant tissues are suitable for DNA-based forensic examination, the forensic investigators should collect all samples that may be of use, and later on its suitability for examination is determined on the basis of the age, condition, and original DNA content. The DNA in an improperly preserved specimen can quickly become degraded and its forensic value greatly limited. Therefore, proper collection and subsequent preservation of samples required for successful genetic analysis. Leaves without any evidence of rot, infection, or insects are usually the preferred tissue for plant DNA analysis. The leaves from dead plants can also be used but due to the tendency of degradation of DNA over time, the success rates of these samples may be quite low. Therefore, the dead or dried leaves are avoided during collection and if the plant is dead then other tissues like flowers are taken into consideration for genetic analysis. Although decaying wood is

unlikely to yield suitable DNA, recent progress to isolate DNA not only from living tissue but also from wood and wood products offers new opportunities to test the declared origin of material such as seedlings for plantation establishment or timber (Finkeldey et al., 2010). Seeds and fruits, and even roots, can provide good quality DNA for successful genetic analyses and thus they are collected depending on their quality and availability on the crime scene (Kumar et al., 2003; Walters et al., 2006; Gitzendanner, 2012).

The preserved DNA may get denatured due to some enzymes present in cells and the inhibition of the enzymes that could facilitate the breakdown of the DNA and other cellular components can be achieved by removing moisture from the sample. Therefore, the drying of the botanical sample in silica gel is the easiest method of safe preservation for its DNA analysis. Dried samples are also less vulnerable to fungal growth. A few grams of silica gel is added directly to the small collecting bag, preferably a plastic zipper bag in which the sample has been placed for its preservation. Silica gel storage could be applied for the preservation of various types of samples. Although wood or completely dried leaf samples are capable of survival for their prolonged storage without silica gel, the addition of silica gel may help in the inhibition of sample's deterioration and increase the length of time for which DNA can be successfully extracted. The exhaustion and need for its replacement can be identified by adding color indicating desiccant silica gel into it. The silica gel in which high moisture containing plant materials like succulents are preserved should be replaced several times to achieve sufficient drying. In the cases where silica gel cannot be applied for preservation, the samples should be refrigerated or frozen for their safe storage without deterioration. The samples that are supposed to be analyzed within a few days can be stored at 4°C, while at 20°C if they are supposed to be stored for a few months, and 80°C ultracold storage is essential for several years' preservation. In all cases, samples should be stored in airtight plastic bags or containers. However, these techniques are only suitable for small quantities of samples, as freezer space is typically far more limited and costly than room temperature storage. Therefore, the desiccation method using silica gel is more preferred than refrigeration (Gitzendanner, 2012).

Evidence Collection from the Gut

Digestive tract contents of the human body such as stomach wash, intestinal content, vomitus, and fecal matter are collected for detection of the presence of ingested plant materials, drugs, poisons, pollen/spores, diatoms, etc. The conventional techniques of stomach content examination encompass the light microscope for observation of unknown samples from the evidence and comparing them with known reference samples for assessment of total stomach contents. The identification and individualization of evidentiary material found in these contents are usually done with genetic analysis or DNA sequencing methods (Lee et al., 2004).

Stomach and Intestinal Content

A medical examiner generally scoops out the matter found inside the dissected stomach during post-mortem examination and collects the stomach content. In case of impracticability to collect the entire sample, a portion of thoroughly mixed samples retained for later analysis or several sub-portions can be selected to represent the entire contents. This is especially important if the meal is in the early stages of digestion and there are many clumps of solid or semisolid material present. For intestinal contents, several samples should be preserved that reflect the various regions. A standard preservative may be used (e.g. 10% formalin) to denature enzymes and kill bacteria. The use of preservatives is fine for microscopic use, however, for later DNA typing methods may be inhibitory for PCR amplification. It is recommended that a fraction of the stomach contents be frozen for potential DNA usage later in the case (Lee et al., 2004; Bock and Norris, 2016).

Vomitus and Fecal Material

Vomitus and fecal matter are typically found in the cases of rape, robbery, and homicide. The fresh or sometimes dried vomitus or fecal matter could be obtained directly from the crime scene or during post-mortem examination. The clothing retained from a suspect is most vulnerable to the occurrence of fecal matter as well as vomitus. Preferably glass or plastic containers are used to collect and store feces and vomit samples found on crime scenes. The fecal material or vomitus that adhered to clothing should be carefully retained as there are chances of it sloughing off during handling. The swatches of clothing stained biological or

excrement material should be cut and stored in a sealed paper, glass, or plastic container with ensuring the presence of plant material in it. The seeds should be removed from excrement matter using sterile forceps, then rinsed with sterile water, air-dried, and observed under a light microscope (Norris and Bock, 2000).

The excrement-stained clothing samples are examined for the presence of plant cell content and compared to the excrement retained from the clothes of the victim. These unknown plant cell traces from excrements are compared with known food or vegetable reference samples. The plant cell composition of the fecal matter on both individuals' clothes showed remarkable similarity. Furthermore, a similar linkage was made when examining feces-stained clothing from a robbery suspect and comparing it to fecal matter left at a crime scene. In most cases, the excrement matter adhere with the clothing is usually dried, and thus preservatives are not necessary for its storage. In the case of a damp sample, it should be dried prior to sealing it in the container. However, as per need and feasibility, these fresh excrements could be stored fresh using a preservative or refrigerated at 4°C for prolonged storage of a few days for forensic examination (Norris and Bock, 2001; Bock and Norris, 2016).

Botany Field Datasheet

The botany field datasheet helps to maintain the record of several types of information for processing crime scenes. This ultimately provides the detailed documentation of description and details of each and every piece of evidence collected for forensic analysis. This datasheet also encompasses the general environmental conditions along with other relevant information about scene conditions. The types of information that are documented in the botany field datasheet are given in Figure 7.7 and Figure 7.8.

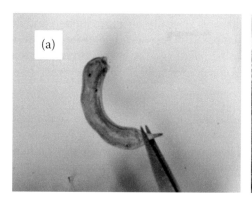

FIGURE 7.7 Botanical sample collected from the crime scene (a) and reference sample collected from similar plant present in the surrounding environment of scene (b).

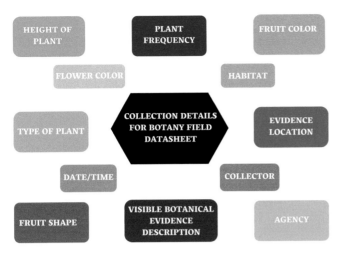

FIGURE 7.8   Collection details for botany field datasheet.

CONCLUSION

The botanical materials associated with crime are very significant to investigate that crime and find the preparator. As proper searching, collection, and packaging of plant evidence is needed for accurate analysis, a professional and trained botanist is preferred for this challenging job. This chapter focuses on collection and packaging guidelines for botanical evidence present on the scene of crime or body or outfits of the preparator. The collection methods and essential equipment can be varied according to the type of crime or crime scene. For the later study and analysis, every evidence should be photographed before collection. The plant material present in fecal matter, vomit, injuries, or body orifices should be collected during autopsy with proper equipment. Sometimes, it is challenging for botanists to search and collect evidence and he/she fails to collect them properly; this can lead to false results also.

REFERENCES

Adams-Groom, B. (2012). Forensic palynology. In *Forensic Ecology Handbook: From Crime Scene to Court* (pp. 153–167). New Jersey, USA: John Wiley and Sons, Ltd. 10.1002/9781118374016.ch10

Armstrong, E. J., and Erskine, K. L. (2018). Investigation of Drowning Deaths: A Practical Review. *Academic Forensic Pathology*, 8(1), 8–43. SAGE Publications Inc. 10.23907/2018.002

Bever, R., Golenberg, E., Barnes, L., Brinkac, L., Jones, E., and Yoshida, K. (2000). Molecular analysis of botanical trace evidence: development of techniques. In *Proceedings of the American Academy of Forensic Sciences Annual Meeting* (pp. 21–26).

Bock, J., and Norris, D. (1997). Forensic Botany: An Under-Utilized Resource. *Journal of Forensic Sciences*, 42(3), 364–367. 10.1520/JFS14130J

Bock, J. H., and Norris, D. O. (2016). *Forensic Plant Science*. 10.1016/C2013-0-19012-5

Brinkac, L., Cimino, M., Gross, N., Hopkins, E., Jones, E., and Bever, R. (2000). Analysis of botanical trace evidence. In *Proceedings of 11th International Symposium on Human Identification* (pp. 10–13).

Bryant, V. M. (2009). Palynology. In *Wiley Encyclopedia of Forensic Science*. New Jersey, USA: John Wiley and Sons, Ltd. 10.1002/97804 70061589.fsa085

Bull, P. A., Morgan, R. M., Sagovsky, A., and Hughes, G. J. A. (2006). The Transfer and Persistence of Trace Particulates: Experimental Studies Using Clothing Fabrics. *Science and Justice - Journal of the Forensic Science Society*, 46(3), 185–195. 10.1 016/S1355-0306(06)71592-1

Carll, L., and Lee, H. (2004). The Use of Biological and Botanical Evidence in Criminal Investigations. In *Forensic Botany*. 10.1201/9780203484593.ch7

Chandra, R., and Sharma, V. (2014). Forensic botany: an emerging discipline of plant sciences. *Indian Botanists Blog-o-Journal*, 2–8. http://www. indianbotanists.com/2014/03/forensic-botany-emerging-discipline-of.html

Cox, E. J. (2012). Diatoms and Forensic Science. In *Forensic Ecology Handbook: From Crime Scene to Court* (pp. 141–151). John Wiley and Sons, Ltd. 10.1002/9781118374016.ch9

Coyle, H. M., Divakaran, K., Jachimowicz, E., Ladd, C., and Lee, H. C. (2001). Individualization of marijuana (cannabis sativa) samples for forensic applications and narcotics enforcement. In *Proceedings of the American Academy of Forensic Sciences* (Vol. 7, p. 30).

Coyle, H. M., Lee, C. L., Lin, W. Y., Lee, H. C., and Palmbach, T. M. (2005). Forensic botany: Using plant evidence to aid in forensic death investigation. *Croatian Medical Journal*, 46(4), 606–612.

Coyle, H. M. (Ed.). *Forensic botany: principles and applications to criminal casework*. CRC Press, 2004.

Dormontt, E. E., Boner, M., Braun, B., Breulmann, G., Degen, B., Espinoza, E., Gardner, S., Guillery, P., Hermanson, J. C., Koch, G., Lee, S. L., Kanashiro, M., Rimbawanto, A., Thomas, D., Wiedenhoeft, A. C., Yin, Y., Zahnen, J., and Lowe, A. J. (2015). Forensic timber identification: It's time to integrate disciplines to combat illegal logging. In *Biological Conservation*, 191, 790–798). 10.1016/j.biocon.2 015.06.038

Finkeldey, R., Leinemann, L., and Gailing, O. (2010). Molecular genetic tools to infer the origin of forest plants and wood. In *Applied Microbiology and Biotechnology*, 8(5), 1251–1258. 10.1007/s00253-009-2328-6

García-Mozo, H., Beltran-Aroca, C. M., Badu, I. K., Jimena, I., and Girela-López, E. (2021). Airborne pollen and spores' deposition in alveolar tissues as a tool in drowning forensic diagnosis. *Aerobiologia*, 1(11). 10.1007/s10453-021-09690-y

Gitzendanner, M. A. (2012). Use and Guidelines for Plant DNA Analyses in Forensics. In *Forensic Botany: A Practical Guide* (pp. 93–106). John Wiley and Sons. 10.1002/9781119945734.ch5

Gressel, J., and Ehrlich, G. (2002). Universal inheritable barcodes for identifying organisms. In *Trends in Plant Science*, 7(12), 542–544. 10.1016/S1360-1385(02)02364-6

Hall, D., and Byrd, J. *Forensic botany: a practical guide*. John Wiley and Sons, 2012.

Hall, D. W. (2012). Introduction to Forensic Botany. In *Forensic Botany*: A Practical Guide (pp. 1–11). 10.1002/9781119945734.ch1

Horton, B. P., Boreham, S., and Hillier, C. (2006). The development and application of a diatom-based quantitative reconstruction technique in forensic science. *Journal of Forensic Sciences*, 51(3), 643–650. 10.1111/j.1556-4029.2006.00120.x

Krstic, S., Duma, A., Janevska, B., Levkov, Z., Nikolova, K., and Noveska, M. (2002). Diatoms in forensic expertise of drowning - A Macedonian experience. *Forensic Science International*, 127(3), 198–203. 10.1016/S0379-0738(02)00125-1

Kumar, A., Pushpangadan, P., and Mehrotra, S. (2003). Extraction of high-molecular-weight DNA from dry root tissue of Berberis lycium suitable for RAPD. *Plant Molecular Biology Reporter*, 21(3). 10.1007/bf02772807

Ladd, C. A. R. L. L., and Lee, H. C. (2004). The use of biological and botanical evidence in criminal investigations. *Forensic Botany: Principles and Applications to Criminal Casework*. New York: CRC Press, 97–115.

Lee, C.-L., Hsu, I., and Miller Coyle, H. (2004). DNA and the Identification of Plant Species from Stomach Contents. In *Forensic Botany*. 10.1201/9780203484593.ch9

Liu, M., Zhao, Y., Sun, Y., Wu, P., Zhou, S., and Ren, L. (2021). Diatom DNA barcodes for forensic discrimination of drowning incidents. *FEMS Microbiology Letters*, 367(17). 10.1093/femsle/fnaa145

Margiotta, G., Bacaro, G., Carnevali, E., Severini, S., Bacci, M., and Gabbrielli, M. (2015). Forensic botany as a useful tool in the crime scene: *Report of a case. Journal of Forensic and Legal Medicine, 34*, 24–28. 10.1016/j.jflm.2015.05.003

Miller, J. (2017). Forensic Botany and Stomach Contents Analysis: Established Practice and Innovation. In *Taphonomy of Human Remains: Forensic Analysis of the Dead and the Depositional Environment* (pp. 187–200). John Wiley and Sons, Ltd. 10.1002/9781118953358.ch14

Miller Coyle, H., Ladd, C., Palmbach, T., and Lee, H. C. (2001). The green revolution: Botanical contributions to forensics and drug enforcement. *Croatian Medical Journal*, 42(3), 340–345. 10.1201/9780203484593-16

Milne, L., Bryant, V., and Mildenhall, D. (2004). Forensic Palynology. *Forensic Botany: Principles and Applications to Criminal Casework*. New York: CRC Press, 217–252.

Norris, D. O., and Bock, J. H. (2000). Use of Fecal Material to Associate a Suspect with a Crime Scene: Report of Two Cases. *Journal of Forensic Sciences*, 45(1), 14657J. 10.1520/jfs14657j

Norris, D. O., and Bock, J. H. (2001). Method for examination of fecal material from a crime scene using plant fragments. *Journal of Forensic Identification*, 51(4), 367–377

Pollanen, M. S. (1998). Diatoms and homicide. *Forensic Science International*, 91(1), 29–34. 10.1016/S0379-0738(97)00162-X

Robbenblatt, A. C. G. M. (2016). Digging for the Disappeared: Forensic Science After Atrocity by Adam Rosenblatt. *Human Rights Quarterly*, 38(1), 224–228. 10.1353/hrq.2016.0011

Robertson, B., Vignaux, G. A., and Berger, C. E. *Interpreting evidence: evaluating forensic science in the courtroom*. John Wiley and Sons, 2016. 10.1002/9781118492475

Rohn, E. J., and Frade, P. D. (2006). The role of Diatoms in medico-legal investigations II: a case for the development and testing of new modalities applicable to the diatom test for drowning. *The Forensic Examiner*, 15(4), 26.

Saferstein, R. Criminalistics: *An introduction to forensic science* (p. 73). Upper Saddle River, NJ: Pearson Prentice Hall, 2007.

Scott, K. R., Morgan, R. M., Jones, V. J., and Cameron, N. G. (2014). The transferability of diatoms to clothing and the methods appropriate for their collection and analysis in forensic geoscience. *Forensic Science International*, 241, 127–137. 10.1016/j.forsciint.2014.05.011

Singh, R., Singh, R., Kumar, S., and Thakar, M. K. (2006). Forensic analysis of diatoms-a review. Anil Aggrawal's *Internet Journal of Forensic Medicine and Toxicology* [Serial Online]. http://anilaggrawal.com/ij/vol_007_no_002/papers/paper002.html

Virtanen, V., Korpelainen, H., and Kostamo, K. (2007). Forensic botany: usability of bryophyte material in forensic studies. *Forensic Science International*, *172*(2–3), 161–163. 10.1016/j.forsciint.2006.11.012

Walters, C., Reilley, A. A., Reeves, P. A., Baszczak, J., and Richards, C. M. (2006). The utility of aged seeds in DNA banks. *Seed Science Research*, *16*(3), 169–178. 10.1079/ssr2006246

Wiltshire, P. E. J., and Black, S. (2006). The cribriform approach to the retrieval of palynological evidence from the turbinates of murder victims. *Forensic Science International*, *163*(3), 224–230. 10.1016/j.forsciint.2005.11.019

Wiltshire, P. E. J. (2006). Hair as a source of forensic evidence in murder investigations. *Forensic Science International*, *163*(3), 241–248. 10.1016/j.forsciint.2006.06.070

Wiltshire, P. E. J. (2009). Forensic ecology, botany, and palynology: Some aspects of their role in criminal investigation. In *Criminal and Environmental Soil Forensics* (pp. 129–149). Springer Netherlands. 10.1007/978-1-4020-9204-6_9

Wiltshire, P. E. J. (2015). Forensic Botany. In *Encyclopaedia of Forensic and Legal Medicine: Second Edition* (pp. 520–527). Elsevier Inc. 10.1016/B978-0-12-800034-2.00180-4

Wu, C. L., Yang, C. H., Huang, T.-C., and Chen, S.-H. (2006). Forensic Pollen Evidence from Clothes by the Tape Adhesive Method. *Taiwania-Taipei*, *51*(2), 123–130. 10.6165/TAI.2006.51(2).123

CHAPTER 8

Toxicological Evidence Collection

Amarnath Mishra[1]*, Sourabh Kumar Singh*[2]*, and Shrutika Singla*[2]

[1]Worldwide Association of Women Forensic Experts (WAWFE-Caribbean), School of Forensics, Risk Management & National Security (SFRMNS), Rashtriya Raksha University, Lavad-Dahegam, Gandhinagar, Gujarat, India
[2]Amity Institute of Forensic Sciences, Amity University, Noida, Uttar Pradesh, India

CONTENTS

INTRODUCTION

The term "forensic toxicology" is a branch of forensic science that deals with poison and its effects on living organisms. According to Paracelsus, "All substances are poison, there is none which is not poison. The right dose differentiate between a poison and a remedy." According to Peter Mere Latham, "Poisons and medicines are oftentimes the same substance given with different intents." Mathieu J. B. Orfila was the first successful scientist in the field of forensic toxicology, which led him to be the "father of toxicology" (Fisher et al.).

Forensic science is a growing field and each passing day we are solving cases with the help of forensic knowledge. In forensic toxicology, we deal with the blood, drugs, poisons, and pesticides in viscera, tissues, body fluids, stomach contents, and organs. These exhibits are utilized for the purpose of identification of poisoning and confirming the cause of death (Mishra, 2017a).

A poison is a substance which deliver antagonistic impacts on a person consuming it. It may include drugs, nutrients, pesticides, contaminations, and proteins. Indeed, even radiation is a toxic substance. Although not normally viewed as "synthetic," most radiations are created from radioisotopes, which are synthetic substances. The idea that even a substance as harmless as water is poisonous if an excess is ingested. Regardless of whether a medication goes about as a treatment or as a poison relies upon the portion.

The forensic toxicologists are the experts with skills and knowledge in the field of forensic toxicology. They visit the crime scene that is related to suspected poisoning case for collection of evidence present at the crime scene such as various instruments used to inject the poisons, tablets, vomit, drugs, drinks, etc. Toxicological evidences are not only collected during crime scene investigation, but a forensic pathologist also collects and preserves viscera and stomach contents from the dead body during the autopsy. A forensic pathologist then sends the samples collected to the forensic science laboratory for the detection and analysis of poison present in the body fluid. The samples collected from the crime scene and during autopsy are handled with care, and then packed, marked, and sent to a forensic science laboratory with proper labelling. A chain of custody is maintained while transferring evidence from the crime scene to the laboratory.

Forensic toxicology includes different types of poisoning: accidental, suicidal, and homicidal. In accidental poisoning, a person took a poison accidently without knowing its harmful effects. In suicidal poisoning, a person took a poison to inflict harm to himself/herself, knowing all the possible causes of poison that can ultimately lead to death. In homicidal poisoning, a person is given poison by another in order to take revenge or any other reason.

Different types of samples could be found at the crime scene, such as tablets, syrups, soft and hard drinks, drug powder, etc. These different samples are handled in different ways (Trestrail, 2007).

ROLE OF FORENSIC INVESTIGATOR AND FORENSIC TOXICOLOGIST

A forensic investigator visits the crime scene to collect the information and evidence related to the event that happened. He/she is generally the first person to visit the crime scene. They recognize early signs and symptoms of poisoning during life or immediately after death and can provide the best information about the crime scene. They can provide the information about the signs and symptoms to the lab analyst, which will help him/her in the detection of the poison. A forensic toxicologist can be a forensic investigator who visits a crime scene related to toxicology.

A medical officer or forensic pathologist conducts the post-mortem, which certifies the death and also whether the death has occurred due to poison. He/she preserves the body fluid and viscera for the detection of poison.

A forensic toxicologist deals with different types of chemicals and poisons. He/she isolates and identifies the poison in the body fluid. He/she needs to prove that if there is an involvement of a poison in a particular death, and the accused that was in possession of the poison administered it to the victim. They also need to prove which poison is responsible for the death of the individual and in what quantity the sample was taken.

A forensic toxicologist gets a hint about the poison from the wrapper or container containing the chemical, if it was found at the crime scene or the signs and symptoms of the dead individual (Siegel, 2017).

CRIME SCENE INVESTIGATION

Crime scene investigation is a crucial step in solving any crime scene. A forensic toxicologist gets to know many clues related to the event at the crime scene. Different items and points must be looked at carefully at the crime scene by a forensic toxicologist. Some of these are given below:

- Location of the victim
- Location of vomit material, poison residues
- Location of vials, syringes, food, drinks
- Receipts of purchase of the material
- Search of trash cans
- Search of wash basin
- Search for fingerprints and trace evidences such as hairs and fibers

The investigating officer plays an important role as he/she needs to look closely at the environment of the crime scene. They need to see if the crime scene has been manipulated or if some foul play is happening at the scene. By looking at the environment, one gets to know about the number of individuals involved in the event (Adelson, 1974).

The analysis of the crime scene and whether it is organized or not often gives information about the mind-set of the criminal. If the crime scene is organized, that means the criminal had a full plan of conducting the crime and in this case, he/she will not leave any evidence or weapon at the crime scene. But if the crime scene is disturbed, then evidence could be found at the crime scene related to the criminal and the poison used for conducting the crime (Department of Army: Crimes involving poison, 1967).

A forensic toxicologist who visits the crime scene also needs to answer some important questions:

- Does the position of the body give the possibility of unnatural death?
- Is there any unusual odor at the crime scene?
- Is the evidence present at the crime scene useful or misinterpreting?
- Is the evidence present related to forensic toxicology?

There are some points that a forensic investigator or toxicologist must keep in mind:

1. He/she should not presume something about the event that happened.
2. He/she should pick only the necessary evidence leaving things that can lead to misinterpretations.
3. He/she should not manipulate evidence.
4. He/she must collect facts and information to determine the cause of death (Mishra, 2018).

In general, all the deaths involving the use of poison are considered homicides in the beginning until the facts are proved in other ways. In some cases, the victim may be alive after consuming the poison. The investigator or toxicologist should ask questions about the signs and symptoms after consuming poison, how he/she consumed it, and how they felt. In some cases, if the victim is dead, the investigator must ask questions from the individual who contacted the victim just before the incident or the individual who saw the victim first after death.

After interrogating, if the investigator found the involvement of poison at the scene, then he/she must determine the source of it. There may be some receipt from a medical store that can tell the costumer name, purchase date, name of the substance consumed, manufacture and expiration date, etc. This information may lead to the criminal.

If some vials or syringes are found at the crime scene, there might be fingerprints on them. By using methods for development of fingerprints, criminals may be identified (Schuman, 1970).

DIFFERENT TYPES OF EVIDENCE AT THE CRIME SCENE

Different types of toxicological evidence can be found in forensic toxicology cases such as drugs, poisons, and viscera. Some of them are given below:

- *Food and Drinks*: In most of the cases, food and drinks are contaminated with the poison so that the consumer will not know about the contamination.
- *Drugs*: It includes any substances that can be found in the form of powder, pill, capsule, vial, etc. It may also include illegal and seized substances that may be used for trafficking and sold and manufactured against the law.
- *Poison*: Poisons are the substances that directly affect the functioning of the body and mind. These substances are harmful and may result in the death of an individual. These substances are mainly restricted for use in our homes.
- *Medicines*: Medicines are the chemicals taken to prevent and to treat any disease.
- *Viscera*: Viscera include body fluid and body organs such as blood and stomach and intestinal content submitted for the detection of toxicological substances.
- *Hairs*: Hairs are very useful pieces of evidence in cases of toxicology. Drugs and heavy metals can be detected in hairs.
- *Pesticides*: Pesticides are one of the most common pieces of evidence in forensic toxicology. Individuals consume these pesticides and the substances are most commonly available at their homes to harm themselves.
- *Bottles and Vials*: These are the materials in which chemicals involved in the crime scene are stored.
- *Spoons, Syringes, Glasses*: These are the materials that are used to take the chemicals inside the body (Levine, 2006).

If we talk about toxicological evidences, these substances can be isolated into three general groups: horticultural and modern synthetic compounds; medications and medical care items; and natural toxins i.e. plant and creature sources. Radiation is also harmful to an individual. It leads to various illnesses and skin diseases (Mishra, 2017b). These three groups, alongside a fourth class, radiation, are discussed below (Figure 8.1).

Agricultural Chemicals

These are the chemicals used in agriculture to prevent manifestation by insects and pests. The majority of agricultural chemicals are pesticides, which include herbicides, insecticides, fumigants, fungicides, and rodenticides (Figure 8.2).

- **Insecticides**
  The four fundamental classes of insecticides are organophosphates, carbamates, chlorinated hydrocarbons or organochlorides, and insecticides got from plants (herbal). Organophosphate and carbamate insecticides act on acetylcholinesterase, the catalyst that corrupts acetylcholine (the courier of the parasympathetic sensory system). Thus,

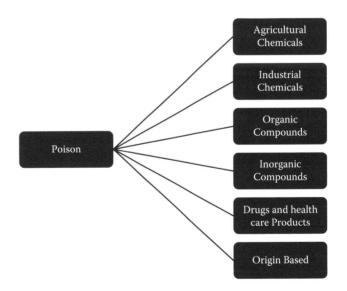

FIGURE 8.1   Classification of poison found at crime scene.

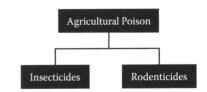

FIGURE 8.2   Classification of agricultural poison.

acetylcholine levels stay high, misrepresenting the ordinary elements of the parasympathetic framework. Impacts, for example, salivation, lacrimation, pee, poop, jerking of the skeletal muscles, delirium, confusion, and in extreme harming, passing from respiratory discouragement happens.

Chlorinated hydrocarbons utilized as insecticides, for example, DDT and Endosulfan, are bigger atoms than the chlorinated hydrocarbons utilized as natural solvents, chloroform. The major harmful impact created by these insecticides is seizures. The utilization of DDT is prohibited in numerous nations because of its ecological impacts and because it might cause malignancy in people. DDT is a profoundly fat-dissolvable synthetic that gathers in fish, and, when fowl eat such fish, the substance additionally aggregates in their fat tissues. The DDT in the fowl brings about delicate eggs, which are inclined to breakage. This will, at last, diminish the number of inhabitants in fish-eating fowl.

As a rule, insecticides from plants are less harmful. Pyrethrins are generally utilized in insecticides in the home, such as Mortein and Baygon. They have a fast "knockdown" for bugs and have a low potential for creating harmfulness in people. The significant harmfulness of pyrethrins is hypersensitivity. Rotenone is a mellow aggravation and an oncogen.

- **Rodenticides**
  Warfarin was initially evolved as a medication to treat thromboembolism, an illness brought about by blood clots, as it hinders the blend of a factor that is basic for the thickening of the blood. The restraint of blood coagulating by warfarin can prompt interior dying, notwithstanding. Due to its capacity to instigate inside dying, warfarin is additionally utilized as a rodenticide (Saputra, 2019).
- **Industrial chemicals**
  The term *mechanical synthetic compounds* is utilized to allude to synthetic compounds utilized either in farming or as medications. In this manner, it incorporates synthetic compounds utilized in industry, just as synthetics found in or close to families. Harming with mechanical synthetic substances happens frequently by either percutaneous or inward breath courses (Kumari and Mishra, 2021).
- **Plant Poisons**
  Various plant poisons are harmful to the human body and can cause major toxicity, which may lead to death. Certain examples of plant poisons are *Abrusprecatorius*, *Digitalis pupurea*, Dhatura, etc. (Das et al., 2016).

Organic Compounds

- Most hydrocarbon and organic compounds, such as toluene, heptanes, n-hexane, and benzene affect the focal sensory system. The hydrocarbons are lipid soluble and get broke in the layer of nerve cells in the cerebrum. Furthermore, a large number of the hydrocarbons causes heart disease. The hydrocarbon n-hexane additionally harms PNS. Benzene is harmful to organs like bone marrow and also can cause leukemia.
- Alcohols also affect the focal sensory system and a few alcohols cause poisoning at high levels. Major alcohol includes methanol, ethanol, isopropanol, ethylene glycol, and phenol. Methanol can deliver visual impairment after being utilized to formic acid, which likewise prompts acidosis, portrayed by an acidic pH in the body (lower than the ordinary pH of 7.4). It likewise creates fetal liquor condition, a significant reason for mental impediment in offspring of moms who drink during pregnancy. Ethanol is harmful to the liver and is a significant reason for cirrhosis, a condition described by solidifying the liver. Phenol varies from different alcohols in creating harm to various organs. And last, ethylene glycol, which is broadly utilized as a liquid catalyst specialist in cars, causes renal harm when it is biotransformed to oxalic acid.
- The significant damage delivered by aldehydes, for example, formaldehyde, is irritation. Formaldehyde can likewise cause unfavorably susceptible responses in individuals who have been exposed to it. Instances of other basic aldehydes incorporate acetaldehyde, glutaraldehyde, and acrolein. The poison levels of ketones and esters are like those of aldehydes in causing principally a disturbance of the respiratory plot whenever breathed in and the gastrointestinal parcel whenever ingested.
- Sweet-smelling amines and nitro compounds, for example, aniline, toluidine, and nitrobenzene, produce depression in focal sensory system and methemoglobinemia. Methemoglobinemia is a condition where the ferrous particle in hemoglobin, which carries oxygen, is oxidized to the ferric structure. Oxidized hemoglobin, called methemoglobin, can even now convey oxygen, but with low efficiency, so the body will have an absence of oxygen. Some sweet-smelling amines and nitro bunches are known to cause bladder disease.
- Since the two anhydrides and isocyanates are profoundly receptive, they are very aggravating to the upper respiratory parcel. However, the

airborne focus is adequately high, the upper respiratory plot can't eliminate the entirety of the isocyanate or anhydride particles, and pneumonic injury (basically edema) results. Such an event happened in Bhopal, India, during the 1980s, when methyl isocyanate from a synthetic plant was exposed to the air, killing and harming more than 2,500 individuals. Since they are synthetically receptive, anhydrides and isocyanates also result in asthma and hypersensitive contact dermatitis. A few examples of anhydrides include maleic anhydride and phthalic anhydride and that of isocyanates are methyl isocyanate and toluene diisocyanate.

- Various natural synthetics are phosgene, carbon disulfide, and halogenated sweet-smelling mixes. Phosgene acquired a reputation when it was utilized in substance warfare in World War I. Like anhydrides and isocyanates, phosgene is profoundly receptive. Rather than responding with the mucosal linings of the upper respiratory parcel, in any case, it will in general respond with the lungs, causing edema. Accordingly, the lungs' guard against microscopic organisms are debilitated, and pneumonia may happen.

- Halogenated sweet-smelling substances with more than one ring, for example, polychlorinated biphenyls (PCBs), polybrominated biphenyls (PBBs), and 2,3,7,8-tetrachlorodibenzodioxin (TCDD), can deliver various harmful impacts in lab creatures, including malignancy, birth defects, liver injury, porphyria, and immune toxicity. The PCBs have been widely utilized as cooling specialists in electrical transformers. People are more impervious to these poisonousness substances, and the primary harmful impact seen in people is chloracne, like adolescent skin inflammation (Figure 8.3).

Inorganic Compounds

- Instances of metal compounds harmful to people incorporate manganese, lead, cadmium, nickel, and arsenic mixes; beryllium oxide; and the basic fumes, inorganic salts, and natural mixes of mercury. Manganese toxicity can harm the mind, bringing about a condition with diseases like Parkinson's illness; for example, slurred discourse, mask-like face, and inflexibility. Mercury can likewise harm the cerebrum, prompting social changes; in any case, mercury is additionally poisonous to the fringe sensory system, causing tactile and engine indications. Furthermore, mercury is poisonous to the kidneys. Methyl mercury is particularly poisonous to the mind of a baby.

- Lead is presumably the most omnipresent metal toxin. Utilized for various purposes, before World War II it was a significant constituent in paint, and it has been utilized in gas. Like mercury, lead is harmful to the sensory system and kidney; however, its poisonousness is age-subordinate. In youngsters, the blood–cerebrum boundary isn't completely evolved, and more lead enters the mind. The degree of harm relies upon the concentration; at a lower concentration, little declines in knowledge and conduct changes may result, while significant levels bring about extreme cerebrum harm and demise. In grown-ups, the lead will in general reason loss of motion or shortcoming, demonstrative of fringe sensory system harm.

- In intense cadmium harming by ingestion, disturbance of the gastrointestinal track leads to sickness, spewing, loose bowels, and stomach cramps.

- Arsenic aggravates harm to numerous organs. They cause skin sores, a decline in heart contractility, vein harm, and wounds of the sensory system, kidney, and liver. Arsenic mixes additionally produce skin and lung tumors in people (Chaurasia et al., 2012).

- Certain nickel and hexavalent chromium mixes, just as beryllium oxide, are poisonous to the lungs and can cause a cellular breakdown in the lungs.

- Acids, for example, sulfuric and hydrochloric acids, and unequivocally soluble mixes, sodium hydroxide, and potassium hydroxide, are destructive to tissues on contact and can cause extreme tissue wounds. Sulfuric acids, sodium hydroxide, and potassium hydroxide are dynamic fixings in channel cleaners, the ingestion of which can cause extreme substance consumption of the mouth and throat.

- Hypochlorites are regularly utilized as blanching specialists. In low focuses, as in family unit fades,

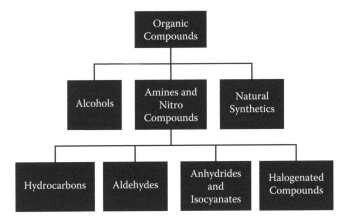

FIGURE 8.3 Classification of organic compounds.

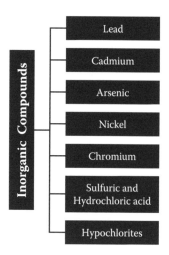

FIGURE 8.4   Classification of inorganic compounds.

hypochlorites have little harmfulness yet might be aggravating to tissues; they can be destructive at high fixations. Cyanide particles poison the oxidative metabolic apparatus of cells so deficient energy is created. The impact is as though oxygen was absent for the cells, even though there is a lot of oxygen in the blood. Hydrogen sulfide and chlorine profoundly disturb the respiratory track, with pneumonic edema the major poisonous impact. Ongoing fluoride harming is called fluorosis, which is described by tooth mottling and expanded bone thickness. These changes, particularly of the bone, are identified with an adjustment in body calcium brought about by fluoride. Silica and asbestos stay in the lungs for significant periods, and both produce lung fibrosis. Moreover, asbestos is a notable human cancer-causing agent (Arquitecture et al., 2015) (Figure 8.4).

Drugs and Healthcare Products

Harming with drugs overwhelmingly includes oral openings. With drugs, along these lines, disturbance of the respiratory parcel is rare, yet anorexia, queasiness, and regurgitation because of gastrointestinal aggravation is normal (Figure 8.5).

- **Painkillers**
  Painkillers (analgesics) are the most commonly utilized medications for some harming cases. Models incorporate ibuprofen and acetaminophen. Anti-inflammatory medicine meddles with the oxidative consumption of fuel by cells. To get energy, the cells change to a less proficient method of consuming fuel that

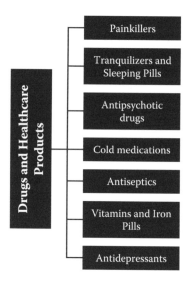

FIGURE 8.5   Classification of drugs and healthcare products.

doesn't utilize oxygen yet produces a ton of warmth. Expanded sweat happens to neutralize an ascent in internal heat level, prompting parchedness and thirst. Ibuprofen likewise modifies the pH in the body, influencing the focal sensory system. The significant poisonousness of acetaminophen is liver harm.

The significant poisonousness from opiate analgesics, similar to morphine, is melancholy of the focal sensory system, particularly the cerebrum community controlling the breath. The reason for death in morphine gluts is normally respiratory disappointment. Sickness is brought about by morphine's incitement of the chemoreceptor trigger zone in the cerebrum, and blockage is brought about by morphine's downturn of a strong movement in the digestive tract.

- **Tranquilizers and sleeping pills**
  Benzodiazepines, for example, diazepam, clonazepam, and chlordiazepoxide, have a wide edge of well-being when utilized at endorsed dosages. Their major poisonous impact is the misery of the focal sensory system, which brings about solid incoordination and slurred discourse. For sleeping pills containing barbiturates, chloral hydrate, paraldehyde, and meprobamate, nonetheless, the edge of well-being is much smaller, and the significant poisonousness is extreme wretchedness of the focal sensory system, prompting respiratory and cardiovascular disappointment.

- **Antipsychotic drugs**
  Like benzodiazepines, antipsychotic drugs, for example, chlorpromazine, perphenazine, and

haloperidol, have a moderate effects, rarely causing fatalities. These obstruct the activity of the parasympathetic and brain sensory systems and accordingly produce such undesired impacts as dry mouth and obscured vision from the previous and a drop in circulatory strain after standing in the last mentioned.

- **Cold medications**

  Nasal decongestants, antihistamines, and hack medication, which are found in over-the-counter arrangements for treating the diseases of colds, have a low potential to deliver harmfulness. Nasal decongestants, for example, ephedrine, impersonate the activity of epinephrine by animating the thoughtful sensory system, and therefore, an excess of ephedrine produces manifestations identified with incitement of the brain and focal sensory systems. The gloom of the focal sensory system and parasympathetic bar are two basic poison levels of antihistamines; for example, diphenhydramine. Depression of the focal sensory system is likewise the significant harmfulness of dextromethorphan and codeine, both used to stifle hacking/coughing.

- **Antiseptics**

  Most antiseptics (e.g. hydrogen peroxide, benzoyl peroxide, resorcinol, benzalkonium chloride, parabens, and cetylpyridinium chloride) produce gastrointestinal aggravation whenever ingested. Benzoyl peroxide and parabens applied to the skin might be harmful. Among the most poisonous antiseptics are hexachlorophene, benzalkonium, and cetylpyridinium chloride, any of which can wound inner organs. Foundational poisonousness (twofold vision, sluggishness, quake, seizures, and demise) with hexachlorophene is bound to happen in children because the moderately dainty layer corneum of their skin is profoundly penetrable.

- **Vitamins and iron pills**

  Insufficiencies just as abundances of vitamins are hurtful. Inordinate nutrient A (retinol, or retinoic corrosive), known as hypervitaminosis A, can bring about skin sores, edema, and liver harm. Overconsumption by Alaskan locals of the polar bear liver, a rich wellspring of nutrient A, has delivered intense poison levels, portrayed by overpowering drowsiness and serious migraines. Constant harming with nutrient A can cause neurological side effects, including torment, anorexia, exhaustion, and peevishness.

  Overabundance of nutrient C can prompt kidney stones. Aside from disturbance of the skin and respiratory plot, the most serious poisonousness of nutrient K abundance is the expanded obliteration of red platelets, which prompts iron deficiency and the collection of bilirubin, one of the results of hemoglobin corruption. Overabundance of bilirubin can bring about brain harm in babies, a condition known as kernicterus. Since the blood–brain boundary isn't all around created in babies, bilirubin enters and harms the cerebrum. Because of the blood–brain hindrance, kernicterus isn't found in grown-ups.

  Iron, a metal that is vital for ordinary wellbeing, can likewise cause harm. The harmfulness of iron is a consequence of its destructive activity on the stomach and digestive system when present in high foci. Accordingly, intestinal draining happens, which can prompt the improvement of stun.

- **Antidepressants**

  Among tricyclic antidepressants, amitriptyline and imipramine represent the vast majority of the deadly instances of harm. These drugs have various impacts, including blockage of the parasympathetic framework and harm to the focal sensory system, for example, exhaustion, shortcoming, brought down by the internal heat level, seizures, and respiratory wretchedness. Death is generally brought about by damage to the heart. Lithium salts, used to treat hyper-depression, generally have low recuperative characteristics.

Origin Based

Poisons are of microbial, plant, creature, or engineered. Microbial poisons are created by minute living beings; for example, microorganisms and growths. Botulinus poison, for instance, is delivered by the bacterium *Clostridium botulinum* and is equipped for inciting shortcoming and loss of motion when present in underprocessed, nonacidic canned nourishments, or different food sources containing the spores. An illustration of a plant poison is the belladonna alkaloid hyoscyamine, which is found in belladonna (*Atropa belladonna*) and jimsonweed (*Datura stramonium*).

Creature poisons are normally moved through the bites and stings of venomous earthbound or marine creatures, the previous gathering including poisonous snakes, scorpions, arachnids, and ants, and the last gathering including ocean snakes, stingrays, and jellyfish. Engineered poisons are answerable for most poisonings. "Engineered" alludes to synthetic compounds fabricated by scientific experts, for example, medications and pesticides, just as synthetic substances filtered from regular sources, for example, metals from minerals and solvents from oil. Engineered poisons incorporate pesticides, cleaners, beautifying agents, drugs, and hydrocarbons (Kobilinsky, 2012).

COLLECTION AND PRESERVATION OF EVIDENCE

Toxicological evidence is very difficult to handle and must be handled with proper care and attention. There are two types of samples in cases of forensic toxicology:

- Ante-mortem Samples: These are the samples taken from the live individual, such as blood, gastric lavage, urea, defecation, milk, hair.
  - In case of a live individual, blood and urine must be collected. About 25 mL of blood is enough for the detection of poison.
  - Liquid samples must be sealed in an air-tight container so that these cannot be degraded by bacteria present in the atmosphere. Samples should be frozen and dispatched on ice to the laboratory, except blood. Blood should not be frozen.
  - Samples like hair can be packed in druggist folds or in a paper envelope in a way that the sample does not slip away from the packaging.
  - It will be better if additives not be added in the samples.
- Post-mortem Samples: These are the samples taken during the autopsy of a dead individual by a forensic pathologist such as blood, viscera, intestinal, and stomach content. These samples are packed with preservatives such as formalin or sodium chloride in a proper manner in a container. Samples are then frozen at 4°C to prevent degradation. These samples are transferred to a forensic science laboratory in frozen form.
  - Different organs can be collected for the detection of poison, such as brain, kidney, and liver. About 100 g brain, 100 g liver, and 50 g kidney is enough for identification and detection of poison.
  - If possible, vitreous humor can be collected.

The following precautions must be followed while preserving the samples:

- The container must be labeled with the name, age, sex, police station, medical examiner, hospital name, mortuary, investigating officer, date of autopsy, and seal of doctor with the signature by an official or medical examiner.
- The content from different organs must be preserved in different containers; stomach content and intestinal content should be taken in two separate glass or plastic air-tight containers.
- Blood and urine must be packed separately and no preservative should be added in it.
- Containers should not be filled completely to prevent bursting of the container due to the gases formed in it.
- The container should be sealed as soon as the content is poured in it to prevent release of volatile substances from the sample.
- The container containing the sample must be kept at low temperature and also be transported at low temperature to a forensic science laboratory.
- **Natural samples:** If the origin of the consumed intoxicant is known, one should take the known sample from the source. The sample should be refrigerated and preserved in a cool environment. Plants can be preserved in moist towels and refrigerated, frozen, or squeezed and dried. Then the sample must be sent to the laboratory on the same day, if possible (Benjamin, 2010).

Analysis/Tests for Toxicological Evidences to Be Performed at the Scene of Crime

Forensic toxicologist need to perform some tests at the crime scene. Such tests are known as spot tests or presumptive tests. These tests give an indication about the poison that could be present. One should not rely on the presumptive test for the confirmation and must go for confirmatory tests. Confirmatory tests are performed in the laboratory (Mishra, 2020) (Figure 8.6).

In this chapter, we will study presumptive or spot tests as we are focusing on crime scene investigation (Table 8.1).

Given below are presumptive tests performed for various poisons:

- **Reinsch's test**
  Around 20 ml of concentrated hydrochloric acid and 100 ml of water are taken in a porcelain bowl in which a brilliant copper foil, of around 3 × 1/4 inch, is set with one of its closures fixed on the edge of the bowl in the structure of a circle. It is bubbled for about 30 minutes to check whether the copper, bowl, and acid are liberated from the metal to be tried (here it is arsenic).

  On the off-chance that a stain on copper foil shows up, the clear investigation is to be completed again with new materials. On the off-chance that the clear is negative, the speculated material is added and bubbled for about an hour or more with the random option of water

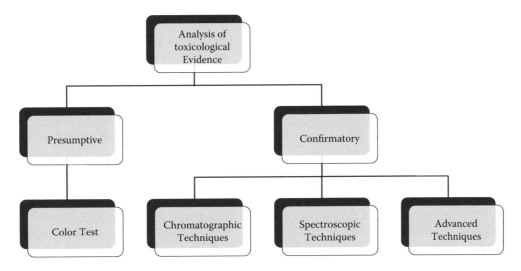

FIGURE 8.6 Tests performed to detect the poisons.

TABLE 8.1 Presumptive Tests for some of the Poisons

Tests	Poison
Reinsch's Test	Arsenic, Antimony, Mercury
Gutzeit Test	Arsenic
Marsh's Test	Arsenic
Copper Sulphate-Pyridine Test	Cyanate
Prussian Blue Test	Cyanide
Fuchsine Test	Sulfites
Zwikker's Test	Thiobarbiturates and Non-thiobarbiturates Test
Dille-Koppayani Test	Barbiturates
McNally's Test	Salicylates and Salicylic Acid
Liebermann's Test	Cresols and p-amino Phenols
Mandelin's Test	Strychnine
Gerrard's Test	Hyoscyamine
Gunzberg's Test	Hydrochloric Acid
Ammonium Molybdate Test	Arsenites and Phosphates

and acid to compensate for the misfortune due to vanishing. A sparkling steel grain stain shows up in no time flat, which becomes thick gradually. The stained copper strip from by the Reinsch test is washed carefully with water followed by alcohol and at long last with ether to eliminate the fat if the matrices are organic materials. The strip is dried by keeping it between channel paper sheets, cut in little bits of 0.2 mm × 0.2 mm size, and taken into a Reinsch tube. The cylinder is warmed gradually on the fire of soul light. The dark store on the copper strip volatilizes and is saved on the cooler piece of the cylinder. The cylinder is cooled and seen under the magnifying lens. Trademark octahedral gems of arsenious oxide are seen. Natural arsenicals don't react if the natural issue isn't wrecked. Some natural sulfur intensities produce dark stains of copper sulfide, which might be taken out by oxidation. The convergence of hydrochloric acid ought not be excessively low or excessively high. This test is for the most part utilized for fast screening of arsenic, antimony, and mercury.

• **Gutzeit Test**
The arrangement acquired from the wet digestion measure is tried by this technique. One ml of the arrangement is taken into a Gutzeit device, and two pellets of unadulterated zinc metal are placed into it. Five ml of weakening sulphuric acid is poured over the substance. The advanced gas is cleaned by ignoring lead acetate

paper (to retain hydrogen sulfide gas) and is responded at last with mercuric chloride test paper. A yellow stain on the paper shows the presence of arsenic.

- **Marsh's Test**

  The electrolytic Marsh Berzelius test is done over a regular zinc-sulphuric acid technique for the development of early hydrogen as these reagents are regularly sullied with arsenic and so on insufficient materials like consumed bones, hair, and nail peelings containing minute hints of arsenic and for testing the weak hints of arsenic present as a characteristic constituent in tissues. The Swamp's test seems, by all accounts, to be the solitary dependable procedure accessible. The test is acted in the arrangement got from the wet absorption measure. The arrangement containing arsenic in the pentavalent state is diminished to the trivalent state by overflowing with pyrogallol arrangement and sulphurated water. One ml of the test arrangement is taken into a porcelain bowl, blended in with 2 to 3 drops of 0.5% pyrogallol arrangement and 1 ml of soaked sulphurated (water immersed with SO_2), and bubbled for 30 minutes.

  The pentavalent arsenic is decreased to the trivalent state. A clear control test is controlled by taking weakened sulphuric acid in the cathode and anode offices of the Marsh device by passing a current of roughly 4.5 Amp at 6 V for 30 minutes. There ought to be no stain on the Swamp tube at this stage. The test arrangement containing arsenic in the trivalent stage has at that point filled the contraption and the cycle is rehashed for 30 minutes. A reflection of dark metallic radiance is seen at the cooler side of the Marsh tube if arsenic is available. To affirm that the mirror kept in the Marsh tube is simply because of arsenic, both finishes of the cylinder are fixed after supplanting hydrogen with air. The cylinder is then warmed gradually on the fire of soul light by keeping the smaller segment of the cylinder cooler. The mirror vanishes and the octahedral precious stone of arsenous trioxide is saved on the cooler, smaller finish of the cylinder that is distinguished under the high force of the magnifying instrument.

- **Copper Sulphate-Pyridine Test**

  One ml of the concentrate is added to a weakened arrangement of copper sulfate to which a couple of drops of pyridine have been recently added. A lilac-blue accelerate is shaped, affirming the presence of cyanate. This is a solvent in chloroform with the creation of a sapphire-blue arrangement.

- **Prussian Blue Test**

  One ml of a newly arranged 10% arrangement of ferrous sulfate in newly bubbled and cooled water is added to 2 ml of the concentrate. A greenish accelerate is shaped. Hydrochloric acid is added drop by drop to break down the accelerate. A blue coloration or hastening (in some cases accelerate is shaped on keeping) shows the presence of cyanide.

- **Fuchsine Test**

  One drop of Fuchsine reagent (arranged by dissolving 0.015 g. Fuchsine in 100 ml of water) is set on a spot plate. One drop of the impartial arrangement of concentrate is added. The red tone of the reagent is released showing the presence of sulphites.

- **Zwikker's Test**

  The buildup of concentrate is taken up in chloroform. To 1 ml of chloroform separate, 2–3 drops of 0.5 ml of 5% pyridine in chloroform is added and shaken. The shade of the chloroform layer becomes purple. At that point, 1 drop of glacial acetic acid is added. If the shade of the chloroform layer changes from purple to frail blue, the presence of non-thiobarbiturates is shown. On the off chance that the chloroform layer becomes green after adding pyridine in chloroform, the presence of thiobarbiturates is shown. This green shade changes to light green on adding acidic acid.

- **Dille-Koppayani Test**

  Preparation of Reagent:

  Reagent 1: Cobalt acetate solution 1 gm of cobalt acetate (tetrahydrate) is broken up in 100 ml of supreme alcohol followed by expansion of 0.2 ml of acetic acid.

  Reagent 2: Isopropylamine solution 5 ml of isopropylamine is blended in with 100 ml of methanol.

  Strategy 1: A limited quantity of separated material is put on a spot plate. Three to four drops of cobalt acetate arrangement and 3–4 drops of isopropylamine arrangement are added. The appearance of a purple or blue-violet tone shows the presence of barbiturate.

  Strategy 2: The buildup of concentrate of the test is taken in 1 ml of chloroform. To a segment of Chloroform concentrate of the example, 2 drops of newly arranged 1% cobalt acetate in methanol is added trailed by 1 lithium hydroxide in methanol drop by drop. A blue ring at the intersection demonstrates the presence of barbiturates.

- **McNally's Test**

  To the buildup of concentrate of organic materials, a couple of drops of acetone and 1–2 ml of water are added. Two drops of 0.5% copper sulfate arrangement in 10% acetic acid are added followed by a spot of strong sodium nitrite. It is shaken and warmed progressively to bubbling and kept up in bubbling condition for a couple of moments. A red tone is framed if salicylates and salicylic acid are available.

- **Liebermann's Test**
  The antacid distillate vanishes to dryness over a little fire in a porcelain dish and cooled. A spot of sodium nitrite is added. From that point concentrated sulphuric acid is added. On blending cautiously, blue or green coloration is noticed. It goes to red on adding water to it, which turns green whenever made soluble by sodium hydroxide or ammonia arrangement. Blue-red shading shows the presence of phenol while violet's tone demonstrates Resorcinol. Green shading shows the presence of alpha-naphthol and beta-naphthol. Earthy colored to dark hue shows the presence of cresols and p-amino-phenol.

- **Mandelin's Test**
  To the Brucine free buildup, one drop of Mandelin's reagent (1% arrangement of ammonium vanadate in concentrated sulphuric acid) is added. A profound violet-blue or profound purple tone shows up which at last changes to yellow on a long-standing characteristic of the presence of strychnine.

- **Gerrard's Test**
  One to two ml of 2% mercuric chloride arrangement in half of the alcohol is added to a part of a buildup of the concentrate. A red tone grows right away. Hyoscyamine creates a yellow tone which gets red on consumption, while hyoscine doesn't create any difference in shade.

- **Gunzberg's Test**
  A couple of drops of Gunzberg's reagent (arranged by dissolving 2 gm of phloroglucinol and 1 gm of vanillin in 100 ml of 95% alcohol) is taken in a porcelain dish and vanished to dryness over a little fire and cooled. A glass pole along with the material to be tried is added to the dried reagent and warmed delicately. A purplish red tone creates the presence of free hydrochloric acid.

- **Ammonium Molybdate Test**
  To 2 ml of concentrate, ammonium molybdate and nitric acid are included in significant excess. A yellow glasslike hasten of ammonium arsenomolybdate is acquired on bubbling (qualification from arsenites, which give no hastening, and from phosphates, which yield an accelerant neglected or upon delicate warming). The

accelerant is insoluble in nitric acid, yet breaks up in an ammonia arrangement and arrangements of harsh salts (Mebs, 1987).

PREVENTIVE MEASURES TAKEN UP BY FORENSIC TOXICOLOGIST

There are many preventive measures that a forensic toxicologist must consider while solving a crime scene:

1. While visiting a crime scene, he/she must not disturb any material present there. He/she must not smoke, should not consume any food or drink, and should not use washrooms and wash basin.
2. He/she should pack and label the evidences carefully so that it does not escape from the packaging.
3. Liquid samples must be packed in air-tight containers to prevent it from decomposition.
4. Proper labeling is required.
5. Chain of custody should be maintained.
6. When the sample reaches the laboratory, the labeling should be checked carefully.
7. Sometimes the sample that reaches the laboratory is in very small quantities, so it must be used carefully for detection.
8. If possible, hair and nail samples from the victim must be collected. There are certain drugs and poisons that do not stay in the body. Those chemicals can be detected with the help of hairs and nails.
9. Forensic toxicologist must not consume any sample delivered to the laboratory for identification and detection (Saferstein, 2015).

CONCLUSION

Forensic toxicology is a very important part of science that supports a wide variety of medico-legal applications. Primary for the medical practitioner is to get a robust background knowledge in analytical chemistry, including the isolation, extraction, and detection methods for poisons, mainly those involving the mass spectrometer and other instrumentation methods. The collection of the variety of samples will differ on the application but it will always require proper certification, transportation, and preservation to assure the reliability of the items for the analysis. Understanding of drug effects as well as the pharmacokinetics, along with an awareness of the possible constraints in the analysis of results, confirm the credible evidence that has not been overemphasized.

REFERENCES

Adelson, L. (1974). Murder by poison. In: *The Pathology of Homicide*, Charles C. Thomas, IL:Springfield, 725– 875.

Arquitecture, E. Y. et al. (2015). No Covariance Structure Analysis of Health-related Indicators in the Elderly at Home with a Focus on Subjective Health Title, *Acta Universitatis Agriculturae et Silviculturae MendeliannaeBrunensi, 53* (9), 1689–1699.

Benjamin, David M. (2010). Forensic pharmacology. In R. Saferstein (ed.), *Forensic Science Handbook, vol. 3*, 2nd Edition. Upper Saddle River, N.J.: Patience Hall.

Chaurasia, N., Mishra, A., & Pandey, S. K. (2012) Fingerprint of Arsenic Contaminated Water in India- A Review. *Journal of Forensic Research, 3*, 10.

Das, A., Jain, V., & Mishra, A. (2016). A Brief Review on a Traditional Herb: AbrusPrecatorius (L.). *International Journal of Forensic Medicine and Toxicological Sciences, 1*, 1.

Department of Army: Crimes involving poison. *Department of Army Technical Bulletin TB PMG 21.* Washington, DC: Department of Army, 1967, 11–13.

Fisher, B. A. J., Tilstone, W. J., & Woytowicz, C. *Introduction to Criminalistics: The Foundation of Forensic Science.* Academic Press.

Kumari, S., & Mishra, A. (2021). Heavy Metal Contamination, Soil Contamination- Threats and Sustainable Solutions, Marcelo L. Larramendy and Sonia Soloneski, IntechOpen.

Kobilinsky, L. (2012). *Handbook of Forensic Chemistry.* New Jersey, USA: Wiley Publications.

Levine, B., ed. *Principles of Forensic Toxicology,* 3rd Edition Washington, D.C.: AACC Press, 2006.

Mishra, A. (2017a). Advances of Forensic Science. *International Journal of Forensic Medicine and Toxicological Sciences, 2*, 1.

Mishra, A. (2017b) Impact of Radiation on Health: Clinical and Forensic Allusion. *Annals of Life Sciences,* 001/01.

Mishra, A. (2018). Poisoning Trends and their Forensic Investigation Poisoning Trends, their Investigation and Development of Improved Isolation Method. Deutsche Nationalbibliothek. ISBN: 978-613-7-34847-5.

Mishra, A. (2020). Forensic Chemistry and Toxicology, Medical Toxicology, Pinar Erkekoglu and Tomohisa Ogawa, IntechOpen.

Mebs, D. (1987). *Toxicity Testing. Strategies to Determine Needs and Priorities, Toxicon.*

Saputra, R. (2019). The relationship between leaf tissue characteristics and the level of resistance to leaf rust disease (Puccinia polysora) in several varieties of shelled maize (Zea mays L.). *Journal of Chemical Information and Modeling, 53* (9): 1689–1699.

Saferstein, R. (2015). Criminalistics: An Introduction to Forensic Science. 11th Edition. ISBN: 978-1-292-06867-1.

Schuman, A. Sparrow G: Women Who Murder, New York, 1970.

Siegel, J. *Forensic Chemistry Fundamentals and Applications.* Wiley Blackwell, 2017.

Trestrail, J. H. (2007). Criminal Poisoning: Investigational Guide for Law Enforcement, Toxicologists, Forensic Scientists, and Attorneys. 2nd Edition. ISBN: 1-58829-821-3.

CHAPTER 9

Digital Evidence Collection

Chintan Singh[1], *Harshita Tara*[2], *and Amarnath Mishra*[3]

[1]Amity Institute of Forensic Sciences, Amity University, Noida, Uttar Pradesh, India
[2]Nextechno Gen Private Limited, Patparganj, Delhi, India
[3]Worldwide Association of Women Forensic Experts (WAWFE-Caribbean), School of Forensics, Risk Management & National Security (SFRMNS), Rashtriya Raksha University, Lavad-Dahegam, Gandhinagar, Gujarat, India

CONTENTS

INTRODUCTION

Computer forensics deals with the various processes of finding/gathering evidence data related to the digital crime to find the culprits.

Objectives

1. To identify, gather, and preserve the digital evidence.
2. Track the culprits in the court.
3. Interpret, document, and present those pieces of evidence that can be admissible in court.
4. Perform incident response to prevent loss of intellectual property, finances, etc.
5. To know the different processes of handling various platforms, data types, and multiple operating systems.

A forensic examiner keeps in their mind the certain rules that must be followed during computer/digital forensic examination as well as to handle and analyze the digital evidence. This will maintain the authentication and the integrity of the digital evidence to be accepted in the court (Hassan).

Digital evidence that can be found at the crime scene are hard drive, thumb drive, memory card, smart card, Dongle, digital camera, server, scanner, etc.

Before the investigation, it is mandatory for the investigator to understand the rule of evidence, the submission of those evidence in the legal proceeding, especially in the digital crime cases that can have major challenges. Proper and specific knowledge is required to collect, preserve, and transport the digital evidence because the evidence obtained from the crime scene might vary from the traditional forms.

Ensure that the digital evidence is properly collected, preserved, examined or transferred in a manner that maintains the accuracy and the reliability of the digital evidences.

Standard Operating Procedures (SOPs)

SOPs are being documented and quality control guidelines should be supported by complete case records and widely accepted procedure and equipment.

Implementation of standard operating procedures allows us to operate company-compliant policies and plans.

It is mandatory that no modification should be done to the SOPs before implementing them.

All the investigators that seize, investigate, or examine digital evidence must maintain an appropriate standard operating procedure document. The use of standard operating procedure is fundamental to both law enforcement agencies and forensic science investigators.

Standard operating procedure should be generally accepted in the field and supported by the data that have been gathered in a forensically sound manner (Powell & Haynes, 2020).

The investigators should use different hardware and software that are appropriate and effective for the seizer and examination procedures of the digital evidence. Hardware that will be used in the seizing and examination procedures of the digital evidence should be in good operating condition in the field and be tested. Software that will be used to ensure the reliable result should be tested in seizing and examination procedures of the digital evidence.

All the activities that will be done by the investigators related to the seizure, storage, examination, or transfer of various digital evidence should be recorded in writing and should be available for review. There should be a chain of custody maintained for all the items that have been seizure by the investigators in the field.

Any activity that can have the potential to alter, destroy, or to damage any part of original evidence should be performed by qualified technical person in the forensically sound manner.

Forensic Readiness:

> It refers to an organisation ability to make optimal usage of digital evidence in a specific period.

It consists of both technical and non-technical actions that can increase an organization, competence to use the digital evidence. It also includes the establishment of different specific incidence response process/procedure and designated trained officer or investigator to handle those procedure in case of any breach. It helps the investigators to collect and preserve the digital evidence efficiently (Gogolin, 2021).

A forensically trained investigators and well-prepared incident response team ensures that there will be proper reaction against any misfortunes and the ability to handle the digital evidence according to the proper legal procedure that can be admissible in the court of law.

An incident response team who are forensically ready offers the investigators the following advantages:

1. It helps in proper digital evidence gathering.
2. It enables the use of complete digital evidence collection to act as an obstacle to insider threats.
3. It enables the investigators to conduct the efficient investigation in a limited time.
4. It facilitates the well designed and structured approach towards the collection and storage of digital evidence to reduce any type of investigation expenses.
5. It also facilitates the structured approach towards the collection and storage of all the information from digital evidence.
6. It also helps in the protection from the various threat of cyber crime such as fraud or extortion by an information security policy.
7. It also demonstrates the due diligence.
8. It also makes sure that the investigation done by the investigators should meet all the regulatory requirements.
9. It ensures the improvements in the interface to the law enforcement.
10. It also ensures the improvement in the prospects of successful legal actions.
11. It also makes sure that the evidence does not have any commercial or privacy disputes.
12. It ensures the prevention of attackers from covering their tracks.

Forensics readiness planning refers to the set of different processes or procedures that are required to collect and store the digital evidence.

These are the following steps that describe the key activities in forensics readiness planning:

1. Identify the potential digital evidence at the crime scene.
2. Determine the source of the evidence and its impact while retrieving the information.
3. Define the specific policies that will determine the process to legally extract the information from the digital evidence with minimal disruption.
4. Establish another specific policy to securely handle and store the collected digital evidence.
5. Train the officers or the investigators to handle the incident and collect the digital evidence that established the process to document the whole procedure for the chain of custody.
6. Establish the legal advisory board to guide the whole investigation process.

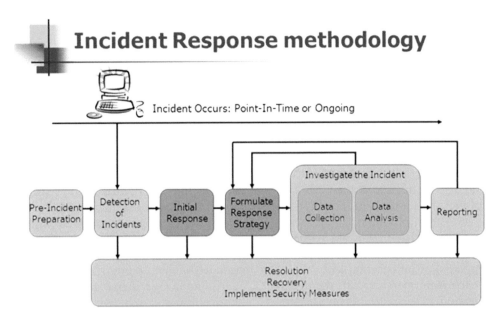

FIGURE 9.1   Showing incident response methodology.

Incident Response

1. It is the process of developing the strategy to address the occurrence of any kind of security breach in the system.
2. It consists of the formulation of security policies and goals, creation of the incident response team, analysis of different threat, and establishing the different method to detect any kind of breach (Zjalic, 2020).
3. Different governmental departments create an incident response plan, as shown in Figure 9.1, to complete goals such as
   a. To implement the strong security policies.
   b. To effectively monitor and analyze the network and system traffic.
   c. To ensure operational logs.
   d. To handle the incident in the way that decreases the damage and reduces the recovery time.
   e. To establish the process for extracting the information from the digital evidence in a forensic sound manner.

A digital forensic investigator by virtue of their skills and experiences helps the law enforcement agencies to investigate the cybercrimes.

Digital forensic investigators perform the following tasks:

- Evaluates the different damages of the security breach.
- Identifies and recovers the datathat have been required for the investigation.

- Extracts the digital information from digital evidence in a forensically sound manner.
- Ensures the proper handling of the digital evidence.
- Creates the reports and documents the whole investigation process to be presented in the court of law.
- Reconstructs any damaged storage devices and uncovers the information that can be hidden in the digital evidence.

Cybercrime investigators need to obtain the warrant from the concerned authorities to search the crime scene. The warrant should maintain all the digital devices that should be investigated. When dealing with the digital evidence related to the internet usage, the investigators must preserve the anonymity of the other users.

Code of ethics are the different principles that are stated to describe the expected behaviour of the investigator while handling the case at the crime scene (Hayes).

Computer forensic investigators should perform the investigations that are based on well-known standard procedures.

Computer forensic investigators perform the assigned tasks with high commitment and diligence.

Computer forensic investigators examine the digital evidence carefully within the scope of agreement.

The computer investigation team plays a major role in solving the case. The team is responsible for evaluating the crime scene for different digital pieces of evidence. Every team member of the investigation team should be assigned a specific task with the equal roles and responsibilities that let the investigation team analyze the incident easily.

There are a few guidelines to build the computer investigation team, as follows:

- To determine the person who has to respond first at an incident so that a proper internal computer investigation can be performed with the specific procedures.
- To organize the other team members and then give responsibility to each one of them.
- To a point of person as a technical head to lead the whole investigation procedure.
- The computer investigation team has to be as small as possible to maintain the confidentiality and avoid any kind of information leak.
- To provide each team member with the necessary authorization to complete their assigned tasks.

Computer or digital forensics is that branch of forensic science that basically deals with the criminal offences that have been performed using the different technical or digital devices such as computers, laptops, mobile phones, CDs, DVDs, USBs, iPods, etc. (Le-Khac, N.-A., & Choo).

To find and gather the appropriate digital evidence from the scene, the following people or the team may be involved:

- Attorney – helps in giving any kind of legal advice about how to carry the investigation.
- Photographer – photographs the crime scene and any kind of digital evidence that have been gathered.
- Incident responder – responsible for the measures that have been taken when an incident occurs; first person who is responsible for securing the incident and collecting any kind of digital evidence that is present at that crime scene.
- Decision maker – responsible for the authorization of the procedure during the whole investigation process.
- Incident analyst – analyzes is the incidents based on their occurrence.
- Evidence examiner – examines the digital evidence that have been acquired and sort those useful evidence.
- Evidence documenter – documents all the digital evidence present in the investigation process.
- Evidence manager – manages the evidence and has all the information about the digital evidence.
- Expert witness – offers the formal opinion as a testimony in the court of law.

In the field of computer or digital forensics, the digital evidence places an important role in tracking the perpetrator. Digital evidence that is tampered in any way in the forensic investigation process is not at all admissible in the court of law.

To conduct a computer or digital forensic investigation that is legally sound, it is necessary to employ skillful, experienced, licensed investigators (Kävrestad).

The computer forensic investigator implements the various tools and different techniques to retrieve and analyze the information from the digital evidence. However, these standalone procedures can affect the resultant evidence and the case outcomes. Thus, there is the specific need for the forensic unit to establish and follow the well-documented systematic process to investigate the crime scene that ensures the quality assurance.

Computer or digital forensics investigation can be done efficiently only when the forensic investigators follow the specific standard quality assurance procedures.

Some of the quality assurance practices are as follows:

- Digital forensic tools that are meant for the digital forensic examination process should undergo validity testing to check the accuracy of results.
- The final computer forensic reports must be technically reviewed by another forensic examiner prior to be presented in the court of law to ensure that the tools and techniques used in the process were sufficiently documented and should be in the forensically sound manner.

After obtaining the required permissions the investigators are ready to investigate the crime scene. The investigation phase includes various processes that need systematic execution to obtain better results.

The computer or digital forensic investigation is a process of collection of the wide variety of the processes that starts from the incident response to the analysis of the crime scene gathering the digital evidence for the analysis and then from documenting the whole investigation to reporting.

Every case is unique and needs a different method of approach, and there are a variety of tools that differ depending upon the platform, operating system, and type of target evidence.

Digital forensic tools can either be software or any hardware or commercial or open source or it can be designed for a specific purpose or with a broader functionality (Tamma et al. 2020).

It is better to consider the commercial tools to extract the information from the digital evidence in comparison to the open-source tools.

Using the digital forensic tools for a specific purpose will allow in-depth investigation.

No single tool is all inclusive; thus, it is recommended to have multiple tools on hand.

Computer Forensics Investigation Methodology

- First response refers to the first action that should be performed after occurrence of the incident.
- The term *first responder* means the person who first arrived at the crime scene and access the victim's computer system or any kind of digital evidence after the victim has reported that incident.
- A first responder can be a network administrator or any law enforcement officer or any computer investigator.
- Generally, a first responder is the person who comes from the forensics laboratory for the initial step in the investigation.
- If the incident occurs in any company or on individual computers, the victim first contacts the forensic laboratory for the cybercrime investigation.

Roles of First Responders

- The first responder is responsible for protecting integrating, collecting, and preserving the digital evidence obtained from the crime scene.
- First responders have the complete knowledge of the computer or digital forensics investigation. They preserve and store all the discovered digital evidence in a simple protected and forensically sound manner (Satpathy, S., & Mohanty).
- First responders are the people who investigate the crime scene in a forensically sound manner so that the obtained digital evidence can be acceptable or admissible in the court of law.
- The first responder plays a very crucial role in the computer or digital forensic process because they are the very first people who arrive at the crime scene for the initial step in the investigation.
- The investigation process starts after collecting all the digital evidence from the crime scene effectively and efficiently.

The main key roles or the responsibilities of the first responders are as follows:

- Identifying the crime scene – after arriving first at the crime scene, the first responder identifies the scope of the crime scene and then establishes the perimeter. They define the parameters by

including the area or the room, depending on the network digital evidence. After that, they start listing down all the digital evidence that is involved or presented at the incident from which the information can be collected.

- Protecting the crime scene – in any cybercrime case, a search warrant is mandatory for searching and seizing digital evidence; therefore, a first responder protects all the digital evidence and waits for the officer in charge to come to the crime scene.
- Preserving temporary and fragile evidence – in the case of any temporary or fragile evidence that can be damaged or disappear or altered, such as monitor or screen information or any running program, the first responder at the crime scene does not wait for the officer in charge to come, they can take the photographs of all the evidence and take the necessary steps towards it.
- Collecting complete information about the whole incident – for collecting the complete information about the whole investigation procedure, the first responder is responsible for conducting the preliminary interviews of all the suspects and the persons that have been present at the crime scene and ask the various questions about the incident that happened.
- Documenting all the findings – the first responder starts documenting all the information about the collected digital evidence to maintain the chain of custody document sheet.
- Packaging and transporting all the collected digital evidence – after collecting all the digital evidence from the crime scene, the first responder labels them and places them in the evidence storage bags, which protects the digital evidence from any kind of damage, sunlight, or high temperatures. These storage bags can be the Faraday bags that block the wireless signals so that the wireless devices cannot acquire the data or wipe the data from the digital evidence. Then the first responder transports all these packed storage bags to the forensics laboratory for their examination.
- Gather preliminary information at the crime scene – at the time of the cybercrime incident, securing the crime scene and surrounding area to avoid any tampering of the digital evidence is mandatory. Preliminary information at the crime scene provides the basics for the cybercrime investigation and helps in finding the information from the digital evidence easily if there is no third-party interference at the crime scene.

COMPUTER FORENSICS INVESTIGATION PROCESS

The computer or digital forensics process consists of the methodological approach for the investigation, collection, and analyzing of different digital evidence and managing the investigation process right from the time of reporting to its conclusion.

There has been the rapid increase in cybercrimes, including the theft of intellectual property to cyber terrorism along with litigations involving large organizations. This process has led to the development of various laws and different standards that define the different cybercrimes, various digital evidence, search and seizure methodology, recovery of the evidence, and the various investigation processes.

The cybercrime investigators should follow the different forensics investigation process that complies with local laws and established standards.

Digital evidence is very fragile in nature when present at the crime scene so proper and thorough forensic investigation methods that ensure the integrity and authentication of the evidence is mandatory to prove their admissibility in the court of law.

The computer forensics investigators should follow the repeatable and well-documented standard operating procedures, as in Figure 9.2, so that the findings of the

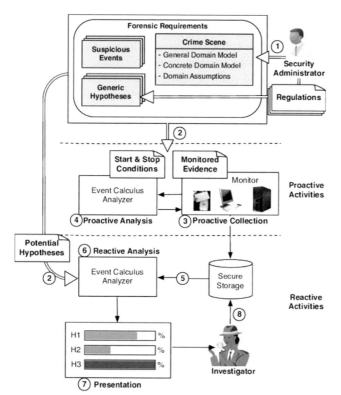

FIGURE 9.2 Showing the various stages of digital forensic investigation process.

investigation can be invalidated during cross examination in court.

PHASES IN COMPUTER/DIGITAL FORENSIC INVESTIGATION PROCESS

There are three phases involved in the computer or the digital forensics investigation process:

1. Pre-investigation phase – this is the phase that includes all the tasks that have been performed prior to the commencement of the actual investigation that takes place. It basically involves the setting of the computer forensics lab building, the computer forensics workstation toolkit, and the whole investigation team getting approval from the concerned authority, etc.
2. Investigation phase – this phase is considered the main phase in the computer or the digital forensics investigation. It consists of the acquisition preservation and the analysis of the digital evidence data to identify the actual source of the crime and the main culprit. This phase also involves the implementation of the technical knowledge to find the evidence, examine the document, and preserve the information for the evidence. A computer forensics expert performs all these tasks to ensure the authentication and the integrity of the evidence (Johansen).
3. Post-investigation phase – this is the last phase that basically involves the reporting and documentation of all the actions undertaken. Every jurisdiction has set the standard operating procedures for reporting the findings and the evidence and the report should comply with all these standard operating procedures as well as it should be admissible in the court of law.

A framework for forensic investigation process is described in Figure 9.3.

Digital forensics investigation methodology:

1. First response at the scene
2. Search and seizure of the digital evidence
3. Collect the evidence
4. Secure the digital evidence
5. Data acquisition from the digital evidence
6. Data analysis
7. Evidence assessment
8. Documentation and reporting
9. Testify as an expert witness

The digital forensics investigation process is the collection of a wide variety of the processes that starts from

Computer Forensic Investigation Process model

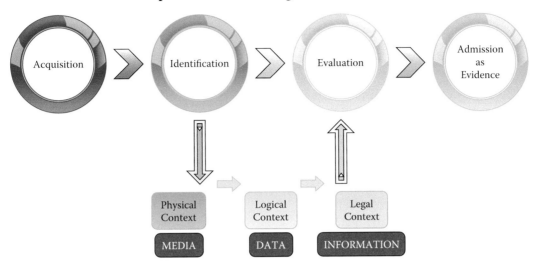

FIGURE 9.3 Showing the computer forensic investigation process.

basically the incident response to the analysis of the crime scene and then the collection of the digital evidence to its analysis and then from the documentation to reporting each step in the process is equally important for acceptance of the digital evidence in the court of law.

Examination or the Investigation Goals:

The cybercrime investigators must have a clear idea about the goals of the examination prior to conducting the investigation at the scene.

Investigators should have the in-depth technical knowledge and understanding about the inner workings of what type of evidence is being examined.

Investigators should have the capability to take the systematic approach and methods to examine the digital evidence based on the request made, for example by an attorney.

Hypothesis or the formulation criteria:

The cybercrime investigators should have the consideration and established the form of reasoning that assist to form the hypothesis.

TOOL SELECTION

Digital forensics tools can be software or hardware, commercial or open source, or they can be designed for the specific purposes.

It is better to have the consideration of the commercial tools that have a greater market value than the open-source tools.

Using the commercial tools designed for the specific purposes will allow the in-depth investigation to take place.

Since no single tool is all inclusive, thus it is recommended to have the multiple tools in hand.

Forensic tools must undergo the validation process prior to using it at the scene or for casework.

Results Review and Their Evaluation

Review the results from the different points of view and then communicate the findings to the client with the realistic expectations.

Conclusion and the Opinion Formulation

The conclusion is judgment based on the various facts.

Checklist to prepare for the computer or digital forensics investigation:

1. Do not turn off the computer off or on or run any programs or attempt to access data on the computer or the mobile phones that have been present at the crime scene. An expert should have the appropriate tools, be it software/hardware, and have knowledge to data overwriting and damage from static electricity.
2. Secure any relevant media including the hard drives of the cell phones, DVDs, USB drives, etc.
3. Wheather a person automatically communicates a section and recycling restrictions that may apply to any relevant media.

4. Form the preliminary assessment of the crime scene and then identify the type of data that is sought or information that can be relevant to the case.

5. Once the machine or the digital evidence have been secured, then obtain the information from that evidence and the peripherals and turn off the network to which it is connected.

6. Obtain the passwords to access the encrypted or the password-protected files or the systems.

7. Compile a list of names, mobile numbers, and the email addresses or any other information to whom the subject might have communicated.

8. If the computer has been accessed before the forensic expert is able to secure the mirror image, note down the user who has accessed it, what files they have accessed, and when they have accessed those files. If possible, try to find out why the computer has been accessed.

9. Maintain the chain of custody for each digital evidence.

10. Create a list of various key words or any phrases to use when there will be a need to search for the relevant data.

First response by the Digital Forensics laboratory staff:

Securing and evaluating the electronic evidence at the crime scene:

This involves the protection of the crime scene from any type of unauthorized access and keeps the digital evidence away from any kind of damage or harm. It consists of:

- search warrant for the search of the crime scene and seizure of the digital evidence
- planning the search and seizure
- conducting the initial search at the crime scene

Conducting preliminary interviews at the crime scene:

This involves these cybercrime investigators to identify all the people or the subjects who are present at the crime scene along with their position at the time of entry and the exit and the reason for being at the crime scene. It consists of:

- asking various questions
- checking the consent issues
- witnessing the signatures and initiatives taken and present at the crime scene

DATA COLLECTION FROM MOBILE PHONES

Mobile phone technology is basically a complicated technology. Innovation in the technology of mobile phones makes forensics of mobile devices more complex and complicated. A major contributor that increases complexity of the forensics of mobile devices is the variety of mobile manufacturers on the market with each having proprietary software and hardware formats and standards. Presently, mobile devices are used by millions of people. The advancements in the technology not only focus on features, but also design and size, which attract the common public. Advanced features of mobiles have not only made it convenient in use for the common public, but on other hand, criminals use it for their illicit purposes. Therefore, this device has become a part of investigation to reach the miscreants.

The new era of smart devices has evolved in the last few years that has facilitated the public in fulfilling their need with fast and efficient communication devices. These devices in the hands of antisocial activists can cause great harm to the public. Due to a wide range of smartphones available on the market, an ultimate forensics investigation framework is very difficult to reach. This paper outlines a review of some of the previously used mobile forensics investigation models and compares the NIST guidelines of cell phone forensics with the other SOPs and available models. Also, important stages of the data acquisition as well as for further investigation are identified and used in the new unified mobile devices forensics investigation model.

Handling Evidence and Securing the Evidence

All the evidence should be handled according to the strategy mentioned at the start of the investigation. A chain of custody forms should be maintained to ensure the integrity of the evidence. An important step is to isolate the device from the network. Also, the need of any traditional forensics process should be kept in consideration. Isolation of the crime scene from the people not required at the crime scene because the integrity of the evidence can be ensured if there is no unauthorized access at the crime scene.

The mobile phone forensic is broken into three main categories:

1. **Seizure**
2. **Acquisition**
3. **Examination**

Forensic examiners face some challenges while seizing the mobile device at the place of the crime scene as evidence.

At the crime scene, if the mobile device found is switched off, the examiner should place the device to automatically power on. Faraday bags are specifically designed to isolate the phone from the network. If the phone is found switched on, switching it off has a lot of concern attached to it. If the phone is locked by a PIN or password or encrypted, the examiners will be required to bypass the lock or determine the PIN to access the device. Mobile phone are networked devices and can send and receive data through different sources, such as telecommunication system, Wi-Fi access points, and Bluetooth.

So, if the phone is in a running state, a criminal can erase the data stored on the phone by executing a remote wipe command. When a phone is switched on, it should be placed in a Faraday bag.

If possible, prior to placing the mobile device in the Faraday bag, disconnect it from the network to protect the evidence by enabling the flight mode and disabling all network connections i.e. Wi-Fi, GPS, hotspot, and so on. This will also preserve the battery, which will drain while in a Faraday bag and protect against any leak in the Faraday bag.

Once the mobile device is seized properly, the examiner may need several forensic tools to acquire and analyze data stored on the phone.

Mobile data collection is a method of compiling qualitative and quantitative information with the help of a mobile device (e.g. mobile phone, tablet, etc.). This approach has been proven to increase the speed and accuracy of data collection, service delivery effectiveness, and program staff performance.

DOCUMENTATION

The phase of documentation is interconnected with all the other devices as the documentation is to be done at all the stages of the investigation. Chain of custody is an important document to maintain from starting the investigation till the representation of the evidence in court. Further, the whole crime scene is to be documented. The documentation should include the following:

- Legal authority letter.
- Chain of custody.
- Photographs and manual documents of the visible as well as digital evidence.
- Information about the mobile device, if obtained from the owner.
- All the carried-out investigation should be documented as if to be handed over to any other examiner.
- Formulated strategy to carry out the investigation.
- Report of the findings.

REVIEW

The final phase is the review phase. This phase is specifically for the investigator. The review phase gives the examiner an opportunity to improve their expertise as well as analytical skills. All the steps followed before are analyzed in this phase and a peer review of the investigation is carried out. This results in efficient investigation and facilitates finding the criminals.

DATA COLLECTION FROM SOLID STATE DRIVE (SSD) IN DIGITAL FORENSICS

Evidence of vital importance can be located on digital exhibits such as USB drives, external hard disks, and other devices found at the crime scene. Digital forensic imaging of evidence offers not only all active files and folders, but also deleted or concealed data from the storage device, and is an essential aspect of digital forensic analysis. Data from digital exhibits can be acquired using a variety of open-source and private forensic techniques. However, the exhibit may be wiped, erased, or overwritten several times, or data may be permanently deleted. As a result, a key concern about the type and amount of data that might be retrieved arises (Raychaudhuri, 2019). Digital evidence integrity must be accessible, displayed, and guaranteed so that it can be accounted for in a court of law. Solid-state drives (SSDs) are one of the options for storing data files. Because of three technology enhancements, including the Training Records Information Management (TRIM) feature, garbage background collection, and wear levelling, which can automatically erase data files that have been deleted, facts and problems were discovered on the SSD (Iqbal & Soewito, 2020).

SSD Features: The TRIM feature, garbage background collection (GBC), and wear levelling are three updated technologies on SSDs that can erase data files that have been destroyed; however, they cause substantial challenges for forensic investigators (Nisbet & Jacob, 2019; Aldaej et al., 2017). As a result, the number of cases requiring digital forensic competence is expected to rise in the future (Van Houdt, 2013). In just a few minutes, use of the TRIM functionality, garbage background collection, and wear levelling on the SSD to clean files have been permanently removed from that sector (Iqbal & Soewito, 2020).

METHODS

Static forensics and active forensics are the two methodologies used in digital forensics. Static forensics uses traditional processes and approaches to conduct the forensic process, in which electronic evidence is processed in a bit-by-bit image. The forensic process takes place on a computer that isn't turned on or functioning (off). Live forensics, on the other hand, uses analytical processes in which electronic evidence can be studied directly in the state of digital equipment in living situations, although it does not produce useful results (Rafique & Khan, 2013). Digital forensics must make use of forensic technologies, which forensic investigators utilize to seek for digital evidence by analyzing and extracting data from digital evidence (Rasjid et al., 2017).

Based on the aforementioned issues and challenges, the question is how to retrieve digital evidence such as files on SSDs with TRIM enabled and deep freeze configurations that could be utilized for digital crimes. We proposed employing static forensic methods to process a copy of SSD (imaging of SSD) using two programmes: FTK Imager and DD. Association of Chief Police Officers (ACPO) framework and digital forensics should analyze using four tools: FTK, Autopsy, OSForensics, and Photorec to produce the following contributions and novelties in digital forensics:

- The imaging process of SSD with TRIM feature enabled and deep freeze configuration using two forensic tools, namely FTK Imager and DD, which can be used as references.
- The scenario testing should be done three times to see how many files could be recovered on an SSD with the TRIM feature activated and deep freeze setup.
- As a result of the implementation, Autopsy and Photorec were able to successfully recover and extract files from three test cases. We should use in SSD data collection also.

THE COPYING PROCESS (IMAGING OF SSD)

Imaging of SSD includes static forensic methods, which is technique of forensic imaging (copying data byte by byte) to be carried out while the computer is turned off. All of the requirements for forensic analysis are met in static forensics by employing various types of external devices, such as USBs. A static forensic tool searches for digital evidence on storage media (Rafique & Khan, 2013). Static forensics is concerned with checking duplicate copies of drives in order to recover data such as deleted files, web browsing history, network connections, and user login history, among other things (Albanna & Riadi, 2017). The imaging of a solid-state drive (SSD) utilizes two forensic tools: FTK Imager and DD. Figure 9.4 shows the steps in the copy (SSD imaging) process.

ANALYSIS AFTER IMAGING OF SSD

The process of digital forensics analysis begins with the study and analysis of the resulting image file of SSD

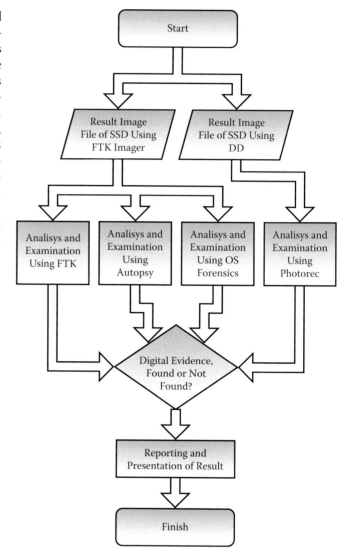

FIGURE 9.4 Static method for imaging of SSD.

utilizing FTK Imager employing FTK, Autopsy, and OSForensics. Employing Photorec, the result image file of SSD using DD will be examined and analyzed (Iqbal & Soewito, 2020).

STEPS OF IMPLEMENTATION

The test scenario will be implemented three times in total. Turning on the computer simulation that has a SSD is the first step in the **first test scenario**. The next step is to verify that the TRIM feature is active. The third step entails putting it in a deep freezer. The fourth step is to copy data such as document files, images files, audio files, and videos files from the created flashdisk to the SSD. The simulation computer should be turned off for step five. Step six is to connect a 180 GB SSD to an examiner PC with a 1 TB HDD. The seventh step is to perform write blocking on the examiner computer to prevent data from being exchanged. The eighth stage entails using two tools, FTK Imager and DD, to perform process imaging on the SSD. Step nine involves analyzing and examining the resulting file image using four different tools: FTK, Autopsy, OSForensics, and Photorec, as well as validating digital evidence discovered using the hashing technique. The final stage is to present and report on the digital evidence that has been successfully recovered and extracted (Marupudi, 2017).

Because the TRIM feature and deep freeze configuration were checked in the first test scenario, there is no need to check them in the **second and third test** cases. So, in the second and third test scenarios, the first step is to turn on the computer simulation, which contains a 180 GB SSD. The second step is to copy data such as document files, photographs, audio files, and video files from the 16 GB flash-disk to the 180 GB SSD. The simulation computer must be turned off in the third phase. Step four is to connect a 180 GB SSD to an examiner PC with a 1 TB HDD. The fifth step is to perform write blocking on the examiner computer to prevent data from being exchanged. The sixth phase entails using two tools, FTK Imager and DD, to perform process imaging on the SSD. Step seven involves analyzing and examining the output file image with four tools: FTK, Autopsy, OSForensics, and Photorec, as well as validating digital evidence discovered through the hashing approach. Reporting and presenting digital evidence that has been effectively retrieved and extracted is the final stage.

COMPLETION OF DATA EXTRACTION FROM SSD

After implementation Photorec and Autopsy data can be analyzed. Photorec takes less time than Autopsy to complete an analysis. The Photorec analysis takes 1–2 hours. However, Autopsy takes 6–10 hours to complete (Dwivedi, 2019). From the first to the third test scenario, the percentage of success rate for data recovery and extraction has reduced. It can be concluded that the more times a computer that has been configured for a deep freeze is shut down or restarted, the less likely the files will be retrieved or the lower the percentage that can be obtained.

REFERENCES

Albanna, F., & Riadi, I. (2017). Forensic Analysis of Frozen Hard Drive Using Static Forensics Method. *International Journal of Computer Science and Information Security (IJCSIS), 15*(1), 132–138.

Aldaej, A., Ahamad, M. G., & Uddin, M. Y. (2017, March). Solid state drive data recovery in open source environment. In *2017 2nd International Conference on Anti-Cyber Crimes (ICACC)* (pp. 228–231). IEEE.

Dwivedi, A. Singh C, Mishra A, Mishra V. (2019). "Comparative analysis of data mining in criminal and fraud detection," *International Journal* of *Psychosocial Rehabilitation*, 2020, doi: 10.37200/IJPR/V24I6/PR260137

Gogolin, G. (2021). Digital Forensics Explained Second Edition.

Hassan, N. A. Digital Forensics Basics: A Practical Guide Using Windows OS.A press; 2019 Feb 25.

Hayes, D. (2020). Practical Guide to Digital Forensics Investigations.

Iqbal, M., & Soewito, B. (2020). Digital Forensics on Solid State Drive (SSD) with TRIM Feature Enabled and Deep Freeze Configuration Using Static Forensic Methods and ACPO Framework. *International Journal of Computer Science and Information Security (IJCSIS), 18*(11), 322–332.

Johansen, G. Digital Forensics and Incident Response,Incident response techniques and procedures to respond to modern cyber threats, 2nd Edition.

Kävrestad, J., Fundamentals of Digital Forensics,Theory, Methods, and Real-Life Applications.

Le-Khac, N.-A., & Choo, K.-K. R., Cyber and Digital Forensic Investigations, A Law Enforcement Practitioner's Perspective.

Marupudi, S. S. R. (2017). Solid State Drive: New Challenge for Forensic Investigation.

Nisbet, A., & Jacob, R. (2019, August). TRIM, Wear Levelling and Garbage Collection on Solid State Drives: A Prediction Model for Forensic Investigators. In *2019 18th IEEE International Conference On Trust, Security And Privacy In Computing And Communications/13th IEEE International Conference On Big Data Science And Engineering (TrustCom/BigDataSE)* (pp. 419–426). IEEE.

Powell, A., & Haynes, C. Social media data in digital forensics investigations. In *Digital Forensic Education* (pp. 281–303). Cham: Springer, 2020.

Raychaudhuri, K. (2019). A Comparative Study of Analysis and Extraction of Digital Forensic Evidences from exhibits using Disk Forensic Tools. *International Journal of Cyber-Security and Digital Forensics, 8*(3), 194–206.

Rafique, M., & Khan, M. N. A. (2013). Exploring Static and Live Digital forensics: Methods, Practices and Tools. *International Journal of Scientific & Engineering Research, 4*(10), 1048–1056.

Rasjid, Z. E., Soewito, B., Witjaksono, G., & Abdurachman, E. (2017). A Review of Collisions in Cryptographic Hash Function used in Digital

Forensic Tools. *Procedia computer science, 116,* 381–392.

Satpathy, S., & Mohanty, S. N. (Eds.). (2020). Big Data Analytics and Computing for Digital Forensic Investigations (1st ed.). CRC Press. https://doi.org/10.1201/9781003024743

Tamma, R., Skulkin, O., Mahalik, H., & Bommisetty, S. (2020). *Practical Mobile Forensics: Forensically investigate and analyze iOS, Android, and Windows 10 devices.* Packt Publishing Ltd.

Van Houdt, B. (2013). Performance of Garbage Collection Algorithms for Flash-based Solid State Drives with Hot/cold Data. *Performance Evaluation, 70*(10), 692–703.

Zjalic, J. (2020). *Digital Audio Forensics Fundamentals: From Capture to Courtroom.* Focal Press.

CHAPTER 10

Forensic Entomology: Overview and Application Considerations

Jason Byrd, Lerah Sutton, and Adrienne Brundage

Maples Center for Forensic Medicine University of Florida Gainesville, Florida, USA

CONTENTS

HISTORY AND CURRENT STATUS OF FORENSIC ENTOMOLOGY

Historical Association of Flies and Medicolegal Death Investigations

The relationship between flies and death is not a new concept. Though there are myriad examples throughout history demonstrating the association flies and death in both a medicolegal and purely observational context, a few of the earliest landmark applications will be explored here. As early as the second millennium B.C. in what is considered the first encyclopedia ever written, flies – specifically the "green and blue flies" (*Diptera: calliphoridae*) – were documented to associated with death (Poebel, 1936). However, it was not until several millennia later that the first documented medicolegal application of entomology occurred. In 13th century China (some translations listing the year as 1235 A.D. and others listing it as 1247 A.D.), the investigator Sung Tz'u detailed the homicide by sickle of a villager in a rice field. In an effort to identify the murderer, Tz'u requested all villagers lay their sickles down in front of them, hypothesizing that flies would be attracted to the sickle used in the commission of the crime due to the residual bits of blood and tissue on the blade. When the flies indeed behaved as Tz'u expected they would, the suspect confessed to his crime (Tz'u & McKnight, 1981; Benecke, 2001).

In 1668, the Italian scientist Francesco Redi set out to disprove the previously widely accepted theory of

DOI: 10.4324/9781003129554-10

spontaneous generation. Prior to his experiment, the relationship between flies and maggots – then often referred to as "worms" – was not well understood. Redi designed a simple experiment utilizing three jars of rotting meat with a series of barriers between the meat and the flies. The first contained rotting meat with no physical barrier between the flies and the meat, thus allowing unrestricted access to the meat. The second contained rotting meat but had a gauze-type barrier that allowed the smells of decomposition to reach the flies but prevented the flies from making physical contact with the meat. The third contained rotting meat with an air-tight barrier that prevented both olfactory and physical contact with the meat. In the first container, flies laid their eggs directly on the rotting meat, thus producing maggots. In the second container, the flies were still attracted to the smell of the rotting meat but due to the gauze-barrier they were unable to make contact with the meat, so they laid their eggs on the gauze instead. In the third container, no insect activity was observed. Thus, the theory of spontaneous generation of maggots from the decomposition process of rotting meat was disproved (Redi et al., 1675; Byrd & Sutton, 2020).

Western society did not begin to utilize forensic entomology as it is known today until 1850 when the death of an infant near Paris, France, was investigated by pathologist Dr. Bergeret d'Arbois. The mummified body of an infant was discovered within the plastered wall of a home under renovation. Investigation into the development timeline of insect evidence associated with the remains – a pupal casing of *Musca carnaria* (Linnaeus) – was used to determine that the colonization of the body occurred many years earlier, prior to the current tenants occupying the home (Bergeret d'Arbois, 1855).

FIGURE 10.1   Jean Pierre Mégnin was a French Army veterinarian and entomologist. In 1879, he was elected president of the Société Entomologique de France and published *La faune des cadavres application de l'entomologie à la médecine légale in 1894*. (Photo credit: Public Domain).

The Relationship Between Taxonomy, Ecology, and Insect Succession

Although numerous medicolegal death investigations were aided by the use of entomological evidence, it was not until the late 1800s that forensic entomology began to gain a solid foundation. Scientific exploration into insect taxonomy and ecology provided the basis upon which all modern forensic entomology has been built. One of the most critical components of the advancement of forensic entomology has been the study of insect succession within the context of decomposition ecology. One of the first individuals to specifically recognize and document the process of insect succession and how species changed throughout the decomposition process was Pierre Megnin. In his 1894 publication, he explained the concept of insect succession as a predictable wave of carrion-feeding insects unique to various stages of decomposition that can be used to determine a

timeline of death. Notably, he documented eight distinct waves of insects for terrestrial decomposition and two waves of insects for buried remains (Mégnin, 1894) (Figure 10.1).

Despite the general understanding that insects colonize remains in unique waves of succession, true application of forensic entomology to medicolegal death investigations requires the identification of individual species of insects associated with decomposing remains. One of the first and most important texts that perpetuated this field was *The Blowflies of North America*, published in 1948. This text detailed adult identification of calliphorid species in great detail, along with information on how to collect and preserve them for reference (Hall, 1948). This landmark text laid the groundwork for all future studies in forensic entomology relating to basic insect taxonomy – including the subsequent publication of morphological identification keys of various insect species (Whitworth, 2006; Marshall et al., 2011; Jewiss-Gaines et al., 2012).

Once species identification has been established, then the ecological impact of succession within the decomposition process can be studied. Jerry Payne pioneered research into the use of insect succession for postmortem interval estimation beginning in the mid-1960s. Specifically, he studied the decomposition process of pig carcasses and how the presence or absence of certain species of insects could be linked to the time of death. His work was uniquely applicable to forensic casework as he also catalogued over 500 individual species of insects that colonize decomposing remains (Payne, 1965; Payne et al., 1968).

Casework Applications

The ultimate goal of the application of forensic entomology to medicolegal casework is generally to aid in the estimation of the post-mortem interval, most typically through determination of the minimum time since colonization. This requires a comprehensive understanding of insect identification, succession, and rates of development. While morphological identification through the use of dichotomous keys has been frequently utilized as the standard of identification over the last several decades of forensic entomology casework, it is not always a viable option. In many cases, morphological identification may not be possible due to either degradation of the specimen itself (potentially as a result of improper collection and/or preservation) or absence of morphological keys for a particular species/life stage in question. As a result, current research efforts have been focused on molecular identification of insects that yield a much greater accuracy of species identification as compared to morphological identification. The first such study was published in 1994 on three of the more common blowfly species in North America – *Phormia regina* (Meigen), *Phaenicia (=Lucilia) sericata* (Meigen), and *Lucilia illustris* (Meigen), which led to the continuation and increased frequency of molecular studies for insect identification and application to forensic casework (Sperling et al., 1994) (Figure 10.2).

FACTORS AFFECTING INSECT COLONIZATION

General Effects of Differing Environments

When remains begin to decompose, they release chemical signals that are attractive to insects, including putrescine, cadaverine, and methyl mercaptan (Cammack et al., 2015; Tabor et al., 2005). The discovery and subsequent colonization of decomposing remains can occur as quickly as a few minutes after death and insect colonization is often responsible for the majority of soft tissue loss in

FIGURE 10.2 Many species of fly larvae are visually similar in the larval stage, which makes conclusive species identification based on their morphology difficult. (Photo credit: Jason Byrd).

decomposition cases (Early & Goff, 1986; Kreitlow, 2010). However, there are many factors which can prevent, inhibit, or slow, the initial colonization of insects on decomposing remains. These factors may include mechanical barriers, seasonal/environmental differences, urban vs. rural environments, aquatic environments, and many others – all of which have the potential to alter both the species present on and the pattern of insect succession of the remains (Anderson, 2020).

Mechanical Barriers

One of the most common and obvious factors that affects the ability of insects to colonize remains is that of mechanical barriers. Many cases that entomologists are involved in are homicide investigations which are frequently associated with attempts to hide or conceal the remains. Whether as a result of direct (e.g. wrapping a body in a sheet or tarp) or indirect (e.g. keeping a body inside a house with tightly sealed windows or doors or burial of remains), any mechanical barriers between the remains themselves and the environment in which insects would be able to access them will change the colonization pattern. For the purposes of understanding the effects of mechanical barriers on insect colonization patterns, direct barriers are defined as intentional efforts to conceal remains and prevent insect colonization and indirect barriers are defined as unintentional effort that still result in prevention of inset colonization of remains.

Direct barriers associated with wrapping a body can be in the form of either natural fibers (e.g. cotton and silk), synthetic fibers (e.g. polyester and nylon), and plastics. The composition of the wrapping material affects the ability of insects to colonize the remains as natural fibers may provide less of a barrier than synthetic fibers or plastics due to the weave of the material. Newly hatched larvae may have greater success in permeating the weave of natural fibers than synthetic fibers. Tightly wrapped, sealed, and unbroken plastics typically present an impenetrable barrier for insect colonization unless oviposition occurred prior to wrapping or concealment of the remains in this fashion. Indirect barriers associated with concealing a body from discovery may include storing of the body in a location unlikely to be seen by other individuals such as inside buildings, larger freezers, or clandestine graves. Although less obvious than the concept of tight wrapping in direct barriers, indirect barriers may still inhibit or delay insects from being able to access remains. In cases such as these, it is often difficult for an entomologist to determine the length of the delay caused by direct or indirect barriers which subsequently affects the ability to accurately estimate time since death based on time since colonization. As such, it is crucial for investigators to document the presence of any mechanical barriers and convey that information to an entomologist so it may be taken into consideration within the context of a minimum post-mortem interval estimation (Anderson, 2020).

Seasonal and Environmental Differences

Temperature plays a critical role in both insect development and the decomposition process in general. As such, seasonal and temperature differences must be documented and conveyed to an entomologist for inclusion in any post-mortem interval estimation. Various insect species are active at different times throughout the year, so the season(s) in which decomposition occurred may alter the species present on the remains. Some insect species are more cold-tolerant than others, so the season in which decomposition occurred and the threshold temperatures for development of the insect species present play an important role in post-mortem interval estimation (Donovan et al., 2006). For the decomposition process in general, the seasons in which the process begins plays a critical role in the rate at which decomposition occurs. As such, a universal model assessing decomposition rates is not realistic. Specifically, decomposition that begins in near-freezing or freezing temperatures and then extends into warmer months (i.e. Winter into Spring) will experience a slower rate of decomposition in the early phases followed by a more rapid acceleration as environmental temperatures increase. Decomposition occurring in steadily warm temperatures (i.e. spring, summer, and fall) will occur as a steadier rate. Decomposition that begins in warmer temperatures but the extends into colder temperatures (i.e. fall into winter) will experience rapid decomposition but will often result in incomplete or dramatically slowed tissue loss in the later stages of decomposition (Sutton, 2017).

Water as a different type of barrier to insect colonization than mechanical barriers as differing species of insects will colonize remains submerged in water. Terrestrial insects (e.g. blowflies, beetles, etc.) cannot penetrate an aquatic barrier; thus, submerged remains will not be colonized by terrestrial insect species. However, there are aquatic insect species that will utilize the body as an ephemeral ecological resource within their environment. Some insect species within these aquatic environments will feed on tissues of the body (i.e. using it as a food resource), whereas others will use the body as a habitat. These aquatic insect species can then be utilized to provide submergence interval estimations which can be correlated to post-mortem interval estimations (Wallace & Merritt, 2020).

Lighting Patterns

The activity level of flies is typically regulated by lighting conditions. The majority of blowfly species require both light and warmth to oviposit or larviposit, but there are some species of blowflies that are willing to enter into darker or colder conditions to do so (Greenberg, 1990). Thus, documentation of the availability of both light and warmth is critical information for an entomological assessment. This includes external conditions of sun vs. shade and internal conditions such as artificial lighting. The diurnality of most species of flies generally prevents nocturnal oviposition/larviposition, but in some urban environments where there is adequate artificial light and temperature control, this behavioral tendency can be overcome, thus leading to nocturnal oviposition/larviposition (Stamper et al., 2009; George et al., 2014).

ENTOMOLOGICAL EVIDENCE COLLECTION, ANALYSIS, AND REPORT WRITING

Collection

Proper collection and preservation of entomological evidence is critical in order to ensure the success of subsequent analysis. Equally important is appropriate and thorough documentation of the crime scene. An attempt to document and collect insect evidence directly from a crime scene should always be made as that will provide the entomologist the most representative sample of entomological evidence present at the scene. Paramount to this is documentation and collection of a representative sample of all insects present. That is, documenting all relevant environmental conditions that may affect the colonization and development of insects on the scene – temperature being the most critical – and documentation and collection of all areas of insect colonization of both the body and the scene itself. Some insect species will wander away from the remains after the feeding stage of their life cycle is complete, so investigation on scene to search for insects that may have left the body will further aid in providing a complete collection of all insects relevant to the scene and investigation. This includes the search for pupal casings which can demonstrate additional life cycles that the insects on scene may have completed, thus aiding in a more accurate estimation of the minimum post-mortem interval.

While collection from and documentation of the crime scene itself is best practice for entomological evidence assessment, in some cases collection from the scene is not possible and instead must be conducted at autopsy. Even if a collection is able to be made from the crime scene, ever effort to perform a collection at autopsy should be made as well. Importantly, collection from a crime scene is limited to collection of externally accessible insects in order to prevent disturbance of the remains themselves until an autopsy can be conducted. Performing a collection at autopsy may provide access to additional areas of colonization that were otherwise inaccessible at the crime scene, thus adding to the representative sample collection for entomological analysis (Figure 10.3).

There are numerous guides published regarding proper collection crime scene evidence collection techniques and methods including a comprehensive chapter by Sanford et al., in Byrd & Tomberlin's (2020) *Forensic Entomology: The Utility of Arthropods in Legal Investigations,* which contains step-by-step instructions on the proper methods for evidence collection, including numerous photographic examples (Sanford et al., 2020). The aforementioned chapter is the first entomological evidence collection protocol that has been reviewed and approved by the American Board of Forensic Entomology, thus making it the standard by which all entomology collection should occur; however, it was not the first publication attempting to standardize collection protocols. Attempts to standardize entomological collection procedures have been in progress for several decades, with the first suggested protocol for the collection and preservation of insect evidence published in the early 1980s (Lord & Burger, 1983). The European Association of Forensic Entomology developed a protocol for best practice in forensic entomology in general – which included elements of collection and documentation – that was published in 2007. It also included definitions of key terms and methods used for estimation of the minimum post-mortem interval based on entomological evidence (Amendt et al., 2007). As such, detailed explanations of collection and documentation methods beyond what have already been addressed will not be explored in this chapter as we instead refer the reader to investigate the published and approved standards by the EAFE and ABFE.

Analysis

Forensic entomology can be utilized for numerous applications within a medicolegal investigation, but the most common question asked of entomologists by law enforcement is how insects and entomological evidence can be used to assist in a time of death determination. Most entomologists rely on the concept of time since colonization (TOC) in order to assist in answering this question (Catts, 1990). It is important to understand that forensic entomologists cannot and should not attempt to determine time since death or a post-mortem interval. Rather, the most appropriate determination they can seek to make is a *minimum* post-mortem interval (mPMI). There are numerous limitations associated with entomological evidence as it relates to estimation of the mPMI that will be explored in greater detail in a subsequent section (Nuorteva, 1977; Erzinclioglu, 1983; Smeeton et al., 1984; Anderson & VanLaerhoven, 1996; Smith, 1986; Catts & Goff, 1992; Dillon & Anderson, 1997; Wells & LaMotte, 2001; Capobasso et al., 2005). Despite these limitations in application, there is still much that can be gleaned from entomological evidence analysis within a medicolegal death investigation. Two primary methods of analysis are used to aid in determination of the mPMI: insect succession methods and thermal accumulation methods. These methods may be used separately or together to better aid in mPMI estimation but the determination of which method to use depends on the availability of specific types of evidence and associated data (Goff, 1993; Wells & LaMotte, 2020).

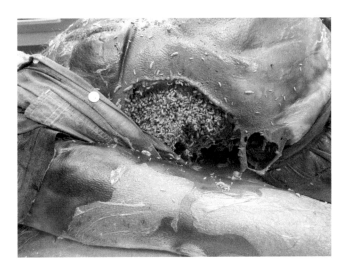

FIGURE 10.3 When collecting entomological evidence for forensic analysis, is it important to collected a representative sample of the insects that are present. Different body shapes, sizes, and colors can indicate different species. (Photo credit: Lerah Sutton).

Insect Succession Methods

The simple presence or absence of particular insects within various stages of decomposition can – in some cases – help entomologists and forensic investigators determine a basic time since death estimation. Many publications throughout the history and application of forensic entomology to medicolegal death investigations suggest that each stage of decomposition is associated with a distinct set of insect species (Mégnin, 1894; Schoenly, 1992; Goff, 1993; Goff, 2010; Anderson, 2010). However, some research suggests this method is unreliable and may not be of as much value to a forensic investigation as other methods of analysis (Schoenly & Reid, 1987; Moura et al., 2005). Particularly, it is not an especially useful method for estimation of the mPMI in the early stages of decomposition (i.e. days vs weeks/ months) and is instead better applied to cases with a more extended time since death or a more advanced stage of decomposition (Payne, 1965; Smith, 1986; Goff, 1993). Comparisons of presence or absence of certain expected species with the observed stage of decomposition may provide valuable information to investigators. If a body is in a particular stage of decomposition, but the insect assemblage is inconsistent with the degree of decomposition observed, this could provide support for the idea that the body was subject to conditions that inhibited insect colonization at the time of death. For example, if a body is in a more advanced state of decomposition, but only insect oviposition is observed, this could indicate that something interfered with or interrupted the expected pattern of colonization (smith, 1986). While insect succession can be a valuable tool to supplement a time of death estimation, caution should be exercised when using it in the absence of other methods for an mPMI estimation. Particular attention should be paid to the context and comparison of the species of insects observed and their correlation to the observed state of decomposition of the remains (Wells & LaMotte, 2020).

Temperature-Dependent Development Methods

The most accurate and reliable method to-date for determining mPMI using insects is using development data to correlate the age of an insect with the time of colonization of decomposing remains. This is accomplished through the use of development data of the observed insect species and correlating the size and life stage of said insects with the TOC (Greenberg, 1990; Catts & Goff, 1992). Because insect development is a temperature-dependent process, much of this information relies on obtaining accurate temperature data from the crime scene and/or the location where the decomposition occurred. That is, insects develop faster in warmer climates and slower in colder climates. Thus, climate- and geographic-

region specific development data is critical for appropriate application to an mPMI estimation (Byrd & Sutton, 2020). The mechanism used to accomplish this method of analysis is based on the accumulated degree-day model (Briere et al., 1999; Worner, 2008). This method helps to standardize temperature against time which helps to correlate the complex process of thermally dependent insect development to an investigatively relevant time since death. More simply put, although insect development data may be expressed in terms of "degree-hours or degree-days" that does not necessarily directly correlate to numbers of hours or days within a post-mortem interval. Rather, it provides the baseline for a minimum amount of time that it would have taken the insects observed on and collected from the decomposing remains to reach their particular stage of development at the time of analysis (Greenberg, 1990; Catts & Goff, 1992). However, it is important to remember – and to exercise caution when expressing these results within an entomological report – that there are many factors which could inhibit insect colonization at the time of death which would, in turn, delay the time of colonization as it relates to the time of death (Byrd & Sutton, 2020).

Report Writing

Once insect evidence has been collected and analyzed, it falls to the forensic entomologist to detail their actions and findings in a scientific report that will be submitted to the case investigators and likely also to a court of law. There are certain considerations that must be made when choosing an entomologist to work with and what constitutes a high-quality and reliable forensic entomology report. The specific methods an entomologist may choose to use will differ on the type of analysis being requested, the availability of reference data for the specie(s) in question, and the questions being asked by investigators. In any case, all entomology reports should include certain elements in order to be considered a comprehensive report. They should include a brief summary of the case itself – typically based on a police report provided to the entomologist that is supplemented with any on-scene observations they may have made if they travelled to the scene to do evidence collection themselves. This should also include case findings including what evidence was collected, what was situationally observed on scene, and other relevant information. Relevant findings often include environmental factors such as indoor vs. outdoor locations, sun vs. shade exposure, or others that may influence the colonization and development of insects. An explanation of how the insects were identified must be included along with the methodology used to do so and references to the relevant peer-reviewed literature that supports said methodology.

Inclusion of temperature data and weather information is critical, particularly if temperature-dependent development methods were used for estimation of the mPMI. If this method was used, the specific calculations used must be included along with an explanation of how the mPMI was determined. A summary and qualifying statements should also be included that contextually explain the relevance, statistical uncertainty, and appropriate application of the information included in the report. Any report that claims to be able to definitively pinpoint the time of death within a number of hours should be viewed with caution as there is not currently sufficient scientific evidence to support such specific claims with adequate certainty (Wells & LaMotte, 2020; Byrd & Sutton, 2020).

THE FUTURE OF FORENSIC ENTOMOLOGY

Professionalism in Forensic Entomology

In order to perpetuate the continued growth of the field of forensic entomology – and in order for it to gain widespread acceptance as a legitimate scientific discipline – professionalism standards and standard operating procedures must be put into place and strictly adhered to by all practicing forensic entomologists. Although historically entomologists have been somewhat resistant to the concept of licensing, all other major professional fields such as physicians, veterinarians, and lawyers have adopted professionalism standards and certifying exams; thus, it became imperative that entomologists follow suit in order to obtain their desired professional credibility (Perkins, 1982; Hall & Hall, 1986). The purpose of such endeavors is to provide quality assurance within a discipline through standardization of both training and practice. This encompasses all aspects of forensic entomology from the foundations of education to the standard operating procedures on scene to the evidentiary analysis conducted in the laboratory. In an effort to help further the professionalization of forensic entomology and the creation and implementation of standards, the American Board of Forensic Entomology (ABFE) was created. It offers both board certification for practicing entomologists as well as technician certification for those who collect entomological evidence on crime scenes. Both educational and performance criteria are evaluated when determining the eligibility of an individual to sit for either form of ABFE exam. Peer review is highly recommended by the ABFE when authoring forensic reports such that two independent evaluations of the same batch of evidence is conducted to ensure accuracy and integrity of results (Byrd & Tomberlin, 2020). Beyond the ABFE exist two organizations dedicated to the furtherance of professionalism and education within forensic entomology:

the European Association of Forensic Entomology (EAFE) – founded in 2002 – and the North American Forensic Entomology Association (NAFEA) – founded in 2003. Both organizations seek to foster an atmosphere and platform for learning and collaboration within the forensic entomology community (Gemmellaro & Weidner, 2020).

New Advances and Applications in Forensic Entomology

The applications of forensic entomology to casework throughout history have ranged from the most rudimentary associations of flies to decomposition to species identification using molecular techniques. There is little doubt that – as it has throughout the last several centuries – forensic entomology will continue to grow and develop in both its methods and applications. The newest and most rapidly growing field of study is the use of molecular techniques and DNA for species identification (Stevens et al., 2020). An accurate identification is of utmost importance in forensic casework as the development data – and then, by extension, the application to questions of time since death – can vary greatly between species. This is of particular concern for species of insects that do not have comprehensive identification data through traditional methods such as the Sarcophagidae (Smith, 1986). Molecular genotyping of insects provides an alternative to traditional morphology-based methods of identification. This rapidly developing field of research works by comparing an unknown evidentiary specimen such as one obtained from a crime scene to a known reference standard used for identification (Wells & Stevens, 2008).

The value of this new area of study cannot be understated; the breadth of its potential application is vast. Advances in forensic entomology will continue to hold value for application to human medicolegal death investigations but will also begin to be more applicable to other areas of study within the forensic sciences. In particular, the field of wildlife forensic services stands to uniquely benefit from molecular identification studies as they apply to concepts of population genetics and identification of geographic variation amongst specimens of evidentiary value (Picard & Wells, 2011). Furthermore, issues of animal poaching and other wildlife crime within the context of conservation law enforcement can be aided by the molecular identification of unknown samples (Cronin et al., 1991; Dizon et al., 2000). Specific applications of forensic entomology to wildlife crime may include the movement or disturbance of a carcass; the presence or position of wounds; estimation of the time since death; assessment of poisons, pesticides, or other toxins; and cruelty or abuse (Anderson & Byrd, 2020).

CONCLUSION

Forensic entomology has existed within the general scientific community for centuries and will continue to widen its field of application with the advent of new and novel research methods. Despite the great strides that have been made to advance forensic entomology thus far, there are numerous opportunities to continue enhance the science. Paramount within these opportunities is species specific research. While it is common knowledge within the entomology community that certain species of blowflies are commonly found and associated with decomposing remains, many of these species do not yet possess adequate identification and/or development data that would allow them to be utilized within a forensic investigation to their fullest potential. Furthermore, with the application of forensic entomology to cases of wildlife crime, an understanding of potential differences between the substrates of colonization (i.e. human vs. non-human) must be definitively explored in order to more fully understand how the species being colonized may affect the insect species present, their rates of development, and the potential effects all of this may have on estimation of the post-mortem interval. Efforts toward standardization of investigative and analytical procedures coupled with continued future research endeavors will ensure that the field of forensic entomology remains viable, professional, and sustainable.

REFERENCES

Amendt, J., Campobasso, C. P., Reiter, G. E., LeBlanc, H. N., & Hall, M. J. (2007). Best Practice in Forensic Entomology: Standards and Guidelines. *International Journal of Legal Medicine, 121*(2), 90–104.

Anderson, G. S. (2010). Insect succession in a natural environment. In J. H. Byrd & J. L. Castner (Eds.), *Forensic entomology: The utility of arthropods in legal investigations*. Boca Raton, FL: CRC.

Anderson, G. S. (2020). Factors that influence insect succession on carrion. In J. H. Byrd & J. K. Tomberlin (Eds.), *Forensic entomology: The utility of arthropods in legal investigations*. Boca Raton, FL: CRC Press, Taylor & Francis Group.

Anderson, G. S., & VanLaerhoven, S. L. (1996). The Initial Studies on Insect Succession on Carrion in South Western British Columbia. *Journal of Forensic Sciences, 41*, 617–625.

Benecke, M. (2001). A Brief History of Forensic Entomology. *Forensic Science International, 120*(1–2), 2–14.

Bergeret d'Arbois, M. (1855). Infanticide, Momification Naturelle du Cadavre. *Ann.d' Hyg. Publique Et De Med. Leg, 4*, 442–452.

Briere, J. F., Pracros, P., Le Roux, A. Y., & Pierre, J. S. (1999). A Novel Rate Model of Temperature-Dependent Development for Arthropods. *Environmental Entomology, 28*(1), 22–29.

Byrd, J. H., & Tomberlin, J. K. (2020). Licensing and auality assurance. In *Forensic entomology: The utility of arthropods in legal investigations*. Boca Raton, FL: CRC Press, Taylor & Francis Group.

Byrd, J., & Sutton, L. (2020). Forensic Entomology for the Investigator. *WIREs Forensic Science, 2*(4), DOI: 10.1002/wfs2.1370

Cammack, J., Pimsler, M., Crippen, T., & Tomberlin, J. (2015). Chemical Ecology of Vertebrate Carrion. *Carrion Ecology, Evolution, and Their Applications*, 1st ed. 187–212.

Capobasso, C. P., Linville, J., Wells, J., & Introna, F. (2005). Forensic Genetic Analysis of Insect Gut Contents. *American Journal of Forensic Medical Pathology, 26*(2), 161–165.

Catts, E. P. (1990). Analyzing entomological data. In R. E. Williams, N. H. Haskell, & E. P. Catts (Eds.), *Entomology & death: A procedural guide*. SC: Clemson.

Catts, E. P., & Goff, M. L. (1992). Forensic entomology in criminal investigations. *Annual Review of Entomology, 37*, 253–272.

Cronin, M., Palmisciano, D., Vyse, E., & Cameron, D. (1991). Mitochondrial-DNA in Wildlife Forensic-Sciences – Species Identification of Tissues. *Wildlife Society Bulletin, 19*, 94–105.

Dillon, L. C., & Anderson, G. *Forensic Entomology — Use of Insects towards Illegally Killed wildlife* (p. 12, Rep.). Toronto, Ontario: World Wildlife Fun, 1997.

Dizon, A., Baker, C., Cipriano, F., Lento, G., Palsboll, P., & Revees, R. (2000). Molecular Genetic Identification of Whales, Dolphins, and Porpoises: Proceedings of a Workshop on the Forensic Use of Molecular Techniques to Identify Wildlife Products in the Marketplace. *NOAA Technical Memorandum: US Department of Commerce, 52*, 671–685.

Donovan, S. E., Hall, M. J., Turner, B. D., & Moncrieff, C. B. (2006). Larval Growth Rates of the Blowfly, Calliphora Vicina, over a Range of Temperatures. *Medical and Veterinary Entomology, 20*(1), 106–114.

Early, M., & Goff, M. L. (1986). Arthropod Succession Patterns in Exposed Carrion on the Island of O'ahu, Hawaiian Islands, USA. *Journal of Medical Entomology, 23*(5), 520–531.

Erzinclioglu, Y. Z. (1983). The Application of Entomology to Forensic Medicine. *Medicine, Science, & Law, 23*(1), 57–63.

Gemmellaro, M. D., & Weidner, L. (2020). Professional history of forensic entomology. In J. H. Byrd & J. K. Tomberlin (Eds.), *Forensic entomology: The utility of arthropods in legal investigations.* Boca Raton, FL: CRC Press, Taylor & Francis Group.

George, K. A., Archer, M. S., & Toop, T. (2014). Correlation of Molecular Expression with Diel Rhythm of Oviposition inCalliphora vicina (Robineau-Desvoidy) (Diptera: Calliphoridae) and Implications for Forensic Entomology. *Journal of Forensic Sciences, 60,* S108–S115.

Goff, M. L. (1993). Estimation of the post-mortem interval using arthropod development and succession patterns. *Forensic Science Review, 5,* 81–94.

Goff, M. L. (2010). Early Postmortem Changes and Stages of Decomposition In J. Amendt (Ed.), *Current concepts in forensic entomology.* Dordrecht: Springer.

Greenberg, B. (1990). Nocturnal Oviposition Behavior of Blow Flies (Diptera: Calliphoridae). *Journal of Medical Entomology, 27*(5), 807–810.

Hall, D. G. (1948). *The Blowflies of North America.*

Hall, D., & Hall, R. (1986). Entomologists, Taxonomists, Public Opinion, and Professionalism. *Bulletin of the Entomological Society of America, 32,* 8–21.

Jewiss-Gaines, A., Marshall, S., & Whitworth, T. (2012). Clister flies (Calliphoridae: Polleniinae: Pollenia) of North America. *Canadian Journal of Arthropod Identification, 19.*

Kreitlow, K. (2010). Insect Succession in a Natural Environment. In J. H. Byrd & J. L. Castner (Eds.), *Forensic entomology: The utility of arthropods in legal investigations* (2nd ed.). Boca Raton, FL: CRC.

Lake, P. S. (1988). Dynamics of heterotrophic succession in carrion arthropod assemblages. *Oecologia, 76*(3), 477–480.

Licensing and Quality Assurance [Introduction]. (2020). In J. H. Byrd & J. K. Tomberlin (Authors), *Forensic entomology: The utility of arthropods in legal investigations.* Boca Raton, FL: CRC Press, Taylor & Francis Group.

Lord, W. D., & Burger, J. F. (1983). Collection and Preservation of Forensically Important Entomological Materials. *Journal of Forensic Science, 28*(4), 936–944.

Marshall, S., Whitworth, T., & Roscoe, L. (2011). Blowflies (Diptera: Calliphoridae) of eastern Canada with a key to Calliphoridae subfamilies and genera of eastern North America, and a key to the eastern Canadian specias of Calliphorinae, Luciliinae and Chrysomyiinae. *Canadian Journal of Arthropod Identification, 11,* 1–93.

Mégnin, P. (1894).*La fauna de los cadáveres: Aplicación de la entomología a la medicina legal.*

Moura, M. O., Monteiro-Filho, E. L., & De Carvalho, C. J. (2005). Heterotrophic succession in carrion arthropod assemblages. *Brazilian Archives of Biology and Technology, 48,* 477–486.

Nuorteva, P. (1977). Sarcosaprophagous insects as forensic indicators. In C. G. Tedeschi, W. G. Eckert, & L. G. Tedeschi (Eds.), *Forensic medicine: A study in trauma and environmental hazards* (pp. 1072–1095). Philadelphia: W.B. Saunders Company.

Payne, J. A. (1965). A Summer Carrion Study of the Baby Pig Sus Scrofa Linnaeus. *Ecology, 46*(5), 592–602.

Payne, J. A., King, E. W., & Beinhart, G. (1968). Arthropod Succession and Decomposition of Buried Pigs. *Nature, 219*(5159), 1180–1181.

Perkins, J. H. *Insects, experts, and the insecticide crisis.* NY: Plenum Press, 1982.

Picard, C. J., & Wells, J. D. (2011). A Test for Carrion Fly Full Siblings: A Tool for Detecting Postmortem Relocation of a Corpse. *Journal of Forensic Sciences, 57*(2), 535–538.

Poebel, A. (1936). The Beginning of the fourteenth tablet of Harra hubullu. *The American Journal of Semitic Languages and Literatures, 52*(2), 111–114.

Redi, F., Bourdelot, P., Lachmund, F., Magalotti, L., Redi, F., Redi, F., & Redi, F. (1675). Francesci Redi, nobilis Aretini, Experimenta circa res diversas naturales, speciatim illas, quae ex Indiis adfernatur.: Ex Italico Latinate donata.

Sanford, M. R., Byrd, J. H., Tomberlin, J. K., & Wallace, J. R. (2020). Entomological Evidence Collection Methods In J. K. Tomberlin (Ed.). In J. H. Byrd (Ed.), *Forensic entomology: The utility of arthropods in legal investigations* (pp. 63–85). Boca Raton, FL: CRC.

Schoenly, K. (1992). A Statistical Analysis of Successional Patterns in Carrion-Arthropod Assemblages: Implications for Forensic Entomology and Determination of the Postmortem Interval. *Journal of Forensic Sciences, 37*(6).

Schoenly, K., & Reid, W. (1987). Dynamics of heterotrophic succession in carrion arthropod assemblages: Discrete seres or a continuum of change? *Oecologia, 73*(2), 192–202.

Smeeton, W. M., Koelmeyer, T. D., & Holloway, B. A. (1984). Insects associated with exposed human corpses in Auckland, New Zealand. *Medicine, Science, & Law, 24*(3), 167–174.

Smith, K. G. *A manual of forensic entomology.* Ithaca, NY: Cornell University Press, 1986.

Sperling, F. A., Anderson, G. S., & Hickey, D. A. A DNA-Based Approach to the Identification of Insect Species Used for Postmorten Interval

Estimation. *Journal of Forensic Sciences*, *39*(2), 1994.

Stamper, T., Davis, P., & Debry, R. W. (2009). The Nocturnal Ovipositing Behavior of Carrion Flies in Cincinnati, Ohio. *Journal of Forensic Sciences*, *54*(6), 1450–1452.

Stevens, J., Picard, C., & Wells, J. (2020). Molecular Genetic Methods for Forensic Entomology. In J. H. Byrd & J. K. Tomberlin (Eds.), *Forensic entomology: The utility of arthropods in legal investigations*. Boca Raton, FL: CRC Press, Taylor & Francis Group.

Sutton, L. (2017). Declassifying Decomposition: Estimation of the Postmortem Interval Using Total Body Score and Accumulated Degree Days. *University of Florida Doctoral Dissertation*, p. 148.

Tabor, K. L., Fell, R. D., & Brewster, C. C. (2005). Insect fauna visiting carrion in Southwest Virginia. *Forensic Science International*, *150*(1), 73–80.

Tz'u, S., & McKnight, B. E. (1981). *The washing away of wrongs: Forensic medecine in 13th-century China*. Ann Arbor: University of Mich., Center for Chinese studies.

Wallace, J. R., & Merritt, R. W. (2020). The Role of Aquatic Organisms in Forensic Investigations. In J.

H. Byrd & J. K. Tomberlin (Eds.), *Forensic entomology: The utility of arthropods in legal investigations*. Boca Raton, FL: CRC Press, Taylor & Francis Group.

Wells, J. D., & LaMotte, L. R. (2001). Estimating the post-mortem interval. In J. H. Byrd & J. L. Castner (Eds.), *Forensic entomology: The utility of arthropods in legal investigations* (pp. 367–388). Boca Raton, FL: CRC.

Wells, J. D., & LaMotte, L. R. (2020). Estimating the postmortem interval. In J. H. Byrd & J. L. Castner (Eds.), *Forensic entomology: The utility of arthropods in legal investigations* (pp. 213–224). Boca Raton, FL: CRC.

Wells, J. D., & Stevens, J. R. (2008). Application of DNA-Based Methods in Forensic Entomology. *Annual Review of Entomology*, *53*(1), 103–120.

Whitworth, T. (2006). Keys to the Genera and Species of Blow Flies (Diptera: Calliphoridae) of America North of Mexico. *Proceedings of the Entomological Society of Washington*, *108*(3), 689–725.

Worner, S. P. (2008). Bioclimatic models in entomology. In *Encyclopedia of Entomology* (pp. 476–481). Springer.

CHAPTER 11

Fiber Evidence Collection

Prashi Jain[1], Vaishali Omi[1], and Amarnath Mishra[2]

[1]Amity Institute of Forensic Sciences, Amity University, Noida, Uttar Pradesh, India
[2]Worldwide Association of Women Forensic Experts (WAWFE-Caribbean), School of Forensics, Risk Management & National Security (SFRMNS), Rashtriya Raksha University, Lavad-Dahegam, Gandhinagar, Gujarat, India

CONTENTS

DOI: 10.4324/9781003129554-11

INTRODUCTION

A fiber is a thread of any material that is longer than its width. It is important trace evidence that can be found at crime scenes like sexual assault, murder, burglary, and in many other cases. It can help in establishing a link between the suspect, crime scene, and the victim. The fibers from the clothes of the individuals fall off or adhere to the clothing of the other individual or to any other furniture. These fibers may be of evidential value for the investigators as they can provide a link to the suspect as this is the trace evidence and hence get unnoticed by the suspect.

Fibers may get transferred from clothes, carpets, car upholstery, sofa, etc. and can be transferred from the victim to the suspect or the suspect to the victim. There are two types of transfers: direct transfer and indirect or secondary transfer. Direct transfer is from the suspect to the victim or the victim to the suspect when in direct contact. Indirect transfer or secondary transfer means when there is a transfer of fiber from an object to the suspect and then it is transferred to the victim or vice versa; for example, when a suspect sits on sofa, the fibers from the sofa adhere to the suspect's clothing and then during commitment of the crime when the suspect came in contact with the victim it then transferred to the victim.

Fiber is not as conclusive evidence as a fingerprint and DNA; thus, they are not specific to an individual. However, the forensic scientists, by analysis of the fiber, can narrow down the list of suspects. The fibers that are less common aid in the investigation. For example, a suspect wearing a blue shirt of angora fiber is more rare than a blue shirt of cotton fiber. With this, the composition of the dyes used and many other properties may help in narrowing down the list of suspects.

TYPES OF FIBERS

Depending upon their source, fibers are broadly divided into many categories:

1. Natural fibers
2. Semi-synthetic fibers or regenerated fibers
3. Synthetic fibers
4. Mineral fibers
5. Miscellaneous and unusual fibers

Natural Fibers

Natural plant fibers may be more ribbon shaped and may contain twists at irregular intervals. Natural fibers from an animal source look like hair and will often have rough external scale patterns and medulla. Natural fibers are the oldest fibers and are made up of cells; they have a better ability to absorb moisture. A natural fiber is considered to be very comfortable and the clothing that directly touches our skin is mostly made up of natural fibers.

Natural fibers are further divided into many categories:

Plant Fibers

Plant fibers or vegetable fibers are characterized by anatomical feature. Cotton fibers are typically used in textile material. The type of cotton, fiber length, and the degree of twist contributes to the variness of these fibers and color application in addition influences the value of cotton fiber identification. Completely different fibers embrace jute, linen, etc. Identification of less common plant fibers found that crime sites or on suspected commodity can really increase importance; examples are cotton, jute, hemp, flax, sisal, fiber (fruit fiber), etc. (Figure 11.1).

Plant fibers are specialized plant cells. A polarized lightweight micrograph of wool fibers. A vicinity of the plant from that they are out there. Seeds, fruits, stems, and leaves all manufacture natural plant fibers. Plant fibers vary greatly in their physical characteristics; some ar terribly thick and stiff, whereas others are sleek, fine, and versatile. Some are amorphous, a loose arrangement of fibers that is soft, elastic, and absorbent. However, all plant fibers share the common compound of sugar. Sugar is additionally a compound that's created from easy monosaccharide units, and isn't a super molecule. Proteins and sugar have completely different chemical and physical properties that permit a rhetorical mortal to tell animal and plant fibers apart. As an associated example, sugar will absorb water, however it is insoluble (will not dissolve) in water. It is immune to damage from

FIGURE 11.1 Balls of cotton (Andhra – South India) ready for harvest (Mamichaelraj, 6 September 2020).

harsh chemicals and will alone be dissolved by sturdy acids, like oil of vitriol. Cotton is the foremost typical fiber used in textiles.

Stem fibers, hemp, jute, and flax are all made from the thick region of plant stems. They are doing not grow as single, unconnected fibers like cotton, however in bundles. These bundles are also six feet long and extend the complete length of a plant. Throughout the process, the bundles are separated from the stem and overwhelmed, rolled, and washed till they separate into single fibers. Flax is that the most typical stem fiber and is most typically found within the textile linen. This material isn't as well-liked because it once was as a result of its high price. Linen may be a terribly swish and sometimes shiny cloth that resists wear and feels cool in weather condition. Pants, jackets, and shirts are the most common garments created from linen. Sometimes a murder victim's body is burned to hide the proof, but rarely the unit the stays; therefore, it is destroyed and no fibers stay.

Animal Fibers

Animal fibers, which are mostly used in textile material, are wool and the most common wool fibers come from sheep. The finer wool fibers are used in making clothing while coarser wool fibers are used to make carpets. The diameter of the wool fibers holds importance in the analysis of the fiber from the crime scene; examples are wool, silk, mohar, angora, camel, etc.

Animals give fibers from three sources: hair, fur, and webbing. All animal fibers are manufactured from proteins. They're employed in consumer goods, carpets, ornamental hangings like curtains, and bedding (Figure 11.2).

Fur may be a smart donor of fibers; however, it's not a textile. Rather, an animal like a beaver or fox is trapped, and the skin removed and treated. This leads to a versatile skin that retains the fur. Fur is employed nearly solely for coats and gloves.

Hair fibers are the foremost widespread of animal fibers. Animal hair is brushed out of the animal's coat, shed naturally and picked up, or clipped. The foremost common animal hair employed in textiles is wool from sheep; however, there's additionally cashmere and material from goats, angora from rabbits, likewise hair from members of the even-toed ungulate family – alpacas, llamas, and camels. Hair fibers are used for articles of consumer goods, bedding, significant coats, carpets, bags, and articles of furniture upholstery. Once animal hair fibers are created into textiles, they're typically loosely spun to feel softer, creating textiles that shed fibers.

Silk, another fiber, is collected from the cocoons of the caterpillar bombycid. The caterpillars are reared in captivity, and every cocoon should be rigorously

FIGURE 11.2 Cashmere scarf (Ryz, 7 February 2007).

straightened by hand. The shimmering look of silk is caused by the triangular structure of the fiber that scatters light because it passes through, rather like a prism. Materials made up of silk are unremarkably employed in consumer goods and a few beddings. As a result, silk fibers are terribly long and they have a tendency to not shed as simply as hair fibers.

Semi-synthetic Fibers

A semi-synthetic fiber is a machine-made fiber obtained by regenerated cellulose from cotton, wood, or other plant material; examples are rayon, acetate, triacetate, etc.

Regenerated fibers (or changed natural fibers) are an area unit derived from polyose and area unit principally plant in origin. The foremost common of this sort are textiles. It's a fiber that may imitate natural fibers and customarily is sleek and silk in appearance. Polyose with chemicals combined with acetate produces the fiber celanese that's utilized in carpets. Once polyose is combined with three acetate units, it forms polymeric amide nylon – a breathable, lightweight material – utilized in superior consumer goods.

Synthetic Fibers

Synthetic fibers are those manufactured from materials that are not fibers; examples are nylon, polyester, acrylic, teflon, polypropylene, etc.

FIGURE 11.3   Microscopic view of polyester.

Synthetic compound fibers originate with oil products and area unit non-cellulose-based fibers. The fibers area unit whole unreal polymers that serve no alternative purpose except to be woven into textiles, ropes, and also the like. These fibers will have completely different characteristics. They need no definite form or size, and many, like polyester, could also be simply bleached. Characteristic among the artificial fibers is straightforward during a forensics research lab, victimization either a polarizing magnifier or infrared spectrometry (Figure 11.3).

Synthetic fibers could also be terribly long, or cut, and used short. Their form is set by the form of the spinneret and will be spherical, flat, cloverleaf, or perhaps a lot of advanced. However, beneath magnification, all artificial fibers have terribly regular diameters. They are do not have any internal structures; however, they could also be solid or hollow, twisted, and faveolate on the surface. Looking on what's placed into the combo, they'll be clear or semi-transparent.

Polyester is a really common fiber, and represents a really massive cluster of fibers with a typical chemical makeup. It's found in polar fleece, crease-resistant pants, and extra-value-added to several natural fibers to supply additional strength.

Nylon has properties just like polyester, except it's simply diminished by lightweight and targeted acid. Polyester is immune to each of those agents. Nylon was initial introduced as a man-made silk, and artificial tights still elapse the name nylons.

Acrylic is usually found as a man-made wool or imitation fur, and includes a lightweight, downy feel. However, acrylic articles of clothing tend to ball or pill simply. This is often a reasonable fiber.

Olefins are employed in superior articles of clothing, like thermal socks and carpets; as a result, they are fast drying and immune to wear.

Mineral Fibers

Synthetic fibers are those manufactured from materials that are not fibers; examples are nylon, polyester, acrylic, Teflon, poly propylene etc.

Synthetic compound fibers originate with oil product and area unit non- cellulose-based fibers. The fibers area unit whole unreal polymers that serve no alternative purpose except to be woven into textiles, ropes, and also the like. These fibers will have terribly completely different characteristics. They need no definite form or size, and many, like polyester, could also be simply bleached. Characteristic among the artificial fibers is straightforward during a forensics research lab, victimization either a polarizing magnifier or infrared spectrometry.

Synthetic fibers could also be terribly long, or cut and used short. Their form is set by the form of the spinneret and will be spherical, flat, clover- leaf, or perhaps a lot of advanced. However, beneath magnification, all artificial fibers have terribly regular diameters. They are doing not have any internal structures, however could also be solid or hollow, twisted, and faveolate on the surface. Looking on what's place into the combo, they'll be clear or semitransparent.

Polyester a really common fiber, polyester represents a really massive cluster of fibers with a typical chemical makeup. It's found in polar fleece, crease-resistant pants, and extra value-added to several natural fibers to supply additional strength.

Nylon has properties just like polyester, except it's simply diminished by lightweight and targeted acid. Polyester is immune to each of those agents. Nylon was initial introduced as a man-made silk, and artificial tights still elapse the name nylons.

Acrylic usually found as a man-made wool or imitation fur, acrylic includes a light-weight, downy feel. However, acrylic article of clothing tends to ball or pill simply. This is often a reasonable fiber.

Olefins square measure employed in superior article of clothing, like thermal socks and carpets, as a result of their terribly fast drying and immune to wear. (Table 11.1)

TABLE 11.1 Charactistics of Fibers

S. No.	Fiber	Characteristics
1.	Acetate	• synthetic fiber resembles silk • shiny, soft, and luxurious fabric • does not shrink and gets wrinkled • wide range of colors and lusters • used for home décor, furniture, drapes, curtains, and also for clothing
2.	Acrylic	• synthetic fiber made from polymer called acrylonitrile • warm, thus used in making sweaters etc. • dries quickly • soft in nature • lightweight • chemical and moth resistant • used for carpet, jumper, gloves, etc.
3.	Aramid	• synthetic fiber and heat resistant • maintains its shape at high temperatures • strong and resistant to stretch • used in ropes and cables, tires, protective clothing, etc.
4.	Bicomponent	• made using two types of materials • the end product may contain only one material and the second one might dissolve during the process or contain both materials • contains very fine fibers • they have unique cross section • self-bulking • used as crimping fiber
5.	Cotton	• natural fiber obtained from cotton plant • type of cellulose fiber • soft and fluffy in nature • it is absorbent • have a long durability • used to make bedsheets, curtains, in clothing, etc.
6.	Lyocell	• semi-synthetic fiber which can be used as a substitute of cotton or silk • it is a type of cellulose fiber • lightweight • soft in nature • absorbent • have a good dyeability • used in dressing, conveyer belts, clothing, etc.
7.	Silk	• natural fiber obtained from the mulberry silkworm *Bombyx mori* • have good moisture retaining capacity • smooth, soft, and lightweight • used in clothing, surgical suture, parachutes, etc.
8.	Jute	• natural fiber and 100% biodegradable • called as golden fiber because of its golden and silky shine • it has moderate moisture regain and low thermal conductivity • have good antistatic and insulating properties • heat resistant • used in making ropes, rugs, carpets, twine, etc.
9.	Linen	• natural fiber and type of flax • smooth and wrinkles easily • have absorbency of about 20% • second strongest fabric • it is abrasion resistant and antiallergic • used in making table clothes, bath towels, bedsheets, etc.

(Continued)

TABLE 11.1 (Continued)

S. No.	Fiber	Characteristics
10.	Wool	• natural fiber and obtained from the animals like sheep, rabbit, camel, etc. • soft and warm • it is fire resistant • can absorb large quantity of moisture • used in clothing, blanket, upholstery, insulating, etc.
11.	Hemp	• natural fiber and is stronger than cotton • resistant to heat and does not fade in sunlight • longer life span • dyes colors are long lasting • used in making bags, shoes, paper, building materials, etc.
12.	Asbestos	• mineral fiber and is heat resistant • have high tensile strength, wear and friction characteristics • have electrical and sound insulation capacity • it also has capability to adsorb • used in making suits of firefighters, etc.
13.	Melamine	• it can resist physical and chemical degradation • resistance to high temperatures • possess properties like scratchiness, hardness, and moisture resistant • used in industrial fabrics, stuff toys, filters, etc.
14.	Modacrylic	• synthetic copolymer • soft, easily dyed, and strong • resistant to chemical and solvents • have good dimensional stability • used in making carpets, workwear, paint roller cover, scatter rug, etc.
15.	Nylon	• synthetic fiber and stronger than polyester fibers • abrasion resistance, elastic, tough, and easy to wash • they are smooth and soft • lightweight fabric of high resilience and low in moisture absorbency • used in making dresses, raincoats, carpets, sleeping bags, ropes, parachutes, etc.
16.	Olefin	• synthetic fiber and resistant to abrasion, stain, sunlight • dries quickly • heat sensitive • low melting point • textiles can thermally bonded • used in making laundry bags, sandbags, slipcovers, etc.
17.	Polyester	• synthetic fiber and resistant to many chemicals • strong and lightweight • resistant to stretching and shrining • dries quickly • easy to wash • used in clothing, fire hoses, carpets, tire cord, pillowcases, etc.
18.	Rayon	• synthetic fiber similar to cotton and linen • smooth, soft to touch, and comfortable texture • shiny and drapes easily • capacity to absorb moisture • used in clothing, tire cord, medical surgical products, industrial products, blankets, draperies, sheets, etc.
19.	Spandex	• can be stretched over 500% without breaking • it is soft and smooth • lightweight • resistant to abrasion • more durable than rubber but have poor strength • resistant to body oils • used in foundation garments, golf jackets, ski pants, slacks, bathing suits, etc.

FIBERS OBTAINED FROM THE HAIRS OF ANIMALS

The fibers are obtained from the hairs of animals by various methods and then they are manufactured in the factories to make fabric from them. Many animal fibers have good properties; they provide warmth, soft touch, etc. which make them highly expensive. The fibers like wool, silk, cashmere, angora, etc. are obtained from various animals.

Hair is the slender outgrowth from the skin of the individual. Animal hairs contain large amounts of proteins. The morphology of animal fiber is different from other fibers. In these we can see the medulla under the microscope and thus can be differentiated from other fibers.

Silk

Silk is a natural animal fiber and some forms can be woven into textiles. The silk contains the protein called fibroin. The silk is obtained from the larvae that form cocoons and the most common silk is obtained from the mulberry silkworm *Bombyx mori*. The structure of the silk fiber is a triangular prism, which produces a shimmering effect.

It has triangular shape with rounded corners in the cross-sectional view and has smooth surface and longitudinal lines passing along the filament in the longitudinal view of the fiber under the microscope (Figure 11.4).

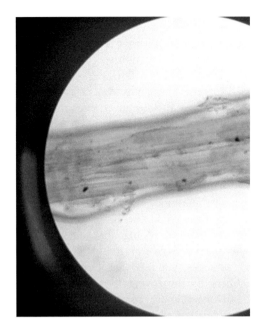

FIGURE 11.5   Microscopic view of wool fiber (40x).

Wool

Wool is a natural fiber that is obtained from sheep mostly and from other animals also like angora from rabbit, cashmere from goat, etc. It contains the protein along with some parts of lipids.

Wools are basically produced by the follicles that are embedded in the skin of the animals. There are two types of follicles: primary follicles and secondary follicles. Primary follicles produce three types of fibers: kemp, medullated fibers, and true wool fibers. Medullated fibers have similar characteristics like hair and kemp fibers are coarse and shed out. Secondary follicles only produce true wool fibers (Figure 11.5).

SAMPLING AND TESTING

Fiber proof is gathered with special vacuums, sticky tape, and extractors. It's necessary to be correct in recording wherever the fiber square measure is found. Inaccurate or incomplete recording could cause the evidence to be inadmissible in court.

Often, the rhetorical person of science can get little amounts of fibers from against the crime scene, maybe even simply one fiber. The primary task is to spot the sort of fiber and its characteristics (such as color and shape). Then the investigator makes an attempt to match it to fibers from a suspect supply, like an automobile or home. After you have only one fiber as proof, you can't do tests that injure or alter the fiber in any approach. Two strategies that will analyze fibers while not damaging them are square measure polarizing lightweight research and infrared chemical analysis.

FIGURE 11.4   Microscopic view of silk fiber (40x).

Polarizing lightweight research uses a magnifier that contains a special filter in it that enables the person of science to see the fiber exploitation specific lightweight wavelengths. However, the fiber will tell the person of science the sort of fiber. Natural fibers, like wool or cotton, need solely a standard magnifier to look at characteristic shapes and markings. Infrared chemical analysis emits a beam that bounces off the fabric and returns to the instrument. However, the beam of sunshine as modified, reveals one thing of the chemical structure of the fiber, creating a straightforward distinction between fibers that look greatly alike. If massive quantities of fiber area units are found, a number of the fibers could also be subjected to straightforward, however harmful, testing—burning them in a flame or dissolving them in numerous liquids. Within the research laboratory activities, you'll have a chance to look at and compare fibers by employing a magnifier. Additionally, perform burn testing to assist in determining fibers. Ultimately, you're asked to check your ability to unravel against the law by examination fibers found on completely different suspects with a fiber found at the crime scene.

COLLECTION AND PRESERVATION OF FIBER EVIDENCE

- A fiber is a trace evidence that can be overlooked by the investigators if not searching for that particular evidence.
- They are found in the micro traces and should be handled with care.
- They can be collected using forceps, tweezers, can be tape lifted, or by using a vacuum.
- The fibers should be collected carefully in the paper bags and in separate bags to prevent the cross contamination from other evidence.
- If the sample is wet, then it should first be air-dried at room temperature and then packed in the suitable container.
- The fiber on any clothing should be preserved in a paper bag as it is by folding the paper bag with the cloth to avoid contamination between different areas of that cloth.
- Care should be taken while collecting different samples from different locations so that they don't come in contact with other samples and contaminate them.
- Similarly, there can fibers present on the carpet, bedding, and rug that should be folded carefully and prevent areas suspected of having fibers present on them.
- If fibers are found on the car seats, then they have to be covered with the polyethylene and the fibers that sometimes adhere to other objects like a knife, doorknob, wooden stick, shoes, etc.

and that should be covered to protect the adhering clothing.

- Fibers on the dead body should only be collected and preserved by the medical examiner and then sent to the forensic laboratory for further examination.
- Always clean the surface on which the collection procedure has to be carried on so as to prevent any cross contamination from the surface or from any other evidence.
- The evidence should be collected in clean paper bags or small paper bundles, small pill boxes, glass vials, tightly sealed containers, or druggist folds, etc.
- Do not disturb the samples like soil, blood, paint, or any other evidence on which the fiber is adhered.
- Fibers can also be extracted from the fingernails of the victim and suspect, which can be collected using a toothpick or fingernail file. This can be found in cases like sexual assaults, where there is a struggle between the victim and the suspect.
- After packaging all the evidence, label the container with the collector's name, date, time, location, item number, investigator's name, signature, etc. and then seal the package.

EXAMINATION OF FIBER EVIDENCE

Physical Examination

Physical examination of the fiber is carried out by examining the fiber with the naked eye.

The fiber samples are observed for various characteristics. The suspected sample and the control or admitted sample is compared for characteristics like type of fiber, color, texture, weaving pattern, design, any defect, and any additional information about the fiber if present.

After observing these characteristics, the fabric is also examined for the thread counting in a particular area for both samples.

Physical Characteristics

Type – The examiner should first identify the type of the fiber which the most important characteristic to identify. There are many types of fibers and an examiner should be able to categorise all the samples which are found on the crime scene.

Color – The color of all the samples should be noted down. The matching of the colors is made and if the dye color is same is observed.

Texture – The texture of the fiber is either smooth, rough, coarse, etc. is observed.

TABLE 11.2 Observation Table for the Examination of Physical Characteristics of the Fiber

S. No.	Characteristics	Questioned Sample	Known Sample	Inference
1.	Type of fiber			
2.	Color			
3.	Texture			
4.	Weaving pattern			
5.	Type of textile the fiber originated from			
6.	Design			
7.	Any additional information			

Weaving pattern – The weaving pattern of the fabric obtained from the crime scene is compared with the sample collected from the suspect.

Design – Pattern or any design or print on the fabric is noted down and compared among the samples.

Type of textile the fiber originated from – Examiner should be able to identify the type of textile fiber; for example, carpets, rugs, car upholstery, etc.

Additional feature - If the fiber contains any specific logo or brand name, tag, etc. is observed in this category (Table 11.2).

Thread Counting

Thread count – The number of threads in the fabric obtained from the crime scene is compared with the number of threads in a particular area of the control or admitted sample.

The thread count is horizontal and vertical. In the about 3 mm^2 fabric taken, the threads are counted both vertically and horizontally (Table 11.3).

Microscopic Examination

A microscopy test helps to determine the origin of the fiber used in making the cloth.

Procedure: Test the fiber sample under a microscope and observe the structure of the fabric (Table 11.4).

Chemical Examination

In chemical examination, different fibers chemically react differently with different chemicals.

Burn Test

It is the simplest way to identify the fibers of fabric. This test is done to check the fabric origin, whether it is natural or man-made.

In the burn test, we observe the following characteristics:

1. Flame color
2. Smoke color

TABLE 11.3 Observation Table for Thread Count of a Fabric

S. No.	Thread count	Questioned Sample	Known Sample	Inference
1.	Horizontal			
2.	Vertical			

TABLE 11.4 Observations of Microscopic Examination

Fibers	Longitudinal Section Appearance	Cross-section Appearance
Silk	Smooth with distinct lengthwise striations.	A hollow structure is present with mostly triangular, irregulars outline.
Wool	Rough surface with scales protruding out.	Irregular in size, and nearly round.
Cotton	Flat, Irregular, cotton is smoother and less irregular.	Fiber appears twisted and thick walled from alteration of bright and dark portions.
Synthetic	Smooth and regular.	A cylindrical structure with fragmented cortex.
Jute/Bamboo/Bagasse	____	Node and internodes like structure.

TABLE 11.5   Observations of Burning Test of Fibers

Fiber	Flame Color	Smoke Color	Smell	Rate of Burning	Residue
Silk	Black	Grey	Burning hair	Medium	Globular structure formed at base
Wool	Black	Grey	Burning hair	Medium	Forms black bead
Synthetics	Black	Black	Pungent	Slow	Fiber on burning melts
Jute	____	____	Burning paper	Fast	Black and greyish ash
Cotton	____	____	Burning paper	Fast	Small amount of light grey ash

3. Smell
4. Residue
5. Rate of burning

Advantage: It requires less time to conclude a result (Table 11.5).

Solubility Test

The solubility test of fiber provides a definite identification. There are different types of solubility tests that must be carried out for examination of specific fibers from a large group of fibers (Table 11.6).

Chemical Test

Different fibers chemically react with different chemicals (Table 11.7).

Instrumental Analysis of Fiber

Pyrolysis Gas Chromatography This technique is used to analyze the fiber and it can even examine the 1/8th inch of a fiber. A pyrogram is generated at the end of the process, which helps in interpretating the type of fiber being analyzed. It is a destructive technique. It is also sensitive to small differences in the chemical nature of the fibers; thus, it is more superior than FTIR.

TABLE 11.6   Observation of Solubility Test

Fiber	HCl	NaOH	Bleach	Acetone
Cotton	NR	Shrinks slight reaction	NR	NR
Wool	Slight yellowish	Dissolves to "glob"	Bubbles slight yellowish	Slight reaction slight yellowish
Silk	Crumpled/shrunk	Dissolves to "glob"	Yellowish	NR
Polyester	NR	NR	NR	NR
Rayon	Slight yellowish	Reaction to "glob"	Slight reaction whiter	Slight fade
Nylon	NR	NR	NR	Slight reaction dissolving ...
Acetate	NR	Slight dissolving	Shrink slight reaction	TOTAL dissolving

TABLE 11.7   Observation of Chemical Test

Fiber	Solvent	Identification
SILK + WOOL	Concentrated hydrochloric acid	Silk will dissolved in the solvent. Wool fiber becomes swells.
VISCOSE RAYON + ACETATE	Sulfuric acid and equal amount of iodine.	Dark blue color indicates viscose rayon. Yellow color indicates acetate.
NYLON + WOOL	Sodium hydroxide	Wool will dissolve. Nylon will not dissolve.
COTTON+ LINEN	Sulfuric acid and weak ammonia Iodine and zinc chloride Caustic soda	Cotton dissolved and linen unaffected. Cotton stain reddish purple and linen stained blue to purple. Cotton remain white and linen turns to yellowish.
POLYESTER	Hot meta cresol/acetone/formic acid	Polyester soluble in hot meta cresol but insoluble acetone and formic acid.
ACRYLIC	Ammonium thiocyanate	Dissolved

In this technique, an instrument called a pyrolyzer is used in which the fiber is heated at a high temperature and instead of burning the fiber it decomposes it in smaller fragments, which is then mixed with the mobile phase.

Gas chromatography is not capable of heating the substance to a higher temperature at a stationary phase and many analytes might decompose if the temperature will be higher than 300° C. So, therefore, a pyrolyzer is introduced in the system, which can raise up to temperature 700°–1000° C. The pyrolyzer is connected to the injector of the GC. The solid fiber is put in the pyrolyzer and then it is heated and decomposed into smaller fragments and it vaporizes and then mixes with the mobile phase, which then swept into the stationary phase.

The fragments are stable and are characteristic to that material. These fragments are separated by GC and then are displayed in the chart called a pyrogram. The pyrogram obtained is characteristic to the material examined; for example, a pyrogram of nylon would be different from a pyrogram of acrylic.

Fourier Transform Infrared Spectroscopy This technique is non-destructive and is mostly use in forensic laboratories. It can not only broadly classify the group of the fiber but also classify the fiber into a sub-group or sub-class; for example, by FTIR we can also differentiate nylon 66 from nylon 6-12. A single fiber can also be examined under the microscope.

Scanning Electron Microscopy Scanning electron microscopy is a method of photography. This type of microscope uses electrons rather than light to form an image. There are many advantages of using SEM rather than of light because it allows a large amount of sample to be in focus at one time.

Atomic Force Microscopy Atomic force microscopy is a method performed using an atomic force microscope; it is an instrument to analyze and characterize samples at the microscopic level. The instrument will allow an analyst to look at the surface characteristics with very accurate resolution ranging from 100 micrometers to even less than 1 micrometer.

Chemical or Dye Analysis The chemical analysis will involve the extraction of the dye from the fiber sample and then characterize and identify its chemical structure.

It is actually difficult to extract a dye from the fiber sample as these samples are typically small and this method of dye analysis is a destructive method that leaves the fiber useless for further color examination. But, since some fibers have similar colors, chemical analysis becomes a necessity.

SIGNIFICANCE OF FIBERS AS TRACE EVIDENCE

1. Fibers are a form of trace evidence and easily transferable. These are very useful in crime scene investigation as they can be easily identified under a microscope.
2. They are easily transferred from the clothing of a suspect to that of the victim.
3. They are capable of multiple transfers; for example from carpet, bed, etc. to the suspect's clothing.
4. These transfers can be direct or indirect. By direct transfers, we mean that the fiber is transferred directly from a fabric onto a victim's body. While by indirect transfer, we mean that the already transferred fibers on the clothing of a suspect are transferred to a victim's body.
5. Whenever two people come in contact with each other, there may be transfer of fibers or there may not be. The construction and the fiber composition of the fabric, the duration, and the force of contact and the condition of the clothing with regard to the damage are important considerations.
6. Another important consideration is the time delay between the actual physical contact and the collection of clothing items from the suspect or victim. If the victim is immobile, very little fiber loss will be there, whereas the suspect's clothing will lose the transferred fibers quickly.
7. The possibility of finding transferred fibers on the clothing of the suspect a day after the actual contact had been made will be very remote, depending upon the use and the handling of that clothing.

CRIME FILES

Murder of George Marsh (1912)

George Marsh was the retired president of Goodwill Soap Company. He was found dead with four bullets in his head in an embankment in Lynn, MA. There were no signs of robbery as well. The wallet and gold watch he was wearing were found intact and thus no evidence of robbery was there. The family of Marsh also cannot gain anything from his death as all of his money has to be given to the charity after his death.

On the embankment there was only a piece of fabric and a matching grey button. When an investigation was carried out, by getting information from the public they came to know that a light blue car was seen near Marsh's house. When police traced the car they reached Willis A. Dorr. He had spent a good time in studying the rear portion of the George Marsh's house as told by the boarding keeper. Dorr rented another room in which he left his overcoat from which all the buttons were removed.

The piece of cloth found was woven with different pearl grey buttons attached to it. The overcoat that was found at the motel room was sent to the Lowell Textile School for the examination of the fabric found at the crime scene and the fabric of the overcoat. After examination, it was observed that the weave of the overcoat was similar to the weave pattern of the fabric found at the crime scene. This evidence was used to convict Willis Dorr for murder, who was the previous renter of that motel room.

In the examination, both fabrics were compared under the microscope. The fragment on the button matched with that of the coat in both weave pattern and texture, and also the torn area of the coat was clearly visible.

The jury decided that Dorr was guilty and ignored Dorr's plea of mitigation. Dorr was executed on March 24, 1914, in Charlestown, Massachusetts.

Ted Bundy Case

Ted was a charming, articulate, and intelligent person. He was born on November 24, 1946, in Burlington, Vermont. When Bundy was in his adolescence stage, he developed the signs of a sadistic serial killer.

In the interviews, Bundy told how he roamed the streets in search of discarded pornography and he also spied on women through the open windows. He was antisocial and had many juvenile records of theft that were dismissed when he turned 18. By 1972, he graduated college and showed interest in a career in law and politics. In 1974, he diverted from his career and discovered his true passion, when he ferociously assaulted his victims.

He started to prey the young and attractive women near his home in Washington and then he gradually moved to Utah, Colorado, and finally Florida. Bundy preyed on these women by faking a disability by either putting his arm in a sling or leg in a fake cast and walking on crutches and then he asked the women to help in carrying his books or unload objects from his car. Sometimes he also impersonated authority personnel like police officers or firefighters to gain the trust of the victim before attacking. After winning their trust, when the victim got in his Volkswagen, he then struck their head with a pipe or crowbar and then tied their hands with a handcuff and forced them into the car. Bundy had removed the passenger seat of his car so that he could lay down the victim in the car properly without getting noticed by others.

In this way, Bundy was able to rape the victims. He strangled his victims and also mutilated them after the death. He then prolonged the events by returning to visit the corpses at their dump sites or even taking them home in order to gain further sexual gratification. In some cases, he also placed their heads in his apartment and also slept with the corpses until they putrefied.

As a witness description spread, Bundy was suspected by several people and they contacted to the authorities but no common evidence was found at that time, but Bundy was under surveillance.

First, he was convicted for kidnapping but he escaped after two years and moved to Florida. He then killed three people in 1978, but then got arrested in February. He murdered 12-year-old Kimberly Leach and the fibers were found in his car, which matched the girl's clothing and showed his contact with the girl. He was put to death in 1989.

Leanne Tiernan Case

In August 2001, someone walking his dog in Lindley Woods, near Otley, in West Yorkshire, found the body of 16-yearold Leanne Tiernan, buried in an extremely shallow grave. This was ten miles from her farm in Landseer Mount, Bramley, Leeds. She had been walking home from a Christmas party, wanting a trip when she disappeared.

How She Was Found

She had a black bag over her head, kept in place with a dog collar, with a scarf and cable tie around her neck, and cable ties holding her wrists. Her assailant had then wrapped her body in plastic bin liners tied with twine.

Length of Time Since Her Death

The specialist examining her body siad that it had not been there since the New Style calendar month. She had been smothered and her body held at low temperatures at intervals during the interim.

The Dog Collar, the Twine, and the Cable Ties

Police caterpillar-tracked down suppliers of the dog collar and determined that someone from Bramley had bought several like the one found around Leanne Tiernan's neck. His name was John Taylor, and he was a poacher UN agency that had been seen around the woods where the body was found.

The twine was an uncommon kind, used for rabbit netting, and was caterpillar-tracked all the way down to a supplier in Devon, that had exclusively created one batch and matched the twine found in John Taylor's home. The variety of cable ties used on Leanne Tiernan were of a form used nearly exclusively by the Royal Mail, the patent company of John Taylor's leader, Parcel Force. Once the police searched John Taylor's house, they found loads of the cable ties and one in each of the dog collars.

DNA Examination

Police searched the woods and recovered around 400 things, along with cans and magazines, and rhetorical scientists compared polymer samples from these, the quilt cowl, and conjointly the bin baggage with samples from friends, family, residents on the council estate where Leanne lived, and known sex offenders.

Hairs Found at Intervals on the Headband

The scarf tied around Leanne Tiernan's neck had some hairs caught at intervals in the knot. Sadly, there wasn't enough polymer at intervals of the roots for traditional polymer identification. However, the scientists found really small amounts of polymers at intervals in the hair shaft and used mitochondrial polymer testing to match it to John Taylor.

First British Murder Investigation Exploitation Dog Polymer Identification

There were dog hairs on Leanne Tiernan's body, and scientists in the state created a partial dog polymer profile; this was the first time a British murder investigation had used dog polymer identification. However, John Taylor's dog had died, so this may not be used in proof.

The Carpet and Bloodstains Beneath Floorboards

Forensic scientists found a strand of pink carpet fiber on her clothes, with specific patterns of dye. Though John Taylor had destroyed the carpet by burning it, police found strands around a nail that matched the fiber on her jumper. Beneath the floorboards, police found bloodstains that the rhetorical scientists referred to as happiness to Leanne Tiernan.

The Arrest

John Taylor was inactive in New Style calendar month 2001, and sentenced to a pair of life sentences in Gregorian calendar month 2002. In New Style calendar month 2003, he was condemned of two rapes, supported polymer proof, and given a pair of additional life sentences.

REFERENCES

Bertino, A. J., & Bertino, P. N. (2015). The study of fibers and textiles. In *Forensic science: Fundamentals and investigations* (pp. 76–105). Australia: South-Western.

Bisbing, R. E. (2006). Trace evidence in the real crime laboratory. In *The Forensic Laboratory Handbook* (pp. 265–290). Totowa, NJ: Humana Press.

Crossley, J. A. A., Gibson, C. T., Mapledoram, L. D., Huson, M. G., Myhra, S., Pham, D. K., ... & Watson, G. S. (2000). Atomic Force Microscopy Analysis of Wool Fiber Surfaces in Air and Under Water. *Micron, 31*(6), 659–667.

De Forest, P. R., & DeForest, P. R. *Forensic Science: An Introduction to Criminalistics*. New York, NY: McGraw-Hill Humanities/Social Sciences/Languages, 1983.

Mamichaelraj. (6 September 2020). "Balls of Cotton (Andhra -South India) Ready for Harvest," [Photograph] Retrieved From: https://commons.wikimedia.org/wiki/File:BALLS_OF_COTTON_(ANDHRA_-SOUTH_INDIA)_READY_FOR_HARVEST.jpg. Creative commons license abbreviation

Peças, P., Carvalho, H., Salman, H., & Leite, M. (2018). Natural Fiber Composites and Their Applications: A Review. *Journal of Composites Science, 2*(4), 66.

Robertson, J., Roux, C., & Wiggins, K. G. *Forensic Examination of Fibers*. Florida, USA: CRC Press, 2017.

Ryz. (7 February 2007). "Cashmere Scarves", [Photograph] Retrieved From: https://commons.wikimedia.org/wiki/File:Kaschmirschal_1.jpg

Saferstein, R. (2004). Criminalistics: An introduction to forensic science.

Saferstein, R. (2019). Trace evidence I: Hairs and fibers. In *Forensic science: From the crime scene to the crime lab* (2nd ed., pp. 319–343). Hoboken: Pearson.

Sharma, B. R. (2018). *Scientific Criminal Investigation* (Vol. 5). Gurgaon, Haryana, India: Universal/LexisNexis.

Siegel, J. A., & Mirakovits, K. (2018). Fibers, paints, and other polymers. In *Forensic science the basics* (2nd ed., pp. 405–430). Jaipur: Oxford Book Company.

Wikipedia contributors. (2021, February 12). Cotton. In *Wikipedia, The Free Encyclopedia*. Retrieved 20:46, February 22, 2021, from https://en.wikipedia.org/w/index.php?title=Cotton&oldid=1006427813

Wikipedia contributors. (2021, February 20). Silk. In *Wikipedia, The Free Encyclopedia*. Retrieved 20:47, February 22, 2021, from https://en.wikipedia.org/w/index.php?title=Silk&oldid=1007823810

Wikipedia contributors. (2021, February 22). Jute. In *Wikipedia, The Free Encyclopedia*. Retrieved 20:48, February 22, 2021, from https://en.wikipedia.org/w/index.php?title=Jute&oldid=1008244733

Wikipedia contributors. (2021, February 19). Linen. In *Wikipedia, The Free Encyclopedia*. Retrieved 20:49, February 22, 2021, from https://en.wikipedia.org/w/index.php?title=Linen&oldid=1007777319

"10 Famous Criminal Cases Cracked by Forensics." Criminal Justice. Inner Vision Ultrasound Blog, 05 Feb. 2011. Web. 14 Jan. 2016.

CHAPTER 12

Fingerprints

Leggie L. Boone

Polk County Sheriff's Office, Keiser University Florida, Sherlock Institute of Forensic Science (SIFS) India Pvt. Ltd., Editorial Board of Fashion and Law Journal Legal Desire Media and Insights, Worldwide Association of Women Forensic Experts (WAWFE-US), International Association for Identification Florida Division of IAI Generation ForSciTe, LLC Lakeland, Florida, USA

CONTENTS

WHAT IS A FINGERPRINT?

A fingerprint is the impression left by a finger's friction ridges upon contact with a surface. Fingerprints have been found on surfaces dating back over 3000 years. Cave walls and artifacts recovered through archaeological exploration have uncovered handprints, fingerprints with visible patterns, and footprints. Friction skin, called such due to the folds, ridges, and valleys of detail present for grasping, skidding, and braking capacity, exists on different areas of the body. The palmar side of the hands and the soles of the feet are the prevalent areas of friction skin, but we also have this type of skin on our elbows and knees. Although the friction skin

patterns are different, the purpose of the surface of folds is the same (Figure 12.1).

Fingerprints begin to develop during the third to fourth month of fetal growth. Within the womb, when the fetus is approximately 4–5 inches long (10–12 cm), between the size of an apple and an avocado, the *volar pads* on the tips of the web-like protrusions of the hands move, push against the wall of the uterus, and settle into patterns (loops, arches, or whorls). These volar pads are present on the fingers, areas of the palms, toes, and soles of feet (see Figure 12.2).

As the fetus continues to grow, the movement within the uterus, genetic factors, and health of the mother contribute to the intricate ridge detail that will remain with the individual throughout life and even into

FIGURE 12.1 Four fingers. Image by Leggie Boone.

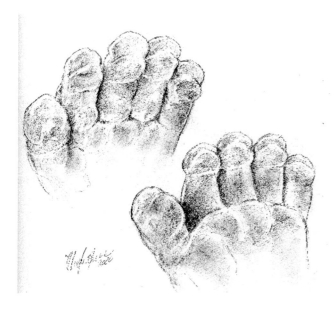

FIGURE 12.2 Volar pads of hand (left) and foot (right) of developing fetus. Image by Hugh Jones.

decomposition. No two people have been determined to have the same fingerprints. Closely related family members may have similar patterns and ridge flow; however, there will undoubtedly be minute details in each finger, palm, and foot that are unique to each individual. The fingerprint details we are born with remain with us throughout life, regenerating when injured, and establishing additional characteristics when scarred. There are reasons why a fingerprint pattern may be damaged:

- Amputation: a portion of the fingers or hand may be surgically or accidentally removed.
- Mutilation: portions of the fingers or hands are intentionally damaged in an effort to cover, alter, or distort existing fingerprints.
- Injury: a deep cut, puncture, or another type of open wound may create a scar within the ridge detail.

In actuality, any of these occurrences will add details to that individual's fingerprint record that make their fingerprints more easily identifiable.

REFLECTION

I went to a residential burglary and dusted the home in the areas that the victim noted as being disturbed by the intruder. After getting several latent lifts, I asked the homeowner if I could roll his fingerprints for the purpose of elimination when the examiner does their comparisons. The homeowner was okay with this step and I gathered my ink pad and fingerprint and palm cards. As I passed him my pen to sign his name on the print card, I saw that he had no fingers. Medically speaking, the distal and intermediate phalanges of both hands were gone. This man was functional with the proximal phalanges, which he explained were lost in a cherry bomb accident as a teenager and what remained had healed into rounded nubs. From the crime scene investigator perspective, these nubs still had details and the potential to leave prints; therefore, they were inked and rolled for the investigation.

Mutilations have been performed by some criminals who believed that removing or surgically covering their fingertips would lessen their chances of being identified. A problem with that manner of thought: fingertips are not the only areas of the hand with identifiable ridge detail. Criminals have had skin grafted from another part of the body, applied acid, burned, or sliced the epidermis off to hide their identities. Depending on the depth or degree of the injury, the ridge detail may heal and regenerate. The addition of a scar or scar tissue provides more detail for the examiner to compare and identify. Mutilation may also occur through occupational abrasions. Masonry workers and those who frequently handle rough surfaces and harsh chemicals/cleansers with their bare hands tend to wear down the ridged surfaces and new creases may develop over time. Aging also impacts the friction ridge surfaces, reflected in drier skin and arthritis in the joints, making the collection of prints a little more difficult.

Conditions Impacting Fingerprints and Fingerprinting

There also exists a condition, *Adermatoglyphia*, which is a very rare genetic disorder resulting in people being born without fingerprints or ridge detail on the palms and soles of the feet. The disorder is associated with the lack of development of sufficient pores on the palmar side of the hands and soles of the feet (Nousbeck et al., 2011).

Other genetic mutations may result in polydactyly, oligodactyly, or syndactyly. *Polydactyly* refers to the development of one or more extra digits on the hands or feet. Commonly found on the ulnar (little finger side) or radial (thumb) side of the hand, the extra digit(s) may have varying degrees of functionality. *Oligodactyly* is a result of underdeveloped muscle and bone, leaving the subject with less than five fingers or toes on the hand or foot. *Syndactyly* is the full or partial fusion of digits. During fetal development, the webbing of the fingers and toes dissolves, but in the subject with syndactyly, the webbing remains. These and other malformations that impact the hands and feet are rare in humans, yet may occur more frequently in specific regions of the world and also in multiple animal species.

As a professional investigator, understand that the mutations are rare, yet you may have to be careful and creative in obtaining elimination prints or booking records if you should have a situation involving fingerprints of this nature. In the complete absence of fingerprints, due to amputation or full hand burns, for example, footprints may be considered as source of individual details for identification.

HISTORY

Fingerprints have been noted in history for over 3000 years. Portions of fingerprints or full handprints have been located impressed in clay, on the exterior of a sarcophagus, in art, and architectural structures all around the world. Some cultures, including ancient Babylonia, Greece, and parts of China, incorporated fingerprints in wax seals as a mechanism for signing important documents or for business transactions. In the late 1800s, fingerprints had just begun to be infused as a part of the intake process of criminals in penal institutions. Prior to fingerprints, a tattoo index existed in some countries, as a means of recording details on some inmates, at least until the tattoo was obliterated or covered with an alternate image. Branding by burning a symbol or message on subjects was also a method of identifying, or at minimal, associating a person with an owner, a location, a crime, or an institution. Also, photography was growing in its popularity and technical advancements. Thus, methods for maintaining records, documenting inmate demographics and fingerprints, and an efficient system of tracking current and former inmates were among the motivators for some scientific contributions. Several authorities in fingerprint history are commonly mentioned in forensic textbooks and journals for their efforts and theories shared and applied in law enforcement conferences and scientific consortiums (Table 12.1).

Amazing Find

Dr. Henry Faulds stumbled into fingerprint peculiarities by finding ancient pottery shards on a beach in Japan (Lee & Gaensslen, 2001). His interest led him to study the regenerative nature of fingerprint detail by slicing skin from the fingertips of patients and examining the regrowth of the same detail (Lee & Gaensslen, 2001). Faulds was a close cousin to Charles Darwin, the well-known evolution scientist and the two often communicated by letters.

TABLE 12.1 Contributors to Fingerprint Science and Forensic Discipline

Name	Contributions
Jan Evangelist Purkyn (Purkinje)	1823, Established the first rules for classifying fingerprints and organized nine fingerprint patterns
Sir William Hershel	1856, Fingerprints are permanent; 1858, In Jungipoor, India, required residents to sign documents with fingerprints
Henry Faulds	1880, Fingerprints are individual; In an article to *Nature*, suggested that fingerprints may be useful in criminal identification (Lee & Gaensslen, 2001)
Alphonse Bertillon	1883, Anthropometry, mugshot photography, "God's eye" perspective photography, and dynamometer applications (for measuring use of force)
Sir Francis Galton	1888, pointed out minutiae within fingerprint patterns (Maltoni et al., 2003); 1892, published *Fingerprints*, after performing the first detailed study on fingerprint classification, dividing the patterns into arches, loops, and whorls, as well as their sub-patterns (Galton, 1892)
Sir Edward Richard Henry	1888, Henry Classification System, using Galton's foundations; 1900, *Classification and Uses of Finger Prints*
Juan Vucetich	1892, First criminal fingerprint identification, developed fingerprint classification system

HOW ARE FINGERPRINTS LEFT?

When a surface is handled by the fingers or palms, there is a chance that there will be a transfer of the ridge detail onto that surface. Multiple factors are involved with the deposition of a fingerprint. Although this list is not all encompassing of every scenario, the following contributing factors will be discussed:

- Components of a Fingerprint
- Patterns
- Minutiae
- Types of Prints
- Surfaces
- Absence of Prints

Components of a Fingerprint

As a crime scene investigator, knowledge of how fingerprints are left is an important tool. Morphologically, a fingerprint is left when the oils, minerals, and water that are produced in the dermal layers of the skin rise to the outer layer through the pores, spread across the epidermis, and are transferred to a surface. Varying sources will show the secretions of the skin to contain between 95% and 99% water. The remaining components include fatty acids, amino acids, and minerals, such as sodium, potassium, calcium, and magnesium. Trace amounts of metals, including zinc, copper, iron, chromium, nickel, and lead, may be present; however, the quantities will vary for each individual depending on what they have ingested. The combination of water, acids, and minerals generated by the eccrine sweat glands appear on the skin as a mechanism to aide in regulation of the body temperature or may be the internal response to an infection. The skin is a complex system of multiple layers of cells. Each layer has a specific function in the continual regeneration of skin, particularly when an injury has occurred. A cross-section of skin, in Figure 12.3, shows the sweat glands within the dermal layer. The dermal papillae, between the dermis and epidermis, determines the ridge detail that is visible on the outer surface of the epidermis. The sweat glands send the cocktail of perspiration to the surface through ducts that open as pores distributed all over the outer surfaces of the hands and feet, as well as the rest of the body.

Several factors can increase the generation of perspiration on the hands – emotions, nervousness, fear, physical activity – and the rate of sweat production is determined by genetic components, gender, and age. As we reach our 50s and beyond, we tend to perspire less and our skin dries more quickly. Thus, recording fingerprints of the elderly may be a bit more challenging, yet there will still be ridge detail and creases helpful in the comparison process. Since the perspiration is primarily water, the

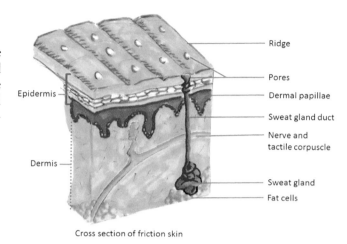

Cross section of friction skin

FIGURE 12.3   Cross section of friction skin. Image by Hugh Jones.

conditions of the environment play a significant role in the discovery, development, and collection of latent fingerprints. The water in the fingerprint evaporates quickly, decreasing chances of recovering latent ridge detail. Higher temperatures will tend to dry areas with potential fingerprints, and moist, cooler temperature will potentially damage fingerprints.

Patterns

As mentioned, during fetal development, the volar pad movement and final location for settlement determines the fingerprint pattern. There are three main classifications of fingerprint patterns: loops, whorls, and arches.

The loop pattern, in Figure 12.4, is the most common pattern of fingerprint, appearing on between

FIGURE 12.4   Loop pattern (right slant). Image by Leggie Boone.

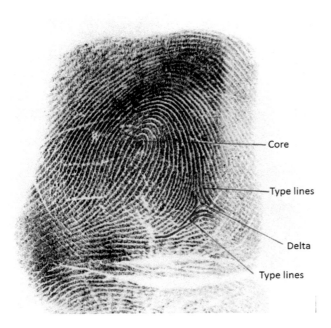

FIGURE 12.5   Loop pattern with core, delta, and type lines accentuated. Image by Leggie Boone.

FIGURE 12.6   Whorl pattern. Image by Leggie Boone.

60–70% of the fingerprint population. A loop is formed when ridges enter on one side of the finger, curve upward, creating the *core* of the pattern, and exit on the same side entered. Loops have one *delta*, which is a triangular area where *type lines* run parallel and split, around the delta. Loops are further defined by the examiner as ulnar or radial loops. An ulnar loop slants downward in the direction of the little finger (ulnar bones) and the radial loop slants downward in the direction of the thumb (radial bones). The slant of the loop is described as a left slant or right slant to aid in classification and in fingerprint searches. Figure 12.5 illustrates the characteristics that define a loop pattern.

Whorl patterns appear on roughly 30–35% of the fingerprint population. A whorl, Figure 12.6, is formed when type lines enter each side and ridges form a circular or spiraling pattern in the core.

Whorl patterns have two deltas and may appear as a plain whorl, a central pocket whorl, a double loop whorl, or an accidental pattern containing two or more deltas. See Figure 12.7 and Figure 12.8.

Arch patterns are the least common, appearing in roughly 5% of the fingerprint population. Arches have ridges that flow on one side, with a raise near the center, and exit from the opposite side. Arch patterns have no core and no delta, and may appear as a plain arch with a slight central raise or as a tented arch with a more pronounced raise. See Figure 12.9.

Minutiae

As the layer of perspiration connects with any surface, there is a chance that the ridges on the epidermis will leave a representation of the detail on that surface. The ridges and furrows, also called grooves, represent the minutiae of the friction skin. *Minutiae* are small details and make up the intricate, unique design of the fingerprint and palm print. When a fingerprint is left on a surface, the lines of the pattern are imprints of the raised

Plain Whorl   Central Pocket Whorl   Double Loop Whorl   Accidental Whorl

FIGURE 12.7   Whorl patterns. Image by Hugh Jones.

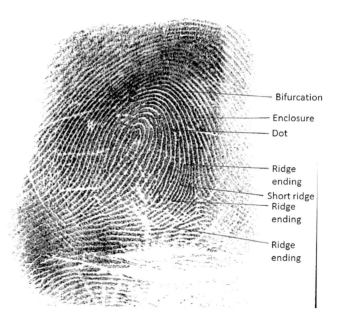

FIGURE 12.8 Whorl pattern with two deltas. Image by Leggie Boone.

FIGURE 12.10 Fingerprint minutiae. Image by Leggie Boone.

ridges and the voided spaces between the ridges represent the furrows. There are several minutiae that may be found in a fingerprint. The position, thickness, and relative location of the ridges help the examiner to identify or eliminate the contributor of fingerprints developed or recorded. Below, Figure 12.10, displays examples of such details.

Types of Prints

Inked Prints

Inked prints are intentional representations of the friction ridge details on the palmar side of the hands. Ink is applied to the fingers and palms, which are then pressed on a card or in the appropriate place to record the imprint. Inkless methods are available from vendors of

forensic supplies. Both inked and inkless methods are performed to capture the details of the ridge detail, joints, and creases of all areas of the hands. The records may be acquired during the booking process when a subject is apprehended during a criminal investigation. Individuals may be fingerprinted for background checks for hiring purposes (i.e. law enforcement, education system, daycare, etc.). Other instances may occur when fingerprints may be recorded – check cashing, firearms acquisition or permit to carry, or elimination prints. Live scan instruments are used as an inkless method of electronically capturing and storing fingerprint

FIGURE 12.9 Plain arch (left) and tented arch (right) patterns. Image by Leggie Boone.

and palm print detail to an authorized law enforcement entity. The live scanned records may be used in the place of inked records for the aforementioned purposes.

Latent Prints

Latent prints are the chance impressions not always visible on surfaces that have been touched by the hands. Latent prints may be partial, leaving a portion of the finger or palm, or may completely display the full finger or palm. Latent prints require powder or chemical processing methods to make them more visible for photographing or lifting. Several factors may affect the development of quality latent prints. An understanding of how latent prints are left on a surface helps the crime scene investigator better determine the techniques needed to recover latent prints. Various conditions may occur- pressure applied may create distortion, movement may reduce quality, and the matrix or surface factors may impact the acquisition of prints. Smooth, *nonporous* surfaces, including glass, some metals, and plastic tend to receive latent prints at a greater degree than textured or *porous* surfaces (paper, cloth, and untreated wood). The surface and the environmental conditions will dictate which processing technique is appropriate for latent print development.

Processing

"Physical evidence cannot be intimidated. It does not forget. It sits there and waits to be detected, preserved, evaluated, and explained." Herbert Leon MacDonell

- Powder processing uses a brush of fiberglass, animal hair, or synthetic fibers; black, silver, grey, and white of varying consistencies; fluorescent powders are available; and magnetic powder is another option. Traditional powders have percentages of resin polymers and vary in color for contrast. The choice of powder to apply is based on the surface and the tools available for processing and collection.
- Chemical processing is performed by applying individual or combined chemicals to adhere to the amino acids, fatty oils, or other minerals in fingerprint residue. Ninhydrin is a commonly applied chemical for latent print development on porous surfaces, such as paper products, producing a color change as a reaction where amino acids have been absorbed. Silver nitrate, iodine, physical developer, and chemical stains are available for development of prints. Several chemical development compounds and techniques have emerged to meet the challenges of the varying surfaces, substrates, and matrices that

friction skin may encounter. Ardrox – a secondary fingerprint stain; amido black and coomassie blue- for the development of friction ridges in blood; small particle reagent- for developing fingerprints on wet surfaces; and many more are accessible for latent print development primarily in controlled conditions.

- Cyanoacrylate or super glue fuming is a chemical process that requires closed conditions and proper ventilation. The object, typically one that has a nonporous surface, is placed in a sealable cabinet, tank, or closable space. The item should be placed so that most or all of its surfaces can be exposed to the fumes. Drops of super glue are poured onto an aluminum cup, which is then placed on a hot plate. The container is sealed and a timer should be set to avoid over-processing. As the super glue warms, fumes rise and adhere to the amino acids, proteins, and fatty acids of fingerprints, creating a white, chalky coating. If the inside of a vehicle is processed or a tented space is processed, the vehicle or space should be allowed sufficient time for fumes to dissipate before handling the evidence and exposing your eyes, lungs, and skin to lingering fumes. Fuming chambers of different sizes can be purchased, and have timed mechanisms for efficient fuming and safe air filtration. If ridge detail is visible, photographs should be taken and the surfaces may be further processed with powder to enhance the detail. Super glue fuming has been successfully performed to develop latent prints on skin in some cases.
- Vacuum Metal Deposition (VMD) is another process requiring a closed chamber. A thin mist of gold vapor and a layer of silver or zinc are heated and the vapors that arise adhere to fingerprint residue. The amounts of the metals and the multi-step vacuum process require a calibrated chamber and the technique can be used for varying surfaces.
- Another technique is electrostatic dust lifting, which is often used in conjunction with powders or chemicals. Photography is a supplement to latent development using chemicals, powders or the aforementioned methods. Other processes are useful and may be successfully applied based on the surface, environment, and individual training and skill. Practice on non-evidentiary items is necessary prior to exposing fragile fingerprint evidence to inappropriately used chemicals. There may only be one opportunity to develop the detail that could lead to an identification. Inclusion of a control sample with known prints is recommended in order to confirm the chemicals and delopment processes are functioning properly.

Plastic or 3-D Prints

Plastic prints or three-dimensional prints are prints found in moldable or soft surfaces. A 3-D print might be found in a bar of soap, soft caulk, putty, chocolate, paint that has not fully dried, and any number of similarly impressionable surfaces. Collection of the item with the impression is best so that the prints can be developed and photographed in controlled conditions. If the evidence cannot be recovered, examination of quality photographs are necessary to allow for comparison.

Examination quality photography is high-resolution photography that includes a scale (inches or centimeters). The camera must be held securely or mounted on a tripod parallel to the plane of the evidence. Also, the scale must be positioned on the same plane as the evidence. If the fingerprint is impressed in clay on the ground, the scale must be placed on the ground at the same depth as the impression, so that the information captured can reflect the measurement tool clearly and can be reproduced accurately when printed, enlarged, or enhanced. Lighting must be considered, as there may be shadows on portions of the print. Use *oblique* lighting and take photos while altering the angle and direction of the lighting so that you will have all shadowed areas brightened in your photos. The oblique lighting technique, also called side lighting, refers to holding your light source at a low angle to provide greater visibility of surfaces and areas in shadows. The photos captured require a scale because the image needs to be comparable in size to the known finger or palm print when placed side-by-side. The scale also aides when enlarged images are printed. High resolution allows the enlargement and enhancement without losing clarity and quality. A low-resolution image will become pixelated when enlarged.

Patent Prints

Patent prints are prints that occur as the result of the transfer of a medium. If the hand touches oil, paint, blood, or other residues, then touches a surface, the hand carries that residue and leaves an impression of the ridge detail on the surface. Distortion, by pressure or movement, may occur with or without a residue; therefore, locating and preserving the minutiae in a patent print are very significant. Again, examination of quality photography is necessary for any evidence with fine, fragile details such as those in fingerprints. When possible, recover the item displaying the patent print. Be careful to package the item in such a way as to reduce movement in the container or damage to the ridge detail.

Surfaces

Porous and nonporous surfaces have been described. What happens when there are both types of surface on an item of evidence? Determine if the processing technique can be performed to develop prints on both types of surface. An example is tape. Cyanoacrylate fuming of the non-adhesive side may be performed after sticky-side powder is applied to the adhesive side.

If the CSI cannot process the item at the scene, the evidence may be recovered for processing in more labor-intensive conditions, such as within a laboratory under a hood with a controlled environment for fumes or powder dispersal.

Other Surface Issues

A wet surface can be processed with *small particle reagent* (*SPR*). The solution of SPR is prepared when needed and can be applied by spraying, pouring, dipping, or immersion. The effective chemical (dependent on the manufacturer) in SPR reacts with the oils or fats in fingerprint residue (Bumbrah, 2016). Sticky-side powder is another resource, used for most types of tape, labels, and surfaces that have adhesive compound. The sticky-side powder is mixed into a paste and brushed onto the adhesive side of tape, allowed setting time, and lightly rinsed.

Absence of Prints

"I am one of the few people in the world who can murder you and leave no forensic evidence." Abby Scuito

Eventually, you will have to go to court. You may be asked to explain what tasks you performed while working at a crime scene or while performing additional duties associated with investigating an offense. Whether during a deposition or giving your testimony in the courtroom, an attorney will ask, "If no fingerprints were found (or identified to her/him), doesn't that mean the defendant did not touch that surface?"

The answer is no. Latent prints are chance impressions. Finding latent prints is a great aide to the investigation; however, several scenarios are possible to explain why the defendant's prints were not recovered or identified.

- The surfaces processed may not have been conducive to prints. Some surfaces just do not receive and keep fingerprints well. For example, the textured surfaces of several electronic devices. Touching the item does not ensure that a latent print will be retrievable. When powder-processed, a textured surface will yield a copy of the texture. Chemical processing and photography may assist in latent development on some textured surfaces.

- The subject may not have touched the surface with adequate pressure to leave ridge detail. Everyone does not produce the oils in perspiration at the same rate and if the subject is not secreting those oils sufficiently and touches a surface lightly, minimal ridge information may be left. When handling something that is typical to handle, there is little chance for the higher degree of perspiring that comes with doing something uncommonly done (breaking in a door, for example). The homeowner's fingerprints are expected to be found on the door of their own residence, yet, they may not appear there because their sweat glands may not be actively moving those oils to the surface of their hands. As stated, fear and nervousness (and doing wrongful acts) stimulate the sweat glands for many people.
- Additionally, movement while touching the surface may damage any ridge detail left. Turning a round doorknob may suggest that there should be fingerprints, however, the motion of turning may smear any fingerprint residue left there.
- The surface may have been cleaned. We have seen it done in movies and on television. After a crime has been committed, the perpetrator wipes the surfaces they touched. Wiping the surface can remove prints. Be aware: most criminals do not take the time to clean up behind themselves, particularly in the commission of property crimes.
- Another reason no prints may be found is that the subject may have had a barrier over their hands. A sock, a rag, a glove, or any covering over the hands will reduce the chances of leaving fingerprints. Reducing the chances is not eliminating. There have been instances where a subject wore latex gloves and fingerprints were found on the surfaces touched. If the level of perspiration is heavy enough, the oils may build up inside of the gloves and an impression may be pressed through, onto the surfaces handled. It is important to note that you should always, always take all used gloves and other materials with you when leaving a crime scene. Improper disposal of gloves may lead to embarrassing moments of explaining why your fingerprints were identified inside of the gloves found by another investigator at the scene. The inside of latex and nitrile gloves can be successfully processed for fingerprints.
- You may not have processed the item(s) the subject handled. Crime scene investigation requires training and the experiences you gain

during your tenure will help develop your intuition for observing what needs to be processed, photographed, or collected.

Your response to the attorney may be, "The absence of fingerprints does not mean that the subject did not commit the crime."

You could also acknowledge that the presence of fingerprints does not necessarily prove that the defendant committed the crime either. Remember, the age of a latent print cannot be determined in many instances. Identification of a latent print on a surface means that the individual touched it at some point in time. It is the job of the detective to determine if that point in time was during the commission of a crime.

NO FINGERPRINTING ALLOWED

If you lived in Fall River, Massachusetts, in the 1890s, you would not have had fingerprints as a consideration in crime scene processing. Because of this, Lizzie Borden, the notorious Hatchet Woman suspected of killing her father and stepmother, there was no identifiable connection between her and the murder weapon, aside from proximity.

If the murder weapon was suitable for latent print development, there may have been a different ending in the trial of Lizzie Borden.

CLASSIFICATION OF FINGERPRINTS

Fingerprints can be classified by their patterns as loops, whorls, or arches. Classification allows the examiner to group each fingerprint into a category by class characteristics. When a latent print is obtained, the presence and absence of ridge flow and features (core, delta, and type lines) help to determine whether it is an arch, a loop or whorl. Some latent prints will provide enough information to determine the pattern. If known prints are available, the subject may be eliminated based on the pattern. For example, if the latent print is a whorl pattern and the known prints have arches and loops, the known prints can be eliminated as having made the latent impression.

It is important to also be aware that having a similar pattern does not mean that the prints originated from the same source. Pattern classification cannot determine identification. In the early years of fingerprint record-keeping, criminal identification through photographs, Bertillonage measurements, and law enforcement or witness memory were the collaborative mechanism for determining whose records to compare. As fingerprints became the primary means of criminal identification, systems were developed to organize the growing number of records. As mentioned, Sir Edward Richard Henry was a forerunner in the explanation of the significance of fingerprints. While working with the Indian Civil Service in 1896–1897, Henry developed the fingerprint classification system utilized for several decades. Henry was assisted by two officers of the Inspector General, Azizul Haque and Hemchandra Bose. The men devised the system initially based on the presence of the whorl and loop patterns.

PALM PRINTS

A single fingerprint may have over 150 details of interest to the latent examiner. Palm prints are just as unique as fingerprints. A palm print could have over 2000 pieces of information, including the joints, creases, deltas, and variations of ridge flow in the area beneath the fingers (interdigital or triradius), surrounding the thumb (thenar), and outer edge (hypothenar). See Figure 12.11. The position of the palm on objects for grasping a bottle or can or writing on a check or paper may require obtaining a more thorough record of the thenar area, called a thenar roll, and the hypothenar area, called the writer's palm.

The palm has three major creases. The *distal transverse crease* is present beneath the interdigital padding. This crease typical extends from the hypothenar edge of the hand and branches slightly below the index and middle fingers before fading into smaller creases. The *proximal transverse crease* crosses the middle of the palm from the edge of the hand below the index finger and thins in the hypothenar area. The *radial longitudinal crease* often begins with the proximal transverse crease, and curves toward the middle of the heel of the hand.

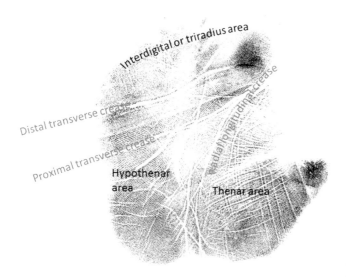

FIGURE 12.11   Palm print. Image by Leggie Boone.

Loops, whorls, and deltas may be present in the palm. A variety of creases and scratches may be visible all over the palms and the joints of each finger. Using the hands for occupational movements, dryness, age, genetic factors, and health contribute to the addition of creases in the hands.

COMPARISON-ACEV

Latent print comparisons are performed by trained examiners. Several forensic associations offer training and tests for competence in latent print examination. Examiners must be prepared to report and testify to their process for comparisons and their findings. A derivation of the scientific method has been applied to the steps involved in latent print examination. David Ashbaugh, a renowned expert in the world of fingerprints, coined the methodology as ACE-V, to name the four major components of the examination of fingerprints. Analysis, Comparison, Evaluation, and Verification (ACE-V) provides a format for performing and explaining how fingerprint evidence is reviewed, and how conclusions are established.

In the **Analysis** phase, the unknown/latent print is inspected for sufficient detail that could potentially aide in the comparison step. Orientation of the impression is decided, if possible. The examiner surveys the impression for levels of detail that lead to the next step, comparison. There are three levels of details (Ashbaugh, 2000):

- Level 1 Detail includes the ridge flow within the impression. Establishing the direction of the ridge flow may assist with determining the pattern as a loop, arch, or whorl (depending on how much information is available in the impression).
- Level 2 Detail includes minutiae, as well as the absence of minutiae. The short ridges, bifurcations, ridge endings, and other details, provide target areas on which the examiner can focus.
- Level 3 Detail includes the pores (poroscopy), ridge edges (ridgeology), and incipient ridges (narrow ridges between the mature or fully developed ridges) of the impression. Creases and scars are also associated with Level 3 Detail.

The latent print development process may contribute features that could inhibit clarity in the impression. Powder processing may deposit excess grains within the furrows of a latent print, therefore, care and practice are needed to minimize damaging the already fragile latent impression. Use of cyanoacrylate fuming may contribute excess flaking between ridges as well. Deposition pressure, how heavily the impression is made on or into a surface, impacts the clarity of detail in the impression. Also, distortion may occur in the impression. If the fingers or palms move while touching the surface, the remaining residue will potentially be wiped, distorting the ridge detail. If the fingers or palms touch, lift, and retouch a surface, uneven overlapping of detail may occur.

In the **Comparison** phase of examination, two impressions are viewed side-by-side using visual aid equipment. Tools including magnifiers and ridge counters, as well as computer enlargement and enhancement software, may be used to view the unknown to known or the known to known impressions. The examiner will choose a group of minutiae or a focus area of one impression and look for similarities or dissimilarities in the known impression. Levels of detail (pattern, ridge flow, creases, size, core features, pores, ridge edges, and scars) are compared for agreement or disagreement. Distortion in either impression, caused by pressure, the medium in which the impression is deposited, the development technique, movement or overlapping lays may present explainable differences.

In the **Evaluation** phase of examination, the examiner determines a conclusion based on the analysis and comparison. The language of the latent examination conclusion has changed over the history of fingerprint evaluations, yet the meanings are the same. An *identification* is concluded when the examiner determines that there is sufficient agreement between the unknown and known impression to confidently report a single source contributor. A *nonidentification* or an *exclusion* is concluded when there is disagreement between the ridge detail of the unknown and known impression. Limited detail may aid in the elimination of subject prints. When there is insufficient ridge information to determine if there is agreement or disagreement between the questioned and known impressions, the examiner may report *inconclusive* findings. Provision of elimination prints or prints displaying an area previously not clearly recorded may be requested.

The determination of "how much" information is sufficient to form a conclusion is based on the training, experience, and knowledge of the examiner. The examiner must make an objective decision as a result of the factual information (minutiae and visible detail) in the evidence impression.

The fourth and final phase of the impression examination process is **Verification**. Another competent latent examiner is enlisted to analyze, compare, and evaluate the impressions in question. Verification offers a second view and opportunity for the conclusion to be confirmed or revisited. The verification step also is a mechanism to eliminate or highly reduce bias in the conclusion. When the conclusion is confirmed by the verifying examiner, the determination may be reported. In the event of conflicting conclusions, the primary examiner may review the comparison and, if needed, apply the conflict resolution protocol established within the agency or laboratory. Latent print examination is a human process and proficiency comes through practical experience, personal skill, and training. All efforts are made to offer the accurate and credible conclusion, as the result could impact the apprehension or freedom of a subject, the lives of those associated with the investigation, and the members within the fingerprint discipline of forensic science.

"It is better that ten guilty persons escape, than one innocent suffer." William Blackstone

AUTOMATED FINGERPRINT IDENTIFICATION SYSTEM (AFIS)

The Henry Classification System was an effective means of organizing the hundreds of thousands to millions of fingerprint records that were obtained through criminal and civil record keeping. Locating a fingerprint record among the current millions to billions of records in existence today would be an enormous feat if the Henry system was the only mechanism being applied. In the 1960s, the National Institute of Science and Technology (NIST), in collaboration with the Federal Bureau of Investigation (FBI), oversaw the project of automating the process of fingerprint records searching (AVISIAN Staff, 2014). As the new technology improved, fingerprint searches that once took more than 30 days to manually review thousands of records were taking approximately 30 minutes, depending on the size of the database (AVISIAN Staff, 2014). By the early 1980s, AFIS had grown to worldwide use and continues to make improvements in the search and encoding algorithms and additional biometric capabilities accessible to law enforcement organizations. AFIS is an excellent tool for investigative leads, but the eyes of the analyst are the means by which an examination must be completed. IAFIS (Integrated Automated Fingerprint Identification System) emerged in 1999 as an upgrade to AFIS and IAFIS houses criminal records, civil records, and terrorist records totaling over 100 million and is maintained by the FBI (FBI, 2020).

CASES IN FINGERPRINT HISTORY

On March 27, 1905, an art shop owner, Thomas Farrow, opened his store to would-be early morning customers. Moments after entering, he and his wife, Ann, were brutally attacked and their cashbox robbed. Few witnesses and circumstantial evidence were available, but a bloodied fingerprint on the cashbox and the new investigative tool of fingerprint examination were the essential factors in this double homicide. The conviction and execution of the guilty Stratton brothers was a first for London (Wood, 2017).

On September 19, 1910, Thomas Jennings entered the home of his third break-in of the night in Chicago, Illinois. Clarence Hiller, hearing noises in the late night, rose to check the source. He met Jennings on the stairs and in the midst of their brawl, Hiller was shot. Jennings was caught a short distance away with a revolver and wearing bloodstained clothing. There were fingerprint impressions discovered on the freshly painted railing which were identified to Jennings, and along with the cartridges in his revolver, the evidence contributed to his conviction for murder. Still a new form of evidence, the conviction based on fingerprint evidence made this the first case of its kind in U.S. history (Uenuma, 2018).

In 2008, in Gwinnett, Georgia, a teacher was murdered during a robbery. The investigation of witness statements, video surveillance, and DNA analysis led to the arrest of Donald Smith. Adamant denial and, finally, fingerprint comparisons to crime scene evidence confirmed that Ronald Smith, identical twin brother to Donald, was the actual culprit (Ferran, 2010). This case re-confirmed that although identical twins have the same DNA, their fingerprints are different. Prior to fingerprint records for incarcerated persons, photographs, demographic data, and body measurements (anthropometry) were maintained in files. In 1903, when the Leavenworth prison personnel encountered William and Will West, the system of anthropometric and demographic detail was challenged and fingerprint recording prevailed.

Cold cases continue to be solved with AFIS and IAFIS technology, as well as the capabilities within other forensic disciplines, evolve. Options for fingerprint searching that did not exist in the 1970s are now available and accessible. Wrongfully convicted persons are being exonerated and culprits are being apprehended.

"It is a capital mistake to theorize before you have all the evidence. It biases the judgment." Sherlock Holmes, *A Study in Scarlet*, 1887

REFERENCES

Ashbaugh, D. *Quantitative –Qualitative Friction Ridge Analysis: An Introduction to Basic and Advanced Ridgeology.* Boca Raton, FL: CRC Press, 2000.

AVISIAN Staff. (2014). A history of AFIS. Secure ID News. Retrieved from https://www.secureidnews.com/news-item/a-history-of-afis/

Bumbrah, G. S. (2016). Small Particle Reagent (SPR) Method for Detection of Latent Fingermarks: A Review. *Egyptian Journal of Forensic Sciences*, 6(4), 328–332. Retrieved from 10.1016/j.ejfs.2016.09.001

Federal Bureau of Investigation. (2020). Next Generation Identification (NGI). Retrieved from https://www.fbi.gov/services/cjis/fingerprints-and-other-biometrics/ngi

Ferran, L. (2010). Rare Twin Murder Case Echoes Bizarre Fingerprint Origins. Retrieved from https://abcnews.go.com/TheLaw/atlanta-twin-murder-case-echoes-fingerprint-origins/story?id=9909586

Galton, F. *Finger Prints.* New York, NY: MacMillan and Co., 1892.

Maltoni, D., Maio, D., Jain, A., & Prabhakar, S. *Handbook of Fingerprint Recognition.* New York, NY: Springer Science+Business Media, Inc, 2003.

Nousbeck, J., Burger, B., Fuchs-Telem, D., Pavlovsky, M., Fenig, S., Sarig, O., Itin, P., & Sprecher, E. (2011). A Mutation in a Skin-specific Isoform of SMARCAD1 Causes Autosomal-Dominant Adermatoglyphia. *American Journal of Human Genetics*, 89, 302–307.

Uenuma, F. (2018). The First Criminal Trial that Used Fingerprints as Evidence. Retrieved from https://www.smithsonianmag.com/history/first-case-where-fingerprints-were-used-evidence-180970883/

Wood, J. M. (2017). In 1905, Fingerprints Pointed to Murder for the First time in London. Retrieved from https://www.mentalfloss.com/article/62532/112-years-ago-fingerprints-pointed-murder-london

CHAPTER 13

Firearms Evidence Collection

Mohammad A. AlShamsi

Head of Firearms and Toolmarks Section, Gen. Dept. of Forensic Science and Criminology, Dubai Police, UAE

CONTENTS

DOI: 10.4324/9781003129554-13

INTRODUCTION TO FORENSIC FIREARMS EVIDENCE

Firearms have been around since black powder was invented back in the 13th century (Dillon, 1991). Their ignition system was developed and improved throughout time from hand-cannons, matchlocks, wheel-locks, Snaphaunce, "true" flint-locks, percussion cups, and now modern firearms (Bydal, 1990; Greener, 1910). After modern firearms came into play, different types of firearms and mechanisms were seen by the end of the 19th century (Greener, 1910; Davis, 1958). Handguns, rifles, machine guns, and shotguns are different general types of firearms (Greener, 1910). There are always various firearms that come in different forms, such as combination guns, improvised or homemade guns, cane or knife guns that are also different objects with a firearm mechanism incorporated in them (Davis, 1958).

The types of firearms depend on the operations their particular mechanisms do. The main four mechanisms that can be seen in different firearms are single-shot, repeating, semi-automatic, and automatic firearms (Davis, 1958). Where in most single-shot firearms, only one cartridge is loaded and chambered by hand then fired. The extraction and ejection are mostly done by hand, but some firearms may have an ejector mechanism incorporated, which assists the firearm's operator in doing so (Greener, 1910). Repeating firearms can load more than one cartridge at a time with magazines that vary in design. They load, fire, extract, and eject using the operator's muscular force one cartridge after another (Davis, 1958). However, in semi-automatic cocking, loading, extracting, and ejecting a cartridge is done by the explosion force caused by the propellant's combustion. The difference between a semi and an automatic firearm is the number of bullets that are projected every time the trigger is pulled. In a semi-automatic firearm, only one bullet is fired for every trigger pull (Greener, 1910). On the other hand, automatic firearms will continue to fire as long as the trigger is pulled and there are still cartridges in the magazine (Davis, 1958; Heard, 1997).

Handguns, rifles, and machine guns mostly use a cartridge to fire a bullet. A cartridge is a case that holds together the primper assembly or priming depending on whether it is a centerfire or rimfire cartridge, respectively, the propellant, and the bullet (Davis, 1958). On the other hand, shotguns use shotgun shells, also known as shotshells. Shotshells contain similar components to a cartridge with the addition of a wad that separates the propellant from the shots. In most instances, a cartridge contains a bullet, where a shotshell contains multiple shots, also known as pellets (Hatcher et al., 1957; Heard, 1997).

The class and individual characteristics transferred by firearms come in the form of striations and impressions to cartridges and shotshells (Hatcher et al., 1957). This allows firearms examiners to determine whether a specific bullet or cartridge case has been fired from a specific firearm and may link it to previous shooting incidents (Davis, 1958). The discharged cartridge expels gunshot residue (GSR) from the muzzle, which allows firearms examiners to determine the distance from muzzle to target, which may indicate whether a suicide, homicide, or an accidental crime happened (Hatcher et al., 1957). Firearms examiners may examine the internal parts of a firearm to determine whether an accidental incident occurred or another tail to the story that needs to be uncovered (Hatcher et al., 1957). A firearms examiner may also reconstruct shooting-related crime scenes to determine the area of origin and the firing sequence. Everything mentioned above can be found at different crime scenes, whether it is a cartridge case on the ground or a bullet in a victim, and even a firearm in a pond (Davis, 1958). That said, a firearms examiner can assist investigations in many ways (Hatcher et al., 1957).

Firearm Evidence Considerations

A point worth mentioning is a firearms examiner examines physical evidence and does not link a bullet and a cartridge case to a person. A firearm examiner can identify a bullet or a cartridge case to a firearm and does not know whether a specific person operated a firearm. For example, a shooting incident occurred where a victim was shot five times in front of his/her house (Davis, 1958). Assume the firearms examiner identifies all five bullets as having been fired from the same firearm. On the other hand, the firearms examiner cannot be specific as to whether the firearm might have been operated by only one person or might have been operated by five people sharing the same firearm (Davis, 1958; Heard, 1997).

However, a firearm examiner should be aware of other potential evidence that may be found on firearms-related evidence but can be associated with the suspect or victims, such as biological, trace evidence, latent fingerprints, and gunshot residue.

Handling firearms safely, keeping in mind other evidence such as biological and fingerprints.

Always treat any firearm as if it was loaded, always point the muzzle of any firearm in a safe area, and the handler should not place his/her finger in the trigger guard unless intended to fire (Heard, 1997). Depending on the type of firearm, the safety procedure might change slightly; however, they all follow the same idea. Remove the ammunition from the firearm by ejecting the magazine or emptying the revolver's cylinder; make sure to check the chamber and remove any cartridge if in place; a cable zip tie or similar objects can be placed in a firearm's action securing it in place, if cartridges are found in the magazine, handlers should not attempt to empty the magazine to count the cartridges for biological and fingerprint evidence purposes. Firearms should be secured in a cardboard box or similar; preferably in a see-through box sealing it from all directions to avoid any kind of tampering (Davis, 1958; Gunther & Gunther, 1935). However, suppose a firearm or firearm-related evidence is found underwater, such as bullets or cartridge cases. In that case, a secure container shall hold the evidence with the same water medium it was found in to minimize oxidation, which may affect the individual characteristics, which result in identification or elimination (Davis, 1958). Handlers should always consider using new packaging to avoid any cross-contamination; rendering a firearm safe may be done by certified personnel who have gone through some training in firearm documentation and handling (Heard, 1997).

Some crime scenes might involve an area where ammunition is reloaded. Crime scene personnel should note that fired bullets and cartridges cases can be linked to such tools, which may assist in an investigation (Davis, 1958).

Crime scene investigators need to know what a firearms examiner can do in order for them to know how to utilize the available tools to assist the investigation in any way possible. That said, a firearm examiner can provide but is not limited to the following services (Hatcher et al., 1957):

- Firearm examination and identification: A forensics firearms examiner can determine whether a particular bullet was fired from a particular gun or whether a particular cartridge case or shotshell was fired in a particular gun.
- Automated ballistics identification system: A forensics firearms examiner can link a particular bullet, cartridge case, or shotshell to a particular firearm that has been registered in the system previously or used in other crimes.
- Serial number restoration: A forensics firearms examiner is capable of retrieval, recovery, and revisualization of the manufacturer's identifier on a firearm in cases where the serial number has been obliterated.
- Distance determination: A forensics firearms examiner uses gunshot residues to determine the distance of a firearm's muzzle from a target at the time of discharge.

Search and Recovery Equipment

A metal detector can help search for metallic-related evidence such as a firearm, cartridge case, or even a bulletin of different crime scenes, for example, sandy, grassy, and underwater (Gunther & Gunther, 1935).

However, proper recovery and handling techniques are just as crucial as searching and locating evidence. Handling and packaging best practices related to firearm evidence will be discussed in more detail in the next section. However, all recovered evidence needs to be packaged and documented and may include but is not limited to the following (Hatcher et al., 1957):

- Case number
- Date
- Item number
- The location where evidence was recovered
- Address, room, wherein the room
- Detailed description of item being recovered
- Name and initials of the person who located/collected evidence item
- Name and initials of the second person who observed evidence in place

FIREARM EVIDENCE PACKAGING AND HANDLING

Firearm Safety and Handling

To package a firearm at a crime scene, all firearms need to be rendered safe first. Firearms vary based on different ignition systems, makes, and models (Heard, 1997). Nevertheless, rendering a firearm safe is almost the same for every kind (Mathews, 1962). Any kind of repeating firearm will have a magazine type of storage, whether internal such as tubular magazines or external such as boxed magazines to load and feed cartridges is in the firearm (Hatcher et al., 1957). To render a firearm safe, follow the steps mentioned below:

1. Always assume every firearm is loaded and ready to fire, control the muzzle direction at all times, and do not forget the trigger finger must be kept off the trigger and out of the trigger guard.
2. Always point the firearm in a safe direction.
3. If the magazine is detachable, then remove it. If it is not, then empty the magazine from the cartridges.
4. Inspect the firing chamber/s, and empty them if any cartridges are found.
5. Examine the bore to make sure that there is no object stuck in the barrel that may endanger the next firearm operator (aka squib).
6. It is recommended when possible to insert a plastic wire tie (aka zip-tie) through the locking mechanism to ensure it is safe and can be

FIGURE 13.1 Rendering firearms safe using wire tie (ready to package).

FIGURE 13.2 Inoperable 3-D printed firearm parts.

visually noticeable, as depicted in Figure 13.1. (Note: DO NOT insert the wire tie in the barrel. This may affect the examination and identification process done by the firearms examiner.)

Secondly, after rendering a firearm safe, it needs to be documented sufficiently to prevent any kind of intended or unintended accidents (Mathews, 1962). Documentation of recovered firearms may include the following:

- Make
- Model
- Serial number
- Caliber
- Type of firearm (e.g. single-shot, repeating, shotguns, self-loading)
- Other, such as the condition of the weapon when found (e.g. broken, disabled)

Rendering a firearm safe is of utmost priority, as mentioned previously. However, an authorized crime scene investigator or other authorized personnel shall render a recovered firearm safe. Whether by in-house training or else, competency needs to be reflected by successfully passing some sort of training. The authorized personnel rendering the safe firearm need to be reflected in the chain of custody (Mathews, 1962).

Finally, packaging and handling packing allow evidence to travel securely from a crime scene to another destination, such as a forensics laboratory (Mathews, 1962). Many packaging options include using evidence boxes, manila envelopes, paper bags, canvas bags, jewelry cardboard boxes, item tag only, and more. That said, when it comes to packaging a firearm after it being secured and documented sufficiently, it is recommended to package a firearm in a cardboard box and use wire ties aka zip ties to secure it in place (Mathews, 1962; Heard, 1997). It is also recommended for a firearm cardboard box to have a see-through panel. Finally, the signature of the packager and the date across evidence tape is recommended to insure no tampering with the tape or seal has occurred.

3-D Printed Firearms Handling and Collection

3-D printed firearms have been around since around 2012. They might be seen in certain crime scenes already and may increase shortly. A 3-D printed firearm can be recovered in conditions such as intact and operable, partially, or destroyed. (AlShamsi, 2019). That said, in order to recover a 3-D printed firearm successfully, the following steps should be followed:

If the 3-D printed firearm is intact and operable:

- Handle and transport similarly as traditional firearms (mentioned in the previous sub-section "Firearm Safety and Handling") (AlShamsi, 2019).

If the 3-D printed firearm is partially or entirely damaged "inoperable":

- Collect any intact and damaged components found, especially the metal pieces (which may be mechanical parts of the firearm such as a nail that might operate as the firing pin, as depicted in Figure 13.2) (AlShamsi, 2019).

Homemade Firearms and Other Miscellaneous Firearms

Homemade firearms, aka country-made firearms or zip guns, are constructed with pre-existing materials with no certified firearms manufacturing or gunsmith's supervision. These firearms can be extremely dangerous to their operators or anyone in their surroundings (Mathews, 1962). They may explode or perform unexpectedly (Gunther & Gunther, 1935). Nevertheless, if encountered with such guns at crime scenes, then handle and transport them similarly to traditional firearms (mentioned in the previous sub-section "Firearm Safety and Handling").

Moreover, various firearms have gun mechanisms incorporated into them, which are usually seen in an umbrella, or cane, or even a knife (Mathews, 1962; Heard, 1997). Even if such firearms come in the form of a tree, check the feeding mechanism and follow the same steps mentioned previously in the sub-section "Firearm Safety and Handling."

Fired Ammunition

Fired ammunition is divided into two parts: the projectile/s and the cartridge case or the shotshell. Fired projectiles are frequently found in two locations, either at random places at a crime scene (e.g. in a wall, which usually a crime scene investigators recovered, or if found in a body, then it is recovered by a medical examiner during an autopsy.) Either way, when recovering a projectile, non-metallic tools or plastic-covered tools such as plastic tweezers or plastic-tipped tongs should be used (Burrard, 1962). This is done not to affect or alter the individual characteristics associated with the ballistics features, making firearms examination and identification possible.

Do not forget fired bullets may contain bloodborne pathogens such as COVID-19 or AIDS virus, which may be transferred after striking, passing through, or recovering from a shooting victim. That said, crime scene investigators should always consider potential biohazards (Welch, 1981).

Additionally, recovered cartridge cases or shotshells should be handled with non-metallic tools not to manipulate or damage pre-existing characteristics transferred by a firearm.

Finally, all the evidence must be packaged separately (e.g. if three bullets are recovered from a crime scene, they should be placed in three different packages.). This is done not to create any additional marks or alter existing marks by bullets or cartridge cases striking each other within the same package (Burrard, 1962). The marks required for firearm examination and identification come in the form of microscopic striations, "scratches," and impressions. This illustrates how delicate and small in size these marks are in assisting any investigation. That said, handling them with care is very important. Packaging of fired projectiles and cartridge cases is recommended to be in cardboard jewelry boxes or similar to cotton-padded paper boxes (Welch, 1981).

Unfired Ammunition

Any cartridge consists mainly of a cartridge case/ shotshell, propellent (aka gun powder), projectile/s, and a primer assembly or priming (Burrard, 1962). To fire a cartridge, the primer or the priming material is struck by a firing pin or a hammer. That said, crime scene investigators should pay attention to package the unfired cartridges securely to avoid any loose rounds that may accidentally strike one of the primers, resulting in a cartridge going off. Cartridges can be packaged together; however, biological and fingerprint evidence should be considered (Burrard, 1962). Also, unfired ammunition should be packaged separately from firearms. Unfired ammunition most of the time can be recovered either from a magazine or in a box of ammunition. If found in a magazine, leave the live rounds inside if possible. Then package the magazine containing the ammunition securely, making sure it cannot be tampered with. If found in a box of ammunition, the same should be applied (Heard, 1997; Welch, 1981).

Underwater Firearm Evidence Collection

We have discussed firearm evidence and discussed best practices with regard to handling them. However, when firearm evidence is found underwater, it is dealt with a little differently. Most firearm evidence is made up of metallic components, and when metallic components are submerged underwater, the oxidation process starts to increase, causing them to corrode. This weakens or even destroys the marks associated with the examination and identification of a firearm. The oxidation process accelerates even faster when brought out of the water. That said, the best way to deal with this is to recover the firearm evidence with the same water. For example, suppose a firearm is found underwater. In that case, it should be rendered safe as soon as it leaves the water, if possible, and placed in a plastic box containing the same water it was found in, similarly if projectiles or cartridge cases are found underwater. Underwater crime scene investigators should also consider other evidence and biological and fingerprints that may be recoverable.

Do not attempt to handle metallic firearm-related evidence with any metallic tipped tong, forceps, and similar tools because they may produce unnecessary tool marks on the evidence or even manipulate or damage significant pre-existing evidence beneficial to an investigation.

GUNSHOT RESIDUE

When a firearm expels a projectile, the propellant powder is burned, producing heat and gas inside the cartridge case.

That said, gunshot residue (GSR) is composed of the following:

- The combustion of the priming mixture produces primer residues.

- The residues caused by burning propellant.
- Excess trace material caused by erosion caused by a bullet and the interior of the barrel.
- Unburned as well as partly burnt powder.

GSR is made up of primer residues and propellant residues. Partially or fully burned propellants and other gunshot residues are expelled from the muzzle during the firing process and can be used to determine the muzzle's distance to the target, which will be discussed in detail later. This section will focus on primer gunshot residues that are deposited, particularly at close range. These residues can be visible; however, some may require chemical treatment (Lee & Pagliaro, 2014; Di Maio, 1985; Di Maio & Vincent, 2015).

Primer residue is produced by striking the hammer or the printing pin of the primer mixture in a cartridge (Burrard, 1962). Thus, it causes microscopic particles to leak through various openings in a firearm. GSR, a particle characteristic of primer residue, is defined as a particle with a spherical or non-uniform structure containing the elements lead styphnate, antimony sulfide, barium nitrate, and other chemicals (Burrard, 1962).

Different reasons may cause primer gunshot residue to be deposited, such as firing or handling a firearm, being within close range of a gun being discharged, or even contacting an object that already has primer gunshot residue on it (Di Maio, 1985; Di Maio, 1985). However, a crime scene investigator needs to know that the examination cannot determine these listed circumstances' relative likelihood (Burrard, 1962) (Welch, 1981).

A person not firing a firearm will not have primer gunshot residue on their hands. Also, negative results could be produced when washing or wiping, wearing gloves (Burrard, 1962). Plus, sweating extensively, or even environmental factors such as rain and wind, bloody hands, excessive debris on the sample, significantly more than 2 to 6 hours passing between firing and sampling, or the weapon that does not contain primer residue hands when discharged (Lee & Pagliaro, 2014; Allen, 1983; Di Maio, 1985; Di Maio, 1985).

When recovering primer gunshot residue, note the following (Lee & Pagliaro, 2014):

- Microscopic primer gunshot residue particles have been found to follow the bullet's direction and are commonly found on the victim's hands.
- Primer gunshot residue cannot be used to determine the distance from the muzzle to the target.
- It is impossible to determine if the primer GSR has been collected from an inanimate object or a hand.
- The primer GSR may be from handling a firearm or even unloading it.

In order to collect primer GSR from a suspect's hands, follow the guidelines mentioned below (Lee & Pagliaro, 2014):

- Always sample the hands of a suspect promptly. Collect primer residue samples at the scene when feasible.
- If collection at the scene is impossible, then bag the suspect's hands with paper bags or similar before transporting.
- Secure paper bags around the suspect's wrists with rubber bands or similar; secure bags around the suspect's wrists with rubber bands or even tape.
- Photograph and document the hands, especially if any blood spatter patterns are present, before inspecting the hands for primer GSR.
- Always clean your hands before sample collection.
- Wear latex barrier gloves, not nitrile. Hold the suspect's hand by the wrist, and keep clear from contacting the required surface.
- If the examination is required to be performed on a dead body, avoid wet or bloody areas.

In order to collect primer GSR from clothing, follow the guidelines mentioned below (Lee & Pagliaro, 2014; Di Maio, 1985):

- Collecting samples from clothing highly depends on the lab's policy. Note: Clothing similar to the skin (vinyl, leather) is best.
- Photograph with standard and IR camera with scale (will be discussed later).
- Carefully remove clothing.
- Package flat on paper, so particles are not disturbed.
- Do not fold or cut clothing items.
- Place in a box or on flat cardboard covered with paper.

If a firearm was used from a vehicle, samples may be collected to determine the presence of primer GSR. In order to collect primer GSR from vehicles, follow the guidelines mentioned below:

- The collection should be done from leather, vinyl, or plastic surfaces.
- Avoid sampling fabric surfaces. (Note: This depends on the lab's policy wheather fabric surfaces should be considered or not.)
- If a firearm was discharged inside a vehicle, a great place to sample would be areas where small amounts of settled dust can be visualized.
- Areas exposed to the wind are less likely to retain primer GSR.

Use a single primer residue kit to sample the areas of interest. Document the area currently being sampled "right hand" or "top of dashboard near driver window."

Any evidence, including GSR, should be recovered by a trained and authorized personnel.

Muzzle to Target Distance Determination

For the past seven decades, firearm examiners have been using muzzle-to-target determination successfully in solving shooting crimes. However, this process has undergone numerous refinements in detection levels and instrumentation, which have been critical in improving the destructive and non-destructive methodologies (Burrard, 1962). In muzzle-to-target distance determination, a comparison is made between the gunshot residue distribution from the item collected at the crime scene to gunshot residue patterns prepared in a laboratory-based on different distances (Chaklos & Davis, 2005) (Di Maio, 1985). During this process, it is essential that each step right from preparing, detecting, and comparing the gunshot residue be carefully documented (Burrard, 1962).

Some of the necessary steps of the muzzle-to-target distance determination process include but not limited to (Burrard, 1962; Brown, 1985):

- Thorough crime scene documentation (weather, rain, humidity, wind, etc.).
- 90-degree photography (when possible).
- Distance of photography should be mentioned if evidence is not recovered.
- Infrared photography (non-destructive visualization technique especially on dark surfaces).
- Using the lead and nitrites chemical reaction to help with mapping and enhancing the distribution of GSR particles.
- Measuring the shotgun patterns in case a shotgun was used in a crime scene.

It is crucial to approach the interpretation of gunshot residue patterns with extra care due to specific factors that might affect the expected pattern results (Lindman, 1989). For example, the target surface composition will determine the surface's ability to hold and retain the gunshot residue (Dillon, 1989). If the target surface is soaked from rainwater or blood, the chance to recover the residue diminishes greatly (Burrard, 1962). Finally, a critical angle incident can also influence the amount of residue left on the target surface. In such a scenario, a trajectory reconstruction can be used to determine the angle of incidence.

Infrared and Ultraviolet Camera in Gunshot Residue

Crime scene investigators use digital photography for documentation. One of the advanced applications of crime scene photography is infrared and ultraviolet photography to document gunshot residue (Chaklos & Davis, 2005; Bailey, 2007).

Crime scene investigators can use digital infrared photography as a non-destructive test for examining GSR on dark and multi-colored fabrics. When a firearm has been discharged, GSR exits the muzzle of the firearm and creates a visible powder pattern on light-colored clothing at specific muzzle-to-target distances (Chaklos & Davis, 2005). However, when GSR patterns are found on dark or multi-colored clothing, the pattern is not clearly visible because of the background color. The detection and enhancement of GSR patterns are commonly demonstrated nowadays by a digital camera that produces infrared images (Bailey, 2007). Digital infrared photography reveals GSR details on dark and multi-colored fabric because the human eye is not sensitive to this region of the electromagnetic spectrum. (Note: Lead-free ammunition with smokeless powder will not show GSR under IR light.) (Bailey, 2007).

Gunshot residue is one of the easiest items of evidence to photograph and takes very little time and effort. Gunshot residue can be visualized using infrared reflected photography in some circumstances by following the steps mentioned below (Chaklos & Davis, 2005; Bailey, 2007):

1. Place the item of evidence on a flat surface with good lighting such as a photo-flood lamp or some other emitter of infrared energy.
2. Place the camera on a quadra-pod or tripod.
3. Set camera in the manual mode.
4. Set image quality to highest resolution, recommend raw + jpeg.
5. Turn off auto ISO.
6. Set ISO to 200–400.
7. Achieve 1:1 ratio with macro lens relevant to make and model of digital camera.
8. Position camera at a distance of 30 centimeters then 1 meters (12 inch then 30 inches) to achieve close-up view and wide view.
9. Turn off camera and lens auto focus.
10. Focus lens on GSR pattern.
11. Attach an infrared filter.
12. Select shutter speed for the particular lighting used and F-stop combination f/22 to start for maximum depth of field.
13. Take a series of photographs using all of the available visible pass filters for the evidence. Varying modes black/white and comparing them with colored may yield better results visually.

SHOOTING SCENE INVESTIGATION AND RECONSTRUCTION

During crime scene reconstruction, all the actions and events in a crime scene are eliminated or determined by analyzing the laboratory examination of physical evidence, position and location of the physical evidence, and the crime scene pattern. During reconstruction, the laboratory examination of physical evidence, interpretation of the scene pattern evidence, and scientific scene analysis come into play and the logical formulation of a theory and systematic study of related information (NA, 2019).

Importance of Crime Scene Reconstruction

Crime scene reconstruction is critical in the determination of the exact course that a crime took. This is done by limiting possibilities that might have culminated in the crime scene or based on the encountered physical evidence. This is why the integrity of a crime is preserved so that it helps with reconstructing the crime. With reconstruction, the investigator uses logical approaches in theory formulations, has the ability to examine physical evidence scientifically, and make observations at the crime scene (Burrard, 1962).

Crime scene reconstruction is essential for crime scenes that involve a shooting to help determine the manner of death (whether accidental, suicide, and homicide), which would be difficult to determine under conventional means. One way to differentiate a suicide from a homicide is the muzzle-to-target distance, which is possible through crime scene reconstruction. Reconstruction also allows trajectory reconstructions to prove or disprove the witnesses, victims, and suspects of a shooting scenario. However, while crime scene reconstruction should be a routine procedure for investigating shoot cases, its maximum ability has not been utilized fully over the years (NA, 2019).

A successful shooting investigation is made up of the following components: reconstruction experiments, the laboratory examination of pattern and physical evidence, medical and autopsy records, crime scene processing, and the use of investigative information. Like most investigations, crime scene reconstruction is heavily dependent on the quality of the crime scene documentation. That is the search, collection, and preservation of the required evidence. Evidence such as gunshot residue in shooting cases can be lost or destroyed if efforts to locate and preserve such evidence are not made. Additionally, the required evidence might not be located and collected before losing or releasing the crime scene in many cases (Heard, 1997).

Preliminary Steps for Shooting Incident Investigations

Any investigative information such as statements from parties present during the crime scene is vital to both the crime scene personnel and the overall investigation. Since the crime scene investigator needs to remain objective and open-minded during the investigation process, they can rely on investigative information for help across specific vital duties (Welch, 1981).

Gunshot residue analysis is vital in shooting cases to determine the approximate muzzle to target distance and those involved in the shooting. However, gunshot residue is likely to be destroyed and lost if not collected and stored correctly. In such cases where critical pieces of evidence are missing or lost, the hands of both the potential shooter and the victim should be sampled as soon as possible. The victim's clothing can also be a valuable source of information about gunshot residue distribution patterns and, therefore, should be preserved and used in distance determinations (Welch, 1981). The clothes should be removed carefully from the victim, dried, and should not be folded, as mentioned in the previous section.

Additionally, it is crucial for clothing from the potential shooters and victims to be seized. It might contain gunshot residue, soil patterns, damage, tears, and transfer elements such as glass fragments and blood spatter. Critical in the reconstruction process. Damage to trace evidence on clothing can be used to corroborate a witness statement regarding the events or movements during and after the incident (Di Maio, 1985; NA, 2019).

Suppose an incident involved more than one shooter or multiple shots. In that case, the investigator must:

- Locate and account for all associated firearm evidence by conducting an inventory of the witnesses account regarding the number of shots fired.
- Type and number of wounds sustained, bullet strikes and deflections.
- Number of bullet holes (with the entry and exit points).
- Number of recovered shell casings.
- Number of bullets each firearm can hold and how many of the bullets are missing.

The investigator's next logical step is to reconcile the collected data and account for all recovered firearms and possible shots.

Crime scene investigators should also not release the crime scene until after all the evidence has been collected and reviewed. An x-ray and an autopsy should be conducted to gain insight into how many fragments and bullets hit the victim or ricocheted inside the body (Di Maio, 1985).

Role of Markings on Projectiles

In crime scenes, projectiles are examined by forensic laboratories to help provide information that is critical to the reconstruction process. Carrying out a forensic examination on the firearms will yield information regarding the rifling characteristics, the type of ammunition used, and the caliber characteristics. These help determine the model and manufacture of the gun with databases such as the Association of Firearms and Toolmarks Examiners AFTE online database, or the Federal Bureau of Investigation's Gun Rifling Characteristics GRC or other. On the other hand, a microscopic examination will offer information about the surfaces that the projectile contacted immediately after firing (Burrard, 1962).

Firearm Specific Markings

Markings present on fired projectiles can be classified as either received after leaving the muzzle, individualizing characteristics, or class characteristics (Hamby, 1974). The class characteristic classification are features that are predetermined to manufacturing and are specific to a particular type of firearm, its model, and manufacturer such as the number of lands and grooves, their widths, degree of pitch, and the twist's direction. Individualizing characteristics classifications are not predetermined to manufacturing and are marked on fired projectiles or cartridge cases resulting from the erosion and/ or corrosion caused by firing the firearm. These include uneven wear markings that are produced during manufacturing, shavings, skid marks, and the striations made on the projectile as it passes through the firearm's barrel (Hamby, 1974).

Post-Muzzle Markings and Trace Evidence

Markings made on a projectile as it leaves the muzzle can also be used in reconstructing its trajectory. These markings result from the terminal trajectory or final impact surface, intermediate target impacts. When a fired projectile comes into contact with an intermediate target, it maintains the Locard Exchange Principles (Hamby, 1974). It collects some material traces from this target, which can be identified and traced to an individual in the crime scene such as fabric or blood. Whenever a projectile passes through an intermediate target, it creates a direction of the direction, facilitating reconstruction (NA, 2019). Other types of trace evidence from intermediate targets that can help with the reconstruction process include gun residue on both clothing and hands. The terminal trajectory shape and size can help in crime scene reconstruction and can be confirmed using the projectile markings after it went through the terminal surface (Hamby, 1974).

Geometric Projection Methods for Trajectory Determination

There are three main geometric projection methods available to a crime scene investigator in determining the trajectory of a projectile. These include physical (strings, rods, and probes) and optical projection methods (low-power lasers and visual sightings), and crime-scene 3-D scanning and software reconstruction.

Physical Projection Methods

Entry Hole Geometry The estimated angle of entry of a projectile can be measured using the shape of its entry and exit holes. Since most projectile holes feature an elliptical shape, their angle of impact can be determined with trigonometry; that is, finding the cosine of the ratio of the hole's width to that of its length.

Probes and Rods Probes are critical in establishing a projectile trajectory in cases where the holes of the projectiles are close together, which impedes access to one of the projectile hole's blind side. However, the investigator must approach this with care to prevent damage to the projectile holes when using the probe.

Some of the materials used for this type of reconstruction include hollow metal tubes, solid metal rods, and wooden rods. Ensure that the rod used has a width similar to the hole's diameter and should not be thick to force the rod into the projectile hole.

Strings When working with projectile holes that are far apart, one can align this distance by using probes attached by strings. However, the strings from sagging or being deflected by either side of the hole can lead to an error (NA, 2019).

Optical Projection Methods

Optical Sighting Optical sighting is one of the simplest means investigators can use to assess how projectile holes align during reconstruction and is made by visual observation. However, the resulting alignment lacks precise direction and only preliminary. Using this method, the investigator should attempt to photograph the trajectory reconstruction alignment through one projectile hole.

Low Power Lasers Compared to an optical sighting, the use of low-power lasers has proved more effective due to their ability to define a straight line, especially where long distances are involved. However, since projectiles' trajectory can be influenced and gravity, extra care should be taken as the projectile curve might be curved, mainly when a lower velocity projectile was used (NA, 2019).

Laser Path Alignment with the Projectile Holes in Walls   In a scenario where a projectile trajectory ends within a wall, the observer has to ensure that he or she does not disturb the projectile's entry hole when accessing the termination point. The investigator can opt to cut into the whole close to the projectile hole to gain access or use a laser probe in cases involving a blind projectile hole. When using a laser probe, the investigator should insert it carefully into the projectile hole while preventing any damage to it. Once the probe is inserted into the hole, the investigator should attach the laser to the probe, effectively extending the probe.

Laser Beam Documentation   While both photographic and video documentation should be done continuously throughout this method, it should only be done after aligning the laser beam with the projectile holes. Adding dust or smoke to the setup can also help enhance the visualization of the laser beam. However, it is imperative to note that using visualizing smoke in areas with air circulation or outdoors can be quite tricky (NA, 2019).

Positioning Stages   The investigators can also rely on commercially manufactured positioning platforms for help with positioning the laser. The laser's head should be mounted on a multi-axis stage with the requisite scales for documentation and calculation purposes (NA, 2019).

Using the Aligned Laser Beam to Determine the Angle Information   Investigators can also rely on tape measures and protractors to establish the presence and document the projectile hole's location based on fixed points at the crime scene. To ensure correct angle measurement, the investigator can also use levels, inclinometers, and plumb bobs. Finally, once the investigator obtains and documents the projectile trajectory, they should carry out a second determination of trajectory.

Intermediate Target Placement in the Laser Beam   The use of a laser beam allows the investigator to interpose people and objects to check reconstruction scenarios. However, when encountering soft intermediate targets such as cushions, pillows, or mattresses, it would be ideal to use a hollow probe. Either way, the investigators should be careful to prevent deflection, which is likely to cause errors (NA, 2019).

Dual-Opposed Co-axial Laser   Reconstructing the alignment of projectile holes for soft objects can be done using a hollow probe. However, when relying on a substitute object, the investigator should ensure that the object bears a similar weight, size, and shape to the hollow probe. These can be useful in duplicating scenarios without having to tamper with the actual evidence. If objects in the crime scene, such as bodies, have projectile holes, two lasers should be used to determine the projectile's alignments. Once the first laser's alignment is established, the investigator should mount the second laser on the first laser beam. By using a second laser, the investigator has the ability to use it on the moveable placement of subject' bodies.'

Lighting Auxiliary Alignment Targets   The light in outdoor scenes makes it challenging to use lasers in reconstructing trajectory alignment. The ideal time for using such setups for reconstruction outdoors is during night time. However, with auxiliary and temporary targets, experimentation in the daylight can be done using reflective strips and white index cards. Successful outdoor reconstruction during day time can now be achieved by placing the strips or cards across various laser beam locations (NA, 2019).

Crime Scene 3-D Scanning and Software Reconstruction

Crime Scene 3-D Scanning   3-D scanning tools are available to measure with high resolution the details in a certain area specially in applications such as crime scene investigation. Certain requirements are needed to be achieved in order to scan a shooting crime scene.

1. Scan the crime scene with no alterations (raw documentation).
2. A rod with two probes should be used for every bullet hole according to the angle of impact.
3. Rescan the crime scene with the probes in the bullet holes to clearly visualize the angle of impact in the crime scene. This can be done more than once to scan areas that are not visualized from one area of a crime scene.
4. Upload the software with crime scene data, and insert requirements to visualize bullet/s trajectory, area of origin, and more.

Sources of Error and Precautions

During reconstruction, one is likely to face errors caused by the projectile's post-impact trajectory. Developing predictions can be difficult if the project ricocheted or grazed on a target. The same can also be said when the projectile hits the target from an angle of impact (Burrard, 1962).

Therefore, deflection has to be taken into account in reconstructing trajectory alignment with an intermediate target (NA, 2019). That is, a projectile gains some degree of deflection once it goes through an object. The degree of deflection will be determined by the projectile's interaction with the object, the object, and its shape (Burrard, 1962).

While two points are enough to determine a projectile trajectory, this can be difficult when deflection has occurred. Therefore, the investigator should stick to using a minimum of three points to increase trajectory reconstructions' accuracy (NA, 2019). The investigator should also consider the possibility of some degree of deflection. This can be done through several experiments involving firing the weapon multiple times to determine the variability and deflection (Burrard, 1962).

Shell Casing Ejection/Cartridge Case Pattern Analysis

Valuable information can also be gathered from shell casings at the scene of the crime. The casings can be matched back to the suspect's guns to ascertain the specific cartridge source. When the weapon is not found, the information on the shell casings can be kept in a database where they will be compared to other cartridge cases (NA, 2019). The shell's location on the crime scene can also provide insight into the shooter's location. Even with most automatic and semi-automatic firearms ejected to the right, the investigator must carry out experiments using either the same model or a similar one to gain insight into the gun's ejection pattern. However, the following factors should be taken into consideration when determining the gun's ejection pattern: environmental factors such as wind and rain, the ground surface where the casings fell, the position of the shooter (was he/she standing or was he/she moving), the shooter's body position and hand, and the type of ammunition used. However, caution has to be practiced when making conclusions on the casing location as they might have been moved by traffic or kicked away after their ejection (Heard, 1997).

OTHER SHOOTING RECONSTRUCTION CONSIDERATIONS

Application of Chemical Reagents in Shooting Reconstruction

Before digging into the reagents that may be used to determine whether a hole was produced by a bullet or not, a note worth mentioning is the failure to detect lead, copper, or nickel using the reagents mentioned below does not eliminate the presence of a certain metal in a bullet's composition. Also, verification of the effectiveness should be checked before applying any of the reagents on evidence. Finally, precautions must be exercised to minimize or eliminate the possibility of absorption or inhalation of the chemical reagents (Haag, 2006).

Dithiooxamide (DTO)

The dithiooxamide test (also known as the Rubeanic Acid Test) is a chemically specific chromophoric test for the presence of cuprous (copper-bearing) material. Copper-jacketed bullets represent a considerable percentage of ammunition evidence in criminal cases.

The test identifies a bullet wipe or bullet splash caused by the copper-bearing particulate in the form of bullet jacket fragments found around the perimeter of a bullet hole. While the test is not particularly useful for distance determinations, it can detect residue consistent with the discharge of a firearm or the passage or impact of a copper-jacketed bullet. Thus, the copper particles will react with dithiooxamide to become a dark mossy-green color (Haag, 2006).

2-nitroso-1-naphthol

The 2-nitroso 1-naphthol test also known as 2-NN, is a supplemental test for the presence of copper. Thus, the iron, copper, and zinc particles will react with 2-NN to become green, pink, or orange color, respectively (Haag, 2006).

Sodium Rhodizonate (Soro)

The sodium rhodizonate test is a chemically specific chromophoric test for the presence of lead in any form. The presence of particulate lead is a random non reproducible phenomenon dependent on many uncontrolled variables that may be caused by leading, metal fouling, or a dirty barrel at the time of discharge (Bashinski et al., 1974). If both DTO and sodium rhodizonate tests are required to be performed, the DTO test for copper should be performed first. The presence of lead around a hole may establish it as a bullet caused but not necessarily from a lead bullet. Also, the test may uncover "lead splash" phenomenon when a lead bullet or a soft point bullet strikes a surface. If the bullet comes incontact with a surface at a shallow angle the direction can be determined by the splash direction. Thus, the lead particles will react with sodium rhodizonate to become a purple-blue color (Haag, 2006).

The presence of vaporous lead is very useful in that it typically is found at closer ranges. Although the sodium rhodizonate test cannot be used to determine precise muzzle-to-target distances, it is possible to determine the maximum distance to which it will be deposited using the firearm and ammunition in combination. note: this is not applicable to lead free ammunition (Bashinski et al., 1974).

Dimethylglyoxime (DMG)

Dimethylglyoxime, also known as DMG, is a test to detect nickel. This reagent is useful for bullets that are jacketed with nickel similar to DTO for copper (Haag, 2006).

Vehicle Dynamics in Shooting Reconstruction

Vehicle motion and dynamics have to be factored in during reconstruction if a vehicle was involved in a shooting. Vehicles present a level of complexity due to the irregular shapes, and non-static location and orientation (NA, 2019; Haag, 2006). The squaring technique of vehicles presents a good frame of reference with respect to a crime scene. Several phenomenons associated with shooting incidents on vehicles should always be considered when bullets come in contact with metal such as "lead-in" mark, "pinch point," fracture lines in painted metal surfaces, and bullet holes in tires.

Moreover, the crime scene investigators should be able to identify bullet hole characteristics in laminated glass compared to tempered glass. The fracture lines from the impact of a bullet penetrating or striking can help the investigator determine the projectile hole's location, the number of subsequent projectiles and their sequence, the angle of incidence, and the projectile's direction essential for reconstruction (NA, 2019; Haag, 2006).

Firearm-Associated Blood Spatter Patterns

Analyzing the patterns exhibited by blood spatter can help in the reconstruction of shooting incidents. Crime scenes with a high-velocity impact spatter will point towards a high-energy injury. This impact spatter can also help shed some light on the victim's location, critical for reconstructions. Blood patterns associated with firearms such as misting and blowback can aid an the investigation to differentiate between a murder and a suicide (NA, 2019).

REFERENCES

AlShamsi, M. A. (2019). 3D Printed Firearms Comparison. *AFTE Journal*, *51*(4), 242–245.

Allen, D. E. (1983). Effects of Blood on Gunshot and Gunpowder Residue. *AFTE Journal*, *15* (2), 102.

Bailey, James A. (2007). Digital infrared Photography to Develop GSR Patterns. *Australian Journal of Forensic Sciences*, *37* (1), 33–40.

Bashinski, J. S., Davis, J. E., & Young, C. (1974). Detection of Lead in Gunshot Residues on Targets Using the Sodium Rhodizonate Test. *AFTE Journal*, *6* (4), 5.

Brown, C. G. (1985). Detection of Nitrites and Lead in Gunpowder Residue Patterns. *AFTE Journal*, *17* (2), 118.

Burrard, G. *The Identification of Firearms and Forensic Ballistics*. New York: A.S. Barnes & Co, 1962.

Bydal, B. A. (1990). Percussion Primer Mixes. *AFTE Journal*, *22* (1), 1–26.

Chaklos, D., & A. Davis. (2005). Visualization of Gunpowder Residue Patterns Using a Digital Infrared Camera and Optical Filters. *AFTE Journal*, *37* (2), 117–122.

Conrad, W. E. (1980). Firing Pistol Ammunition in a Revolver. *AFTE Journal 12* (1), 33.

Davis, J. E. *Introduction to Tool Marks, Firearms and the Striagraph*. Springfield: Charles C Thomas Pub Ltd, 1958.

Di Maio, J. M. (1985). Gunshot Wounds: Practical Aspects of Firearms, Ballistics, and Forensic techniques, 37–40.

Di Maio, Vincent, J. M. (2015). Gunshot Wounds: Practical Aspects of Firearms, Ballistics, and Forensic Techniques 292.

Dillon, J. H. (1989). Graphical Analysis of the Shotgun/ Shotshell Performance Envelope in Distance Determination Cases. *AFTE Journal*, *21* (4), 593–594.

Dillon, J. H. (1991). Black Powder Background. *AFTE Journal*, *23* (2), 689–693.

Dillon, J. H. (1991). The Manufacture of Conventional Smokeless Powder. *AFTE Journal*, *23* (2), 682–688.

Greener, W. W. *The Gun and Its Development*. New York: Cassel and Company, 1910.

Gunther, J. D., & Gunther, C. O. *The Identification of Firearms*. New York: John Wiley and Sons Inc, 1935.

Haag, Lucien C. *Shooting Incident Reconstruction*. Cambridge, MA: Academic Press, 2006.

Haag, M. G. (1997). 2-Nitroso-1-naphthol Versus Dithiooxamide in Trace Copper Detection at Bullet Impact Sites. *AFTE Journal*, *29* (2), 204–209.

Hamby, J. (1974). Identification of Projectiles. *AFTE Journal*, *6* (5/6), 22.

Hatcher, J. S., Jury, F. J., & Weller, J. *Firearms Investigation, Identification, and Evidence*. Harrisburg: Stackpole Books, 1957.

Heard, B. *Handbook of Firearms and Ballistics – Examining and Interpreting Forensic Evidence*. West Sussex: John Wiley & Sons, Inc, 1997.

Lee, C. L., & Pagliaro, E. M. (2014). Crime Scene Guidebook. *Institute of Forensic Science*, *1*, 48–49.

Lindman, D. A. (1989). Weathering Time Factor in GSR Proximity Determinations. *AFTE Journal*, *21* (3), 500–502.

Mathews, J. H. *Firearms Identification, Volume I.* Springfield: Charles C. Thomas, 1962.

NA. (2019). Crime scene reconstruction. Jagannath University 1-27.

Welch, N. E. (1981). Matching a Bullet to a Cartridge Case. *AFTE Journal*, *13* (4), 79.

CHAPTER 14

Trace Evidence

Hillary Mullings-Williams

Worldwide Association of Women Forensic Experts (WAWFE-Caribbean), Institute of Forensic Science and Legal Medicine, University of the West Indies, Jamaica Caribbean Association of Forensic Sciences

CONTENTS

SOIL

Soil is material that is formed at the interface between the atmosphere and the earth's crust. It is also defined as the top layer of the earth surface. Soil is formed by the combined action of biological, chemical, and physical processes and is composed of organic (live and dead animal, plants, and microorganisms) and inorganic (mineral) matter, air, and water and these are found in varying proportions, as seen in Figure 14.1. Soil is considered dynamic as the materials within the soil are always combining and changing (Fitzpatrick, 2013). Soil formation usually determines the color soil has; however, in some areas, the color of the soil may be determined by the composition of minerals in its parent rock. Soil tends to have individual layers that vary in organic matter and physical and chemical characteristics. These individual layers can be distinctively identified in a cross section of the soil and these layers from

the soil surface to the underlying parent rock are called the soil profile as seen in Figure 14.2. Each layer may be different in color, size of particles, biological matter present, and chemical composition. Soil is also comprised of remnants of man-made activities to include fragments of man-made material e.g., concrete or brick; and these materials give soil unique properties that can make it forensically significant (Strahler, 2013).

Forensic Significance

Soil can be one of the under-utilized pieces of evidence at a crime. Soil can be found everywhere and as such it tends to be overlooked as a valuable source of evidence at a crime scene. Based on Locard's Exchange Principle: *Every Contact leaves a trace*, soil evidence may be transferred from or deposited on a suspect/perpetrator or victim at a crime scene. Soil evidence may be recovered on the surfaces to

FIGURE 14.1   Soil sample with biological matter.

FIGURE 14.2   Soil profile showing the varying layers of the soil.

FIGURE 14.3   Soil sample on sneakers.

Methods of Recovery and Collection

It is important to take detailed notes on the general surroundings and the area immediately surrounding the soil sample to be collected. The number, size, and type of samples to be collected are dependent on the nature of the location being investigated and the activity that may have occurred at the scene. Care must be taken to ensure that adequate samples are collected to represent the soil composition of the entire scene location.

Generally, the amount of soil to fill an average pill bottle would be enough soil to ensure comparative analysis can be done. Soil samples must be packaged dry therefore wet soil samples should be air dried at room temperature before packaging. Samples should preferably be placed in "rigid plastic containers" rather than polythene bags or paper bags because the package must keep soil lumps intact. Paper envelopes should not be used because they easily tear and leak. Photographs and written notes must be taken of soil adhering to clothing or shoes; the information should include the location of the soil then the entire item should be packaged. Wet items of clothing should be air-dried in the laboratory as soon as possible.

Control samples are collected depending on the circumstances of the crime that had occurred. If the unknown samples are that which was collected on the suspect's shoes or clothing, the control samples collected should be surface soil samples approximately a quarter inch depth. These samples must be collected at various locations within the crime scene in order to collect a representative sample of

include clothing, shoes (Figure 14.3), or tires. Soil evidence is usually composed of extremely fine grains to large, clumpy particles and tend to have an affinity to stick and transfer especially the fine particles. Forensic examination and analysis of soil evidence may determine class characteristics that may either refute or corroborate victim or witness statements. Most of these analyses provide information through comparative analysis of unknown samples and control or reference samples. The forensic analyses that will be done is dependent on the circumstances of each individual case. The significance of soil evidence is to locate area where person or object met the soil.

the entire area. Each area must be packaged separately and be properly labelled. Instances where there was digging or excavation (e.g. burying of a body), samples must be taken from each layer identified to the depth of the hole. Record the description of soil at the various layers and measure each depth where the sample was collected. Each layer should be air-dried and packaged and labeled separately. Tools used for digging should be thoroughly cleaned before and after use and should not have any remnants of the previous sample remaining on it. Examples of tools that can be used are stainless-steel shovels, spades, trowels, and artist's palette knives. The artist palette knives can be used in instances of separating very thin layers of soil.

Personal protective gear must be worn at all times on the crime scene and non-powdered latex gloves must be worn as the talc powder in powdered gloves can result in contamination of the soil sample as talc can be found naturally in the soil as a silicate mineral. Dried soil samples must be stored at room temperature in a sealed container. If biological material is present in the collected soil sample, these samples should be packed in unused paper bags or preferably unused cardboard boxes as biological material degrades at a faster rate in plastic or nonporous containers.

Forensic Analysis

Forensic analysis of soil samples involves comparative analysis that usually begins with macroscopic and microscopic examination of the physical characteristics of soil samples. These characteristics include color of the soil; presence and type of vegetation in the soil, grain size, etc. Soil samples are also compared by analyzing the gradient density of the samples and determining the chemical composition of the samples using instrumentation such as X-ray Fluorescence (XRF), Scanning Electron Microscope (SEM), and Attenuated Total reflection-Fourier Transform Infrared (AT-FTIR).

PAINT

Paint is a man-made liquid that forms into a thin, hard coating when it dries after being spread over rigid surfaces. Paints function as a decorative and protective coating for buildings, motor vehicles, and many other objects. Pigments, binders, and solvents are the three main components of paint. Binders provide the support medium for pigments and additives that result in the attachment and retention of the pigments on the surface being painted. Pigments give the paint its color and lack of transparency. Solvents are used to provide a suspension of binders and pigments for application on surfaces and will be lost during the application process. The application of

FIGURE 14.4 Image of multilayers of a paint fragment seen on Fourier Transform Infrared (FTIR).

paint is usually done in multiple layers called coats; see Figure 14.4; each coat may contain components different from the other coats (Bentley, 2001).

Forensic Significance

Paint can be found at crime scenes in various forms such as fragments, chips, or smears and are encountered in instances such as hit-and-run accidents, paint transfer, and tool marks in burglary cases. Paint evidence may provide investigative leads that provide investigators clues to narrow down searches, and may also provide associative evidence that is evidence that may link a suspect with the victim or the crime scene.

Methods of Recovery and Collection

The ability to detect and collect paint samples on the crime scene is very important as every sample forgotten or missed may be lost forever. The ability to conduct forensic paint analysis is dependent on the quantity, quality and type of the paint samples collected. Detailed documentation must be made of the surface from which the paint sample will be collected and of any relevant areas surrounding these surfaces. Surfaces where sample may be collected include but not limited to motor vehicles, window frames, door jambs, walls, and crow bars. The possibility of cross-contamination must always be considered when searching and collecting paint samples at crime scenes.

Paint chips or fragments are collected with tweezers; the chips can then be wrapped in a paper fold and labeled. Paint smears or powders are recovered by scratching using

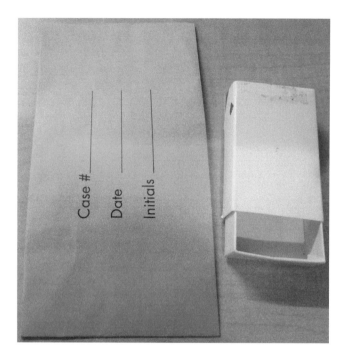

FIGURE 14.5 Paper envelope and cardboard box for packaging glass fragments.

a knife or a scalpel or a razor blade and then wrapped in a paper fold or small cardboard box (Figure 14.5) and labeled. If paint chips or fragments are not visible or too small to be collected with a tweezer, then a tape lift of the sample area should be done to collect paint samples. As a caveat, tape lifts should only be used if other collection methods are not possible. Items (e.g. crowbars or tools) that can be transported should have the areas with paint traces or smears covered with a clean sheet of paper and then packaged and labeled and transported to the laboratory as soon as possible. A large immovable object should be sampled, collecting as much if not all the available paint sample present.

Clothing and fabrics containing paint chips should be collected and transported to the laboratory. In the laboratory, these items may be searched with a stereomicroscope and paint samples collected with tweezers. Clothing and fabrics may also be shaken over a clean sheet of paper and the chips dislodged collected.

A designated filtered vacuum cleaner may be used to collect paint chips on large surfaces such as carpets, bed linens, etc. The filter and nozzle must be thoroughly cleaned after each collection to prevent cross contamination. This technique can be used when tape lifting is not practicable (e.g. on wet surfaces). Unfortunately, the vacuuming method is indiscriminate in that it collects everything on the surface of the item and will therefore require extensive sorting to identify paint samples. Also, the risk of cross contamination is high, especially if the vacuum is not thoroughly cleaned after each use.

Control or known paints samples must be collected near to but not within the zone of contact where the foreign paint transfers are found. This is required as the paint found on motor vehicles or large surfaces (e.g. wall) can be highly variable over its entire surface.

Forensic Analysis

Forensic paint analysis is comparative analysis that compares crime scene samples with known or control samples. Manufacturers of paint tend to use their own unique mixture of pigments and binders and this will allow for discrimination of paint among manufacturers. Instrumental analysis using instruments such as a Raman Spectrometer and X-ray Fluorescence (XRF) and Attenuated Total reflection-Fourier Transform Infrared (ATR-FTIR) are used to identify these pigments and binders. Comparative analysis of paint samples is also done by comparison of the physical characteristics of paint. The physical examination of paint would include color assessment; determining the number, sequence, and thickness of the layers of the sample; surface texture of the paint and physical fit of two samples of paint chips or fragments. Chemical analysis of the solubility of paint samples is another comparative analysis that can be performed. As the composition of paint varies, paint samples may demonstrate different solubility with varying solvents e.g., methanol and acetone.

GLASS

Glass is technically defined as "The inorganic product of fusion which has cooled to a rigid condition without crystallizing." Glass is made by heating mostly silica sand with soda and lime to a liquified form then cooled quickly so that there are no crystals to form in the glass. Glass is composed of mixtures of inorganic components present in different concentrations; some of the components are added intentionally to ensure proper glass structure, to decrease manufacture cost, or to provide required properties such as heat resistance, color, safety, and some of the components are added unintentionally in trace amounts as contamination from the manufacturing process or from the raw material used.

Glass can be classified based on its intended use, such as containers which are jars, bottles, and glasses; flat glass used in architecture and cars; glass fibers used for insulation and specialty glass. Glass can also be classified based on its main raw material; these include soda lime used to make containers and windows; leaded glass used for making housewares and decorations; borosilicate glass used in industry and to make lamps and cookware; and special glass used to make optical and electronic products (Copley, 2001).

Forensic Significance

When a glass object breaks, fragments can be ejected from the object in all directions, including backward toward the direction of the breaking force. Glass fragments can be transferred onto any surface that is within the zone of breaking. The number of glass fragments that can be transferred within this zone of breaking is governed by certain factors. These factors are:

1. Objects or items closest to a breaking glass will most likely have glass fragments being transferred to it, and the number of fragments transferred will depend on the distance of the object or items from the breaking glass.
2. The greater the damage to the glass, the greater the number of fragments that can be transferred.
3. The number of glass fragments transferred is more likely be greater on the individual breaking the glass than someone standing nearby.
4. The number of fragments transferred will increase as the number of hits to the glass increases.

The ability of the glass fragments to persist on surfaces is dependent on many factors. Glass fragments are easily lost on smooth surfaces and tend to persist longer on rough surfaces. Rough clothing, for example, wool, tends to retain glass fragments longer than smooth clothing, for example, silk. Wet clothing will allow retention of glass fragments than dry clothing. The loss of fragments from clothing will be greater the more active the wearer and larger fragments of glass will be lost more quickly than smaller fragments of glass.

Methods of Recovery and Collection

Collection should be done by hand if the location of the glass is important, which is usually the case.

Hand Picking with Tweezers or Forceps

Glass fragment visible to the naked eye can be collected with tweezers or forceps. The use of white light or specialized light sources and hand lenses can assist in the visualization of fragments and facilitate their collection.

Tape Lifts

Cellophane tape or double-sided tape can be used. The adhesive surface of the tape is contacted once or multiple times on the area to be sampled. The adhesive surface of the tape is then stuck to another suitable surface such as microscope slide, acetate sheet or to itself. This is done in order to keep the surface that was sampled free from contamination. It must be noted that tape lifting from an object or a surface might also yield fingerprints that may be destroyed if not handled carefully.

Vacuuming

Vacuums contain special attachments that direct a stream of air that is drawn into a nozzle onto a paper or fabric filter. A special filtered vacuum cleaner may be used to collect trace evidence (e.g. glass from carpet, bedding, etc.). This technique can be used when tape lifting is not practicable (e.g. on wet surfaces). However, it is indiscriminate in what it collects as it collects all debris present, therefore requiring the tedious task of sorting to recover glass fragments.

Scrapings

A forceps or spatula is used to scrape the surface of clothing to recover debris on a clean sheet of paper. However, one will have to be contamination conscious when using this method; the forceps or spatula must be thoroughly cleaned after use on each item of evidence.

Shaking Clothing Over a Large Metal Cone

A sheet of paper is placed on a flat surface with the cone above it. The item of evidence is shaken over the top of the cone and the glass fragments that are present will be collected on the sheet of paper below the cone. To prevent contamination, the cone must be cleaned thoroughly after each item of evidence.

Recovered glass is then either packaged in folded paper and then placed inside an envelope or small cardboard box, as seen in Figure 14.5. Control or known samples are collected from known sources, which in most instances, are the remaining portion of the glass that was broken. As many fragments as possible should be collected from the control or known source. Glass fragments collected from the control or known source should be collected and packaged separately from those fragments collected at the scene. In collecting fragments from the control or known source, it is recommended to label to identify the inner and outer surfaces of the glass; this is particularly useful when dealing with glass from windscreens, which tend to be laminated glass. Items located near the glass source that was broken may contain fragments of glass; these items, if moveable, should be packaged and sent to the laboratory for testing. Care must be taken to ensure that these items are not excessively shaken during collection and packaging as fragments can be easily lost during movement.

The victim and suspect should be sampled for glass fragments, as transfer onto their clothing, footwear, and head hair is possible during the commission of the crime. Clothing and footwear should be collected over clean sheets of paper and the item wrapped in the paper and packaged in evidence bags or envelopes. Head hair should be combed onto a clean sheet of paper and packaged and labeled and submitted to the laboratory for analysis. Items or tools used to break glass may contain glass fragments and should be packaged and sent to the laboratory for testing. Glass fragments are transient evidence that can be easily transferred or lost. Care must always be taken to prevent transfer or loss of glass fragments.

Forensic Analysis

After application of the force, the glass bulge on the side opposite to the impacting force and radial fracture begins, a concentric fracture will then form. Cone fracture is when a high-velocity projectile penetrates glass. The fragments of glass should be analyzed to determine fracture patterns. Physical properties of glass fragments can be analyzed and compared; these properties include glass thickness, glass density, color of the glass, glass curvature, and refractive index of glass fragments. Instrumental analysis of glass samples can be done to identify and compare their elemental composition.

REFERENCES

Bentley John Composition, Manufacture and use of Paint Caddy Brian Forensic Examination of Glass and Paint: Analysis and Interpretation Taylor and Francis London 2001.

Copley, G. *The Composition and Manufacture of Glass and its Domestic and Industrial Applications (Chapter 2) Forensic Examination of Paint and Glass*. Taylor and Francis, 2001.

Fitzpatrick, R. W. *Soil: Forensic Analysis*. Chichester: Wiley Encyclopedia of Forensic Science, 2013.

Strahler, A. *Introducing Physical Geography*. New Jersey: Wiley, 2013.

CHAPTER 15

Rapid DNA Analysis at Crime Scenes

Mohammed Naji[1] and Hanan Almulla[2]

[1]Senior DNA Analyst, Dubai Police – General Department of Forensic Sciences and Criminology, UAE
[2]Forensic Genetics Expert, Dubai Police – General Department of Forensic Sciences and Criminology, UAE

CONTENTS

HISTORY OF DNA TYPING

DNA analysis plays an important role in criminal investigation and it serves as evidence for the prosecution. The application of DNA analysis technology to the biological samples and forensic evidence in criminal casework has revolutionized forensic science (Roewer, 2013). Over the years, DNA analysis passed through different phases and improvements.

By the mid 19th century, ABO typing techniques became a standard method in forensic laboratories and has since been used for solving many cases related to personal identification and paternity testing (Mohammed, 2019); however, it has some limitations, one of which is that it can just be used in forensic typing as an exclusion tool to exclude suspects to be the source of blood samples deposited at a crime scene. However, this test does not clearly identify the suspect involved because many people share the same blood type.

In 1980, the first development of Restriction Fragment Length Polymorphisms (RFLPs) occurred, which allowed Alec Jeffreys to apply this technique during his research in hereditary diseases to visualize the unique patterns in DNA fragments to differentiate between organisms (Thompson et al., 2012). In forensic science, RFLP technique was used as an important tool to differentiate between individuals by visualizing length polymorphisms after treating genomic DNA samples with one or more restriction enzymes that cleave the DNA to produce a number of fragments of different lengths. The RFLP technique has been very useful as markers for genomic DNA and it became the first scientifically accepted forensic DNA analysis method in the United States with a few limitations. One of these limitations was that it needed large amounts of DNA, which is difficult to obtain when dealing with crime scene samples (Butler, 2015).

In 1986, Kary Mullis invented polymerase chain reaction (PCR). It was considered the gold standard and the most important invention in molecular biology and was a widely supported technique for analyzing DNA (Watson, 2012). PCR facilitates the duplication of a specific DNA segment, in which a small quantity of DNA can be duplicated in large amounts over a short period. Kary Mullis was awarded the Nobel Prize in Chemistry in 1993 for his effort in developing this technique (Wrublewski, 2019). The advantages of using PCR technology compared to other technologies are the analysis of a small quantity of DNA within a sample and the analysis of degraded DNA samples.

Despite the success of PCR of RFLP between 1986 to 1990, forensic scientists switched their DNA forensic typing methods to PCR of short tandem repeats (STRs) in the beginning of 1990 (McDonald & Lehman, 2012). Short tandem repeats (STRs) is a microsatellite with much smaller repeat units, with the number of repeats varying between individuals, making STRs valuable and effective for human identification purposes and other forensic applications. The short length of the repeat units gives them the ability to be amplified more easily, and they are less prone to problems with degraded DNA.

SHORT TANDEM REPEATS (STRS) AND CODIS

Short tandem repeats are considered the backbone of forensic DNA analysis and are widely used today for human identification and different DNA forensic applications. Short tandem repeats (STRs) are stretches of DNA with core repeat units that are two to seven nucleotides in length (Krishnan et al., 2017). There are many different types of STRs. The main two differences are the variety of the number of repeats and variety of the repeat patterns. The diversity of the number of repeats happens when some DNA sequences have two nucleotides repeated alongside each other and that type of sequences are called dinucleotide repeats. Other types of sequences have three nucleotides in the repeat unit and that type of sequences are called trinucleotides repeats, tetranucleotides have four, pentanucleotides have five, and hexanucleotides have six nucleotides in the core repeat unit (Gettings et al., 2015).

The variety of the repeat pattern, on the other hand, occurs when some DNA sequences comprise two or more adjacent simple repeats (e.g. TCTATCTG TCTA TCTG). These sequences called compound repeat STRs and examples of these types are FGA, VWA, D3S1358, D8S1179, D2S1338, D19S433, D12S391, and D6S1043 (Mohammed, 2019). The other types of sequences are called complex repeats that may contain several repeat blocks of variable unit length as well as variable intervening sequences. An example of such repeats is D21S11 (Dash et al., 2020).

CODIS is the abbreviation for the Combined DNA Index System and is the specific term used to describe the FBI's program that focuses on DNA forensic databases (Grogan, 2019). In addition to that, it could be used as a software to run these databases. The contribution of federal, state, and local forensic laboratories was considered the main feature of this database. In 1997, the FBI announced the selection of 13 different STR loci to constitute the core of the U.S. national database, CODIS. All CODIS STRs are tetrameric repeat sequences (Chatumal et al., 2010). On January 1, 2017, the FBI announced an expansion of the original thirteen short tandem repeats (STRs) to become 20 STR loci

(Dash et al., 2018). This expansion would help the law enforcement to get greater discrimination potential for human identification and different forensic applications.

Forensic DNA typing proceeded through many developments that help forensic scientists achieve their role in investigating crimes and serve as evidence for the prosecution and courts, but the main limitation from previous technologies happens when the biology forensic experts have to transfer evidences to the forensic laboratories (Mapes, 2017). Transportation consumes a lot of time and effort, which might affect the progress of some forensic cases. Traditional methods of DNA analysis require a certified laboratory with five or six expensive instruments. It also needs at least two certified and trained technicians and it takes at least a day for processing the samples.

In last years, technological developments in the field of forensic DNA analysis have soared, with the latest advances forecasting a future in which DNA traces can be analyzed at the crime scene using a single instrument. In addition to that, the forensic biology expert can compare the profile of evidences traces and a suspect's profile in the DNA database in the crime scene area within a few hours.

Rapid DNA analysis technology is a new development that can significantly shorten analysis times. It is less expensive, easy-to-use, and portable at the crime scene. This type of technology would be more effective in the field locations thus it would increase the speed of specific forensic cases and that would help relieve the work of the main laboratories that are still needed for complex DNA analysis.

There is specific relationship combining rapid DNA analysis and CODIS STRs. The FBI describes rapid DNA analysis as a specific process of producing a CODIS Core Loci STR profiles from a reference sample (Della Manna et al., 2016).

INTRODUCTION OF RAPID DNA ANALYSIS

Rapid DNA analysis is a fully automated process of developing a short tandem repeat (STR) profile from a reference sample buccal swab (Tan et al., 2013). This type of process has many advantages, for example, it takes place without any human intervention and it is a non-invasive way to collect DNA samples from an individual's cheek.

In 2010, the FBI established the Rapid DNA Program Office to facilitate the role of forensic experts in crime scenes by creating fully integrated DNA analysis systems to speed up the current DNA analysis process (Mapes, 2017). The Program Office works with various types of departments and agencies such as the Department of Defense, the Department of Homeland

Security, the National Institute of Standards and Technology (NIST), the National Institute of Justice, and other federal agencies to ensure the coordinated development of this new technology among federal agencies. This type of program was set up to analyze the reference sample of a suspect while the arrestee is still in police custody and also to compare his/her DNA profile with the other DNA profiles in the database of unsolved crimes.

In the beginning of 2011, the first mobile rapid DNA technologies were developed that have the ability to analyze short tandem repeat (STR) of different types of samples such as human tissue samples, direct reference samples (buccal Swab) and even objects with low DNA copy numbers, allowing for the potential analysis of crime scene samples (Shapiro, 2010). With these developments and by the end of 2012, researchers in the Netherlands decided to start one of the big projects to study the effectivity of implementing this new technology in crime scenes to examine biological evidences and obtain DNA analysis results within two hours. The project went through several phases and faced many obstacles until mobile rapid DNA technology options came into view and appeared in the field of forensic science.

IMPLEMENTATION OF RAPID DNA

The standard DNA analysis workflow is designed to perform optimally with crime scene samples since it is not an uncommon occurrence for them to be exposed to degrading factors. Moreover, some of these samples naturally contain less amounts of DNA and require sensitive procedures in order to get interpretable results. The first step in forensic DNA analysis is cell lysis, a process that breaks the cells open in order to release the DNA along with the rest of its contents. Some of these cellular components possess inhibitory characteristics for the downstream processing of the DNA analysis, which would therefore require the DNA to be extracted and purified from the solution as much as possible. Additional inhibitors could be present on the substrate on which the biological fluid is found and also depending on the type of the sample itself. Some examples include heme in blood, indigo dyes in denim, humic acids in soil, and melanin in hair.

Following DNA extraction, DNA quantitation is performed, which serves a significant purpose for the subsequent stages of the analysis. Firstly, knowing the amount of DNA present in each sample helps predict and understand the resulting DNA profile. Secondly, samples that contain insufficient or undetectable amounts of DNA can be identified and excluded from the subsequent steps, which would save some time in the

downstream analysis and would contribute to a more cost-effective process. Furthermore, since samples can contain non-human DNA such as those from plant, animal, and microbial origins, DNA quantification kits focuses on identifying human DNA to ensure that the read profile is of human origin. In the next step, called normalization, the known concentrations of DNA in all the samples are adjusted to match the required range of DNA input that is critical for the following amplification process.

The polymerase chain reaction (PCR) follows, in which the amount of DNA present in the sample is exponentially copied or amplified through around 25–35 thermal cycles in a thermocycler instrument where the end product would contain sufficient amounts of genetic material for detection. This amplification is performed only at selected STR sites depending on the used kit, so that specific DNA fragments are produced, and the different lengths within these sets of fragments are determined by the genetic construction of the unique individual to which the DNA sample belongs. Afterwards, detection is done by a method called capillary electrophoresis (CE) in which these fragments are separated by size through a polymer solution. The CE instruments and their software identify the specific STR alleles as a function of time, as the larger fragments would require a longer time to migrate through the polymer solution due to their heavier molecular weight. Eventually, an entire DNA profile is constructed out of those data.

Under this standard DNA analysis workflow, the time needed to get from the initial lysis step all the way to obtaining a profile can take up to two days. Even with the available automated procedures, a single process such as cell lysis can take up to 3.5 hours depending on the instrument used and the number of samples run per batch. This meticulous workflow is consequently time-consuming, especially for cases that are urgent or that requires the detention of involved parties. Consequently, in order to achieve rapid DNA analyses that would require no more than a couple of hours, the conventional stages of forensic DNA analysis must either be sped up or excluded. The general workflow of current rapid DNA analyses go by the following framework: cell lysis → DNA extraction → DNA amplification → fragment detection.

There are several implications of this summarized workflow that need to be considered. Firstly, in the absence of a thorough DNA purification process, inhibitory compounds may affect the efficiency of DNA amplification and would hinder the production of a more accurate DNA profile. Therefore, the samples from which we could expect a sufficient amount of end product for detection are those that already began with an expectedly larger quantity of DNA such as blood or saliva. With blood samples, however, the greater the amount present, the more heme there will be as well, which could obstruct the DNA analysis workflow. There will also be reductions in the number of sample runs per batch and the entire process will probably work on a fully automated system that will require minimal or no human intervention even with data interpretation.

PCR was one of the main foci of rapid DNA analysis. In 2008, an advance was made in terms of amplifying multiple STR loci where the usual Identifiler process was modified to consume 36 minutes instead of the usual 2.5–3 hours (Vallone, 2008). In this instance, the enzyme that synthesized the newly amplified DNA copies, called the AmpliTaq Gold^{TM} polymerase enzyme was replaced with a set of two enzymes that do not require an additional start-up time in order to be heat-activated. One of the two enzymes included was the SpeedSTAR™ HS DNA polymerase, which had a significant effect in reducing DNA profile artifacts that resulted from the enzyme substitution. The advantage that the SpeedSTAR™ HS DNA polymerase possesses is that it synthesizes the new DNA strands with an extension rate of 1000 base pairs per 10 seconds, which is six times faster than the standard Taq polymerase used in conventional PCR (Takara Bio). Moreover, unlike other polymerases enzymes, its function is not restricted to the use of a specific PCR instrument. Moreover, the time taken for each step of the PCR was reduced so that the total final time went down by 78%. By the following year, improvements were made by adding one more polymerase, which helped in reducing the artifacts that were previously present in the DNA profile that had resulted from an incomplete amplification reaction (Vallone, 2009).

In another study in 2012, the PCR time for the same kit was reduced to 26 minutes. In addition to using SpeedSTAR™ HS DNA, the PCR instrument was replaced for one with a more efficient ramp rate, which helped to reduce the total PCR time by using a quicker transition rate going from one temperature to another. Moreover, two steps from this reaction were combined into a single step, and by 2014, the reaction was reduced to a mere 14 minutes by additionally using the Streck Philisa® Thermal Cycler, which had the fastest effective temperature transition compared to five other thermocylers in the same study (Butts, 2014).

RAPID DNA TECHNOLOGY MANUFACTURERS

Many companies are racing to develop innovative and efficient criminal investigation solutions; one of these is Rapid DNA Technology. Various manufacturers have developed different instruments for Rapid DNA analysis. IntegenX, which is now part of Thermo Fisher Scientific, and ANDE are considered the most important companies

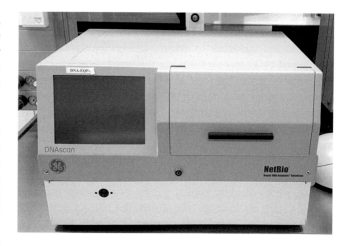

FIGURE 15.1   DNAscan Rapid System.

around the world in the rapid DNA technology industry (Romsos & Vallone, 2015).

In March 2016, DNAscan Rapid System was considered the first Rapid DNA instrument to earn the National DNA Index System (NDIS) approval from the FBI (Della Manna et al., 2016) Figure 15.1. This approval represented a pioneer move toward widespread adoption for the concept of use rapid DNA analysis to analyze crime scene samples. After attaining FBI Approval, accredited NDIS laboratories have the right to match between DNA samples examined by the DNAscan system with different DNA profiles linked to the FBI's Combined DNA Index System (CODIS) program, without any human intervention.

The DNAscan System is fully automated, provides high-quality data, and is validated by seven different external laboratories with the main developer. The system generates DNA profiles in less than two hours. The main advantage of this system is obtaining STR profiles from up to five buccal swabs in one run.

In March 2018, Thermo Fisher Scientific announced that it has acquired IntegenX, which was considered as the market leader of Rapid DNA technology for various applications related to forensics and law enforcement. This partnership sparked a scientific breakthrough in the Rapid DNA Industry (Kim, 2019). In 2019, Thermo Fisher Scientific developed their Rapid DNA platform and called it the Rapid HIT ID System as displayed in Figure 15.2 and by 2020 the FBI has approved their system for use by accredited forensic DNA laboratories to analyze DNA reference samples and compare DNA profiles against the U.S. National DNA Index System (NDIS) CODIS database without any human intervention (Hakim et al., 2020).

The Rapid HIT ID System is fast, simple to use, and fully automated, from entering the sample to receiving the result, as shown in Figure 15.3. This system is used for analyzing DNA reference samples in 90 minutes.

FIGURE 15.2 Rapid HIT ID system.

This type of system integrates many steps, including sample preparation, STR analysis, obtaining a DNA profile that is then combined with specific softwares to be uploaded to a database for comparison purposes and analysis.

Thermo Fisher Scientific created two versions of this technology. One of them is the RapidHIT ID System and the other is the RapidHIT 200 System (Amick & Swiger, 2019). The main difference between these two instruments is the number of samples included in a single run. The RapidHIT ID System uses just one sample in a run, whereas the RapidHIT 200 System uses eight samples in

FIGURE 15.3 Rapid HIT ID system processing.

one run, which gives it a strong advantage, especially when the forensic scientist has many samples and wants to proceed in limited time. Table 15.1 illustrates the main differences between different instruments.

TABLE 15.1 Comparing between Different Rapid DNA Technology Instruments

Instrument	ANDE	RapidHIT™ 200	RapidHIT™ ID System
Manufacturer	NetBio	IntegenX by Thermo Fisher Scientific	Thermo Fisher Scientific
Dimensions	75 × 45 × 60 cm (29.5 × 17.6 × 23.6 in)	73 × 71 × 48 cm (28.5 × 28 × 18 in)	48 × 53 × 27 cm (19 × 21 × 10.5 in)
Weight	54 kg (117 lbs)	81.5 kg (180 lbs)	28.5 kg (63.8 lbs)
Cartridges	• I-Chip for crime scene samples • A-Chip for reference samples	Sample cartridge and Control cartridge with four chambers each	• INTEL for crime scene samples • ACE for reference samples
STR assay	FlexPlex® STR Assay (23 autosomal loci, 3 Y loci, amelogenin)	• PowerPlex® (16 markers) • AmpFℓSTR® NGMSElect™ Express (17 markers) • GlobalFiler™ Express (24 markers)	GlobalFiler™ Express (21 autosomal loci, 2 Y loci, amelogenin)
No. of samples per run	• 5 samples (A-Chip) • 4 samples (I-Chip)	5 samples along with a positive control, a negative control and a ladder	One sample
Run Time	< 2 hours	< 2 hours	~90 minutes
Data Analysis	• ANDE Expert System Software (DNA profile generation and analysis) • ANDE FAIRS™ Software (includes database comparisons and biological relatedness analysis)	GeneMarker® HID (DNA profile generation and analysis)	• RapidLINK™ Software (includes database comparisons and biological relatedness analysis) • GeneMarker® HID Software (DNA profile generation and analysis)

RAPID DNA INSTRUMENTS AND THEIR DEVELOPMENTAL VALIDATION

ANDE™, developed by Network Biosystems, also known by the name NetBio, is a fully automated, ruggedized portable system that is able to analyze DNA samples including blood, tissue, bone, and various crime scene samples in under 2 hours. It weighs 54 kg and measures at 75 × 45 × 60 cm or 29.5 × 17.6 × 23.6 in. The one-time use I-Chip (A-Chip for reference buccal swabs from known donors) contains all the consumables needed for DNA purification, amplification, and detection, and is inserted into the instrument along with up to four crime scene samples. The chip's 6-month shelf life at room temperature eliminates the need for any cooling equipment and the military standard ruggedization tests performed on both the instrument and its chips deem them safe for constant transportation so as to be used as a decentralized laboratory. ANDE™ utilizes the FlexPlex® STR Assay, developed in 2017 (Grover, 2017), that contains 24 STR markers including the 20 CODIS core loci, plus 4 others internationally used. Moreover, it covers 3 additional loci that are specific to the male Y-chromosome, which are also targeted by other Y-DNA typing kits approved for NDIS CODIS databasing. The accompanying Expert System data interpretation software generates the profile following DNA fragment detection and is designed to interpret the profiles according to a set of rules similar to those followed by a forensic expert in order to accomplish complete automation of the rapid DNA analysis system. As a simple example, any peaks lower than the set threshold for signal strength is indicated by a color-coded warning box. The Expert System also generates an Excel file for the profile ready to be uploaded to CODIS if no issues on them were encountered.

Rapid and condensed DNA analysis systems could originally only cater to reference samples from known donors with high DNA abundance since the traditional DNA analysis workflow is elaborately designed to tend to the sensitive nature of crime scene samples. Still, applications of rapid DNA analysis on crime scene samples were developed in light of the benefits it would serve case investigations. Thus, initially approved by the FBI in 2018 for use on reference samples, the ANDE™ system has since gone through developmental validations to support the approval of casework samples as well as the application of the automated Expert System data analysis software on such samples. For these analyses, NetBio developed a Low DNA Content BioChipSet that incorporated an additional sample concentration module within the I-Chip. This added module uses microfluidics ultrafiltration between the DNA purification and PCR steps and contains a concentration membrane for each sample allowing for a higher DNA content to flow into the PCR chamber and consequently into the fragment detection stage. Additionally, the entire product of cell lysis is forwarded for extraction and the binding of the genetic material to the purification filter is enhanced. These modifications cater to the minute amount of DNA usually obtained from crime scene samples as opposed to the overly concentrated samples from buccal swabs that would usually require dilution of the DNA for profiling.

In their validation study, tested mock samples included cells from mobile phones, drinking containers, swabs from chewing gum, cigarette end cuttings, swabs taken from bloodstains on tiles and on fabric, swabs taken from semen stains on fabric, and a solution of bone power dissolved in a demineralization buffer. Full and accurate DNA profiles were obtained with blood samples down to 1 μL in volume and from crime scene items containing saliva and semen, whereas touch items of lower DNA input such as those from mobile phones, even with full profiles, showed some flagged markers by the Expert System due to low detection signal. DNA profiles from bone samples, as those found in disaster victim identification, also showed full and accurate profiles. Overall, the system demonstrated an applicable workflow for rapid DNA analysis on samples attained from crime scenes (Turingan, 2016). A similar study was conducted in 2020 aiming to measure up to the criteria for NDIS approval following the FBI's Quality Assurance Standards on the developmental validation (Turingan, 2020).

The RapidHIT™ 200 was initially intended, as was typical for such systems, for use on reference buccal samples of high DNA content. The instrument measures at 73 × 71 × 48 cm or 28.5 × 28 x 18 in and weighs around 80 kg. It allows the simultaneous run of 5 samples along with a positive control, a negative control and a ladder, in the span of about 2 hours. The ladder provides a standard against which the size of the DNA fragments are measured, whereas the controls, a strict requirement in every conventional forensic DNA analysis run, act as additional verification indicating that the system components are working properly and that no contamination in it is present. These eight samples are placed in a set of two cartridges containing the consumables required for cell lysis, DNA extraction, and amplification, providing the choice of PowerPlex® (16 markers), AmpFℓSTR® NGMSElect™ Express (17 markers) or GlobalFiler™ Express (24 markers including the CODIS core loci) assays.

In 2013, IntegenX tested a newly developed protocol for the application of its RapidHIT™ 200 Human DNA Identification System on mock casework samples that contained blood and saliva. These samples included soda cans, cigarette ends, chewing gums, seed husks, drinking straws, and dry bloodstains on various tools, fabrics, and common flat surfaces. On similar sets of samples, the new protocol produced more accurate profiles compared to the original standard buccal protocol, and exhibited profiles that were also suitable enough to be compared to a database (Gangano, 2013). The following studies in 2019 were also conducted where three additional protocols were developed that experimented with various parameter values concerning the extraction process. This enhancement aimed to analyze a wider range of DNA concentration, akin to the ones usually dealt with from crime scenes. These protocols showed improved profiles with lower DNA concentrations even though it still did not compare to the results of conventional methods, as is the case with the other available systems. Moreover, the protocols were problematic with higher DNA input samples since the amount of DNA entering the PCR reaction was more than the ideal amount, not to mention that the overall reaction time increased from under 2 hours to around 2.5 hours (Shackleton, 2019).

In 2015, IntegenX launched the RapidHIT™ ID System, measuring at a much smaller 48 × 53 × 27 cm or 19 × 21 × 10.5 in and weighing at around 28.5 kg. It runs one sample at a time in a span of 90 minutes and uses INTEL single-sample GlobalFiler™ Express cartridges specific for crime scene samples (as opposed to the ACE cartridges for reference samples) and includes a number of similar one-time use cartridges for positive and negative controls. The system incorporates a data management software called the RapidLINK™ software which is an intuitive interface that centralizes information on all the RapidHIT™ ID instruments that are connected in a given region and also manages the hierarchy of users who are granted access to the system.

Four main applications are additionally available in the software to be used by forensic experts. The RapidLINK Match application allows to compare a run sample to any connected database in search for a matched profile, whereas the RapidLINK Staff Elimination Database application automatically compares the newly run sample to a saved database containing staff DNA profiles to alert the user in case a possible DNA contamination from a staff member is present in the sample. The forensic expert also has the option to use the RapidLINK Familial or Kinship applications to conduct biological relatedness analyses such as those used in disaster victim identification (DVI), where an additional option is available to automatically produce a final report containing statistical figures on the applied analysis. The forensic expert will also be granted access to the GeneMarker® HID software, which is essentially equivalent to the GeneMapper™ ID-X software that is used internationally with the capillary electrophoresis instruments in the normal workflow, allowing the expert to see, edit, interpret and print the profiles. An internal version of this software is also used by the instrument itself to perform primary analysis on the run sample for the end

user to see. Samples pass the primary analysis when they display a green tick on the instrument screen once the run is over and it indicates that all peaks in the DNA profile has passed the threshold criteria. The system might also display a yellow tick where one or more peaks are below the threshold, which is where secondary analysis by an expert will be needed using the RapidLINK™ or the GeneMarker™ HID software. Finally, a red "X" mark from the primary analysis informs the end user that an error prevented the profile from being generated.

Developmental validation on the INTEL system tested mock crime scene samples including blood droplets on fabrics and various surfaces, saliva on coffee cups, soda cans, cigarette ends and chewing gum, as well as pulled hair containing their roots. Although the cartridge is only recommended for use on blood and saliva samples, touch samples were also tested and included firearms, face masks, hats and pens. Results show that hair root samples had the greatest number of passed primary analyses, followed by blood then saliva samples, while none of the touch items passed the primary analysis. For all sample types, however, manual secondary analysis increased data recovery of the profiles. The performance of the ACE cartridges was also examined for crime scene samples, where they produced less concordant results compared to the more sensitive INTEL cartridges even after secondary analysis. Overall, the validation showed that the RapidHIT™ ID platform along with the INTEL cartridge is an accurate system to analyse crime scene samples containing high to moderate DNA content (ThermoFisher Scientific).

CASE STUDIES ON RAPID DNA ANALYSIS

Due to the recognized shortcomings and consequent lack of validation of the application of rapid DNA analysis on real crime scene samples, no forensic laboratory thus far has adapted this technology as a regularly used tool despite some prospects of success with specific, albeit limited, types of biological materials such as blood. Regardless, in 2015, the DNA profiling laboratory of the Health Sciences Authority of Singapore in cooperation with the National University of Singapore began to test the application of the RapidHIT™ 200 platform on some of its more concerning cases. Automated initial data interpretation was utilized but was followed by an expert manual review prior to database comparison. Moreover, because of court admissibility and report validity issues, each sample had a parallel running under the conventional workflow for concordance analysis. In total, 36 samples were tested from 9 urgent cases of various offences including rape, homicide, assault, burglary, fire outbreak, and discovery of an unidentified corpse. These samples comprised semen on tissue paper, cigarette ends, blood, and a sample of bone marrow. In accordance with pervious validation studies, 80% allele calling success rate ranged from 75% for cigarette ends to 100% for blood samples while the standard workflow achieved 100% in all sample types. The main issue with the system was encountered with mixed profiles as, compared to the normal workflow, identification of the alleles that were contributed by the minor donor was significantly reduced (Thong, 2015). This reflected the discussed need to increase the sensitivity of the assays adopted in the Rapid DNA analysis platforms in a manner suited to the irreplaceability of the crime scene samples that are already complicated or weak in nature.

BENEFITS AND DRAWBACKS OF RAPID DNA ANALYSIS

Rapid DNA analysis technology is considered an unprecedented breakthrough in the forensics DNA field. As with any new technology, there are benefits and drawbacks associated with implementing it at crime scene. The main benefit of implementing Rapid DNA technology at the crime scene is the speed of the whole process which would help the policeman or the forensic expert to determine if a suspect's DNA matched DNA previously found at a crime scene. The traditional process of DNA analyses takes a long time to obtain an accurate analysis and get the final report. Some labs need days to weeks to analyze some DNA testing, whereas Rapid DNA analysis can do the same process within two hours while suspects are still in police custody (Dash et al., 2020).

The second benefit is the less chance of the DNA sample being contaminated in the Rapid DNA analyses compared to the traditional analysis process. The evidence sample in traditional DNA testing must go through different phases beginning from identified, collected and transported to the main forensic DNA lab, then to be handled by the forensic experts. This process would increase the probability of contamination. On the other hand, by using Rapid DNA technology at the crime scene, fewer processing steps and fewer people are involved. The handling process is complete once a sample has been placed in a Rapid DNA machine, which will lower the risk of contamination.

However, there are several challenges facing law enforcement agencies regarding the implementation of rapid DNA analysis at crime scenes. One of them is that rapid DNA testing requires a sufficient amount of individual DNA in order to give a complete analysis and obtain full DNA profile. That means that these machines were designed to test samples taken directly from individuals for identification purposes more than any crime scene case sample. Most of the crime scene samples cannot be analyzed by rapid DNA platforms and needs a trained technician to analyze and interpret the results because these types of samples contain mixtures of DNA profile from more than one individual. For these reasons, most crime scene samples must be processed by an accredited forensic DNA laboratory Murphy, 2018). Table 15.2 shows the advantages and drawbacks between Rapid DNA analysis and conventional DNA workflow.

TABLE 15.2　Advantages and Drawbacks between Rapid DNA Analysis and Conventional DNA Workflow

	Conventional DNA Workflow	Rapid DNA Analysis
Advantages	• A comprehensive workflow, with the capacity to edit analyzes options during any step as deemed needed • Sensitive for the identification and analysis of inhibited, degraded or low content DNA samples such as touch cells • Validated for the analysis and interpretation of samples of mixed DNA sources • Quantifies DNA before amplification; a condition for analysis quality and court admissibility	• Fully Automated • Summarises the DNA analysis process in 1.5–2 hours, which helps produce faster intelligence for critical or urgent cases • Decentralized; operable at the crime scene location and any criminal justice entities or offices • Short manual handling time lessens the chances of contamination • Operated by any trained individual besides forensic DNA experts, with controlled user accessibility • A portable system that occupies a compact space
Drawbacks	• Takes about 1–2 days • More chances of contamination with each step or analyst involved • Analysis is only done by forensic DNA experts in a centralized laboratory, where sample transport adds to the time needed to obtain results	• Analysis is only sensitive enough for high DNA content samples (e.g. blood, saliva) • Analysis is aimed at single-sourced DNA samples only • A limited number of samples is analyzed per run, depending on the instrument • Still in need of proper validation for use in real cases

PAST EFFORTS AND FUTURE OF RAPID DNA ANALYSIS

The Rapid DNA act of 2017, announced in august of that year, amended the DNA Identification Act of 1994 by extending CODIS access to the Rapid DNA analysis systems. This was done in hopes of the time it takes to capture or eliminate suspects, exonerate the innocent and help forensic experts by allowing them to focus more of their time and resources on more complicated cases. The act, however, also restricted this access to include only reference samples taken for identification purposes and not crime scene samples, including rape kits. The Rapid DNA act of 2017 further assigned the FBI the responsibility to issue standards according to which procedures must be followed by criminal justice entities when using a Rapid DNA instrument in order for them to be eligible to utilize CODIS (Congress, 2017).

Around a year following the act, the FBI established the Non-CODIS Rapid DNA Best Practices/Outreach and Courtroom Considerations Task Group, whose aim was to align the goals, responsibilities, and recommendations of the different fields of the criminal justice system including forensic DNA experts, law enforcement, and prosecutors, for the proper implementation of Rapid DNA analysis of crime scene samples in the court system without, for the time being, any focus on the eligibility for use on CODIS nor the NDIS. The guides developed by the task force include those pertaining to administrative practices, instruments and consumables, crime scene and reference samples, staff, training and reporting of results (FBI, 2019).

An agreement statement between the Scientific Working Group on DNA Analysis Methods (SWGDAM), the European Network of Forensic Science Institutes (ENFSI), and the FBI's Rapid DNA Crime Scene Technology Advancement Task Group was contracted in 2020 (Hares, 2020). It highlighted five main concerns that represent hurdles in the way of validating the use of rapid DNA technologies on crime scene samples and also comparing these sample to the database. Firstly, specific technical considerations are needed in order to warrant the validity of the sample analysis, including simultaneously running a human-specific positive control with each sample, which helps identify and distinguish those that are inhibited, degraded, or present at low quantities by comparison. As done in the normal workflow, the quantification of the DNA sample is deemed a necessary measure of sample quality, but it is a feature yet to be implemented on a Rapid DNA platform. It is worthy to note at this point the differences in validation requirements between crime scene and reference samples, as the latter do not require a DNA quantitation step since it is certainly known to contain a great amount of DNA and that such samples, taken in the present of an official, are not subjected to any degrading factors.

Moreover, raw data unprocessed by the automated interpretation software must be available for analysis by the trained experts themselves since, as mentioned already, DNA profiles from crime scenes are more complicated in terms of mixtures and degradation. The automated process of data interpretation by the software must, and with high accuracy, identify artifacts and label alleles that will require the manual interpretation of the expert, even with single-sourced samples. In any case, the agreement still requires the system to improve the generated profiles of samples containing mixtures and low DNA input by improving the technical aspects within the different stages of DNA extraction and amplification, which will eventually aid the manual interpretation with a greater level of confidence. Finally, it is obligated for the platform manufacturers to perform a well-defined validation study that accurately reflects the types and conditions of samples commonly found at crime scenes and covers the standards mentioned in the FBI's Quality Assurance Standards for Forensic DNA Testing Laboratories (Board 2000) including, but not limited to, the publication to be peer-reviewed, inclusion of a comprehensive study on mixture analyses, identifying the detection limits of the system, recommendations on the appropriate types of samples to be analyzed, and comparison studies against the conventional workflow. Furthermore, each laboratory adopting this new technology has to perform internal validations including development of interpretation guidelines, quality assurance parameters, mixture interpretation, and statistical considerations. According to SWGDAM, these separate and individual sets of regulations for validating reference and crime scene samples are set so that the CODIS database would only contain data of the highest quality in order to maintain the public's confidence in the integrity of the forensic DNA analysis and eventually, the preservation of an individual's rights (SWGDAM, 2017).

REFERENCES

Amick, G. D., & Swiger, R. R. (2019). Internal Validation of Rapid HIT® ID ACE Sample Cartridge and Assessment of the EXT Sample Cartridge. *Journal of forensic sciences*, 64(3), 857–868.

Board, D. A. (2000). Quality Assurance Standards for Forensic DNA Testing Laboratories, *Forensic Science Communication*, 2(3).

Butler, J. M. (2015). The Future of Forensic DNA Analysis. *Philosophical Transactions of the Royal Society B: Biological Sciences*, 370(1674), 20140252.

Butts, E. L., & Vallone, P. M. (2014). Rapid PCR Protocols for Forensic DNA Typing on Six Thermal Cycling Platforms. *Electrophoresis*, 35(21–22), 3053–3061.

Chatumal, W., Markalanda, D. A., Illeperuma, R. J., Ranawaka, G. R., & Fernandopulle, N. D. (2010). Population Study of the Combined DNA Index System (CODIS) Core Loci D3S1358, D5S818, D8S1179 Short Tandem Repeat (STR) Polymorphisms in Sri Lanka. *Journal of the National Science Foundation of Sri Lanka, 38*(1).

Congress.gov, H. Rept. 115–117 – Rapid DNA Act of 2017 (2017). https://www.congress.gov/congressional-report/115thcongress/house-report/117/1 (accessed October18, 2020).

Dash, H. R., Rawat, N., Kakkar, S., & Swain, A. K. (2018). *Fundamentals of Autosomal STR Typing for Forensic Applications: Case Studies. In DNA Fingerprinting: Advancements and Future Endeavors* (pp. 209–221). Singapore: Springer.

Dash, H. R., Shrivastava, P., & Das, S. (2020). *Introduction to Forensic DNA Analysis. In Principles and Practices of DNA Analysis: A Laboratory Manual for Forensic DNA Typing* (pp. 3–11). New York, NY: Humana.

Della Manna, A., Nye, J. V., Carney, C., Hammons, J. S., Mann, M., Al Shamali, F., ... & Turingan, R. S. (2016). Developmental Validation of the Dnascan™ Rapid DNA analysis™ Instrument and Expert System for Reference Sample Processing. *Forensic Science International: Genetics, 25*, 145–156.

FBI.gov, Non-CODIS Rapid DNA considerations and best practices for law enforcement use (2019). https://www.fbi.gov/file-repository/non-codis-rapid-dna-best-practices-092419.pdf/view (accessed October19, 2020).

Gangano, S., Elliott, K., Anoruo, K., Gass, J., Buscaino, J., Jovanovich, S., & Harris, D. (2013). DNA Investigative Lead Development From Blood and Saliva Samples inLess than Two Hours Using the RapidHIT™ Human DNA Identification System. *Forensic Science International: Genetics Supplement Series, 4*(1), e43–e44.

Gettings, K. B., Aponte, R. A., Vallone, P. M., & Butler, J. M. (2015). STR Allele Sequence Variation: Current Knowledge and Future Issues. *Forensic Science International: Genetics, 18*, 118–130.

Grogan, L. (2019). Ethical Implications of CODIS.

Grover, R., Jiang, H., Turingan, R. S., French, J. L., Tan, E., & Selden, R. F. (2017). FlexPlex27—Highly Multiplexed Rapid DNA Identification for Law Enforcement, Kinship, and Military Applications, *International Journal of Legal Medicine, 131*(6), 1489–1501.

Hakim, H. M., Khan, H. O., Lalung, J., Nelson, B. R., Chambers, G. K., & Edinur, H. A. (2020). Autosomal STR Profiling and Databanking in Malaysia: Current Status and Future Prospects. *Genes, 11*(10), 1112.

Hares, D. R., Kneppers, A., Onorato, A. J., & Kahn, S. (2020). Rapid DNA for Crime Scene Use: Enhancements and Data Needed to Consider Use on Forensic Evidence for State and National DNA Databasing-An Agreed Position Statement by ENFSI, SWGDAM and the Rapid DNA Crime Scene Technology Advancement Task Group, *Forensic science international: Genetics, 48*, 102349.

Kim, A. (2019). The Evaluation of the RapidHIT™ 200 on Degraded Biological Samples.

Krishnan, J., Athar, F., Rani, T. S., & Mishra, R. K. (2017). Simple Sequence Repeats Showing 'Length Preference'Have Regulatory Functions in Humans. *Gene, 628*, 156–161.

Mapes, A. A. *Rapid DNA Technologies at the Crime Scene 'CSI'fiction Matching Reality*. Amsterdam:University of Amsterdam, 2017.

McDonald, J., & Lehman, D. C. (2012). Forensic DNA analysis. *Clinical Laboratory Science, 25*(2), 109.

Mohammed, M. N. (2019). Study of Autosomal STR Markers in United Arab Emirates Population.

Murphy, E. (2018). Forensic DNA typing. *Annual Review of Criminology, 1*, 497–515.

Roewer, L. (2013). DNA Fingerprinting in Forensics: Past, Present, Future. *Investigative genetics, 4*(1), 1–10.

Romsos, E., & Vallone, P. M. (2015). Rapid DNA maturity assessment. *Forensic Science International: Genetics Supplement Series, 5*, e1–e2.

Shackleton, D., Pagram, J., Andrews, N., Malsom, S., Ives, L., & Vanhinsbergh, D. (2019). Development of Enhanced Sensitivity Protocols on the RapidHIT™ 200 with a View to Processing Casework Material. *Science & Justice, 59*(4), 411–417.

Shapiro, J. A. (2010). Mobile DNA and Evolution in the 21st Century. *Mobile DNA, 1*(1), 1–14.

SWGDAM, Scientific Working Group on DNA Analysis Methods Position Statement on Rapid DNA Analysis (2017). https://1ecb9588-ea6f-4feb-971a73265dbf079c.filesusr.com/ugd/4344b0_f84df0465a2243218757fac1a1ccffea.pdf (accessed October19 2020).

Takara Bio, SpeedSTAR HS DNA Polymerase. https://www.takarabio.com/products/pcr/fast-pcr/speedstar-hs-dna-polymerase (accessed July21, 2020).

Tan, E., Turingan, R. S., Hogan, C., Vasantgadkar, S., Palombo, L., Schumm, J. W., & Selden, R. F. (2013). Fully Integrated, Fully Automated Generation of Short Tandem Repeat Profiles. *Investigative genetics, 4*(1), 16.

ThermoFisher Scientific, RapidINTEL™ Sample Cartridge for blood and saliva samples. https://www.thermofisher.com/document-connect/document-connect.html?url=https%3A%2F%2Fassets.thermofisher.com%2FTFS-Assets%2FLSG%2Fmanuals%2FMAN0018979_RapidINTEL_RHIT_v1_1_3_Validation_UB.pdf&title=VXNlciBCdWxsZXRpbjog

UmFwaWRJTlRlRFTCBTYW1wbGUgQ2FydHJpZG-dlIGZvciBibG9vZCBhbmQgc2FsaXZhIHNhbXBsZ-XM= (assessed October 20, 2020).

Thompson, R., Zoppis, S., & McCord, B. (2012). An overview of DNA typing methods for human identification: past, present, and future. In *DNA Electrophoresis Protocols for Forensic Genetics* (pp. 3–16). Humana Press.

Thong, Z., Phua, Y. H., Loo, E. S., Shue, B. H., & Syn, C. K. C. (2015), Investigative leads from DNA: Casework Experience from the IntegenX RapidHIT™ 200 System. *Forensic Science International: Genetics Supplement Series*, 5, e69–e70.

Turingan, R. S., Tan, E., Jiang, H., Brown, J., Estari, Y., Krautz-Peterson, G., & Selden, R. F. (2020). Developmental Validation of the ANDE 6C System for Rapid DNA Analysis of Forensic Casework and DVI Samples. *Journal of Forensic Sciences*, 65(4), 1056–1071.

Turingan, R. S., Vasantgadkar, S., Palombo, L., Hogan, C., Jiang, H., Tan, E., & Selden, R. F. (2016). Rapid DNA Analysis for Automated Processing and Interpretation of low DNA Content Samples. *Investigative genetics*, 7(1), 1–12.

Vallone, P. M., Hill, C. R., & Butler, J. M. (2008). Demonstration of Rapid Multiplex PCR Amplification Involving 16 Genetic Loci. *Forensic Science International: Genetics*, 3(1), 42–45.

Vallone, P. M., Hill, C. R., Podini, D., & Butler, J. M. (2009). Rapid Amplification of Commercial STR Typing Kits. *Forensic Science International: Genetics Supplement Series*, 2(1), 111–112.

Watson, J. *The Double Helix*. UK: Hachette, 2012.

Wrublewski, D. T. (2019). Analysis for Science Librarians of the 2018 Nobel Prize in Chemistry: Directed Evolution of Enzymes and Phage Display of Peptides and Antibodies. *Science & Technology Libraries*, 38(1), 51–69.

CHAPTER **16**

Crime Scene Investigation for Veterinarians: Practical Vision

Víctor Toledo González[1]*, Esther Espejo Alvim*[2]*, Carlos Muñoz Quezada*[3]*, and Rodrigo Marcos Quezada*[4]

[1]International Scientific Working Group of Animal Forensic Sciences (ISWG-AFS); Worldwide Association of Women Forensic Experts (WAWFE), Spain
[2]Experimental and Comparative Pathology Program of the Faculty of Veterinary Medicine and Zootechnics, University of Sao Paulo; Brazilian Association of Legal Veterinary Medicine, Brazil
[3]Iberoamercan Association of Medicine and Forensic Veterinary Sciences, Chile
[4]Chilean Association of Criminalists (COLCRIM AG); Forensis SpA, Chile

CONTENTS

DOI: 10.4324/9781003129554-16

VETERINARY MEDICINE AND FORENSIC SCIENCES

Veterinary medicine associated with forensic sciences arises in response to the need to have qualified professionals to face the growing social demand that requires effective sanctions in cases of direct or indirect abuse, wilful or culpable, exercised against animals. Known is that certain events may be associated with other acts of interpersonal abuse. The veterinary forensic investigator must be aware that they can face cases where animals are victims and as eventual perpetrators/aggressors used to commit crimes and even as silent witnesses.

However, veterinary forensic science work transcends much further in its actions and is not only limited to abuse. There is an infinity of governmental interest facts such as illegal animal trafficking and poaching, bioterrorism, national security, public health (zoonosis), environmental crimes, (Cooper and Cooper, 2008) or others of lesser disclosure, but no less critical, such for example, crime in the food industry. Colleagues and friends have already described many of these, in other publications, in current times where the concept of ONE HEALTH and ONE VIOLENCE take on meaning and importance.

Even so, despite the existing literature, so much of veterinary doctors in the world feel oblivious to the subject, defenseless and ignorant as to what to do or not to do, when called to participate in a civil or criminal investigation, unaware of their abilities, capacities, and rights. Training in animal forensic science will become essential when conducting an investigation related to animals that participate as victims, perpetrators, or witnesses of an event.

Lack of knowledge, skills, and other factors that we will comment on later, and the need to fulfil the assigned task in relatively limited times, ultimately translate into ineffective and inefficient work on the part of all those who participate in an investigation. That undoubtedly generates personal and professional frustration, especially in those who recognize non-human animals as sentient beings capable of modifying the environment and, therefore, intelligent beings. When we refer to the environment, we include the human, who has benefited from the use of animals as work and entertainment tools and the emotional and therapeutic aspect. We must not forget that the human-animal relationship carries with it various degrees of interconnections and situations. The complexity of this relationship must be admitted in each investigation, and those who can best understand them or at least consider them are professionals linked to animals.

So why train in a discipline where we may never be able to access the crime scene and see what is happening with our own eyes?

The answer is easy to answer from our point of view. If we do not know how to work in the crime scene, what questions might be asking to the officers when they ask for help? Would it analyze "evidence" without knowing if it met the essential collection, preservation, and conservation requirements to maintain its integrity?

The problem increases by not attending the crime scene in person. In general, each forensic veterinarian, including investigators, should not base their hypothesis only on the evidence but also on the context of the crime scene in which the evidence was found. A trained veterinarian's participation in the team will allow identity, collection, and maintainenance of the integrity of signs of an animal action for forensic analysis (Merck, 2013). This would increase the probability that said indications would become evidence presented in court and constituted as evidence. Let us remember that good practices in the crime scene will allow having pieces of evidence/vestiges that explain and demonstrate, in a logical way, what happened (interpretation), beyond any reasonable doubt.

TRACES, SIGNS, EVIDENCE, AND MEANS OF PROOF

These should not be confused, the concepts of traces, evidence, and means of proof. Traces are elements or imprinted signs left consciously (to mislead) or subconsciously by the perpetrators of an event through their actions (e.g. a fibre, a bloodstain, etc.).

The signs are the acts, facts, circumstances, and effects from which the existence of other facts can be inferred, through logical reasoning. That is, what makes us think about something, allows us to imagine the existence of a certain circumstance linked to the event or crime under investigation.

Evidence, on the other hand, is the means that allow the acceptance or rejection of a fact. It can be defined as anything (tangible or intangible) that can help to refute or corroborate a particular fact in dispute (Gardner and Krouskup, 2019). The evidence arises from the forensic study carried out on an element, to detect traces in it that allow it to be elevated to a solid means of proof. They come from testimonies, objects, documents, antecedents, etc., and they demonstrate, clarify, or confirm facts (see below). They must also comply with the rules of relevance (be directly related to the case), of validity (adequate, sufficient, reliable), and of competence, within physical, mental, legal, scientific parameters, etc. In short, they allow us to relate findings found or collected.

Finally, Means of Proof serves to demonstrate the veracity or falsity of a fact. They are made up based on conclusions and results of the analyses of the evidence, which allow confirming or disproving a hypothesis or a statement.

VETERINARIANS AND CRIME SCENE

In many countries, the regulations do not contemplate the mandatory presence of a veterinarian in the crime scene. Generally, to contain live animals or for emergency care of one of them, injured/dying, they are called (triage, see below). Currently, this situation is slowly changing.

The veterinarian who goes without knowledge will generally alter the context of the crime scene, moving, destroying, or incorporating evidence that could turn into "false evidence," even if guided by personnel in charge. The tension experienced in many cases leaves no room to think quickly. If we add ignorance, tension, eventual insecurity at work, or physical and psychological conditions (e.g. phobias) inappropriate for work, etc., without a doubt, the forensic report's result will not be up to what expected. This is a critical point since an innocent personality could be unjustifiably blamed or a real aggressor be released.

It is unnecessary to be a veterinarian to understand that non-human animals, of any species, behave in a special manner and very different from humans. We are not talking about those animals who suffer anthropomorphization. However, considering and recognizing aspects that can be attributed to a particular species is the task of a veterinarian and related professionals such as biologists, zoologists, etc., leaving the clinic pathological aspects to the veterinarian.

Knowing all the aspects related to the work carried out in the crime scene (context), in cases where animals are involved, will allow the veterinarian to identify, more effectively, the critical points or most relevant aspects related to the victim, its behaviour, and its environment. The same happens if the aggressor is another animal.

It does not mean that a veterinarian should know about all species or all specialties, but can recognize the need for a particular specialist in certain circumstances.

We already suggest that the knowledge and training in this discipline will allow ask pertinent questions specific to the officers when the veterinarian was not called to the crime scene, trying to obtain as much useful information as possible. It could eventually help interpret the findings found during the exam. However, we must reiterate that their presence in the crime scene will provide vital elements for interpreting these findings: the context in which the events occurred.

The forensic veterinarian work is only one part of the judicial process. Our job is not to do justice but rather to seek the truth, based on the analysis of scientific and judicially robust evidence.

This chapter aims to guide and provide tools to veterinarians and related professionals to face a civil or criminal case, where part or all of the evidence reveals the participation of live or dead animals. In most of the world, a veterinarian's training incorporates a range of medical knowledge about various species, domestic and wild, among others. One of them is the pathological anatomy.

For this reason, we will not delve into the process of taking samples of animal origin and analyses of results. However, we will do a brief summary of the literature related to sampling. Information that is more extensive can be consulted in publications mentioned in the references section.

Based on the vast existing literature directed at human research (Miller & Massey, 2016), much less devoted to animals, and insights forged by the authors' experience over the years, we will focus on what, in our view, is one of the most critical and unknown points in an forensic investigation involving animals: the work in the crime scene.

This chapter does not aim to replace criminal investigators. However, it supports self-conviction that the presence of a veterinarian with forensic knowledge will always be necessary in cases involving animals or their vestiges into the crime scene. Nobody sees what they do not know, and only multidisciplinary work will allow us to meet the objectives set in a professional, efficient, and effective way.

It should be remembered that science advances vertiginously, and it is the duty of those who participate in this discipline to be continuously updated, both in concepts and methodologies. This will allow us to make the best decisions, discuss and interpret a fact in an informed way, with knowledge and property.

TYPES OF EVIDENCES

Testimonial Evidence

It originates from interviews and interrogations of victims, witnesses, suspects, or any other person present or not in the crime scene (Miller & Massey, 2016; Gardner

& Krouskup, 2019). Animals will not give a testimony of what happened, whatever their participation in an event. However, we must remember that animals may be training and used as instruments of aggression against people that could bear witness to what happened. There may also be people who saw a particular event, who know the characteristics of an individual animal or a particular past event.

The significant disadvantage of this evidence is the subjectivity and relativity of the stories. Many factors can influence those testimonies: Degree of perception, ability to remember, perspective, personal interests, self-belief in what others say, etc. Despite all this, this collected information must not be discarded and this must be evaluated, along with the physical evidence (Gardner & Krouskup, 2019).

Physical Evidence

They constitute all the specific, tangible physical elements found, documented (photography, planimetry, mainly when they cannot be transported), and collected in a crime scene for later analysis. These can be partial or totally incorporated into the expert report and eventually exposed to a court as evidence. Either way, the physical evidence is objective, factual, exists, and cannot be denied. The only interpretation obtained from it, by the person who analyzes it, permeates that degree of subjectivity. Nevertheless, that is the fault or misfortune of the person who interprets it, not of the evidence. This physical evidence, protected under the chain of custody, must be subjected to various forensic analyses by many professionals to deliver as much useful information as possible (Miller & Massey, 2016; Gardner & Krouskup, 2019). The researcher must interpret these results considering, previously, the full analysis of all the findings, avoiding issuing conclusions with high degrees of certainty about what happened based on partial analyses. It is also essential to know that evidence may or may not prove something. We must remember that the purpose of the scene investigation is to identify traces/evidence related to the crime. This must include probative and exculpatory evidence (Merck, 2013).

Physical evidence creates an objective knowledge structure with which testimonial evidence can be refuted or corroborated (Gardner & Krouskup, 2019).

Circumstantial Evidence

It is evidence that arises when "telling facts" (Gardner & Krouskup, 2019) (Fisher & Fisher (2012) include this evidence into real/ physical evidence. These facts are analyzed together and reveal a third particular fact. For example, Mr. Prim could use his dog to attack a person in a rural area near a lake on a sunny day. When the investigator arrives at the suspect's house, he/she watch mud on the dog's paw present into the house. This mud could be the same type of mud found next to the lake (on a dry day when it has not rained). With this only information, we can infer and assume, with a high probability, that this dog was in the crime scene. An analysis of the evidence, comparing the material found in the feet of the dog and in the lake, will corroborate or not, our assumption, with a greater degree of certainty.

Not every trace found in the crime scene can be considered evidence. For this, an interpretive and significant value must be assigned to each trace. It is not enough to find an element of criminal interest. This must be evaluated according to a determinate context.

Based on the principles of criminalistics/forensic sciences (see below), the investigator must reconstruct a history of what happened with the elements found. To do this, it must place them within a sequence of events (temporality of events) and relate them to the environment. It must functionally locate an element found within of the crime scene and relate it to its environment.

Let Us Look at an Example Concerning Context

A dog hanged in a residence has been reported (Figure 16.1). The dog was dead, tied tightly with a rope around its neck. A red puddle around the dog was identified as blood, generating spots that covered much of the body. The presence of blood and its analysis in the laboratory is essential to define any particularity of it,

but it only tells a piece of the story. This does not talk about context where the traces were found. The owners declared that the dog died due to a haemorrhage by parvovirus.

Let us analyze the crime scene in more detail:

The blood had bubbles on its surface, and there was also a projection of blood on the walls. Is it possible that a dog with profuse diarrhoea can project blood towards the walls, as observed in the case? (Imagine the mood of the animal).

Instead, it appears that the blood patterns are produced by shaking by the dog, trying to get loose. Did the pathologist know that there were bubbles that could indicate suffocation?

The context of the crime scene is almost everything!

We have mentioned the concept of chain of custody above. It could briefly be defined as the procedure by which the sample's integrity assures its collection to the report's issuance. It guarantees the authenticity, security, preservation, and integrity of the physical evidence found, obtained, collected, and examined, continuously and interruptedly, until delivered as evidence before a legal court. Generally, each body in charge of acting in the crime scene has its chain of custody formats.

EFFECTS ON CRIME SCENE

During the investigation, it is necessary to consider that some specific changes or effects may occur in the place,

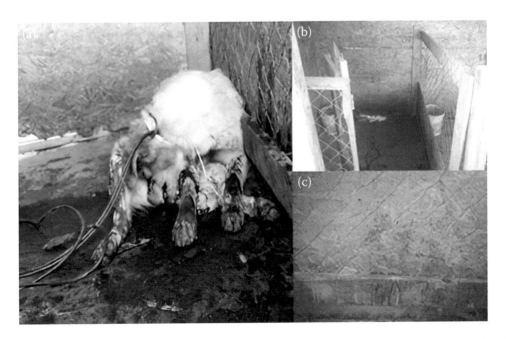

FIGURE 16.1   (a) Dead dog hanged and a large volume of blood lost; (b) the same place after it has been clean to hide the evidence; (c) blood projection. Property: Carlos Muñoz Quezada.

altering the context of crime scene and, therefore, promoting an incorrect interpretation of it. The first to consider are transitory effects. These can disappear quickly from the crime scene and therefore must to be recognized early in the investigation (Gardner & Krouskup, 2019). They commonly found when searched intentionally and not casually (e.g. the heat emitted by a cigarette, smell of perfumes, disinfectants, urine, food in a trough, etc.).

Others are unpredictable or unexpected effects that occur randomly (Gardner & Krouskup, 2019). An example of these effects occurs when researchers enter a closed space with a high ammonia concentration. The "noxious" environment prompts the first arrivals to the crime scene to open windows, doors, or turn on extractors to reduce the level of contamination.

When they unconsciously turn on lights and then do not remember or do not know if those lights were on when they arrived or who turned them on; in addition, when someone accidentally moves an object from the original position. If no one documented the condition of the place or the condition/position of an item when arriving, the original context is lost forever. For this reason, it is essential to know who did what (Gardner & Krouskup, 2019)! At all times, everything we do must be documented.

The predictable effects are the third group. They are those changes that occur with a certain regularity, under specific and general conditions. As an example, the determination of the approximate time since death (*post-mortem interval, PMI*) through the appearance of *rigor*, *livor*, and *algor mortis* (role of a forensic pathologist) or the presence and development *status* of cadaveric fauna (role of an entomologist) (Adapted from Gardner & Krouskup, 2019). In both cases, the regularity of these changes will depend on internal factors (characteristics of the corpse) and external factors present in the environment (temperature, humidity, pH, salinity, human action, etc.).

BASIC PRINCIPLES OF CRIMINALISTICS

During crime scene processing, the so-called "basic principles of criminalistics or basic principles of forensic sciences" must be continuously applied. Through them, we will try to associate the findings (traces, evidence) found in the crime scene and the environment, in a given context. It will allow us to elaborate one or more logical hypotheses of what, eventually, happened. This must be objectively demonstrated. Here is a brief description of them (Montiel, 2003):

- **Principle of Use.** It is to determine the type of element/tool and weapon used to commit the crime. Physical elements must be considered (heat, cold, radioactive elements, radio frequencies, etc.); chemical elements (herbicides, pesticides, toxins, poisons, etc.); biological elements (viruses); and mechanical elements (anything that can cause trauma).

- **Principle of Production.** It consists of determining how the element was in question manipulated. A chain could hang an animal and suffocate it, leave it tied up in the sun, tie its legs, throw it into a lake, etc. Elements used to commit a crime are not always used in the form for which they were built.

- **Principle of Exchange.** The most used and known. It is the well-known principle of Edmund Locard (1877–1966). It establishes that every time two individuals or elements come into contact (direct), there is a transfer of elements between them, allowing for a connection. It is crucial to consider it in those crimes where a hand-to-hand confrontation is necessary. Now, we can add that this "contact" can occur remotely and not necessarily directly. We could call it "indirect contact or just "tranfer"

Let's See an Example

One person murders three people who live with a cat. The latter flees upon hearing the shots. The murderer sits for a few seconds to rest in front of the switched-on fan and then leaves. As veterinarians, we know that a domestic cat leaves hair behind when it walks every corner. Therefore, the probability that the murderer collected hair from the cat on his clothes when he sat down? (indirect exchange or tranfer). The degree of adherence and permanence of the trace element on the individual's clothing will depend on other factors such as texture, sample size, etc. However, it is also likely that hair that is normally suspended in the air has adhered to the killer's clothing or drawn to him by the fan's airflow (indirect exchange). Direct contact would be given by coming into contact with the cat's body. All this possibilities must be analyzed. We cannot fail to mention the possibility that someone has put an item on the scene in order to mislead investigators or incriminate someone. For this reason, the context of the crime scene is so important and allows us to associate the findings more logically and comprehensively.

- **Principle of Correspondence.** It occurs when an element (e.g. lit a cigarette, cutting tools, weapons, etc.) with which the damage was caused leaves its characteristics imprinted on the body on which it impacts or overlaps. It can be determined by comparing a suspect element found in the crime scene and an item in possession of the suspect or accused.

(a) (b)

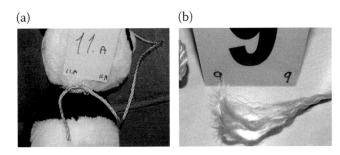

FIGURE 16.2 Ends of the rope near the neck (a), and the opposite end (b) must be protected for analysis. Avoid cutting the rope before removing it, evaluating the possible presence of trace elements, and recording possible marks. Ideally, the neck rope should be removed during necropsy if the corpse moves to the laboratory in a reasonable time. Property: Víctor Toledo González, José María González.

Let's see an example

The rope used has two ends. One end is close to the knot on the neck (Figure 16.2a), and the other end was fixing the rope in height (Figure 16.2b). In this case, we can analyze the rope's characteristics (the type of material, type of interlacing of its fibres, colour, texture, etc.) and its cut-end characteristics. If we have a suspicion, we look in the places where a rope resembles the one found in the habitats of the crime scene. If we can demonstrate that both have the same characteristics and the ends of the rope in the suspect's possession coincide with those found in the crime scene (we got a match). Then, we can infer (circumstantial evidence) that the rope used to hang the animal came from that other rope in the suspect's possession. In addition, we must try find the instrument used to cut the rope and compare the cutting zone. However, this is not proof that the suspect committed the crime.

- **Probability Principle.** After elaborating on a hypothesis and sequential reconstruction of the events, we must ask ourselves, is it likely that this has happened like this? How sure am I?

It is an approximation to the truth. We refer to it as null, low, medium, or high probability. It is not convenient to pronounce with "this happened exactly like that" due because some factors may not have been considered during investigation.

- **Principle of Certainty.** By analyzing data using an appropriate methodology, procedures, technology, and tools, it will be possible to originate information that must interpret correctly. This

information will serve to refute or corroborate the hypotheses raised. This information will be written in the expert report.

- **Principle of Reconstruction.** It is based on the generation of a hypothesis of what happened sequentially, based on the analysis of the elements present in the crime scene and its context. We should not confuse with recreation, which constitutes only part of the reconstruction.

Example of reconstruction of the facts with the accused:

"... I left home at 06:00 after arguing with a relative. I took the car and went to the canine rehabilitation centre, where I work. I was very upset. When I entered, I realized that two animals had escaped during the night. I was enraged. I took the rope to catch them. One of them bit me and in my desperation, I choked him."

Example of recreation of the events:

Imputed: "I took the rope and hanged him like this ..."

It should be observed that some authors talk about just five principles: transfer, identification, classification/individualization, association, and reconstruction (Inman & Rudin, 2001).

With these principles in mind during the investigation, we must ask ourselves:

What is this clue? (Nature of the element/instrument)

How the instrument was used?

What purpose it served during the crime?

Has this evidence connection with others?

After identifying the traces/vestiges/evidence, an attempt should try to determine when the event occurred or when the weapon was used it. For this, we can consider the characteristics of the victim and the environment. For example, to determine the *PMI*, we can determine the presence of food in containers or the content of food in the animal stomach. It is necessary to try to determine if both foods have the same origin and characteristics. We can also check the characteristics of plants in the crime scene (e.g. dry, wet, etc.) or the presence of flies, larvae, etc. All this determines temporality aspects of the event. Finally, the sequence of events must be determined, that is, order logically and chronologically how the facts unfolded (Gardner & Krouskup, 2019). It is necessary to imagine how the perpetrator of a crime acted, considering the elements found, their relationship, and their characteristics. For example, running dog bloody fingerprints can tell where the dog ran after the attack.

MANAGING THE EVIDENCE

Frequently, the literature mentions the forensic linkage triangle. This reminds investigators, in a very general way, of the need to link the suspect, the victim, and the crime scene. However, another graphical way of representing all the components, which must be investigated and linked, is proposed in this chapter (Figure 16.3).

We must be aware that physical evidence may or may not be linked to one or more elements. Furthermore, the degree of linkage may differ between them. The mere link between the physical elements may

not necessarily be useful to incriminate someone. Besides, each element has its history, independent of the others. This story can be of great value in the investigation and contribute or not, as evidence. The testimonial and circumstantial evidence related to each element must be part of the bonding exercise. The evidence's interpretation should be done when we have all the possible information and not part of it. The great effort is to collect all this information, try to demonstrate its probative value, and try to give a logical explanation of that possible link.

An Example Where It Shows That Physical Evidence Is Not Always Enough

A dead animal was found in a prohibited hunting area, with a projectile wound on its body. Among the bushes are the shotgun and the case of a cartridge. Fingerprint and blood patterns on the barrel of the gun, and the trigger. What appears to be a piece of fingernail was found on the hilt of the weapon.

The time of death of the animal was calculated between May 13 and 16 by the veterinary medical pathologist and all DNA tests pointed to a single person. That person was serving a child support penalty and had already be detained for petty theft.

When the visit is made at the suspect's house, the man denies participation in the event. When his weapon is needed to be handed to investigators, he realized that it had disappeared. He was aware that he had the same weapon registered to hunt, but he claimed that he had not done so for a long time. He stated that he had been away those days in search of work. Investigators noted that he was wearing a bandage on his right hand. He pointed out that he had gotten the manicure to be presentable and that the person who performed it injured him.

Investigators corroborated the alibi. Indeed, he was away waiting to interview for more than two weeks, and that he had attended the manicure before his trip. So how did so much physical evidence appear that places him in the crime scene? After that, possible suspects were investigated.

The alimony plaintiff (ex-wife), who turned out to be friend of the hairdresser, obtained the blood and nail chunk from the manicure. Even though all the physical evidence focused attention on that man, this testimonial and circumstantial evidence generated a reasonable doubt regarding his participation in the events. Eventually, it discovered that her ex-wife had put all that evidence to blame him.

The determination of the *PMI* depends on many factors that, in our opinion, make it difficult to determine an exact moment of death. We believe it is more

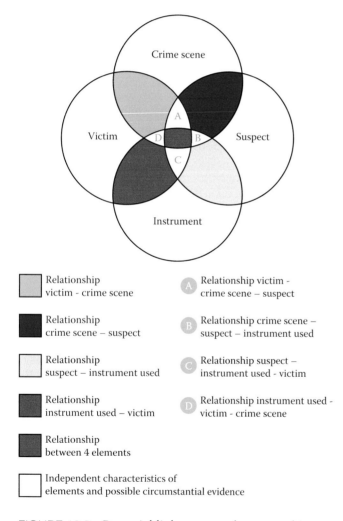

Relationship victim - crime scene

Relationship crime scene – suspect

Relationship suspect – instrument used

Relationship instrument used – victim

Relationship between 4 elements

Independent characteristics of elements and possible circumstantial evidence

(A) Relationship victim - crime scene – suspect

(B) Relationship crime scene – suspect – instrument used

(C) Relationship suspect – instrument used - victim

(D) Relationship instrument used - victim - crime scene

FIGURE 16.3 Potential links among elements subject to forensic investigation and analysis. Big white zones in each circle show the individual history of the used instrument (Nature of the element), victim, suspect, and crime scene.

prudent to describe the findings. Besides, in a few or almost no cases, it is possible to have all the necessary information to risk giving such an exact diagnosis. Nevertheless, this is already a specialty of pathologists, and this is only an appreciation based on experience.

CRIME SCENE

Physical spaces where events occur compromises the health, well-being, life of any animal mediated by an action contrary to a legal system, is known as the crime scene, etc. The name given to the crime scenes varies according to the country's regulations. In general, there are single or multiple crime scene and each of them may or may not be related to each other.

For example, a bird prey intoxicated by ingesting a poison deposited on a dead animal. Depending on poison, the animal can die in the same place of consumption or move before dying in another place. In the first case, we speak of a single or straightforward crime scene. In the second case, there is a primary crime scene, where he poisoned, and a secondary crime scene, where he died.

In this chapter, reference will be made to the "crime scene" as a synonym for "scenography" because, generally, we are not eyewitnesses to the criminal activity. Instead, we find a place where there are traces, indications, and possible pieces of evidence of the criminal act necessary to collect.

If we witnessed the illegal action, we could speak of the "crime scene," associating the concept of flagrant crime with said action. This condition allows agents to act quickly, preventing the criminal act from being carried out without requiring the authority's official permission. After this period, which can vary depending on the country, the investigator just can act with a court order. This forces us to know the local regulations.

According its physical location and its physical condition four types of crime scenes are described: indoor (closed), outdoor (open), mixed, and aquatic/underwater, respectively (Lee & Pagliaro, 2013; Harris & Lee, 2019). Their classification will depend on the characteristics of each one of them and to the type of crime (Harris & Lee, 2019).

The outdoor crime scene is located in a space with no restrictions on entry or leakage of elements. There is a lack of total control of all or the vast majority of the components present in the place. It constitutes places like forests, oceans, deserts, etc. Its extent or perimeter tends to be imaginary and exists only for spatial planimetry purposes. Poaching and crimes against the environment are generally associated with this kind of scene (Figure 16.4a).

The indoor crime scene is opposed to the one described above. Here there is greater control of the elements within the surrounding perimeter and the airspace. It avoids, more efficiently, the departure of elements from the crime scene or the entry of new elements (e.g. veterinary clinics, hotels, a room, clandestine

(a)

(b)

(c)

(d)

FIGURE 16.4   Crime scenes: (a) Outdoor; (b) indoor; (c) mixed; (d) aquatic/subaquatic.

Property: Víctor Toledo González.

breeding or slaughterhouses, inside a factory, etc.) (Figure 16.4b).

A **mixed crime scene** has the characteristics of an indoor and outdoor crime scene. It is possible to avoid, to a certain degree, the entry of new elements or exit from them. It is associated with places with closed areas or facilities within a land, with a naturally or artificially defined perimeter (fences, walls, riverbank, ravines, etc.) (Figure 16.4c).

Finally, an **aquatic and underwater crime scene** is one in which the investigated evidence is total or partially underwater (ocean, lakes, rivers, streams, etc.). For example, the damage caused to marine fauna as a result of oil spills, damage caused by sonars, destruction of coral reefs, etc.) (Figure 16.4d).

Whatever the type of crime scene investigated, the function is the same:

Examine and evaluate the crime scene in a comprehensive, methodological, systematic, and balanced (objective) manner (Miller & Massey, 2016; Gardner & Krouskup, 2019), with the specific purpose of:

1. Collecting objective, scientific, and judicially useful physical evidence
2. Collect testimonial and circumstantial evidence
3. Recognize, record, and document the context of the crime scene in the least disturbed condition as possible (Merck, 2013; Harris & Lee, 2019; Gardner & Krouskup, 2019).

In animal forensic sciences, the most critical point of the investigative process is the crime scene processing. Any result obtained will largely depend on the quality of the work carried out in the crime scene.

Among the leading causes that lead to inefficient and ineffective processes, we can point out:

1. The lack of knowledgeable investigators and veterinary doctors with criminal/forensic knowledge.
2. Lack of tools and skills.
3. The lack of organized, coordinated, and multidisciplinary work (ethologists, clinicians, anatomists, pathologists, officials, park rangers, etc.). Coordination is essential to avoid ambiguous or contradictory actions, thus avoiding improvisations that put the investigation at risk.
4. The lack of organization and flexible methodologies (each crime scene is unique and must act conscientiously) (adapted from Gardner & Krouskup, 2019).

When the crime scene is processed, we must be aware that any action taken within site will alter its integrity will occur until processing is complete. By dynamic action, elements present in the crime scene can be added, moved or destroyed, generating artifacts and modifying its context. It would be best if it always worked concentrated and methodologically to reduce these alterations and evidence loss. Using a camera on the forehead upon arrival at the crime scene may help recognize these types of artifacts in later stages of the investigation (Gardner & Krouskup, 2019).

There is also the risk of altering the crime scene when live animals require immediate attention by a veterinarian. It can enter without knowledge or instructions, altering and destroying the context in its entirety. Any action taken must report it and document it. This action will decrease the probability of a wrong interpretation. In addition, live animals that roam it can make the alteration of the crime scene; always have to know who did what and determine why. For example, someone arriving at the crime scene and avoiding an imminent accident, for the team, pulls a branch that was about to fall. Later, during photographic analysis, the branch appears in its original position. If the action did not document, the confusion begins.

FIRST RESPONDER

Commonly, the investigator in charge of the case is not the first to arrive at the crime scene. Usually, the report of a fact is made by someone related to the affected animal or by third parties, especially when it comes to wildlife. They go to the closest police authorities to the crime scene (e.g. police officers, park rangers, etc.). Depending on the personnel of each entity, the reaction time will vary. In most cases, the first to arrive to the crime scene is known as first responder (FR).

A FR is probably not the most suitable person to act where there are animals. However, at the beginning of the investigation, their performance and decisions will be essential for their success (Fisher & Fisher, 2012; Fisher & Fisher, 2014; Miller & Massey, 2016; Rogers & Stern, 2018; Harris & Lee, 2019; Gardner & Krouskup, 2019).

The FR will have the following functions:

1. Verify/confirm the complaint to open an investigative process.
2. Verify the need for emergency teams for medical care (save lives, if possible or by advising veterinary/rescue professionals).
3. Define the central element of the crime scene and everything that is within it for its protection.
4. Identify "weak evidence" that can be altered or lost in a short period.
5. Coordinate the resources to control the place (people, witnesses, etc.).

6. Document everything and then deliver the crime scene and its annotations to the corresponding authorities (investigator/officer in charge of the crime scene).

Due to the need to act quickly in this initial stage, the use of an audio recorder is very useful (Harris & Lee, 2019), but it does not replace the documentation.

Under regular conditions, its function is not the processing of the crime scene (Gardner & Krouskup, 2019).

To fulfil these functions, the FR must have adequate knowledge to ensure the integrity of the process.

The first step that an FR should consider and the future research team (CSI team) is safety, before any intervention in the crime scene and must continually be attentive to surroundings so as not to become another victim. This security includes:

1. Safety of possible live or dying animals present on site (provide primary care, triage (see below).
2. Security for the FR or CSI team itself.
3. Safety of persons/witnesses present at the scene.
4. Security of evidence.
5. Security against potential risks that may arise in the future during the processing of the crime scene (Espinoza et al., 2013; Fisher & Fisher, 2014; Miller & Massey, 2016; Rogers & Stern, 2018; Gardner & Krouskup, 2019; Harris & Lee, 2019; Toledo et al., 2020).

With so many functions, it is logical to think that it will create artifacts during its performance, altering the context of the crime scene. For this reason, we should document your actions, thus avoiding errors in interpretation, during work in the crime scene or later periods of the investigation (Miller & Massey, 2016; Gardner & Krouskup, 2019).

Security/Biosecurity Considerations

Potential risks include:

- Dangerous climatic and physical agents: heat, cold, rain, snow, wind (e.g. falling trees or other structures), flash floods, time of day (light, dark), noise, lightning, waterspouts, fog, fires, traps for animals, volcanic and seismic activity, unexploded explosives or unsafe environment (e.g. suspect present in the crime scene), firearms, radiation, electricity, avalanches, mined land, tide levels, cliffs, vehicular, air, marine traffic and railroad, hunting grounds, presence of needles and syringes, sharp instruments such as cock-fighting blades, etc.).

- Presence of dangerous animals and insects, dangerous plants. A certain degree of hypersensitivity to the bite can enhance the harmful effects with a specific substance, etc.
- Chemicals: Pesticides, herbicides, gases, toxic baits, elements found in the crime scene (e.g. in clandestine laboratories), ammonia levels, or the chemicals used as part of the investigation.
- Biological: Pathogens transmitted by various routes: viruses, bacteria, parasites, fungi/mould, body fluids, zoonotic diseases (Espinoza et al., 2013; Toledo et al., 2020; Norris, 2020).

Zoonosis

A Zoonosis is an infectious disease naturally transmitted from vertebrate animals to humans (definition based on the World Health Organization, WHO, 2020). https://www.who.int/es/news-room/fact-sheets/detail/zoonoses

It is important to emphasize that the direct ingestion of contaminated material in veterinary forensic/criminalistics work is unlikely and generally occurs due to poor personal hygiene. However, small-contaminated airborne particles can use this route of entry. Abrasions or punctures can generate when handling animals with sharp beaks, claws, or nails. The presence of areas of unprotected skin or with the presence of wounds can be a route of infection. We must not forget the environment where the event occurs. It can present a risk of zoonosis, due, for example, to the accumulation of contaminated bird droppings, contaminated debris, or where rat infestations are present, among others (WHO, 2020).

WHO points out that there are more than 200 known types of zoonosis, among which are: anthrax, psittacosis, botulism, rabies, leishmaniosis, toxocariasis, toxoplasmosis, leptospirosis, brucellosis, Lyme disease, pasteurellosis, salmonellosis, sarcoptic mange, avian influenza, giardiasis, cryptococcosis, among many others. Some are equally dangerous to humans and animals in terms of health, while others only cause significant diseases in humans (even death) and minor effects in non-human animals (WHO, 2020).

As soon as possible and after verifying/confirming a crime that is a reason for the investigation, the FR must notify the investigation team by providing the exact location of the place. He must prepare written records, photo, and video graphics that will later serve as support during the completion of the respective report.

Preliminary Report or Initial Documentation

The header of the report must contain at least:

1. Name's agent.

2. Authority and institution it represents.
3. Location.
4. Date and time when you receive a call to the service and your arrival at the place.
5. Time of call to the investigation team and time of arrival (Fisher & Fisher, 2012; Miller & Massey, 2016; Rogers & Stern, 2018; Gardner & Krouskup, 2019).

In the body of the report, it is useful:

- Record weather conditions (temperature, humidity, wind direction, degree of light, etc.).
- Describe or identify odours, sounds, air flows, degrees of irritation of the ocular and nasal mucosa (if any), respiratory capacity due to the presence of elements in the environment (e.g. ammonia); visual capacity (which can be related to the degree of contamination). In short, recognize the transitory effects present in the place.
- Identify those persons/witnesses/suspects present when arriving, leaving, or arriving.
- Carefully identify who said what to corroborate or refute future statements.
- Identify and describe vehicles or means of transport directly or indirectly linked to the denounced event.

The use of a camera head mount, upon arrival, can allow capture the crime scene in its original condition quickly. It is imperative, especially when it comes to the emergency team, to care for people or live animals. The emergency will generate unavoidable alterations, forever losing the initial context.

The Life of Animals and People Prevails Over the Protection of Evidence

The degree of knowledge and control on the part of the FR will allow the emergency team to enter more cautiously, reducing the deleterious effects in cases where animals participate. It would help if you never lost patience.

Working and respecting the work of the other entities will ensure better performance of the entire investigative team. It will allow better quality work if these teams are called later to declare or confront the evidence. These suggestions extend ate the moment of controlling and isolating people/witnesses/suspects present in the place to obtain their collaboration. It is recommended to instruct them not to discuss the case with each other and avoid cross-contamination of stories. They can interview individually and separately (Gardner & Krouskup, 2019).

Triage

The presence of live endangered or dying animals is the priority in any crime scene, even on the possible evidence present in the place. There are animals that, despite their serious condition, may present a non-urgent condition. Triage, therefore, is a system whose objective is to prioritize medical care for any living/dying animals present in the crime scene. A veterinarian to avoid moving, destroying, or incorporating new evidence into the crime scene must be guided by the FR. Any procedure performs (clinical or not), as well as any input you use (e.g. syringes, drugs, muzzles, etc.), must be reported, documented, recorded, and preserved as part of the investigation (Figure 16.5). The same goes for the animal's belongings (e.g. collars, chains, etc.).

During this initial inspection of crime scene the presence of veterinarian can be useful evaluate the situation and start the animal triage planning (Touroo & Fitch, 2018; Norris, 2020). Each animal must be identified using necklaces, bracelets, ribbons with different colours/numbers/letters, etc. They also they must be photographed and prepared for transport (Touroo & Fitch, 2018).

Although it is not the specific responsibility of the FR to process or collect evidence from the crime scene, it could intervene in it, applying the chain of custody system, in cases where:

1. It is not possible to notice the group of competent investigators to process the place
2. When they cannot appear in a reasonable time
3. When there are well-founded reasons to believe that the evidence will be damaged or lost in a short period (fragile/weak – transitory evidence)

After controlling the general safety aspects, the care of live animals, and the collection of flimsy evidence, the FR must:

FIGURE 16.5   All medical supplies used during urgent care are part of the investigation and kept protect under the chain of custody. Property: Víctor Toledo González, José España Báez, Ángel Iglesias, Isaac Navarro, Elena Iglesias.

1. Establish an initial perimeter/cordon off the place according to the central element of crime scene
2. Establish a single point of entry, and exit to the incident. The person managing this checkpoint will be responsible for documenting who enters and leaves the scene and the reason for their entry
3. Arrange areas for the preparation of resources and create an effective link with researchers (Miller & Massey, 2016; Rogers & Stern, 2018; Gardner & Krouskup, 2019).

To define the perimeter, a FR must consider:

1. The primary focal point (s): Generally, where a body is found (e.g. cat hanging from a beam, a dead animal next to a human corpse, etc.)
2. The natural entry and exit point(s): Logical routes through which those who committed the crime entered and exited. This zone usually contains footprints of physical evidence that can destroy at the time of first entry. If possible, begin the search and identification of clues before entering the primary focal point.
3. The secondary scene(s) or branches: They are peripheral areas to the principal crime scene. For example, some authors point out that dead dogs as a result of clandestine fights are thrown or buried in neighbouring places, close to the "competition" area. Physical evidence (e.g. blood, hair, etc.) may be present in areas outside of the central crime scene. Besides, we may find the vehicles that transported them are located. These means of transportation will also be part of the investigation (Gardner & Krouskup, 2019).

The perimeter must extend beyond the area of interest, allowing better work by the future research team. This must be re-evaluate it upon arrival and continue to evaluate it permanently during the process. This is common when we are in an outdoor crime scene. The limitation of the perimeter cannot be conditioned by natural elements (e.g. a water channel, a shrub hedge, etc.). More evidence can be present outside these natural limits. Artificial boundaries (e.g. tapes, fences) are usually effective when people/witnesses are present (Rogers & Stern, 2018; Gardner & Krouskup, 2019).

THE ARRIVAL OF THE INVESTIGATIVE TEAM

The arrival of the CSI team begins by contacting the FR who must:

1. Report on the security aspects of the place

2. Report on the status of victims (alive or dead), witnesses, and suspects
3. Report on all activities carried out for the control of the crime scene
4. Report any flimsy evidence collected under the chain of custody
5. Explain the reasons for the scope or area of the scene defined
6. Must provide a personal opinion on the nature of the crime and what it led to thinking so
7. Report any alteration suffered into the crime scene before the arrival of the CSI team, due to witnesses, rescue teams, etc. (duly identified) (Fisher & Fisher, 2012; Gardner & Krouskup, 2019).

After this process, the FR functions can be reduced to control the people present, control the perimeter, collect testimonies, and coordinate new resources (Gardner & Krouskup, 2019).

CRIME SCENE PROCESSING BY CSI TEAM

As noted above, the purpose of the CSI team is

1. Collect the most significant amount of evidence present in the crime scene
2. Capture the context of it.

Specific steps must be carried out in an established order, from the least intrusive to the most intrusive. These procedures will validate or refute the possible hypotheses and theories of what happened after the investigation and analysis of all the evidence. This established order will reduce the possibility of altering or destroying the value of both procedures (Gardner & Krouskup, 2019).

A crime scene is dynamic, which forces researchers to evaluate each activity and action they perform continually. These activities include:

- Technical/ocular inspection (observation) and planning (coordination).
- Perimeter or cordon off (protection of the crime scene, safeguarding the evidence).
- Search for vestiges.
- Fixation by photography/videography, diagrams, sketches, and mapping.
- Collection, conservation, preservation, storage, and transfer of evidence.
- Analysis of the evidence.
- Reconstruction of events (Fisher & Fisher, 2012; Espinoza et al., 2013; Merck, 2013; Miller & Massey, 2016; Rogers & Stern, 2018; Gardner & Krouskup, 2019; Toledo et al., 2020).

FIGURE 16.6 Graphic summary activities to be carried out in the crime scene, highlighting the need for their execution under the chain of custody. Property: Víctor Toledo González.

Figure 16.6 graphically summarizes the sequence of activities in a crime scene.

It should be noted that many tests and analyses performed in the crime scene are orientation tests. These will help to determine its importance for laboratory analysis quickly, for example. If we find a red stain, the orientation test could tell us that it is a possible bloodstain and not ketchup.

The last two activities mentioned are an exercise generated continuously, in a transversal way, during the crime scene processing or subsequent procedures.

We reiterate that each procedure must be carried out from the least intrusive to the most intrusive, and the actions within each activity must comply with the same precept.

Some procedures are carried out in mind simultaneously, such as observation and planning, analysis of the evidence found to generate associations between them and the context of the crime scene. Is generating hypotheses of what happened, which try to reconstruct the events. These hypotheses are also dynamic and may vary as research progresses, and new evidence and associations are found.

The process ends with the preparation of the expert report and eventual presentation in court.

For the crime scene processing, it is required to have adequate implementation and instrumentation to fulfil the tasks. A list of them can be found at the end of the chapter (Appendix).

Technical/Visual Inspection (Assessment – Observation)

Before any measure, the complexity, extent, and security of the crime scene, ways to mitigate risks, and the need for a new human team must be evaluated (Espinoza et al., 2013; Merck, 2013; Rogers & Stern, 2018; Gardner & Krouskup, 2019; Toledo et al., 2020). The answers to these questions will continuously determine the methodology to follow.

The three priority functions that the FR and the investigative team must fulfil upon arrival at the crime scene are the same:

1. Determine the central elements into the crime scene.
2. Establish security aspects.
3. Recognize and collect weak evidence (Harris & Lee, 2019; Gardner & Krouskup, 2019).

In confined spaces with live and dead animals, high levels of ammonia are usually concentrating. As will be discussed later, these levels can diminish the investigator's work capacity, causing him to take rapid palliative measures. Never alter the context of the crime scene by opening windows, turning on extractors, or lights without first recognizing those transient elements. The level of contamination with gases, dust, etc. is evidence that must be recorded quantitatively or qualitatively. It could also make sense of future circumstantial evidence (e.g. degree of eye irritation from researchers or animals present at the site, respiratory distress, visual impairment, etc.).

After the three main functions are controlled, and the scene is stable, it will be possible to start processing under an established methodology. During the observation, the investigator must move around and, in some cases, very close to the central crime scene (primary focus). Although it does not seem an intrusive action, it may be necessary to move an object to get a better view of something in particular (e.g. an element under a sheet, etc.). All field activities need to be documented.

To document and describe the presence of some aspects in a concise and precise manner, present in the crime scene during the initial observation, the researcher may consider: the item found, quantity, colour, type of construction, approximate size, identification of characteristics, condition, location (e.g. three black-handled, silver-bladed knives, about 20 cm long, metallic-looking, brand X, worn on the body of a victim) (adapted from Gardner & Krouskup, 2019).

If any change is suspected in the crime scene, the FR must be included in this preliminary search activity (Miller & Massey, 2016).

Planning and Coordination

There must be prior planning to meet the objective of the investigation. It is obvious to think that the movement of people within the crime scene will inevitably alter its integrity and context. For this reason, the researcher must consider the degree of modification that her actions will generate when defining an action plan. The leader must assign defined and concrete functions for each member of her team, avoiding contradictions, duplications, and overlapping functions (Rogers & Stern, 2018; Gardner & Krouskup, 2019). Coordination ensures that all actions are made in the correct order and those essential aspects of the scene examination mast not sacrificed without prior consideration. Before acting, all legal and scientific aspects must be considered (e.g. authorizations, confirm the complaint, etc.) (Fisher & Fisher, 2012). In animal cases, a veterinarian with significant experience should be present during this step (Merck, 2013; Norris, 2020).

During planning, consider:

1. The number of professionals that make up the team.
2. The tools available.
3. Available resources.

Although these three elements should respond to the scene's nature and scope, in reality, this is not the case, especially when the victims are non-human animals.

There are crime scenes processed by a single team of researchers, regardless of their extent, as is known as an area focus. However, there are other crime scenes where specialized personnel (functional approach) carry out each task (e.g. photography, collecting, mapping, etc.) (Gardner & Krouskup, 2019). The use of one or the other approach will depend on many factors, among them, recurrent is the availability of resources (human and technical) and the media of the case.

Perimeter (Evaluation/Reassessment)

The CSI team must re-evaluate the limit of the perimeter established by the FR using the same criteria, but now, in a new, controlled, more stable scenario and about which there are additional information. The new scenario allows the use of tools that improve visibility during processing (e.g. use of artificial light). If there was no FR, the CSI team must establish it (Figure 16.7) (Gardner & Krouskup, 2019).

We have already pointed out that the crime scene can vary in type, number, and extension. When defining the perimeter, these factors must be considered. In general terms, and whenever possible, the multilevel isolation system is recommended (Miller & Massey, 2016; Rogers & Stern, 2018; Gardner & Krouskup, 2019) (Figure 16.8).

Includes at least two protection levels, one internal that will protect the core elements of a crime (real crime area). This perimeter's outer part will be arranged as an investigator's work area, equipment area, evidence, and waste storage. Along with a second external perimeter, this work zone will provide a physical barrier between the crime scene and unauthorized persons or the media.

When a crime is committed in an enclosed area or a single crime scene, cones, fences, or simply closing a door makes the control of real o false evidences more effective.

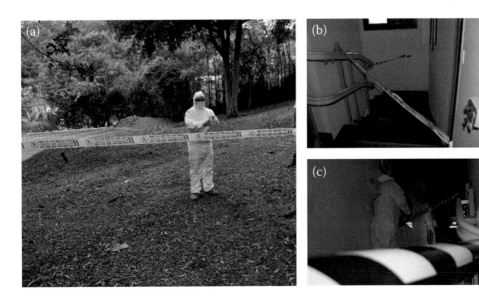

FIGURE 16.7 (a) Perimeter in outdoor crime scene; (b) and (c) two perimeter views of the same indoor crime scene. Property: Víctor Toledo González, Carlos Jaramillo Gutiérrez.

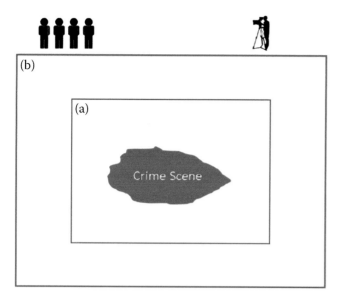

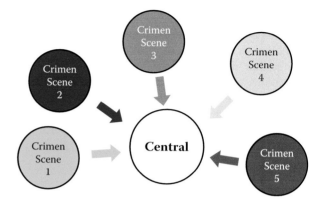

FIGURE 16.9 Multiple scenes. The evidence collected in each scene must be correctly identified and labelled. After that, can be centralized in an established point. Later all evidences must be sent to the reference laboratories duly preserved, preserved, and packed. Property. Víctor Toledo González.

FIGURE 16.8 Multilevel isolation system. It allows us to guide investigators' actions effectively, organize efforts (human and technical, and keep witnesses, people, and the media in safe areas. Crime scene. Primary focus; (a) Interior zone for individuals of CSI team; (b) External zone (more resources). Property. Víctor Toledo González. (Adapted from Miller & Massey, 2016; Rogers & Stern, 2018; Gardner & Krouskup, 2019).

However, we must never forget the eventual presence of secondary crime scene outside a property that will require protection. If functionally necessary and adequately staffed, more perimeters could be established. Generally, as the extent of crime scene increases, multilevel isolation becomes more significant. The perimeters are intended to guide the investigation team more effectively to decide who should or should not pass beyond the perimeter (e.g. police officers, experts, rescue teams, doctors, prosecutors, etc.). There are pressing situations that do not allow a job as ideal as this. There are areas where crime levels are so high that police forces' mere presence generates tension. In these cases, the priority is to take care of the primary focus of the crime scene (Gardner & Krouskup, 2019).

If the crime scene is gigantic or consists of multiple scenes, it is possible to perimeter each of them separately. Generally occur in crimes committed against wildlife and the environment. Various crime scenes may or may not be related to each other. As the research progresses, it is possible to reduce the number of crime scenes by merging those related. A work point can be established to centralize the evidence. Each evidence

must be, duly labeled, and associated with the corresponding crime scene (Figure 16.9).

Subsequently, it is necessary to determine the access roads in the perimeters. In the case of closed or mixed crime scenes, the door's presence does not mean that it is the best entry point due to its ease of use. The perpetrator's logical used routes (entry/exit) must be determined since they could contain traces/physical evidence useful for the investigation. We already pointed out that an emergency team's abrupt entry could destroy these findings and the context. For this reason, an alternative route for entry and exit of the forensic team should be sought until both possible routes used by the perpetrator are adequately processed. We must avoid that the chosen entry is not exposed to the public to avoid the unofficial disclosure of photographs (adapted from Gardner & Krouskup, 2019).

If there are no entry alternatives and live animals, they must act quickly by fixing the access routes with a photo or video during entry. The use of white lights and alternatives light sources (ALS) directed on the entry route can show us some possible indication of dodging, photographing, and protecting.

Check-In

Once the access points have been defined, it is necessary to record each person's entry and exit, especially in the perimeter that corresponds to the primary crime scene (Figure 16.10). This record should include:

Name of agent	Identification	Institution	Purpose	Time check-in	Time Check-out

FIGURE 16.10 Check-in. People who trespass a security perimeter must be identified, indicating the purpose of their presence. Above all, in the perimeter that protects the primary focus of the crime scene. Property: Víctor Toledo González, Ángel Iglesias, José España, Isaac Navarro, Elena Iglesias.

If necessary, the same can be done in external perimeters trying not to obstruct the different professionals' fluid action. In practical terms, the fundamental thing is to keep track of who was in the primary focus. Documents must be complemented with the one provided by the FR, which should indicate who was in the crime scene before the arrival of the CSI team (Gardner & Krouskup, 2019).

Crime Scene Processing

Searching for Traces and Evidence

Since the search begins with the observation of the place, it could be indicated that it is not intrusive. However, since the search must be carried out several times to be successful, it becomes increasingly intrusive with the consequent alteration of the crime scene. It is already pointed out that both the crime scene activities and the steps within each of them must be carried out from the least intrusive to the most intrusive (Gardner & Krouskup, 2019).

Any search method used must be methodical and systematic, allowing for a thorough and detailed search. Systematic and methodological does not mean rigidity.

The determination of one searching method or another may be subject to certain factors such as:

Characteristics of the place: It is not the same to look for on a smooth ceramic floor as in a garden covered with grass (Figure 16.11a and 16.11b, respectively). It is also difficult to search for evidence in the home of a person suffering from Diogenes syndrome (Figure 16.11c). In the first case, the field vision of the researcher will be better. In the second case, the researcher must be more careful and reduce his search space. On the other hand, more complex or broad surfaces could require the help of more researchers. We must consider the conditions or place's climatic characteristics may affect the search's effectiveness (high/low temperatures, contamination, odours, etc.).

Luminosity: A place under good lighting conditions will allow an investigator to focus his search on a larger surface (Figure 16.12). However, we must consider the type of lighting present in the place and its directionality. There are elements that are better viewed with a light of a specific wavelength. White light is usually is the best. The use of ALS can improve identification (Miller & Massey, 2016). In summary, if lighting conditions are poor, the investigator must narrow the search area (Figure 16.13).

There may also be elements that shine only when a beam of light hits them at a certain angle. It is expected in outdoor crime scene where certain pieces of evidence are located only during the entry/exit process due to the sun's rays' refraction at a specific moment. Given the rotation of the earth, the brightness can be transitory. For this reason, it should be identified as soon as possible

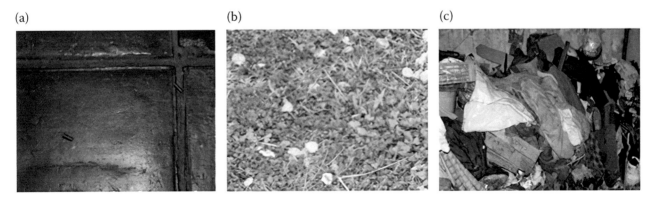

FIGURE. 16.11 Search place characteristics. (a) Clean and smooth floor with good visibility; (b) the existence of any evidence is not seen; (c) disorganized, dirty place where it becomes difficult to find evidence. Property: Víctor Toledo González, Carlos Muñoz Quezada, José María González.

FIGURE 16.12 (a) Photography without flash; (b) flash photography; (c) photography with natural light through windows; (d) photography with artificial light (fluorescent). Property: Víctor Toledo González, José María González.

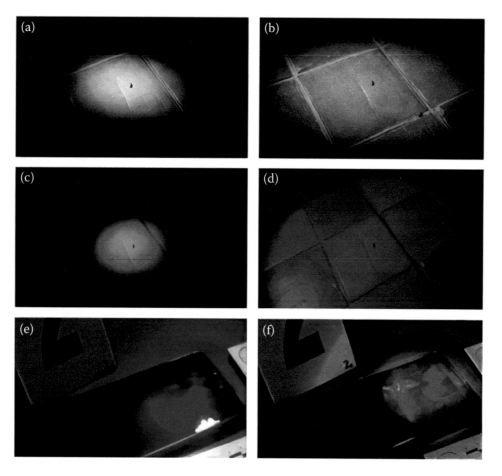

FIGURE 16.13 (a) and (b) Use of a white light source on a smooth floor. (a) The diameter of the light beam is concentrated in a smaller area; (b) the search area is enlarged by enlarging the diameter of the beam; (c) and (d) show the same effect as (a) and (b) but using an ALS; (e) and (f) search for evidence on a mobile phone, using ultraviolet (UV) light and ALS, respectively. Property: Víctor Toledo González, José María González.

without altering the search methodology. This reinforce, as we have already pointed out, that the methodology must also be flexible to achieve the objectives pursued. Each crime scene is unique and dynamic (Miller & Massey, 2016). Therefore, the researcher must respond to these changes to ensure the success of the search and collection of evidence, avoiding altering the crime scene. Although they can be advantageous to illuminate, halogens have the disadvantage that it generates much heat in small places. This reduces the researcher's ability to concentrate and comfort during the work. In most cases, natural light is usually the best, especially in open crime scenes. If it is possible to wait for processing, it is advisable to protect the crime scene and wait for daylight (Gardner & Krouskup, 2019).

Size of the article sought and visual capacity of the researcher. Although an element's size may not be such a determining factor when searching on a specific surface (e.g. a nightstand), it is when searching a larger, less delimited surface (Gardner & Krouskup, 2019). Besides, it is essential to consider each researcher's visual capacity and the presence of some other psychic and/or physical factor that reduces their ability to search (e.g. phobias).

These factors can be presented in combination or individually. Either way, the best response to this scenario is by decreasing the search area (Gardner & Krouskup, 2019).

Search Patterns

Various search patterns can be used. The choice will depend on the same factors described above and on experience or custom of use by the investigator in charge. There are usually cases in which a search modality is the one that gives the best results and confidence to an investigator. However, flexibility in the search methodology will be possible only if we know them.

There are five basic search patterns to achieve completeness:

Search for lines and stripes: Most often used in open (large-area), mixed, or outdoor crime scenes. The area is subdivided into strips with a functional size that allows an operator an efficient search. The searching starts at a point by moving forward and searching only in the strip in which it is until the end of its journey. The search continues in the contiguous strip, in reverse direction. The process is repeated until the entire area is covered. If necessary, the stripes can be delimited with indicators, ropes, etc., without altering the crime scene. Some experienced professionals often use the extension of their arms as an imaginary division of the crime scene (Figure 16.14). This form requires much concentration since it is natural to always see beyond what is functionally possible (Fisher & Fisher, 2012; Espinoza et al., 2013; Miller & Massey, 2016; Rogers & Stern, 2018; Gardner & Krouskup, 2019, Toledo et al., 2020).

Linear search: It is quite useful in open and large areas. It is a variation of the stripe search. One group heads in a straight direction, arms outstretched, at the slowest seeker's pace until they finish their assigned slot. As they advance, they must search in all directions. Remember that the crime scene is three-dimensional. When someone finds evidence, the search stops until it is marked or numbered. There will be a person in charge of keeping up with the search. When the entire area is covered, the process is repeated in reverse. As a disadvantage, the need for a more significant number of people than previous method (Figure 16.15).

Circular or spiral search: They are used more frequently in indoor crime scenes. The seeker begins at an external point of the crime scene, and as it advances, it rotates towards the centre (concentric) (Figure 16.16a).

(a)

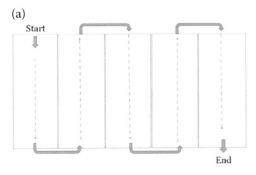

(b)

FIGURE 16.14   (a) Search for lines and stripes; (b) demonstration using arms to define surface analyzed during searching. Property: Víctor Toledo González, Carlos Jaramillo Gutiérrez. (Scheme adapted from Miller & Massey, 2016; Rogers & Stern, 2018; Gardner & Krouskup, 2019).

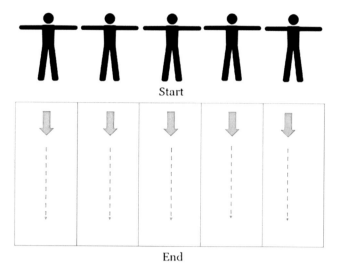

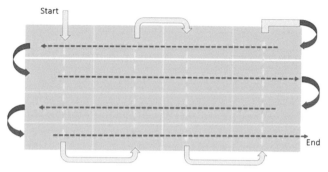

FIGURE 16.17 Grid search. Property: Víctor Toledo González. (Adapted from Miller & Massey, 2016; Rogers & Stern, 2018; Gardner & Krouskup, 2019).

FIGURE 16.15 Linear search. Useful in outdoor crime scenes. Property: Víctor Toledo González. (Adapted from Miller & Massey, 2016; Rogers & Stern, 2018; Gardner & Krouskup, 2019).

The rotation can be clockwise or counter clockwise. It can also be carried out from the centre outwards (eccentric) (Figure 16.16b). The same distance must be maintained between each lap and the speed rhythm regularly. It is natural that as the radius of the circle decreases, the researcher accelerate the pace.

The disadvantage of the eccentric spiral is the need to traverse the crime scene until starting point, thus significantly altering the evidence or the context of the place. In the centre, you can find any evidence, not just a corpse.

Grid Search: The crime scene/area is divided into horizontal and vertical stripes (Figure 16.17). Searching begins in one of the two orientations and moves straight

through it, until completing the search. Then it does it in reverse for the adjoining strip. After covering all the stripes oriented in one direction, it does so on the other stripes oriented in the other direction. The change of orientation allows the re-evaluation of the same area by a seeker from a second perspective. This would increase the chances of finding elements that shine due to the incidence of solar rays and temporarily in a determinate angle.

Zonal Search

Used in small and generally compartmentalized spaces (e.g. a desk, a bookcase, a car).

Each area's space will be identified with a number/letter and evaluated in depth by a person. It allows an exhaustive search and a better overlapping of spaces, avoiding forgetting elements hidden in corners or with little visibility (Figure 16.18).

A variation of this, in an extensive crime, is to divide the land into smaller zones. Each one will become a small crime scene and a search pattern will be defined in

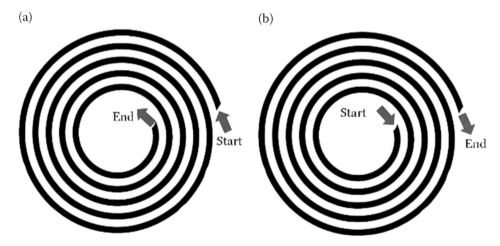

FIGURE 16.16 Linear search. (a) Concentric; (b) eccentric. Property: Víctor Toledo González. (Adapted from Miller & Massey, 2016; Rogers & Stern, 2018; Gardner & Krouskup, 2019).

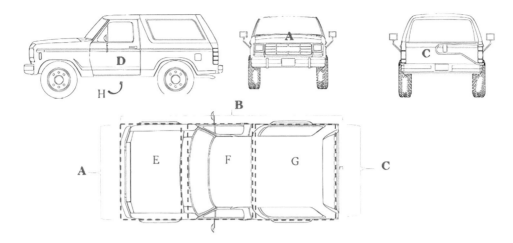

FIGURE 16.18 Zone search. Useful in compartmentalized structures Property: Víctor Toledo González. (Adapted from Gardner & Krouskup, 2019).

each of them (e.g. circular, fringe, etc.). The boundaries and reference points (e.g. angles and edges) of each "new scene" must be well identified and recorded and will allow the articulation of all of them in later research processes (Figure 16.19).

Point-to-Point Search

Despite being a little-used method, some circumstances deserve its application. It consists of going from one focal point (e.g. a corpse) to another focal point without an established pattern—the results in random movements within the crime. The main distinction is that walking and working trails are clear from each point of interest, and the team does not deviate from these cleared areas (Gardner & Krouskup, 2019). In spaces as Figure 16.20, there are two important considerations: a) due to the staircase's width, there is not enough space to apply any of the search patterns indicated before. Therefore, as we move forward, we can discover elements that are of interest to us at any point. This access road may be the only existing one, and the entry of emergency teams or others can damage any element arranged on this road. As we

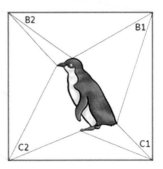

FIGURE 16.19 Variation of the zonal search on very extensive crime scene. Various points of the analyzed element are fixed at the angles of each grid. Property: Víctor Toledo González. (Adapted from Gardner & Krouskup, 2019).

FIGURE 16.20   Search point to point. Property: Víctor Toledo González.

pointed out before, the use of a camera on the head and lights will allow capturing at least the original image of possible elements present in the place.

There are also other less common methods, such as a global positioning system (GPS) coordinates (Rogers & Stern, 2018) and others such as Glonass, Beidou, and Galileo. They can be useful in very large crime scenes that cover vast areas. With these systems, a predetermined sequence of coordinates is established and prioritized to create a search pattern (Gardner & Krouskup, 2019).

Crime Scene Processing

Identification of Traces/Vestiges and Evidence

Before the CSI team can process a scene, they must have a working understanding of the nature of physical evidence (Gardner & Krouskup, 2019) and to know what a forensic laboratory is capable of doing with it. Always keep close contact with the laboratories officially designated for forensic analysis in case of doubts to establish the protocols for collecting evidence according to the procedures and instrumentation existing in each one of

them. This practical knowledge will help in the generation of hypotheses when looking for relationships between the findings and deciding if that object is strange in the crime scene. No way presupposes that they are experts in all forensic disciplines.

During the search for clues and evidence, the principles of criminalistics above must be constantly considered, trying to identify the article, consider its use, function, or purpose in the scene, and generate possible associations between the elements found under a specific context.

During the initial observation, evidence of interest will be marked with any striking element that is easy to see, and that contrasts with the background (e.g. a flag, coloured cards, etc.) (Figure 16.21).

Initially, photos will be taken from a panoramic, general, medium, close-up, and detail plane without recording metric witnesses (without measurements or distances) (see below). You can also use a camcorder. The goal is to record everything as it was when it arrived.

The elements finally considered evidence for a forensic analysis, will be identified with numerical indicators/placard in a correlative manner during the search (Figure 16.22). Our experience indicates that marking before numbering allows us to formulate, at the end of the initial search, a hypothesis without tunnel vision, more holistic than what eventually happened considering the scene's general context. This exercise will also allow, objectively, deciding which elements marked will become evidence and which one or which will be discarded from the investigation or not included in the final report.

Above we pointed out the brightness of individual elements that are only seen from a certain angle. Some objects can be seen with the naked eye during entry, but not during exit. If this were the case, the numbering would force us to use a number that alters the correlativity from the beginning in a correlative way. Now, if during advanced stages in the processing of the crime

FIGURE 16.21   Identification of vestiges and evidence. (a) Use of flags; (b) use of eye-catching and easily recognizable elements. Property: Víctor Toledo González, Carlos Jaramillo Gutiérrez, José María González

FIGURE 16.22   Numbering of the vestiges considered evidence for subsequent forensic analysis. Property: Víctor Toledo González, José María González, Carlos Jaramillo Gutiérrez, Valentina Restrepo G., Mónica Rocío Cifuentes C., Jacobo Alzate Z., Josué Donado Z., Ricardo Montes R., Carlos Moreno R.

scene and, therefore, more intrusive, new elements are discovered (e.g. hidden under other clues), we propose a form of identification to avoid altering the numerical correlation of the findings already considered as evidences. It is essential before photograph to assign a unique number to each piece of evidence. The number will be the same during all investigation process.

Various elements can be used for numerical identification. Some of the most commonly used are those shown in Figure 16.23.

FIGURE 16.23   Most used elements to identification. (a) Plastic V marker (double-sided); (b) flat plastic marker; (c) cone. In all cases, the elements may or may not have printed numbers. The use of the cone has the advantage that its numbering can be seen from any angle. Property: Víctor Toledo González, Issaura Sister Campos, Rodrigo Marcos Quezada, Rubén Lozano.

(a)

(b)

(c)

FIGURE 16.24   (a) Use of flat indicator for evidence on vertical surfaces; (b) and (c) unstable identification placard. Property: Víctor Toledo González, Carlos Jaramillo Gutiérrez, Valentina Restrepo G., Mónica Rocío Cifuentes C., Jacobo Alzate Z., Josué Donado Z., Ricardo Montes R., Carlos Moreno R.

All plastic indicators should be cleaned and sanitized between procedures to avoid cross-contamination. Disposal of disposable items is part of the crime scene processing in receptacles designed for each type of waste (e.g. sharps, paper, plastics, etc.)

When the evidence found in height (e.g. walls, trees, etc.), the use of flat indicators can be beneficial (Figure 16.24a). Before choosing the evidence marking and numbering tools, consider the position and type of support they are located (e.g. wall, ceiling, rock, tree, at an angle, etc.). Also, consider the environmental conditions of the place. These factors can affect the stability and positioning of the indicators, as shown in Figures 16.24b and 24c.

It is good to have a set of indicators without a printed number (Figure 16.25). This will allow assigning an adequate identification, manually, to those pieces of evidence found after the initial assignment of numbers.

Many of the evidence may be not seen in the first research due to lack of brightness, because they are latent (that is, more sophisticated methods (e.g. chemical) must be used to visualize them), they are very hidden or other causes. These can be found at any time during processing.

These "new pieces of evidence" can be identified with letters and/or numbers. For example, if this new evidence is associated with other previously numbered evidence (e.g. a knife under the corpse, an imprint on a revolver or a latent lip imprint on glass) can be assigned a letter that accompanies the number of the indicia/substrate to which it is associated (e.g. 1.a; 1. c) (Figure 16.26a). Suppose the new evidence, not previously identified, is not associated with another. In that case, it can be assigned a number that accompanies to the nearest evidence previously numbered (e.g. 1.1, 1.2, etc.) (Figure 16.26b). It should be noted the importance of using numerical indicators with colour that contrast with background, especially during the fall season where the foliage of trees and leaves tends to vary with the incidence of the sun's rays.

Crime Scene Processing

Documentation

This process is critical as it will be used to explain and support in front of a jury, which was not on the scene, "a story" of what happened or not, understandably and

FIGURE 16.25   Manual number assignment on a flat marker for evidence found on flat surfaces or at height. Property: Víctor Toledo González, Isaac Navarro.

 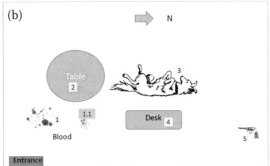

FIGURE 16.26 (a) Glass is identified with the number 5. To the lip print associated with the glass is assigned a letter "A". Therefore, the "new evidence" is identified as 5A. If there are also latent fingerprints, they can be identified as 5B and so on; (b) new evidence found at the end of the correlative numbering and not associated with other evidence can be assigned a number that accompanies the closest evidence (e.g. 1.1, orange rectangle). This means that the new evidence is located between evidence number 1 and 2. Property: Víctor Toledo González, José María González.

Note: NEVER touch or move evidence unless approved by the judicial police to minimize contamination or to tamper with the crime scene.
NEVER handle firearms without the necessary experience because there may be a projectile not yet struck in the chamber or magazine; this is the expert officer's function (if any) (Rogers & Stern, 2018).

logically. Besides, it will allow supporting the procedures carried out by the investigator.

Four elements can be used for documentation (Espinoza et al., 2013; Miller & Massey, 2016; Rogers & Stern, 2018; Gardner & Krouskup, 2019):

1. Written documents (notes).
2. Photographs and videos.
3. Sketches/mapping.
4. Reports.

Each of these procedures is complementary and, in no case, exclusive. Together they constitute the researcher's blog. That is, what it did and what it did not do.

Let us remember that the documentation process had begun with the FR response (if there was one). Otherwise, it will begin with the arrival of the investigative team.

Remember that both dead and live animals must be photographed *in situ* prior to any manoeuvre and their location documented in the scene sketch or otherwise mapped (Touroo & Fitch, 2018).

Written Documents (Notes)

The crime scene notes will tell a story, as will the photographs. Narrative description made by FR (if any) or the officer in charge from the beginning of the investigative process. In both cases, it begins with a Criminal Notice or Crime Notification. If no indication/evidence warrants a deeper investigative process, this report will suffice. If additional efforts such as photography, sketches, etc. are

required, these procedures and results must be explicitly documented.

It must be carried out in a way:

- Detailed (indicating all the facts and actions carried out during the investigation and pertinent conditions of the place)
- Accurate (avoiding including subjectivity and many inferences)
- Understandable (logical and organized)

As the written documentation will be available in its entirety to the parties involved in the case, it will be thoroughly reviewed by the lawyers (especially by the defence), trying to find the shortcomings/errors/gaps in the investigation (Gardner & Krouskup, 2019).

It ust provide information about what the investigator saw in the crime scene that is not evident in the photograph. Therefore, a procedure complements the photographs. Actions and all efforts to find useful elements for the investigation must be accurately reflected. It should also include actions and efforts that did not yield positive results, that is, those where no evidence was found. To avoid the possibility of defence for the failure of efforts, in addition to indicating the places investigated, it must specify the methodologies used in each of them (Gardner & Krouskup, 2019).

If there is a victim, you must describe it, considering: identification (e.g. dog, cat, etc.), location within into the crime scene, and the orientation of its body or parts of it (position of members, etc.).

Let's look at an example A dead body of cat is found in a dining room about 300" away from the door that connects kitchen. The victim is of medium size (3–5 kilograms), white with black spots on the chest. The victim lies on his right lateral ulna on the ground with his head facing north and his tail facing south. The right forelimb is extended and oriented to the east. The left forelimb lies under the body. Both hind limbs are tied, extended, and west- facing. On the chest, you can see a lesion with irregular edges. It has a circle of dark brown liquid, approximately 20" in diameter. Three extensions (like tentacles), with the same characteristics, are projected towards the sternal area and the floor from the injury. No other elements, lesions, stains, or fluids are observed.

Similarly, it is done with all the other elements found, transitory, predictable, unpredictable, etc., including in the narrative the relationship of the new evidence with the one already described (e.g. A pistol found about 240" from cat's head, black in colour, with its muzzle facing towards ... and so on).

PHOTOGRAPHS

Forensic photographs are not artistic photos and have the function of "guiding" those who were not present through the scene, showing all the elements of evidence and its context, from the general to the particular. They should "speak for themselves". Photographs/videography can constitute the key tool to corroborate, refute, and complete the rest of the procedures reflected in the final expert report before its presentation in court. The photographer must know the operation of their equipment and take care of the photograph's composition aspect, trying to draw attention, directly, to the elements that they contribute to the investigation (Gardner & Krouskup, 2019). Information such as day/hour may be reflected in the photograph.

Although the information is stored in the metadata, some prefer that it appear in the photo. Its presence must not distract attention from the jury.

It is recommended never to delete files (e.g. blurred, out of focus photos, etc.) that may be requested during the investigation. The JPG format will be used, as a universal format, and the RAW format for detailed photographs, for comparison purposes, or another similar one that allows guaranteeing the traceability of any changes in the image (Rogers & Stern, 2018; Gardner & Krouskup, 2019).

Although it is common for everyone to carry a mobile with which they can take photographs, the authors of the chapter promote the idea of not using them for forensic work. A mobile phone contains personal information from the investigator, or their environment. Only when they find unexpected crime scenes should the mobile phone be allowed. Besides, the mobile could become part of the chain of custody.

Before starting the activity and at the end of it, the procedure will be identified, using a blackboard, clapperboard, or letter, with necessary information next to the case number (location (address), photographer in charge, institution to which it belongs, weather conditions, start time, and end time) (Figure 16.27) (Miller & Massey, 2016).

In addition to official documents (e.g. a record of the photographic procedure), the essential photography equipment will include: a portable photographic camera, video camera, multiple lenses, filters, charged batteries, memory cards (formatted for the case), flash, tripod, rain protection elements, identification numbers, metric witnesses and indicative arrows (*ad hoc* in size, scale and colour for contrast (e.g. Figure 16.26a- the lip print on the glass) (Miller & Massey, 2016; Rogers & Stern, 2018; Gardner & Krouskup, 2019).

In the scene, five types of photographs must be registered, from the wider to the closer perspective and the least intrusive to the most intrusive. In no photo should appear the researchers working or elements that are not of interest to the investigation.

Panoramic photography: It allows locating or locating the crime scene in space and geographic context. It gives an overview of the place and its relationship with other areas/dependencies, etc. If possible, photographs should be shutter from the four cardinal points. The uses of aerial photography with drones facilitate the work (Figure 16.28).

General photo: A general view (plane) shows the essential aspects of the crime scene. It captures the orientation of the crime scene and some clue patterns, the main reference elements (e.g. doors, windows, paths, etc.), and general relationships (Gardner & Krouskup, 2019). One must be taken before the place's intervention and later, when the pieces of evidence have been identified and numbered (Figure 16.29). In the first case, its purpose is to show the state in which the crime scene was found, and everything found within it (e.g. animals, people/witnesses, etc.). In the second case, it is to show the defined limits of the crime scene and the inputs and outputs. Aerial photographs are useful to show pathways and other nearby structures (Miller & Massey, 2016).

When the place is an outdoor crime scene and it is not too big or when the scene is closed, the photographs must be captured from different fixed points from the outside. They are recorded consecutively from left to right or vice versa, superimposing an image on the one previously captured. It is useful to use general supporting photos taken from different angles and incorporate reference elements in each of them (e.g. a chair, a tree, a rock, etc.). This method allows placing an image next to another and observes the place in 360°

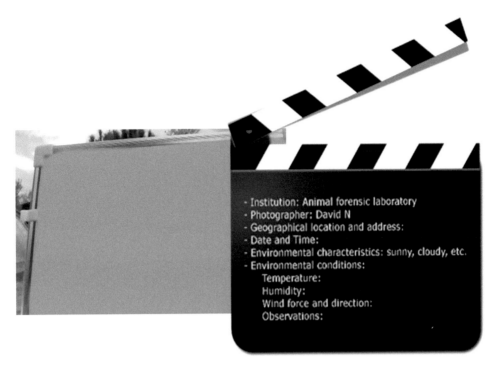

FIGURE 16.27   The first photograph of the case with general information on the process and location. This information must also be documented in the notes. Number case not shown. Property: Víctor Toledo González, Isaac Navarro.

FIGURE 16.28   General photo. (Note: The investigator only appears for educational purposes). Property: Víctor Toledo González, José María González.

(Figures. 16.30 and 16.31) (Espinoza et al., 2013; Miller & Massey, 2016; Rogers & Stern, 2018; Gardner & Krouskup, 2019). The same procedure must be carried out at different heights, considering the possible observation by a witness. It is good to ask some of them from where they saw the event and take a photo from there and then refute or corroborate the witness's version.

If there are spaces or crime scenes connected, the available photo must show the relationship and forms of connection between them. For example, an animal carcass in a room next to another we must show how the two rooms are connected (Adapted from Gardner & Krouskup, 2019).

Evidence/Relationship Establishment Photograph

Commonly referred to as medium plane photography; however, this photograph has nothing to do with distance. It is not the photograph taken between a wide plane and a close-up plane. Its function is to show the positional relationship between one element and others, especially with some obvious reference point in the general photo (Figure 16.32. a, b and c). There are times when the general photograph can be used as a photograph of relationships (Figure 16.32d). (Rogers & Stern, 2018; Gardner & Krouskup, 2019). The use of relationship photographs combined with a general photograph can help the viewer better position

(a)   (b)

(c)   (d)

FIGURE 16.29   General photos of a crime scene: (a) and (b) Outdoor crime scene before and after of evidence identification process, respectively; (c) and (d) indoor crime scene before and after of evidence identification process, respectively. Property: Víctor Toledo González, José María González.

themselves within of the crime scene (Gardner & Krouskup, 2019).

Even though pieces of evidence are registered and identified in official formats and the chain of custody, it is good to use posters with necessary information about the photograph that have been registered (Figure 16.33).

Exam or Forensic Quality Photograph

This corresponds to the commonly called close-up photography. Only the element of interest, the identification number, and an *ad hoc* metric witness (in size, scale, and contrast colour and correctly positioned) should appear in the photograph's composition. The goal is to provide as much detail as possible while preserving identity. The evidence must be able to be clearly identified and separated from all the others. Photographs must be shut at a 90° angle (Figure 16.34) Espinoza et al., 2013; Miller & Massey, 2016; Rogers & Stern, 2018; Gardner & Krouskup, 2019). This will avoid distortion in the size of the object during the reconstruction (Miller & Massey,

2016). Up to now, photos have been taken from the elements exposed on surfaces, avoiding altering the crime scene. It is possible to find a new clue below other evidence. In this case, the entire procedure must be stopped, assigned an identifying number to the new finding, and processed in the same way as the previous ones. That is, identify it with a number and letter, take photos of relationships and forensic quality, measurements, etc. (Gardner & Krouskup, 2019).

In this type of photography, it is mandatory to use and *ad hoc* scale to know its exact dimensions (Gardner & Krouskup, 2019). The use of the identification number is also mandatory (Miller & Massey, 2016). There are L-scale (e.g. Figure 16.34b) and horizontal ones. They have different lengths, scales, and colours to contrast with the background. Many of these scales are numerical with a graphic scale (black/white rectangles). This helps to size an object when numbers do not allow it due to its size (e.g. Figure 16.34 and 16.34c).

Whenever possible, the scale should be positioned the same plane as the object being photographed and at the same angle to the evidence (Espinoza et al., 2013). In

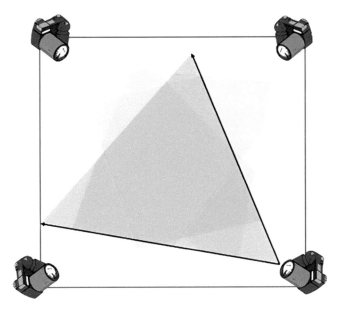

FIGURE 16.30 Photos taken of the crime scene from different angles from left to right or vice versa. Photos overlapping side by side should cover the entire crime scene. It resembles a 360° photo. Property: Víctor Toledo González. (Adapted from Rogers & Stern, 2018; Gardner & Krouskup, 2019).

this way, a reference will be established in standardized measurement units. This will allow dimensioning of the size of the evidence.

When the evidence is very small, is on a support, or over other evidence, it can be combined with a photograph of relationships to give clarity (Figure 16.35). (Miller & Massey, 2016; Gardner & Krouskup, 2019).

The use of combined photographs can help the viewers to better position themselves within of the crime scene. It is essential to avoid frequent errors of depth of field, positioning, presence of artefacts.

Videography

The procedures are similar to those performed in photographs. However, it is essential to note some particular observations (Rogers & Stern, 2018; Gardner & Krouskup, 2019):

1. A tripod must be used to give stability.
2. Recording begins with the camera still for a few seconds. During this time, it is possible to record information on the case number, name of the person in charge, organization, environmental conditions, data, and time. There should be no

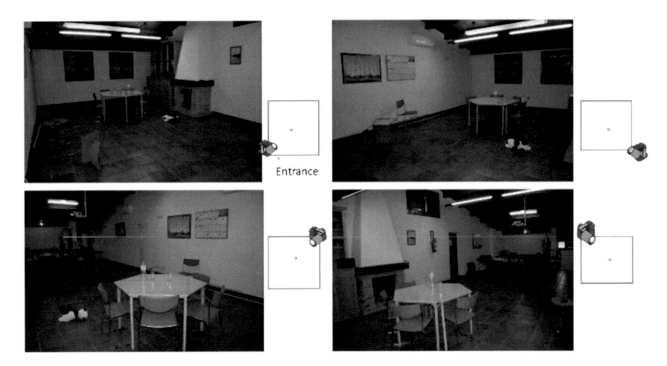

FIGURE 16.31 General photos of indoor crime scene taken from four angles. Property: Víctor Toledo González, José María González.

FIGURE 16.32 Relationship photos: (a) and (b) Relationship between evidences located at the same height incorporating a fixed point (tree). In addition, the order of the numbering can tell me the type of search carried out (here a linear search was carried out in stripes); (c) relationship between evidence located at different heights incorporating a fixed point (e.g. chimney angle); (d) general plane photograph used as a photograph of relationships. (Note: The investigator only appears for educational purposes). Property: Víctor Toledo González, Carlos Jaramillo Gutiérrez, José María González.

FIGURE 16.33 Basic information associated with the evidence and its identification number like the number case, the photographer identification, institution, date and time. Property: Víctor Toledo González, Isaac Navarro.

external noise during the recording that interferes with the voice of responsible.

3. Panning must be slow to understand the context of the place. At the end of the panning, the camera must be immobile for 10 seconds before cutting the recording. During this time, the person in charge must indicate that the recording of that shot is over. If it is necessary to cut a recording urgently, the reason for said action must be recorded orally and in writing.

4. If you use a head camera, remember to make slow movements with it.

5. Take always care to have your video camera in the correct mode (on/off).

SKETCHING AND MANUAL MAPPING

The sketch can be very simple or very complex. It can go from a freehand drawing to going through measuring process and fixing the elements present in the scene (what we call mapping). It will allow the viewer to

FIGURE 16.34 Perpendicular photo to the evidence; (a) and (c): Photo at 90° and use of numerical and graphic scale. The unit used in scale can be inches, centimetres, meters, etc. The circles indicate the inclination/angulation of the core. Therefore, they help to correct the inclination of the shot. (b) Photo taken in incorrect angle. (Note: The investigator only appears for educational purposes). Property: Víctor Toledo González, Isaac Navarro.

understand the design, the orientation, the inter-relationships of the objects into the scene, as well as the spatial limitations of the place (it resembles a general photo). It complements the other documentation methods but does not replace them. Although the initial sketch may be elementary, it must accurately represent the crime scene. It is generally not to scale but should incorporate a design of the place, significant elements

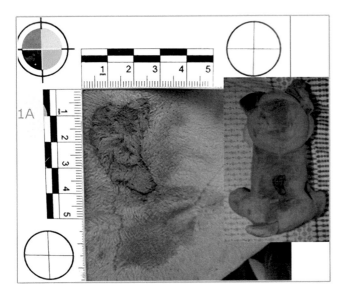

FIGURE 16.35 Combined photo. Red stain. (a) L-scale is used indicating identification number of evidence (surface) and a letter for stain over the surface (1A). The support is the evidence number 1 (the dog). The forensic quality photo is displayed next to the general photo to understand the position and orientation of the stain. Property: Víctor Toledo González.

(house, water source, furniture, etc.), and specific details about the evidence and measurements.

To avoid confusion due to excessive information, it is possible to make several sketches, even some more specific with some hint or pattern of interest (some point it out as a sketch of details). You can also add a legend that indicates the nature of the elements together with their previously assigned number/letter (Figure 16.37). The final outline to present in court should be simple and easy to understand. For this, it is common not to incorporate measures or distracting elements. Less important elements can be described in a legend.

Before making any sketch, it is required to determine the magnetic north's geographic position by using some device (e.g. compass) to orient the various elements within of the crime scene (Figure 16.36). This information must be graphed in the sketch (Figure 16.37). It must also include the report number, the physical address of the place, name of the person responsible and creator of the sketch, and date and time of the creation of the sketch. In summary, the sketch must have at least five elements: heading (for each sketch, indicating the purpose of it); research information (noted above); drawing area (diagram); legend (description of the elements labelled and present in the diagram; and scale and direction notations. For the description, the labels, numbers, and letters present in the diagram must coincide with those assigned in the investigation (Miller & Massey, 2016; Harris & Lee, 2019; Gardner & Krouskup, 2019). The legend allows avoiding excess information within the diagram, scale information, and direction (Gardner & Krouskup, 2019).

There are various methods to make a sketch. However, in this chapter, we will only address some of

FIGURE 16.36   Location of magnetic north for positioning of the scene and the existing evidence in it. There are various tools but the compass is the least expensive and the most widely used. Property: Víctor Toledo González, Isaac Navarro.

them. The simplest and most used is the sketch drawn from above (standard aerial plan, plan view), where the main vestiges/patterns, of importance in the investigation, stand out, and positioned on horizontal surfaces (e.g. floor, roof, etc.). This method is also known as the floor plan or bird's-eye view sketch (Miller & Massey, 2016) (Figure 16.37). Other elements located on vertical

and oblique surfaces can be drawn and described in the legend. In these cases, to simplify the understanding of the sketch, you can choose to use variations of the standard aerial view.

Elevation sketch: This is used to fix objects found in height on vertical or oblique surfaces (e.g. on trees, walls, buildings, etc.) and are useful to indicate uneven terrain (e.g. roads, riverbeds, and riverbanks) (Miller & Massey, 2016) (Figure 16.38).

Cross Projection Sketch: This method is a combination of the previous two (Figure 16.39). It is an excellent option to show elements present on horizontal and vertical surfaces simultaneously, achieving a better understanding of the relationship between them. On the sides of the horizontal surface (e.g. the floor of a room), the lateral surfaces (e.g. walls) are necessary for a better understanding of the crime scene are projected. The

FIGURE 16.37   Aerial sketch of crime scene. It is a simple sketch with the representation of the main elements of the investigation positioned on horizontal surfaces. Blue arrow indicates magnetic north. Property: Víctor Toledo González.

FIGURE 16.38   Elevation sketch of crime scene. It is a useful sketch to position evidence (yellow star) over vertical or inclined surfaces, in height (h). Property: Víctor Toledo González, Carlos Jaramillo.

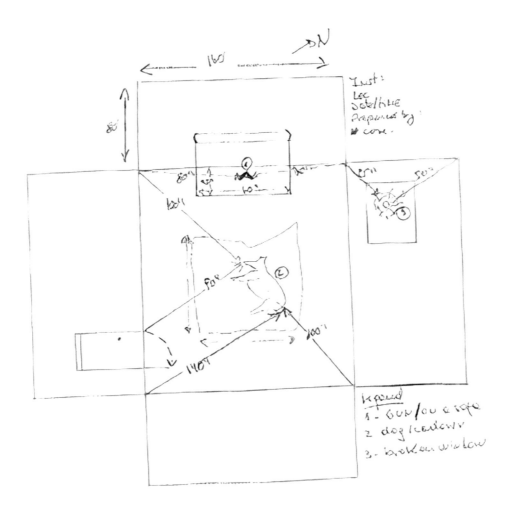

FIGURE 16.39 Cross projection sketch. Useful for representing evidence positioned on horizontal and vertical surfaces at the same sketch. Property: Víctor Toledo González.

elements can be fixed in the same way as on the horizontal surface (Miller & Massey, 2016; Gardner & Krouskup, 2019).

Mapping the Crime Scene

When drawing up the sketch, whatever the view used, it is recommended to take measurements of the crime scene and its associated components. In all cases, the various pieces of evidence found should be established considering fixed or reference points. Measuring tapes, rulers, odometers, laser distance meters, and other adequately calibrated instruments can be used.

Rectangular Coordinates

Rectangular coordinates are very useful in closed crime scenes or with well-defined limits. A centre point of the evidence is determined, from which a straight line is

projected to two adjoining walls at a right angle. For this, the use of laser meters is beneficial. If the object is regular (e.g. a ball) it will be easy to position it the way it was found in the crime scene (Miller & Massey, 2016; Gardner & Krouskup, 2019). Nevertheless if the evidence is irregular (e.g. a weapon, an animal, etc.), considering the central point can locate it in the crime scene but it will not be able to position it correctly as it was during the investigation (Figure 16.40). To correct lack of accuracy, it is possible to use a variation of this method, performing the same procedure from two defined evidence points, generally from well-defined extremes (Gardner & Krouskup, 2019) (Figure 16.41). Limits are clearly identified with numbers, letters, cardinal points, or axes (X and Y). Subsequently, the measurements are recorded in a table for each of them.

It consists of fixing a selected point of evidence to two fixed, immovable points (e.g. corner of a room, doorframe, etc.) or identified and determined reference points (RP) (Figures. 16.42 and 16.43). This allows the correct positioning of the element within the scene.

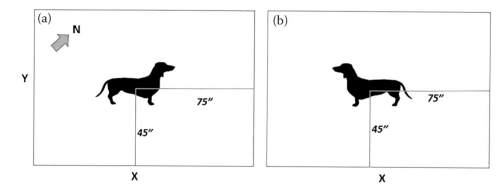

FIGURE 16.40   Rectangular coordinates with one-point fixation of irregular evidence to a reference point or fixed point. Property: Víctor Toledo González.

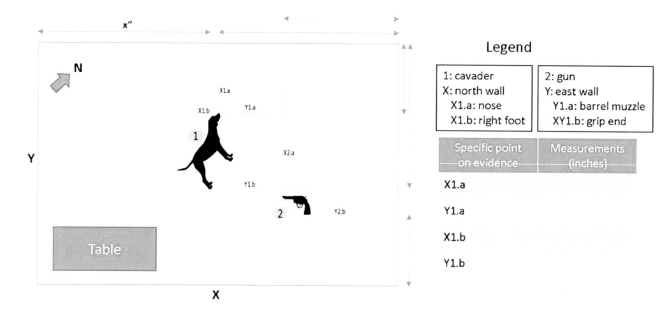

FIGURE 16.41   Rectangular coordinates with two-point fixation of irregular evidence to a reference point or fixed point. This fixation allows us to correctly locate and position the evidence within of the crime scene. Property: Víctor Toledo González.

It can also be used in open crime scenes, although it is better to use the fixation at three fixed points because of the typical absence of clear limits (Espinoza et al., 2013). If we want to position evidence using only the distances of two reference points, it will result in two probable location points (intersection points) (Figure 16.44). Using a third reference point, the radius of fixed points will give us only one intersection point. Again, we find that it only places it within of the crime scene, but does not position it correctly if the evidence is irregular. Remember that the researcher can use several sketches for his work, so knowing these and other methods will help achieve the objective. You can consult the references section for enlarge information.

Whatever the method used, the information must be recorded concisely and clearly in a form designed for it.

It should contain necessary information on the location of the place, day and date, case number, agent assigned to the sketch function, and institution to which it belongs (Miller & Massey, 2016; Gardner & Krouskup, 2019). Besides, the recorded distances between landmarks and fixed points/reference points should be included (Figure 16.45). In addition, a record must be kept of the distance between fixed points and between reference points (not shown)

Photos and video recordings are simple methods for visual registration of crime scene. Currently more sophisticated tools (scanning equipment) can be used to get a three-dimensional video or sketches given a more realistic perspective (Harris & Lee, 2019; Gardner & Krouskup, 2019).

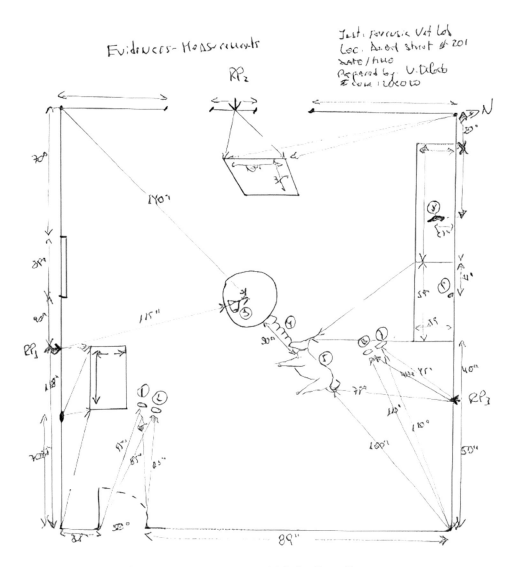

FIGURE 16.42 Scheme of triangulation. Property: Víctor Toledo González.

SAMPLING

We already mentioned that sampling is discussed in length in several and previous publication. However, we will remember some points concerning it related to the investigative aspects. Below is a summary of information from Espinoza et al., 2013; Toledo & Carvallo, 2017; Rogers & Stern, 2018; Brooks, 2018; Harris & Lee, 2019; Barbaro, 2020 and Toledo et al., 2020. Remember, always to wear *ad hoc* biosecurity suit and a double layer of gloves.

According Viner (2020), the animals subjected to abuse, neglect, and cruelty can present degrees of malnutrition or suffer opportunistic infections. Live animals captured in a forensic investigation must undergo routine blood chemistry tests, a urinalysis, and a complete blood count to establish their metabolic and physiological health. Whether dead or alive, all animals should undergo full-body orthogonal radiographs to look for broken bones or foreign bodies. In addition to these standard samples and tests, and based on the physical examination or necropsy findings, the veterinarian and the investigator can choose other factors involved in the case.

Poisons

The animals might be accidentally or non-accidentally poisoned. The clinical examination of the animals, the context of the crime scene, and the samples will be vital for interpreting the findings.

Heavy metals like lead, zinc, and mercury; iff bait or feed is available, for analysis, should be collected approximately 500 g of sample.

To avoid evaporation of the contents of gastric samples, it should be wrapped separately (primary packaging) in aluminium foil. This is available in plastic

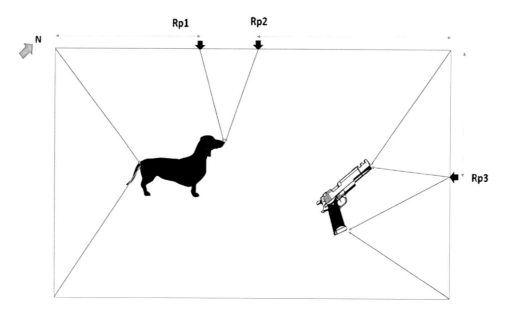

FIGURE 16.43　Triangulation. Barrel muzzle and grip end fixed to corners of the room and one reference point (Rp3). Rp3 is to a known distance from both corners. Property: Víctor Toledo González.

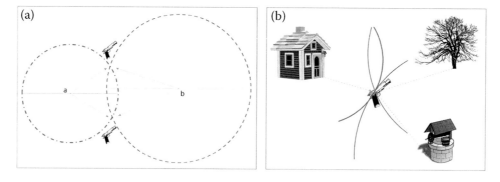

FIGURE 16.44　(a) Using only two fixed points yields two probable points of location of the evidence can be found (intersection points); (b) the use of a third fixed point allows the location of the evidence in a single place within of the crime scene (adapted from Espinoza et al., 2013). Property: Víctor Toledo González.

Location:	Case #:	
Case agent:	Date and time:	
Institution:		
From Evidence#/ description	to	distance
9mm pistol	Point 1 (tree base)	450″
Bullet case	Rp1	80″
Dog (cadaver)	Northeastern corner of room	550″

FIGURE 16.45　The distance between evidence and the different fixed and reference points (RP), the distance between fixed and/or reference points are registered. The measurements will allow the elaboration of a scale map. Property: Víctor Toledo González.

envelopes or an airtight container (secondary packaging). Place all the containers, previously labelled, in a single polystyrene bag or container.

Rodenticides: Phosphine/phosphide rodenticides are as solid granules or blocks. Bait samples for testing should be in dry packed in air-tight containers when wearing a chemical respirator.

Samples of body fluids (whole blood, serum, plasma, and others), must be collected in a leak-proof tube sealed.

Organs should be stored in air-tight containers.

If the analysis is to be performed promptly, the samples can be kept cool before testing. If there is a delay in the start of the test or the sample has to wait for shipment or transportation, the sample may be frozen before packaging.

It is essential to continuously check with the methodology with laboratory before taking samples.

Firearms

A wide variety of firearms and ballistic projectiles made of different metals that can be used against animals. In the crime scene, where a firearm has been used, in addition to describing injuries, it is critical to observe if the place is orderly or disorderly, look for bloodstains, locate the weapon, sheaths and projectiles, and determine entry and exit holes on the body or clothing. Regardless of the projectile or fragment's metallic composition or whether it has been fragmented or not, the elements should never be manipulated with metallic instruments. Ballistic elements should be retrieve from tissues with fingers or plastic tweezers. Animals shot at close range (within a few meters) may have gunshot residue on their hair or skin. Metallic objects and particles extracted from the wound should be cleaned as much as possible, with water or alcohol and a soft cloth or gauze. Air-dry and wrap in breathable material, such as gauze and paper. This will allow it to continue evaporating residual moisture and remain dry.

Bloodstains

We must establish whether a stain found in the crime scene is blood or not. For this, we must take into account the type of support where it has been found and the physical characteristics of sample (dry or liquid). After confirmation, we can used it for identification. It is crucial to establish whether the support on which the stain is located is transportable or not, to proceed to take the sample.

Transportable Items: Dry Spots in Small Samples

These samples will be collected and placed separately in paper or cardboard bags, single and disposable.

It is possible to put several small bags in a larger plastic security bag as secondary packaging and seal with security/evidence tape. All evidence should be always attached to the respective chain of custody record.

Non-Transportable Item

That item that, due to its characteristics and size, cannot be taken entirely to the laboratory; in these, in turn, the stain can be found on a hard surface or a soft surface. An example of these elements can be a car, a wall, a carpet, or a mattress. None of them are taken to the laboratory; once they have been registered by photography, the sample was taken as follows.

Dry stain on non-absorbent surfaces (crystals, metals): moisten a sterile swab with sterile distilled (or deionized) water and wipe it over the surface. Use another dry swab to try to recover as much sample as possible, allow to dry at room temperature, and pack each swab in its tube—labeled tube with the same number or letter with which the evidence has uniquely marked at the crime scene.

Special swabs for forensic use (COPAN) are commercially available that do not fray, contain an antibacterial, and allow preserving the trace for a long time at room temperature.

Then put the swabs in a plastic security bag as secondary packaging and seal with security tape and attach the respective chain of custody record.

If the researcher does not have swabs, they can use gauze or filter paper, although this cannot ensure the same level of sterility as a swab and, therefore, runs the risk of adding contaminating material that later hinders the amplification processes (PCR), when the sample goes to genetic analysis.

Dry stain on absorbent surfaces (e.g. fabrics, upholstery, carpets, etc.).

In cases, the stain is cut out with a scalpel or scissors, placed in a paper or plastic bag, and the wrapper is market with the same number or letter with which the evidence has been a unique market in the crime scene attached to the chain of custody record.

Wet Signs (Clothes or Other Objects)

In these cases, the complete samples or the stains under study should be dried in a protected place on a clean surface (paper). Please avoid direct contact of the sample with a plastic bag because it favours the presence of humidity, and this, in turn, the growth of microorganisms that affect the sample. Suppose animals are found wrapped in bloody garments. In that case, they must be dried at room temperature, avoiding exposing them to pollutants, rodents, insects, direct sunlight to air currents, or any artificial drying equipment such as fans, dryers, irons, and ovens. UV rays and high temperatures affect the biological material and these changes, in turn, affect the quality of the sample for analysis.

Additionally, air currents can detach or eliminate trace evidence such as hairs, fibres, remains of gunpowder, paint, among others that may be present on the garments. Once dry, put the stain (sample) in a plastic bag, mark it with the same number or letter with which the evidence has been uniquely marked in the crime scene. Remember, add it to the chain of custody record. It is essential to collect evidence safely and adequately in suitable containers to avoid breakage and avoid contamination, alteration, or destruction. The integrity of the physical evidence must be preserved. A tertiary packaging (e.g. a box) can be used to simultaneously hold several secondary-type packages.

Burns

These can be caused by direct contact such as hot water, a heat source (e.g. cigarettes, heaters, etc.), or exposure to electrical or radiation sources. Heat source patterns generate patterns with sharp edges and generally reflect the characteristics of the object. Liquid burns show irregular fluid patterns. In this case, the point of the first contact is usually where the damage is most severe. The investigation of the crime scene and the context of the evidence will be of great importance. In fire cases, the crime scene analysis is vital, along with other signs such as odours. Always sample injured and uninjured areas as controls. Microwave burns tend to generate a "cooked chicken" smell. It is vital to verify the presence of trace elements inside the microwave, applying the exchange principle. Skin sections should be stored in 10% neutral buffered formalin and analyzed by a veterinary pathologist.

Other Samples

Fresh or decomposed tissues: Extract 2 cm cube (200 g) in the area where the tissue appears freshest and transport in plastic envelopes or containers. Transport refrigerated (less than three hours) or frozen.

Stools: Only if they are not more than two/three days old (depending on the season). Collect them completely or in pieces in sealed containers or envelopes. Transport in a few hours to the laboratory using cold bags or freeze.

Hair, fibers, feathers, and nails: use paper envelopes: Keep at room temperature, chill, or freeze. If the hair is damp, it should be allowed to dry on non-printed absorbent paper at room temperature, protected from drafts. They should never be cut or torn. It should never be attached to tape (do not use metal clips).

Biological fluids: Wet samples: First, dry the samples at room environment, and protected from direct light or heat sources. If they are in macro elements or real estate, they should be collected with a swab, gauze, or filter paper and packed once documented. Avoid cross-contamination with human, microbiological, or chemical

biological material. Avoid using preservatives such as formaldehyde, sodium hypochlorite, and absolute alcohol, except for formaldehyde for organs or organ fragments that require histopathology studies. When tubes or small bottles are used as containers, they should be marked on the body of these and packed in plastic bags. For samples of semen, saliva search, and vitreous humour use the red cap tube.

Corpse or parts of it: Use disposable gloves (double) and a mask (with a filter if necessary). Put in a resistant bag (one corpse per bag). They can be collected in a hermetically sealed drum. Ideally, a cooler. Never remove the elements used in medical-surgical treatment from the corpse, such as endotracheal tubes, catheters, etc. Any injury generated during procedures must be clearly documented.

Skeletons: Use disposable gloves (double) and a mask (with a filter if necessary) Put in a resistant bag (one corpse per bag). Collect samples from the soil and up to 15 cm deep, below the bone remains. Store in an airtight container. If there are garments next to the remains, include them in the same container. If there are several bodies during an exhumation, they must be packed individually after fixing their position if found in a common grave.

Sharps and Blunt Weapons: These should be inspected for the presence of recent or dry biological evidence. The packaging must ensure that the element is fixed in order to avoid accidents during transport and storage.

Packaging

Whatever type of container is used, it must present an identifying label with the following information:

- Case number
- Brief description of the evidence
- Classification of evidence
- Date, place, time of collection
- Name of the person who collected the evidence
- Institution to which it belongs

All this information must be attached to the respective chain of custody record (Barbaro, 2020).

When the evidences stored in their corresponding containers, they must be sealed using a tape that indicates that it is evidence. Basic information (e.g. date, agent, etc.) is written on the tape and the container simultaneously, as shown in Figure 16.46. This process will allow recognizing if the seal and thus chain of custody was broken (Espinoza et al., 2013).

FIGURE 16.46 Whatever the packaging or container used, they must be labeled, sealed, and sent under chain of custody to maintain the integrity of the evidence. Property: Víctor Toledo González.

APPROACH THE CORPSE

We must remember that the FR or CSI team usually does not consider the active participation of a veterinarian from the early stages in the investigation. However, the authors and many other colleagues' experience indicates the need for one, from the beginning of the investigation, for the broad reasons discussed in this chapter. The presence of a live or dead animal in a crime scene should activate the protocol of "immediately contact veterinarians or specialists" for collaboration in conjunction with the corresponding authorities. Although at present, in many cases non-veterinary medical personnel are the ones who determine the condition of the animal at the crime scene. It should be the exclusive function of a veterinarian.

In any case, and waiting for the official procedures to incorporate this possibility, there are a series of activities inherent to the investigation in the crime scene we need to know. We will not talk about the job done by the clinician (in crime scene or clinic) or the pathologist at the necropsy table.

After verifying the crime scene safety, there are a series of processes to do, ranging from the least intrusive to the most intrusive.

1. Identify the species and number of animals (alive or dead)
2. Evaluate and document the health and degree of the welfare of the animal (alive or dead), without altering the condition of any evidence present on the body. Physical examination of the body is essential in the crime scene, including examining using an ALS (e.g. UV, infrared, etc.)
   If the animal is alive/dying, its condition should be recorded in video or photography and promptly seek help from professionals for its primary emergency care, if you are not a veterinarian. I did not try to lift or move it until the emergency team arrives. Remember that animals behave differently from humans with unexpected reactions, even under conditions that seem safe to handle. You must also consider the possible risk that this animal may pose to the people present in the place.
3. You should NOT turn the animal, especially if the body is over fluids that can generate new evidence where there was none. Any implement used and any procedure performed during urgent care must be documented and recorded. These elements are not eliminated as they will be part of the investigation.
4. While the emergency team or veterinarian arrives, as much information as possible should be documented, initially through photographs and videos, without moving the victim. These images will have the function of recording the animal's initial condition upon arrival at the crime scene and register any temporary visual vestige/effect. Remember that there will also be others such as odours, heat, etc. You will only perceive if you search for them and they will not appear in the photos. The use of videography could allow the capture of sounds that may be the product of the degree of discomfort or degree of injury and damage to the animal. Images of the animal should be recorded from different angles and positions (e.g. head, body, limbs, etc.)
5. The veterinarian evaluation in the crime scene and/or in the clinic includes its clinical examination and external appearance. However, in the crime scene it is essential to verify that that animal had the basic conditions of well-being such as being free from hunger or thirst; freedom from discomfort; free from pain, injury, or illness; freedom to express normal behaviour; and freedom from fear or anguish. The evaluation of these points is verified according presence/absence/quantity and quality. This includes access to adequate food and water (in quantity, quality, and periodicity); type and quality of housing; periods in which it is tied up (time, periodicity, type of chain, etc.); shaded spaces, etc. (Merck, 2013).
6. The appearance of the wound(s) and its characteristics must be described. For this, consider:
   - Shape: use similarities to geometric figures when you can (e.g. circular, rectangular, etc.)
   - Margins: use concepts such as regular or irregular, fuzzy, etc.
   - Surfaces: smooth, porous, cracked
   - Consistency: soft, with or without content, hard and spongy

- Colour: use primary colours (e.g. white, yellow, green, blue, etc.)
- Determine severity (severe, moderate, mild/slight); distribution (focal, multifocal, or diffuse) and duration (acute, recent, or old). The laboratory will determine whether it is acute, subacute, or chronic.
- Size: size should be described based on the use of metric cores
- Location, positioning, and orientation: locate and position wounds in a manner using known landmarks. One can use, among others, protractor techniques that allow the generation of a reference axis (e.g. the column) from which a lesion or group of lesions is oriented (Figure 16.47). In addition to positioning, information on the orientation of the wounds is required. The direction of its longitudinal axis (e.g. in cases of cuts by cutting element). This could help determine how the cut occurred (Merck, 2013).

For cases with ballistic projectile wounds, the introduction of ruled/semi-rigid elements into the wound is promoted to determine the trajectory. However, introducing this type of element without adequate expertise can cause projectile displacement within the wound, generate a false trajectory, or add contaminating elements. Of this, the pathologist must have full knowledge to not attribute a "false trace" as evidence.

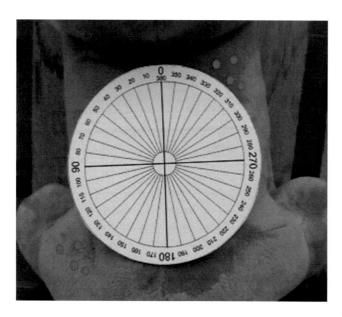

FIGURE 16.47 Lesions (red points) can be registered as a group using a protractor and establishing the column as the main axis. This in a dorsal view, we must be the same from a caudal vision. Property: Víctor Toledo González.

How to register a wound and describe its orientation will depend on the user. However, we believe that a description using the correct anatomical animal concepts can add certainty to the report and avoid interpretations and future discussions.

After collecting possible vestiges/evidence present in any part of the body, the head, hands, and feet should be protected with paper bags and then with plastic bags to avoid loss of any trace present in the mouth, teeth, and nails.

It is suggested to comb the animal to find vestiges on the coat. This should be done by placing the animal on a cloth, white sheet that allows better visualization of any vestiges that the comb is dragging and avoid its loss. The cloth should wrap the victim during their transfer so that the pathologist repeats the procedure in the laboratory

If the animal has fresh wounds, after sampling, put towels over them. Do not forget to photograph before since, through the wounds, during the transfer, extra liquids could be emptied generating new stains.

It is good that an officer who was on the scene accompanies the body during the necropsy, informing the pathologist, which are the vestiges found in the crime scene and not those generated by manipulation.

COMPLETION OF FIELDWORK

Once the field activities are finished and before leaving the crime scene, the investigator assigned to the case will hold the closing meeting in order to establish that all the pieces of evidence were collected and will be sent to the respective reference laboratories. In this meeting, the hypothesis(s) will be evaluated. Possible new additional activities will be determined, and the reports will be finalized with their respective formats.

EXPERT REPORT (ADAPTED FROM GARDNER & KROUSKUP, 2019)

The expert report is part of the narrative documentation process of a process. Since it is the final stage of the investigation, we will discuss it here.

The final report is a summary of all the information collected by the researchers. However, most of them only reflect the most relevant aspects of the research necessary to be discussed, concisely, and to understand the context of the crime scene.

Introduction: It is briefly specified who is in charge of the investigation, institution to which it belongs, case number, date, time, location, reasons for requesting the investigation, observations on the conditions of the place, and actions taken.

Scene characteristics: Describe the stable and static elements of the scene and elements associated with it (e.g. buildings, constructions, presence of windows, doors, furniture, etc.). The external scenes and their relationship to the surrounding area are also described. Describe in some detail.

Scene conditions: Includes the description of the transitory evidence, the level of organization, and the cleanliness of each place investigated separately, even from those sectors where no evidence was found. The description must be objective and far from subjectivity or interpretation.

Environmental conditions: Record temperature, humidity, wind speed, and direction (natural or artificial), degree of visibility and illumination, possible degree of contamination (e.g. measurement of ammonia, CO_2, etc.). Document weather conditions and intensity (e.g. heavy rain, cloudy/clear day, etc.). An attempt should be made to determine the type and degree of relationship of these conditions with the evidence found and the characteristics they present (e.g. after a rain a bloodstain can be diluted by altering its colour; the animals presented conjunctival irritation due to exposure to high levels of ammonia present at the site).

Factors pertinent to entering and leaving the site: It relates to determining, with a high probability, the approach routes to the crime scene and exit. For this, a certain degree of inference is required.

Documentation of the scene: The actions carried out in the crime scene is described. Typically, there are formats for each process (photography, sketches, taking samples, etc.). Each evidence must be identified, individualized, and described. The tool and methodology used are also identified (e.g. photograph taken with an "XX" camera, 50–100 mm objective, UV filters, etc.).

Collection of physical evidence: Generally, official formats are used to record the collected evidences, previously identified and briefly described. In the report, it is necessary to include those of importance and the place from which they were obtained.

Additional exams: Used to describe any additional tests or exams and their results. For example, entomology, analysis of blood patterns, trajectories, use of chemicals for latent prints, etc.

GENERAL CONSIDERATIONS

General considerations result from the observations made directly in the crime, from the comprehensive and objective analysis of the evidence (physical, circumstantial, and testimonial), and the information recorded in notes, photographs, or sketches.

Next, we will give a list of suggestions that we consider vital to consider when working at the crime scene.

1. Be organized, thorough, and systematic at work.
2. Consider always biosafety aspects first.
3. It is essential to document everything you see and you do not see. Sometimes the absence of evidence is the best evidence.
4. Remember that the environment can provide valuable information about what happened (context). Follow all procedures in order and do not rush. The absence of a corpse does not mean that there is no evidence.
5. The crime scene is three-dimensional and not two-dimensional. Therefore, look in all directions while observing and searching for vestiges (Gardner & Krouskup, 2019).
6. Use always the principles of criminalistics to associate elements found into the crime scene considering the context.
7. Constantly re-evaluate your actions and that of your team. Remember that the crime scene is dynamic and methodologies must be flexible.
8. Always be objective and base your interpretations on concrete facts that can be proven.
9. Don't do more than you know how to do. Remember that it is a multidisciplinary work.
10. Be cautious in your arguments. Do not opine. Just discuss and interpret.

FINAL WORDS

The discipline of animal forensic sciences is growing exponentially to solve abuse and acts associated with animals. Veterinarians must be prepared to assist in investigations and collaborate from the first moment. We cannot be passive actors. For our work to meet the necessary skills, we must: 1) train and promote multidisciplinary work; 2) provide education and development for forensic veterinary practitioners; 3) promote and develop regulation in forensic veterinary science and practice; 4) support and encourage research and development in forensic veterinary science and practice; and 5) work in a multidisciplinary way.

REFERENCES

Barbaro, A. (2020). Escena del crimen. In Tebar Flores (ed.), *Manual de Criminalística y Criminología*. Cap. 11: 330–353.

Brooks, J. (2018). *Veterinary Forensic Pathology*. Brooks (ed.), Volume 1 and 2. Pennsylvania USA: Springer.

Cooper, J. E., & Cooper, M. E. *Introduction to Veterinary and Comparative Forensic Medicine*. Wiley-Blackwell. 432 p, 2008.

Espinoza, E., Scanlan, M., Reinholz, A., & Baker, B. (2013). The Wildlife Crime Scene. An Introduction for First Responders. In J. E. Cooper, & M. E. Cooper (eds.), *Wildlife Forensics: Principles and Practice*. CRC Press. Taylor and Francis.

Fisher, B. J., & Fisher, D. R. Techniques of crime scene investigation, 8th ed. Boca Raton, FL: CRC Press/ Taylor & Francis, 2012.

Fisher, J. T., & Fisher, J. Crime Scene Investigation Case Studies Step by Step from the Crime Scene to the Courtroom. Routledge; N.º 1 edición. 236 p, 2014.

Gardner, R., & Krouskup, D. *Practical Crime Scene Processing and Investigation*, Third Edition (Practical Aspects of Criminal and Forensic Investigations). CRC Press. 431 p, 2019.

Harris H., & Lee, H. (2019). *Introduction to Forensic Science and Criminalistics*. 6th Edition CRC Press.

Inman, K., & Rudin, N. Principles and Practice of CRIMINALISTICS. The Profession of Forensic Science. CRC Press, 2001.

Lee, H., & Pagliaro, E. (2013). Forensic Evidence and Crime Scene Investigation. *Journal Forensic Investigation*, 1(2), 1–5.

Merck, M. *Veterinary Forensics: Animal Cruelty Investigations* 2nd Edition. Wiley-Blackwell, 2013.

Miller, M., & Massey, P. *The Crime Scene A Visual Guide*. 1st Edition. Elsevier, Academic Press, 2016.

Montiel, S. J. Criminalística Tomo I Y II. En J.

MONTIEL SOSA, *CRIMINALISTICA*, México: LIMUSA, 2003.

Norris, P. (2020). Crime scene investigation. In J. Byrd, P. Norris, & N. Bradley-Siemens (Eds.), *Veterinary Forensic Medicine and Forensic Sciences*. CRP Press.

Rogers, E., & Stern, A. W. (2018). *Veterinary Forensics: Investigation, Evidence Collection, and Expert Testimony*, 1st Edition. Boca Raton. CRC Press.

Toledo, G., Tremori, T., Martin Orozco, U., Reis, S. T. J., Juri, J., & Viner, T. (2020). Veterinaria forense. In Tebar Flores (ed.), *Manual de Criminalística y Criminología*. Cap 21. 613–647.

Toledo, V., & Carvallo, F. (2017). Forensic veterinary science and medicine. In A. Barbaro (ed), *Manual of Forensic Science. An international Survey*, (pp. 235–254). Boca Ratón: CRC Press.

Touroo, R., & Fitch, A. (2018). Crime Scene Findings and the Identification, Collection, and Preservation of Evidence. In Brooks (ed.), *Veterinary Forensic Pathology*. Volume 1. Pennsylvania USA: Springer.

Viner, T. (2020). Veterinaria forense. In Tebar Flores (ed.), *Manual de Criminalística y Criminología*. Cap. 21. 613–647.

World Health Organization, WHO. (2020). Zoonosis. https://www.who.int/es/news-room/fact-sheets/detail/ zoonoses

APPENDIX

Materials or items required (forensic briefcase)

- Formats of official judicial procedures
- Plastic clamps or tapes to fix guns, knives (avoid movement inside their packaging).
- Data logger or instrumentation to record environmental conditions
- Protective glasses
- Scale
- Colour elements to mark evidence (flags, rods, etc.)
- Paper and plastic bags of different sizes
- Paper envelopes (various sizes)
- Airtight seal bags
- Camera protection bags
- Compass
- Cardboard boxes of different sizes
- Evidence tape.
- Tape measure and laser.
- Sample packing tape.
- Perimeter tape or rope.
- Clips, graphite pencil.
- Live and dead animal identification collars.
- Plastic / glass containers for liquid samples.
- Anti rain notebook
- Communication equipment.
- Shields for marine animals

- Edge support stakes
- Documentation labels.
- Sterile transparent glass bottles with screw cap.
- Hooks.
- Cap.
- Blue vinyl gloves.
- Multipurpose tool.
- Swabs and swabs.
- Sterile syringes.
- Binocular lenses.
- White light flashlight with charged batteries and extra batteries.
- Magnifying glass.
- UV light flashlight.
- Waterproof case.
- First aid veterinary case.
- Evidence markers (numbers, letters).
- Permanent markers.
- Simple masks with filters.
- Cooling medium.
- Biosecurity suit with hood, protective boots, vinyl/rubber occlusive gloves, safety glasses, mask or respirator, and heavy leather gloves to avoid scratches and bites when handling animals.
- Metal and plastic clips.
- Sterile plastic pipettes used to obtain liquid samples.
- Entomology set
- Support table for annotations.
- Horizontal and square graphic/metric witness (different scales/colours) - Arrows of different sizes and colours
- Scissors.
- Silicate tubes (blotter).
- Clean plastic tubes.
- A disposal box for biosecurity equipment.
- Thread to grid the crime scene.

CHAPTER **17**

Forensic Odontology

Alan Diego Briem Stamm[1]*, Marta Alicia Fernandez Iriarte*[1]*, and Juan Esteban Palmieri*[2]

[1]Worldwide Association of Women Forensic Experts (WAWFE-Caribbean), Unidad Académica Odontología Legal, Universidad de Buenos Aires, Argentina
[2]White Helmet Dentist, United Nations, Argentina

CONTENTS

INTRODUCTION

Forensic odontology can be defined as the application of dental expertise to the justice system. Growing utilization of forensic odontology in mass disasters (aviation, earthquakes, tsunamis), in crime investigations, in ethnic studies, and in identification of decomposed and disfigured bodies like that of drowned persons, fire victims, and victims of motor vehicle accidents. Other areas of application include criminalistics, in cases involving abuse of children and elderly. Bite marks also help in detection of culprits. It also renders its service in probing of dental malpractice. Forensic odontology has become an integral part of forensic medicine. The role of forensic odontology has increased as often teeth and dental restorations are the only means of identification. Each case is different and even the seemingly routine case may test the dentist's ingenuity in applying his dental knowledge.

Dental identification takes on two forms. First, the most frequently performed examination is a comparative identification used to establish that the remains of a decedent and a person represented by ante-mortem (before death) dental records are the same individual. Information from the body or circumstances usually provides clues as to the identity of the decedent.

Second, in those cases where ante-mortem records are not available and no clues to the possible identity are available, a post-mortem (after death) dental profile is completed by the forensic dentist, suggesting characteristics of the individual likely to narrow the search for the ante-mortem materials.

The various methods employed in forensic odontology include tooth prints, radiographs, photographic study, rugoscopy, cheiloscopy, and molecular methods. Investigative methods applied in forensic odontology are reasonably reliable, yet the shortcomings must be accounted for to make it a more meaningful and relevant procedure. Most dental identifications are based on restorations, caries, missing teeth and/or prosthetic devices, such as partial and full removal prostheses, which may be documented in the dental record.

The crime scene is one of the most crucial aspects of an forensic investigation. The high-quality and useful evidence leading to accurate and fair criminal justice outcomes can only occur if the scene is processed effectively and professionally. There is only one opportunity to examine the scene of crime, so it is crucial that it is processed as precise and correct as possible. One of the tasks of a crime scene investigator is to reconstruct what may have happened and, based on the reconstruction, to decide which traces are relevant and must be secured. In this context, the recognition of the evidence dental is problematic role. For example, post-mortem dental losses during the inappropriate manipulation in the transport of the body, the underestimation in the search of the dental fragments produced by strong violence, bruises, or thermal action on fire scenes or losses of other evidence (bite marks, lip marks, dental prostheses, etc.) originate unfortunate situations in research, some negligent, others mostly due to ignorance of its value as potential evidence.

Also, mistakes made during the investigation of the crime scene are impossible to rectify in hindsight. Once the crime scene is processed, it will be released, meaning that the crime scene will no longer be protected. Trace evidence can be damaged and items can be removed or added to the scene, making it impossible to restore it to its original state.

FORENSIC ODONTOLOGY

Occasionally, forensic odontology deals with legal issues on behalf of the dental profession. But, most often, the odontology answers questions posed by the justice system and provides answers to legal authorities and expert opinions in courts of law. Significantly, much of the odontology's work is on behalf of grieving family members that have lost a loved one and need to have closure to come to terms with their grief (Avon, 2004; John, 2006). All persons possess an identity during their lifetime and the dignity of confirming and maintaining this identity after death is a strong, compelling societal need. Forensic odontology assists society to accomplish this through comparison of ante-mortem (AM) and post-mortem (PM) data to identify the corpse. There are also legal requirements for confirmation of a deceased person's identity, including religious issues, matters surrounding the estate, remarriage of a surviving partner, and insurance or financial affairs (John, 2006). Of particular legal importance is a case in which a person is the victim of violent crime. Identification of the victim's body becomes circumstantial evidence during the police investigation into cause of death, and is later used in the prosecution of the person responsible for the death (Chandra Shekar & Reddy, 2009; Pretty & Sweet, 2001a).

Worldwide, dentists qualified in forensic science are giving expert opinion in cases related to human identification, bite mark analysis, craniofacial trauma, and malpractice. Human identification relies heavily on the quality of dental records; however forensic odontology can still contribute to the identity investigation in the absence of dental records through profiling the deceased person using features related to teeth. Along with other healthcare providers, dentists encounter cases of injuries that could be non-accidental (Avon, 2004). Detection, interpretation, and management are important from a

legal and humanitarian point of view. Dentists should be aware of the legal impact those cases have, and should refer them to the appropriate authorities for suitable action. Dental identification is a comparative technique, where the PM dental records are analyzed and compared against AM records to confirm identity and establish the degree of certainty that the dental records obtained from the remains of a decedent and the AM dental records of a missing person are for the same individual (Pretty & Sweet, 2001a). Currently, the identification is carried out manually by comparing extracted features from a post-mortem (PM) dental record to extracted fractures from a database of ante-mortem (AM) records. Several individual teeth may get missed or filled after its AM record is taken; hence, dental features need to be recorded based on the contour/shape of individual teeth rather than the contour of the whole jaw (Senn & Stimson, 2010; Sweet, 2010). The new millennium has brought new challenges of terrorism, natural disasters, and high rate of crime. The teeth and dental restorations are the strongest elements in the human body and survive the destructive influences of fire and exposure to the elements and can be survivor remains after an extended period of burial (Figure 17.1).

Since 1897, forensic dentistry has gradually established itself as important, often indispensable, in medico-legal cases, in particular for identification of the dead (Leung, 2008; Bernstein, 1997). The specialty of forensic dentistry generally covers three basic areas what identifications of human remains, litigation relating to malpractice, and criminal proceedings, primarily in the areas of bite-mark evaluation and abuse cases, especially child abuse. Methods to identify the deceased must be reliable and accurate. When ante- and post-mortem registrations have been compared and the result must be evaluated. A conclusion must be drawn where the reasons are stated. The police must be informed about the result as soon as possible.

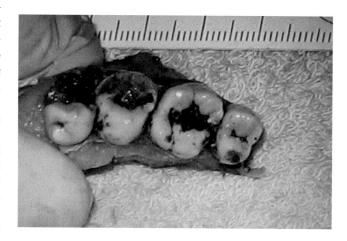

FIGURE 17.1 Dental remains with amalgam fillings.

Credit: The authors.

The adult dentition is comprised of 32 teeth; each tooth possesses five surfaces visible on oral examination. The innumerable combinations of missing teeth, filling materials, carious lesions, and prostheses involving 160 surfaces form the basis for dental identification (Bernstein, 1997; Bernitz, 2009). Specific morphologic patterns of individual restorations (fillings and crowns), features incorporated within root canals, per apical and surrounding bone enhance characterization (Adams, 2003a). The concept that no two dentitions are alike is the base premise of dental identification.

Other approaches include visual identification, which is known to be unreliable due to a high rate of false positives, comparison of medical records and data, such as serial numbers on prosthetic joints and breast implants, fingerprints if ante-mortem data are available, and DNA analysis (Deplama, 2005; Adams, 2003b). The contours and extensions of dental fillings and the crowns for example produce unique identities in the radiographic examine. These are used in forensic comparisons. The decrease in caries rate and the subsequent decline in the use of amalgam restorations over the past few decades have resulted in loss of these important identifiers in some cases (Sweet & Di Zinno, 1996). These situations create a challenge for forensic odontology (Appelbaum, 2010; Acharya, 2006). Still, radiographs show many other anatomical features, such as root shape, surrounding bone trabecular, root canal filling materials, retentive pins and posts, pulp size and shape, and periodontal and per apical inflammatory disease that can be of significant value in identification cases (Scott, 2001; Clement, 1998; Bell, 2001) (Figure 17.2).

Dental identification assumes a primary role in the identification of remains when post-mortem changes, traumatic tissue injury, or lack of a fingerprint record invalidate the use of visual or fingerprint methods. The identification of dental remains is of primary importance when the deceased person is skeletonized, decomposed, saponified, mummified, burned, or dismembered.

The principal advantage of dental evidence is that, like other hard tissues, it is often preserved after death (Clement, 1998). Even the status of a person's teeth changes throughout life and the combination of decayed, missing, and filled teeth is measurable and comparable at any fixed point in time. The fundamental principles of dental identification are those of comparison and of exclusion (Clement, 1998; Bell, 2001).

Considering that there are two types of discrepancy: those that can be explained and those that cannot. Explainable discrepancies normally relate to the time elapsed between the AM and PM records (Pretty & Addy, 2002). Examples include teeth extracted or restorations placed were found in post-mortem records only. If a discrepancy is unexplainable, for example a tooth is not present on the ante-mortem record but is present on the post-mortem record, then an exclusion must be made (Pretty & Addy, 2002; Griffiths & Bellamy, 1993).

If there are no ante-mortem dental records, a post-mortem dental profile will typically provide information on the victim:

1. Age:
   - In children: The patterns of tooth eruption, the root length, tooth can be were assessed.
   - In young adults: The third molar development.
   - In middle-aged and older adults: Periodontal disease progression, excessive wear, multiple restorations, extractions, bone pathosis, and complex restorative work were assessed. Recently, dentine composition and cement deposition were examined in relation to age determination.
2. Etnic:
   - Can be assessed from skull shape and form.
   - Other characteristics, such as Carabelli's cups, shovel-shaped incisors, and multi-cusped premolars.
3. Gender can be assessed from:
   - Skull shape and form, (no gender differences regarding teeth morphology).
   - Presence or absence of Y-chromatin in teeth.
   - DNA analysis.
   - Mandibular canine's size.
4. Socio-economic status can be assessed through the quality, quantity, and presence or absence of dental treatment.
5. Occupation, dietary habits, and dental or systemic diseases. The presence of erosion can suggest alcohol or an eating disorder while stains can indicate smoking or tetracycline. Unusual wear patterns may result from pipe stems or cigarette

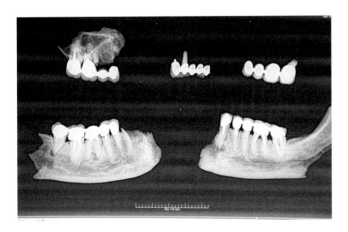

FIGURE 17.2   Details of bone, teeth, and restorations by forensic radiographic study.

Credit: The authors.

holders. A range of conclusions can be drawn following a comparison of ante-mortem and post-mortem records.

The American Board of Forensic Odontology (ABFO), however, recommends these to be limited by four conclusions (American Board of Forensic Odontology):

1. Positive identification: the ante-mortem and post-mortem findings match in sufficient details, without any unexplainable discrepancy, to establish that they are from the same individual.
2. Possible identification: the ante-mortem and post-mortem data have consistent features but, because of the quality of either the post-mortem remains or ante-mortem evidence, it is not possible to establish identity positively.
3. Insufficient evidence: the available information is insufficient to form the basis for a conclusion of any sort.
4. Exclusion: the ante-mortem and post-mortem data are clearly inconsistent.

Because enamel is the hardest substance in the human body, teeth survive fires, mutilation, and decomposition. In 2004, during the tsunami in Thailand, 73% of the victims were identified using forensic odontology (Grupo de Evaluación de INTERPOL sobre el Maremoto, 2011). Teeth can persist long after other skeletal structures have succumbed to organic decay or destruction by some other agencies, such as fire (Borrman et al., 1995). Dental identification of humans occur for a number of different reasons, and in number of different situation like for the body of victim of violent crime, fire, road traffic accident, and workplace accident (Brannon & Morlang, 2001). Bodies of people who have been deceased for some time prior to discovery and those found in water also present unpleasant and difficult in identification. The odontology can play a significant role in this process. By identifying the victims of crime and disaster (Figure 17.3) through guidelines and standards, can assist those involved in crime investigation (Sarode et al., 2009; BriemStamm, 2011).

The information provided by a multidisciplinary team can lead police investigators to possible identities for the unknown individual. Comparisons between possible identities and the unknown individual can direct investigators to a presumptive or positive identification (Sarode et al., 2009). Presumptive identification may also be made based on tattoos, circumstantial evidence, personal effects, or facial reconstruction. This type of identification is not scientifically confirmed, but can be accepted as final when foul play is not suspected and no other reason for doubt exists (Sarode et al., 2009).

It's pointed to the potential use of pulp chamber and root morphology in process of identification. Furthermore,

FIGURE 17.3   Oral autopsy on aircrash victim.

Credit: The authors.

it is possible to use the pulp chamber to distinguish approximate age of the individual. It has also been indicated that the root morphology, besides the pulp chambers, can help in determining whether the tooth is from the maxillary or mandibular arch, and distinguishing if it is an anterior or posterior tooth.

It's very important to use computer identification through databases including Plass Data© or WinID©, which are used nowadays to compare AM and PM data in the identification of deceased or missing individuals (Sarode et al., 2009; BriemStamm, 2011).

DENTAL EVIDENCE IN CRIME SCENE INVESTIGATION

The process of reconstructing a crime begins with an aalysis walk-through of the scene. This preliminary round is done to give the investigator a rough idea of what happened, why it happened, and how it happened. The importance is on preventing crime scene contamination and how to secure the different types of physical evidence in an appropriate manner. The forensic dentistry is commonly required to identify tooth marks from a crime scene. The finding at the crime scene of ejected teeth or fragments of them often cause situations controversial in research. Not having a dentist in this first approach to the crime scene is a great problem at the inadequate recognition and manipulation of the evidence them by untrained personnel, they can cause their irremediable loss as eventual evidence. In the oral cavity, fragmentations that result from high-impact energies is necessary to establish protocols in the criminal scene for the correct identification and collection of these fragments. It has been mentioned the confusion of pieces of teeth with pieces of quartz or simple rocks as traces that should be considered in the investigation (Bowers, 2011).

The methodology can be protocoled according to the guidelines of American Board of Forensic Odontology (ABFO) (American Board of Forensic Odontology), using proper techniques for collection and preservation of evidence for the last stage of comparison of suspects. The dental impression and model materials are very important to preserving the physical evidence present on inanimate materials to later on compare with the teeth of a suspect and make a conclusion (Bowers, 2011).

Tooth marks can be found in foods but also in other objects such as wood, plastic, or metal (Bernitz et al., 2006). Indentations in the teeth can leave marks, in most cases by impressions of the incisors of the upper and lower jaw. Such traces can serve as evidence. Such marks may be found on, for example, food (apple, cheese, chocolate, etc), chewing gum, and skin (Bernitz et al., 2008). The identification is based on the individuality of a dentition, which is used to match a tooth mark to a suspected dentition. Parameters like size, shape, and alignment of teeth are used (Bowers, 2011; Bernitz et al., 2006). These variables are including in the analyzing a tooth mark, pattern association and metric analysis (Bowers, 2011). The teeth may also leave marks during a fall or because of a punch against the teeth. In such cases, the teeth often are damaged or fractured. Then, the scene must be searched for the dropped or fractured teeth. Most often, tooth marks occur in the skin. Identifying unknown human remains by dental science is second in effectiveness only to fingerprints (Stimson, 1980).

Dental photography mainly shows dental remains and features bite marks. Proof of the photographs' authenticity starts at the crime scene itself. Under no circumstances should both the negatives and prints be out of the possession of the photographer (Bowers, 2011).

The physical evidence of a tooth mark must be preserved until there is a suspect. It is important to choose and use proper dental materials to take impression of the tooth marks and for making models of the marks from inanimate material.

The tooth mark identification is based on the individuality of a dentition. The first step is to reconstruct the dental profile from the marks by using anatomical features and after that if the police have a suspect for comparison with their teeth, either exclude the suspect or judge how likely it is that they made the mark (Marshall et al., 1974; MacFarlane et al., 1974).

To preserve physical evidence for a long period of time need proper use and understanding of dental materials to perform the impressions and make models. Impression materials are used to make an accurate replica of the tooth mark. The impression gives a negative reproduction of the tooth mark (Figure 17.4), and by filling it with dental stone or other material, such as epoxy resin, a positive cast (Figure 17.5) is made for study of the tooth and the profile of the mark. The

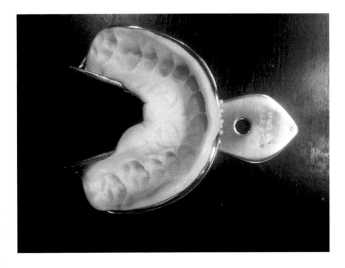

FIGURE 17.4 Negative reproduction of the tooth's marks with alginate.

Credit: The authors.

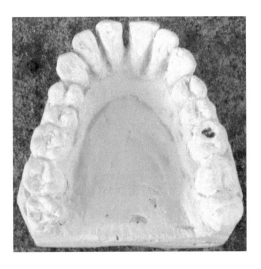

FIGURE 17.5 Plaster model of the mandibular denture.

Credit: The authors.

accuracy, detail, and quality of this final replica are of greatest importance for the results. Between the various types of impression materials currently available and the qualities they possess, the elastic impression rubber materials may be the choice (MacFarlane et al., 1974). Alternatively, silicone may be the preference because of its physical and mechanical properties, such as lowest dimensional change on setting, lowest permanent deformation, and highest detail reproduction.

The evaluation of tooth marks is difficult and considerable caution is required when conclusions regarding such evidence are to be drawn in criminal cases. The value of the evidence is greatly enhanced if comparable results are obtained by using several different methods.

BITE MARKS

Bite mark evidence recovery and analysis is the most complex and demanding role that the forensic dentist plays in the criminal justice system. Complex issues when bite marks are found on human skin, such as in cases of sexual homicide, sexual assault, and rape and in domestic violence cases of abuse, require a high level of training and expertise. Unfortunately, there are no areas of this aspect of the discipline that the forensic dentist can be involved in, primarily because of the urgency of the cases that require an almost immediate deployment. Also, there is a legal requirement that warrants, court orders, and legal consent for the seizure of evidence from suspects only include specific personnel possessing specialized training and skills (Vale, 1996). Currently, photographic protocols exist (Golden, 2011), in which the presence of a reference scale (ABFO n.2) is required and must be in the same plane as the bite mark. These two elements have to be perpendicular to the digital camera. However, if protocols are not strictly respected, some distortions can appear and interfere with correct analysis. Bite marks found at crime scenes show an array of angled indentations, abrasions, micro-lacerations, and contusions. The tooth patterns observed on skin and in inanimate objects generally reflect the incisor surfaces of the suspect's dentition present in the dental arch. Skin bite marks are generally present on the body of the victim and inflicted by the assailant, but in some cases the wounds are self-inflicted or inflicted by the victim on the assailant (Golden, 2011). A variety of foodstuffs and inanimate objects with bite marks have been investigated as part of crime scenes (Figure 17.6).

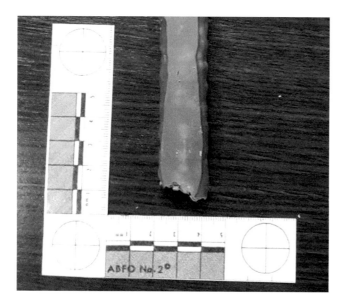

FIGURE 17.6   Bite mark on cookie chocolate.

Credit: The authors.

The bites may be inflicted as a result of differing degrees of anger, revenge, sexual frustration, wrath, righteous indignation, and punishment (Bowers, 2006).

It is important to decide initially to attempt to define the term *bite mark*. In a forensic sense, it is suggested a mark is caused by the teeth either alone or in combination with other mouth parts (Bowers, 2006). This definition merely implies that the marks were made by the teeth. It does not require that the material in which the mark was registered was either seized or torn by the teeth and indeed the force causing the teeth to leave a mark need not have been derived from the individual whose teeth caused the mark (Bowers, 2006; Martin de Las Heras et al., 2007).

Bite marks may be penetrating or non-penetrating. Whether or not such penetration occurs is probably a function of several factors such as the sharpness of the biting part of the tooth, the force applied, the rate of application of the force, and the amount of movement between the teeth and the tissue bitten (Pretty & Sweet, 2001b).

Bite marks in flesh can be considered as forming a spectrum from amorous bites to aggressive bites. All features of a mark must be considered. In some cases tooth pressure marks alone may not allow a decision that a mark is a definite bite mark, but taken in combination with tongue pressure marks such a lesion may be diagnosed as a definite bite mark (Souviron, 2006). At some point after the processing of the bite mark, the alleged perpetrator will be located. Impressions of the teeth will be made, and stone casts poured for comparison to the bite mark. At this time, intraoral photographs of the anterior teeth in centric and protrusive relationship as well as incisal/occlusal views of the maxillary and mandibular anterior teeth are to be made (Souviron, 2006; Giannelli, 2008). Legally, it is important to obtain informed consent duly witnessed, or a court order. Otherwise, the dentist could violate due process, thereby invalidating the evidence and subjecting themself to assault charges. The use of 2-D and 3-D scanning of the bite marks seems to be a satisfactory means of preserving the shape and form of the bite marks prior to investigation procedures. It's very important to use the 3-D method because it allows for the elimination of problems related to the distortions arising from 2-D photographic documentation (Pretty & Sweet, 2001b; Giannelli, 2008).

EFFECTS OF THE FIRE IN THE ORAL CAVITY

Fire investigation involves the examination of all fire-related incidents once firefighters have extinguished the fire. The practice is similar to the examination of crime scenes in that the scene must be preserved and evidence collected and analyzed, but with numerous additional difficulties and dangers (Hill et al., 2011). The

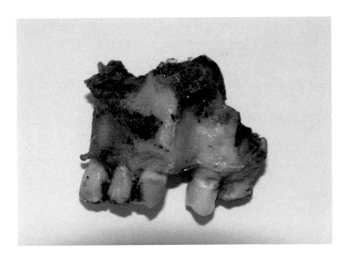

FIGURE 17.7   Teeth and bone suitable for DNA analysis.
Credit: The authors.

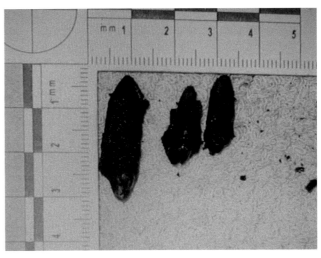

FIGURE 17.8   Teeth with dark or charred appearance.
Credit: The authors.

maintenance of integrity of extremely fragile structures is crucial to the successful confirmation of identity. In such situations, the forensic dentist must stabilize these teeth before the fragile remains are transported to the mortuary to ensure preservation of possibly identification evidence (Berketa et al., 2015). It is a probability that police personnel are untrained in the recognition of body parts. Thus, while dealing with any incinerated dental remains, a systematic approach must be followed through each stage of evaluation of incinerated dental remains to prevent the loss of potential dental evidence (Berketa et al., 2015). In several situations, teeth and bones are frequently the only sources of DNA available for identification of degraded or fragmented human remains (Figure 17.7).

The effects of fire on teeth are particularly evident on the anterior dentition, which has less protection from soft tissues. The enamel crown of a tooth may separate from the body of the tooth if exposed to extreme temperatures and surviving structures can become extremely fragile and susceptible to crumbling from even minor forces (Berketa et al., 2015; Berketa, 2014).

Separation of tooth crowns lead to a loss of information for comparison with ante-mortem dental records. In these cases, root morphology placement and angulations and the bony features are the only information for comparison (Berketa, 2014). Posterior tooth crowns while less likely to be lost, often fracture, and may dislodge, becoming wedged against the neighboring or opposing crowns. The color changes that occur during incineration may be useful in order to predict the degree of fragility of the dental tissues (Berketa et al., 2015; Berketa, 2014). In general, the teeth that have a dark or charred appearance (Figure 17.8) are not as delicate as those that are "porcelain white" in appearance. It would be prudent to employ a stabilization technique as a matter of course in this scenario (Grevin et al., 1998).

RADIOLOGY EVIDENCE

The use of radiological investigation is well accepted in forensic odontology practice. They provide an objective assessment and recording of the hard tissues of the teeth and jaws as well as surgical or restorative features that may be of interest to the examiner. Furthermore, they provide a visual image that can be used to demonstrate intricate details to a lay audience (Nomir & Abdel-Mottaleb, 2007; Chen, 2007; Jain & Chen, 2004). Radiography being a non-destructive method also plays a vital role in forensic dentistry to uncover the hidden facts which cannot be seen by means of physical examination. Dental examination and comparison between ante-mortem and post-mortem dental records and radiographs produce results with a high degree of reliability and relative simplicity (Lee et al., 2004; Hinchliffe, 2011).

The radiographic study is a very important forensic investigative procedure and is advantageous over photographic evaluation because external and internal anatomical features can be analyzed. Unique root curvatures, restorations, and endodontic treatments can be compared in ante-mortem and post-mortem radiographs of incinerated dental remains (Grevin et al., 1998). Also, they are an excellent tool as they can identify an enormous amount of information in the roots of the teeth, existing dental treatment including the presence of surgical plates, or dental implants and bony anatomical landmarks (Berketa, 2014; Grevin et al., 1998). If the facilities are available, then taking an

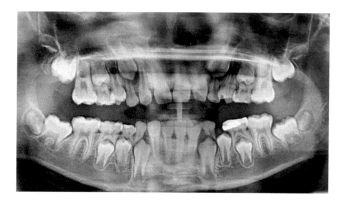

FIGURE 17.9   Orthopantomagram radiograph.

Credit: The authors.

FIGURE 17.10   Portable x-ray equipment in the mortuary.

Credit: The authors.

orthopantomagram radiograph would be considered a better method (Figure 17.9).

Panoramic radiographs are also helpful to determine the age of the individual by assessing the stage of eruption (Nomir & Abdel-Mottaleb, 2007; Chen, 2007). X-ray equipment will be of great advantage in both internal and dental examinations, particularly when an estimate of a victim's age is required, and also to discover fractures or other unique identification information. The use of radiographs is characteristic of techniques that involve observation of morphologically distinct stages of mineralization. Age estimations are also based on the degree of formation of root and crown structures, the stage of eruption, and the intermixture of primary and adult dentitions (Hinchliffe, 2011). The size of dental pulp cavity is reduced as a result of secondary dentin deposit. The measurements of this reduction can be used as an indicator of age (Nomir & Abdel-Mottaleb, 2007; Jain & Chen, 2004). Using radiographs, the pulp length and width are measured. These ratios are found to be significantly correlated with age. Results show the strongest correlation with age to be in ratio between the width of the pulp and the root. This indicates that the rate of deposition of dentine on the mesial and distal walls is more closely related to age than that on the roof of the pulp cavity. However, the limitation of the technique is that the correlation between age and the ratios between pulp and the root length was found to be significant for only maxillary cuspids and premolars (Hinchliffe, 2011). X-ray examination is also a very effective method of locating and identifying evidential material such as bullets or bomb fragments. X-ray equipment, preferably portable, should always be made available in the mortuary (Chen, 2007; Hinchliffe, 2011) (Figure 17.10).

Advances in computer technology coupled with improvement in sensor technology over the past 25 years have resulted in the adoption of digital radiography systems in dental practice. These now include the ability to image orthopanographic, cephalographic, and computed tomographic images for nearly instant delivery to clinical workstations (Lichtenstein et al., 1988). This stands in marked contrast to film-based dental radiography, particularly in forensic applications, and holds many advantages for the forensic dentist. The dentist-investigator is able to speedily discern whether or not features that might serve to confirm or refute a suspected identification are visible and order re-imaging if needed while the specimen is available. In addition, PM and AM images can be rapidly transmitted across great distances without any loss of fidelity, questions of orientation (left versus right side), or acquisition date and other provenance issues. In the past, film-based images were first reproduced or copied onto additional film substrates and then hand-delivered (mail, courier, etc.) for comparison (Nomir & Abdel-Mottaleb, 2007; Lee et al., 2004; Hinchliffe, 2011). Loss of detail and possible loss of the original image were not uncommon (Lichtenstein et al., 1988). Older, film-based images can, by the use of optical scanning hardware and software, be converted to an electronic image (data set) which can be treated similarly to original digital radiographs (transmission, optimization, storage, etc.) (Schulze & Drage, 2020; Jain et al., 2019).

Digital radiographic imaging software also allows the investigator to optimize or enhance the image as viewed on-screen, resulting in visualization of greater detail in the captured image – again increasing the likelihood of an identification or exclusion. Many investigators are working to perfect comparative systems (digital image-subtraction, image rectification, point-to-point analysis, etc.) to assist the forensic dentist in analyzing radiographic images (Jain et al., 2003). Several sophisticated computer applications are now available for use in collating and comparing large amounts of dental data (Piotrowski & Szczepaniak, 2000). These applications are effective at sorting large numbers of ante-mortem records to reduce the number of potential matching post-mortem records to only a few. This allows the forensic odontology's to complete the manual comparison of the actual charts and radiographs to determine if a match exists (Jain et al., 2003; Hu et al., 2001). Although there are many avenues available to authorities to arrive at the identity of unknown human remains, dental identification is rapid, reliable, readily available in most situations, and relatively inexpensive in comparison. For example, DNA requires time-consuming testing and collection of samples. Fingerprinting requires that the unknown remains retain soft tissue suitable for lifting print exemplars as well as the availability of fingerprint records on file. Nowhere is this more evident than in cases involving multiple fatalities. DVI (disaster victim identification) situations tax the resources of the medical examiner. In today's fast-paced world, rapid identification is expected, if not demanded, by the next of kin and the press. This would require reliable automatic segmentation techniques that can extract the contour of each individual tooth for latter retrieval purposes to allow for retrieval based on teeth shapes.

CHEILOSCOPY

Cheiloscopy (from the Greek words *cheilos, lips, e skopein* (Caldas et al., 2007) is the name given to the lip print studies (Sharma et al., 2009a). The importance of cheiloscopy is linked to the fact that lip prints are unique to one person, except in monozygotic twins (Negré Muñoz, 2004). Like fingerprints and palatal rugae, lip grooves are permanent and unchangeable (Suzuki & Tsuchihashi, 1970; Coward, 2007; Suzuki & Tsuchihashi, 1975; López Palafox, 2001). It is possible to identify lip patterns as early as the sixth week of uterine life (Caldas et al., 2007). From that moment on, lip groove patterns rarely change, resisting many afflictions, such as herpetic lesions. In fact, only those pathologies that damage the lip subtract like burns, seem to rule out cheiloscopic study (Caldas et al., 2007). Lips are two, highly sensitive mobile folds, composed of skin, muscle, glands, and mucous membrane.

They surround the oral orifice and form the anterior boundary of the oral cavity. Anatomically, whether covered with skin or mucosa, the surface that forms the oral sphincter is the lip area. There is an upper lip (from under the nose and extending laterally toward the cheek from the nasolabial sulcus) and a lower lip (bound inferiorly by a prominent groove, the labiomental sulcus); the two lips are joined at the corners of the mouth, the commissures, and separated by the buccal fend (Caldas et al., 2007; López Palafox, 2001). There are two different kinds of lip coverings: skin or mucosa. When the two meet, a white wavy line forms the labial cord, which is quite prominent in African Americans. Where identification is concerned, the mucosal area holds the most

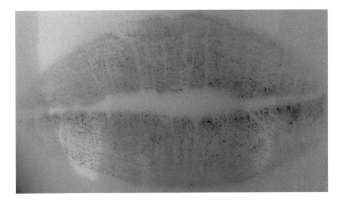

FIGURE 17.11   Lip mark on a porcelain surface.

Credit: Lic. YulianaArezo.

interest. This area, also called Klein's zone, is covered with wrinkles and grooves that form a characteristic pattern: the lip print (López Palafox, 2001; Ball, 2002) (Figure 17.11).

In 1950, Le Moyne Snyder, in his book *Homicide Investigation*, mentioned the possibility of using lip prints in the matter of human identification (Snyder, 1950). The first cheiloscopic expertise was made in Poland in 1966 when a lip print was revealed on window glass at the scene of a burglary. The examination was carried out and the expert concluded that the trace of lips revealed at the scene did not belong to the suspect (Kasprzak, 1990). Renaud, in 1972, studied 4000 lip prints and confirmed the singularity of each one, supporting the idea of lip print singularity (Renaud, 1973). Two years later, Suzuki and Tsuchihashi developed another study that resulted in a new classification for lip prints. This study, made over a long period of time, enabled the authors to confirm not only lip print singularity, but also lip response to trauma; in fact, these authors observed that after healing, the lip pattern was equal to that before the injury occurred. In the last years, studies were carried out by several researchers in India and other countries (Saraswathi et al., 2009; Sivapathasundharam et al., 2001; Sharma et al., 2009b). Different aspects of the lip prints like stability, sex determination (Patel et al., 2010; Augustine et al., 2008), and various morphological patterns using lip prints among different groups of population were studied. A study on post-mortem changes of lip prints (Utsuno et al., 2005) was also carried out to find out the changes in anthropometric measurements of the lip region before and after fixation. All these studies were in agreement with the Japanese research and thus helped in concluding that the cheiloscopic studies can be implemented as an auxiliary method of identification.

Fingerprints are developed by a number of methods that rely on the fact that sweat and body oils that have been transferred from the body to an object react with a

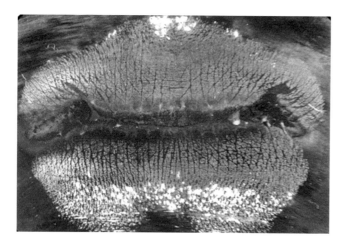

FIGURE 17.12 Lip latent print revealed with cyanoacrylate.

Credit: Lic. Noralí Herrera.

number of reagents to become visible. Fingerprint powders adhere to sweat and body oils, iodine when heated reacts with sweat, ninhydrin reacts with the amino acids in sweat, heated cyanoacrylate (Figure 17.12) reveals latent prints, and sweat fluoresces when illuminated by a laser.

Other authors (Castello et al., 2004) tested developing the latent lip prints using a similar method. According to them, the vermilion borders of the lip shave minor salivary glands and sebaceous glands. These glands are associated with hair follicles, with sweat glands in between, and secreting oils. With these secretions and continual moisturizing, it makes the latent lip prints available at most of the crime scenes. In the other study (Castello et al., 2002) on luminous lip prints, Nile Red was considered as a potential developer for latent lip prints. They used a property of luminescence for latent lip print development. Luminescence is an especially useful property for the search of invisible evidences at the scene of a crime.

Cheiloscopy is interesting mostly in identifying the living, since it can be the only way to link somebody to someone or to a specific location. However, although lip prints have previously been used in a court of law, its use is not consensual and some authors believe further evidence is needed to confirm their uniqueness (Sivapathasundharam et al., 2001; Augustine et al., 2008). In fact, lip print use is controversial and rare. The case of Lavelle L. Davis in 2007 caused a great controversy in the courts of the United States, discrediting the viability of cheiloscopy. In 2009, the NAS report dealt another severe blow to the admissibility of lip prints (Augustine et al., 2008). The FBI has used this kind of evidence only in a single case in order to obtain a positive identification. Nowadays, new research allows for cheiloscopy use in a court of law in the USA

(Bowers & Bell, 1997; The People of the State of Illinois, 2007). Recent studies also point out other possibilities, namely, DNA detection in latent lip prints where some researchers are trying to relate characteristic lip patterns with a person's gender (Schulz et al., 2004). Another aspect that might be interesting to study is the possibility of using identifiable lip prints obtained from the skin of assault and murder victims, in a similar way to what has already been done with latent fingerprints (Augustine et al., 2008). The lip print is produced by a substantially mobile portion of the lip. This fact alone explains the reason why the same person can produce different lip prints, according to the pressure, direction, and method used in taking the print (Negré Muñoz, 2004). If lipstick is used, the amount can also affect the print. This problem, however, can be solved if recordings are made until all of the substance is used (Negré Muñoz, 2004; Coward, 2007; Schulz et al., 2004). Manual register of the overlay is another problem, due to the possibility of some subjectivity (Negré Muñoz, 2004).

RUGOSCOPY

The palatal rugoscopy refers to the study, recording, and classification of ridges located in the mucous of the palate or roof of the oral cavity. When the characteristics of the body do not allow its implementation, such as the advanced decomposition, carbonization, or skeletonization, the palatal rugae can provide important information about the identity of the investigated subject. The usefulness of rugoscopy as a tool for human identification is mainly founded on the alleged distinctive pattern of the palatal rugae (Senn & Weems, 2013). Moreover, these rugae consist of a fibrous tissue that resists physical and chemical trauma, time, and cadaveric alterations to an extent (Rajendran & Sivapathasundharam, 2012).

It has been reported that even when total toothless victim methods available are more limited, the palatal rugae are important evidence that can be recovered in a practical and simple way, playing their anatomical cost patterns directly from the hard palate or mucosal surface of prosthetic elements (Caldas et al., 2007). This method allows identification by direct comparison of the models of the maxilla in which tissues are duplicates of the hard palate, AM and PM, so it is essential factibility of subject specific information in life (Thomas & van Wyk, 1988). Differentiated palatoscopy terms is the study of the anatomy of the roof of the oral cavity or palatal vault, palatine rugoscopy is study, recording, and classification of palatal rugae (Caldas et al., 2007; Thomas & van Wyk, 1988). These rugas originate between the twelfth- and fourteenth-week in- intrauterine life, remaining unchanged throughout life.

This makes them especially feasible, both living subjects and fresh corpses, which is a tool expert undoubted value (Campos, Perrella et al.,). Rugae are not damaged from trauma due to their internal position in the oral cavity and are insulated from heat by the tongue and buccal fat pads. In one study, it was reported that no two palates are alike in their configuration and that the palatal print did not change. In twins also, the studies indicated that the patterns may be similar but not identical. Embryological palatal rugae appear around the third month of intrauterine life from the covering of connective tissue in the palatal process of maxillary bone. Once formed, they may experience changes in their size due to growth of the palate, but its shape is generally maintained. The cast models and ante-mortem intraoral photographs can be found in dental records and serve as the first protocol to perform the identification process (Buchtová et al., 2003; Limson & Julian, 2004). Furthermore, for at-risk populations (for example, pilot of airplanes and firemen), this first record can be preventively arranged and archived for the possible need of identification. Researchers have found the task of classification a difficult aspect of rugae studies. The subjective nature of observation and interpretation within and between observers pose a problem. Nowadays, there are several known palatal rugae classifications.

Palatal rugae are classified according to their form and the design formula called a rugogram is developed. Other authors (Ohtani et al., 2008) compared the rugosities of university students by an impression with irreversible hydrocolloid and cast models in plaster type II. The rugae were highlighted with well-sharpened graphite pencils. The rugae were photographed and the models were scanned, achieving a 92–97% success rate. The authors claimed that this error rate of 3–8% can be reduced by using an intraoral scanner, with a direct transfer to the computer (Ohtani et al., 2008). Some identification methods are available for edentulous victims, such as comparing the anatomy of the paranasal sinuses and comparing the bone patterns observed in radiographs. In addition to this, the victim's own dentures can also be used, which are found inside the mouth or in their homes. Among the evidence from an edentulous victim, the palatal rugae are considered to be one of the unique morphological features. In another study, (Aparicio Castellanos et al., 2007) analyzed the possibility of identifying edentulous individuals by comparing the rugae in denture molds against models obtained from impressions taken from the patients. There are several ways to analyze palatal rugae. Intraoral inspection is probably the most used and also the easiest and the cheapest. However, it can create difficulties if a future comparative exam is required and a more detailed and exact study, as well as the need to preserve evidence,

may justify oral photography or oral impressions (Kapali et al., 1997). Calcorrugoscopy, or the overlay print of palatal rugae in a maxillary cast, can be used in order to perform comparative analysis. However, due to its simplicity, price, and reliability, the study of maxillary dental casts is the most used technique (Kapali et al., 1997; Hemanth et al., 2010).

In fact, contrary to lip prints, it is possible to have ante-mortem data established, such as records found in dental practice in different forms (dental casts, old prosthetic maxillary devices, and intraoral photographs). However, palatoscopy might not be so useful in crime scene investigations in the linking of suspects to crime scenes. In fact, this kind of evidence is not expected to be found in such circumstances (Hemanth et al., 2010; Kashima, 1990). In a case report, it is described a method where palatal rugae were added to a complete denture in order to improve speech patterns in some patients. This process can lead to false identity exclusion due to misleading ante-mortem data (Gitto et al., 1999; Jain & Chowdhary, 2013).

CONCLUSION

A forensic dentist may play a major role in identification in the globalized world. Forensic dentistry has varying applications that require different levels of readiness both technically and emotionally on the part of multidisciplinary team members. The applications in crime scene investigation include identification and age estimation of living or deceased individuals from their teeth, jaws, or facial bones; analysis of bite marks to identify perpetrators; victims of violent and sexual attacks; cases of family violence (marital, child, and elderly abuse and neglect). Recent tragedies and past and present situations have increased awareness concerning the importance of forensic dentistry in identification of victims. However, forensic dentistry is not yet fully introduced into the dental curriculum as a subject.

Moreover, the likelihood of future disasters due to terrorism, earthquakes, and other causes require the dental profession in the world to prepare for an expanded role that would be in a bioterrorism response, crime, or in civil proceedings. Dentists have a major role to play in keeping accurate dental records and providing all necessary information so that legal authorities may recognize malpractice, negligence, fraud or abuse, and identify unknown humans. Currently, there is no agreement among forensic dentists about the uniqueness of the dentition or behavior of human skin during biting, for example. Although these issues have never been proven scientifically, much research is needed to prove suspicions that human dentition is unique.

REFERENCES

Acharya, A. B. (2006). Teaching for Ensicodontology: An Opinion on its Content and Format. *European Journal of Dental Education*, 10 (3), 137–141.

Adams, B. J. (2003a). Establishing Personal Identification Based on Specific Patterns Of Missing, Filled, And Unrestored Teeth. *Journal of Forensic Sciences*, 48(3), 487–496.

Adams, B. J. (2003b). The diversity of adult dental patterns in the United States and the implications for personal identification. *Journal of Forensic Science*, 48(3), 497–503.

American Board of Forensic Odontology. ABFO Reference Manual. Avalalable from: www.abfo.org

Aparicio Castellanos, D. C., Henríquez Higuera, L. F., Hurtado Avella, A. M., Pedraza Gutiérrez, A. P., & Casas Martínez, J. A. (2007). Identificación positiva por medio del uso de la rugoscop'a en un Municipio de Cundinamarca (Colombia): Reporte de caso. *Acta Odontol. Venez.*, 45(3), e1–e6.

Appelbaum, K. L. (2010). Commentary: The Art of Forensic Report Writing. *Journal of American Academy Psychiatry Law*, 38, 43–45.

Augustine, J., Barpande, S. R., & Tupkari, J. V. (2008). Cheiloscopy as an adjunct to forensic identification: a study of 600 individuals. *Journal of Forensic Odontostomatology*, 27, 44–52.

Avon, S. L. (2004). Forensicodontology: the roles and responsabilities of the dentist. *Journal of the Canadian Dental Association*, 70, 453–458.

Ball, J. (2002). The current status of lipprints and their use for identification. *Journal of Forensic Odontostomatology*, 20, 436.

Bell, G. L. (2001). Dentistry's role in theresolution of missing and unidentifiedpersons cases. *Dental Clinics of North America*, 45, 293–308.

Berketa, J., James, H., Langlois, N., Richards, L., & Pigou, P. (2015). Use of a non-volatile agent tostabilizeseverelyincinerated dental remains. *Forensic Science, Medicine and Pathology*, 11(2), 228e234.

Berketa, J. W. (2014). Maximizing Post-mortem Oral-Facial Data to Assist Identification Following Severe in Cineration. *Forensic Science, Medicine and Pathology*, 10(2), 208e216.

Bernitz, H. (2009). The Challenges and Effects of Globalisation on Forensic Dentistry. *International Dental Journal*, 59 (4), 222–224.

Bernitz, H., Van Heerden, W. F. P., Solheim, T., & Owen, J. H. (2006). A Techniqueto Capture, Analyze, and Quantify Anterior Teeth Rotations for Application in Court Cases Involving Tooth Marks. *Journal Forensic Science*, 51, 624–629.

Bernitz, H., Owen, J. H., Van Heerden, W. F. P., & Solheim, T. (2008). An integrated technique for the Analysis of Skin Bite Marks. *Journal Forensic Science*, 53, 194–198.

Bernstein, M. (1997). Forensic Odontology. In Eckert W. G. editor. *Introduction to Forensic Sciences*, 2nd Edition. Boca Raton, FL: CRS Press, pp. 304–351.

Borrman, H., Dahlbom, U., & Loyola, E. (1995). René. Quality Evaluation of 10 Years Patient Records in Forensic Odontology. *International Journal of Legal Medicine*, 1(08), 100–104.

Bowers, C. (2006). Problem-Based Analysis of Bite Mark Identifications: The Role of DNA. *Forensic Science International*, 159S, 104–109.

Bowers, C. M. (2011). *Forensic Dental Evidence: An Investigator's Handbook*, 2nd Edition. San Diego: Elsevier.

Bowers, C. M., & Bell, G. L. *Manual of Forensic Odontology* (3rd ed.), Ontario: American Society of Forensic Odontology, 1997, pp. 16–18.

Brannon, R. B., & Morlang, W. M. (2001). Tenerife Revisited: Thecritical Role of Dentistry. *Journal Forensic Science*, 43(3), 722–725.

BriemStamm, A. D. (2011). Standars, Protocols and Globalization in Forensic Odontology. *The Forensic Oral Pathology Journal*, 2(4), 9–12.

Buchtová, M., Tichy, F., Putnová, I., & Míšek, I. (2003). The development of palatal rugae in the European pinevole, Microtus subterraneus (Arvicolidae, Rodentia). *Folia Zoo*, 52 (2), 127–136.

Caldas, I. M., Magalhaes, T., & Alfonso, A. (2007). Establishing Identity Using Cheiloscopy and Palatoscopy. *Forensic Science International*, 165 (1), 1–9.

Campos, M. L. Rugoscopia palatina, http://www.pericias-forenses.com.br

Castello, A., Alvarez, M., Miguel, M., & Verdú, F. (April 2002). Long-lasting lip sticks and latent prints, Forensic Science Communications [online], http://www.fbi.gov/ hq/lab/fsc/backissu/Apr2002/verd.html

Castello, A., Alvarez, M., Negre, M. C., & Verdu, F. A. (2003). Revelado de huellas labiales invisibles con reactivos fluorescentes. *Cuadernos de Medicina Forense*, 34, 437.

Castello, A., Alvarez, M., & Verdu, F. (2004). Just lip prints? No: There could be something else. *The FASEB Journal*, 18, 6156.

Chandra Shekar, B. R., & Reddy, C. V. (2009). Role of Dentist in Person Identification. *Indian Journal of Dental Research*, 20 (3), 356–360.

Chen, H. *Automatic Forensic Identification Based on Dental Radiographs*. Michigan State University, 2007.

Clement, Ranson, (1998). Dental identification. In *Craniofacial Identification in Forensic Medicine*, Arnold Press, pp. 63–81.

Coward, R. C. (2007). Thestability of lippatterncharacteristicsover time. *Journal of Forensic Odontostomatology*, 25(2), 40–56.

Deplama, A. M. (2005). Gathering the forensic evidence. *RDM, 25*(2), 79–103.

Giannelli, P. (2008). *Bite Mark Analysis, Case Research Paper Series in Legal Studies 08-06.* Case W. Res. Univ. Sch. of Law.

Gitto, C. A., Esposito, S. J., & Draper, J. M. (1999). A simple method of adding palatal rugaeto a complete denture. *The Journal of Prosthetic Dentistry, 81*(2), 237–239.

Golden, G. S. (2011). Standards and practicesfor bite markphotography, *J. Forensic Odontostomatol, 29*, 29–37.

Grevin, G., Bailet, P., Quatrehomme, G., & Ollier, A. (1998). Anatomical reconstruction of fragments of burned human bones: a necessary means for forensic identification. *Forensic Science International, 96*(2–3), 129e134.

Griffiths, C. J., & Bellamy, G. D. (1993). Protection and radiography of heat affected teeth, *Forensic Science International, 60*, 57–60.

Grupo de Evaluación de INTERPOL sobre el Maremoto. La respuesta del equipo de identificación de víctimas sobre el maremoto del sudeste asiático entre diciembre de 2004 y febrero de 006 [citado 27 Mar 2011]. Disponible en: http://www.interpol.int/Public/Disaster Victim/TsunamiEvaluation20100330ES.pdf

Hemanth, M., Vidya, M., Shetty, N., & Karkera, B. V. (2010). Identification of individuals Using of the Palatal Rugae: Computerized Method. *Journal of Forensic Dental Sciences, 2* (2), 86–90.

Hill, A. J., Lain, R., & Hewson, I. (2011 Feb 25). Preservation of dental evidence following exposure to high temperatures. *Forensic Science International, 205*(1–3), 40e43.

Hinchliffe, J. Forensicodontology, (2011). Part 1. Dental identification. *British Dental Journal, 210*, 21924.

Hu, S., Hoffman, E. A., & Reinhardt, M. (Jun. 2001). Automatic Lung Segmentation for Accurate Quantization of Volumetric X-Ray CT Images. *IEEE Transactions Medical Imaging, 20*(6), 490–498.

Jain, A., & Chowdhary, R. (2013). Palatal rugae and their role in forensicodontology. *Journal of Investigative and Clinical Dentistry, 4*, 1–8.

Jain, A. K., & Chen, H. (2004). Matching of dental X-rayfor human identification. *Pattern Recognition, 37*, 1519–1532.

Jain, K., Chen, H., & Minut, S. (2003). "Dental Biometrics Human Identification Using Dental Radiographs," *AVBPA, UK*, pp. 429–437.

Jain, S., Choudhary, K., Nagi, R., Shukla, S., Kaur, N., & Grover, D. (2019). New Evolution of Cone-beam Computed Tomography in Dentistry: Combining Digital Technologies. *Imaging Science in Dentistry, 49*(3), 179–190. 10.5624/isd.2019.49.3.179

John, M. K. (2006). Justice Through Forensic Odontology. *Dental Asia*, 30–34.

Kapali, G. Townsend, L., Richards, & Parish, T. (1997). Palatal Rugae patterns in Australian Aborigines and Caucasians. *Australian Dental Journal, 42* (2), 129–133.

Kashima, K. (1990). Comparativestudy of the Palatal Rugae and Shape of the hard Palate in Japanese and Indian Children. *Aichi Gakuin Daigaku Shigakkai Shi, 28*, 295–320.

Kasprzak, J. (1990). Possibilities of Cheiloscopy. *Forensic Science International, 46*, 14551.

Lee, S. S., Choi, J. H., Yoon, C. L., Kim, C. Y., & Shin, K. J. (2004). The Diversity of Dental Patterns in the Orthopantomography and its Significance in Human Identification. *Journal of Forensic Sciences, 49*, 7846.

Leung, C. K. (2008). Forensic Odontology. *Hong Kong MedDiary, 13*, 16–20. Available from http://www.fmshk.org/database/ articles/03db05_1.pdf

Lichtenstein, J. E., Fitzpatrick, J. J. & Madeweel, J. E. (1988). The Role of Radiology in Fatality Investigations. *American Journal of Radiology, 150*, 751–755.

Limson, K. S., & Julian, R. (2004). Computerized recording of the Palatal Rugae Pattern and an Evaluation of its Application in Forensic-identification. *Journal of Forensic Odontostomatology, 22* (1), 1–4.

López Palafox, J. (2001). Aplicaciones ignoradas en Odontología forense. Interés de la Queiloscopía en la averiguación de delitos (1st Part). *Maxillaris, 529*, 54–58.

MacFarlane, T. W., MacDonald, D. G., & Sutherland, D. A. (1974). Statistical Problems in Dental Identification. *Journal of Forensic Sciences, 14*, 247–252.

Marshall, W., Potter, J., & Harvey, W. (1974). Bite Marks in Apples – Forensic Aspects. *Criminologist, 9*, 21–34.

Martin de Las Heras, S., Valenzuela, S., Valverde, A., Torres, J., & Luna-del-Castillo, J. (2007). Effectiveness of Comparison Overlays Generated with Dental Print Software in Bite Mark Analysis. *Journal of Forensic Science, 52*, 151–156.

Negré Muñoz, M. C. (2004). *Nuevas Aportaciones al Revelado de Huellas Labiales: los lisocromos en Queiloscopia. Tesis Doctoral.* Universitat de Valencia.

Nomir, O., & Abdel-Mottaleb, M. (2007). Human Identification from Dental X-Ray Images Based on the Shape and Appearance of the Teeth. *IEEE Transactions on Information Forensics and Security, 2*(2), 188–197.

Ohtani, M., Nishida, N., Chiba, T., Fukuda, M., Miyamoto, Y., & Yoshioka, N. (2008). Indication and Limitations of Using Palatal Rugae for Personal Identification in Edentulous Cases. *Forensic Science International, 176*, 17882.S.

Patel, S., Paul, I., Astekar, M. S., Ramesh, G., & Sowmya, G. V. (2010). A Study of Lip Print in Relation to Gender, Family and Bloodgroup. *International Journal of Oral and Maxillo Facial Pathology*, 1 (1), 4–7.

Perrella, M., Costa, F., Vessecchi, S., Moccelin, E., & Daruge, E. Identificação por rugoscopia palatina e dactiloscopia, http://www.ibemol.com.br/forense2000/071.asp

Piotrowski, M., & Szczepaniak, P. S., (2000). Active Contour Based Segmentation of Low-Contrast Medical Images. International Conference on Advances in Medical Signal and Information Processing, pp. 104–109.

Pretty, I., & Sweet, D. (2001b). Digital Bite Mark Overlays—Analysis of Effectiveness, *Journal of Forensic Science*, 46, 1385–1389.

Pretty, I. A., & Addy, L. D. (2002). Associated Post-mortem Dental Findings as Anaidto Personal Identification. *Science Justice*, 42, 65–74.

Pretty, I. A., & Sweet, D. (2001a). A Look at Forensic Dentistry--Part 1: The Role of teeth in the Determination of Human Identity. *British Dental Journal*, 190, 359–366.

Rajendran, A., & Sivapathasundharam, B. (2012). *Shafer'sText Book of Oral Pathology*, 7th Edition. Gurgaon: Elsevier India.

Renaud, M. L'identificationchéiloscopique en médicine légale, Le chirurgiendentiste de France, (October 1973), pp. 65–69.

Saraswathi, T. R., Gauri, M., & Ranganathan, K. (2009). Study of Lip Prints. *Journal of Forensic Dental Sciences*, 1, 2831.

Sarode, S. C., Zarkar, G. A., & Kulkarni, M. A. (2009). Role of Forensicodontology in the World's Major Massdisasters: Facts and Figures. *Dental Update*, 36, 435–436.

Schulz, M. M., Wehner, H. D., Reichert, W., & Graw, M. (2004). Ninhydrin-Dyed Latent Finger Prints as a DNA Source in a Murder Case. *Journal of Clinical Forensic Medicine*, 11, 2024.

Schulze, R. K. W., & Drage, N. A. (2020). Cone-Beam Computed Tomography and its Applications in Dental and Maxillofacial Radiology. *Forensic dentistry*, 75(9), 647–657. 10.1016/j.crad.2020.04.006

Scott, B. (2001). Forensics Experts Lending Aid. *Access.*, 12–15.

Senn, D. R., & Stimson, P. G. *Forensic dentistry*, Boca Raton: CRC Press, 2010.

Senn, D. R., & Weems, R. A. (2013). *Manual of Forensic Odontology*, 5th Edition. Boca Raton: CRC Press.

Sharma, P., Saxena, S., & Rathod, V. (2009a). Comparative Reliability of Cheiloscopy and Palatoscopy in Human Identification, *Indian Journal of Dental Research*, 20 (4), 453–457.

Sharma, P., Saxena, S., & Rathod, V. (2009b). Cheiloscopy: The Study of Lip Prints in Sex Identification, *Journal of Forensic Dental Sciences*, 1, 247.

Sivapathasundharam, B., Prakash, P. A., & Sivakumar, G. (2001). Lip Prints (Cheiloscopy). *Indian Journal of Dental Research*, 12, 2347.

Snyder, L. M. *Homicide Investigation*. Springfield: Thomas, p. 65, 1950.

Souviron, R. R. (2006). Forensic odontology: Bite mark identification. In W. U. Spitz (Ed.), *Medicolegal Investigation of Death: Guidelines for the Application of Pathology to Crime Investigation.* (pp. 255–281).

Stimson, P. G. (1980). Maintaining chain of evidence from beginning of case. In Siegel R., & Sperber N. (Eds.), *Forensicodontology Work Book*. New York: ASFO II, p. 1.

Suzuki, K., & Tsuchihashi, Y. (1970). A New Attempt of Personal Identification by Means of Lip Print. *Journal of Indian Dental Association*, 42 (1), 8–9.

Suzuki, K., & Tsuchihashi, Y. (1975). Two Criminal Cases of Lip print. *Forensic Science*, 41, 61–64.

Sweet, D. (2010). Interpol DVI Best-practice Standards—An Overview. *Forensic Science International*, 201 (1–3), 18–21.

Sweet, D., & Di Zinno, J. A. (1996). Personal Identification Through Dental Evidence–Tooth fragments to DNA. *CDA Journal*, 24(5), 35–42.

The People of the State of Illinois, Plaintiff-Appellant, vs Lavelle L. Davis, Defendant-Appelle. Appellate Court of Illinois, Second District, Case No. 94-CF-76, (November 20, 2007). p. 67.

Thomas, C. J., & van Wyk, C. W. (1988). The Palatal Rugae in Identification, *Journal of Forensic Odontostomatology*, 6 (1), 21–25.

Utsuno, H., Kanoh, T., Tadokoro, O., & Inoue, K. (2005). Preliminary Study of Post Mortem Identification Using Lip Prints. *Forensic Science International*, 149, 12932.

Vale, G. L. (1996). Dentistry, Bite Marks, and the investigation of crime". *Journal Calificate Dental Association*, 24(5), 29–34.

Contextualizing Education of Crime Scene Investigation

Samar A. Ahmed

Worldwide Association of Women Forensic Experts (WAWFE-Egypt), Ain Shams University Cairo, Egypt

CONTENTS

Crime scene investigation is an exciting career that is meaningful, impactful, and worth investing in.

Crime scene technicians provide an important and necessary service to society by assisting in the investigation of frequently challenging crimes. There is a reputation that goes with this job that is an open invitation for young people looking for a challenging career. This is the case that is encouraged by a number of television programs in many different languages that bring CSI to the front of the crime world.

The technology that underpins crime scene investigation (CSI) practices offers a degree of sensitivity that might tamper with the integrity of the information extracted from the crime scene; any small interaction with an innocent person's DNA—in its various forms—could potentially contaminate a crime scene and confound detectives. Nonetheless, the advancement is critical in assisting law enforcement in obtaining evidence needed to convict offenders through the use of specimen, evidence analysis in the laboratory analysis, and meticulous recording.

CSIs are responsible for gathering evidence (e.g. fingerprints, firearm casings and cartridges, glass, paint, footwear and tread impressions, biological samples, trace chemicals, fibers etc.), documentation (e.g. video, photographing, and/or sketching), and processing the evidence collected, as detailed per the International Crime Scene Investigators Association (ICSIA). In addition, they may attend autopsies and death investigations, coordinating with police and other investigative agencies, laboratory staff, pathologists, attorneys, as well as other legal and medical experts. At all times, they must stay current on the latest technologies and practices in the field.

Although there are CSIs who can sometimes perform labs, in addition to having advanced degrees (e.g. bachelor's degrees) in biology, chemistry, or other biological sciences, much of the training takes place on the job and in the field.

Being bold and having a sense of adventure are crucial qualities for crime scene technicians. In their pursuit of justice, these experienced personnel use scientific ideas and cutting-edge technology. CSIs must:

- **Be composed:** A degree of comfort is required when working with different types of suspects. This is a fact that the job comes with a great degree of uncertainty and excitement where the technician needs to be able to keep his/her composure and clarity of mind all through it.
- **Be able to think critically and analyze:** Physical evidence from incidents must be matched to current suspected databases by crime scene specialists. As a result, they need to be familiar with scientific testing and methodologies.
- **Communicate well:** They need to be able to communicate effectively withing the team. This is important for report writing and for testimonials in the court.
- **Possess core math and science competency:** In some cases and certain forms of evidence, such skills may be needed for analysis.
- **Have good attention to detail:** This includes being perceptive, being able to concentrate, and—in certain instances—be able to identify and note potential inconsistencies.

All of the above attributes are the focus of any education needed to graduate crime scene investigators that are a successful part of any crime investigation team.

EDUCATION STRUCTURE AND METHODS

When educating crime scene investigators, it is important to utilize all aspects of adult learning. The concept of adult learning manages learners as potential practitioners and equips them for the future in the workplace. This means that the earlier we can build capacities in the context of the workplace the better. Education and training are both elements of the contextualized learning approach needed to ensure that the graduates of these programs need the least possible time after graduation to adapt to the work environment.

Contextualizing education is a long process that should start from the phase of planning all the way through to execution and evaluation.

The scope of contextualization is not only to ensure training is as close as possible to the context of practice but also it is worth noting that the crime scene professional is a member of a team. This means that in order to execute the best possible practice on the ground, the graduate needs to be equipped to be an effective team member in a multidimensional team. This team is usually comprised of multi-professions: forensic investigators, crime scene investigators, criminalists, criminalistic officers, evidence technicians, and social workers, etc. This means that graduates need to be exposed to as many interprofessional training events as possible. Being exposed to this rich learning experience is very important and changes the perception and spectrum of the CSI. This experience allows for a better understanding and appreciation of the value and quality of the work done by other professions at the crime scene. If this can be achieved, many of the incidents of crime scene contamination and loss of evidence can be avoided.

What would these interprofessional development events look like?

It is a common practice to work togeth on training sessions to cap didactic education sessions with knowledge content. These sessions are usually planned as field practices that are under supervision or, in many cases, artificial intelligence is used to promote a near to real practical experience. In order to make sure that these sessions are interprofessional, this requires a restructure and replan of the session, starting from revision of session objectives, identifying a role clarification process, designing empowering practices, and building an inclusive culture. Interprofessional development practices are time, effort, and money saving when designed properly.

DESIGNING A CONTEXTUALIZED CRIME SCENE INVESTIGATOR TRAINING PROGRAM

In order to be able to design a valuable program that graduates crime scene investigators, we have to answer a few questions first, even before the objectives are identified:

1. What are the prerequisites for trainees entering this program?
2. What types of learners will this program attract?
3. What is the possible hiring body that will attract graduates of this program? What is the career prospect of the graduates?
4. What is the structure of the program?
5. What is the suitable number of trainees per cohort?
6. What teaching or training methods do we want to conduct?
7. What are the required infrastructure and educational tools needed?
8. What kind of assessment will be needed?
9. What investment do we need to do in building the assessment plan?
10. Do we have an aligned view of the teaching methods and assessment together with the objectives?

In total, this is my view of what this program should look like in order to be as contextual as possible. This is a total description in answer to the above guiding questions.

A crime scene investigation program can be a program at the level of higher education accepting graduates of high school diplomas of different types. Learners attracted to this program will generally be those students studying science at a higher education level. This entails a good background in chemistry, mathematics, and physics. As graduates, crime scene technicians can be hired by law enforcement agencies, forensic authorities, and independent consultancy firms.

The program is at least a three-year program structured around trace evidence types, general management of the crime scene, communication skills both written and spoken, personal development, etc. The program should host several training and development sessions of interprofessional nature. The aim of the program is also to build a community of practice among these practitioners to allow for information flow and development and to accommodate lifelong collaborative learning. Therefore, a small class is required, around 20–30 students. Teaching classes can be built and designed around cases; the majority of which will be derived from the context where the program is taught. Using a good percentage of practicalness in relation to the knowledge part is a very good approach. The program can be conducted in a facility with a good laboratory infrastructure and that utilizes partnerships with the community in which it is taught. A big part of this program needs to contain field-based training plans. Assessment of the learners will need to cover both the knowledge base and the skills, whether psychomotor skills like laboratory skills or general and transferable skills like communication capacity. This will require infrastructure for administering paper or computer-based written examinations as well as objective structured practical examinations (OSPEs). Another important aspect of assessment will be workplace-based assessment to assess the skill portion.

REFERENCES

Ahmed, S. A., Hegazy, N. N., Abdel Malak, H. W. *et al.* (2020). Model for Utilizing Distance Learning Post COVID-19 Using (PACT)™ a cross sectional qualitative study. *BMC Medical Education*, 20, 400. 10.1186/s12909-020-02311-1

Ahmed, S. A., Shehata, M. H., Abdel Malak, H. W., El Saadany, S. A., & Hassanien, M. A. (2021). Use of Short Videos for Faculty Development in Adaptation Of Interactive Teaching Strategies for Virtual Classroom. *Journal of Microscopy and Ultrastructure* [serial online] 2020, 8, 211–212. Available from: https://www.jmau.org/text.asp?2020/8/4/211/300358

Abouzeid, E., Wasfy, N., El-Zoghby, S., Atwa, H., et al. (2020). Using Appreciative Inquiry to explore the disruptive effect of COVID-19 on medical student trust in their Schools. *Med Ed Publish*, 9 (1), 285, 10.15694/mep.2020.000285.1

Ahmed, S. A., Kamel Shehata, M. H., Wells, R. L., Ahmed Amin, H. A., & Mohamed Atwa, H. S. [2021]. Step-by-Step Guide to Managing the Educational Crisis: Lessons Learned from COVID-19 Pandemic. *Journal of Microscopy and Ultrastructure* [serial online] 2020, 8, 193–197. Available from: https://www.jmau.org/text.asp?2020/8/4/193/302973

Ahmed, S. A., Omar, Q. H., & Elamaim, A. A. (2016). Forensic Analysis of Suicidal Ideation Among Medical Students of Egypt: a Cross-sectional Study. *Journal of Forensic and Legal Medicine*, 44, 1–4.

Ahmed, S. A., Ashry, S. K., & Widdershoven, G. (2019). Effectiveness of Online Teaching for Development of Resident Beliefs and Understandings: A Study on Breaking Bad News to Patients. *Health Professionals Education*, 5(1), 30–38. https://www.forensicscolleges.com/blog/htb/how-to-become-csi

Vicarious Traumatization and the Crime Scene Investigator

Leggie L. Boone

Polk County Sheriff's Office, Keiser University Florida, Sherlock Institute of Forensic Science (SIFS) India Pvt. Ltd., Editorial Board of Fashion and Law Journal Legal Desire Media and Insights, Worldwide Association of Women Forensic Experts (WAWFE-US), International Association for Identification Florida Division of IAI Generation ForSciTe, LLC Lakeland, Florida, USA

CONTENTS

When a crime scene investigator or anyone working in the field of forensic science talks about their job, listeners' ears tend to perk. The audience of family, friends, students, strangers, and occasional curious eavesdroppers may offer a comment or question, like any of the following:

- "Ooh, that's interesting!"
- "I couldn't do a job like that."
- "I bet you've seen some crazy things."
- "You must have a strong stomach."
- "Doesn't that kind of stuff bother you?"
- "How do you sleep after seeing some of that kind of thing?"
- Some even ask, "What was your worst scene?"
- And, "My ____ wants to be a CSI. Can he/she call you?"

Although we CSIs and forensic professionals love what we do, the questions may trigger flashbacks of scenes or evidence that has found its place among our personal mental slideshow of tragedies. These moments of reminiscence and reflection on morbidity are simply surface layers of vicarious trauma.

What Is Vicarious Traumatization?

Vicarious traumatization was introduced by McCann and Pearlman in 1990 as a psychological response of chronic symptomatic distress to indirect trauma experienced by those close to a critical incident (Pack, 2014; Tuckey & Scott, 2014). Vicarious traumatization can resemble burnout, compassion fatigue, and secondary traumatic stress and occurs in occupations in which interaction with trauma and trauma survivors is a component. Identifying the need for tools to decompress is significant and individual to anyone experiencing vicarious trauma as well-being may be negatively impacted through the occurrence of maladaptive behaviors, such as excessive alcohol intake, smoking, or risky behaviors, cynicism, and diminished job performance. Employers should be aware of the risks of occupations most susceptible to vicarious traumatization and should provide education and training to promote resilience. Vicarious resilience is a progression through vicarious traumatization that occurs by the development of effective coping strategies (Pack, 2014).

Everyone engaged in any level of forensics has been introduced to Edmond Locard's Exchange Principle, noting that "every contact leaves a trace." Our contact with crime scenes, particularly tragic ones, takes some fraction of the psychological reflection of trauma and embeds a trace within our psyche. In other words, yes, the scenes do impact us, but each practitioner is affected differently. Based on the phenomenon of vicarious traumatization, I conducted a study to determine how crime scene investigators view their job performance effectiveness based on their frequency of exposure to traumatic scenes and the support provided (or not provided) by their law enforcement agencies or laboratories.

There are multiple surveys accessible online or upon requests through psychology professionals for determining the impacts of trauma on an individual. Research studies may request input from multiple persons within a population of forensic personnel; leadership within a law enforcement organization may wish to monitor employee perceptions of organizational support or work/life balance; or individuals may wish to monitor their own mental health and responses as they move forward in their careers.

Awareness that frequent or a single instance of exposure to trauma may trigger a psychological or emotional response could motivate the professional to develop habits for self-care. Coping strategies are essential to facing any emotional or mentally taxing situation, however, the CSI and forensic professional should maintain a mental checklist of self-assessment thoughts to make sure there is a comfortable balance between what he or she is viewing or handling at work and their home life.

Are you taking care of the physical CSI?

- Eating properly
- Sleeping regularly
- Taking breaks, time off, vacations
- Stepping away from the electronic devices
- Taking prescribed medications
- Getting any needed medical attention

Are you taking care of the psychological CSI?

- Having alone time
- Reading non-work-related material
- Seeking guidance/counseling when needed
- Engaging in hobbies unrelated to your expertise
- Giving attention to your feelings
- Stimulating your intellect
- Saying "no" to avoid overwhelming yourself

Are you taking care of the emotional CSI?

- Spending time with friends or family
- Doing the leisurely things you enjoy
- Laughing
- Reaching out to those with whom you don't see often
- Speaking positivity

Are you taking care of the spiritual CSI?

- Finding inspiration in music, books, art
- Reflecting on your gifts and talents
- Giving to others
- Connecting with children
- Involvement with community happenings

And, are you taking care of the professional CSI?

- Connecting with peers
- Completing tasks at your own reasonable pace

- Taking time for lunch or other breaks
- Creating a positive space for yourself
- Associate with interests outside of work

Concepts and modified statements are taken from the Self-Care Wellness Assessment Worksheet, developed by Saakvitne, Pearlman & Staff of Traumatic Stress Institute/Center for Adult & Adolescent Psychotherapy (published by Norton, 1996), found in *Transforming the Pain: A Workbook on Vicarious Traumatization.*

Remember that we are each impacted by the tragedies of our field in different ways. Desensitization is also a response for many of us. Over time, we may not feel a tangible or visible affect, but being unaffected or indifferent is still a form of response. Know yourself and be sure to develop positive coping strategies to separate your thoughts or distract you from the trauma of the day.

SOCIAL CHANGE IMPLICATIONS

Awareness of vicarious traumatization is a singular piece of the forensic employment journey. An understanding of the facets of the position is key as you progress in any career. Learn about your employer's stance on stress management prevention and intervention. Identify areas of positivity in your work environment, incentives for education, and the availability of resources, networking opportunities, and training. Educate yourself on the policies for workers' compensation for mental health and how your position is included or excluded. Advise novice forensic personnel on the necessities of self-care and susceptibility for vicarious traumatization. Be the peer support you may eventually need if you recognize signs of distress, diminished job performance, cynicism, or burnout. A CSI has to have these tools and more to endure and be effective.

REFERENCES

Pack, M. (2014). Vicarious Resilience: A Multilayered Model of Stress and Trauma. *Journal of Women and Social Work*, 29(1), 18–29. doi:1.1177/08861 09913510088

Saakvitne, K. W. & Pearlman, L. A. (1996). *Transforming the Pain: A Workbook on Vicarious Transformation.* New York, NY: Norton. Also found at https://www.crisissupport.org/wp-content/uploads/2015/04/trauma_wellness_self-assessment.pdf and https://www.brown.edu/campus-life/health/services/promotion/sites/healthpromo/files/self%20care%20assessment%20and%20planning.pdf

Tuckey, M. R., & Scott, J. E. (2014). Group Critical Incident Stress Debriefing with Emergency Services Personnel: A Randomized Controlled Trial. *Anxiety, Stress, & Coping, 27*(1), 38–54. doi:1.1080/10615 806.2013.809421

ADDITIONAL RESOURCES

Organizations such as the National Alliance on Mental Illness (NAMI) found at www.nami.org; the International Critical Incident Stress Foundation, Inc. (ICISF) found at https://icisf.org/; and the Forensic Technology Center of Excellence (FTCOE) found at https://forensiccoe.org offer resources, training, and membership for guidance on assessment, prevention, debriefing, peer support, and several tools for critical incident stress management, vicarious traumatization, and post-traumatic stress.

Personal Wellness Assessment with 8 Dimensions of Wellness. https://nysba.org/app/uploads/2020/04/Self-Assessment-Well-Being-Worksheet.pdf

Researching online may also generate avenues for leadership support, general self-assessment, and coworker assistance.

Work of Care Individual Workbook. http://workofcare.com/wp-content/uploads/2020/03/Work-Of-Care-Individual-Workbook.pdf

Index

Note: *Italicized* page numbers refer to figures, **bold** page numbers refer to tables